Analysis of Machine Elements Using SOLIDWORKS® Simulation 2026

Based on: SOLIDWORKS® Simulation Premium 2026

Shahin S. Nudehi, Ph.D., P.E.
Valparaiso University

John R. Steffen, Ph.D., P.E.
Valparaiso University

SDC
PUBLICATIONS

SDC Publications
P.O. Box 1334
Mission, KS 66222
913-262-2664
www.SDCpublications.com

Download all needed model files from the SDC Publication website (www.SDCpublications.com/downloads/978-1-63057-787-2).

ISBN-13: 978-1-63057-787-2

ISBN-10: 1-63057-787-1

Printed and bound in the United States of America.

Dedication

To James and John who are constant reminders about the important things in life. Also, for family and friends who have provided guidance, inspiration, encouragement, and much delight. J. Steffen

To my wife and children for their unconditional love and support. Shahin Nudehi

About the Authors

Dr. John Steffen obtained his B.S.M.E. from Valparaiso University, M.S.M.E. from The University of Notre Dame, and Ph.D. from Rutgers, The State University of New Jersey. His areas of interest include Machine Design, Mechanisms and Mechanism Synthesis, Finite Element Analysis, and Experimental Stress Analysis. Dr. Steffen is Professor Emeritus of Mechanical Engineering and the Alfred W. Sieving Chair, Emeritus, in Engineering at Valparaiso University, Valparaiso, IN. He is a life member of the American Society of Mechanical Engineers (ASME) and longtime member and supporter of the American Society for Engineering Education (ASEE).

Dr. Shahin Nudehi received his B.S.M.E and M.S.M.E. from Sharif University of Technology in 1994 and 1996, respectively. He graduated from Michigan State University in 2001 where he received his M.S.E.E. in 2004 and his Ph.D. degree in M.E. in 2005. He has six years of industrial experience. He worked as a CAE engineer at SAPCO Engineering where he used ANSYS™ and NASTRAN™ to design and improve various automotive components. He was also a product development engineer at AVL North America, where he was responsible for instrumentation and development of internal combustion engines' emission testing and measurement products. Currently, he is a Professor of Mechanical Engineering at Valparaiso University, where he teaches courses including Finite Element Methods, Heat Transfer, Thermodynamics, Mechanical Measurements, Automatic Control, Vibrations, and Senior Design.

Acknowledgements

The authors would like to acknowledge the following individuals and corporations for their support, encouragement, and invaluable assistance in preparation of this book:

- The SOLIDWORKS Corporation and the SOLIDWORKS Solution Partner team for their support and assistance.

- Mr. Stephen Schroff, Ms. Mary Schmidt, and Mr. and Mrs. Zach (Karla) Werner of SDC Publications for technical assistance preparing this manuscript.

- Mr. Michael A. Steffen, and Mr. Carl Jurss for their assistance with the preparation of many SOLIDWORKS models and drawings.

- Dr. Gregory Scott Duncan, Professor of Mechanical Engineering, whose reviews and feedback contributed to the improvement of the book significantly.

- Mr. Jay Seaglar, Senior Technical Customer Support at SOLIDWORKS (Simulation Products), whose guidance was a tremendous help in developing Chapter-10 (Fatigue Testing Analysis) of this textbook.

- Valparaiso University, the College of Engineering, and Prof. Eric Johnson, the former Dean, who provided an environment that encouraged and supported this effort.

This publication marks the 16th edition of this learner centered, step-by-step guide to using SOLIDWORKS Simulation. Every attempt has been made to make this book error free so that it best serves first-time SOLIDWORKS Simulation users. In many instances, the software provides alternative approaches to perform the same tasks. Some alternative methods are presented; however, it is not possible to include every option while keeping the text of manageable length. In an effort to improve future editions of this text, the authors welcome error corrections and suggestions to enhance the presentation at shahin.nudehi@valpo.edu.

Table of Contents

Chapter 6
Contact Analysis

Chapter 7
Bolted Joint Analysis

Chapter 8
Design Optimization

Chapter 9
Elastic Buckling

Chapter 10
Fatigue Testing Analysis

Chapter 11
Thermal Stress Analysis

NOTES:

PREFACE

Intended Audience for This Text

This text is written primarily for first-time users of SOLIDWORKS Simulation® who wish to understand finite element software capabilities applicable to stress analysis of virtually any mechanical component or assembly. As such, the focus of this text is upon mastering software use. Mastery is accomplished by exploring problems that students should be familiar with from undergraduate engineering courses in Mechanics of Materials, Design of Machine Elements, or similarly named courses. Because students and practicing engineers already are familiar with topics from these courses, they are able to focus primarily on learning the software capabilities introduced herein. Other novice users of SOLIDWORKS Simulation, possessing background in the above-named courses, will also benefit by using the self-study format employed throughout this text.

Many chapter example problems are accompanied by solutions based on the use of classical equations for stress determination. This approach amplifies two fundamental tenets of this text. The first is that a better understanding of course topics related to stress determination is realized when classical methods *and* finite element solutions are considered together. The second tenet is that finite element solutions should always be verified by checking, whether by classical stress equations or by experimentation.

Although it is assumed that readers have working knowledge of SOLIDWORKS, practicality dictates that some users will be new to SOLIDWORKS and/or the SOLIDWORKS Simulation work environment or are transitioning to it from other solids modeling or finite element programs. For these reasons, this text is organized so that individuals with no prior SOLIDWORKS or SOLIDWORKS Simulation experience will be successful. To assist in overcoming any lack of SOLIDWORKS familiarity, models of parts or assemblies for all examples and end of chapter problems can be downloaded and unzipped from the publisher's web site at www.SDCpublications.com. Before proceeding, download and unzip chapter examples and end-of-chapter problems from the publisher's web site at:

www.SDCpublications.com/downloads/978-1-63057-787-2

Using this SOLIDWORKS Simulation User Guide

Each chapter of this text begins with a list of *Learning Objectives* related to specific features of SOLIDWORKS Simulation introduced in that chapter. Most software capabilities are repeated in subsequent examples so that users become familiar with their purpose and are able to apply them to future problems. However, successive use of repeated steps is typically accompanied by briefer explanations. This approach is used to

While it is fairly common knowledge that virtually anyone with a technical background can become proficient at using a finite element program, what is frequently lacking is the ability to discern and interpret meaningful results from the copious output produced by such programs. To address this perceived weakness, chapter example problems and most end-of-chapter problems request students to compare finite element results with results found using classical stress equations. Instructors can elect to emphasize or de-emphasize this aspect by assigning selected parts of end-of-chapter problems.

To accommodate organizational differences between design of machine elements textbooks and between individual course outlines, chapters of this text can be worked in any order. However, it is strongly recommended that Chapters 1 and 2 serve as a common starting point. Chapter 4 introduces the topic of symmetry boundary conditions (fixtures), which is expanded upon in Chapter 5 and applied again in Chapter 6. Depending upon course goals, either Chapter 4 or 5 should be included at a minimum. While other chapters may refer to techniques mastered in earlier (skipped) chapters, all necessary analysis steps are included so that users are able to complete each example. Also, because default SOLIDWORKS Simulation software output includes von Mises stress plots, von Mises stress is introduced briefly in Chapter 2. Instructors should be aware of this fact and attempt to fill in any gaps in understanding until von Mises stress is addressed in your course.

Selected end-of-chapter problems can be used to introduce additional software capabilities to students. Instructors may want to assign these problems if the additional capability might be considered useful to students. Because new software features introduced in these exercises are not described within the chapter examples, an additional **Design Guidance** section is provided to guide students through the process of applying the necessary steps. Each of these problems is designated by the ╬ symbol adjacent to the exercise number.

Finally, evaluation "check sheets" are provided to facilitate grading end-of-chapter problems. These check sheets are created in MS Word® and, thus, can be edited to emphasize (add or delete) particular aspects of a problem and/or to change point values to emphasize instructor desired importance of specific portions of an analysis. Check sheets can be downloaded at the publisher's web site:

www.SDCpublications.com/downloads/978-1-63057-787-2

This is the same web site where model files for all textbook problems are found. It may be instructional to provide these sheets to students when problems are assigned so that instructor expectations and grading criteria are clearly understood.

INTRODUCTION

Finite Element Analysis

Finite element theory was introduced over sixty-nine years ago. However, implementation of this theory only became practical after the advent of high-speed computers. This section introduces one method of understanding the numerous sets of simultaneous equations that must be solved as part of the finite element method, and therefore, why this technique requires computer solution. Other more refined mathematical formulations exist; however, they are not the subject of this text. Suffice it to say that finite element theory applied to the solution of any realistic problem results in a computationally intensive task. Additional insight into the number of equations that must be solved in a finite element analysis (FEA) is related to the number of nodes and elements in a model as described in the next section.

The following discussion provides a simplified overview of the mathematical basis of a finite element solution based on the *stiffness* approach. Begin by considering a simple member of original length **L** subject to an external axial load **F** as shown in Fig. 1. Due to force **F**, the member undergoes an axial deformation shown as **ΔL**. For this simple case, the well-known equation relating force and deformation is given by equation [1].

$$\Delta L = \frac{FL}{AE} \qquad [1]$$

Notice that the material property (**E** = modulus of elasticity) along with the applied force **F**, length **L**, and cross-sectional area **A**, must be known to solve for **ΔL**.

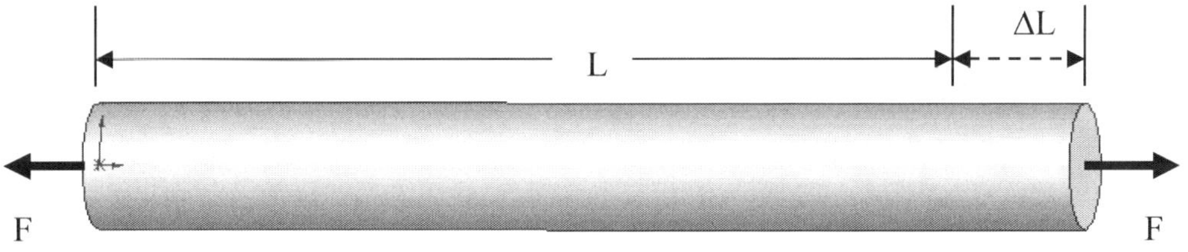

Figure 1 – A simple member subject to axial force **F** illustrates the relationship that exists between the applied force and the resulting deformation Δ**L**.

The next step in a stiffness formulation is used to compute strain based on the deformation determined using equation [1] above. To do so, the simple definition of strain is used where change of length, ΔL, was found above. Strain can be expressed verbally as:

strain = (change of length) / (original length)

or mathematically as:

$$\varepsilon = \frac{\Delta L}{L} \tag{2}$$

Finally, since the goal of analysis is to determine stress in a member, stress can be determined by substituting strain (ε) into the following classic stress-strain relationship.

$$\sigma = E\varepsilon \tag{3}$$

Of course, equation [3] is valid only in the elastic region where stress is proportional to strain. This fact is fundamental to *linear* finite element analysis described in this text.

In summary, the finite element method begins with a mathematical description of deformation, it then proceeds to calculate strain, and finally solves for member stress.

Nodes, Elements, Degrees of Freedom, and Equations

To permit mathematical analysis by the finite element method requires simplification of modeled parts. If the cylindrical member, shown in Fig. 1, were divided into an arbitrary number of *nodes* and *elements*, its model might appear as shown in Fig. 2.

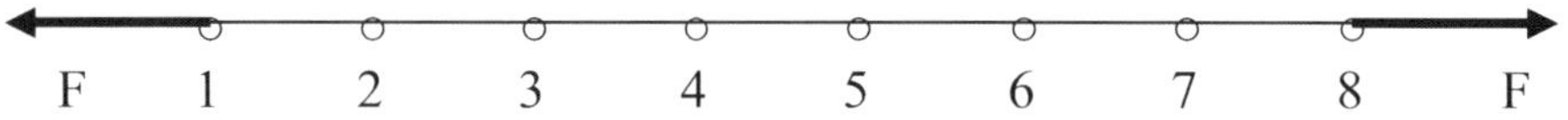

Figure 2 – Simplified model of the cylindrical member sub-divided into a series of nodes and elements.

In Fig. 2, *elements* are represented by short line segments between successive numbered points. The small numbered circles, which represent points of connection between adjacent elements, are called *nodes*. For tracking purposes, elements are also numbered within the finite element software. However, for simplicity, they are not numbered in Fig. 2.

Many different types of elements are found in commercial finite element software. SOLIDWORKS Simulation beam elements *could* be used to model the part shown in Figs. 1, 2 and 3. However, only simple one degree of freedom elements are used here to introduce the concepts of *degrees of freedom* and the *number of equations* that result during a finite element solution. To assist with this understanding, we isolate an arbitrary element and its two nodes located at (n and n+1) from the model in Fig. 2 to obtain an enlarged view of a single element and its two nodes shown in Fig. 3.

Figure 3 – A simple one-dimensional model represented using two nodes and one element.

First, we assume that displacements at nodes n and n+1 are restricted to lie in the X-direction. This restriction ensures that the problem is one-dimensional (i.e., displacements are limited to a single direction, the X-direction). $U_{x(n)}$ and $U_{x(n+1)}$ represent displacements in the X-direction at *each* node. These displacements correspond to one *degree of freedom* at each node. Thus, since displacement at *each* node results in one set of three equations, like equations [1, 2, and 3], it is logical to conclude that two sets of equations result for the element shown in Fig. 3 (one set of equations for each node). If one were to extrapolate the above observation to all seven elements, each with two nodes, for the model shown in Fig. 2, it is evident that:

(7 elements)*(2 nodes/element)*(1 degree of freedom/node) = 14 degrees of freedom [4]

A mathematical solution for the fourteen displacements requires simultaneous solution of fourteen equations to solve this very simple problem. The following section examines primary element types currently available within SOLIDWORKS Simulation.

SOLIDWORKS Simulation Elements

Having established a fundamental understanding of nodes, elements, and degrees of freedom, we next introduce the various types of elements available within SOLIDWORKS Simulation. Basic element types include a *Solid* element, a *Shell* element, various *Beam* elements, and *Truss* elements. *Solid* and *shell* elements are available as either first-order or second-order element types while *Beam* elements have unique characteristics as described in a later section. Descriptions of each element type follow.

Solid Elements

The majority of components analyzed by finite element methods are 3-dimensional models based on solid geometry used to define boundaries of a part or assembly. In this context *solid* refers to parts or assemblies that have significant volume or thickness relative to other component dimensions. The SOLIDWORKS Simulation *solid* elements used to model this type of geometry are named tetrahedral elements. A first-order tetrahedral element, shown in Fig. 4, is comprised of six straight sides, four flat faces, and four nodes that join the edges at each of its four corners. All edges and faces of first-order elements remain straight and flat after deformation. First-order elements are also called “draft quality” elements.

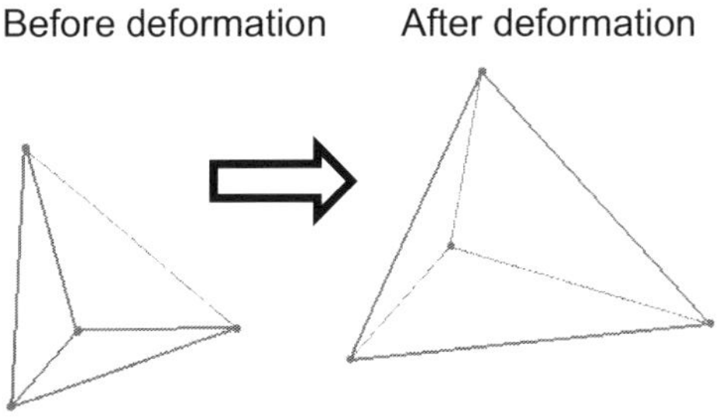

Figure 4 – First-order tetrahedral element before and after deformation.

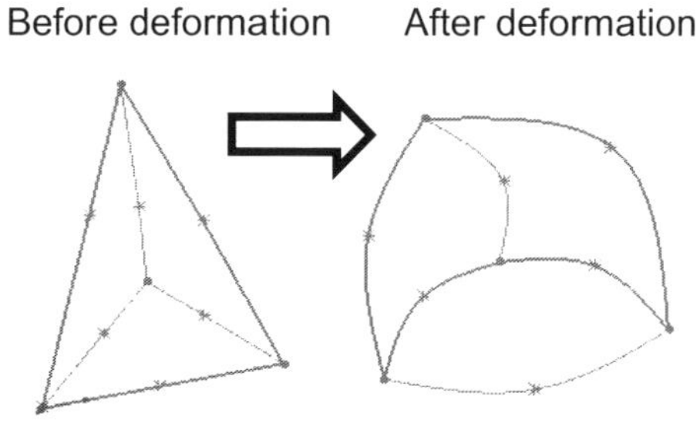

Figure 5 – Second-order tetrahedral element before and after deformation.

A second-order tetrahedral element, illustrated in Fig. 5, is characterized by the addition of another node on each edge of the element for a total of ten nodes per element. These additional nodes, typically called "mid-side nodes," permit element edges and surfaces to deform in a second-order (curved) manner. The obvious advantage of second-order elements is their ability to provide better mapping of curved surfaces. And, a better fit of elements ensures improved modeling of deformations, strains, and hence stresses computed within modeled parts. Whether a first-order (draft quality mesh) or second-order (high quality mesh) is used, the overall mesh density (i.e., total number of elements) is essentially the same for identical model geometry. However, second-order elements yield better results at the expense of greater computational resources.

Solid Element Degrees of Freedom

Both first-order and second-order tetrahedral elements within SOLIDWORKS Simulation allow three degrees of freedom at each node. These degrees of freedom permit *displacements* in the X, Y, and Z directions. The number of degrees of freedom for each element type is summarized below.

First-order (draft quality) element –
A typical first-order element is shown in Fig. 6 (a) along with its three degrees of freedom (i.e., permissible displacements in the X, Y, and Z directions) at each node. For this element, the total number of degrees of freedom is given by:

(3 degrees of freedom/node) * (4 nodes/element) = 12 degrees of freedom/element [5]

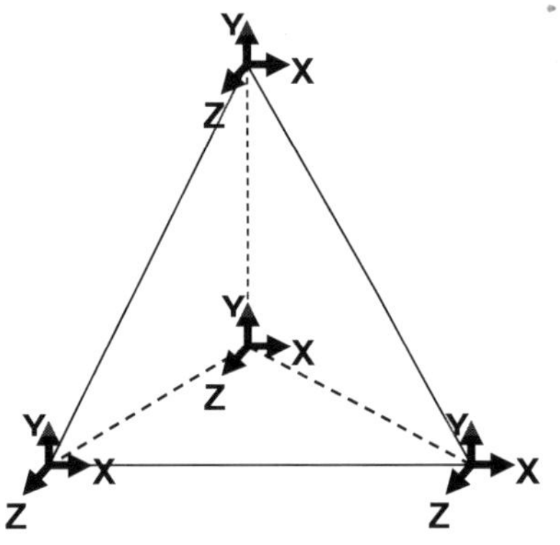

Figure 6 (a) – Draft quality element with three degrees of freedom at each of four nodes.

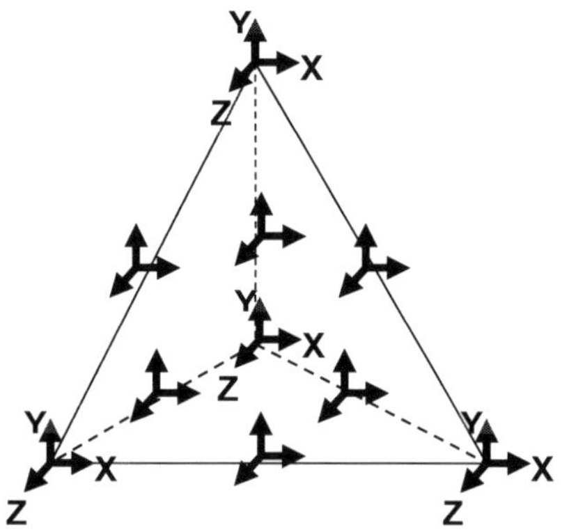

Figure 6 (b) – High quality element with three degrees of freedom at each of ten nodes. (Labels omitted at mid-side nodes.)

Second-order (high quality) element –
Figure 6 (b) shows three degrees of freedom at each of ten nodes on a high quality element. The total number of degrees of freedom for this element is given by:

(3 degrees of freedom/node) * (10 nodes/element) = 30 degrees of freedom/element [6]

Recalling the relationship between degrees of freedom and the corresponding number of simultaneous equations requiring solution for each degree of freedom, it is easily seen that computational intensity increases dramatically as model size and order of the element type increase. Although more computationally intensive, second-order elements yield more accurate results and are almost always recommended for finite element solutions.

Shell Elements

The second type of element available within SOLIDWORKS Simulation is the *shell* element. As implied by its name, *shell* elements are primarily used to analyze thin-walled components such as sheet metal parts or other thin surfaces regardless of material type. Examples of components that might be modeled using shell elements include a propane gas tank, beverage containers, fan blades, a kayak, a cell-phone case, or the oil pan on your car. Although the above examples may appear to present clear-cut differences between uses for *solid* and *shell* elements, in reality there exist numerous situations where a relatively thin member can be modeled equally well using either solid or shell elements. Usually the nature of desired results dictates the choice of element type.

As with solid elements, *shell* elements are also available as first-order "draft quality" or second-order "high quality" mesh types. Figure 7 (a) illustrates a first-order shell element. This element appears two dimensional with straight sides and one flat surface with one node at each of its three corners. Figure 7 (b) illustrates a second-order shell element with its additional mid-side nodes yielding a total of six nodes per element.

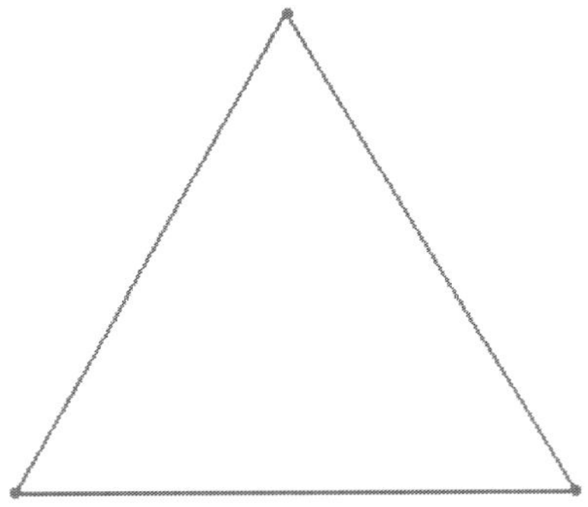

Figure 7 (a) – First-order shell element.

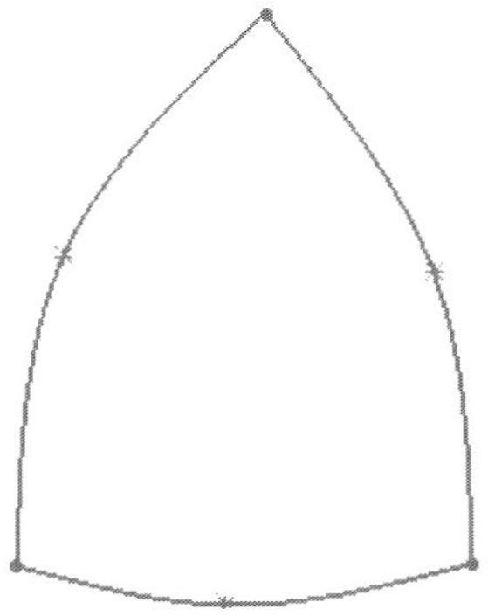

Figure 7 (b) – Second-order shell element showing additional mid-side nodes.

Once again, mid-side nodes permit shell elements to conform to curved geometry of the original component and to better model curvature associated with displacements in deformed parts. Although shell elements are considered two dimensional, a thickness must be defined for them to properly model a part. There are two ways to define a shell mesh. One method creates a shell mesh based on the *mid-surface* of a part while the other approach allows the user to select the surface to be meshed. For example, the 'top' or 'bottom' surface may be specified. Since assignment of mesh thickness varies according to how a shell mesh is defined, this topic is investigated further in Chapter 4.

Element Stress Values

Once again refer to Fig. 15, except this time focus attention on any *one* element. *Element stress* is calculated by averaging stress values from three Gauss points **0**, **0**, and **0'** *within a single element.* Because *element stress* is calculated on a 'per element' basis, an *element* plot of the stress within the model is shown in Fig. 16. Notice that element stress plots typically appear like a "patch work" pattern of discrete colored elements, where each element is all the same color. This occurs because each element shows its own *individual* stress value, which is *not* averaged with surrounding elements. When large differences of stress level occur between adjacent elements, as evidenced by different colored elements, it is a good indication that a smaller mesh size should be used to obtain a better estimate of true stress magnitudes in that area. This phenomenon typically occurs in regions of high stress gradient (i.e., regions where large stress differences occur).

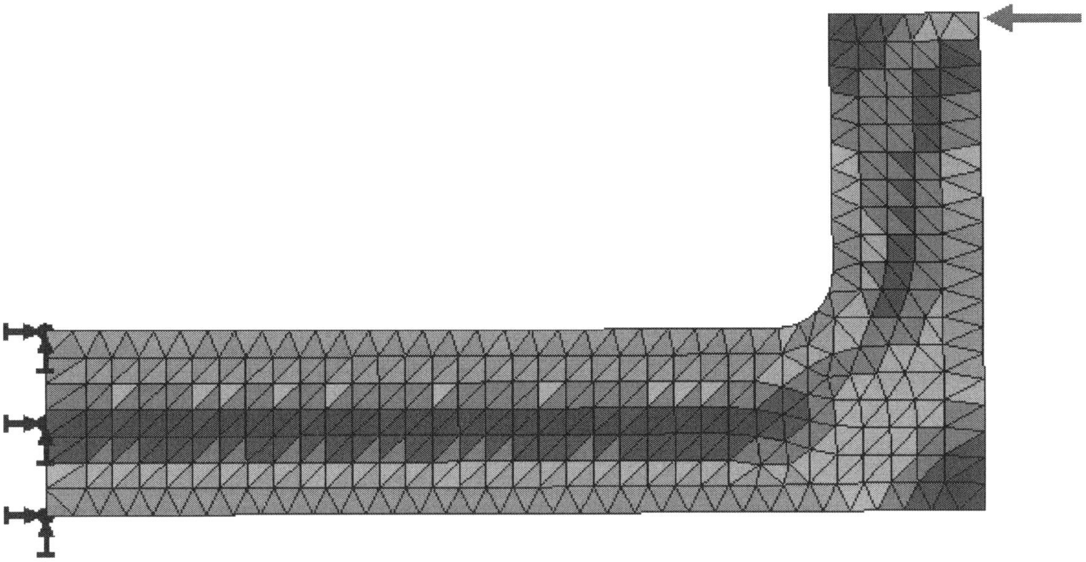

Figure 16 – Element stress plot showing stress magnitudes calculated on a per element basis.

The number of Gauss points varies according to the type of element. Table 1 summarizes the number of Gauss points found in various element types.

Table 1 – Number of Gauss Points Found in Typical Solid and Shell Elements

Element Type	Number of Gauss Points
First order Tetrahedral element (draft quality)	1
Second order Tetrahedral element (high quality)	4
First order Shell element (draft quality)	1
Second order Shell element (high quality)	3

Assumptions Applied to Linear Static Finite Element Analysis

Three limiting assumptions apply to all finite element solutions studied in this text. They are (a) loads are applied statically; (b) materials behave in a linear manner; and (c) deformations are small. Each of these limiting assumptions is reviewed below.

Static Loading

<u>Assumption #1</u>

Loads are applied quasi-statically (i.e., very slowly). Dynamic loads, damping, and inertial effects are not allowed.

Although analyses described in this text are limited to static loading situations, SOLIDWORKS Simulation Premium does provide the capability to solve problems involving dynamic loads, for example a drop test (impact) problem, and to determine the natural frequencies and mode shapes of vibrating systems.

Linear Material Behavior

<u>Assumption #2</u>

Linear assumptions apply to all calculations. This means that system response, such as deformation, strain and stress, is proportional to load.

For example,

- if a 1000 N load causes 0.01 mm displacement,
- then a 2000 N load will cause a 0.02 mm displacement

The linear assumption also implies that parts and assemblies undergo *no* permanent deformation. Or, stated another way, a body returns to its original *un-deformed* shape when loads are removed.

Taken together, the above statements are equivalent to stating that the material of which a body is made does not exceed its yield strength (a.k.a., yield point, or elastic limit). In other words, *all* analyses are presumed to occur on the *linear elastic* portion of the stress strain curve shown in Fig. 17. Recall that the modulus of elasticity "**E**" (a.k.a., Young's modulus) is determined from the slope of the linear portion of the stress versus strain curve.

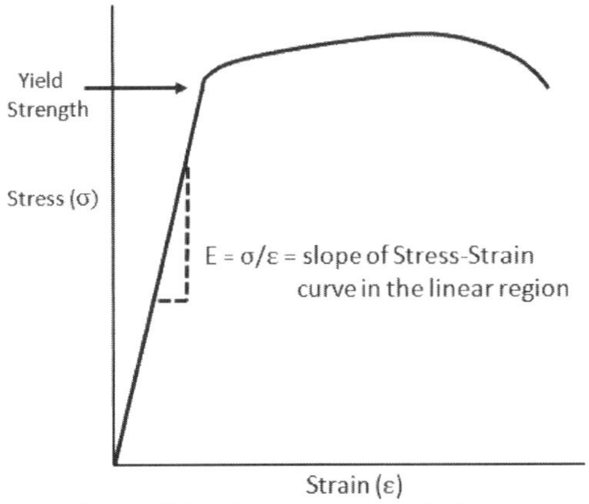

Figure 17 – Stress versus strain curve for a typical ductile material.

The observation stated above for the stress versus strain curve is consistent with the mathematical relationship between stress and strain given by equation [4], which states that stress is proportional to strain.

$$\sigma = E * \varepsilon \qquad [4]$$

In equation [4], modulus of elasticity, **E**, is the constant of proportionality determined from the slope of the linear portion of a stress versus strain graph shown in Fig. 17.

Note that SOLIDWORKS Simulation Premium software includes the capability of solving non-linear problems (also referred to as "post yield" problems). Non-linear problems are not considered in this text.

Small Deformations

Assumption #3

Classification of deformations as "small" is a relative concept. For example, a 7 mm (approx. ¼ in) deformation at the mid-span of a 30 m (approx. 98.5 ft) roof support beam might be considered small for a beam that supports its own weight plus the weight of roofing materials and a significant snow load on the roof exterior. Conversely, a 1 mm (0.04 in) deformation of a small (hand-size) "C"-clamp subject to clamping forces might be considered a relatively large deformation. The Simulation software features a large displacement solver that automatically warns users when large deformations are encountered in a solution. A large displacement solution option can be invoked in such cases.

Closing Comments

Remaining steps of a finite element analysis are analogous to steps involved when solving stress related problems by long-hand methods. In particular, loads and restraints are applied to the model (like creating a free-body diagram), and material properties are selected so that stress levels can be compared to material strength at the conclusion of an analysis. Because these aspects of problem solution are familiar to individuals who have completed a fundamental Mechanics of Materials course, discussion of the equivalent finite element steps is deferred to example problems in subsequent chapters. For these reasons, the remainder of this chapter shifts emphasis to acquaint users with various aspects of the SOLIDWORKS Simulation user interface.

Introduction to the SOLIDWORKS Simulation User Interface

Perhaps the most awkward part of getting started using SOLIDWORKS, SOLIDWORKS Simulation, or any other complex software program, is finding your way around in a new software work environment. Because some users might be new to both SOLIDWORKS Simulation *and* SOLIDWORKS, this introduction begins by providing orientation to the SOLIDWORKS work environment, also known as a Graphical User Interface or GUI.

Proficient SOLIDWORKS users can skip the SOLIDWORKS orientation section below. However, the toolbars and reading associated with Figs. 18 through 20 should be examined. These toolbars are important because many SOLIDWORKS icons are also useful when working in SOLIDWORKS Simulation. Click the SOLIDWORKS icon on your screen to open SOLIDWORKS. Select **[Accept]** when the SOLIDWORKS license agreement appears.

Orientation and Set-up of the SOLIDWORKS Work Environment

First time users of the combined SOLIDWORKS / SOLIDWORKS Simulation software must become acquainted with both the vocabulary and the location of items in the work environment. Thus, we begin by investigating how to add or delete menus to the default SOLIDWORKS graphical user interface. The default 'start-up' SOLIDWORKS screen is shown in Fig. 18. Most menu items, across the top of the screen, are inactive (grayed out) at this time.

Figure 18 – SOLIDWORKS start-up screen showing default menus and toolbars.

Depending upon your work environment, particularly at public access computers, the default SOLIDWORKS work environment may or may not appear as shown in Fig. 18 due to alterations made by other users or individuals who installed the software. Therefore, this section outlines how to return all settings to the factory default settings followed by steps to customize the work environment. Begin by permanently opening and displaying the SOLIDWORKS main menu on the screen as outlined below.

1. If the **Main Menu**, labeled on Fig. 19, appears at the top left of the screen, skip to step 2. Otherwise, move the cursor over the ▶ symbol to the right of the  button at top left of the screen. This action opens the **Main Menu** illustrated in Fig. 19. If the ▶ symbol is not visible, click within the gray

graphics area of the screen. When the ▶ symbol appears, pass the cursor over it and the main menu will open.

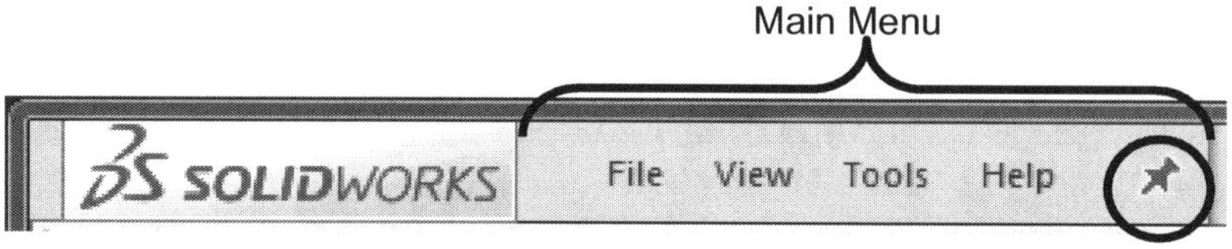

Figure 19 – The SOLIDWORKS button provides access to the **File**, **View**, **Tools**, and **Help** items in the main menu.

2. Because these menu items are used frequently, click to select the "push-pin" icon, circled in Fig. 19. This action permanently displays the main menu.

The next step is to reset to the system default settings. Begin by opening a *new part* file in SOLIDWORKS as follows.

3. In the SOLIDWORKS main menu, click **File**, and from the pull-down menu select **New…**

NOTE: Steps 4 and 5 may or *may not* occur during your first session. Skip to step 6 if step 4 does not appear.

4. The SOLIDWORKS **Units and Dimension Standard** window opens. Within this window, beneath **Units:**, click ▼ to open the pull-down menu and select **IPS (inch, pound, second)** if not already selected.

5. Next, beneath **Dimension Standard:**, click ▼ to open the pull-down menu and select **ANSI** as the dimension standard, if not already selected, and click **[OK]** to close the **Units and Dimension Standard** window.

6. The **New SOLIDWORKS Document** window opens. Within this window, click the **Part** icon.

7. Click **[OK]** to close the **New SOLIDWORKS Document** window. A *new* part file is opened in the graphics area. The default SOLIDWORKS screen appears similar to that in Fig. 20.

Various areas of the *default* SOLIDWORKS start-up screen are labeled in Fig. 20. The **Features** tab, circled in Fig. 20, is *usually* selected by default on the start-up screen. If not, click its tab to select it. Next, explore other *tabs* beneath the **Main Menu** by clicking on the tab name and then examining the contents contained within each tab.

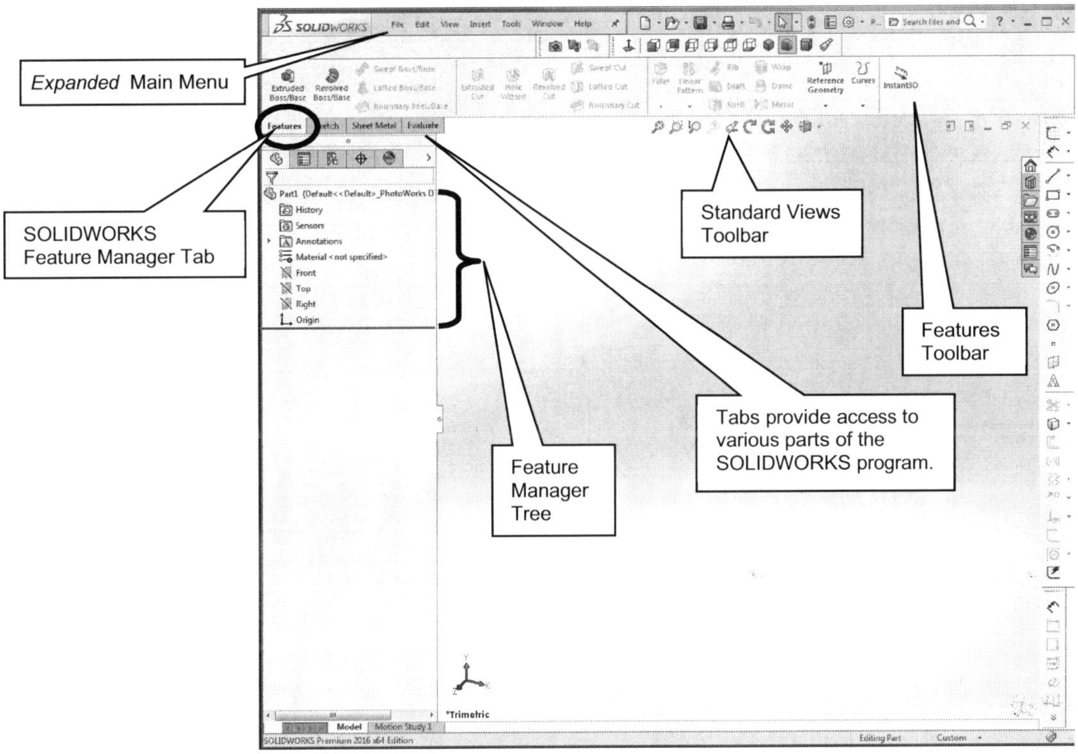

Figure 20 – Definitions identifying basic portions of the SOLIDWORKS screen. Several default toolbars are shown.

If your screen looks like Fig. 20, skip to the section titled **Customizing the SOLIDWORKS Screen** on the next page. If not, proceed to step 8 where the default screen settings are reset.

8. In the main menu, click **Tools**, and near the bottom of the pull-down menu select **Options…** The **System Options - General** window opens (not shown here).

9. At the lower left corner of this window, click the **[Reset…]** button. Immediately a **SOLIDWORKS** window opens as shown in Fig. 21.

10. Select the **[Reset all options]** option to return all settings to the SOLIDWORKS factory default settings.

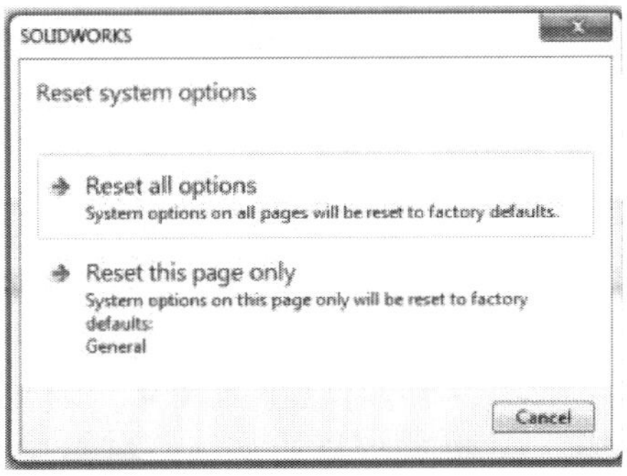

Figure 21 – SOLIDWORKS confirmation window.

11. Click **[OK]** to close the **System Options – General** window. Your screen should now appear like that shown in Fig. 20.

Customizing the SOLIDWORKS Screen

If the large graphics area of the screen appears grey, blue, or some other shaded color as shown in Fig. 20, continue to the next paragraph. However, if the background color is *white*, skip to the sentence following step 7.

Because a shaded background can mask details of a screen image and because printing images on this background wastes considerable ink/toner . . . "think green" . . ., most users prefer to work on a white background. Change the background color as follows.

1. In the main menu, at top left of screen, click **Tools** to open a pull-down menu.

2. Near the bottom of this menu, click **Options...** The **System Options - General** window opens.

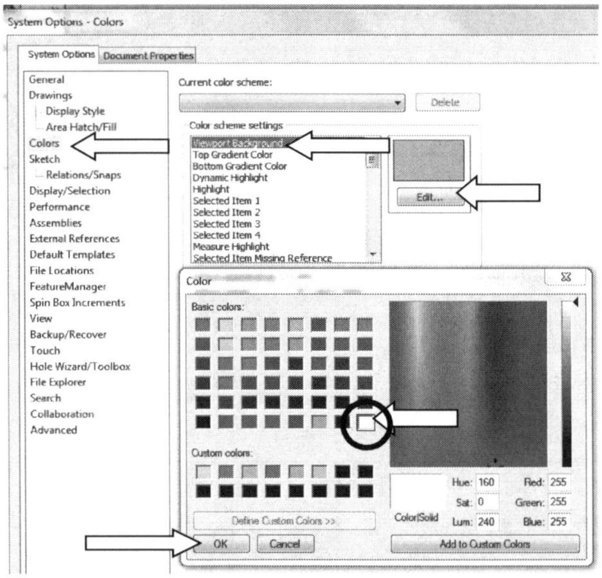

Figure 22 – Selections used to change the **Viewport Background** color.

3. Beneath the **Systems Options** tab, select **Colors** and immediately the right half of the window appears similar to that shown in the *background* of Fig. 22.

4. Within the **Color scheme settings** box, the top entry should read **Viewport Background**. Click to select **Viewport Background** (if not already selected).

5. To the right of this selection, click the **[Edit...]** button. The **Color** window opens as shown in the *foreground* of Fig. 22.

6. Within the **Basic colors:** section of the **Color** window, select the *white* color box circled in Fig. 22; then click **[OK]** to close the **Color** window.

7. Finally, click **[OK]** to close the **System Options - Colors** window. The main graphics area should now appear white. The success of this step depends upon the graphics card in your PC. *(See step 8 if the above procedure failed.)*

8. See **Appendix B** for an alternate way to alter the screen background color.

The next task leads you through the addition of various toolbars to the screen and the modification of some existing toolbars.

9. If the **Standard Views** toolbar, shown boxed in Fig. 23, appears near the top of the screen, skip to the paragraph beneath Fig. 23. Otherwise proceed to step 10.

10. In the main menu, select **View**. Then from the pull-down menu select **Toolbars ►**. This action opens the **Command Manager** pull-down menu shown at the ★ in the partial image in Fig. 23.

11. In the **Command Manager** menu, click the **Standard Views** icon, circled in Fig 23. Immediately the **Standard Views** toolbar appears (shown boxed) in the menu bars above the graphics window. *NOTE: Depending on your screen size, it may be necessary to scroll down the list to locate the **Standard Views** icon.*

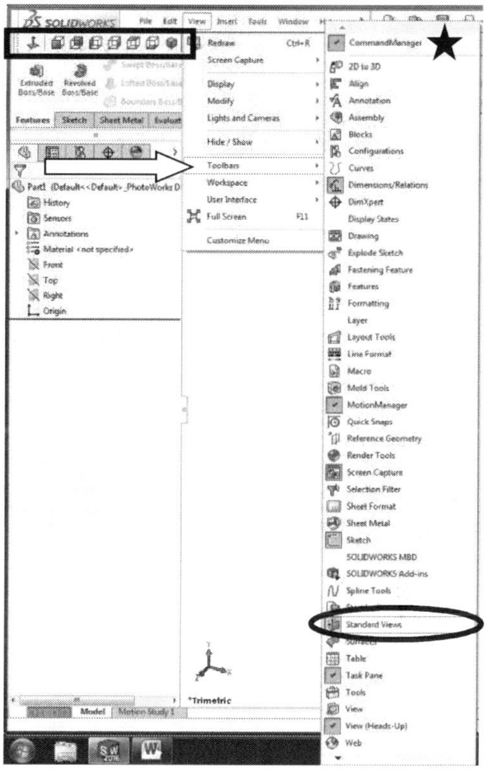

Figure 23 – The Command Manager menu from which toolbars are selected for display.

Although the following steps detail how to add toolbars to the menu, be aware that most necessary toolbars already appear on the screen due to default settings within SOLIDWORKS. Thus, to gain practice with this procedure, follow the steps below to *turn off* the toolbars and subsequently to *turn them back on.*

12. Once again select the **Standard Views** icon (circled in Fig. 23) by selecting **Views / Toolbars ►**, and finally select **Standard Views**. The menu closes and the **Standard Views** toolbar is removed from menus at the top of the screen.

13. Open the **Command Manager** pull-down menu again, but this time use the following shortcut. Right-click anywhere on the top menu bar to immediately open the **Command Manager** menu. *(The menu may be displayed differently.)*

14. Again, locate and select the **Standard Views** icon. The **Command Manager** closes, and the **Standard Views** toolbar is again added to the top of the screen.

15. To gain familiarity with this process, repeat steps 11 and 12, but this time select the **Sketch** icon. The **Sketch** toolbar typically appears along the right edge of the graphics window. If not, its location can be adjusted by clicking-and-dragging a 'drag handle' located at the top or left end of the toolbar.

Finally, observe the icons appearing at the top-middle of the graphics screen as shown in Fig. 24. Because not all of these icons are useful for the purposes of this text, icons that are shown boxed will be kept, new icons will be added (see Fig. 26), and *all others removed* as outlined below.

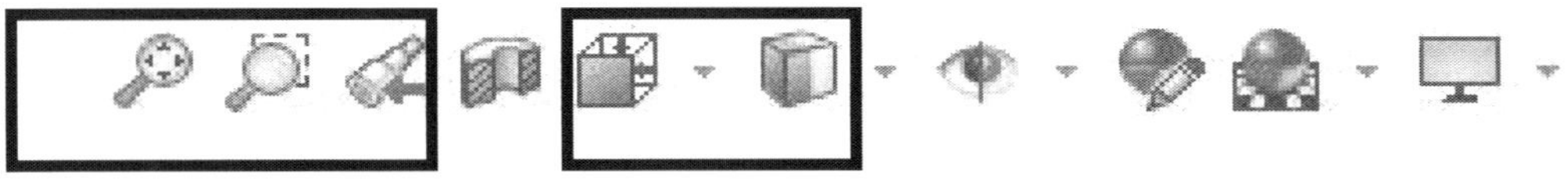

Figure 24 – Default icons appearing at top-middle of the start-up screen.

<u>NOTE</u>: Due to local preferences it is likely that some icons appearing at the top of your screen will differ from those shown above. Thus, as you proceed, eliminate all icons *except those appearing boxed in Fig. 24.*

Proceed as follows.

16. In the main menu, select **Tools** and from the pull-down menu select C**ustomize…** The **Customize** window opens and appears *similar* to Fig. 25.

17. Within this window, select the **Commands** tab. Then, near the bottom, left-side of the **Categories:** scroll list, select **View**. Your screen should appear like Fig. 25.

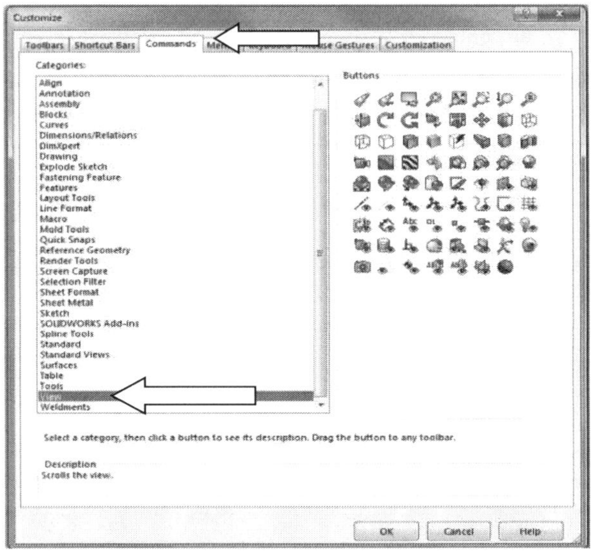

Figure 25 – Menu used to add and delete icons from the **Heads-Up View** toolbar.

18. To remove an unwanted icon from the toolbar, click-and-drag the icon to deposit it into the right side of the **Customize** window shown in Fig. 25. Repeat for each icon to be removed.

19. To add an icon to the toolbar, click-and-drag the icon from the right side of the **Customize** window and deposit it into **Heads-Up View** toolbar.

20. Next, examine images of the desired icons shown in Fig. 26. To add the missing icons, simply click-and-drag the appropriate icon from the right-half of Fig. 25 to its desired location at the top-middle of the graphics area.

21. After updating the icons displayed, close the **Customize** window by selecting **[OK]**.

The icons shown in Fig. 26 are most useful throughout this text. Selecting any of these icons allows the user to perform various graphic manipulations on part models.

Figure 26 – Adjusted listing of icons used most frequently to manipulate models.

A brief description of each icon is provided below.

 **Zoom to Fit** – Resizes the model and places it at the center of the screen.

 **Zoom to Area** – Zooms to an area of the model enclosed in a user defined box.

 **Zoom In/Out** – Move mouse up or down to zoom 'out' or 'in' on the model.

 **Zoom to Selection** – Zooms to a selected location on a part or sub-assembly.

 **Previous View** – Returns image to its previous view.

 **Roll View** – Rotates view about a specific X, Y, or Z axis.

 **Rotate View** – Rotates view about 3-dimensional axes.

 **Pan** – Moves model left/right, up/down, or diagonally without rotation

 **View Orientation** – The ▼arrow provides access to multiple standard views and window display configurations. These views are also accessible using **Standard Views** icons previously added at the upper left of the screen.

22. Additional toolbars can be added to or removed from the screen by right-clicking anywhere on the **Main Menu** and either selecting or deselecting items that appear in the pull-down menu.

23. If the pull-down menu remains open, close it by clicking anywhere outside the menu.

Although short-cut methods for manipulating the model were introduced in the **Preface**, (see **Table 1**, page ix), new users may find the visual display of icon capability helpful.

Seasoned SOLIDWORKS users might choose to place additional toolbars on the screen, or to customize those now appearing by adding or removing specific icons. The procedure to do this is much the same as adding or removing icons in any Windows® program. For this reason, it is not uncommon for slight differences of screen images to occur. The next section outlines steps to add SOLIDWORKS Simulation to the graphics screen.

Orientation to the SOLIDWORKS Simulation Work Environment

Because the primary goal of this text is to master use of the finite element portion of SOLIDWORKS, that part of the program is activated next.

Adding SOLIDWORKS Simulation to the Work Environment

Although SOLIDWORKS (solids modeling software) and SOLIDWORKS Simulation (finite element software) operate seamlessly together, they are different software programs each requiring an individual user license. Thus, it is typically necessary to activate the SOLIDWORKS Simulation portion of the program separately. Below are listed steps required to activate SOLIDWORKS Simulation.

Activating SOLIDWORKS Simulation

Because SOLIDWORKS may have been installed differently on each network or PC, we begin by determining whether or not the Simulation portion of the software is already active.

1. Look for the word "**Simulation**" in both the **Main Menu** (at top left of screen) *and* in the *tab* menu located immediately above and to the left of the graphics screen as labeled in Fig. 27. If "**Simulation**" appears in both locations, skip to step 12 because Simulation is already active on your computer. However, if "**Simulation**" appears only in the **Main Menu**, then skip to the sentence immediately below Fig. 29. Alternatively, if "**Simulation**" does *not* appear in either location, then execute the following steps.

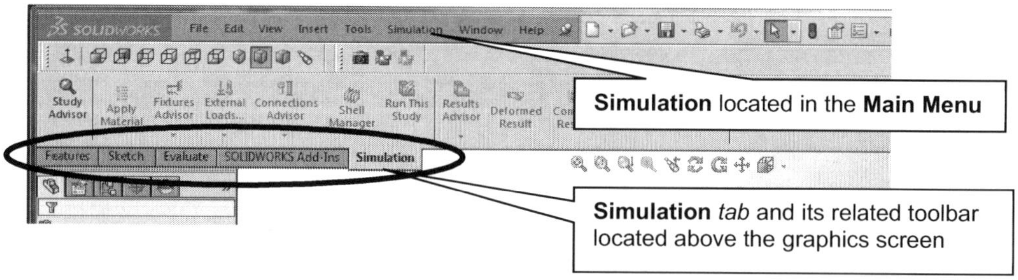

Figure 27 – Seeing the name "Simulation" in both the **Main Menu** and as a *tab* indicates Simulation is already set up on your computer.

2. In the **Main Menu** click **Tools**, and from the pull-down menu select **Add-Ins…** The **Add-Ins** window opens as shown in Fig. 28.

3. Within the **Add-Ins** window place check marks "✓" in both the <u>left</u> *and* <u>right</u> columns adjacent to ☑ **SOLIDWORKS Simulation** ☑. The check mark in the left column activates Simulation for the current session while the check mark in the right column activates Simulation every time SOLIDWORKS is opened.

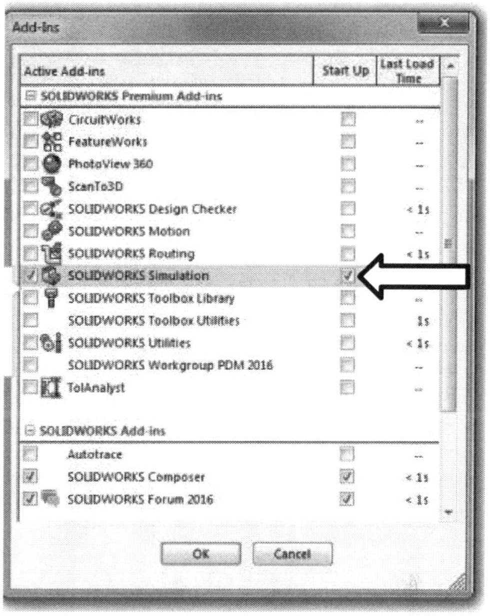

Figure 28 – Window in which SOLIDWORKS Simulation is activated.

4. Click **[OK]** to close the **Add-Ins** window.

5. The SOLIDWORKS **Simulation License Agreement** appears *(for first time users only)*. Click **[Accept]**. See Fig. 29.

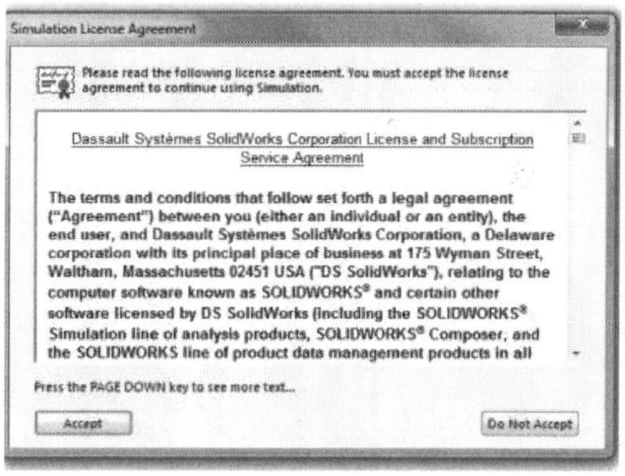

Figure 29 – **Simulation** license agreement.

The word "**Simulation**" should now appear in the **Main Menu** as shown in Fig. 27. If its name also appears on a *tab* above and to the left of the graphics screen, then skip to step 12. Otherwise continue below.

6. Several *tabs* appearing just above the graphics screen are circled in Fig. 27. These tabs *may* include **Features**, **Sketch**, **Sheet Metal**, and **Evaluate** to name a few.

7. Right-click on any of the *tabs* listed in the preceding step and a pull-down menu opens as shown in Fig. 30.

8. Within the pull-down menu, click to select **Simulation** to add its *tab* above the graphics screen. The pull-down menu closes.

The menu in Fig. 30 shows a check mark ☑ adjacent to the name of each tab that is currently displayed at the top left of the graphics area. It also contains a list of other tabs that can be added to or deleted from those currently displayed.

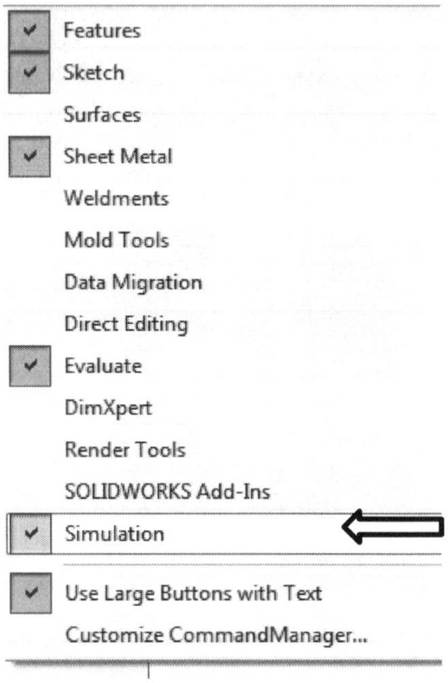

Figure 30 – List of menu tabs that can be added to or removed from the top left of the screen.

The above steps add the name "**Simulation**" to the **Main Menu** located at the top of the screen. Also, a **Simulation** *tab* is located just above the graphics area as shown in Fig. 27. Selecting either of these names provides access to **Simulation** capabilities of the software.

9. In the **Main Menu**, click **Simulation** to open a pull-down menu of capabilities within the finite element portion of the program. Briefly examine this list.

10. Click anywhere outside the menu to close it.

11. Next, click the **Simulation** *tab* to display the Simulation toolbar and the icons used during a finite element analysis. Most icons are initially grayed out.

Next, proceed as follows to remove un-needed tabs.

12. Right-click on any tab *name*. The pull-down menu of Fig. 30 opens. In the pull-down menu clear the check mark "✓" adjacent to ☐ **Evaluate** (if it appears). The menu closes automatically and **Evaluate** is removed from the list of tabs.

13. Repeat step 12 to remove any other tabs except **Features**, **Sketch**, and **Simulation**.

14. Right-click anywhere in the top menu bar to open the **Command Manager** pull-down menu.

15. Near the top of this menu, select ☑ **Use Large Buttons with Text** (if not already selected). This action adds descriptive labels beneath each icon in the currently active toolbar.

The upper portion of the SOLIDWORKS Simulation window should now appear similar to that shown in Fig. 27. The number of icons appearing on a toolbar may vary. Also, because a finite element analysis is not currently active, most icons appear grayed out.

Property Managers and Dialogue Boxes

Property managers and dialogue boxes are, perhaps, the most frequently used items when developing a finite element analysis in SOLIDWORKS Simulation. The importance of these two interfaces cannot be overstated because the specific meaning of each aspect of the finite element modeling process is defined within them. However, these interfaces are only encountered when an actual analysis is being performed. For this reason, this section only attempts to define their location on the screen and provide basic insight to their general role in an analysis. No user interaction is required for the remainder of this chapter.

When opened, a *property manager* is typically located at the left side of the graphics area, shown boxed in Fig. 31. Numerous property managers exist and each is somewhat unique. However, the general observations described below apply to each. The property manager, shown boxed in Fig. 31, is enlarged in Fig. 32.

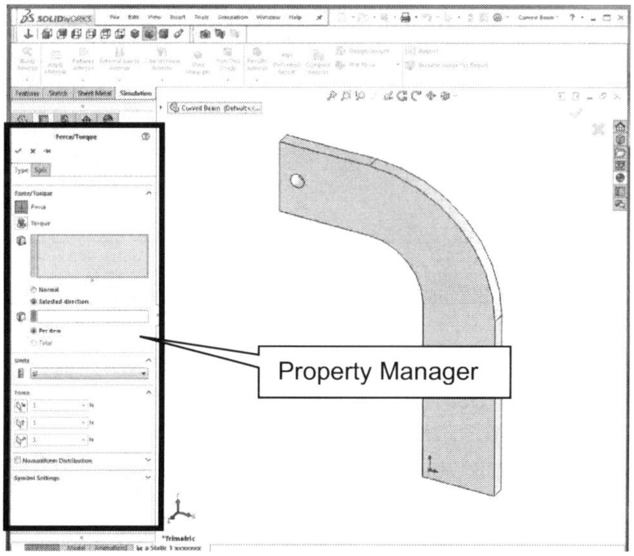

Figure 31 – Image showing the location of a property manager in the SOLIDWORKS Simulation graphical user interface.

Figure 32 shows an example of the **Force/Torque** property manager with its name prominently displayed at the top. This property manager is used when defining different types of loads applied to a finite element model.

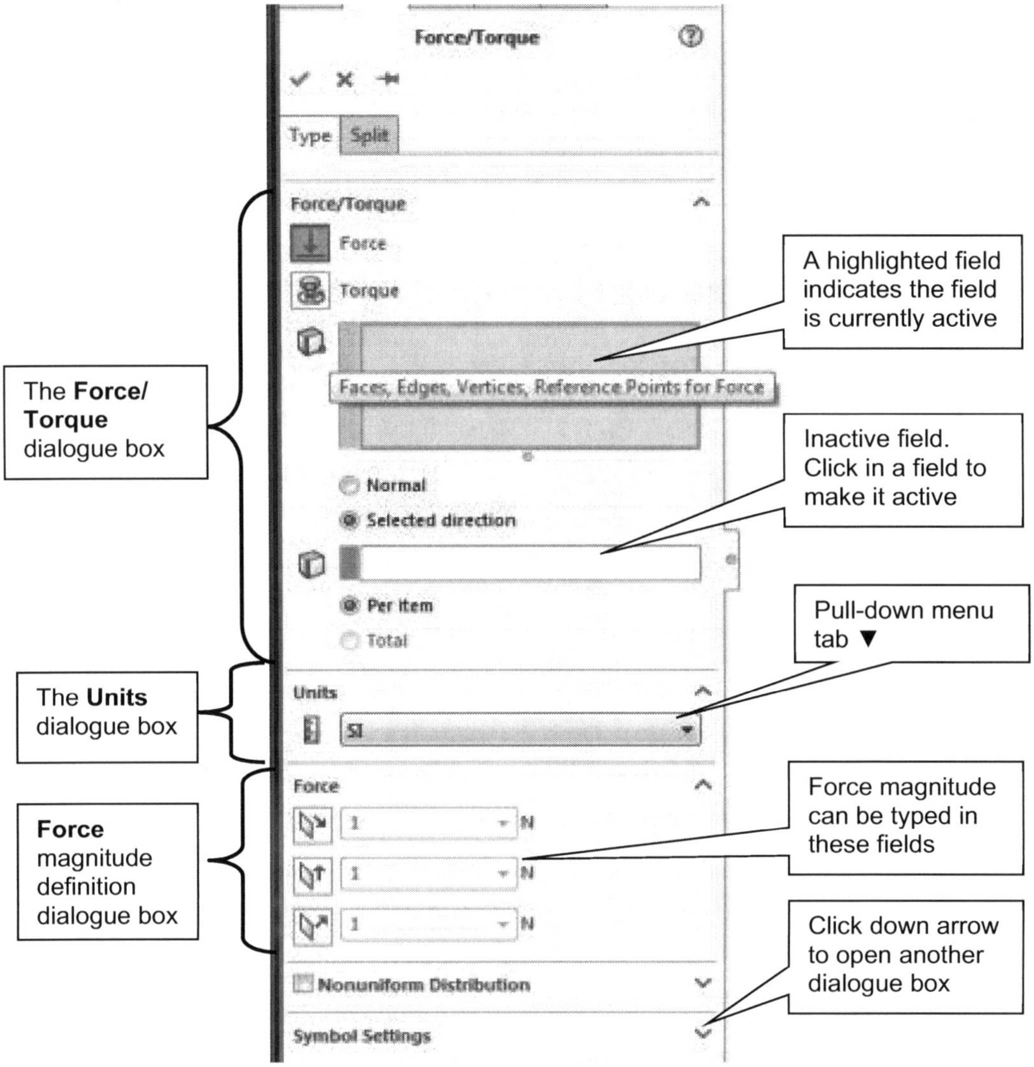

Figure 32– Overview of features common to property managers and dialogue boxes.

Each *property manager* contains several *dialogue boxes*. Five different dialogue boxes appear in the **Force/Torque** property manager shown above; they are **Force/Torque**, **Units**, **Force**, **Nonuniform Distribution**, and **Symbol Settings**. Dialogue boxes group related items in a single location and their names help the user quickly locate items to be defined.

For example, the **Force/Torque** dialogue box lists various types of forces or torques that can be selected by clicking within the ⊙ symbol to the left of a specific load type. Also within the **Force/Torque** dialogue box are two *fields*. Moving the cursor over a field, or the icon adjacent to a field, causes specific field information to appear much like prompts that occur for other Windows® icons. In Fig. 32, the prompt for the upper field is identified as "**Faces, Edges, Vertices, Reference Points for Force**." This field is also highlighted a light blue color (here shown in gray), which indicates it is currently "active" and awaiting user input.

Many dialogue boxes contain pull-down menus that can be accessed by clicking the symbol ▼ adjacent to a field. For example, the **Units** dialogue box in Fig. 32 permits the user to switch between **English (IPS)**, **SI**, or **Metric (G)** units. Some boxes, such as the **Force** dialogue box, permit the user to type a force value into a data box. And finally, as is often the case, insufficient space is available to display the contents of all dialogue boxes simultaneously. Therefore, only the titles of some dialogue boxes appear. In these instances, the user must click the ∨ symbol to display contents of a dialogue box. Such is the case for the ☐ **Nonuniform Distribution** and the **Symbol Settings** dialogue boxes located at the bottom of Fig. 32.

This completes the introduction to underlying fundamentals of finite element analysis and the SOLIDWORKS and SOLIDWORKS Simulation graphical user interfaces. Familiarize yourself with this work environment so that you are able to work comfortably within it.

Step-by-step examples focusing on the application of SOLIDWORKS Simulation to solve finite element modeling problems begin in the next chapter.

Cautions and Other Facts You Should Know

1. Always download example problems and end of chapter problems to the local hard drive of the computer being used. If problem files reside on a remote file server or a USB drive plugged into the computer, execution times that should take a matter of seconds could increase to forty minutes or more.

2. If a SOLIDWORKS Warning window, such as that shown in Fig. 33, appears when a model file is opened, simply click **[OK]** to dismiss the window. The fact that some models were created using the student version of SOLIDWORKS makes no difference; the model files are still valid.

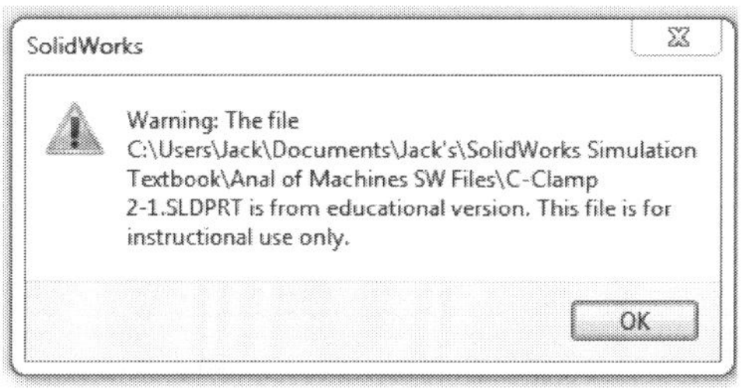

Figure 33 – This SOLIDWORKS warning window can be ignored.

3. Because many finite element results are displayed *graphically* and in *color*, SOLIDWORKS introduced a new color scale option for rendering Simulation

results to assist users with color vision deficiencies (especially red-green colorblindness). Menu selections for setting these options are as follows.

- In the **Default Options** dialog box, select **Plot** > **Color Chart** > **Color options** > **Optimized for Colorblindness**.

While viewing a **Stress Plot** or other graphical results, perform the following steps to switch to the new color scale option.

- Within the **Stress Plot** property manager, select the **Chart Options** *tab*, then click **v** to open the **Color Options** dialogue box. Click **▼** to open **Color Options** field (top field) and from the pull-down menu, select **Optimized for Colorblindness**.

It is suggested that colorblind users bookmark this page for future reference.

4. Because it yields more accurate results a new **Curvature Based Mesh**, shown in Fig. 34 (a), became the system default mesh in 2011. It is recommended for finite element analysis when using SOLIDWORKS Simulation. However, the majority of examples and problems encountered in the first several chapters of this text use a **Standard Mesh**. The reason for using a **Standard Mesh** is that it results in a more *orderly* mesh as illustrated in Fig. 34 (b). A more orderly mesh is useful when selecting nodes at specific locations on a model and to better approximate data along a straight line across a model, such as bending stress distribution from top to bottom of a beam in bending.

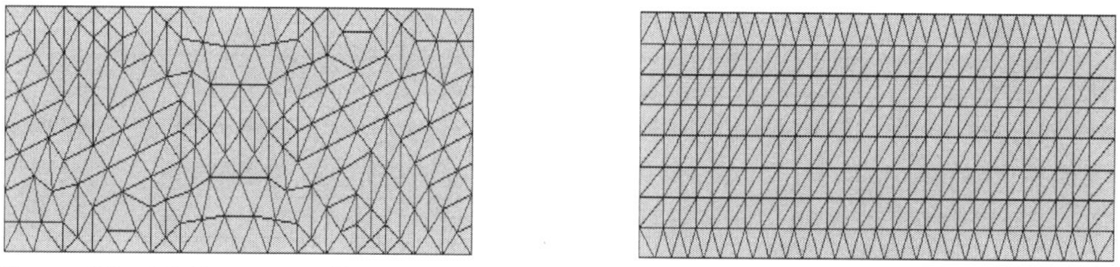

Figure 34 - (a) **Curvature Based Mesh** (b) **Standard Mesh**

5. Problem and exercise statements throughout this text indicate items such as a **Force** applied in the **X**, or **Y**, or **Z** direction. Always refer to the SOLIDWORKS coordinate system triad, Fig. 35, when uncertain about model orientation in the global X, Y, Z coordinate system.

Figure 35 – Cartesian Coordinate system Triad.

CHAPTER #1

STRESS ANALYSIS USING SOLIDWORKS SIMULATION

This chapter is intended to familiarize first-time users of SOLIDWORKS Simulation with basic software capabilities. Particular aspects of the software to be mastered are listed below. This example problem also serves as a model for subsequent Finite Element Analysis (FEA) problems because, once mastered, the sequence of steps is fairly consistent. These steps closely parallel the six learning objectives outlined below.

Learning Objectives

Upon completion of this unit, users should be able to:

- Create and execute a linear, static Finite Element Analysis (FEA). In SOLIDWORKS Simulation this process is named a *"Study."*
- Assign *Material Properties* using the material editor.
- Apply *Fixtures* (i.e., attachment to other bodies) and *External Loads* to a model.
- Use a *Standard Mesh* definition to subdivide a part into nodes and elements.
- Execute a standard *Solution* to a Finite Element Analysis problem.
- Selectively view appropriate stress *Results* of a Finite Element Analysis.
- Use the *Probe* feature to create graphs of stress variation within a part.
- Develop insight into practical decisions that influence how a *Study* is defined to obtain desired results.

Problem Statement

The goal of this example is to determine stresses in the reciprocating cam follower illustrated in Fig. 1. In particular, stresses to be determined are those in the circled region near the upper end of the cam follower where it passes through its support in the frame.

Positions of the cam and follower shown in Fig. 1 and Fig. 2 are assumed to correspond to the location of maximum cam pressure angle and maximum dynamic load on the cam follower. Although not shown here, a dynamic analysis should be performed using SOLIDWORKS Motion and the resulting loads applied to the model.

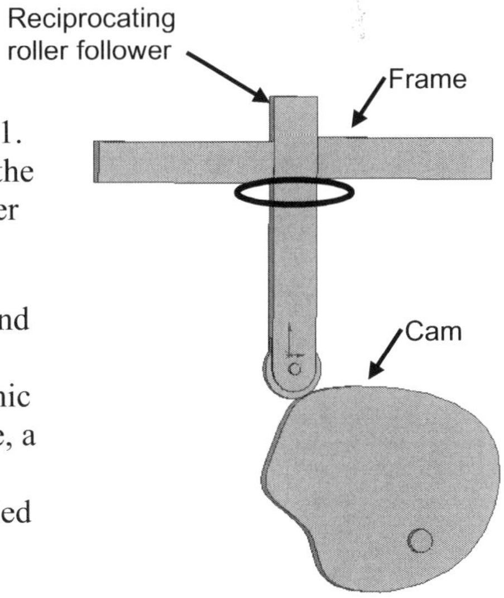

Figure 1 – Concept sketch showing the region of interest on the cam follower.

Figure 2 shows specific dimensions and loads applied to the cam follower. Force components $F_x = -368$ lb and $F_y = 1010$ lb exerted by the cam on the follower in the X and Y directions are applied on the roller-pin at the bottom of the follower. Because a static stress analysis is to be performed, the upper-end of the cam follower is considered "fixed," analogous to the fixed end of a cantilever beam, and corresponding reaction forces R_x, R_y, and a resisting moment M_z are shown at the upper support. We will soon discover one of these end conditions is not possible if solid tetrahedral elements are used to model the cam follower. Do you recall from the element description why this is true?

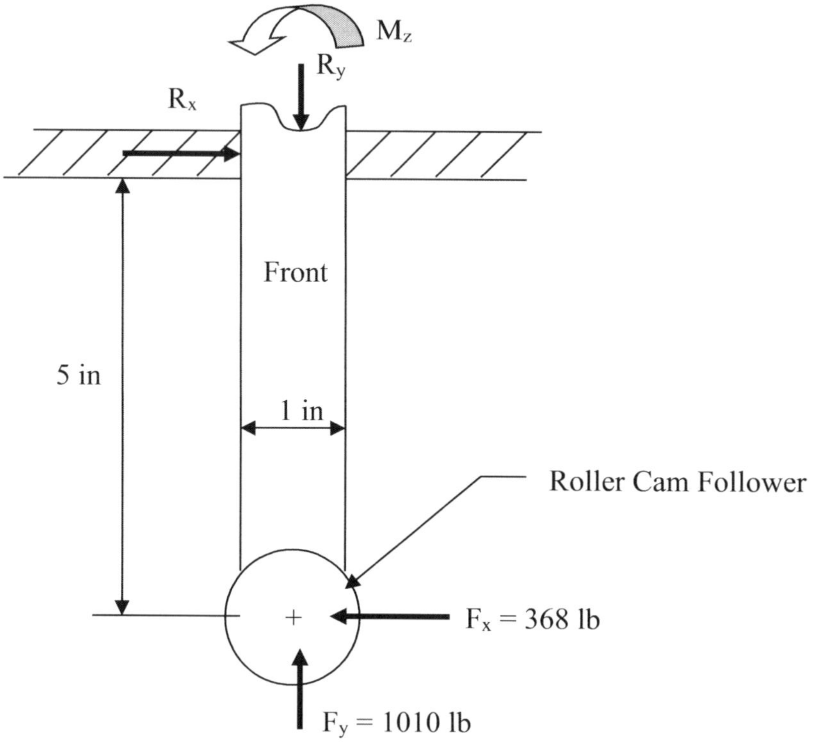

Figure 2 – Two-dimensional model of the reciprocating cam follower. The *Front* surface is labeled for later reference. The follower stem is ½ in thick into the page.

Design Insight

Although finite element programs are powerful computational tools, you should be aware that engineering assumptions are often necessary to advance the design process. In this example, at least three significant engineering assumptions are applied:

- The list of possible materials must be narrowed to a group that provides a strong yet heat-treatable class of steels. Heat treatment is important to produce a hard, long wearing surface for contact between the cam follower and frame in which it slides.
- Because the focus of this analysis is on stress at the *upper end* of the cam follower, modeling of the roller and its pin connection to the follower can be neglected thereby resulting in a considerable saving of modeling effort.

- Assuming that the upper end of the cam follower is "fixed" results in significant simplification for this initial example (i.e., a static rather than a dynamic analysis can be used).

Creating a Static Stress Analysis (Study)

Before proceeding, download and unzip chapter examples and end-of-chapter problems from the publisher's web site at:
www.SDCpublications.com/downloads/978-1-63057-787-2 (see pg. vii for complete details).

1. Open SOLIDWORKS by making the following selections. These steps are similar to opening any Windows program. (*NOTE:* The ">" symbol is used to separate successive menu selections.)

Start>All Programs>SOLIDWORKS 2026> SOLIDWORKS 2026 x64 Edition (OR) Click the **SOLIDWORKS** icon on your screen.

2. After SOLIDWORKS opens, in the main menu, select **File > Open…** and browse to the location where you saved the downloaded problem files. Click the file named **Cam Follower (Part)** and select **[Open]**. A model of the part appears in Fig. 3.

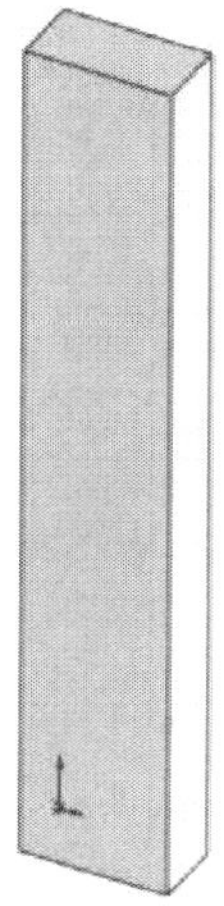

Figure 3 – Solid model of the cam follower.

If a pop-up SOLIDWORKS window appears and states: **Warning: The File C:\Users\Nudehi\Documents\ . . . etc. . . . xxx.SLDPRT is from educational version. This file is for instructional use only**, click **[OK]** to close the window.

NOTE: If SOLIDWORKS **Simulation** is not listed in the main menu of the SOLIDWORKS screen, then in the main menu click **Tools** > **Add-Ins…** Next, in the **Add-Ins** window place check marks "✓" in *both* the left *and* right columns adjacent to ☑ **SOLIDWORKS Simulation** ☑ then click **[OK]** to close the **Add-Ins** window. The **SOLIDWORKS Simulation** License Agreement appears *(for first-time users only).* Click **[Accept]**.

At this point, **Simulation** is added to the main menu displayed at the top of the screen. If the main menu is not displayed, go to the bottom of page I-13 of the Introduction and perform steps 1 and 2. In fact, if the graphical user interface is not set up as outlined on pages I-14 through I-21 of the Introduction, it is *strongly recommended* to do so at this time because instructions below are based on the work environment defined there.

---

3. In the main menu, select **Simulation**. Then from the pull-down menu select **Study...** Alternatively, in the **Simulation** *tab*, near top-left of the graphics area, click the down arrow ▼ beneath the **New Study** icon and from the pull-down menu select **New Study**. A partial view of the **Study** property manager opens as shown in Fig. 4.

4. In the **Name** dialogue box, replace "**Static 1**" by typing a descriptive name. For this example, type "**Cam Follower #1**" as the Study name.

5. Next, in the **Type** dialogue box, verify that the system default **Static** analysis icon appears shaded to indicate it is selected. If not, click to select it. Make sure the **Use 2D Simplification** is unchecked. Our part is a 3D model, and we don't want to simplify (approximate) the analysis by assuming a 2D stress/strain domain to save simulation time.

6. Click **[OK]** ✓ (the green check mark) to close the **Study** property manager.

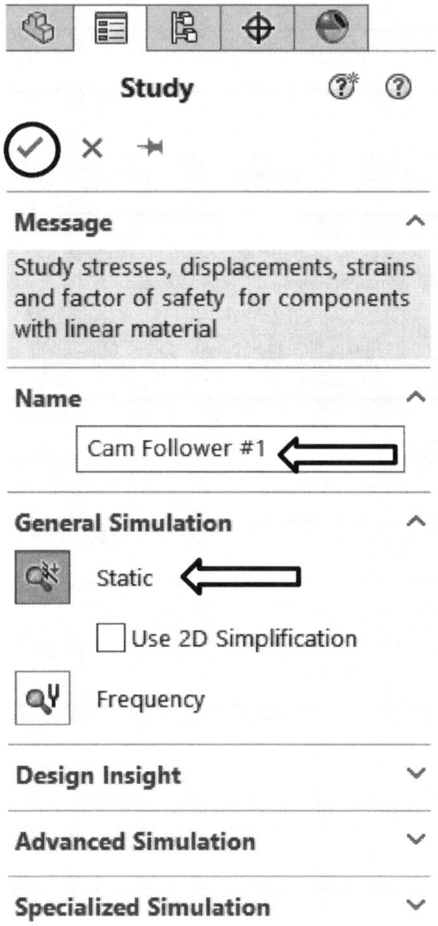

Figure 4 – Initial selections shown in the **Study** property manager.

After completing the above steps, an outline of the current SOLIDWORKS Simulation Study is created in the boxed area of Fig. 5. The SOLIDWORKS feature manager, which contains steps used to construct the solid model, appears above the boxed area.

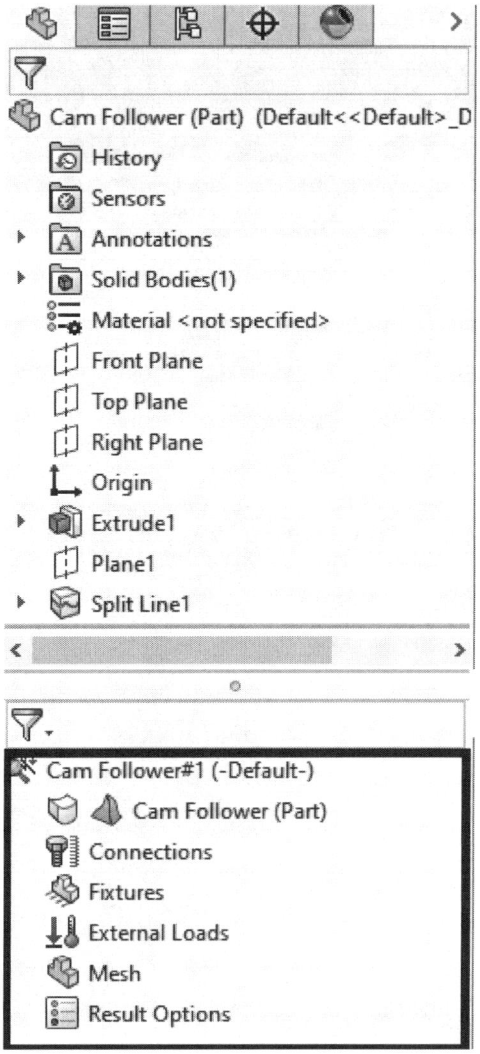

Figure 5 – The **SOLIDWORKS Simulation** manager showing various components used to define a Study.

The Study name, **Cam Follower#1 (-Default-)**, appears at the top of the box. Beneath this name is the **Cam Follower (Part)** folder.

Also shown are:

a. the **Connections** folder; this is where interactions between parts are defined. Connections are not applicable in this example because only one part exists.

b. next is the **Fixtures** folder where restraints are applied to the model,

c. next is the **External Loads** folder where forces, torques, pressures, etc. are applied to a model;

d. the **Mesh** folder appears next. This is where a finite element mesh is created, controlled, and applied to the model.

e. and finally, the **Result Options** folder appears at the bottom of the list. It is not used in this example.

The finite element analysis steps listed in Fig. 5 proceed in a logical order from beginning to end of a Study. Thus, this sequence is followed in all subsequent examples. It is, however, worth noting that these steps can be executed in any order.

Assigning Material to the Model

Begin by defining the material of which the cam follower is made. To do this, proceed as follows. *NOTE: For simplicity in the remainder of this text, the SOLIDWORKS Simulation manager will be referred to simply as the "Simulation manager."*

1. In the Simulation manager *right*-click the **Cam Follower (Part)** folder; see Fig. 6, and from the pull-down menu, select **Apply/Edit Material…** The **Material** window opens as shown in Fig. 7.

2. In the left-hand column of the **Material** window, do the following:

   a) Click the " > " adjacent to **SOLIDWORKS Materials** circled in Fig. 7 (if not already selected).

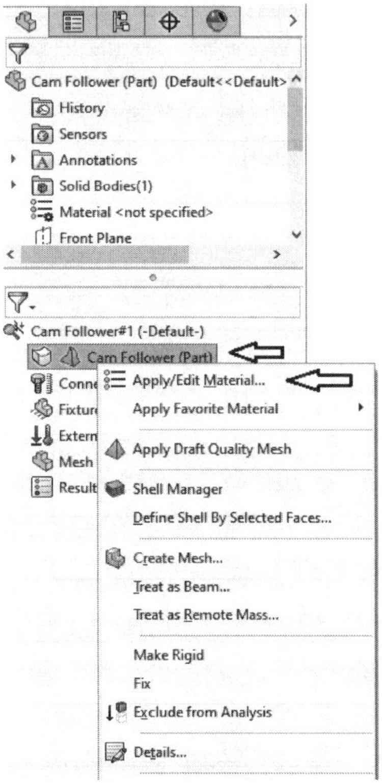

Figure 6 – Selecting the part to which material properties are assigned.

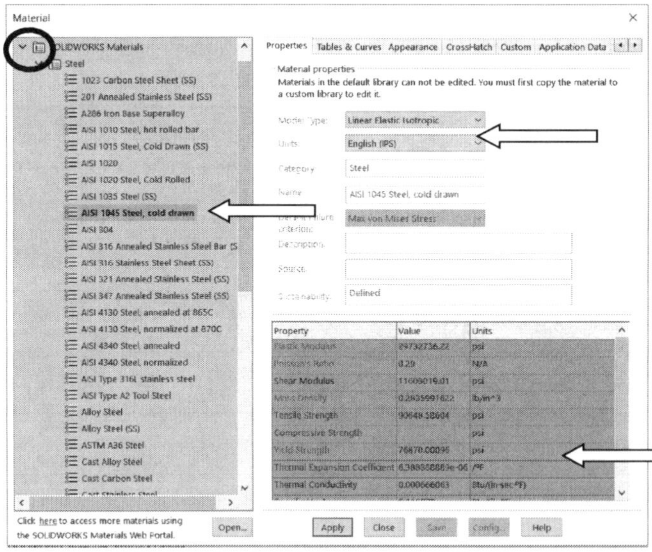

Figure 7 – Material properties of a part are specified in the **Material** window.

   b) Next, click the " > " adjacent to **Steel** (if not already selected) and scroll down the list to select **AISI 1045 Steel, cold drawn**. Immediately, properties of 1045 steel appear in the right half of the table.

c) On the **Properties** *tab*, click ✓ to open the **Units:** pull-down menu. From the list of possible units, select the **English (IPS)**, where IPS indicates units of inches, pounds, and seconds.

Familiarize yourself with information in this table by reading **Property** names listed in the left-hand column and their corresponding magnitudes in the **Value** column. For example, **Yield Strength** = **76870 psi** for AISI 1045 cold drawn steel. Typically, values shown in English units, like yield strength, appear at greater precision than is truly known. This fallacy results because S.I. units are default within Simulation and extra digits frequently occur when values are converted to English units. Examine other material properties listed in the table to become familiar with the types of data available.

3. Click **[Apply]** followed by **[Close]** to close the **Material** window. In the Simulation manager tree, a green check mark "✓" now appears on the **Cam Follower (Part)** icon and **(-AISI 1045 Steel, cold drawn-)** is listed next to the part name. The check mark indicates that material properties have been defined.

Applying Fixtures

Restraints must be applied to stabilize and support the model as it is supported in its actual application. In this example, the top surface of the model, i.e., the location where the cam follower enters the frame, is assumed to be "fixed." This restraint is consistent with a cam follower whose upper end is located in a near-zero clearance slot in the frame and for which a static analysis is assumed. Define fixtures for the model as follows.

1. In the Simulation manager, right-click **Fixtures**, then from the pull-down menu select **Fixed Geometry…** The **Fixture** property manager appears as shown in Fig. 8. Also, the **Example** dialogue box contains an animation depicting the effect of this type of restraint.

2. Within the **Type** tab, locate the **Standard (Fixed Geometry)** dialogue box and select the **Fixed Geometry** icon (if not already selected). This option sets all translations in X, Y, and Z directions to zero. From the Introduction, recall that tetrahedral elements, used to model solid parts, allow only three degrees of freedom (three translations) at each node.

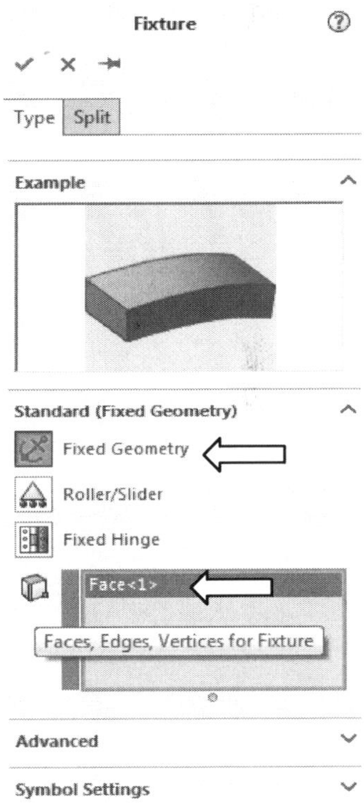

Figure 8 - Selection made in the **Fixture** property manager

As with other Windows® operations, placing the cursor over an icon causes a brief description of the icon to be displayed. Placing the cursor on the icon located to the left of the light-blue colored field in the **Standard (Fixed Geometry)** dialogue box reveals that **Faces, Edges, Vertices for Fixture** can be selected as entities to which restraints can be applied. In this example the top surface of the cam follower is selected as described next.

The light-blue color indicates that the **Faces, Edges, Vertices for Fixture** field is *active* and waiting for the user to specify what part of the model is to be designated as **Fixed**. If, in the following step, selecting the top surface of the model is difficult due to its orientation or size, use the graphics controls to rotate, and/or zoom-in on its top surface. If rotate or zoom icons are used, press **[Esc]** to return to the standard cursor (pointer).

3. Move the cursor over the model and when the top *surface* is indicated by a small green square next to the cursor *and* when **Fixture** symbols appear on the top surface, click to select the surface.

Fixture symbols appear as arrows in the X, Y, and Z directions as shown in Fig. 9 and an information "flag" labels the surface as **Fixed Geometry:**. Also, the notation **Face<1>** now appears in the **Fixture** property manager as shown at the lower arrow in Fig. 8.

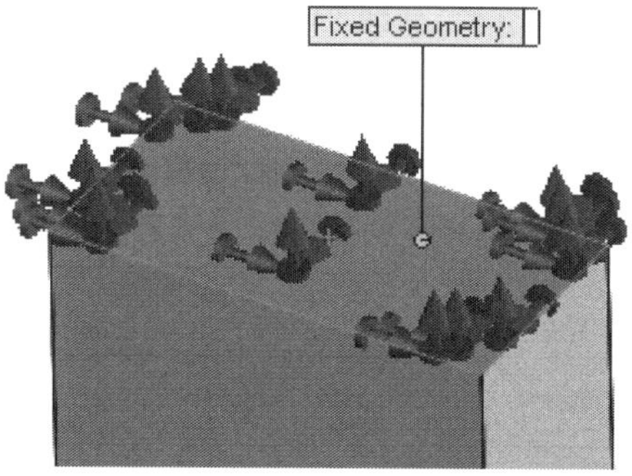

Figure 9 – **Fixed** restraint applied to top surface of the cam follower model.

NOTE: If the *bottom* surface (surface with a line on it) or an edge, vertex, or other surface of the model is selected incorrectly, right-click the incorrect item in the dialogue box (light blue field) and from the pop-up menu, select **Delete**. Then repeat step #3.

4. To change color or size of the restraint symbols, click the down-arrow ⌄ to open the **Symbol Settings** dialogue box located at the bottom of the **Fixture** property manager. Next click the **[Edit Color…]** button to open a color palette. Select the desired color and click **[OK]**. In this example, you are encouraged to leave the fixture color as pre-defined because additional symbols, applied to the model later in this analysis, use different default colors to differentiate fixtures from applied loads. To change symbol size, click the up or down arrows adjacent to the **Symbol Size** spin box. Fixture symbols in Fig. 9 were increased in size to 120 and their color changed for emphasis.

5. Click **[OK]** ✓ (green check mark) at top of the **Fixture** property manager to accept this restraint. The above steps render the top face of the cam follower **Immovable** and create an icon named **Fixed-1** beneath the **Fixtures** folder in the Simulation manager. Click ▶ adjacent to **Fixtures** if the icon is not shown.

Aside:
It is important to note that, although the **Fixture** property manager allows the user to specify **Fixed** restraints at desired locations on a model, the effect of this restraint type produces different restraints when applied to different element types. However, the software recognizes the type of element to which the restraints are applied (solid model [tetrahedral elements], shell elements, truss elements, or beam elements), and applies the proper fixture to each element type.

In the case of a solid model, such as the cam follower, application of **Fixed** restraints prevents translations of the top surface in the X, Y, and Z directions. This type of restraint is referred to as being "immovable" because it prevents only three degrees of freedom at each node selected on the model. Note that the moment acting on top of the cam follower in Fig. 2 is *not* restrained by immovable restraints.

Future examples will reveal that **Fixed** restraints, when applied to shell or beam elements, not only prohibit node translations in the X, Y, and Z directions, but also restrict (i.e., prevent) rotational displacements (i.e., moments) about the X, Y, and Z axes at each restrained node. A shell mesh is investigated in Chapter 4.

Applying External Loads

Following the sequence of steps listed in the Simulation manager, we next apply external forces to the model. Proceed by defining the X and Y force components, one at a time, that act at the bottom center of the cam follower. Begin by applying the vertical component of force F_y = 1010 lb that acts upward on the bottom of the cam follower. Proceed as follows.

1. In the Simulation manager, right-click the **External Loads** folder and from the pull-down menu, select **Force…** The **Force/Torque** property manager appears in Fig. 10.

2. Under the **Type** tab in the **Force/Torque** property manager, click the **Force** icon (if not already selected, indicated by a darker gray).

3. Beneath the light blue colored field, click to choose ⊙ **Selected direction**. This choice is made to define the direction of the Y-force component in step 5 below.

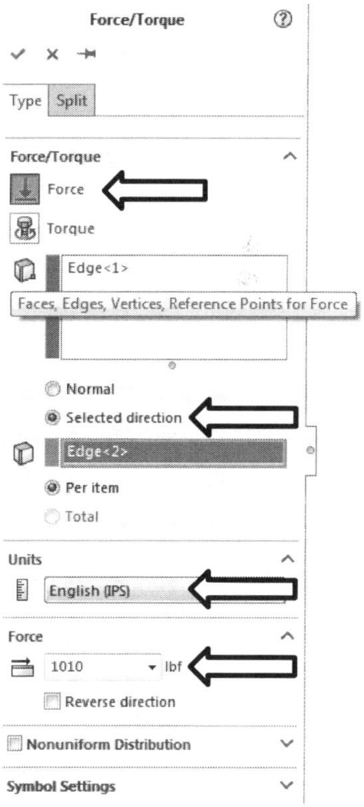

Figure 10 - Definition of force F_y acting on a *Split Line*.

4. In the **Force/Torque** dialogue box, place the cursor in the upper field. If the field does not appear light-blue, click within the box to change its color. Placing the cursor over this box reveals the message, **Faces, Edges, Vertices, Reference Points for Force**. This text prompts the user to select the entity to which the Y-component of force is to be applied. In the graphics area, rotate the model and zoom-in on the bottom face. Notice that a line is located at the center of the bottom surface. As you move the cursor onto this line, the message *(Split Line1)* should appear. Click to select this line since it is desired to place both X and Y force components at the center of the bottom face. After selecting *(Split Line1)*, **Edge<1>** appears in the top field of the **Force/Torque** dialogue box, shown in Fig. 10. *(If any other entity appears in this field, right-click it and select* ***Delete****.)*

5. Next, click inside the bottom field in the **Force/Torque** dialogue box. This action changes the field color from white to light blue. Placing the cursor on this field prompts the user to select a **Face, Edge, Plane for Direction**. In other words, to indicate the direction of the Y-force component it is necessary to select a face, edge, or plane oriented in the desired direction. Click to select *any vertical* **Edge**, of the model shown in Fig. 11. **Edge<2>** should appear in the active field and force vectors should appear on *Split Line 1*. Ignore incorrect Y-directions at this time. If force vectors do not appear, proceed to the next step; otherwise skip to step 7.

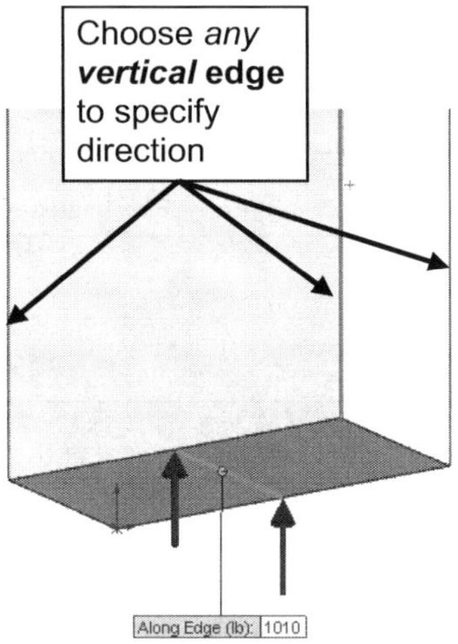

Figure 11 – Vertical force components and the edge used to specify direction of the force acting on Split Line1.

6. Click ⌄ to open the **Symbol Settings** dialogue box located at the very bottom of the **Force/Torque** property manager. Toggle the ☑ **Show preview** check mark "off" and "on" again to display the force vectors.

7. Next, within the **Units** dialogue box select ⌄ to open the pull-down menu to set **Units** to **English (IPS)** (if not already selected).

8. In the **Force** dialogue box, type **1010**, which indicates magnitude of the Y-force component. Examine the direction of vectors appearing in the graphic image and if they are not directed toward the top of the model, check ☑ **Reverse direction.**

9. Click **[OK]** ✓ (green check mark) to accept this force definition and close the **Force/Torque** property manager. SOLIDWORKS Simulation applies the 1010 lb force to the model and creates an icon named Force-1 (:Per item: -1010 lbf:) beneath the **External Loads** folder in the Simulation manager tree.

10. Next, apply the X-force component (F_x = -368 lb) to *Split Line 1* on the bottom of the cam follower. Try this on your own using a procedure similar to the preceding steps. Alternately, a listing of commands is provided below for those desiring guidance.

11. In the Simulation manager tree, right-click the **External Loads** folder and select **Force...** The **Force/Torque** property manager opens.

12. In the **Force/Torque** dialogue box, choose ⊙ **Selected direction**.

13. Click to activate (light blue) the upper field where **Faces, Edges, Vertices, Reference Points for Force** prompts the user to indicate where the force is to be applied. Again, select *Split Line1*. The line is highlighted and **Edge <1>** appears in the active field.

14. Click to activate (light blue) the **Face**, **Edge**, **Plane for Direction** field and proceed to select *any* edge of the model parallel to the X-direction (i.e., parallel to the 1-inch dimension of the cam follower). After selecting an edge, **Edge<2>** appears in the direction field and force vectors in the X-direction appear on *Split Line1*. Ignore incorrect direction at this time.

15. In the **Units** dialogue box set the **Units** field to **English (IPS)** (if necessary).

16. In the **Force** dialogue box, type **368** to define magnitude of the X-force component. If necessary, check ☑ **Reverse direction** to orient force components in the negative X-direction.

17. When the X force component appears as shown in Fig. 12, click **[OK]** ✓ to accept this force and close the **Force/Torque** property manager.

18. A new icon named Force-2 (:Per item: -368 lbf:) appears beneath the **External Loads** folder.

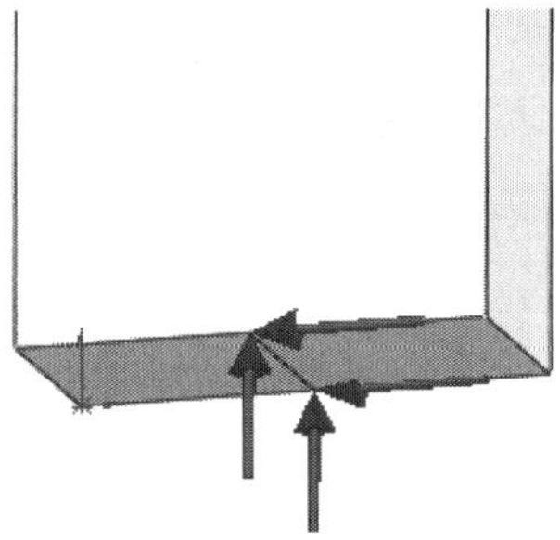

Figure 12 – Front view of cam follower showing force components F_x and F_y applied to the *Split Line 1*.

The model is now complete as far as material property, restraint, and force definitions are concerned. The next step is to Mesh the model as described in the following section.

Aside #1:
Split lines are frequently encountered in the study of SOLIDWORKS. But, this example does not review how they are applied. However, they are also extremely useful in Finite Element Analysis, and for that reason, their application is reviewed in future chapters.

Aside #2:
As noted in the **Design Insight** section at the beginning of this example, stresses at the *upper end* of the cam follower are to be investigated. For this reason, the simplified assumption of force loading at the center of the lower end of the model, where the roller is attached to the follower, might be deemed acceptable. After all, why devote considerable time and effort to model contact stress between the roller-pin and cam follower *if* the focus of analysis is to determine stresses elsewhere in the model? On the other hand, if the focus of this analysis were on stresses in the vicinity of the pin that joins the roller to the cam follower, then details of that geometry must be included in the model. Contact stress between a pin and a hole is investigated in Chapter 6.

Meshing the Model

The final task in preparing the model for analysis is to generate a finite element mesh in the solid model. This section explores the meshing process.

1. In the Simulation manager, right-click the **Mesh** icon and from the pull-down menu, select Create Mesh.... The **Mesh** property manager opens. A partial view of this property manager is shown in Fig. 13.

The **Mesh Density** dialogue box shows a pointer on a sliding scale between **Coarse** and **Fine** mesh sizes. The default setting performs an initial analysis with mesh size set midway between these two extremes.

To learn more about the units, mesh size, and tolerance of the current mesh click to place a check mark "✓" to open the ☑ **Mesh Parameters** dialogue box circled in Fig. 13. At the top of this dialogue box, select ⦿ **Standard mesh** because an *orderly* mesh is desired. Next, inches (**in**) should appear in the **Unit** field. If not, change units by accessing ⌄ to open the **Unit** pull-down menu.

Also, within the **Mesh Parameters** dialogue box observe the **Global Size** of the mesh indicated in the middle field as **0.13576659in**. This value represents the diameter of an *unseen* sphere that circumscribes (surrounds) a typical tetrahedral element in the three-dimensional model. Element size is automatically determined based on geometric features of the model. Values may vary slightly.

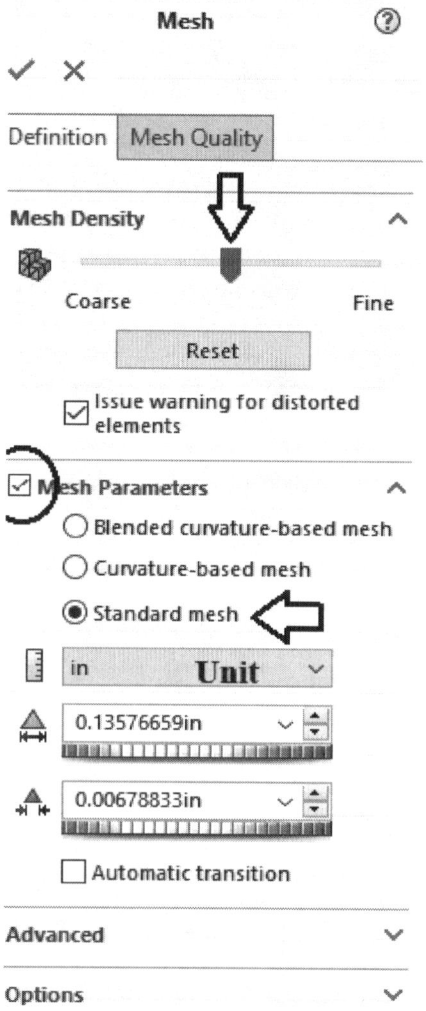

Figure 13- Mesh parameters; can be altered in the **Mesh** property manager.

The third field from the top indicates the mesh **Tolerance**, which is 5% of the global mesh size. In cases where the automatic mesher fails to mesh a model, increasing the tolerance may help. **Tolerance** allows lengths of element sides to deviate from the exact **Global Size** so that the mesh is able to conform to curvature and other irregularities present in geometrically complex models. Default values usually provide sufficient definition of element size to yield acceptable results for an initial finite element analysis.

Although the **Mesh** property manager is essentially unchanged in this example, its use in modifying mesh size is investigated in Chapter 3.

2. Click **[OK]** ✓ to accept the default values and close the **Mesh** property manager.

Meshing starts automatically and the **Mesh Progress** window appears briefly (< 2 sec). After meshing is complete, SOLIDWORKS Simulation displays the meshed model as shown in Fig. 14. Also, a green check mark "✓" appears on the **Mesh** icon in the Simulation manager tree to indicate meshing is complete.

3. To display mesh information, *right*-click the **Mesh** folder and select **Details…** The **Mesh Details** window opens and is also shown in Fig. 14.

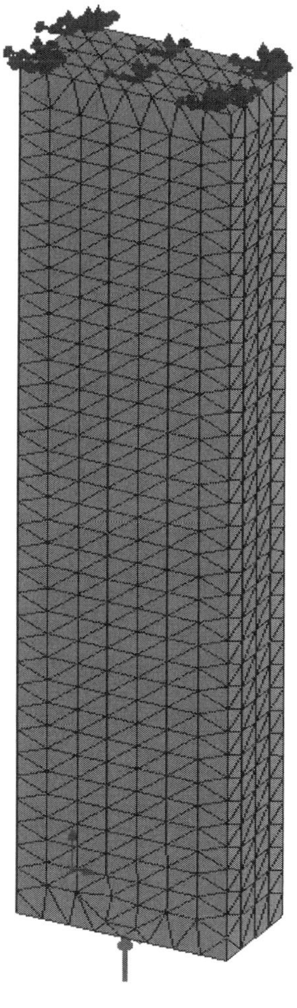

The **Mesh Details** window displays information about the current model such as its **Study name**, **Mesh type (Solid Mesh)**, **Mesher Used (Standard mesh)**, …, **Element size**, **Tolerance** values and other data is repeated. Scroll down in this window and notice that approximately 10539 **Total nodes** and 6546 **Total elements** are created for this model. Because the automatic meshing software attempts to create an optimal mesh for each model, the number of nodes and elements may vary slightly between alternate meshing of complex models.

4. Click ☒ to close the **Mesh Details** window.

Mesh Details

Study name	Cam Follower#1 (-Default-)
Mesh type	Solid Mesh
Mesher Used	Standard mesh
Automatic Transition	Off
Include Mesh Auto Loops	Off
Jacobian points for High quality mesh	16 points
Element size	0.135767 in
Tolerance	0.00678833 in
Mesh quality	High
Total nodes	10539
Total elements	6546
Maximum Aspect Ratio	3.1862
Percentage of elements with Aspect Ratio < 3	100
Percentage of elements with Aspect Ratio > 10	0

Figure 14 – Cam follower with mesh and boundary conditions illustrated. Also shown is the **Mesh Details** window where mesh information can be reviewed.

5. To hide the mesh, right-click **Mesh** and from the pull-down menu select **Hide Mesh**. Conversely, selecting **Show Mesh** in the pull-down menu returns the mesh display to the model. Try this option but Hide the mesh before continuing.

> **Aside:**
> As noted earlier, it is permissible to define material properties, fixtures, external loads, and create the mesh in *any order*. However, all these *necessary* steps must be completed prior to running the Solution portion of a Study.

Running the Solution

After the model has been completely defined, we are ready to proceed to the *Solution* process. This is the second major portion of a finite element program. It is where the numerous equations that define a Study are solved. For all of its complexity, this portion of a Finite Element Analysis is, perhaps, most deceiving in terms of its seeming simplicity from the user's perspective. Time required for an analysis can vary from several seconds to several hours depending upon overall model complexity and the computer hardware used. Most examples in this text should solve in a matter of seconds to five minutes at most. To solve the current example, proceed as follows.

1. To run an analysis, right-click **Cam Follower #1 (-Default-)** located at the top of the Simulation manager tree. Refer to highlighted text at upper arrow in Fig. 15.

2. From the pull-down menu, select **Run** and the solution process begins automatically. A window that tracks progress of the Solution appears, but due to the small size of this example, it is displayed only briefly.

After successful solution of this static analysis, SOLIDWORKS Simulation creates a new folder, named "**Results**," at the bottom of the Simulation manager tree. This folder *may* contain multiple sub-folders, but *only the three sub-folders, shown boxed in Fig. 15,* contain default plots resulting from analysis of the current model. If these folders do *not* appear, follow steps (a) through (f) outlined on the next page. Otherwise skip to the section titled "**Examination of Results**."

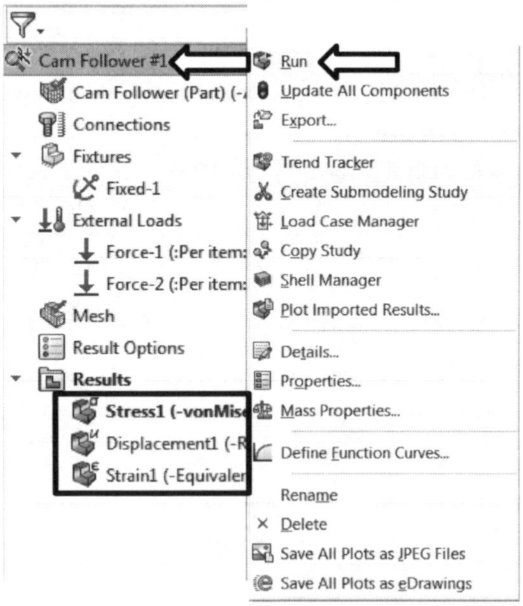

Figure 15 – **Results** folders created as part of the Solution process. Each folder contains solution information indicated by its name.

a) Right-click the **Results** folder and from the pull-down menu, select **Define Stress Plot…** The **Stress Plot** property manager opens.

b) In the **Display** dialogue box, select **VON: von Mises Stress** from the pull-down menu (if not already selected).

c) Also in the **Display** dialogue box, verify that **Units** are set to **psi**. If not, click ⌄ from the **Units** pull-down menu and select **psi** as the units used to display results.

d) Click **[OK]** ✓ to close the **Stress Plot** property manager and immediately a plot of von Mises stress is displayed in the graphics area.

e) Repeat steps (a) through (d), but in step (a) select **Define Displacement Plot…**; in step (b) accept the default display named **URES: Resultant Displacement**; in step (c) change the **Units** pull-down menu to inches (**in**); and in step (d) click **[OK]**✓.

f) Repeat steps (a) through (d) a third time, but in step (a) select **Define Strain Plot…**; in step (b) accept the default display item named **ESTRN: Equivalent Strain**; in step (c) take no action because strain is unitless; and in step (d) click **[OK]**✓. The three sub-folders should now appear beneath the **Results** folder.

Examination of Results

The third major part of a finite element analysis (FEA) is examination of calculated results. The outcome of an analysis, in the form of graphs, plots, and data, can be viewed by accessing computed output stored in the various **Results** folders. These results are the ultimate goal of a finite element analysis. It is where validity of finite element calculations should be investigated by cross-checking them against manual calculations or other verifiable experimental or reference results. *Checking computed results is a necessary step in good engineering practice!*

Understanding Default Graphical Results

1. If a color plot of **Stress1 (-vonMises-)** is *not* displayed on the graphics screen, then right-click the folder labeled **Stress1 (-vonMises-)** and from the pull-down menu select **Show**. Alternatively, double-click the name **Stress1 (-vonMises-)**.

2. In the Simulation manager, right-click **Stress1 (-vonMises-)** and from the pull-down menu, select **Edit Definition...** The **Stress Plot** property manager opens.

3. In the **Display** dialogue box, verify that **Units** are set to **psi**. If not, click ⌄ to open the **Units** pull-down menu and select **psi** as shown in Fig. 16.

4. Next click ⌄ to open the **Advanced Options** dialogue box and verify ⊙ **Node Values** is selected.

5. If necessary, check "✓" to open the ☑ **Deformed Shape** dialogue box. Then, click to activate ⊙ **Automatic** as shown in Fig. 16.

6. Click **[OK]** ✓ to close the **Stress Plot** property manager.

The above actions cause a deformed view of the cam follower along with a color-coded plot of the von Mises stress distribution to be displayed on the model as shown in Fig. 17 and on your screen.

Default information provided near the top of the graphics screen, circled in Fig. 17, includes:

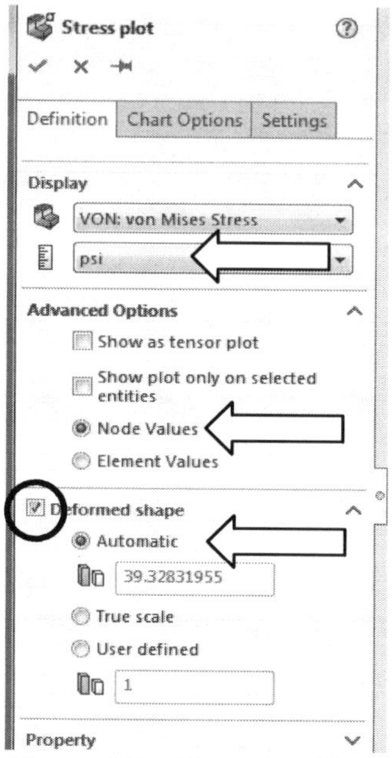

Figure 16 – Changing **Units** and **Deformed Shape** of the model in the **Stress Plot** property manager.

- **Model name:** ← Contains the name of the SOLIDWORKS model opened from the parts file at the beginning of this example; it is named "**Cam Follower (Part)**."

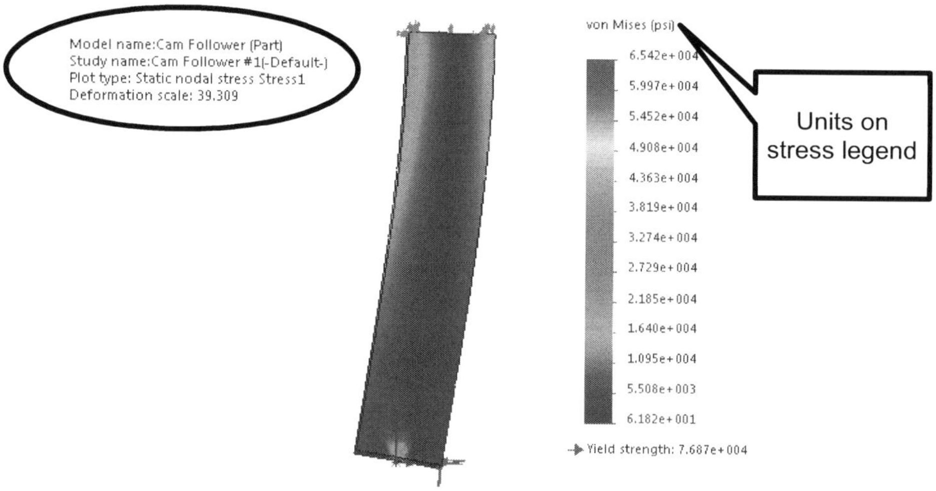

Figure 17 – Default plot of von Mises stress distribution throughout the cam follower. Stress is shown in English units (psi). NOTE: Stress values may be expressed in floating point or scientific notation. Number formatting is covered in a later chapter.

- **Study name:** ← Lists the name you typed into the **Study** property manager at the start of this example. If previous instructions were followed precisely, this name should appear as "**Cam Follower #1**."

- **Plot type:** ← Should indicate "**Static nodal stress Stress1**"

- **Deformation Scale:** ← To illustrate a deformed shape, SOLIDWORKS Simulation scales the maximum deformation of the model to 10% of the diagonal of a bounding box around the model (this box is not visible). A number representing the magnitude of the **Deformation scale** for the current model appears on the bottom line. This value indicates that the part image is deformed 39.309 *times larger* than its actual deformation (values may vary). The intent of a deformed model is to aid visualization of part deflection and does *not* represent the actual deformation magnitude.

- Also appearing on the plot is a color-coded stress scale. Stress magnitudes at various locations throughout the model can be determined by matching colors to those of the color-coded stress scale. Red traditionally corresponds to high stress while dark blue corresponds to *algebraically lower* stress magnitudes.

Results Predicted by Classical Stress Equations

It is assumed that some users may not yet be familiar with von Mises stress.[1] Therefore, the discussion below digresses to examine *other*, more fundamental, stresses that occur within the cam follower model. To accomplish this, a brief but thorough solution to the current problem is included based on use of classical stress equations.

Begin by recalling the original free-body diagram of the cam follower shown in Fig. 2. That figure revealed the part is subject to force components in both the X and Y directions on its lower end. The upward acting force component $F_y = 1010$ lb causes an axial compressive stress in the Y-direction given by $\sigma_y = F_y/A$. Although this stress is shown near the lower end of the cam follower in Fig. 18, classic stress equations assume it is *uniformly distributed* throughout the model from top to bottom. Similarly, the X-component of force, $F_x = -368$ lb that acts perpendicular to the length of the cam follower, causes bending stress given by $\sigma_y = Mc/I$ as shown at the top of the model in Fig. 18. Bending stress is maximum at the top of the model due to maximum length (5 in) of the moment arm acted upon by the X-component of force F_x which is applied at the bottom of the cam follower. Review stress calculations included on Fig. 18 before proceeding. Recall the cam follower is 1.00-in wide by 0.50-in thick.
Because all stresses depicted on Fig. 18 act in the Y-direction, they can be combined simply by adding magnitudes of axial and bending stresses provided proper $\pm$ signs are included. Combining these stresses yields the following results:

[1] It is presumed that use of this SOLIDWORKS Simulation user guide will be introduced near the beginning of a Design of Machine Elements or Mechanics of Materials course. However, most traditional textbooks on these subjects delay introduction of von Mises stress until later chapters. For this reason, early examples in this user guide involve stresses that are more familiar to individuals who have completed a fundamental mechanics of materials course.

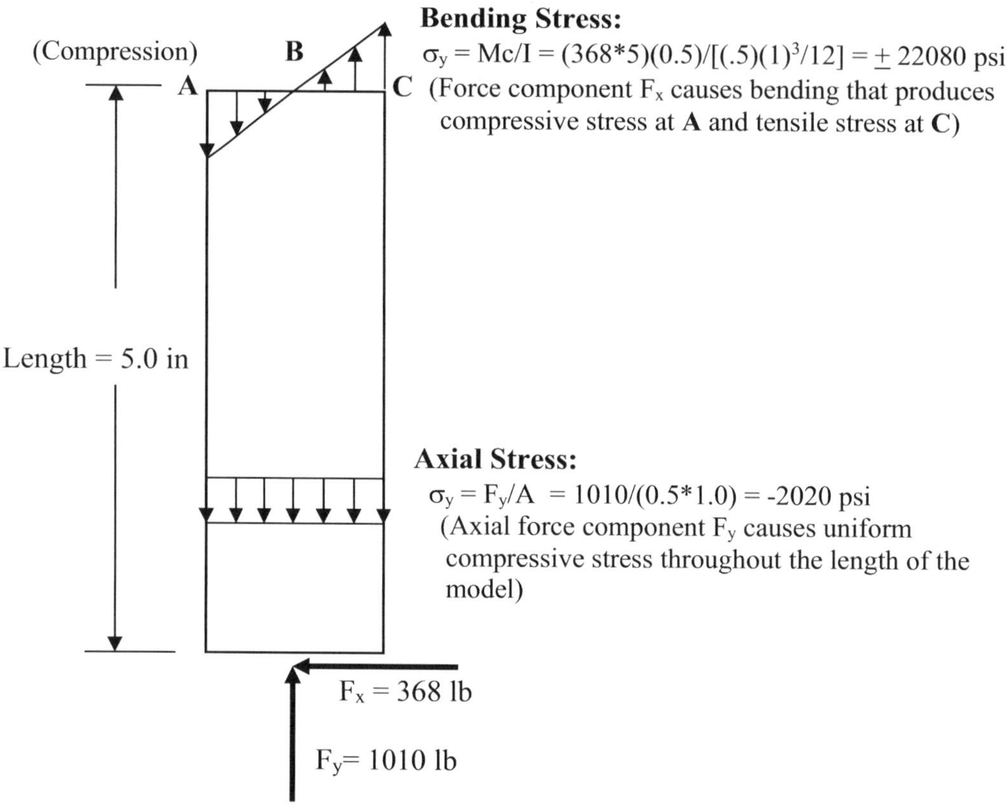

Figure 18 – Schematic of loading and distribution of bending stress (compression on left-side and tension on right-side) and axial stress (compression) in the Y-direction on the cam follower determined using classic stress equations.

Stresses at points **A**, **B**, and **C** *combine* as described below.

Stress at point **A** is in compression due to both axial and bending stresses, thus:

Stress at point **A**: $(\sigma_y)_A = \sigma_{Axial} + \sigma_{Bending} = (-2020) + (-22080) = -24{,}100$ psi

Stress at point **B** is in compression due to axial stress, but bending stress is zero on the neutral axis, thus:

Stress at point **B**: $(\sigma_y)_B = \sigma_{Axial} + \sigma_{Bending} = (-2020) + (0) = -2{,}020$ psi

Stress at point **C** is compressive due to axial stress, but acts in tension due to bending stress. Because the tensile "+" bending stress is greater than the compressive "-" axial stress, the resultant stress at point **C** is:

Stress at point **C**: $(\sigma_y)_C = \sigma_{Axial} + \sigma_{Bending} = (-2020) + (+22080) = +20{,}060$ psi

Simulation Results for Stress in Y-Direction

The above results are next compared with those determined using the finite element analysis performed in this chapter. To do so, it is meaningful to produce a plot of normal stress in the Y-direction (i.e., σ_y). Proceed as follows.

1. In the Simulation manager, right-click the **Results** folder and from the pull-down menu select **Define Stress Plot…** The **Stress Plot** property manager opens as shown in Fig. 19. The property manager does not initially look like Fig. 18.

2. In the **Display** dialogue box, click ⌄ to open the pull-down menu adjacent to the **Component** field. This field shows that **VON: von Mises Stress** is initially selected. From the list of stresses available in the pull-down menu, select **SY: Y Normal Stress**. This selection identifies normal stress in the Y-direction, commonly represented by σ_y, as the stress to be displayed in a new plot. This is the *same* stress previously determined using classical equations.

For future reference it is informative to observe all the other stresses available for analysis within the **Component** field. Briefly return to the pull-down menu and note the list of thirteen stresses included there. Although names rather than Greek symbols are listed, observe what stresses it is possible to select when defining a new plot. Following is a *partial* list of stresses available.

σ_x, σ_y, σ_z = Normal stresses in X, Y and Z directions listed as **SX**, **SY**, **SZ**.

τ_{xy}, τ_{xz}, τ_{yz} = Shear stresses on X, Y, and Z planes, listed as **TXY**, **TXZ**, **TYZ**.

σ_1, σ_2, σ_3 = 1st, 2nd, and 3rd Principal stresses listed as **P1**, **P2**, **P3**.

And, other stresses not listed here.

3. Also in the **Display** dialogue box, change **Units** to **psi** (if necessary).

4. In the **Advanced Options** dialogue box verify that ⊙ **Node Values** is selected.

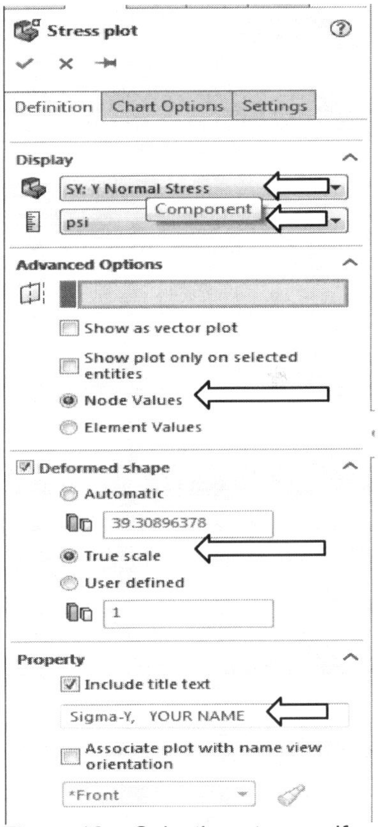

Figure 19 – Selections to specify plotting of a different stress component on the model.

5. Because it is often convenient to turn off the deformed shape when viewing stresses within a model, check "✓" to open the ☑ **Deformed Shape** dialogue box (if not already open) and select ⊙ **True Scale** to display deformation of the

model at its true magnitude. Suppressing display of the deformed shape also proves helpful when using the **Probe** feature later in this example.

6. Open the **Property** dialogue box by clicking ⌄. Within this dialogue box, click to place a check mark next to ☑ **Include title text** and type a descriptive title such as **Sigma-Y, *Your name*.** A descriptive title serves both to identify *what* quantity is plotted and *who* created this new plot.

7. Click **[OK]** ✓ to accept these changes and close the **Stress Plot** property manager. A plot of normal stress in the Y-direction (σ_Y) now appears on the graphics screen and a new plot, named **Stress2 (-Y normal-)**, is listed beneath the **Results** folder. The icon labeled **Stress1 (-vonMises-)** still contains the original plot of von Mises stresses while **Stress2 (Y-normal-)** contains a new plot of normal stress in the Y-direction (σ_Y).

Also note that the plot title and your name entered in step 6 now appears at the top-left of the graphics window. This data helps identify printed output at a public (campus) printer. Next, proceed as follows to modify visual characteristics of the graphics display.

8. Right-click **Stress2 (-Y normal-)** and from the pull-down menu, select **Settings….** The **Stress Plot** property manager opens again except now the **Settings** tab is active as shown in Fig. 20.

9. Within the **Fringe Options** dialogue box, select **Discrete** from the pull-down menu. This action displays stress contours as discrete color bands rather than the rainbow effect created by the **Continuous** display. While on this menu, experiment with other **Fringe Options**, then reset to **Discrete** to correspond with images illustrated on the following pages.

10. In the **Boundary Options** dialogue box, select **Model**. This option outlines model edges with a black line, thereby making its edges easier to view.

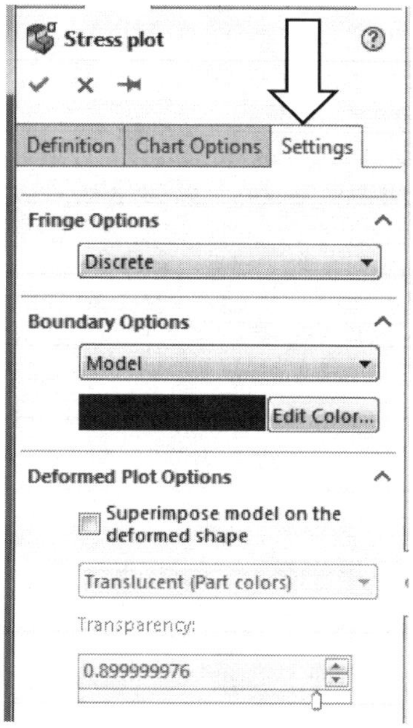

Figure 20 – Altering stress contour display options in the **Stress Plot** property manager.

11. Click **[OK]** ✓ to close the **Stress Plot** property manager. A *partial* image of the **Discrete** fringe plot of normal stress in the Y-direction near the top of the model appears in Fig. 21 (a).

Using the Probe Tool

Although stress contour plots provide a general sense of stress *magnitudes throughout the model*, it is often desirable to determine stress magnitudes *at specific locations*. To accomplish this, use of the **Probe** tool is demonstrated next. To aid in selecting specific points on the model its image is modified by superimposing a **Mesh** on the model.

To alter model appearance, return to the **Stress Plot** property manager and proceed as follows.

1. Right-click **Stress2 (-Y normal-)** and from the pull-down menu select **Settings…** This action returns us to the **Settings** tab within the **Stress Plot** property manager.

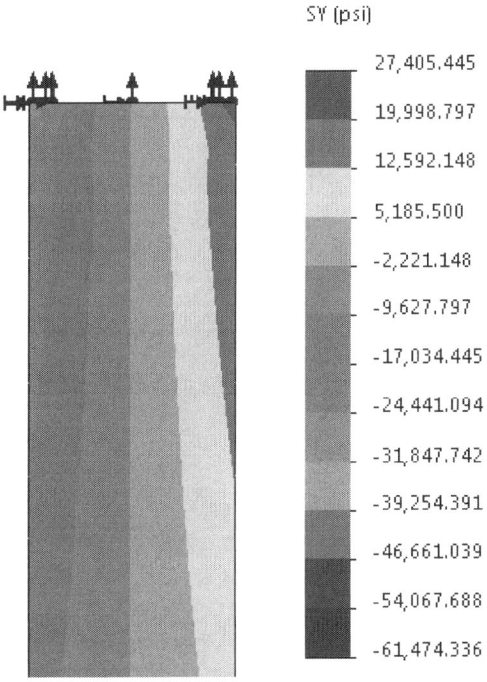

Figure 21 (a) – Upper portion of model showing stress σ_y as **Discrete** fringes.

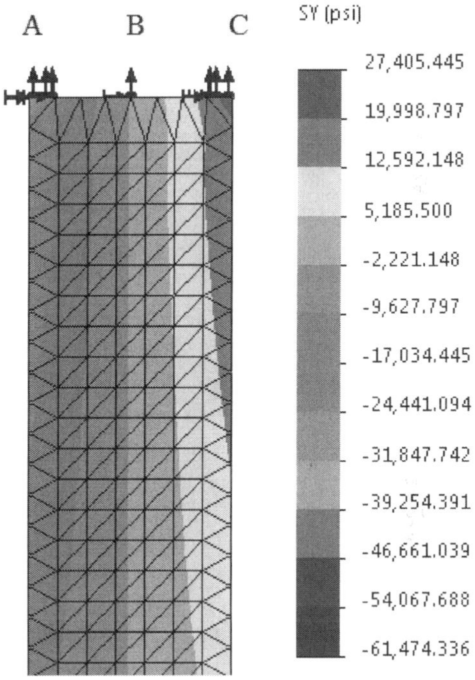

Figure 21 (b) – Upper portion of the model showing the normal stress σ_y and a **Mesh** superimposed on the model. This action facilitates using the **Probe** feature.

2. Within the **Settings** tab, open the pull-down menu ⌄ in the **Boundary Options** dialogue box and select **Mesh**. A mesh is displayed on the model.

3. Within the **Chart Options** tab, open the pull-down menu ⌄ in the **Position/Format** dialogue box for the **Number Format** 111.11 1.1e2 to select **floating** instead of **scientific** and change the number of decimals X.123 to 3.

4. Click **[OK]** ✓ to close the **Stress Plot** property manager. The upper portion of the model should now appear with the mesh shown as illustrated in Fig. 21 (b).

We are now ready to compare manually calculated stresses with stress values determined using a finite element analysis. To facilitate comparisons, manually calculated stress magnitudes at points **A**, **B**, and **C** on top of the cam follower in Fig. 21 (b) are repeated below.

Stress at point A: $(\sigma_y)_A = \sigma_{Axial} + \sigma_{Bending} = (-2020) + (-22080) = -24{,}100$ psi

Stress at point B: $(\sigma_y)_B = \sigma_{Axial} + \sigma_{Bending} = (-2020) + (0) = -2{,}020$ psi

Stress at point C: $(\sigma_y)_C = \sigma_{Axial} + \sigma_{Bending} = (-2020) + (+22080) = +20{,}060$ psi

The **Probe** tool will be used to determine stresses at points **A**, **B**, and **C** on the model and at all points in-between. Occasionally it *may* be necessary to approximate the stress at point **B** on the model's centroidal axis. The reason for this is that the automatically generated mesh size depends on model geometry. Therefore, nodes, which typically are used as measurement points, may or may not lie *exactly* at the desired location on the cam follower centroidal axis. This will be determined as the analysis proceeds.

Begin by zooming-in on the top of the model. An image similar to that shown in Fig. 21 (b) should appear on your screen. Two different methods for using the Probe tool are demonstrated below. Proceed as follows to use the **Probe** tool by the first method.

5. Because stress in the Y direction (σ_y) is to be examined, in the SOLIDWORKS Simulation manager tree right-click **Stress2 (-Y normal-)** and from the pull-down menu, select Probe. A partial view of the **Probe Result** property manager opens but does not initially look like Fig. 22.

6. In the **Options** dialogue box, click to choose ⊙ **On selected entities**. The **Results** dialogue box expands to include a highlighted (light blue) field. This field is active and is awaiting the selection of **Faces, Edges, or Vertices** on the model.

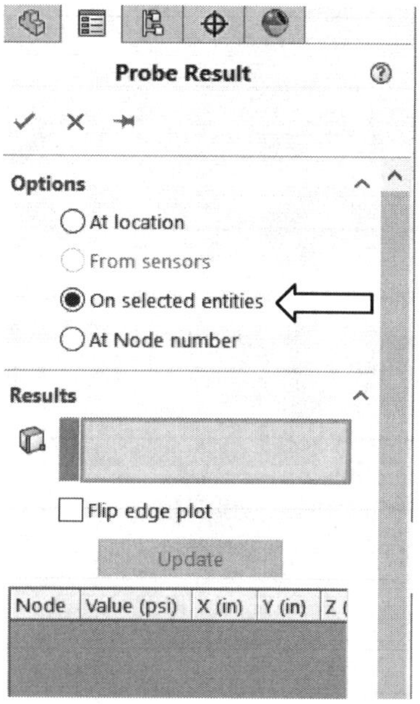

Figure 22 – Partial View of the **Probe Result** property manager.

7. In the graphics screen, slowly move the cursor over faces, edges, and vertices (corners) of the model. The symbol adjacent to the cursor changes to a square, a line, or a small circle to represent selection of a **Face**, an **Edge**, or a **Vertex** respectively. Click to choose the line on the top, front **Edge** of the cam follower. **Edge<1>** appears in the highlighted field and the **[Update]** button (circled) becomes active.

8. Click the **[Update]** button. This action fills the **Results** table with the data seen in Fig. 23 and described below.

*NOTE: To view complete results, <u>it will be necessary</u> to enlarge the table width <u>and</u> width of individual columns within the table by clicking-and-dragging the right boundary of the **Probe Result** property manager and the individual column boundaries respectively.*

Information contained in each column of the **Results** table includes (from left to right):

- **Node**: This column contains the number of each node located (in sequence) across the top front edge of the model. Node numbers are assigned automatically by the software during mesh generation. Seventeen nodes exist across the top edge because high quality tetrahedral elements have nodes at both corner and mid-side locations on each element. Count element sides in Fig. 21 (b) or on your screen.

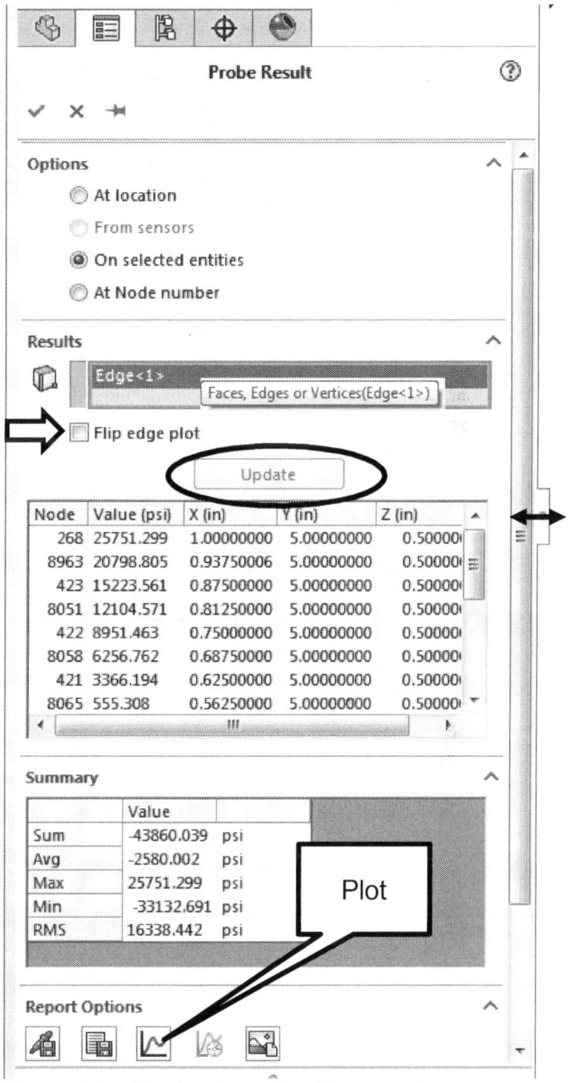

Figure 23 – **Probe Result** table contains stress values at node locations across the top **Edge** of the model.

- **Value (psi)**: This column contains magnitude of the *selected* stress (σ_y) at each node location along the top front edge.

- **X (in)**: This column contains X-coordinates of each node location across the top of the model. The initial value appears as 1 inch and subsequent values decrease in 1/16 inch increments across the model. (Refer to values shown in Fig. 23.)

- **Y (in)**: This column contains Y-coordinates of each node location. Because the original cam follower model was created by locating the origin of a global X, Y, Z coordinate system at its bottom left-hand corner, all points along the top edge lie at a distance of Y = 5.000 inches above that origin.

- **Z (in)**: This column contains Z-coordinates of each node location. Because the original model was extruded ½ inch in the positive Z direction, all Z-coordinates on the top *front* edge are located at Z = + 0.500 inches.

9. In the **Report Options** dialogue box, located near the bottom of the **Probe Result** property manager, click the **Plot** icon; see Plot "flag" in Fig. 23. A graph of stress variation (σ_y) across the top front edge of the model is displayed.

> **Aside:**
> In this user guide, images of stress within the model are referred to as "stress contour plots" or simply "plots." On the other hand, when an image shows the relationship between two variables X and Y, in the form of a line, the image is referred to as a "graph."

Notice, however, that the graph on your screen displays tensile (positive) stress on its left-hand side and compressive (negative) stress on its right-side. This is just the reverse of the actual stress distribution across the top of the cam follower shown in Fig. 24. The reason for this "error" is that the top edge of the model is a line with two different ends, but no means is provided to select data from one end of that line to the other. This logical misrepresentation of data is easily remedied by the following action.

10. First, close the current graph by clicking the ☒ at its upper-right corner.

11. Next, near the top of the **Results** dialogue box, place a check "✓" adjacent to ☑ **Flip edge plot**. See white arrow in Fig. 23.

12. Again, click the **Plot** icon and a corrected graph, showing variation of σ_y across the top edge of the model, from left to right, should appear as seen in Fig. 24. *Do not close the plot window.*

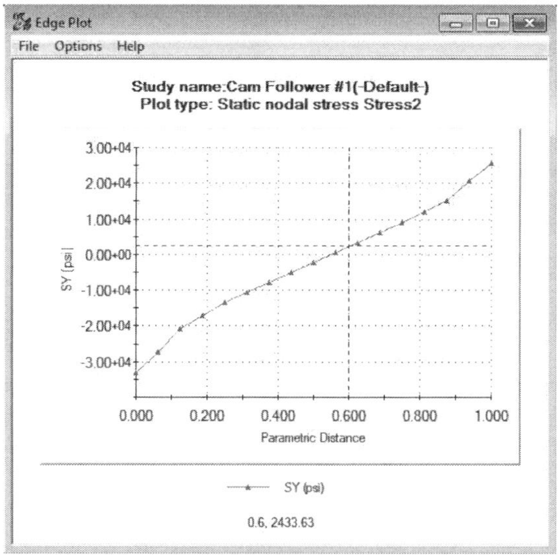

Figure 24 – Graph of stress distribution σ_y from the left side (0.0 in.) to right side (at 1 in.) along top front edge of the cam follower.

The graph in Fig. 24 indicates compressive stress (negative values) along the left side of the model as expected. This stress gradually decreases to zero near the center of the model and then becomes positive, indicating tensile stress on the right side of the cam follower. These results are consistent with our understanding of stress distribution on the top edge of the model. However, we next observe that these results do not agree well with results obtained using classical stress equations.

OBSERVATIONS:
Table 1 below compares results of manually calculated stresses with finite element results obtained using the **Probe** tool at locations **A**, **B**, and **C** on the top-end of the cam follower. Verify results in the Probe Tool Results column in Table 1 below by scrolling through results in the **Values (psi)** column of the **Probe** table on your screen.

Table 1 – Comparison of stress σ_y computed by classical and finite element methods.

Location	Manual Calculation (psi)	Probe Tool Results (psi)	Percent Difference (%)
Point A	-24100	-33132.69	27.26 %
Point B	-2020	-2125.33	4.95%
Point C	+20060	+25751.29	22.10 %

Results in Table 1 indicate significant differences between results calculated using classical stress equations and those determined using finite element analysis methods. How can this be?

The above question can be answered by recalling St. Venant's principle, which states that stress predicted by classic equations exists only in regions *reasonably well removed* from (a) points of load application, (b) support locations, and (c) locations of geometric discontinuity. Any of these conditions typically introduce significant *localized* effects. Thus, in these regions, shortcomings of classical stress equations are at odds with more accurate results predicted by finite element methods. For this reason, the **Probe** tool is used again, but this time it is used to select nodes at locations somewhat removed from the upper support location. Proceed as follows.

13. Begin by closing the **Edge Plot** graph. Click ☒ to close the graph window.

14. Within the **Options** dialogue box of the **Probe Result** property manager, click to select ⦿ **At location**. This action clears all data from the **Results** table and changes the mode of operation to one that enables display of results at user selected node locations.

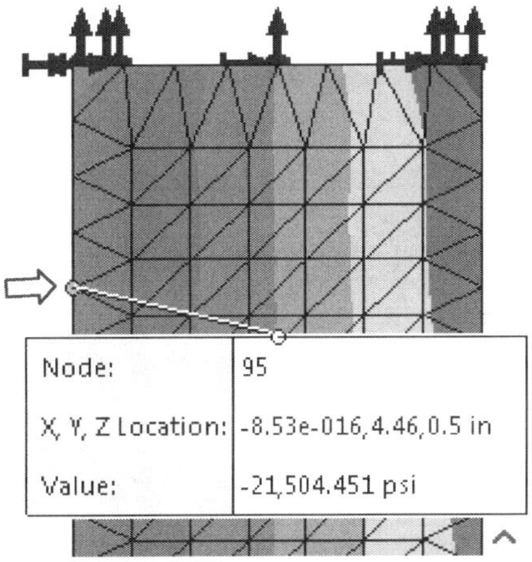

Figure 25 – Close-up view of top end of the model showing the first node selected along an *approximate* straight-line across the model.

Zoom in on top of the model. Move the Probe tool into the graphics area and count down to the 4th node below the top-left corner. See the node selected in Fig. 25. This node is somewhat arbitrarily assumed to be "sufficiently removed" from the *immovable* **Fixture** condition applied on top of the cam follower. This location is chosen to reduce the effects predicted by St. Venant's principle.

As you perform the next step, a small information "flag" will appear adjacent to each selected node, like the "flag" shown in Fig. 25. Information listed in this flag includes the *Node Number* in its top row, node coordinates *(X, Y, Z)* on the second line, and stress magnitude is listed in the bottom line; units are included with all values. These values are also listed in the **Results** table of the **Probe Result** property manager. Unfortunately, these "flags" tend to overwrite one another for closely spaced node selections. Flags can be moved by clicking them and dragging to arrange them as desired; see neatly arranged flags in Fig. 26. Alternatively, in the **Annotations** dialogue box at the bottom of the **Probe Result** property manager, turn OFF *parts* of these flags by clearing the check "✓" mark from ☐ **Show Node/Element Number** and from ☐ **Show X,Y,Z Location**. However, it is suggested that ☑ **Show Value** remain checked.

15. Proceed across the model *from left-to-right* and click to select *only nodes at element corners* as illustrated by small circles in Fig. 26. If an error is made when selecting nodes, simply click the ⊙ **At Location** button again. This action clears the **Results** table, and the selection process can be repeated.

> **Aside:**
> Due to the arbitrary mesh generation scheme, it may not be possible to select nodes in a *straight line* across the model. Despite this inconvenience, it is still possible to compute stresses at each node location and compare classical results with finite element values listed in the **Results** table. Why? Because each node's Y-coordinate is known.

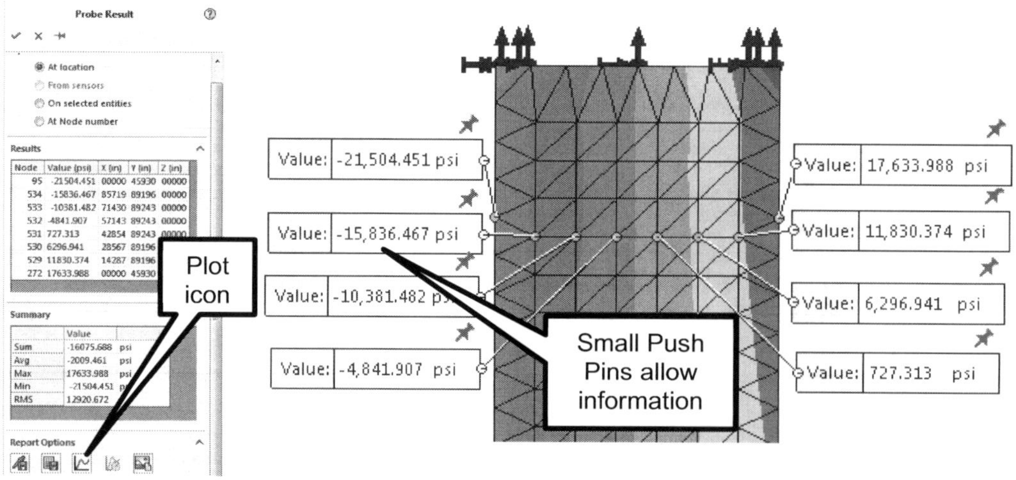

Figure 26 – **Results** table containing σ_y values for each node selection across the model at a distance "sufficiently removed" from support conditions.

16. Within the **Report Options** dialogue box, once again select the Plot icon. The resulting **Probe Result** graph is shown in Fig. 27.

The graph in Fig. 27 reveals the expected variation of stress caused by adding the uniform axial compressive stress to the near linear variation of bending stress. Bending stress varies from compression on left side of the model (negative values) to tension on the right side (positive values).

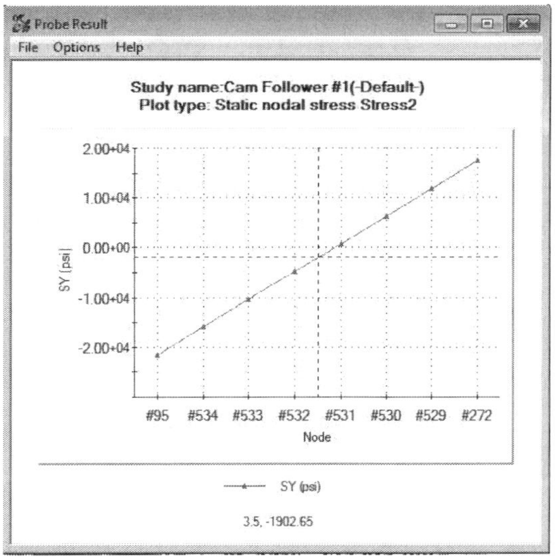

Figure 27 – Plot of combined axial and bending stress variation (σ_y) across the model.

17. Move the cursor onto the graph and note that crosshairs (two intersecting dashed lines) appear and move with the cursor. On the default graph, stress **SY (psi)**, *or possibly **(ksi)**,* is plotted on the ordinate and node numbers are plotted on the abscissa. As the crosshairs move, values of the X and Y coordinates at their intersection update automatically beneath the graph.

18. Move the cursor to the intersection of the curve and the centroidal axis of the model. This location should occur midway between node numbers 531 and 532. Since the cam follower is seven (7) elements wide, its center should lie 3.5 elements from either side of the cam follower.

With the crosshairs on the curve *at* the centroidal axis, the coordinates displayed beneath the bottom-center of the graph should read either (X = 3.5 nodes, Y = -1902.65 psi) or X = 3.5 nodes, Y = -2123.89 psi. Units are *not* shown with values beneath the graph. The reason for uncertainty of the Y-coordinate is lack of accuracy locating the exact crosshair intersection with the curve. Thus, the average of these two values -

$$(\sigma_y)_{AVG} = [-1903 + (-2124)]/2 = -2013 \text{ psi} \quad \text{(rounded values)}$$

is used for comparison in Table 2.

Table 2 shows a comparison between stresses calculated using classical equations and those computed using the finite element analysis. Results of both methods are compared at *approximately* 0.54 inches below the top of the model. Refer to the Y-coordinate, labeled "**Y (in)**," in the **Results** table of Fig. 26 for the exact distance (4.459-in at nodes on left and right sides of the cam follower). Bending stress components at points A and C in Table 2 are computed at this location, while stress at point B is calculated above.

Table 2 – Comparison of stress σ_y computed by classical and finite element methods at an arbitrary distance below the top of the cam follower.

Location	Manual Calculation (psi)	Probe Tool Results (psi)	Percent Difference (%)
Point A	-21710	-21504	0.96 %
Point B	-2020	-2013	0.35 %
Point C	17670	17634	0.20 %

Note the significant improvement in the comparison of manual calculations and finite element results in Table 2. Differences are less than 1 % at all points **A**, **B**, and **C**. Based on these comparisons, several additional observations are included in the Summary section at the end of this chapter.

19. Do *not* close the **Probe Result** graph. Instead, proceed directly to the next section.

Customizing Graphs

Because default information displayed on SOLIDWORKS Simulation graphs is rather terse, as evidenced by graphs of the previous section, this section briefly examines those graphs and explores means to enhance them. Begin by examining differences between graphs shown in Figs. 24 and 27 (repeated below).

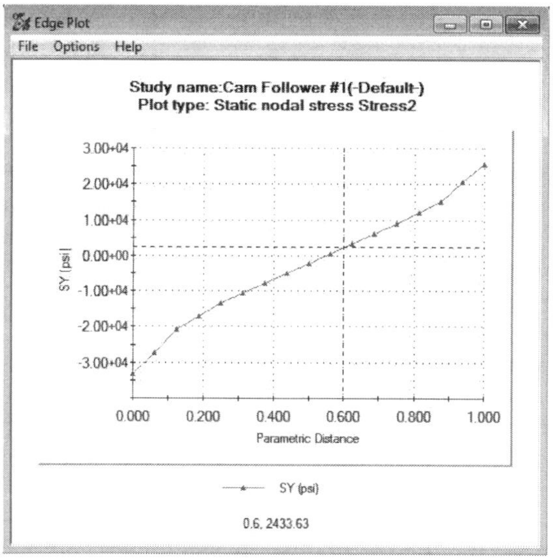

Figure 24 – Repeated

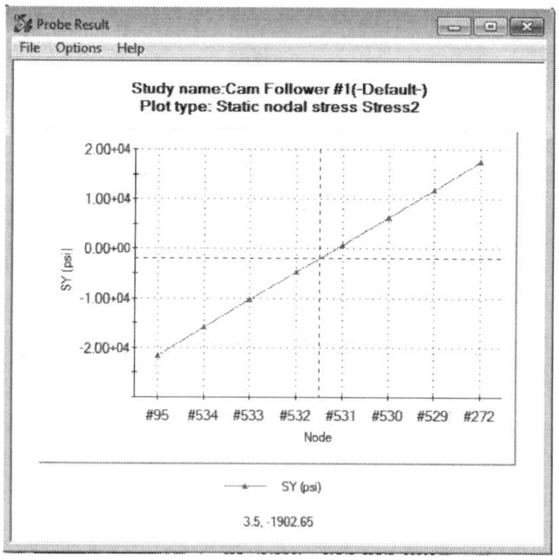

Figure 27 – Repeated

Observations:

- Both graphs bear the same title. Therefore, there is no obvious clue that these graphs represent stress data at different locations on the cam follower.

- The Y-axis label indicates that normal stress in the Y-direction is plotted (**SY** = σ_y), but there is no indication that **SY** is a combination of axial and bending stress.
- The X-axis in Fig. 24 plots the **Parametric Distance**, which in this case begins at 0.0 inches at the left side of the model and increases to 1.0 inch at its right side. Recall, the 1 inch wide top *edge* of the model was selected to create Fig. 24.
- The X-axis in Fig. 27 lists the numbers of each **Node** selected as the **Probe** tool moved across the model from left to right.
- A legend, at bottom middle of the graph, indicates the symbols, line color, and units used to plot **SY**. If other lines were plotted on the same graph, additional symbols and colors would appear. Also, because the model *edge* was selected for the graph of Fig. 24, stress at both mid-side *and* corner nodes was plotted for each element. However, only element corner nodes were selected for the plot in Fig. 27; therefore, fewer data points are displayed.

Because properly labeling various parts of a graph is very informative *and* because ability to accomplish this task can be used throughout the remainder of this text, graph labeling is investigated next. However, be aware that graph labeling capability within SOLIDWORKS Simulation is rather limited and somewhat arduous to use. Therefore, steps below outline *only* the most useful tools for customizing graphs. Because the graph shown in Fig. 27 should still be open, proceed as follows.

1. In the menu at the top of the **Probe Result** *graph*, select **Options**. Then from the pull-down menu select **Properties**. The **2D Chart Control (Unicode) Properties** window opens as shown in Fig. 28.

Begin by replacing the graph title with more descriptive wording.

2. Select the **Titles** tab. Then, within the **Titles** tab, select the **Label** tab.
3. Within the **Text:** box type a descriptive title. *Hint: Type the <u>second</u> line of text first.* Choose wording that fully describes the information displayed on this graph. Press the **[Enter]** key between lines of text. Compare your title to that shown in Fig. 28. Then, click **[Apply]** when done. *Do not close window.*
4. Explore other options within the **Titles** tab as time and interest permit.

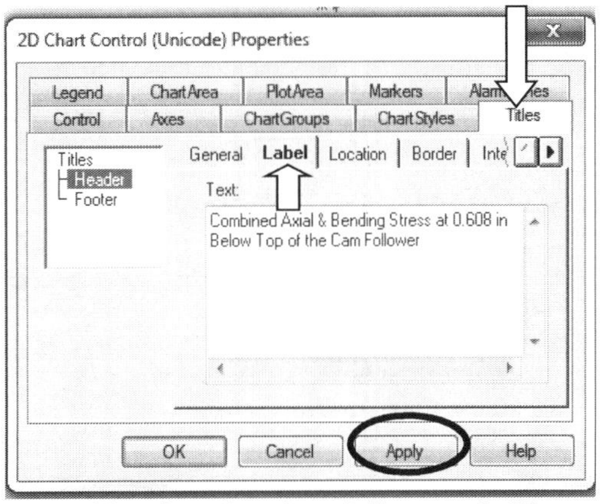

Figure 28 – Creating descriptive graph titles and axis labels within the **2D Chart Control Properties** window.

Next, alter the axis labels. Once again, the goal is to provide more descriptive labels on the X and Y axes. The following step assumes the **2D Chart Control (Unicode) Properties** window remains open. If not, open it again by repeating step 1.

5. Select the **Axes** tab followed by selection of the **Title** tab. (CAUTION: Avoid accidentally selecting the **Titles** tab used in step 2 above). Notice that **X** is highlighted (blue) at the top left corner of the current window to indicate X-axis.

6. In the **Text:** box, replace the current axis label, "**Node**," using wording such as, "**Node Numbers Across the Cam Follower: Left to Right (Node Nos.)**," then click **[Apply]**. Your axis label should appear beneath the X-axis.

Note that node numbers are the default display when the **Probe** tool is used. The task of altering these values to represent distance across the width of the cam follower appears to be impossible. Proceed as follows to enhance the Y-axis label.

7. While still on the **Axes** tab, click to highlight **Y** in the **Axes** box located at top left of the **2D Chart Control (Unicode) Properties** window. The **Text:** box changes to show the current Y-axis label, **SY (psi)**.

8. Type a new, more descriptive label of your own choosing for the Y-axis into the **Text:** box. Then click **[OK]** to close the **2D Chart Control Properties** window.

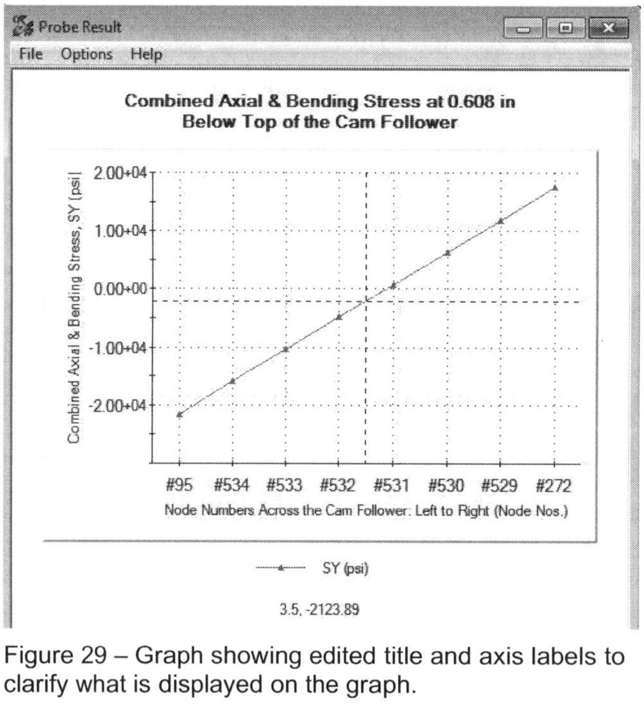

Figure 29 – Graph showing edited title and axis labels to clarify what is displayed on the graph.

An edited version of the graph with a more meaningful title and descriptive axis labels is shown in Fig. 29. **CAUTION: Once the graph is closed, all edits are lost.** Therefore, if a graph is to be printed, proceed to step 9 prior to closing the graph.

9. In the **Probe Result** *graph* window, select **File**. Then from the pull-down menu, select either **Save As…** a filename you designate (or) **Print** the graph immediately.

10. To close the **Probe Result** graph, click ⊠. Users should form the habit of always applying *descriptive titles, axis labels,* and *their name* to every graph.

11. Click **[OK]** ✓ to close the **Probe Result** property manager.

Summary

- The effect of *localized* conditions, also known as "end-conditions" or "boundary conditions," which occur at locations of support, applied loads, and/or areas of geometric discontinuity (locations of stress concentration) upon finite element results can be significant. These effects typically are not predicted by classical equations used in manual stress calculations. For this reason, care must be exercised when checking finite element results in these regions.

- Excellent agreement typically exists between finite element analysis and manually computed results at locations *sufficiently removed* from localized conditions (examples of St. Venant's principle).

- The importance of selecting the *appropriate stress* within a finite element analysis when comparing results cannot be overstated. For example, the SOLIDWORKS Simulation default plot of von Mises stress does not, and should not, agree when compared with manually calculated values of stress in the Y-direction (σ_y) for the cam follower. Simply stated, *like* stresses must be compared when checking validity of finite element results.

The current example concludes at this point. Most of the software capabilities introduced in this example are fundamental to a successful finite element analysis and will be encountered repeatedly in subsequent examples and end-of-chapter problems. This file either can be saved or deleted. See below for further saving guidance.

To SAVE or Not to SAVE Files, that is the Question?

Whether or not to save your SOLIDWORKS Simulation files depends upon a number of factors. Some general guidelines regarding file retention follow.

- It is highly recommended that all chapter example problems be deleted upon completion. Why? (a) You have already benefited from the learning experience; (b) these files are not referred to later in the text, and (c) if a chapter problem must be re-worked, you will discover how quickly a solution can be repeated because of your increased software proficiency.
- Do not delete end-of-chapter problem files until all plots, graphs, and tabular data required for an assignment have been printed.

- In the event your work must be interrupted, it is possible to SAVE a file part way through a solution and to continue the solution at a later time (see Option 1 or 2 below).

A brief description of options for closing a file, with or without saving it, follows. Because a variety of file structures are found in different computer work environments, the guidelines below are quite general. It is suggested that local system guidelines be followed regarding *where* files are saved (i.e., to a personal USB drive, to the hard-drive, or to personal file space allocated on a system network).

To exit SOLIDWORKS Simulation and *save a file and all changes made to that file*, proceed as follows.

OPTION 1 – Close a File and SAVE its Contents Using the Original File Name *(Not recommended for this example.)*

1. From the main menu, choose **File**. Then from the pull-down menu, select **Close.** This action opens the **SOLIDWORKS** window shown in Fig. 30.
2. In this window, select the **Save all** option indicated at the arrow in Fig. 30. This action saves the original SOLIDWORKS file plus all changes made within the Simulation portion of the software.

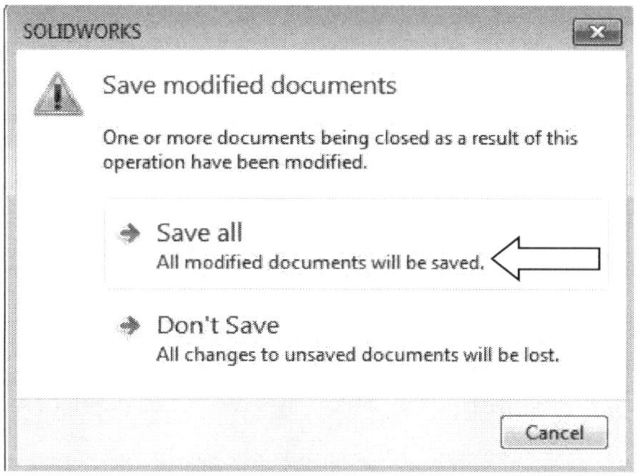

Figure 30 – Saving a file using a previously assigned file name.

3. The above action saves an up-to-date version of the model under its original file name, which in this example is "**Cam Follower (Part)**."
4. See OPTION 4 for instructions to be used when re-opening this file.

OPTION 2 – Close a File and SAVE its Contents Under a Different File Name *(Not recommended for this example).*

1. From the main menu, choose **File,** and from the pull-down menu, select **Save As…** The **Save As** window opens and the current file name, "**Cam Follower (Part),**" appears in the **File name:** field. Simply replace the existing name and click the **[Save]** button at lower right of the **Save As** window.
2. See OPTION 4 for instructions to be used when re-opening this file.

OPTION 3 - Close a File Without Saving Results *(Recommended)*

It is almost universally recommended that files *not* be saved for the simple expedience of (a) not having to rummage through the numerous files created during a finite element solution to find a single desired file, and (b) although computer memory is now rather inexpensive, why waste it saving files that will not be accessed again. To close a file without saving results, proceed as follows.

1. From the main menu, choose **File**. Then from the pull-down menu, select **Close.** This action opens the **SOLIDWORKS** window shown in Fig. 30 (repeated).

2. In this window, select the **Don't Save** option indicated at the arrow in Fig. 30 (repeated). This action discards all finite element results but saves the original SOLIDWORKS model file.

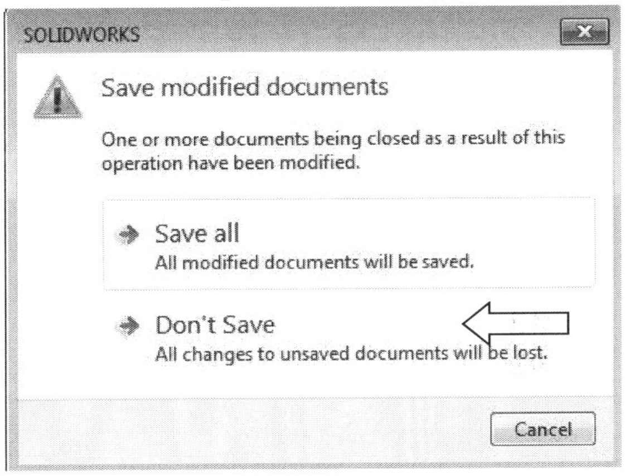

Figure 30 (repeated) – Saving a file using a previously assigned file name.

The only times a file should not be discarded are when (a) a solution must be interrupted and returned to at a later time; or (b) in an academic environment it is suggested that a solution file be retained until one is certain that all assigned problem parts have been submitted; or (c) in one or two rare instances an end-of-chapter problem may be revisited in a later chapter. In these rare instances, users will be instructed to Save the original solution file . . . just in case an extension of the original problem is assigned later.

OPTION 4 – Re-open a SOLIDWORKS Simulation File Saved Using OPTION 1 or OPTION 2

Confusion sometimes results when Simulation files are re-opened within SOLIDWORKS because the Simulation results are not immediately displayed. Follow steps below to overcome this unexpected file re-opening procedure.

1. In the main menu select **File** followed by **Open…** The **Open** window appears. Alternatively, it might be necessary to browse to a USB, or other file storage device in your system network, to locate and click on the file name to be opened.

2. Select the desired file name and click the **[Open]** button. In the case of the **Cam Follower (Part)**, a reduced size image of the SOLIDWORKS screen is shown in Fig. 31. Note, however, that only the SOLIDWORKS model is displayed; Simulation results are not displayed either on the model or in the Simulation manager tree.

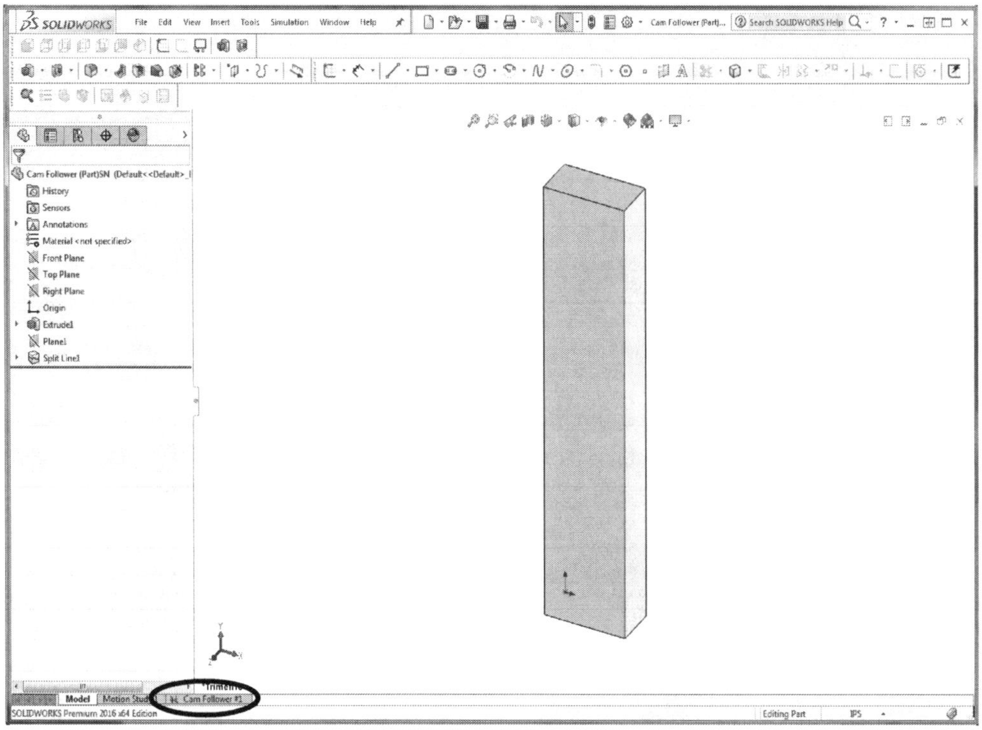

Figure 31 – Screen image after a SOLIDWORKS <u>Simulation</u> model is re-opened.

3. To open the SOLIDWORKS <u>Simulation</u> results file, simply click the *tab* labeled **Cam Follower (Part)** located near the lower left corner of the screen; circled in Fig. 31. It contains the Simulation solution up to the point when it was last **Saved**.

EXERCISES

End of chapter exercises are intended to provide additional practice using principles introduced in the current chapter. Future chapters also build upon capabilities mastered in preceding chapters. SOLIDWORKS part files for all example and end-of-chapter problems can be downloaded from www.SDCpublications.com/downloads/978-1-63057-787-2. To save time, download all the files at one time. Use a USB drive or save files on your PC or network.

Most exercises include multiple parts. In an academic setting, it is likely that parts of problems will be assigned or modified to suit specific course goals.

╬ ***Designates problems that introduce new concepts. Solution guidance is provided for these problems.***

Default Expectations (unless otherwise specified)

- Include a *descriptive* Study name and *your name* when naming each Study. This approach uniquely labels each plot with your name.
- Use *discrete* stress contours (colored fringes) and display all plots on an *un-deformed* view of the model.

RECALL: "Plot" – refers to a stress contour plot (i.e., colored fringes depicting stress magnitudes, displacements, etc. within a model).

"Graph" – refers to an X-Y line graph that depicts a relationship between two variables.

EXERCISE 1 – Shear Due to Bending in a Cantilever Beam

The cantilever beam pictured in Fig. E1-1 is rigidly supported (**Fixed**) at its left-end and is subject to forces F_x and F_y applied to its right-end. Either create a beam model using SOLIDWORKS on your own or open problem file **Cantilever 1-1**, which is available at the publisher's web site (see above). Then, perform a finite element analysis of this beam subject to the following guidelines.

- Material: **AISI 1045 Steel cold drawn**
- Mesh: In the **Mesh** property manager, select **Standard mesh**.
- External Load: Assign an axial **Force** F_x = 830 lb that acts **Normal** to the right-end of the beam in the direction shown. Also, apply a downward **Force** F_y = 760 lb that acts on the top-right **Edge** of the beam. *Split Lines* are not used.

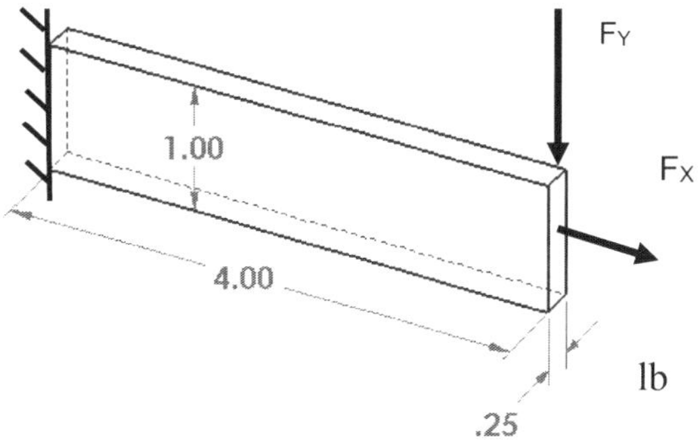

Figure E1-1 – Basic dimensions (in inches) of a cantilever beam subject to loads F_x and F_y.

Assign a **Fixed** restraint to the left-end (left-end face) of the beam in Fig. E1-1.

Determine the following:

a. Create a stress contour plot of shear stress τ_{xy} showing the stress distribution on the front face, which corresponds to the 1.00 x 4.00 inch side of the beam.

b. Use the **Probe** feature to create a graph of τ_{xy} across the left-front edge of the beam. Create this graph by zooming in on the left end of the model and selecting its left edge; use **Flip edge plot** if necessary. Customize the graph title and include your name. Also provide descriptive labels for both the X and Y axes on this graph.

c. Use the **Probe** feature to create a graph of τ_{xy} across the front face of the beam by selecting successive nodes (from top to bottom) at a location approximately 1-in. to the right of the fixed-end of the model. Refer to the **Results** table to ensure the X-value corresponds to approximately 1 in. from the left-end of the model. *Record the actual X- value.* If nodes are not aligned in a straight line across the model, then choose nodes along the best approximation of a straight line at this location. On this graph, manually label the maximum value of τ_{xy} and the X location used to determine shear due to bending. Customize the graph title and include your name. Also provide descriptive labels for both the X and Y axes.

d. Calculate the maximum shear stress due to bending using classical equations at the fixed end *and* at the same distance to the right of the fixed end determined in the **Results** table of step (c). Then, use equation [1] below to compute the percent difference between classical and finite element solutions for maximum shear stress determined half-way between top and bottom surfaces of the beam in parts (b) and (c) above.

$$\% \text{ difference} = \frac{(\text{FEA result - classical result})}{\text{FEA result}} * 100 = \qquad [1]$$

e. Briefly state reason(s) why shear stress determined in parts (b) and (c) differ.

f. Use the **Probe** feature to create a graph of σ_x across the front face of the beam (from top to bottom) at approximately X = 1 in. to the right of the fixed-end. *Record the actual X value.* Select *both* corner and mid-side nodes to yield a more uniform graph. In the **Results** table, observe and record the exact X-coordinate of nodes located on the top and bottom edges of the beam. Assign a descriptive title and axis labels to this graph; include your name in the title.

g. Use classical stress equations to calculate the *appropriate* normal stress on *both* the top and bottom surfaces of the beam at the location determined in step (f) above. Clearly label calculations at each location. Hint: the X-coordinate of node location(s), determined in step (f) above, should help to determine this exact distance.

h. Use equation [1] to compare finite element results for σ_x with manual calculations of the *appropriate* normal stress on both top and bottom surfaces of the beam. Clearly label calculations corresponding to "top" and "bottom" surfaces.

i. If results for the comparison of σ_x at the location from the left end [determined in part (h) above] differ by more than 3%, then locate and correct the error(s) in either the finite element model and/or in manual stress calculations.

EXERCISE 2 – Combined Stress in an "L" Shaped Cantilever Beam

The "L"- shaped cantilever bracket, pictured in Fig. E1-2, is rigidly supported (**Fixed**) at its left end. It is made from **2014-T4** Aluminum and is subject to a concentrated tensile load of F = 6.5 kN applied to a *Split Line* located adjacent to the hole on the right end of the beam. Open the file **Cantilever Bracket 1-2**. Use the model provided at the publisher's website www.SDCpublications.com/downloads/978-1-63057-787-2 (See pg. vii for details and pg. I-25 for "Cautions".) Create a finite element model based on the following information.

- Material: **2014-T4** Aluminum (Use S.I. units)
- Mesh: In the **Mesh** property manager, select **Standard mesh**. Tetrahedral elements are the (system default) high quality elements.
- External Load: Assign a **Force** F = 6.5 kN, directed to the right and applied on the *Split Line* labeled in Fig. E1-2.
- Fixture: Apply a **Fixed** restraint at the left-end of the model.

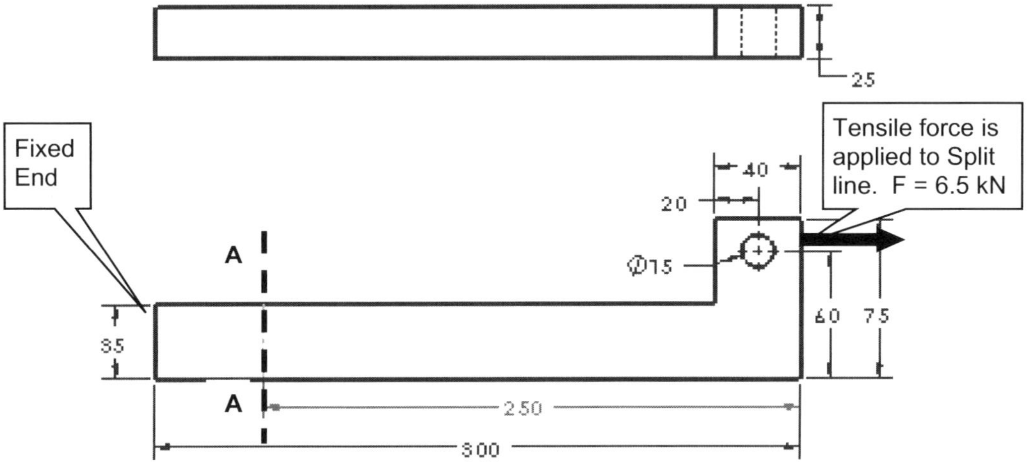

Figure E1-2 – Front and top views of an "L"-shaped cantilever beam "fixed" at its left-end and subject to a horizontal force F = 6.5 kN applied at its right end. (All dimensions in mm.)

Determine the following:

a. Create a stress contour plot of the *most appropriate* normal stress distribution on the front face of the beam. Part (d), below, provides clues regarding the *most appropriate* stress. Consider the lower image in Fig. E1-2 to be the "front" view. Include your name and a descriptive title on this plot; refer to the **Property** dialogue box in Fig. 19 regarding procedure to add your name to a plot.

b. On the plot of part (a), state whether or not the material yield strength is exceeded. If it is exceeded, circle the region or regions where this occurs and state the reason for your conclusion.

c. Use the **Probe** feature to create a graph of the *most appropriate* normal stress across the front face of the beam by selecting successive nodes (from top to bottom) at location A-A. Refer to the **Results** table to ensure the X-value corresponds to approximately 50 mm from the left-end of the model. If nodes are not aligned in a straight line across the model at location A-A, then choose nodes along the best approximation of a straight line. *Record the exact distance on the graph.* On this graph, manually label the value and location of stress on the top, centroidal, and bottom surfaces of the beam. Customize the graph title and X and Y axis labels, and include your name in the graph title. The *most appropriate* normal stresses should correspond to those computed in part (d).

d. Use classical equations to calculate the combined axial and bending stresses on the top, centroidal (middle), and bottom surfaces of the beam at location A-A. In the event that nodes at location A-A do not lie exactly 50 mm from the left end, then use the *exact distance* determined in part (c) above. Clearly label calculations corresponding to each of these surfaces.

e. Use equation [1], repeated below, to compute the percent difference between classical and finite element solutions for stresses determined on the top, centroidal, and bottom beam surfaces determined in parts (c) and (d) above.

$$\% \text{ difference} = \frac{(\text{FEA result - classical result})}{\text{FEA result}} * 100 = \qquad [1]$$

f. If results of part (e) differ by more than 3%, determine the source of error and, in a brief paragraph, describe the source of the error and how it was eliminated.

<u>EXERCISE 3</u> – Stress and Deflection Analysis

The "L"-shaped cantilever beam, shown in Fig. E1-3, is rigidly supported (**Fixed**) at its left end, point **A**, and subject to a downward force of 1500 N applied to the vertical *face* at end **C**. Cylindrical rod **AB** is made of **Alloy Steel** while the material of rectangular member **BC** is **2014-T6** Aluminum. This exercise investigates both displacements and stress at various locations on the model. Open file **L-Part 1-3** found at the publisher's web site (see pg. vii for details and pg. I-24 for "Cautions" when downloading files).

Create a finite element study of this beam based on the following information.

- Material: Cylindrical member **AB**, **Alloy Steel** (Use S.I. units)
  Rectangular member **BC**, **2014-T6** Aluminum (Use S.I. units)

- Mesh: In the **Mesh** property manager, select a ⊙ **Standard mesh**.
  Tetrahedral elements are the (system default) high quality elements.

- External Load: Assign a **Force** F = 1500 N, directed to the downward and applied on the vertical *face* at end **C**, of member **BC**.

- Fixture: Apply a **Fixed** restraint at the left-end **A** of member **AB**.

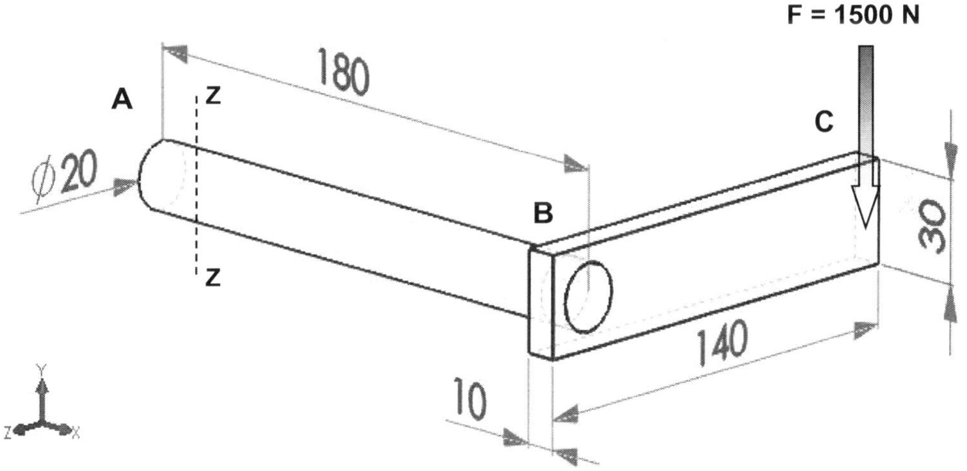

Figure E1-3 – The "L"-shaped cantilever beam is made from two different materials. The beam is fixed at its left end (point **A**) and subject to a downward force F = 1500 N applied to the face at end **C**. (All dimensions in mm.)

Determine the following:

a. Select a Dimetric view to display the model for this plot. Create a stress contour plot of the *most appropriate* stress that best shows bending stress in cylindrical section **AB**. Include the mesh on this plot. Also, include your name and a descriptive title on this plot. The **Property** dialogue box in Fig. 19 outlines the procedure for adding a title and your name to a plot.

b. For the stress plot created in step (a), use the **Probe** feature to create a graph of bending stress variation from top to bottom of beam **AB** at section **Z-Z**. Section **Z-Z** is considered to lie along a line of nodes located four elements from the fixed end. Select nodes starting at the *top-most* node on the cylindrical profile and continue by selecting both corner and mid-side nodes to the *bottom-most* node on the cylindrical surface at section at **Z-Z**. Note and record bending stress magnitude at the top-most and bottom-most nodes listed in the **Results** dialogue box. Also, record the distance of selected nodes from the fixed end. Distance from the fixed end can be determined from the X coordinate listed in the **Results** table. *HINT #1 – Small "information flags" that accompany each node selection can be moved out of the way by clicking-and-dragging anywhere on the "flag." Flags can also be turned off by clearing check "✓" marks from the **Annotations** dialogue box at bottom of the **Probe** property manager. HINT #2 – If an error is made when selecting nodes, clear the erroneous values by clicking ⊙ **At Location** in the **Options** dialogue box of the **Probe** property manager and begin again.* Customize the graph title and X and Y axis labels; include your name in the graph title.

c. Create a plot of shear stress τ_{xy} in the model. Include your name and a descriptive title on this plot.

d. Use the same procedure as outlined in step (b), except this time create a graph of shear stress τ_{xy} variation from the top to bottom of cylindrical member **AB** at section **Z-Z**. Note and record the maximum and minimum values of shear stress τ_{xy} listed in **Results** dialogue box of the **Probe Result** property manager.

e. Manually calculate bending stress at the top and bottom of member **AB** at section **Z-Z** and compare values to those found using the **Probe** tool in part (b). Clearly label calculations corresponding to the top and bottom surfaces.

f. Use equation [1], repeated below, to compute the percent difference between classical and finite element solutions for bending stresses determined on the top and bottom beam surfaces determined in parts (b) and (e) above.

$$\% \text{ difference} = \frac{(\text{FEA result - classical result})}{\text{FEA result}} * 100 = \qquad [1]$$

g. Manually calculate the most appropriate shear stress at the top, centroidal, and bottom surfaces of member **AB** at section **Z-Z** and compare values to those found using the **Probe** tool in part (d). Clearly label calculations corresponding to the top, centroidal, and bottom locations.

h. Use equation [1] to compute the percent difference between classical and finite element solutions for shear stresses determined on the top, centroidal, and bottom beam surfaces determined in parts (d) and (g) above.

i. Manually calculate vertical displacement of the model at location **C**. Use any of these methods: Castigliano's method, superposition, singularity functions, numerical integration, moment-area method, or a method assigned by your instructor. Briefly state any assumption(s) applied to your calculations.

j. Create a finite element plot of the *most appropriate* displacement that corresponds to displacement calculated in part (i). Include automatic labeling of this displacement on the plot. On this plot compute the percent difference between classical and finite element solutions using equation [1] above. Briefly explain why differences greater than 2% (if any) occur.

╬ EXERCISE 4 – Stress Determination in a Bicycle Brake Lever (Special Topics: Using a Fixed Hinge Joint Fixture, model Defeaturing, and Coordinate determination using the PROBE tool)

Basic dimensions and a solid model of a bicycle brake lever are shown in Figs. E1-4 (a) and (b). The brake lever is subject to a downward force of **F** = 70-lb applied on the *Split Line* shown in Fig. E1-4 (b). A solid model of the assembly consists of the brake lever plus a partial view of its cable shown at the left side of the model. The cable connects to caliper brakes at either the front or rear bicycle wheel; only a “stub” length of the cable is shown. Open the file **Brake Lever Assembly 1-4**.

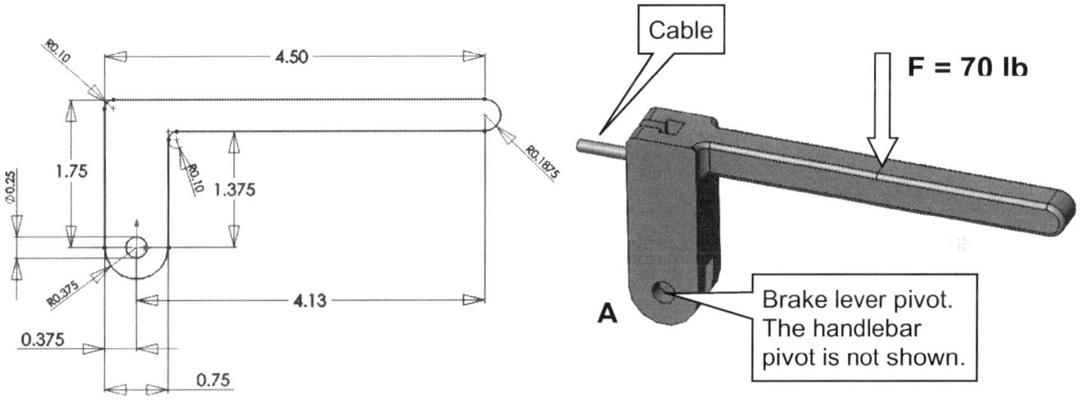

(a) (b)

Figure E1-4 – Dimensioned view of brake lever and solid model view showing external load applied to a split line. (All dimensions in inches.)

When a braking force is applied to the brake lever, the lever pivots (rotates) around a pin that attaches it to the bicycle handlebar pivot (not shown) at the lower hole at **A**. For this reason, a **Fixed Hinge** fixture is introduced in this example. Assume the following:

- Material: Brake lever – Aluminum, **201.0-T7 Insulated Mold Casting (SS)**
  Cable & Cable Anchor – Steel, **AISI 347 Annealed Stainless Steel (SS)**

- Mesh: Select a ⊙ **Standard Mesh**; use the default mesh size. See the **Solution Guidance** section titled **Location/Dimension Determination** before meshing the model.

- Fixture: Apply a **Fixed** (immovable) restraint to the cable free-end. Apply a **Fixed Hinge** to holes **A** at bottom of the brake lever.

- External Load: Apply a **70** lb downward load to the *Split Line* on top surface of the model. Apply load *after partially defeaturing* the model.

Two aspects of this problem are unique, i.e., not introduced in the current chapter. First, because the brake lever is free to *rotate* about hole **A** near its lower extremity, a **Fixed Hinge** is specified at that location. And second, locations (or more specifically, dimensions) must be determined from node locations on the model. Guidance in the application of these two items is provided below.

Solution Guidance

It is assumed that the user has opened the model file and started a Study in SOLIDWORKS Simulation. The following instructions are to serve as a "guide"; they are less detailed than the step-by-step procedure found in example problems.

Fixed Hinge Specification

A **Fixed hinge** joint acts like a door hinge. This joint type allows *rotation* about a fixed axis on the model but prevents translation in other directions. A **Fixed Hinge** joint is applied to holes located at **A** near the bottom of the **Brake Lever Assembly**. This joint prevents translations in the X, Y, Z directions but allows the model to rotate about the selected axis. Proceed as follows:

- Right-click the **Fixtures** folder and from the pull-down menu select **Fixed Hinge**. The **Fixture** property manager opens as seen in Fig. E1-5.

- In the **Standard (Fixed Hinge)** dialogue box the **Cylindrical Faces for Fixture** field is highlighted (light blue).

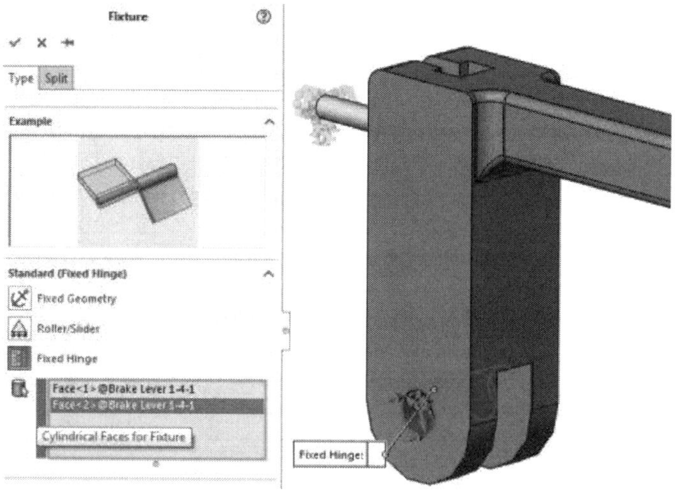

Figure E1-5 – Specifying a **Fixed Hinge** restraint

Solution Guidance (continued)

- Zoom in on the *two* bottom holes in the model and select the *inner surface* of each hole. **Face<1>@Brake Lever 1-4-1** and **Face<2>@Brake Lever 1-4-1** appear in the highlighted field shown in Fig. E1-5. These cylindrical surfaces are free to rotate about an axis perpendicular to the model face.

- Click **[OK]** ✓ to close the **Fixture** property manager.

A **Fixed Hinge** restraint specifies that a cylindrical face can only rotate about its own axis; it cannot translate along the axis or translate perpendicular to the selected axis.

Defeature the Model

The brake lever is to be *partially* defeatured before meshing. Proceed as follows.

- In the SOLIDWORKS feature manager tree, click "▶" to open the folder labeled ▸ **Brake Lever 1-4<1> (Default<<Default>_Photoworks Display State2>**.

- Scroll to the bottom of this folder, right-click Handle Fillet and from the pop-up menu select **Suppress**. Edges of the lever handle should appear square like those in Fig. E1-6 (a) or (b). *Do NOT suppress any other fillets!*

- Apply the **External Load** (**F** = **70** lb) to the split line *before* meshing the model. Otherwise, it may be difficult to locate the split line. In the **Force** dialogue box, select ☑ **Reverse direction** if force vectors do not appear directed *downward.*

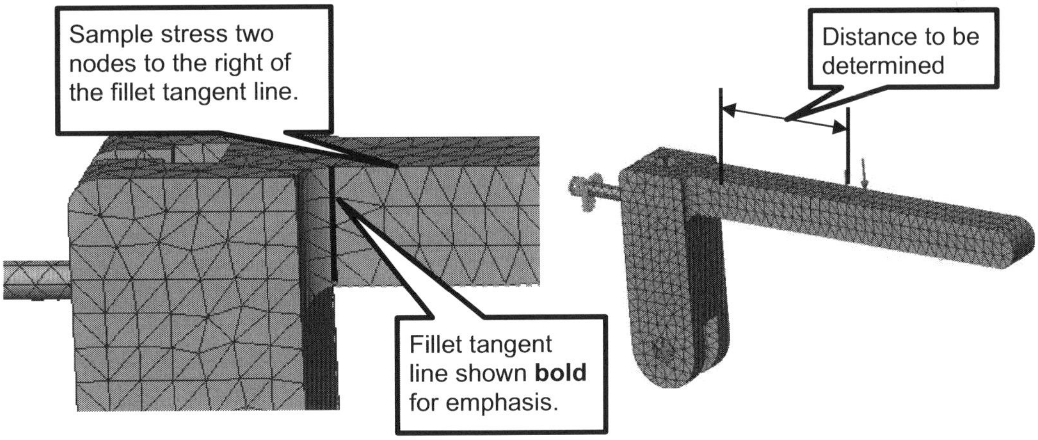

(a) (b)

Figure E1-6 – Model with External **Loads** and **Mesh** applied to the *defeatured* model.

Solution Guidance (continued)

Determine Location Dimension

- **Mesh** the model; set **Unit** to **in** (inches). After meshing the model should appear as shown in Fig. E1-6 (a) and (b).

Bending stress in the brake lever is to be determined at a location two *corner* (not mid-side) nodes to the right of where the fillet tangent line, shown bold in Fig. E1-6 (a) and Fig. E1-7, blends into the straight portion of the brake lever handle. For this reason it is necessary to determine the distance from that location to the applied **External Load**. This distance is needed to permit manual checking of finite element results. Steps below provide hints as to how to determine this distance using results from the **Probe Result** table.

- Small circles in Fig. E1-7 show node locations where bending stress is to be determined. Stress at both corner and mid-side nodes is easily determined using the **Probe** tool within SOLIDWORKS Simulation. However, an accurate *manual* calculation of bending stress requires knowledge of the distance from nodes on top and bottom of the brake lever to the location where the **External Load** is applied.

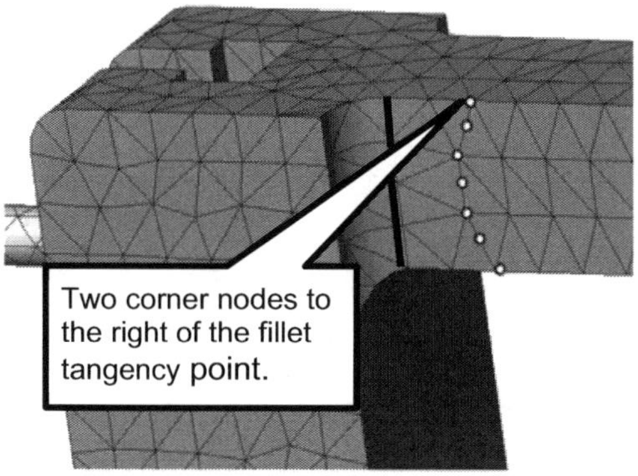

Figure E1-7 – Circles indicate corner and mid-side node locations where bending stress is to be determined.

- Open the **Probe Result** property manager and select ⊙ **At location**. In the **Annotations** dialogue box verify that ☑ **Show X, Y, Z Location** is checked.

- Click to select the top node indicated in Fig. E1-7. In addition to its stress **Value (psi)**, its **X**, **Y**, and **Z** coordinates are displayed in an information "flag" as well as in the **Results** dialogue box. Verify that **Units** are set to **in** (inches).

- Repeat the preceding step at the node where the **External Load** is applied; see Fig E1-6 (b). Length of the moment arm can now be determined from the appropriate coordinates.

Determine the following:

a. Create a stress contour plot of the *appropriate* bending stress in the "handle" of the brake lever; display a front view. Include the mesh superimposed on a model of the entire part. Also, show **Fixtures** and **External Loads** on this plot.

b. Use the **Probe** feature to create a graph of bending stress from top to bottom of the brake lever at a location two *corner* nodes to the right of the fillet tangency line shown bold in Fig. E1-6 (a) and Fig. E1-7. On this graph manually record stress values on the top, middle, and bottom surfaces of the brake lever. Customize the graph title and axis labels and include your name in the title.

c. Use the **Probe** feature to create a graph of shear stress due to bending across the front face of the brake lever at the same location used in the step (b). On this graph manually record shear stress values on the top, middle, and bottom surfaces of the lever. Customize the graph title and axis labels and include your name in the graph title.

d. Manually calculate bending stress on the top and bottom nodes of the model at the same location used in part (b) above. Note and record node coordinates and the horizontal distance between the location of external load application and the second corner node to the right of the fillet tangent line. After defeaturing the model, the brake lever handle is a 3/8-in x 3/8-in square cross section.

e. Use equation [1], repeated below, to compute the percent difference between classical and finite element solutions for bending stresses determined on the top and bottom beam surfaces determined in parts (b) and (d) above.

$$\%\ \text{difference} = \frac{(\text{FEA result - classical result})}{\text{FEA result}} * 100 = \qquad [1]$$

f. Manually calculate the maximum and minimum shear stress due to bending using classical stress equations at the location used in part (c). Then use equation [1] above to determine the percent difference between classical and finite element solutions for maximum shear stress determined in parts (c) and (f). Clearly label locations of all calculations.

g. State the reason for comparing classical and finite element results for bending stress at a location two corner elements to the right of the fillet tangent line.

EXERCISE 5 – Selecting Specific Stress at Locations on a Model

The torque handle, in Fig. E1-8 (a) and (b), functions like many handles found on commercial, high-voltage electrical cabinets. In these applications a force applied to the handle rotates a cylindrical shaft which opens the electrical cabinet while simultaneously disengaging (i.e., "killing") power to components within the cabinet. This action protects workers from potentially dangerous electrical contact when servicing components within the cabinet.

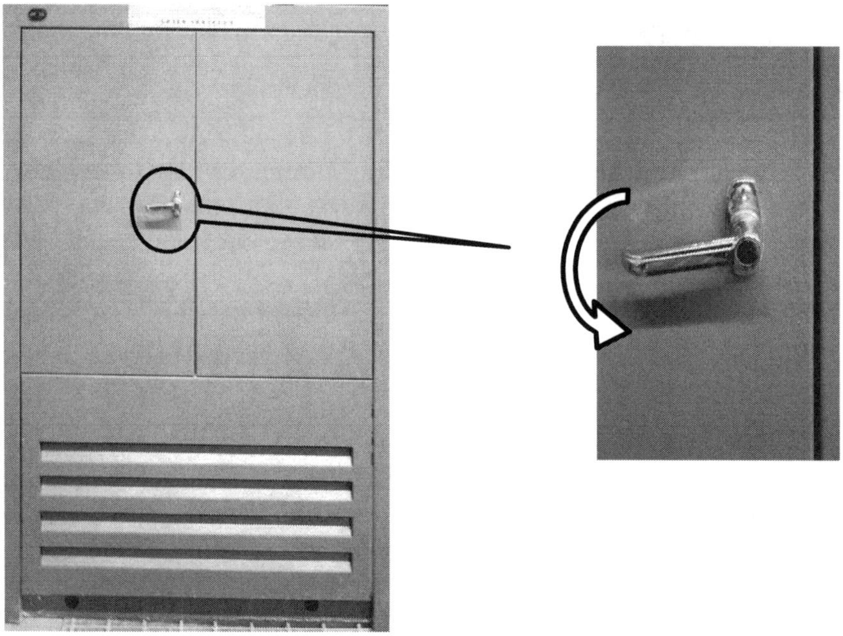

Figure E1-8 - (a) Commercial electrical cabinet. (b) Torque handle and implied rotation.

Dimensioned top and front views of the torque handle are shown in Fig. E1-9 (a). The handle is made from **2024 Alloy** Aluminum. To simulate resistance to rotation a **Fixed** restraint is applied on the circular *face* on the cylinder end. A downward force of 88 N is applied to the vertical *surface* on the free end of the rectangular handle. Open the file **Torque Handle 1-5**. Create a finite element model of this part based on the following information.

- Material: **2024 Alloy** Aluminum (Use S.I. units)
- Mesh: Select a **Standard mesh**. This mesh consists of (system default) high quality tetrahedral elements.
- External Load: Assign a **Force** F = 88 N directed downward on the vertical *face* at the free end of the handle as shown in Fig. E1-9 (b).
- Fixture: Apply a **Fixed** restraint on the circular end *face* of the cylinder.

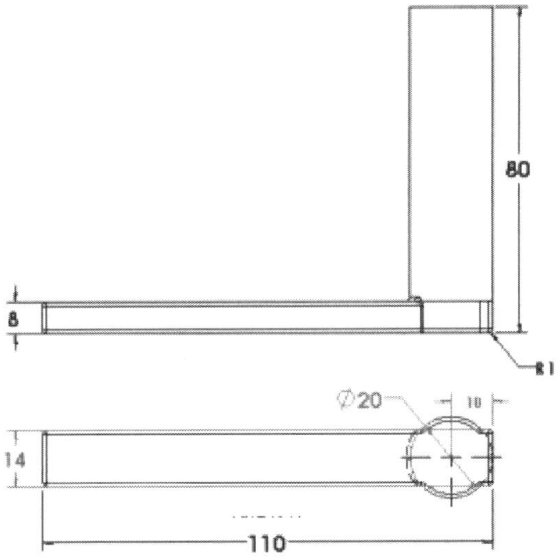

(a)

(b)

Figure E1-9 – (a) Dimensioned views of the torque handle. (UNITS: mm).

(b) **Fixture** and **External Load** applied to torque handle.

Determine the following:

a. Create a plot of the *most appropriate* stress to determine bending stress on the top surface of the handle at a location three nodes to the left of the fillet at the intersection between the straight handle and the cylindrical segment. Refer to location at point **A** in Fig. E1-10. Use the **Probe** tool to determine stress magnitude and node coordinates at location **A**. Include an information "flag" at this location on the plot. If an information "flag" does not appear, it can be turned on by opening the **Probe Result** property manager and within it open the **Annotations** dialogue box. Turn on information "flags" by checking ☑ **Show Node/Element** Number, ☑ **Show X,Y,Z** Location, and ☑ **Show Value**. *NOTE: The X coordinate of the third node to the left of the fillet is a negative value because the handle origin is located at the center of the cylinder. From there the handle geometry is extruded in the negative X direction.*

b. On the plot of part (a), include a manual calculation to determine bending stress at point **A**. Express answer in N/m^2. Also on this page, briefly answer the question: Why is it advisable to determine the finite element value of this stress at some distance from the intersection between the rectangular handle and cylindrical rod?

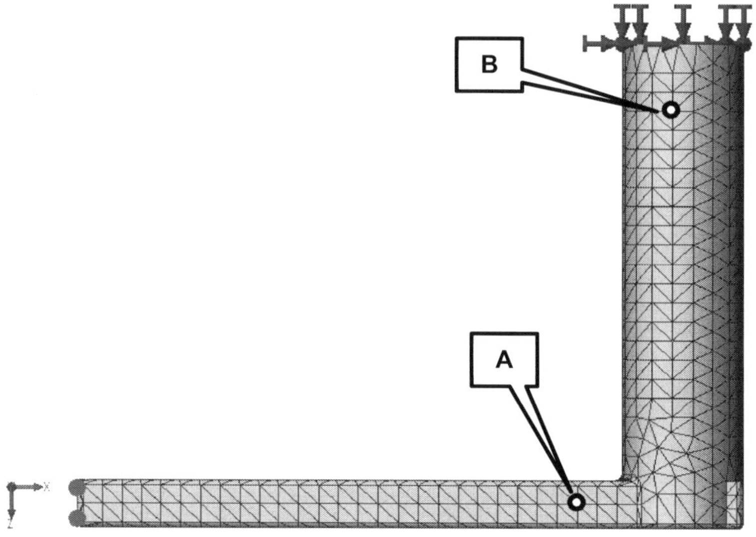

Figure E1-10 – Top view of torque handle showing locations where stress is to be determined.

c. Use equation [1], below, to compute the percent difference between classical and finite element solutions for bending stresses determined on the top handle surface determined in parts (a) and (b) above.

$$\% \text{ difference} = \frac{(\text{FEA result - classical result})}{\text{FEA result}} * 100 = \qquad [1]$$

d. A second goal is to determine the bending stress at point **B** on the top surface of the cylindrical segment at a location three nodes from the **Fixed** end; see location in Fig. E1-10. To accomplish this, generate the *appropriate* stress plot to determine this stress; include an information "flag"showing stress magnitude and X, Y, Z coordinates at the specified node.

e. On the same page as part (d) and corresponding to stress determined by finite element methods, manually calculate bending stress at location **B**. Also, if one were to consider what other stress acts at point **B**, manually calculate that stress and identify it by name. Then sketch a traditional two-dimensional stress element (of the type used in a mechanics of materials course) aligned with the X and Z axes on the top cylindrical surface and label all stress magnitudes.

f. Use equation [1], above, to compute the percent difference between classical and finite element solutions for bending stress determined on top of the cylindrical segment at point **B**.

Textbook Problems

It is highly recommended that the above exercises be supplemented by problems from a design of machine elements textbook. A great way to discover errors made in formulating a finite element analysis is to work problems for which the solution is known by independent calculation or experiment. Typical textbook problems, if well defined in advance, make an excellent source of solutions for comparison.

NOTES:

CHAPTER #2

CURVED BEAM ANALYSIS

This example, unlike that of the first chapter, will lead you quickly through those aspects of creating a finite element Study with which you already have experience. However, where new information or procedures are introduced, additional discussion is included. For consistency throughout this text, a common approach is used for the solution of all problems.

Learning Objectives

In addition to software capabilities studied in the previous chapter, upon completion of this example, users should be able to:

- Use SOLIDWORKS Simulation *icons* in addition to menu selections.
- Apply a *split line* to divide a selected face into one or more separate faces.
- Simulate *pin loading* inside a hole (or other loading on a curved surface).
- Use **Design Checks** to determine the *Factor of Safety* or lack thereof.
- Determine *reaction* forces acting on a finite element model.

Problem Statement

A dimensioned model of a curved beam is shown in Fig. 1; English units are used. Assume the beam is subject to a downward vertical force, F_y = 3800 lb, applied by a cylindrical pin (not shown) through a hole near its upper end. Beam material is 2014 Aluminum alloy. The bottom of the curved beam is considered "fixed." In this context, the *actual* fixed end-condition is analogous to that at the end of a cantilever beam where translations in the X, Y, Z directions and rotations about the X, Y, Z axes are considered to be zero. However, recall from Chapter 1 that **Fixture** types within SOLIDWORKS Simulation also depend on the type of element to which they are applied. Therefore, because solid tetrahedral elements are used to model the curved beam, **Immovable** restraints are used.

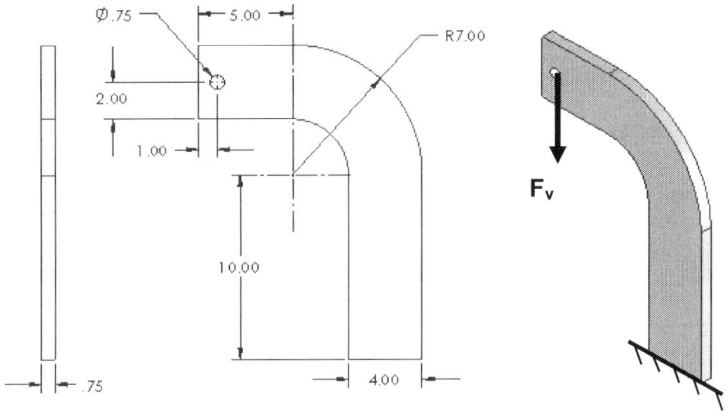

Figure 1 – Three dimensional model of a curved beam. (Dimensions in "inches")

Design Insight
Numerous mechanical elements occur in the shape of initially curved beams. Examples include C-clamps, punch-press frames, crane hooks, and bicycle caliper brakes, to name a few. This example examines stress at section A-A shown in Fig. 2. For cases such as this, where applied load, **F**, acts to one side of the cross section under consideration, classical equations calculate bending moment **M** = **F*L** about the centroidal axis (not the neutral axis) at that location. Reaction force **R** = **F** is also applied here. Accordingly, classical equations for stress in a curved beam can be used to predict stress at section A-A. In this example, the validity of this assumption is investigated while exploring additional capabilities of SOLIDWORKS Simulation software.

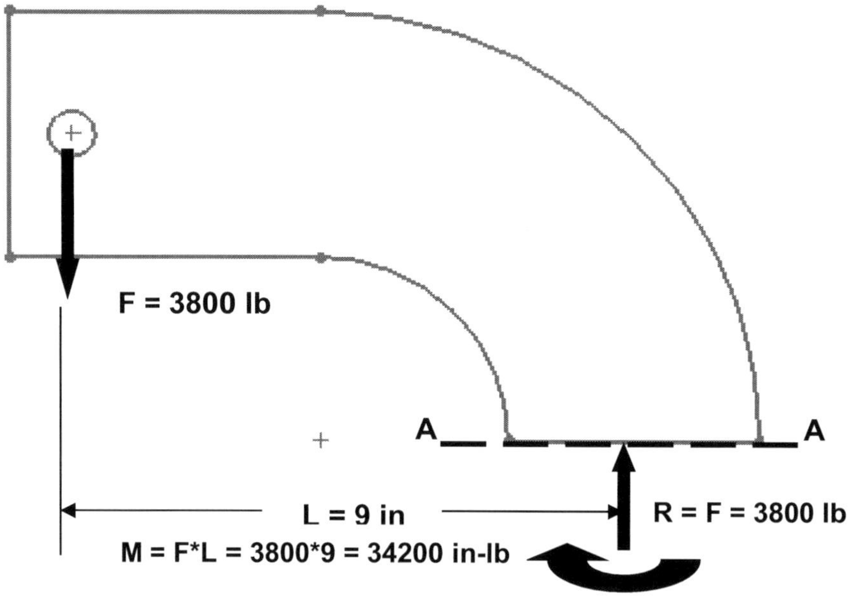

Figure 2 – Traditional free-body diagram of the upper portion of a curved beam model showing applied force **F** acting at a hole, and reactions **R** = **F**, and moment **M** acting on cut section **A-A**.

Creating a Static Analysis (Study)

1. Open SOLIDWORKS by making the following selections. (*NOTE:* The symbol ">" is used below to separate successive menu selections.)

Start>All Programs>SOLIDWORKS 2026 (or) Click the **SOLIDWORKS 2026** icon on your screen.

2. In the SOLIDWORKS main menu, select **File > Open...** Then browse to the location where SOLIDWORKS Simulation files are stored and select the file named "**Curved Beam**," then click **[Open]**.

Reminder:
If you do not see **Simulation** listed in the main menu of the SOLIDWORKS screen, click **Tools** > **Add-Ins...**, then in the **Add-Ins** window check ☑ **SOLIDWORKS Simulation** in both the **Active Add-Ins** and the **Start Up** columns, then click **[OK]**. This action permanently adds **Simulation** to the main menu every time a file is opened.

Because one goal of this chapter is to introduce and to use Simulation icons during the solution process, set-up of the Simulation toolbar is described below. If you previously set up the Simulation toolbar as outlined in the Introduction to this text, the Simulation *tab* should appear near the top left, above the graphics area on your screen. In that case, click on the **Simulation** *tab* and skip to step 5.

Setting up the Simulation Toolbar

If the **Simulation** *tab*, shown in Fig. 3, does not appear at the top left of your screen, then add it to the other tabs as follows. Otherwise, skip to step 2.

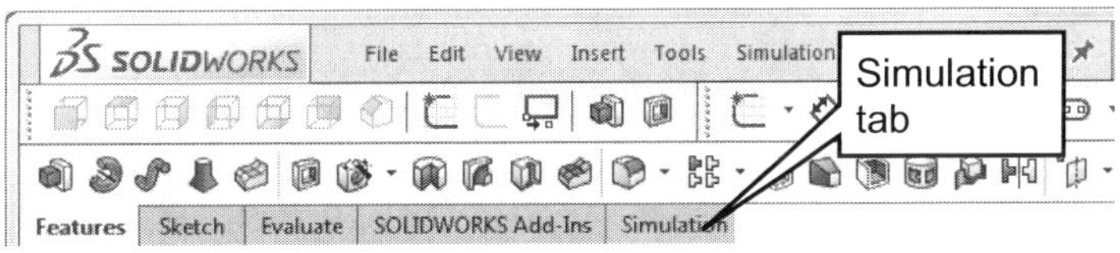

Figure 3 – Useful *tabs* located below the main menu.

1. Right-click on any of the *tab names* (**Features**, **Sketch**, **Evaluate**, etc.) and from the pull-down menu, click to place a check "✓" adjacent to ☑ **Simulation**. This action adds the **Simulation** tab beneath the main menu.

2. Click the **Simulation** tab and its associated toolbar, shown boxed in Fig. 4, opens. This toolbar contains *either* the **Study**  icon or **Study Advisor**  icon. If other icons appear they will be "grayed out" until a Simulation Study is started.

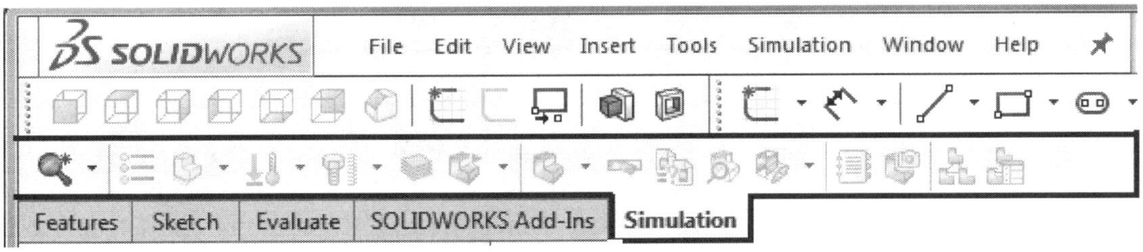

Figure 4 –Common icons found on the **Simulation** tab.

Presuming the **Simulation** icons to be unfamiliar to new users, the icon display mode illustrated in Fig. 6, which includes descriptive captions, is used throughout the remainder of this chapter. To display icons with captions, proceed as follows.

3. Right-click anywhere on any toolbar at the top of the screen to open the **Command Manager** menu shown in a *partial* view in Fig. 5.

4. Just below **Command Manager** at top of this menu, click to select **Use Large Buttons with Text**. This action adds a brief description beneath each icon as shown in Fig. 6. NOTE: Icons shown in Fig. 6 will appear grayed out until a new Study is initiated in step 8 below.

*NOTE: It is also possible to right-click the **Simulation** tab, and from the pull-down menu select **Use Large Buttons with Text**.*

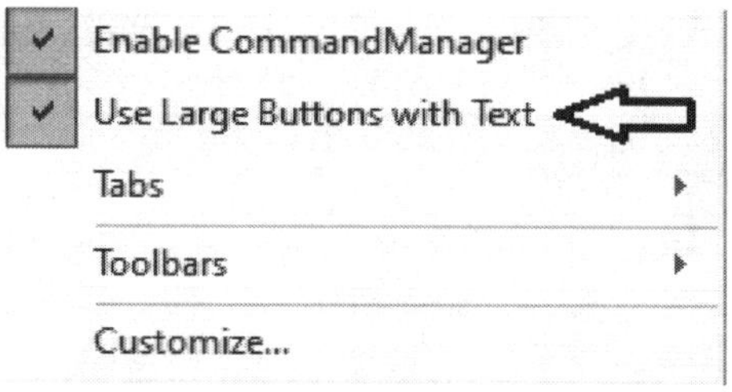

Figure 5 – Partial view of **Command Manager** pull-down menu.

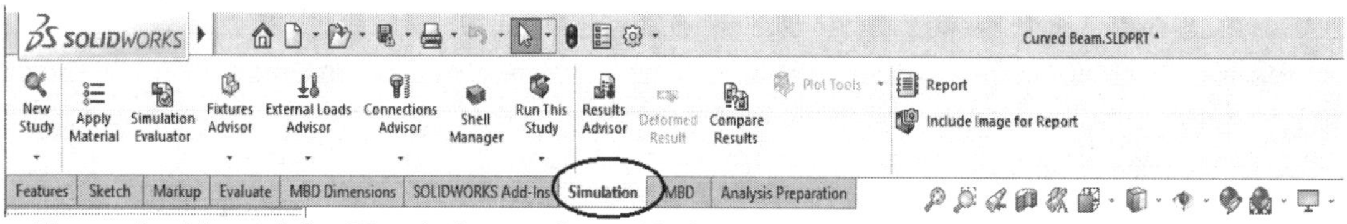

Figure 6 – View of the **Simulation** toolbar with descriptive captions applied beneath each icon.

5. In the **Simulation** tab begin a new study by selecting the ▼symbol located on the **New Study** New Study icon. From the pull-down menu select **New Study**. The **Study** property manager opens (not shown).

6. In the **Name** dialogue box, replace **Static 1** by typing **Curved Beam Analysis - YOUR NAME**. Including your name along with the Study name ensures that it is displayed on each plot. This helps identify results sent to public access printers.

7. In the **Type** dialogue box verify that **Static** is selected as the analysis type. Keep **Use 2D Simplification** unchecked.

8. Click **[OK]** ✓ (green check mark) to close the **Study** property manager.

Notice that an outline of the new Study is now listed beneath the Simulation manager tree and icons on the **Simulation** tab become active as shown in Fig. 6.

Now that an icon-based work environment is established, our Study of stress in the curved beam continues below. As in the previous example, the sequence of steps outlined in the Simulation manager, at the left of your screen, is followed from top to bottom as the current Study is developed.

Assign Material Properties to the Model

Part *material* is defined as outlined below.

1. On the **Simulation** *tab*, click to select the **Apply Material** icon. The **Material** window opens as shown in Fig. 7.

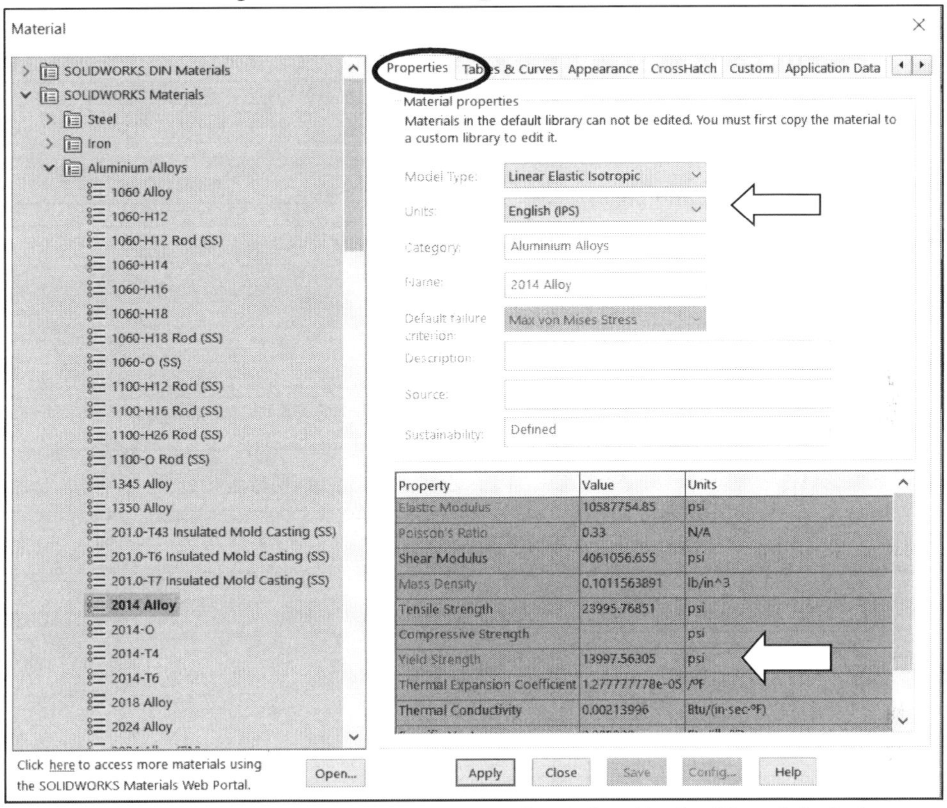

Figure 7 – Material properties are selected and/or defined in the **Material** window.

2. In the left column, select **SOLIDWORKS Materials** (if not already selected). Because the left column typically defaults to **Alloy Steel** or displays the last material selected, click the triangle sign to close the **Steel** folder if necessary.

3. Next, click the triangle symbol next to **Aluminum Alloys** and scroll down to select **2014 Alloy**. The properties of 2014 Aluminum alloy are displayed on the **Properties** tab in the right half of the window.

4. In the **Properties** tab, click to open the **Units:** pull-down menu and change **Units:** to **English (IPS)** if necessary.

In the table, note the material **Yield Strength** is a relatively low 13997.56 psi (essentially 14000 psi). Material with a low yield strength is intentionally chosen to facilitate discussion of *Factor of Safety* later in this example. Examine other values in the table to become familiar with data listed for each material.

Within the table, also notice that some material properties are indicated by red text, others by blue, and some by black. Red text indicates material properties that *must* be specified because a stress analysis is being performed. Conversely, material properties highlighted in blue text are optional values, while those listed in black primarily refer to thermal or vibration damping properties and, as such, are not needed for this stress analysis.

5. Click **[Apply]** followed by **[Close]** to close the **Material** window. A check mark "✓" appears on the **Curved Beam** folder to indicate a material has been selected. Also, the material type **(-2014 Alloy-)** is listed adjacent to the model name.

6. If the "**What would you like to do?**" window opens, click the question mark icon at lower right of the graphics screen to close it.

> **Aside:**
>
> If at any point you wish to *change the material specification* of a part, such as during a redesign, simply right-click the name of the particular part whose material properties are to be changed and from the pull-down menu select **Apply/Edit Material...** The **Material** window opens, and an alternative material can be selected.
>
> However, be aware that when a different material is specified *after* running a solution, it is necessary to run the solution again using the revised material properties.

Applying Fixtures

For a static analysis, adequate restraints must be applied to stabilize the model. In this example, the bottom surface of the model is considered "fixed."

1. On the **Simulation** tab, click ▼ beneath the **Fixtures Advisor** icon, shown boxed in Fig. 8, and from the pull-down menu select **Fixed Geometry**. The **Fixture** manager opens as shown in Fig. 9.

2. Within the **Standard (Fixed Geometry)** dialogue box, select the **Fixed Geometry** icon (if not already selected).

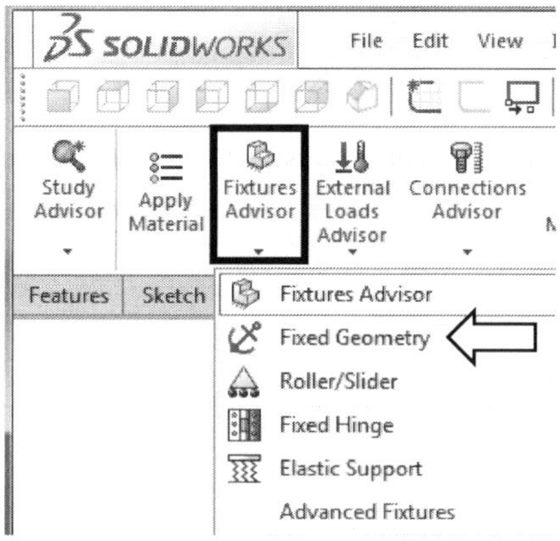

Figure 8 – Selecting the **Fixture** icon

3. The **Faces, Edges, Vertices for Fixture** field is highlighted (light blue) to indicate it is active and waiting for the user to select part of the model to be restrained. Rotate and/or zoom to view the bottom of the model. Next, move the cursor over the model and when the bottom surface is indicated, click to select it. The surface is highlighted, and fixture symbols appear as shown in Fig. 10. Also,

Face<1> appears in the **Faces, Edges, Vertices for Fixture** field.If an incorrect entity (such as a vertex, edge, or the wrong surface) is selected, right-click the incorrect item in the highlighted field and from the pop-up menu select **Delete**; then repeat step 3.

4. If restraint symbols do not appear, or if it is desired to alter their size or color, click the down arrow ⌄ to open the **Symbol Settings** dialogue box, at bottom of the **Fixture** property manager in Fig. 9, and check the ☑ **Show preview** box.

5. Both color and size of the restraint symbols (vectors in the X, Y, Z directions) can be changed by altering values in the **Symbol Settings** dialogue box of Fig. 9. Experiment by clicking the up ^ or down ⌄ arrows to change size of restraint symbols. A box of this type, where values can be changed either by typing a new value or by clicking the ^⌄ arrows, is called a "spin box." Restraint symbols shown in Fig. 10 were arbitrarily increased in size to 200%.

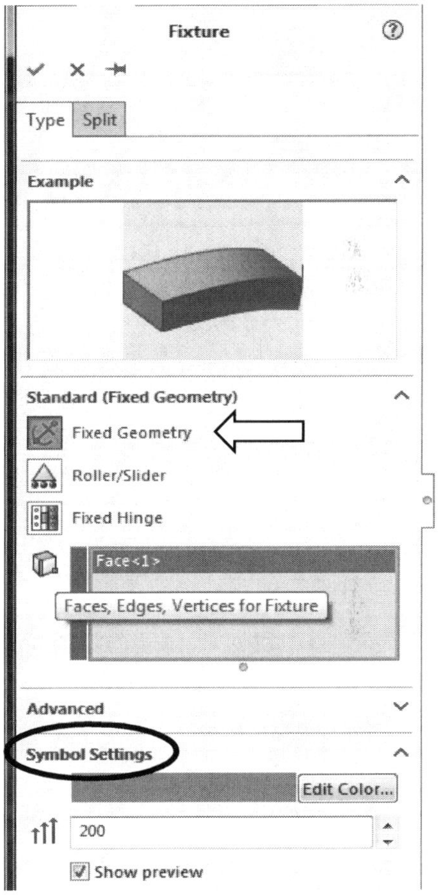

Figure 9 – **Fixture** property manager.

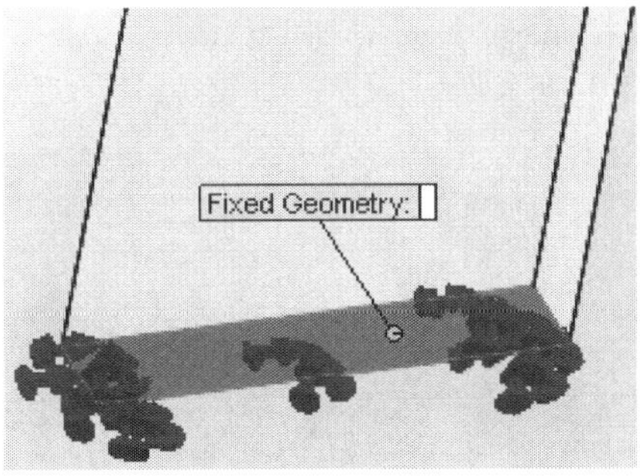

Figure 10 – **Fixtures** applied to bottom of the curved beam model

6. Click **[OK]** ✓ (green check mark) at top of the **Fixture** property manager to accept this restraint. An icon named Fixed-1 appears beneath the **Fixtures** folder in the Simulation manager tree. If the above **Fixed-1** icon does not appear, click the " ▸ " symbol adjacent to **Fixtures** in the Simulation manager tree.

Aside:
Restraint symbols shown in Fig. 10 appear as simple arrows with small disks on their tails. These symbols indicate **Fixed** restraints when applied to shell or beam elements. **Fixed** restraints set both *translational* and *rotational* degrees of freedom to zero (i.e., both X, Y, Z displacements and rotations (moments) about the X, Y, Z axes are zero). However, when applied to either solid models or truss elements, only *displacements* in the X, Y, and Z directions are restrained (i.e., prevented). This latter type of restraint is referred to as **Immovable**. The software applies appropriate fixtures based on element type. Watch for this subtle difference in future examples.

Applying External Load(s)

Next apply the downward force, F_y = 3800 lb, at the hole located near the top left-hand side of the model shown in Figs. 1 and 2. This force is assumed to be applied by a pin (not shown) that acts through the hole.

Analysis Insight:
Because the goal of this analysis is to focus on curved beam stresses at Section A-A, and because Section A-A is well removed from the point of load application, modeling of the applied force can be handled in a number of different ways. For example, the downward force could be applied to the vertical *surface* located on the upper left side of the model, Fig. (a). Alternatively, the force could be applied to the upper or lower *edge* of the model at the extreme left side, Fig. (b). These loading situations would require a slight reduction of the magnitude of force **F** to account for its additional distance from the left-side of the model to the centroidal axis at section A-A (i.e., the moment about section A-A must remain the same).

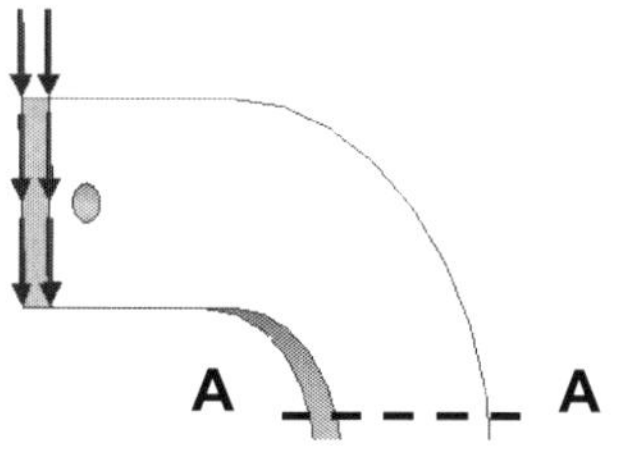

Figure (a) – Force applied to left surface.

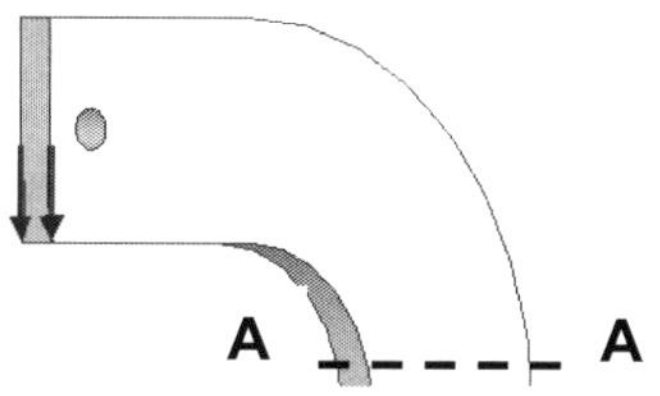

Figure (b) – Force applied to lower edge.

The above loads are simple to apply. However, the assumption of pin loading allows us to investigate use of a *Split Line* to isolate a *portion* of the bottom surface of the hole where contact with a pin is assumed to occur. This surface is where a pin force would be transferred to the curved beam model. The actual contact area depends on a number of factors, which include (a) geometries of the contacting parts (i.e., relative diameters of the pin and hole), (b) material properties (i.e., hard versus soft contact surfaces of either the pin or the beam), and (c) magnitude of the force that presses the two surfaces together. This example arbitrarily assumes a reasonable contact area so that use of a *Split Line* can be demonstrated. If, on the other hand, contact stresses in the vicinity of the hole were of paramount importance, then determination of the true contact area requires inclusion of the actual pin and use of *Contact/Gap* analysis. This type of analysis is investigated in Chapter #6.

Inserting Split Lines

The first task to simulate downward pin loading on the hole bottom is to isolate a small area at the bottom of the hole. This can be accomplished by using a *Split Line*. The method described below outlines use of a reference plane to insert a *Split Line*.

1. In the view toolbar, located above the graphics area, reorient the model by clicking the **Trimetric** or **Isometric** view icon.

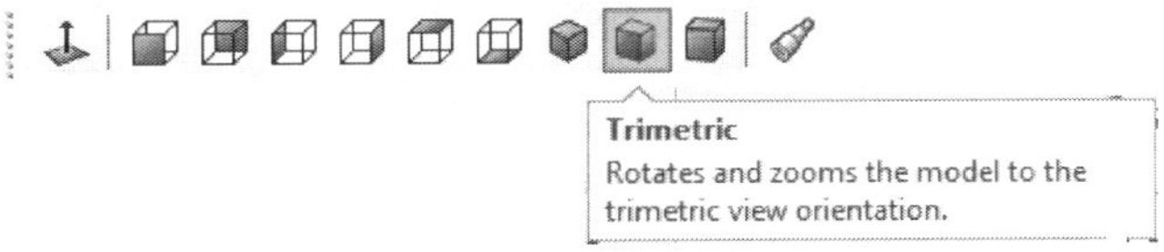

2. From the main menu, select **Insert**. Then, from succeeding pull-down menus make the following selections: **Reference Geometry ►** followed by **Plane...** In Fig. 11 the **Plane** property manager opens to the left of the graphics area. Also, a SOLIDWORKS "flyout" menu appears at the top left of the graphics area to provide access to SOLIDWORKS options; see label in Fig. 11.

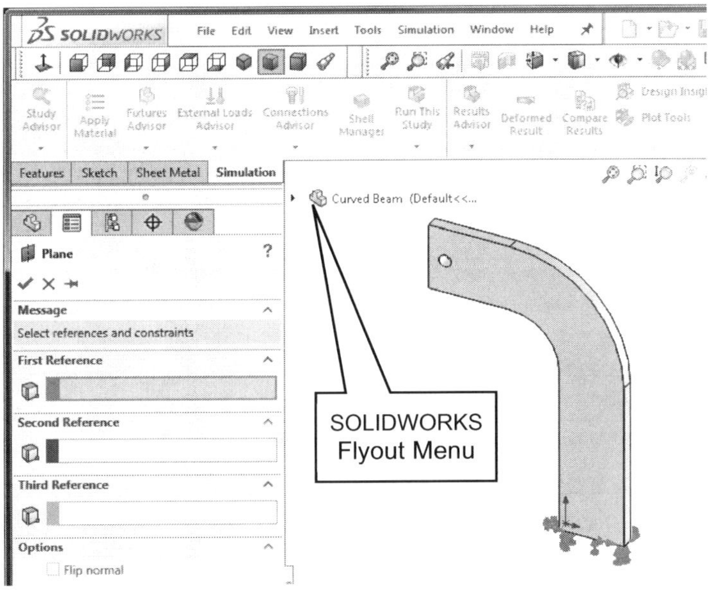

Figure 11 – The **Plane** property manager and SOLIDWORKS flyout menu.

3. Within the **Plane** property manager, under **First Reference**, the field is highlighted (light blue) to indicate it is active and awaiting selection of a plane from which a *new* plane can be referenced.

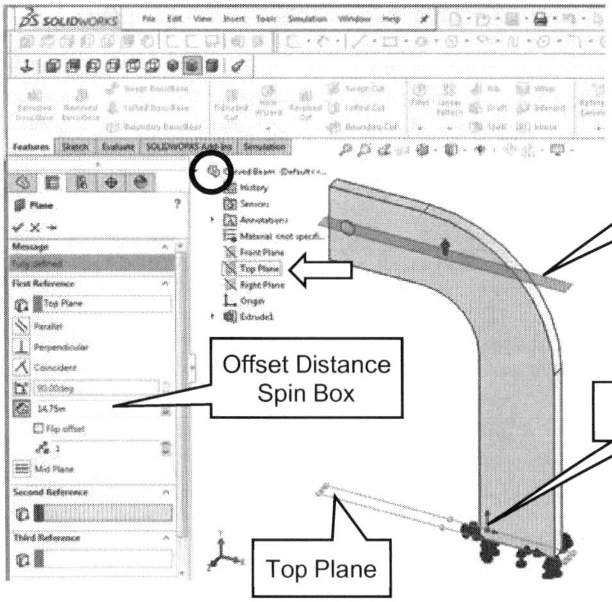

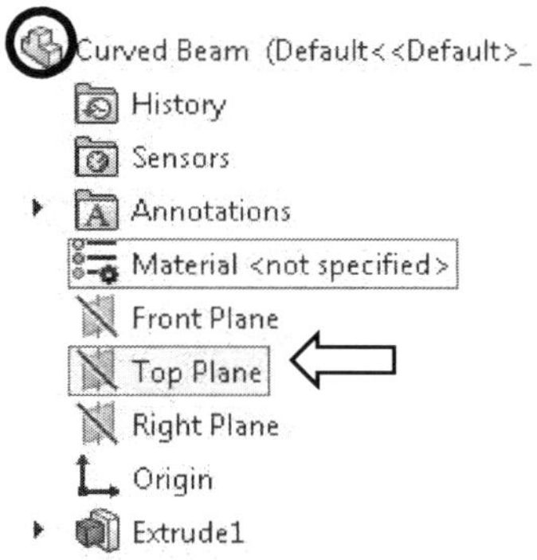

Figure 12 (a) - The **Plane** property manager and selections to create a reference plane passing through the bottom of the hole.

Fig. 12 (b) – Flyout menu (**enlarged view**).

4. Begin by clicking the "▸" symbol to open the SOLIDWORKS flyout menu circled in Figs. 12(a) and (b). Within the flyout menu select the **Top Plane**; see arrows. The **Plane** property manager changes appearance as shown in Fig. 12(a), and **Top Plane** appears in the **First Reference** dialogue box. For those using the **Curved Beam** part file from the textbook web site, the top plane passes through the part origin, which is located on the bottom of the model[1] in Fig. 12 (a).

5. Return to the **First Reference** dialogue box and in the **Offset Distance** spin-box and type **14.75**. This is the distance *from* the **Top Plane** to a **Reference Plane** located so that it intersects the bottom portion of the hole in Fig. 12 (a).

Aside:
The 14.75-in. dimension is determined from the following calculation. Refer to Fig. 1 to determine the source of values used in the equation below.

10 in (height of straight vertical sides) + 3 in (radius of concave surface) + 1.75 in (distance from the horizontal edge beneath the hole and extending an arbitrary distance into the bottom portion of the hole) = 14.75in.

It is emphasized that the area intersected on the bottom of the hole is chosen *arbitrarily* in this example!

[1] Users who created a curved beam model from scratch can also follow these instructions. The *only* difference would be specification of the proper *distance* from the **Top Plane** (used as a reference in *your* model) to the bottom of the hole.

6. Click **[OK]** ✓ to close the **Plane** property manager.

The reference plane created in the previous steps appears highlighted on your screen. If your model is large enough it will be labeled **Plane1**, if not, zoom-in on the top of the model. In the following steps **Plane1** is used to create *Split Lines* near the bottom of the hole. These *Split Lines* enable us to define a small "patch" of area on the bottom of the hole where the downward load will be applied.

7. From the **Main Menu**, select **Insert**. Then, from successive pull-down menus, choose **Curve ▶** followed by **Split Line...** The **Split Line** property manager opens as shown in Fig. 13.

8. Beneath **Type of Split**, select ⦿ **Intersection**. This choice designates the means by which *Split Lines* are defined for this example (i.e., *Split Lines* will be located where the reference plane *intersects* the hole).

9. In the **Selections** dialogue box, **Plane1** should already appear in the **Splitting Bodies/Faces/ Planes** field. If **Plane1** does not appear in this field, click to activate the field (light blue), then move the cursor onto the graphics screen and select the upper plane when it is highlighted. **Plane1** now appears in the top field.

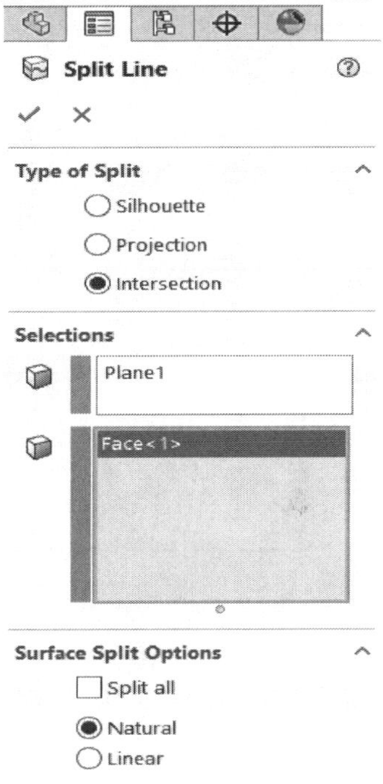

Figure 13 – **Split Line** property manager showing selections.

10. Next, click inside the **Faces/Bodies to Split** field. This field may already be active (light blue). Then move the cursor over the model and select anywhere on the *inside surface* of the hole. It may be necessary to zoom in on the model to select this surface. Once selected, **Face<1>** appears in the active field. Figure 14 shows a partial image of the model with *Split Lines* appearing where **Plane1** intersects the bottom portion of the hole.

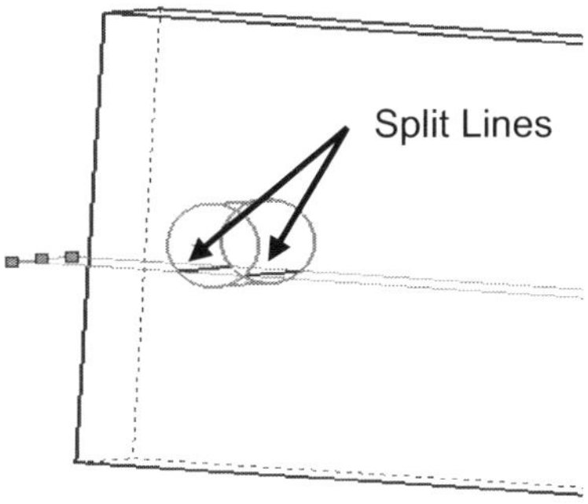

Figure 14 – Close-up view of hole showing *Split Lines* where **Plane1** intersects near the bottom of hole.

Remain zoomed-in on the model to facilitate applying a force to the inside of the hole.

11. In the **Surface Split Options** dialogue box, select ⦿ **Natural**. A **Natural** split follows the contour of the selected surface.

12. Click **[OK]** ✓ to close the **Split Line** property manager.

13. If an information "flag" appears adjacent to the *Split Lines*, click ☒ to close it.

Applying Force to an Area Bounded by Split Lines

Now that a restricted area on the bottom of the hole has been identified, the next step is to apply a downward force, F_y = 3800 lb, on this area. Proceed as follows.

1. On the Simulation *tab*, click ▼ beneath the **External Loads Advisor** icon and from the pop-up menu select the **Force** icon. The **Force/Torque** property manager opens and appears in a partial view in Fig. 15.

2. Within the **Force/Torque** dialogue box, click the **Force** icon (if not already selected). Also, click ◉ **Selected direction**. Then click to activate (light blue) the upper field titled **Faces, Edges, Vertices, Reference Points for Force**.

3. Move the cursor over the model and when the *bottom inside surface* of the hole is outlined, click to select it. **Face<1>** appears in the active field of the **Force/Torque** dialogue box.

4. Next, click to activate the second field from the top of the **Force/Torque** dialogue box. Passing the cursor over this field identifies it as the **Face, Edge, Plane for Direction** field. This field is used to specify the direction of the force applied to the bottom of the hole.

Because a downward, vertical force is to be applied, select a *vertical* edge . . . *any vertical edge* . . . on the model aligned with the Y-direction. After selecting a vertical edge, **Edge<1>** appears in the active field and force vectors appear on the model as seen in Fig. 16.

5. In the **Units** dialogue box, set **Units** to **English (IPS)** (if not already selected).

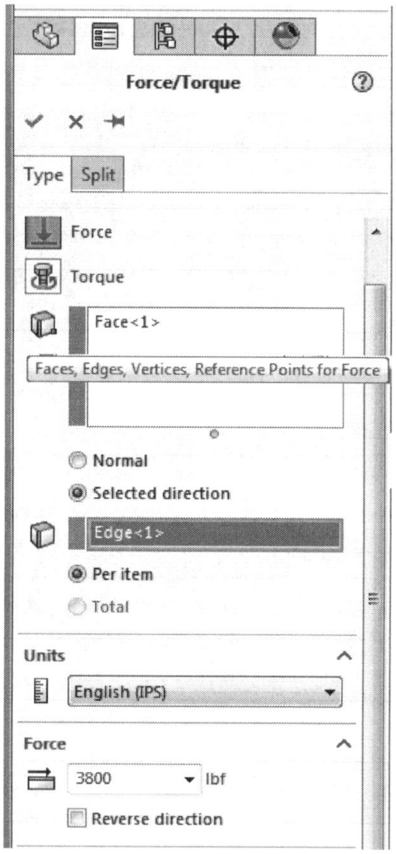

Figure 15 – Specifying a force and its direction on the hole bottom.

6. In the **Force** dialogue box, type **3800**. As noted in an earlier example, it may be necessary to check ☑ **Reverse Direction** if the force is not directed downward.

7. Click **[OK]** ✓ to accept this force definition and close the **Force/Torque** property manager. An icon named **Force-1 (:Per item: 3800 lbf:)** appears beneath the **External Loads** folder in the Simulation manager.

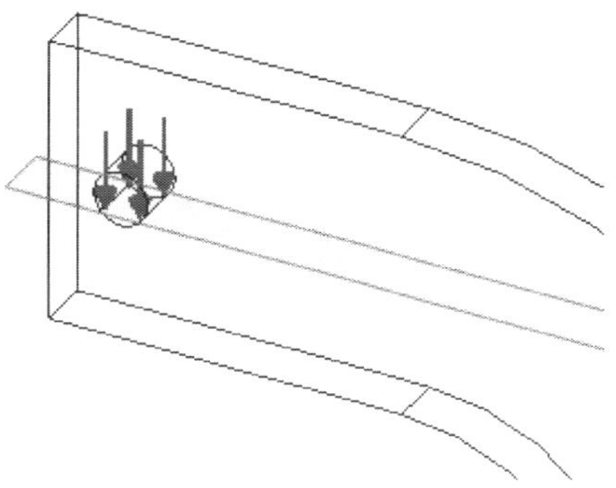

Figure 16 – Downward force applied between *Split Lines* on bottom of hole. A wireframe view of the model is shown.

The model is now complete as far as material, fixtures, and external load definitions are concerned. The next step is to Mesh the model as described below.

Meshing the Model

1. Within the Simulation *tab*, select ▼ beneath the **Run this Study** icon. From the pull-down menu, select the **Create Mesh** icon. The **Mesh** property manager opens as shown in Figs 17 (a) and (b).

2. Check ✓ to open the ☑ **Mesh Parameters** dialogue box and verify that a ⦿ **Standard mesh** is selected. Also set the **Unit** field to **in** (if not already selected). Accept the remaining default settings (i.e., mesh **Global Size** and **Tolerance**) shown in this dialogue box.

3. Click the down arrow ⌄ to open the **Advanced** dialogue box, Fig. 17 (b). Verify that **Jacobian points** is set at **4 points** (this setting indicates high quality tetrahedral elements are used). These default settings produce a good quality mesh. However, verify that the settings are as listed and only change them if they differ.

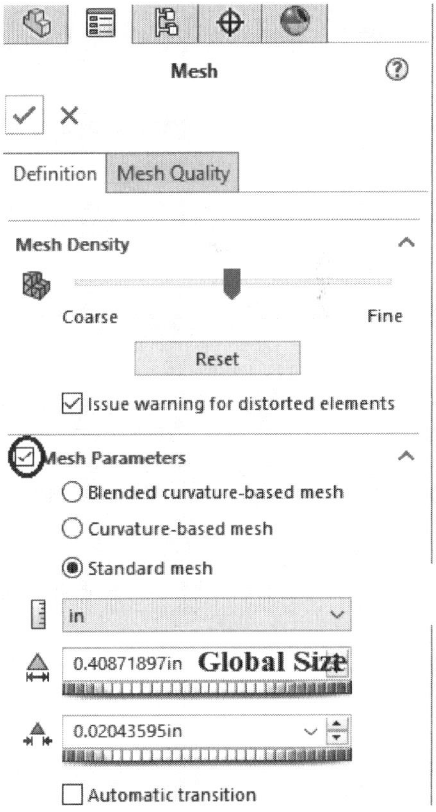

Figure 17 (a) – **Mesh** property manager showing system default **Mesh** settings applied to the current model.

4. Finally, click **[OK]** ✓ to accept the default mesh settings and close the **Mesh** property manager.

Meshing starts automatically and a **Mesh Progress** window appears briefly. After meshing is complete, SOLIDWORKS Simulation displays the meshed model shown in Fig. 18. Also, a check mark "✓" appears on the **Mesh** icon to indicate meshing is complete.

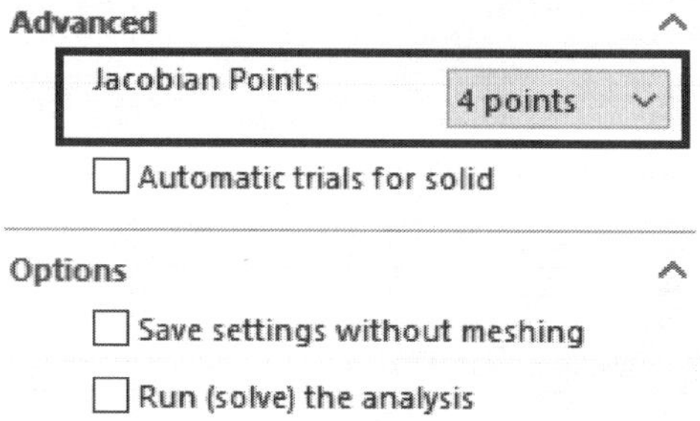

Figure 17 (b) – Views of the **Advanced** and **Options** portions of the **Mesh** property manager.

Since **Plane1** is no longer needed, hide the reference plane by right-clicking it and, from the pop-up menu, select the **Hide** icon.

OPTIONAL:

5. Display mesh information by right-clicking the Mesh folder located in the Simulation manager tree (not the Create Mesh icon); then select **Details...**

The **Mesh Details** window displays a variety of mesh information. Scroll down the list and note the number of nodes and elements for this model is 12578 nodes and 7229 elements (numbers may vary slightly due to the automated mesh generation procedure).

Rotate the model as illustrated in Fig. 18 (a Trimetric view) and notice that the mesh is two elements *thick*. Two elements across the model's thinnest dimension are considered the minimum number for which *Solid Elements* should be used. Thus, two elements are considered an unofficial dividing line between when *Shell* or *Solid Elements* should be used. Therefore, either element type could be used for this model. But, keep in mind that shell elements are typically reserved for thin parts.

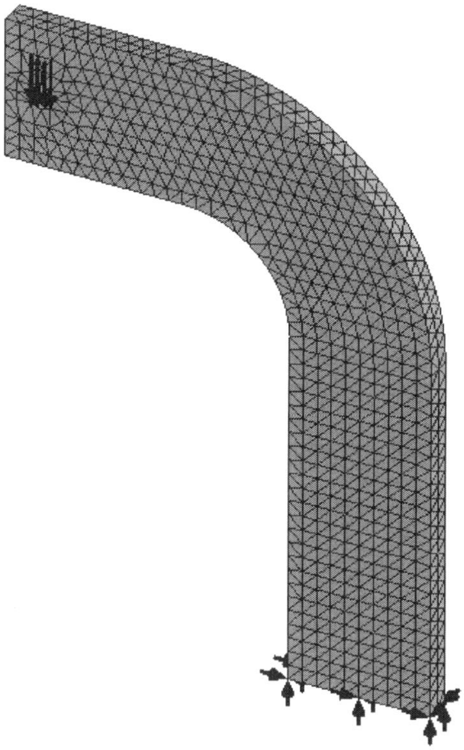

Figure 18 – Curved beam with mesh and boundary conditions illustrated.

6. Click ☒ to close the **Mesh Details** window.

> **Reminder**
>
> Recall that it is permissible to define material properties, fixtures, external loads, and create the mesh in any order. However, all these necessary steps must be completed before running a solution.

Solution

After the model has been completely defined, the solution process is initiated. During a solution the numerous equations defining a Study are solved and results of the analysis are automatically saved for review.

1. On the **Simulation** tab, click the **Run this Study** Run This Study icon to start the Solution.

After a successful solution, a **Results** folder appears below the Simulation manager. This folder should include three default plots saved at the conclusion of each Study. These folders are named as illustrated in Fig. 19. If these folders do *not* appear, follow steps (a) through (f) outlined on page 1-14 of Chapter #1.

If **Units** displayed on the **Stress1 (-vonMises-)** and **Displacement1 (-Res disp-)** plots are not **psi** and **in** respectively, then change them as outlined in steps 2 through 5 below. Otherwise, skip to the next section.

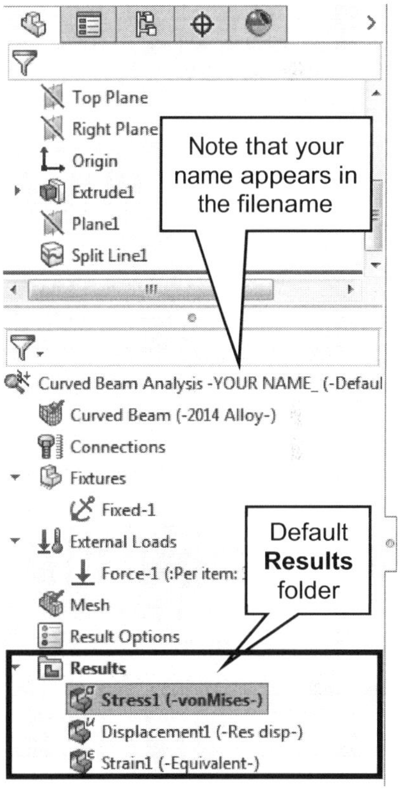

Figure 19 – **Results** folders created during the Solution process.

2. If the von Mises stress plot is not shown, double-click **Stress1 (-von Mises-)** to display the plot.

3. Next, right-click **Stress1 (-vonMises-)** and from the pull-down menu select **Edit Definition…** The **Stress Plot** property manager opens. In the **Display** dialogue box, verify **Units** are set to **psi**. If not, use the pull-down menu to change **Units**.

4. Click **[OK]** ✓ to close the **Stress Plot** property manager.

5. Repeat steps (2) through (4); however, in step (2), double-click **Displacement1 (-Res disp-)** and in step (3) in the **Display** dialogue box alter the **Units** field from **mm** to **in**. NOTE: **Res disp** is short for "resultant displacement."

Examination of Results

Analysis of von Mises Stresses Within the Model

Outcomes of the current analysis can be viewed by accessing plots stored in the **Results** folders listed in the previous section. This step is where validity of results is verified by cross-checking Finite Element Analysis (FEA) results against results obtained using classical stress equations or by experiment. *Checking results is a necessary step in good engineering practice!*

1. In the Simulation manager tree, double-click the **Stress1 (-vonMises-)** folder (or) right-click it and from the pull-down menu, select **Show**. A plot of the vonMises stress distribution throughout the model is displayed.

Figure 20 reveals an image *similar* to what currently appears on the screen. SOLIDWORKS Simulation has a feature that combines all **Results** display options into a single property manager. Access to those display options is accessible via three *tabs* at top of the **Stress Plot** property manager. We will use those tabs in the following steps to convert your current screen image to that shown in Fig. 20.

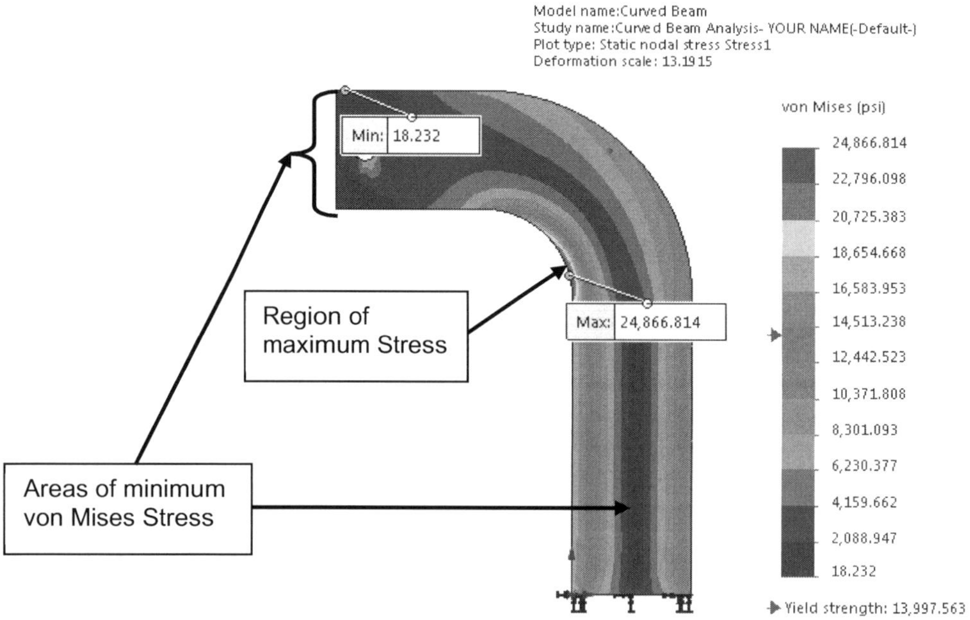

Figure 20 – Front view of the curved beam model showing von Mises stress *after* making changes outlined below. Note arrows indicating Yield Strength on the stress scale at right.

NOTE: *Stress contour plots are printed in black, white, and grey tones. Therefore, light and dark color areas on your screen may appear different from images shown throughout this text.*

2. Right-click **Stress1 (-vonMises-)** and from the pull-down menu select **Chart Options…** The **Stress Plot** property manager opens, a *portion* of which is shown in Fig. 21. Note that the **Chart Options** *tab* is selected.

3. Within the **Display Options** dialogue box, click to place check marks "✓" to activate ☑ **Show min annotation** and ☑ **Show max annotation**. This action labels minimum and maximum vonMises stress locations and magnitudes on the model. *Do not change other checked items.*

4. Within the **Position/Format** dialogue box, change the **Number Format** from **scientific** to **floating** from the pull-down menu. Type **3** for **No of Decimals.**

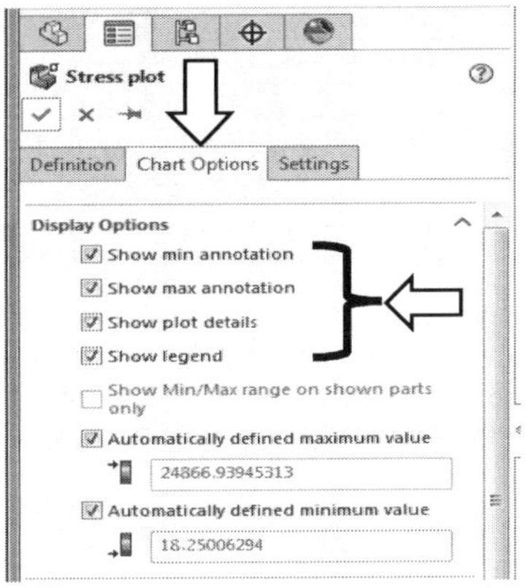

Figure 21 – Upper portion of **Chart Options** tab showing current selections.

5. Next, select the **Settings** *tab*. A partial view of this tab is illustrated in Fig. 22.

6. In the **Fringe Options** dialogue box, open ▼ the pull-down menu and select **Discrete** as the fringe type to be displayed.

7. Next, in the **Boundary Options** dialogue box, select **Model** from the pull-down menu to superimpose a solid outline on the model.

8. Click **[OK]** ✓ to close the **Stress Plot** property manager. If the above changes are not displayed, on the model, double-click **Stress1 (-vonMises-)**.

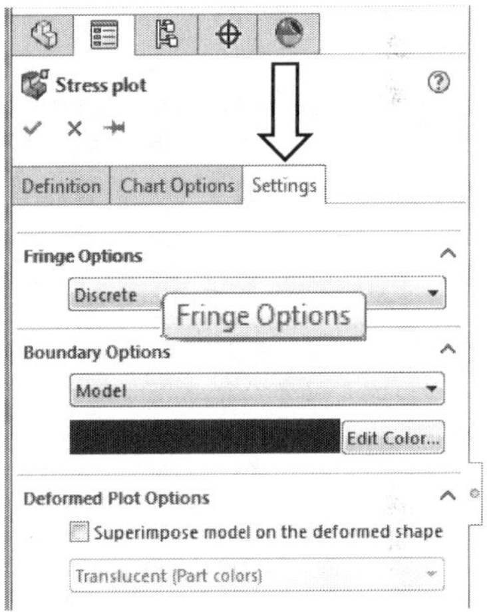

Figure 22 – Selections in the **Stress Plot** property manager.

9. On the **Simulation** *tab*, repeatedly click the **Deformed Result** icon to toggle between a deformed image of the model (default state) and an un-deformed image. See images in Fig. 23 (a) and (b). When done, leave the model in the un-deformed state and rotate it to a front view.

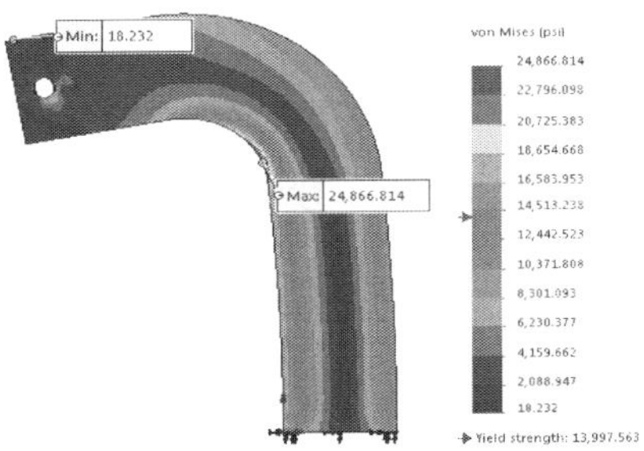

Figure 23 (a) – Deformed model image.

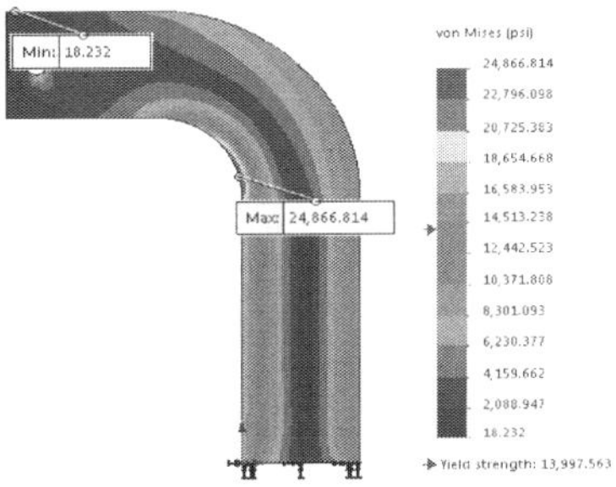

Figure 23 (b) - Un-deformed model image.

The following observations can be made about the figure currently on your screen.

OBSERVATIONS:

- Areas of low stress (dark blue) occur at the top-left side of the model and also through the vertical center of the model. This last region overlaps the neutral axis. The minimum von Mises stress is approximately 18. psi. Regions of high stress are indicated in red. The maximum stress indicated is 24867.6 psi, which occurs along the concave surface (values may vary slightly).

- Material *Yield* Strength =13997.6 ≈ 14000 psi is also listed beneath the color-coded **von Mises** stress legend. A red arrow adjacent to the color chart indicates where the Yield Strength lies relative to all stresses within the model. In this instance, it is clear that some stress in the model *exceeds* the material yield strength. *Yield Strength* and *Safety Factor* are investigated later in this chapter.

Modern software makes conducting a finite element analysis and obtaining results deceptively easy. As noted earlier, however, it is the validity of results and understanding how to interpret and evaluate them properly that is of primary importance. For these reasons, we pause to consider two questions that should be intriguing or, perhaps, even bothering you, the reader.

First, why are all stress values positive in Fig. 20? ("+" stress values typically indicate tension). However, compressive stresses are known to exist along the concave surface for the given loading. Second, why does the solution show stresses above the material yield strength when stresses that exceed the yield strength indicate yielding or failure? These, and many others, are the types of questions that should be raised continually by users of finite element software. Attempts to address these questions are included below.

To answer these questions, we briefly digress to investigate the definition of von Mises stress as a means to determine a *Safety Factor* predicted by the software.

<u>Von Mises Stress</u> -
The example of Chapter 1 avoided the issue about what the von Mises stress is or what it represents. That example further assumed that some readers might not be familiar with von Mises stress. For the sake of completeness and because von Mises stress typically is not introduced until later in a design of machine elements course, its basic definition is included below. Although this SOLIDWORKS Simulation user guide is not intended to develop the complete theory related to von Mises stress, the usefulness of this stress might be summed up by the following statement:

> The equation for von Mises stress "allows the most complicated stress situation to be represented by a single quantity."[2] In other words, for the most complex state of stress that one can imagine (e.g., a three-dimensional stress element subject to a

[2] Budynas, R.G., Nisbett, J. K., <u>Shigley's Mechanical Engineering Design</u>, 9th Ed., McGraw-Hill, 2010, p.224.

combination of shear and normal stresses acting on every face (as illustrated below), these stresses can be reduced to a single number. That number is named the von Mises stress. This number represents a stress magnitude, "which can be compared against the yield strength of a material"[3] to determine whether or not failure by yielding is predicted. As such, the von Mises stress is associated with one of the theories of failure for *ductile* materials; theories of failure are briefly discussed below. Von Mises stress is always a *positive*, *scalar* number.

The above statement answers the question about the positive nature of von Mises stress shown on the model in Fig. 20 and on your screen. It also should provide some insight into why von Mises stress, which is *a single number*, can be used to determine whether or not a part is likely to fail by comparing it to the value of part yield strength *(yield strength is also listed as a single value)*. The method of comparison used is the *Safety Factor,* which is explored later in this chapter.

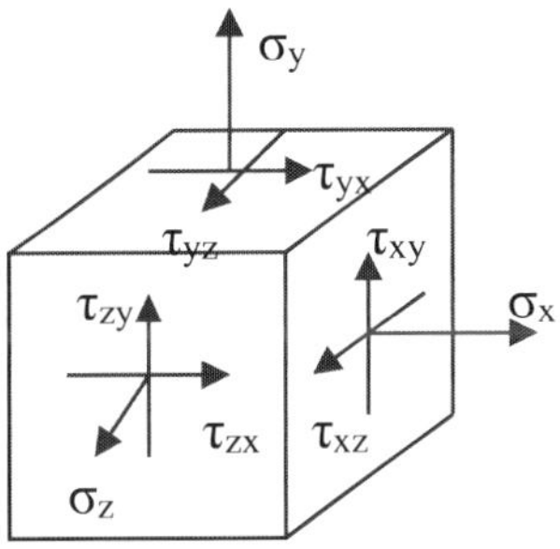

Although the above definition indicates that von Mises stress is always a positive number, that superficial answer might continue to bother readers who intuitively recognize that compressive stresses result along the concave surface of the curved beam.

More fundamentally, the issue in question gets to the heart of every analysis. That question is, "*What stress should be examined* when comparing finite element results with stress calculations based on the use of classical equations?" The answer, of course, is that one must examine the *appropriate stresses* that correspond to the goals of an analysis. For example, in Chapter 1 it was decided that normal stress in the Y-direction (σ_y) was the primary stress component that would provide favorable comparisons with stress calculated using classic equations. The **Verification of Results** section below reveals the *appropriate stress* for the current example. Before continuing, answer the question: "What *is* the appropriate stress?" Then, check your answer below.

Verification of Results

In keeping with the philosophy that it is *always* necessary to verify the validity of Finite Element Analysis (FEA) results, a quick comparison of FEA results with those calculated using classical stress equations for a curved beam is included below.

Results Predicted by Classical Stress Equations

Although not all users may be familiar with the equations for stress in a curved beam, the analysis below should provide sufficient detail to enable reasonable understanding of this state of stress. The first observation is a somewhat unique characteristic of curved beams, namely, for a symmetrical cross-section the beam neutral axis lies closer to the center of curvature than does its centroidal axis. These axes can be observed in Fig. 24. By definition the centroidal axis, identified as r_c, is located half-way between the inside and outside radii of curvature. However, the neutral axis, identified by r_n, lies closer to

[3] Ibid

the inside (concave) surface. Based on this observation, a free body diagram of the upper portion of the curved beam is shown in Fig. 24. Included on this figure are important dimensions used in the following calculations. Dimensions shown are defined below.

w = width of beam cross-section = 4.00 in (see Fig. 1) ***or*** $r_o - r_i$ = 7.00 – 3.00 = 4.00 in
d = depth (thickness) of beam cross-section = 0.75 in (see Fig. 1)
A = cross-sectional area of beam = w*d = (0.75 in)(4.00 in) = 3.00 in^2
r_i = radius to inside (concave surface) = 3.00 in
r_o = radius to outside (convex surface) = r_i + w = 3.00 + 4.00 in = 7.00 in
r_c = radius to centroid of beam = r_i + w/2 = 3.00 + 4.00/2 = 5.00 in
r_n = radius to the neutral axis = $w/\ln(r_o/r_i)$ = 4.00/ln(7.00/3.00) = 4.72 in. [determined by equation for a curved beam having a rectangular cross-section]
c_i = distance from the neutral axis to the inside surface = $r_n - r_i$ = 4.72 – 3.00 = 1.72 in
c_o = distance from the neutral axis to the outside surface = $r_o - r_n$ = 7.00 – 4.72 = 2.28 in
e = distance between the centroidal axis and neutral axis = $r_c - r_n$ = 5.00- 4.72 = 0.28 in

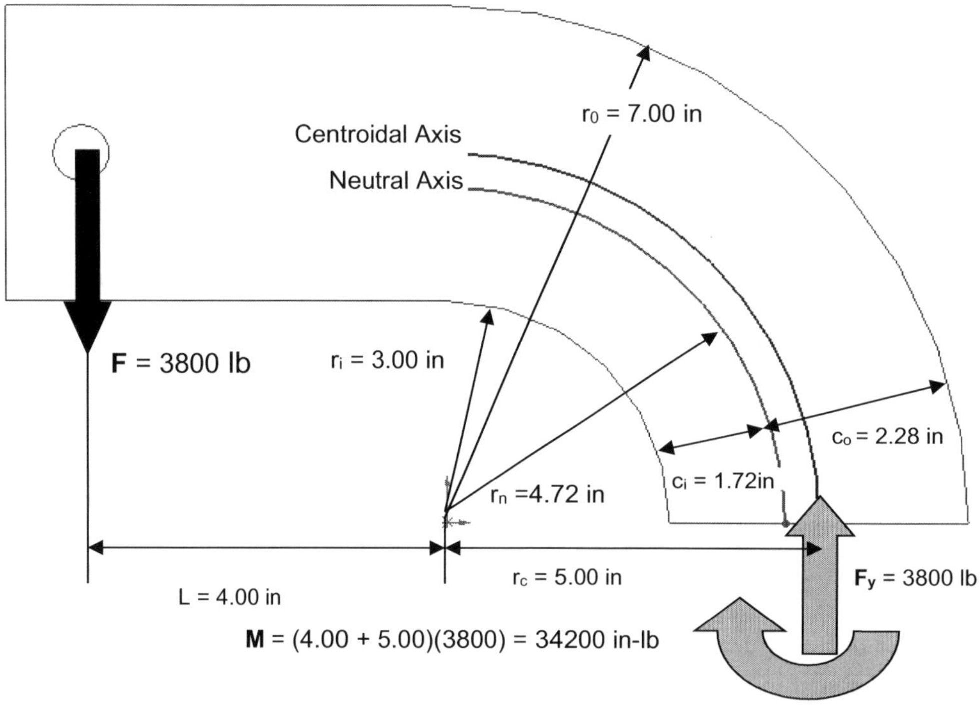

Figure 24 – Geometry associated with calculation of stress in a curved beam.

The reaction force **Fy** and moment **M** acting on the cut section are necessary to maintain equilibrium of the upper portion of the curved beam. Equations used to compute the combined bending and axial stresses that result from these reactions are included below. Each equation is of the general form,

Curved beam stress = $\pm$ bending stress $\pm$ axial stress

Where the "$\pm$" sign for bending stress depends on what side of the model is being investigated. In this case, bending stress caused by moment **M**, is compressive on the concave surface of the curved beam. Hence a minus "-" sign is assigned to the bending stress term in equation [1]. However, on the convex side, bending stress causes tension on the beam surface, thereby accounting for a "+" sign associated with the first term in equation [2]. Reaction force **Fy** acts to produce a compressive stress on the cut section. Therefore, a minus "-" sign is used with the axial stress component in both equations [1] and [2] below. In what *direction* do both of these stresses act?

Stress at the inside (concave) surface:

$$\sigma_i = \frac{Mc_i}{Aer_i} - \frac{F_y}{A} = \frac{-(34200\text{ in-lb})(1.72\text{ in})}{(3.00\text{ in}^2)(0.28\text{ in})(3.00\text{ in})} - \frac{3800\text{ lb}}{3.00\text{ in}^2} = -24610\text{ psi} \qquad [1]$$

Stress at the outside (convex) surface:

$$\sigma_0 = \frac{Mc_o}{Aer_o} - \frac{F_y}{A} = \frac{(34200\text{ in-lb})(2.28\text{ in})}{(3.00\text{ in}^2)(0.28\text{ in})(7.00\text{ in})} - \frac{3800\text{ lb}}{3.00\text{ in}^2} = 11990\text{ psi} \qquad [2]$$

Comparison with Finite Element Results

In addition to serving as a quick check of results, this section reviews use of the **Probe** tool. Both bending and axial stresses act normal to the cut surface in Fig. 24. Therefore, the *appropriate* stress to be used for the finite element analysis is stress acting in the Y-direction. Thus, σ_y should be compared with values computed using equations [1] and [2] above. You are encouraged to produce a finite element plot of stress σ_y on your own. However, abbreviated steps are outlined below if guidance is desired.

1. In the **Simulation** tab, click ⌄ on the **Results Advisor** Results Advisor icon and from the pull-down menu select **New Plot**. Then from the next pull-down menu select the **Stress** icon. The **Stress plot** property manager opens.

2. In the **Display** dialogue box, select **SY: Y Normal Stress** from the pull-down menu. Also in the **Display** dialogue box, set the **Units** field to display **psi.**

3. Click to clear the check "✓" mark from the ☐ **Deformed Shape** dialogue box.

4. Next, within the **Stress plot** property manager, select the **Chart Options** *tab.*

5. In the **Display Options** dialogue box check "✓" to select ☑ **Show min annotation** and also ☑ **Show max annotation**. This action labels both maximum and minimum stress values on the plot of **SY: Y Normal Stress**. Also, within the **Position/Format** dialogue box, change the **Number Format** from **scientific** to **floating** from the pull-down menu.

6. Finally, in the **Stress plot** property manager, select the **Settings** *tab.*

7. Within the **Settings** tab, change the **Fringe Options** pull-down menu to **Discrete**.

8. Click **[OK]** ✓ to close the **Stress plot** property manager.

If a plot of **SY: Y Normal Stress** like that in Fig. 25 does not appear, right-click **Stress2 (-Y Normal-)** and from the pull-down menu select **Show**.

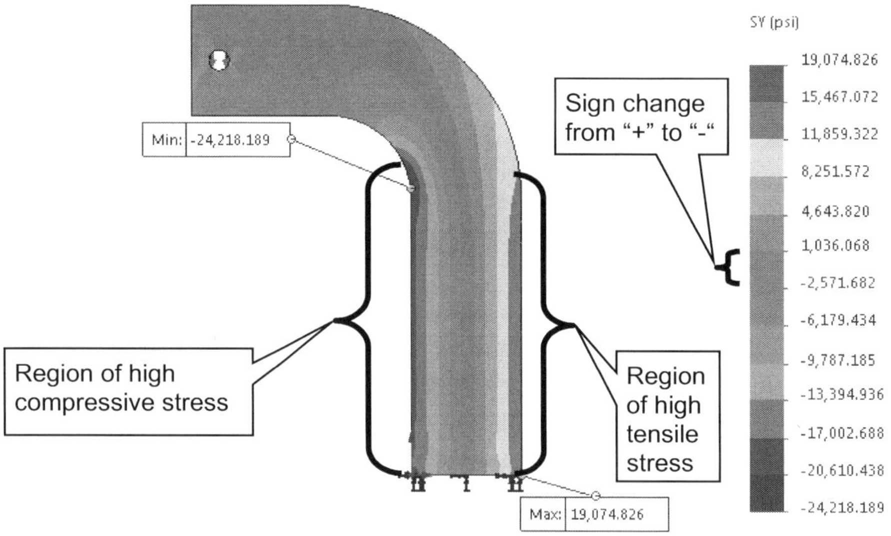

Figure 25 – Plot of **SY: Y Normal Stress** (σ_y) on the curved beam model.

The following observations can be made about Fig. 25.

OBSERVATIONS:

- Tensile (i.e., positive "+") stress is shown in lime green, yellow, orange, and red. This stress occurs primarily along the right vertical side and convex region of the model. Because this region is subject to tensile stress, positive "+" stress magnitudes are expected.
- Compressive (i.e., negative "-") stress is shown by some green, light blue, and dark blue located along the left vertical and concave region of the model. Once again compressive stress should correspond with the user's intuitive sense of stress in that region. Although labeled **Min**, compressive stress is algebraically larger than the maximum tensile stress.
- Low stress regions, corresponding to the neutral axis, or neutral plane, run near the vertical center of the model. Notice the sign change from "+" to "-" in the light green color-coded region of the stress chart. Recall for beams in bending, zero stress occurs on the neutral axis (or) neutral plane.
- Note that **Yield Strength** is *only* labeled on the vonMises stress plot. It does not appear on the current plot. Also, **min** and **max** stress locations are labeled.

The model is next prepared to examine stresses at section **A_i-A_o** shown in Fig. 26.

9. Right-click **Stress2 (-Y Normal-)**, and from the pull-down menu, select **Settings**. Within the **Stress plot** property manager, and set the **Boundary Options** pull-down menu to ▼ **Mesh**. A mesh is displayed on the model.

10. Click **[OK]** ✓ to close the **Stress plot** property manager.

11. Zoom in on the model to where the curved beam section is tangent to the straight, vertical section, shown as **A**i and **A**o in Fig. 26, where subscripts "**i**" and "**o**" refer to the inside and outside surfaces of the model respectively.

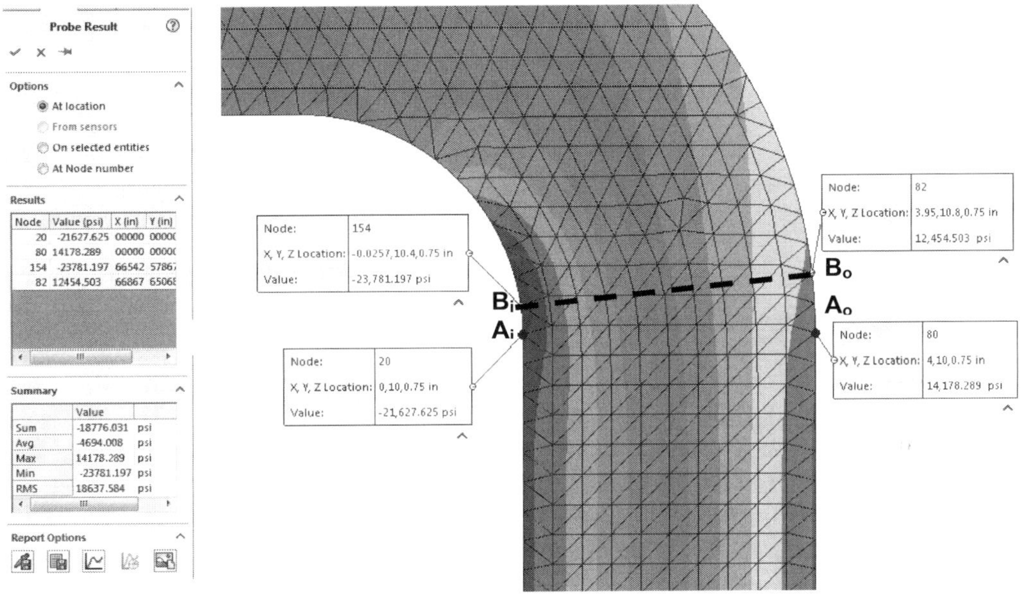

Figure 26 – Use the **Probe** tool to determine stress magnitudes at locations on the concave and convex sides of the curved beam model.

12. On the **Simulation** tab click the Plot Tools icon and from the pull-down menu select the **Probe** tool icon. The **Probe Result** property manager opens as shown on the left side of Fig. 26.

13. In the **Options** dialogue box, select ⊙ **At location** (if not already selected).

14. Move the cursor over the straight vertical edges on the left and right sides of the model. Each edge is highlighted as the cursor passes over it. Click to select two nodes, indicated by a small circle, (one on the left and one on the right) located at the *top* end of each line. These nodes are located at the *intersection* between the straight vertical section and the beginning of the curved beam section. Selected nodes correspond to **A**i and **A**o in Fig. 26. If an incorrect node is selected, simply click ⊙ **At location** in the **Options** dialogue box to clear the current selection and repeat the procedure. *Do not close the **Probe Result** property manager at this time.*

The above action records the following data in the **Results** dialogue box: **Node** number, **Value (psi)** of the plotted stress (σ_y), and the **X**, **Y**, **Z** coordinates of the selected nodes. Also, a small information "flag" appears adjacent to each node on the model and repeats data listed in the **Results** table. *It may be necessary to click-and-drag column edges to view values in the **Results** table.*

Table I contains a comparison of results found by using classical curved beam equations and the finite element analysis results at locations **Ai** and **Ao**. Rounded values are used.

Table I – Comparison of stress (σ_y) from classical and finite element methods at Section A-A.

Location	Manual Calculation (psi)	Probe Tool Results (psi)	Percent Difference (%)
Point **Ai**	-24610	-21628	13.8%
Point **Ao**	11990	14178	15.4%

Examine all values and the **Percent Difference (%)** column. Although differences of this magnitude occasionally do occur, as an engineer you should be disappointed and, in fact, quite concerned at the significant difference between these results given the validity of the curved beam equations. However, when results differ by this magnitude it is always appropriate to *investigate further* to determine if there is a valid cause for the disparity and not simply "write off" the differences as due to the fact that two alternative approaches are used. Can you provide valid reason(s) *why* such large differences exist?

Further thought should reveal that St. Venant's principle is once again affecting the results. In this instance, a traditional engineering approach would dictate using classical bending stress equations for a straight beam in the straight vertical segment of the model below Section **A-A**, in Fig. 1 (repeated at right), and curved beam equations in the portion of the model above Section **A-A**. Therefore, common sense suggests that there is a *transition region* between the straight and curved segments where neither set of classical equations is entirely adequate. In fact, due to the finite size of elements in this region, it is logical to presume that the finite element analysis provides a more accurate solution than do classical equations in this transition region.

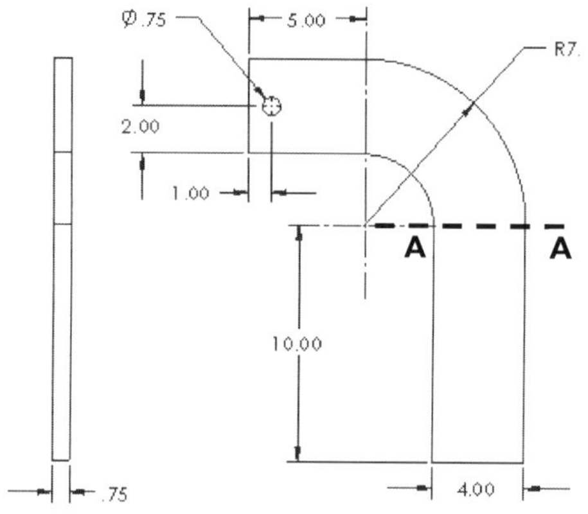

Figure 1 (Repeated) – Basic geometry of the curved beam model.

Given the above observations, we next proceed to sample stress magnitudes at Section **Bi-Bo** in Fig. 26. This new section is located slightly above the transition region. Proceed as follows.

15. Move the cursor over the curved edges of the model. Then, on the concave side click to select the *first* node *above* the previously selected node.

16. Next, on the convex side of the model, select the *second* node *above* the previously selected node. This procedure selects nodes **Bi** and **Bo** in Fig. 26.

Observe the two new stress magnitudes listed in the **Results** dialogue box and compare them to values listed in Table II. Nodes **Bi** and **Bo**, thus selected, lie on a radial line that forms an approximate angle of 7.5° above the horizontal. Stress values calculated using the classical equations are modified to account for a slight shift of the centroidal axis due to beam curvature and for the change in angle of the axial force. Using these values, a comparison of classical and FEA results in Table II reveals that values differ by at most 4.1%, which is a significant improvement over previous calculations.

Table II – Comparison of stress (σ_y) for classical and finite element methods at Section Bi-Bo. (Rounded values are used)

Location	Manual Calculation (psi)	Probe Tool Results (psi)	Percent Difference (%)
Point **Bi**	-24515	-23781	3.1%
Point **Bo**	11940	12454	4.1%

17. Click **[OK]** ✓ to close the **Probe Result** property manager.

This concludes the verification of Finite Element results, but note that even better results are expected at locations further from the transition region.

Assessing Safety Factor

SOLIDWORKS Simulation provides a convenient means to determine and view plots of Safety Factor distribution in the model. To use this capability, proceed as follows.

1. In the **Simulation** tab, click ▼on the **Results Advisor** icon and from the pull-down menu select **New Plot**. Then, from a second pull-down menu, select **Factor of Safety**. The **Factor of Safety** property manager opens as shown in Fig. 27 and displays the first step of a three step procedure.

2. Read text in the yellow **Message** dialogue box *and* at bottom of the **Step 1 of 3** dialogue box. These messages indicate that Safety Factor is based on the failure criterion noted in the **Materials** window. That criterion was specified as **Max von Mises Stress.**

3. In the upper pull-down menu of the **Step 1 of 3** dialogue box, choose either **All** or **Selected Bodies**. Because there is only one part to be analyzed, the result is the same in either case.

4. Next, in the **Criterion** field, click ⌄ the pull-down menu to reveal names of the four failure criteria available to determine the factor of safety.

Figure 27- **Factor of Safety,** Step #1 of safety factor check

A brief overview of the four failure criteria is provided below.

- **Max von Mises Stress** – This failure criterion is used for ductile materials (aluminum, steel, brass, bronze, etc.). It is considered the best predictor of actual failure in ductile materials and, as such, provides a good indication of the true safety factor. This criterion is also referred to as the "Distortion Energy Theory."

- **Max Shear Stress (Tresca)** – This criterion also applies to ductile materials. However, it is a more conservative theory thereby resulting in lower predicted safety factors. As a consequence of its conservative nature, parts designed using this criterion may be somewhat oversized.

- **Mohr-Coulomb Stress** – This failure criterion is applied to the design and analysis of parts made of brittle material (cast iron, etc.) where the ultimate compressive strength exceeds the ultimate tensile strength ($S_{uc} > S_{ut}$).

- **Max Normal Stress** – Also applicable for brittle materials, this failure criterion does not account for differences between tensile and compressive strengths. This theory is also regarded as the least accurate of the methods available.

- Other failure criteria apply for ***shell*** elements made of composite materials. These criteria are not described here.

5. Because the curved beam is made of ductile aluminum and because a good estimate of safety factor is desired, choose **Max von Mises Stress** from the pull-down menu.

Upon making the above selection, the **Factor of Safety** property manager changes to that illustrated in Fig. 28. Immediately below the **Criterion** field notice that the factor of safety check is currently defined as

$$\frac{\sigma_{vonMises}}{\sigma_{Limit}} < 1$$

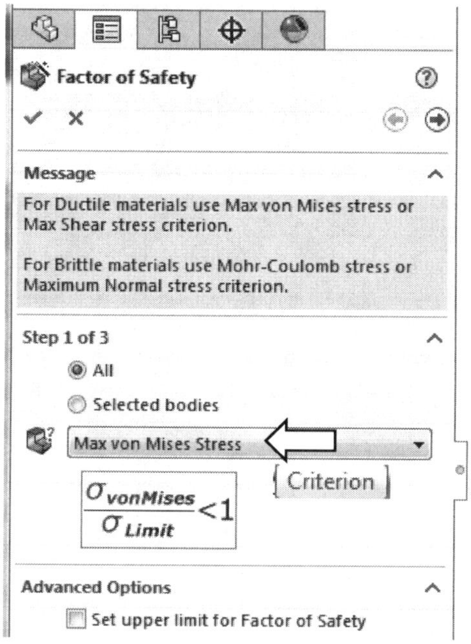

Figure 28 – The failure criterion is selected in **Step 1 of 3** of the **Factor of Safety** dialogue box.

In other words, the above equation is currently set to identify locations in the model where the ratio of von Mises stress to the "limiting" value of stress (i.e., the Yield Strength) is < 1.

Thus, the above criterion identifies locations where yielding of the model is *not* predicted because model Yield Strength, the denominator, is greater than the von Mises stress, the numerator. As initially defined, the above ratio is the *inverse* of the traditional safety factor definition, where:

Safety Factor = n = strength/stress

To plot only critical regions of the part, i.e., regions where the Yield Strength is exceeded and the safety factor is < 1, proceed as follows –

6. Advance to the second step by clicking the right facing arrow button at top of the **Factor of Safety** property manager. The **Step 2 of 3** dialogue box appears as shown in Fig. 29. It may be necessary to click and drag its bottom edge to expand the **Factor of Safety** dialogue box.

7. In the top pull-down menu, select **psi** as the set of **Units** to be used (if not already selected).

8. Under **Set stress limit to**, click to select ⦿ **Yield strength** (if not already selected).

9. Do *not* change the **Multiplication factor**.

Notice that the material, **2014 Alloy** aluminum, and its Yield and Ultimate strengths appear at the bottom of this dialogue box.

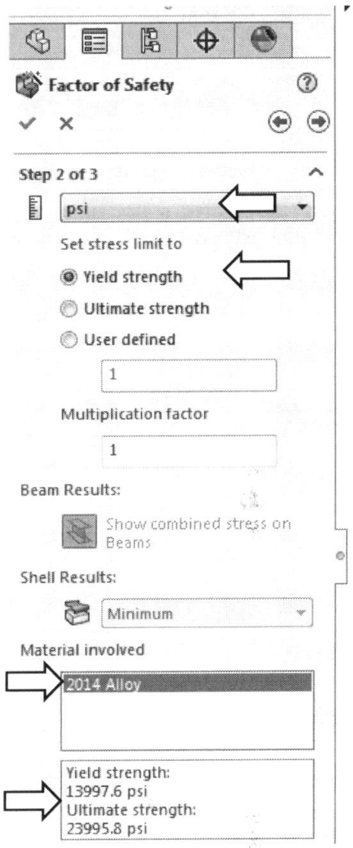

Figure 29 – **Step 2 of 3** in the **Factor of Safety** process.

> **Design Insight** – Focus attention near the top of the **Step 2 of 3** dialogue box.
>
> In the event that a *brittle* material is being analyzed using the Mohr-Coulomb or the Max Normal Stress failure criteria, it is appropriate to select the ⦿ **Ultimate strength** as the failure criterion since brittle materials do not exhibit a yield point.
>
> The O **User defined** option is provided for cases where a user specified material is not found in the **Material Property** table.

10. Click the right facing arrow button at top of this property manager to proceed to **Step 3 of 3** in the **Factor of Safety** property manager shown in Fig. 30.

Two options are available for displaying the factor of safety. Brief descriptions of each are provided on the next page.

- **Factor of safety distribution** – Produces a plot of safety factor variation throughout the entire part.

- **Areas below factor of safety** – A desired value for safety factor is entered in the field beneath this option. The resulting display shows all areas of the model below the specified safety factor in the color red and areas with a safety factor greater than the specified value in blue. This approach easily identifies areas that need to be improved during the design process.

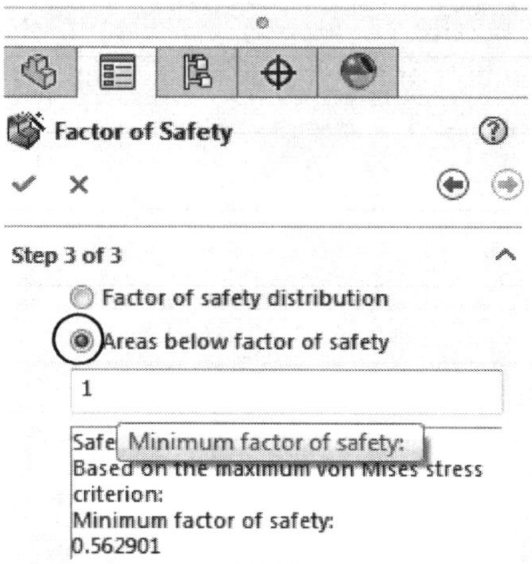

Figure 30 – Redefinition of **Factor of Safety** and values to be displayed on the new plot.

11. Beneath **Step 3 of 3**, select ⦿**Areas below factor of safety** and type "**1**" in the **Minimum factor of safety:** field (if not already "1").

At the bottom of this dialog box the **Safety result** field informs the user that the *minimum* factor of safety is **0.562901** which indicates that the design is *not* safe in some regions of the model. Recall that this value is based on a comparison between Yield Strength and the maximum von Mises stress. *(Values may vary slightly from those shown.)*

Note that the above value of safety factor differs by only .016% from that computed using the reciprocal of the equation appearing in the first **Factor of Safety** window. That is:

$$\frac{\sigma_{Limit}}{\sigma_{vonMises}} = \frac{\text{Yield Strength}}{\text{Max. von Mises Stress}} = \frac{13997}{|-24870|} = 0.5628$$

12. Click **[OK]** ✓ to close the **Factor of Safety** property manager. A new plot folder, named **Factor of Safety1 (- Max von Mises Stress-)**, is listed beneath the **Results** folder. Also, a plot showing regions of the model where the Safety Factor < 1.0 (red) and where the Safety Factor > 1.0 (blue) is displayed.

13. Right-click **Factor of Safety1 (-Max von Mises Stress-)**, and from the pull-down menu select **Chart Options…** The **Minimum factor of safety** property manager opens.

14. In the **Display Options** dialogue box, check ☑ **Show min annotation** and click **[OK]** ✓ to close the **Minimum factor of safety** property manager.

The preceding step labels the location of minimum Safety Factor on the curved beam as shown in Fig. 31. As expected, this location corresponds to the location of maximum compressive stress previously illustrated in Figs. 20 and 25. The figure now on your screen should correspond to Fig. 31. This figure shows regions where the factor of safety (FOS) is less than 1 (unsafe regions) in red. Regions with a factor of safety greater than 1 (safe regions) are shown in blue. Localized regions, along the right and left vertical edges and extending into the concave region, have a safety factor less than one.

The line of text, circled near the top-left in Fig. 31, provides a "key" to interpret safe and unsafe regions on the model.

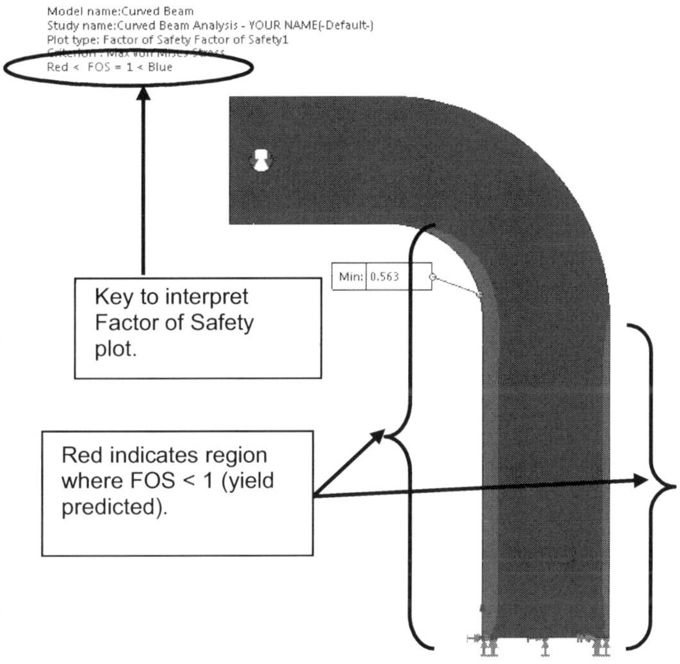

Figure 31 – Curved beam model showing areas where FOS > 1 (safety predicted) and where FOS < 1 (yield predicted).

15. Double-click **Factor of Safety (-Max von Mises Stress-)** and repeat steps 1 through 12 above, but this time set the **Areas below factor of safety** to **2** instead of **1**, in step 11. How does the plot change?

A designer can repeat the above procedure for any desired level of safety factor check.

In summary, an important aspect of the von Mises stress is that it can be used to predict whether or not a part might fail based on a comparison of its stress *magnitude* to the value of yield strength. This topic is aligned with the study of theories of failure found in most mechanics of materials and design of machine elements texts.

Analysis Insight #1:

Faced with the fact that the above part is predicted to fail by yielding, a designer would be challenged to redesign the part in any of several ways, depending upon design constraints. For example, it might be possible to change part dimensions to reduce stress magnitudes in the part. Alternatively, if part geometry cannot be changed due to size restrictions, a stronger material might be selected, or some combination of these or other possible remedies might be applied. Because part redesign might be considered an open-ended problem, it is not pursued here.

Analysis Insight #2:
Return briefly to the vonMises stress plot by double-clicking **Stress1 (-vonMises-)** located beneath the **Results** folder.

Refer to Fig. 32 or your screen and notice that the material yield strength (13997.6 psi) is displayed beneath the color-coded stress scale. Also, an arrow appears adjacent to the stress scale at a magnitude corresponding to this yield strength. Thus, all stresses above the arrow *exceed* the material yield strength. Given this observation it is logical to ask, "What is the meaning of stress values above the material yield strength?"

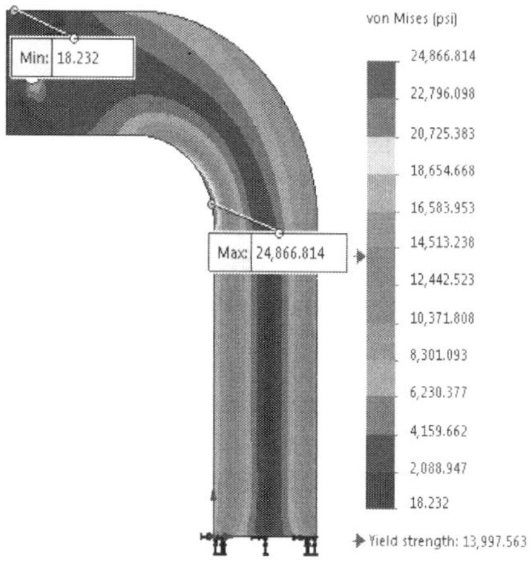

Figure 32 – von Mises stress plot for the curved beam model.

The answer to this question is quite straightforward. Stress values greater than the yield strength are *meaningless!* Why is this true?

Recall that the stiffness approach, described in the Introduction, indicated a finite element solution starts by determining deflection **ΔL** of a part subject to applied loads. Then, based on deflection, strain is calculated as $\boldsymbol{\varepsilon = \Delta L/L}$. And finally, from strain, stress is calculated from the relation $\boldsymbol{\sigma = E*\varepsilon}$. In words, the last equation states that "stress is proportional to strain," where the constant of proportionality **E** (i.e., the modulus of elasticity) is determined from the slope of the *linear* portion of the stress strain curve illustrated in Fig. 33.

Because the FEA solution is based on a *linear analysis*, stress values *above* the yield strength in Fig. 32 are *assumed* to lie along a *linear* extension of the stress-strain curve shown dashed in Fig. 33. However, above the yield strength, the actual stress-strain curve follows the *solid* curved line where stress is no longer proportional to strain. Thus, stress values reported above the yield strength are meaningless.

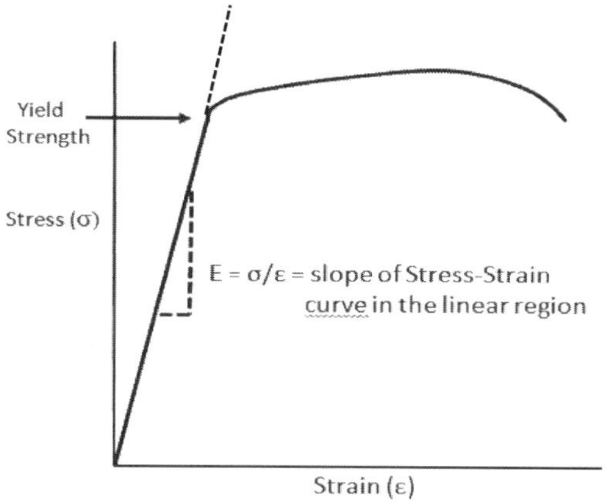

Figure 33 – Stress vs strain curve for a typical elastic material shown by the solid curve.

Problems where stress exceeds the yield strength can be solved in the Professional version of SOLIDWORKS Simulation where *non-linear* analysis capabilities are available to conduct post-yield analysis.

Alternate Stress Display Option

Because some users might prefer more immediate feedback to identify areas where material yield strength is exceeded, this section outlines steps to quickly identify those regions in a part. This option is only valid for von Mises stress plots. Another restriction is that this display option only applies to individual parts. It does not apply to assemblies because individual parts within an assembly might be made of different materials each with their own yield strength. Change the display as follows.

1. Beneath the **Results** folder, right-click **Stress1 (-vonMises-)** and from the pull-down menu select **Chart Options…** The **Stress plot** property manager opens. The bottom *portion* of this property manager is shown in Fig. 34.

2. At the bottom of this property manager, click ˅ to open the **Color Options** dialogue box.

3. Place a ✓ mark to select ☑ **Specify color for values above yield limit** and accept the default gray color specified.

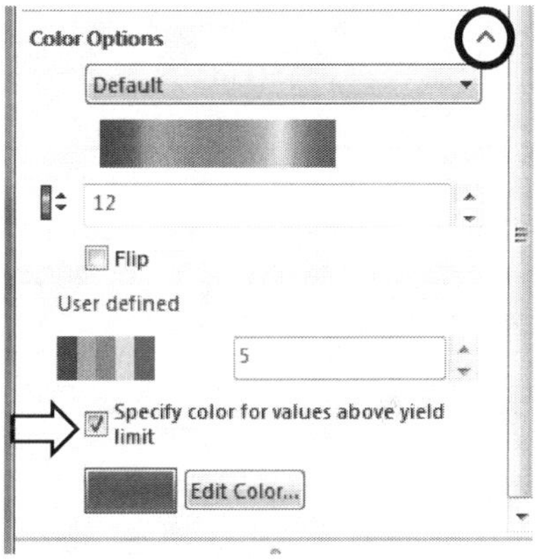

Figure 34 – Customizing displays where stress exceeds yield strength on von Mises plots.

4. Immediately shades of gray are displayed on regions of the model and in the color coded stress chart where von Mises stress exceeds the material yield strength.

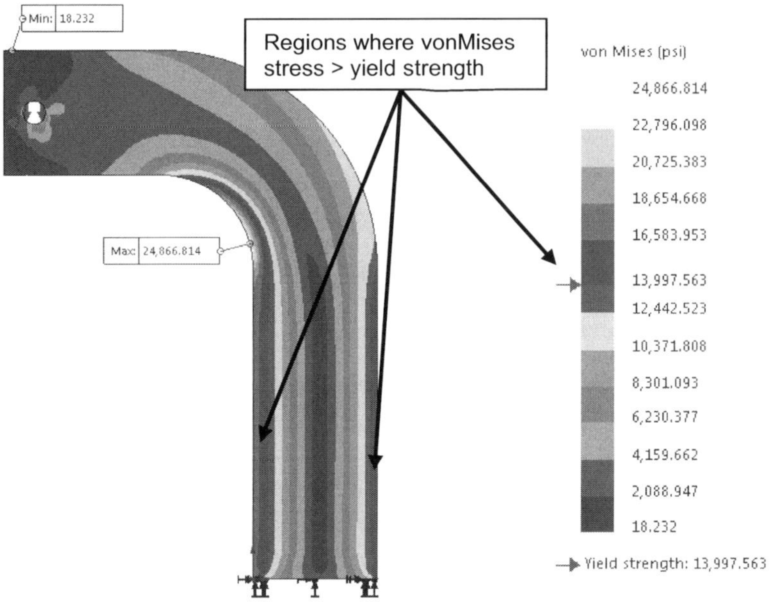

Figure 35 – Altered plot displays stresses greater than the yield strength in shades of grey.

5. Because it is not desired to keep this display, click ✖ to close the **Stress Plot** property manager.

The plot produced using this technique appears in Fig. 35 where all stress magnitudes greater than the material yield strength are displayed in gray tones. Although this plot does not provide insight into magnitude of the Safety Factor, or lack thereof, it does reinforce the concept that stress magnitudes above the yield strength are meaningless. The shades of gray are unimportant.

Determining Reaction Forces

It is always good engineering practice to verify that results obtained correlate well with the given information. One simple way to confirm that results correlate with given information is to check whether or not reaction forces are consistent with external loads applied to the model. This section examines how to determine reaction forces at the base of the curved beam model. To accomplish this, proceed as follows.

1. On the **Simulation** tab, click ▼ on the **Results Advisor** icon and from the pull-down menu, select **List Result Force**. The **Result Force** property manager opens as shown in Fig. 36.

2. In the **Options** dialogue box, verify that **⦿Reaction Force** is selected.

3. In the **Selection** dialogue box, set **Units** to **English (IPS)** (if not already selected).

4. The **Faces, Edges, or Vertices** field is active (highlighted light blue) and awaiting selection of the entity on which the reaction force is to be determined. Rotate the model so that its bottom (restrained) *surface* is visible and click to select it. **Face<1>** appears in the active field. This is the only face where reactions occur.

5. Click the **[Update]** button and the **Reaction force (lbf)** table at the bottom of the property manager is populated with data. Also, X, Y, and Z reaction force components appear at the base of the model and force magnitudes are contained within an information "flag" on the model.

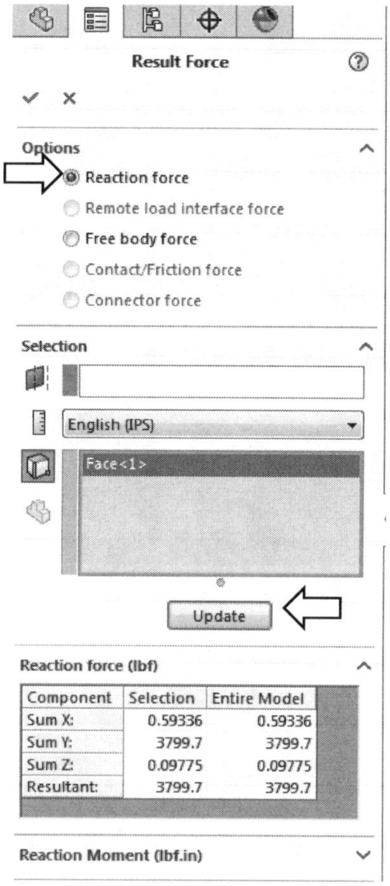

Figure 36 – Data appearing in the **Result Force** property manager.

The **Component** column in this table lists names for the summation of reaction forces in the X, Y, and Z directions and the **Resultant:** reaction. Reaction force magnitudes listed in the **Selection** column are identical to those in the **Entire Model** column. This result is expected because the entire model is restrained at only this one location.

Results interpretation is as follows: (due to mathematical round-off values may vary)

SumX: 0.5934 (close to zero) no force is applied to model in the X-direction
SumY: 3799.7 (essentially 3800 lb) equal and opposite to the applied force
SumZ: 0.0977 (close to zero) no force is applied to model in the Z-direction
Resultant: 3799.7 (essentially 3800 lb = the applied force)

It should be noted that a *moment* reaction at the base of the curved beam is missing from the **Reaction force** table. Also open ▾ the **Reaction Moment (lbf.in)** dialogue box, located below the **Reaction force** dialogue box, and observe it contains no data entries (i.e., no moment reactions). This outcome does not agree with the usual conventions for reactions applied to a free-body diagram used in a traditional engineering statics course and shown in Fig. 2 (repeated at right). However, lack of a moment is consistent with our understanding of **Immovable** restraints applied to three-dimensional tetrahedral elements. Recall, **Immovable** restraints only restrict translations in the X, Y, and Z directions at each restrained node on these elements. This observation accounts for the fact that there are only three force reactions and no moments in the **Reaction force** and **Reaction Moment** tables of Fig. 36.

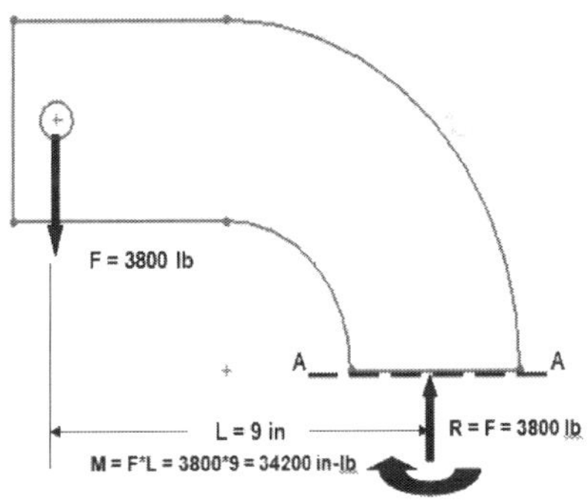

Figure 2 – (Repeated)

The reaction force results above are valid for the *entire model*. However, in many instances a model is supported (i.e., restrained) at more than one location. In those instances, it is necessary to determine reaction forces at other locations on a model. Performing a reaction check is quite simple and can be viewed as an additional means to verify the validity of boundary conditions applied to a model.

Although a surface was selected to examine reaction forces in the above example, it should be evident that other geometric features, such as edges or vertices, can also be selected at other restrained locations on a model.

6. Click **[OK]** ✓ to close the **Result Force** property manager.

Is it Significant That the Model is NOT in Equilibrium?

To answer the above question some additional insight is necessary. Begin by recalling Newton's second law of motion, which states any unbalanced force acting on a body results in an acceleration of that body in the direction of the unbalanced force. This motion is referred to as "rigid body motion" and it follows that such motion is not tolerated in a *static* finite element analysis. Simply stated, rigid body motion refers to motion (displacement) of an entire model irrespective of whether or not the body deforms due to applied loads.

For example, in the case of the curved beam model it is *not critical* that reaction forces *are not equal to zero* in all directions. Although these results indicate that true equilibrium is *not* attained, because $\sum \mathbf{F_x} \neq \mathbf{0}$, $\sum \mathbf{F_y} \neq 0$, and $\sum \mathbf{F_z} \neq 0$, the model cannot move because its base is **Fixed** by **immovable** restraints applied in the X, Y, and Z directions. In summary, if a model is supported by **Fixed** restraints in all possible directions, then the fact that mathematical round-off occurs is of no consequence to equilibrium.

Soft Springs Can Be Applied Where Other Restraints are not Appropriate

Occasionally cases occur where model integrity is compromised by adding extra restraints. Consider for example the model shown in Fig. 37 at right, where the model is subject to "equal and opposite" *forces* applied to its top and bottom holes. In this case it is assumed that the model *cannot be supported by additional **Fixed** restraints* without interfering with accurate modeling of actual forces acting on the model. However, as we saw above, **Reaction Forces** resulting from a finite element analysis typically do not equal zero in the X, Y, and Z directions due to mathematical round-off. The resulting *un*balanced force(s), no matter how small, would cause the model to move with rigid body motion.

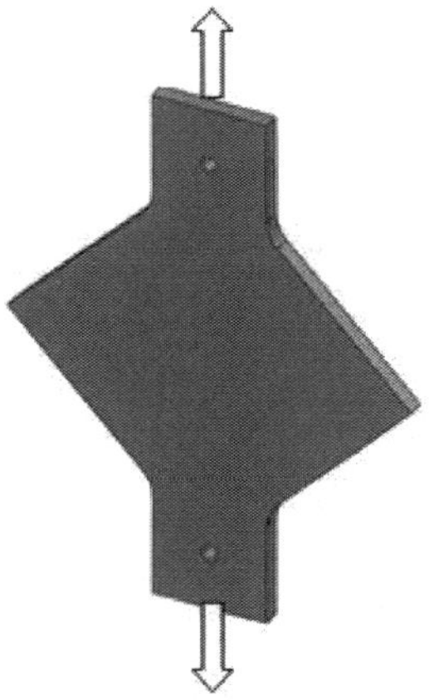

Figure 37 - Model subject to "equal" but opposite forces.

Because model movement with rigid body motion is prohibited within the software, what actually happens is that the Solution *fails to execute* and a message warning that . . . a "singular stiffness matrix" has occurred . . . is displayed. Although this message is fairly obtuse, it simply indicates that the model is insufficiently restrained and, therefore, the resulting equations cannot be solved as presently formulated.

One way to deal with unbalanced forces is to apply *Soft Springs* to support the model. These "springs" serve to stabilize a model against any unbalanced forces; therefore, the analysis can proceed. Look for end-of-chapter problems where a model must be supported by *Soft Springs* to overcome *unbalanced* reaction forces that otherwise would result in rigid body motion. Exercises 3-3 and 5-4 offer guidance regarding how to apply *Soft Springs* in the event they are needed.

Important Caution Regarding Strength and Safety Factor

Earlier discussion in this chapter noted that von Mises stress magnitude is a valid way to represent a complex state of stress within a body by a *single* value. Likewise, material properties such as Yield Strength, Ultimate Strength, etc. are provided as *single* values in the material properties table. As a user of this software, and for manual calculations too, designers must be aware and account for the fact that *statistical variation applies to all values* used. The preceding statement about statistical variation of values applies to, but is not limited to, quantities such as part dimensions, applied loads, load geometry, and material properties. Accounting for statistical variation is an important design/analysis consideration.

Logging Out of the Current Analysis

This concludes an introduction to analysis of the curved beam model. It is suggested that this file *not* be saved. Proceed as follows.

1. On the **Main Menu**, click **File** followed by choosing **Close**.

2. The **SOLIDWORKS** window opens in Fig. 38 and provides the options of either saving the current document or not. Select **[Don't Save]**.

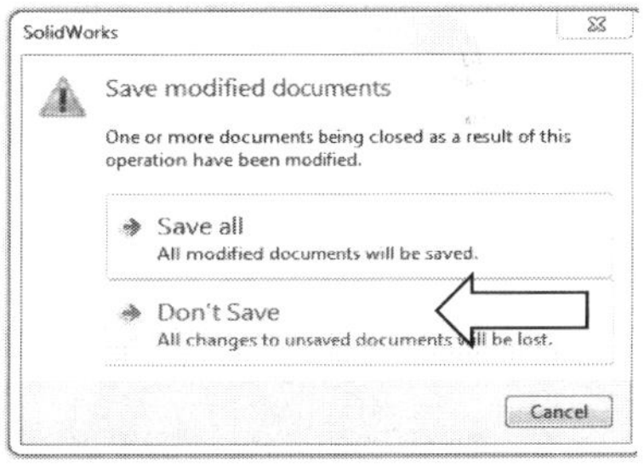

Figure 38 – **SOLIDWORKS** window prompts users to either save changes or not.

EXERCISES

End of chapter exercises are intended to provide additional practice using principles introduced in the current chapter plus capabilities mastered in preceding chapters. Most exercises include multiple parts. In an academic setting, it is likely that parts of problems may be assigned or modified to suit specific course goals.

Designates problems that introduce new concepts. Solution guidance is provided for these problems.

EXERCISE 1 – Curved Beam Stresses in a "C"- Clamp

C-clamps, like that illustrated below, must pass minimum strength requirements before they can be qualified for general purpose use. Clamps are tested by applying equal and opposite loads acting on the two gripping faces. Federal test criteria also requires that the movable (lower) jaw be extended a fixed percentage of the distance of the fully-open state to ensure that column failure of the screw is an integral part of the test. Assume that the movable jaw of the clamp in Fig. E2-1 satisfies the prescribed test criterion, then perform a finite element analysis of the C-clamp subject to the following guidelines.

Open file: **C-Clamp 2-1**

- Material: **Cast Carbon Steel** (use S.I. units)
- Mesh: In the **Mesh** property manager, select **Standard mesh**.
- Fixture: **Fixed** applied to the upper gripping surface of the C-clamp.
- External Load: **950 N** applied downward normal to the lower gripping surface.

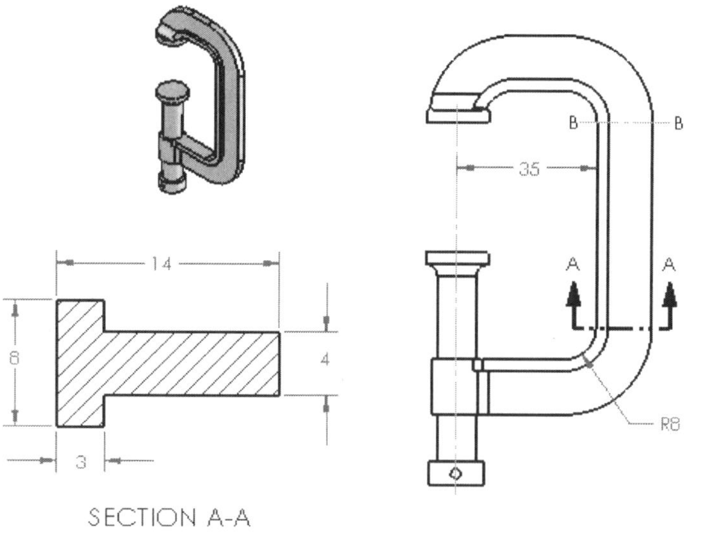

Figure E2-1 (a) – "C"-clamp frame and cross-section dimensions. Stress to be determined at Section A-A. (All dimensions in mm.)

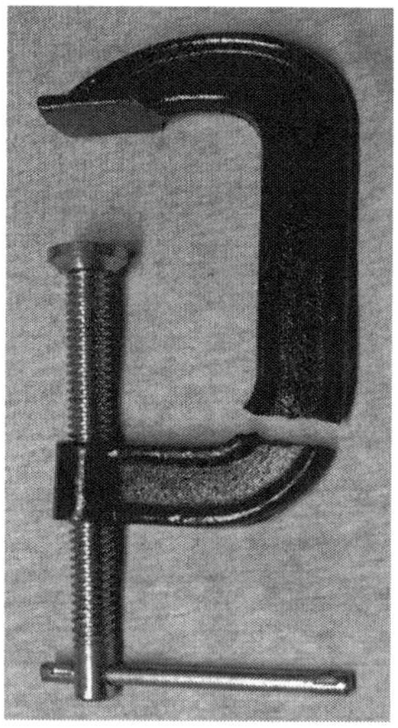

Figure E2-1(b) – Typical failure.

Determine the following:

a. Use classical equations to compute stress at the inside and outside surfaces of the C-clamp frame at section A-A. Section A-A is located where the straight and curved sections are tangent. Include a free body diagram of the lower portion of the clamp and use curved beam equations.

b. Create a stress contour plot of von Mises stress in the frame of the C-Clamp. The plot is to include discrete fringes and show the mesh on the model. Also include automatic labeling of maximum and minimum von Mises stress on this plot.

c. Like part (b), except produce a plot of the *most appropriate stress* in the C-Clamp frame. In other words, because values from this plot are to be compared with manual calculations of part (a), it is necessary to choose the corresponding stress from those available within the **Stress Plot** property manager. Include automatic labeling of maximum and minimum stress on this plot.

d. Use the **Probe** feature to produce a graph of the *most appropriate stress* acting across section A-A. When using the **Probe** feature, begin on the concave (inside) surface at the middle node shown in Fig. E2-2. This location corresponds to the tangent line between the curved and straight segments of the clamp. Then proceed around ½ of the model selecting both corner and mid-side nodes. Continue to the outside of the "T" cross-section. Include a descriptive title, axis labels, and your name on this graph. Beneath the graph, use equation [1] to compare percent differences between classical and FEA determination of stresses at the inside and outside surfaces.

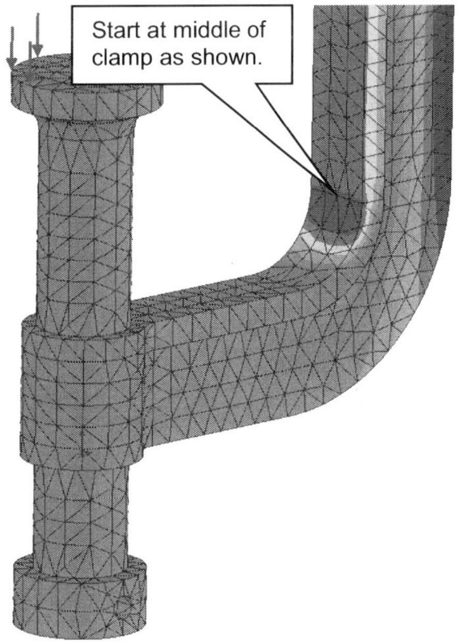

Figure E2-2 – Image shows starting point for use of the **Probe** tool.

$$\% \text{ difference} = \frac{(\text{FEA result - classical result})}{\text{FEA result}} * 100 = \qquad [1]$$

Because there may be several nodes on the inside and outside surfaces of the C-clamp, tell which node or nodes you selected to compare stress values with those computed manually. Also, tell why a particular node(s) was/were selected.

e. Assuming the C-clamp is made of a ductile material, produce a plot showing regions where the safety factor < 1.5. Also, if the safety factor is < 1.0 at any location within the C-clamp, produce a second plot to highlight any un-safe region(s). Manually label region(s), if any, where safety factor < 1.0.

EXERCISE 2 – Curved Beam Stresses in Hacksaw Frame

A common, metal-cutting "hacksaw" is shown in Fig. E2-3. A solid model of the hacksaw is available as file **Hacksaw 2-2**. The model is simplified to include two 0.125 inch diameter holes that pass through the lower left and lower right ends of the hacksaw "backbone" labeled in Fig. E2-3. For analysis purposes, the inside surface of the left-hand hole is to be considered **Fixed** (i.e., immovable). Use split lines to create a small "patch" of area on the inside surface of the hole located at the right end of the backbone. On this surface apply a 50 lb force induced by a tensile load in the saw blade, which is ordinarily held in place between these two holes. Assume the following.

- Material: **AISI 1020 Steel, Cold Rolled** (use English units)
- Mesh: In the **Mesh** property manager, select ⊙ **Standard mesh**; use the default mesh size.
- Units: **English (IPS)**
- Fixture: **Fixed** applied to inside of left hole.
- External Load: **50 lb** applied parallel to the X-direction on the inner surface of the right-hand hole (split lines needed; placement of split lines is user defined).

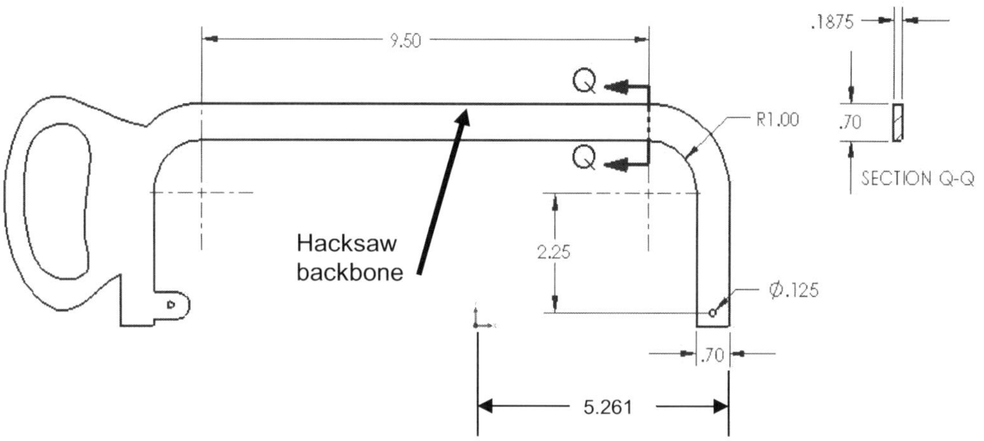

Figure E2-3 – Basic geometry of a hacksaw frame. Stress is to be determined at Section Q-Q.

Determine the following:

a. Use classical curved beam equations to compute stress at the inside (concave) and outside (convex) surfaces of the hacksaw frame at section Q-Q. Section Q-Q is located where the straight and curved sections are tangent. Include a labeled free body diagram of the right-portion of the model.

b. Include a zoomed-in image of the right-hand hole so that the 50 lb applied load can clearly be seen to act between user specified *Split Lines* within the hole.

c. Create a stress contour plot of von Mises stress in the saw backbone. Include automatic labeling of maximum and minimum von Mises stress on this plot.

d. Use the **Probe** feature to produce a graph of the *most appropriate stress* across section Q-Q, beginning at the inside (concave) surface and continuing to the outside (convex) surface of the backbone cross-section. Use the **Stress Plot** property manager to select the *appropriate stress* for this plot to enable comparison with manual calculations of part (a). Include a descriptive title, axis labels, and your name on this graph. Also, below the graph, cut-and-paste a copy of the **Probe Results** table showing values used in this comparison [see Appendix A for procedures to copy SOLIDWORKS images into a Word® document]. Then use equation [1], repeated below, to compute the percent difference between classical and finite element solutions at the inside and outside surfaces of the saw backbone at section Q-Q.

$$\% \text{ difference} = \frac{(\text{FEA result - classical result})}{\text{FEA result}} * 100 = \qquad [1]$$

e. Based on von Mises stress, create a plot showing all regions of the model where Safety Factor < 4.0 and circle these regions on the plot. Include a software applied label indicating the maximum and minimum values for Factor of Safety.

f. Question: If stresses at section Q-Q, calculated using both classical equations and the finite element solution, differ by more than 4%, state the reason for this difference and describe at least one method to reduce the percent difference calculation at this location.

<u>EXERCISE 3</u> – Stresses in a Curved Anchor Bracket

The curved beam shown in Fig. E2-4 is subject to a horizontal load applied by means of a pin (not shown) that passes through a hole in its upper end. A solid model of this part is available as file **Anchor Bracket 2-3**. The lower-left end of the part is attached to a rigid frame (also not shown). Because three-dimensional tetrahedral elements are to be used to model this part, the restraint at this location should be considered **Immovable**. Use split lines to create a small "patch" of area on the inside surface of the 16 mm diameter hole. Locate these split lines 24 mm from the right edge of the model. On this inner surface of the hole apply a horizontal force of 8600 N acting in the positive X-direction (to the right). Assume the following.

- Material: **AISI 1010 Steel, hot rolled bar** (use SI units)
- Mesh: In the **Mesh** property manager, select ⊙ **Standard mesh**; use the default mesh size.
- Fixture: Apply a **Fixed** (immovable) restraint on the inclined surface.
- External Load: **8600 N** in the X-direction applied on the right, inside surface of the 16 mm diameter hole between user defined *Split Lines*.

Determine the following:

a. Use classical equations to compute stress at the inside (concave) surface and the outside (convex) surface of the anchor bracket at section B-B. Section B-B passes through the center of curvature of the curved beam and is considered to be a vertical line. Include a labeled free body diagram of the portion of the anchor bracket to the right of section B-B (show magnitude and direction of all reactions).

b. Include a zoomed-in image of the hole so that the force F_x = 8600 N can clearly be seen to act between user specified *Split Lines*.

c. Create a stress contour plot of von Mises stress in the anchor bracket. Include automatic labeling of maximum and minimum stress on this plot.

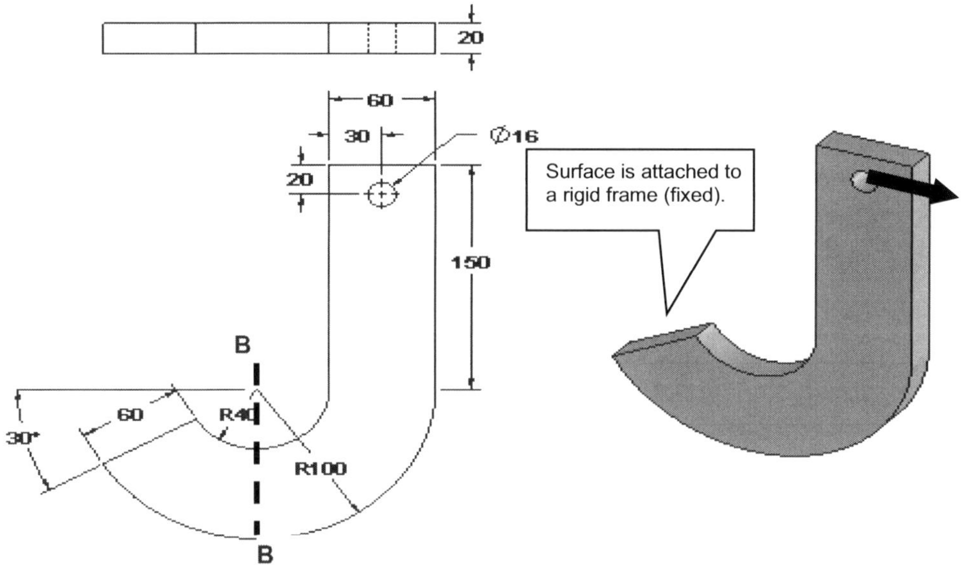

Figure E2-4 - Dimensioned view of the Anchor Bracket. Stress is to be determined at Section B-B.

d. Using von Mises stress, create a plot showing all regions of the model where Safety Factor < 1.5 (if any). Indicate this region(s), if any, by circling its location(s) on the figure and labeling them as "FOS < 1.5." Include a software applied label indicating locations of maximum and minimum values of Safety Factor. Even if region(s) where Safety Factor < 1.5 are found, tell whether or not the entire model can be classified as having no region(s) where safety factor < 1.0.

e. Use the **Probe** feature to produce a graph of the *most appropriate stress* across the bracket at section B-B. Begin at the inside (concave) surface and continue to the outside (convex) surface. (See the *"HINT"* below for guidance when making this graph.) Use the **Stress Plot** property manager to select the *appropriate stress* for this graph to enable comparison with manual calculations of part (a) above. Add a descriptive title, axis labels, and your name to this graph.

   Below the graph or on a separate page either: (a) cut-and-paste a copy of the **Probe Results** table that includes values used for this comparison [See Appendix A for procedures to copy images from SOLIDWORKS Simulation into a Word® document], or (b) click the **Save** icon  located in the **Report Options** dialogue box, to create an Excel spreadsheet containing all values in the **Probe Results** table. [See Appendix A, page A-12.]

   After determining both classical and FEA results at section B-B, use equation [1] to compute the percent difference between classical and finite element solutions at the inside and outside surfaces of the bracket.

$$\% \text{ difference} = \frac{(\text{FEA result - classical result})}{\text{FEA result}} * 100 = \qquad [1]$$

f. If results of part (e) differ by 4% or more, determine the source of error in either the classical solution or finite element solution and correct it. If no error is found, state why results differ by this significant percent difference.

HINT: Because the **Standard mesh** generation scheme within SOLIDWORKS Simulation creates an optimized mesh, it is probable that (a) a straight line of nodes will *not* exist across the model at section B-B (thus, choose the best straight line available), and (b) it is also *unlikely* that node points *occur exactly on a vertical line through the center of curvature.* For these reasons, and to obtain the best estimate of stress on a vertical line through section B-B, proceed as follows.

- Zoom in on a *front* view of the model with a mesh displayed at section B-B.
- On the **Simulation** tab, select the **Plot Tools** icon and from the pull-down menu click the **Probe** tool  icon. This action opens the **Probe Results** property manager.
- In the SOLIDWORKS Feature manager, move the cursor over the **Right Plane** label. This action highlights an edge view of the **Right Plane** at the desired location. This edge view (a line) will assist in locating nodes closest to a vertical line at Section B-B. Unfortunately, the line disappears when the cursor is moved, but it can be re-displayed multiple times by again moving the cursor over the **Right Plane** label. Complete the graph using the **Probe** tool.

EXERCISE 4 – Stresses in a Curved Photoelastic Model (Special Topics Include: Custom material definition, and using a "Hinge" joint for Fixture)

A curved beam model, made from a photoelastic material and subject to axial load **F**, is shown in Fig. E2-5. Beams such as this might be used in an experimental stress analysis laboratory where photoelastic techniques are studied. Photoelastic material has a unique optical property known as birefringence. Thus, when a photoelastic model is subject to applied loads in a field of polarized light, the light passing through the model undergoes changes of wavelength that produce visible "fringes" within the model as shown.

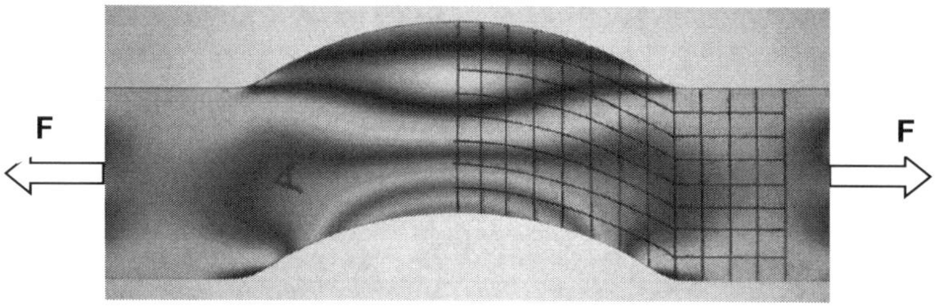

Figure E2-5 – "Fringes" appearing in a photoelastic model subject to a tensile load applied through pin joints (not shown). A grid is superimposed on the model to facilitate locating specific stress magnitudes and directions in the lab.

These "fringes" are analogous to, but not equal to, stress contour plots produced upon completion of a finite element analysis. In this exercise, stresses produced within the curved beam model are examined using finite element methods. Dimensioned views of a typical photoelastic beam are shown in Fig. E2-6.

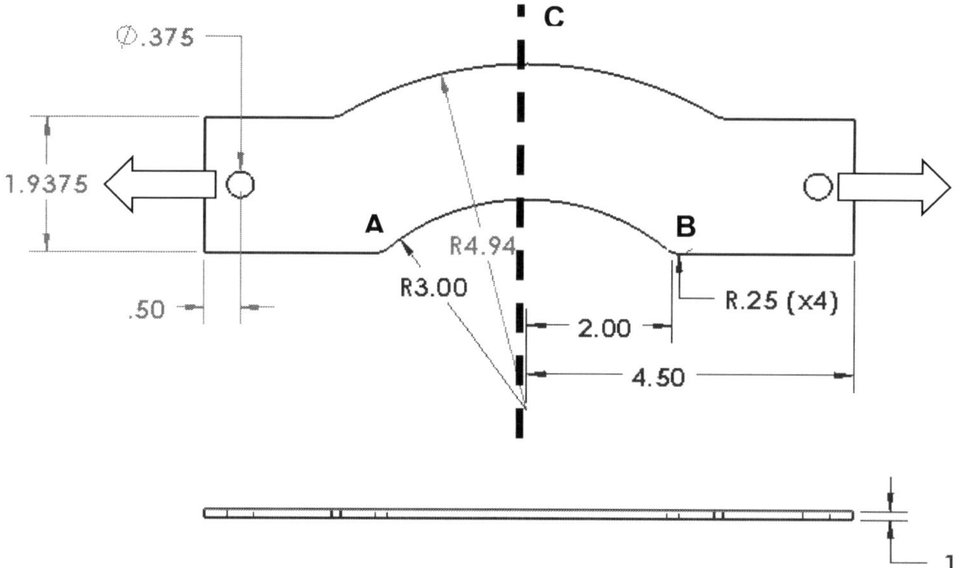

Figure E2-6 – Top view (above) and front (edge) view of a curved beam model. (Dimensions: inches)

Create a finite element model of this part that includes custom material specification, fixtures, external loads, mesh, solution, and results analysis.

Open the file **Curved Bracket 2-4**

- Material: Material properties are not found in the SOLIDWORKS material Library (use custom properties below)
  E = 360e3 psi Modulus of Elasticity (use English units)
  v = 0.38 Poisson's ratio
  S_y = **2200** psi Yield Strength
- Mesh: In the **Mesh** property manager, select a ⊙ **Standard mesh**; use the default mesh size. (Although this model is very thin, use a solid mesh.)
- Fixture: **Hinge Joint** applied at hole on left end of the model.
- External Load: **72** lb in the X-direction applied between user defined split lines on the inner surface of the hole located at the right end of the model.

Two aspects of this exercise are unique. First, properties of the photoelastic material are not available in the SOLIDWORKS material library. And second, the fixture at the left hole of the curved bracket is considered to be a **Fixed Hinge** joint. Guidance in the application of these two items is provided below.

Solution Guidance
It is assumed that the user has opened the model file and started a Study in SOLIDWORKS Simulation. The following instructions are to serve as a "guide"; they are less detailed than the step-by-step procedure found in example problems.

Custom Material Specification
The recommended way to create a custom material definition is to begin with a *similar* existing material and then edit material properties as outlined below.

- Open the **Material** window by right-clicking the **Curved Bracket 2-4** folder and selecting **Apply/Edit Material…**
- Close all open pull-down menu(s) beneath **SOLIDWORKS Materials**.
- Because photoelastic material is a special, clear "plastic like" material, open the **Custom Materials** folder at the bottom of the **SOLIDWORKS Materials** list.
- Next click "►" to open the **Plastic** folder and beneath it select **Custom Plastic**. The right side of the window is populated with property values for an unspecified plastic material.
- On the **Properties** tab, select **Units:** as **English (IPS)**.

- Adjacent to the **Name:** field, change the name "Custom Plastic" to "**Photoelastic Material**." The **Description:** and **Source:** fields can be left blank.

- Within the **Property** column of the lower table notice that red, blue, and black colors are used to indicate different **Property** names. Red lettering indicates information *required* for a stress solution. Blue lettering indicates *desirable, but not necessary* information. And property names appearing in black are used for thermal and vibration studies and are *not required* for the current Study. For each red item, enter the values listed beneath "Material" in the problem statement, but do not change the existing value in the **Mass density** field. Do not alter other values listed in the table.

- Click **[Apply]** followed by **[Close]** to exit the **Material** window. A check "✓" appears on the **Curved Bracket 2-4** part folder and the **Name:** assigned above appears on the part folder. You have successfully defined a custom material.

<u>**Fixed Hinge Specification**</u> A **Fixed Hinge** joint acts like a door hinge. This joint type allows rotation about a fixed axis on the model, but prevents translation along that axis. A **Fixed Hinge** is used at the left end of **Curved Bracket 2-4** to prevent translations in the X, Y, Z directions, but allows the model to rotate thereby maintaining alignment with the external load *as the part deforms*. Proceed as follows.

- Right-click the **Fixtures** folder and from the pull-down menu select **Fixed Hinge…** The **Fixture** property manager opens as shown in Fig. E2-7.

- In the **Standard (Fixed Hinge)** dialogue box, the **Cylindrical Faces for Fixture** field is highlighted (light blue).

- Zoom in on the left hole of the model and select its *inner surface*. **Face<1>** appears in the highlighted field, shown in Fig. E2-7. This cylindrical surface has an axis perpendicular to the model face.

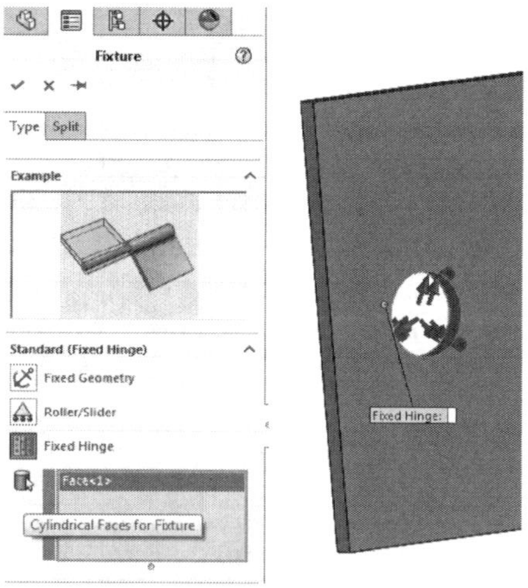

Figure E2-7 – Specifying a **Fixed Hinge** restraint.

- Click **[OK]** ✓ to close the **Fixture** property manager.

Solution Guidance (continued)

A **Fixed Hinge** restraint allows the model to undergo rotations about the selected hole, but no translations perpendicular to the hole. The remainder of this solution uses previously mastered procedures.

Special Solution Note:
Due to specification of a **Fixed Hinge** on this model, it is likely that the following warning message will appear during the **Solution** portion of this analysis.

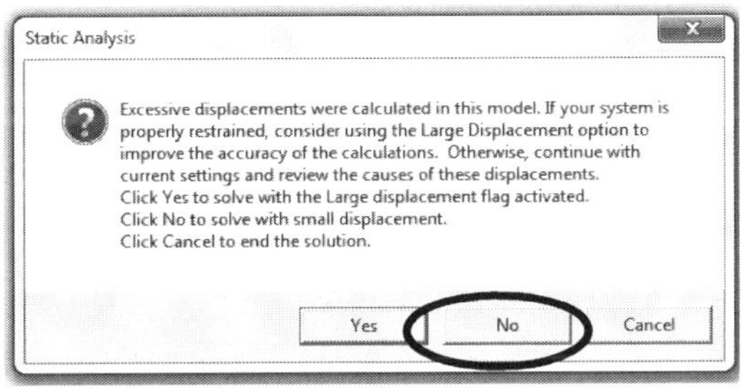

If the above **Static Analysis** window appears, click the **[No]** button, and continue with the "small displacement" Solution.

Determine the following:

a. Use classical equations to compute stress at the inside (concave) surface and the outside (convex) surface of the curved bracket model at section C-C. Section C-C passes through the center of curvature and is considered to be an edge view of the **Right Plane** in the top view of Fig. E2-6. Include a free body diagram of the portion of the model to the right of section C-C; label all magnitudes and directions.

b. Turn *off* the deformed image. Then, include a zoomed-in image of the right hole so that the external load, $F_X = 72$ lb, can clearly be seen to act between user specified *Split Lines* on the inner surface of the hole.

c. Create a stress contour plot showing the *most appropriate stress* that should be analyzed acting across section C-C. The *most appropriate stress* should correspond to the stress calculated in part (a). Do stress fringes on the FEA model loosely approximate those shown in the photograph in Fig. E2-5?

d. Use the **Probe** feature to produce a graph of the *most appropriate stress* across section C-C, begin at the inside (concave) surface and continue to the outside (convex) surface of the model. (See the *"HINT"* near the end of this problem for guidance when making this graph.) Use the **Stress Plot** property manager to select the *appropriate stress* for this plot to enable comparison with manual calculations of part (a) above. Include a descriptive title, axis labels, and your name on this graph.

Below the graph, or on a separate page, either (a) cut-and-paste a copy of the **Probe Results** table that includes values used for this comparison (see Appendix A for procedures to copy SOLIDWORKS Simulation images into a Word® document), or (b) click the **Save** icon, located in the **Report Options** dialogue box, to create an Excel spreadsheet containing all values in the **Probe Results** table. (See Appendix A, page A-12.) This spreadsheet can be inserted onto the page beneath the current graph. In either table, circle and label magnitudes of stress on the concave and convex surfaces at section C-C.

After determining both classical and FEA results at section C-C, use equation [1] (repeated below) to compute the percent difference between these results at the concave and convex surfaces of the model.

$$\% \text{ difference} = \frac{(\text{FEA result - classical result})}{\text{FEA result}} * 100 = \qquad [1]$$

e. On the **Probe** graph created in part (d), label the distance of the neutral axis (neutral plane) from the concave edge of the model at section C-C. Write a brief statement indicating how this value was determined. Compare this value with the location of the neutral axis determined using classical equations.

f. Return to the plot produced in part (c). This time use the **Probe** tool to sample stress magnitudes along the concave edge of the model beginning at point **A** and proceeding from node-to-node until reaching point **B** (see Fig. E2-6). Include a graph of these results with your analysis. Add a descriptive title, axis labels, and your name to this graph.

g. QUESTIONS: Answer the following questions on a separate page.

- Is the variation of stress through the middle of the model shown in the graph of part (d) expected? Why?
- Is the variation of stress shown on the graph of part (f) expected? Why?
- Is the location of the neutral axis determined in part (e) located where it is expected to occur on the curved bracket model? Does the neutral axis of a curved member subject to axial load *always* occur at a location *like* that shown in the plot of part (e)? Explain why or why not.

h. Using von Mises stress, create a plot showing all regions of the model where Safety Factor < 2.5 (if any). Indicate this/these region(s), if any, by circling its/their location(s) on the figure and labeling them as "FOS < 2.5." Include a software applied label indicating locations of maximum and minimum values of Safety Factor.

HINT: Because the mesh generation scheme within SOLIDWORKS Simulation creates an optimized mesh, it is probable that (a) a straight line of nodes may *not* exist across the model at Section C-C, and (b) it is also *unlikely* that node points *occur exactly on a horizontal centerline through the center of curvature.* For these reasons, and to obtain the best estimate of stress on a straight line through the center of the curved section, proceed as follows.

a. Zoom in on a top view of the model at section C-C.

b. On the **Simulation** tab, select the **Plot Tools** icon, and from the pull-down menu click the **Probe** tool  icon. This action opens the **Probe Results** property manager.

c. Open the SOLIDWORKS flyout menu, located at top left of the graphics area, and move the cursor over the **Right Plane** label. This action superimposes an edge view of the **Right Plane** onto the model. This plane will assist in locating nodes closest to a straight line at Section C-C. Unfortunately, the line disappears when the cursor is moved, but this action can be repeated while selecting nodes and can be very useful.

EXERCISE 5 – Curved Beam Stress in a Trailer Hitch (Special Topic Includes: Application of Remote Loads)

The trailer hitch shown in Fig. E2-8 is subject to both vertical and horizontal force components when towing a trailer. The vertical component, or "tongue weight" (**W**), is defined as the downward force due to trailer weight that acts on the hitch. For safety reasons, tongue weight should lie between 9% to 15% of the gross trailer weight (i.e., weight of the trailer plus its cargo). Towing force (**F_T**) is the force required to pull the trailer. Tow force is zero when the trailer is at rest; is reasonably steady when pulling a trailer at constant speed; and is maximum during acceleration or deceleration.

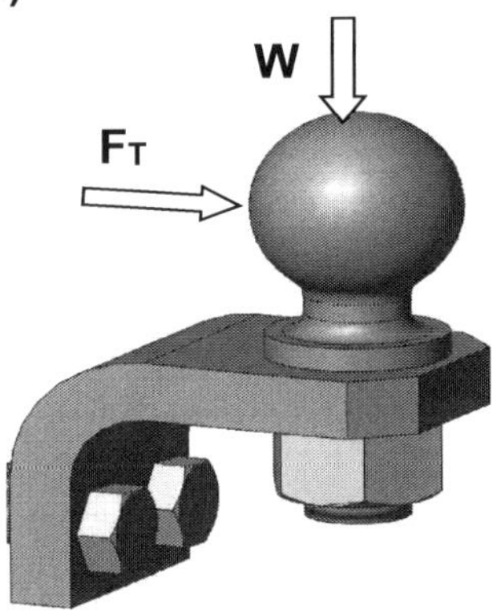

Figure E2-8 – Trailer hitch and ball assembly.

Open file: **Trailer Hitch 2-5**. A drawing of the trailer hitch, minus the ball, appears in Fig. E2-9. The hitch is bolted to a rigid frame on the towing vehicle (not shown) at the two ½-inch diameter holes. Because application of forces to the hitch "ball" may require abilities not yet introduced, and because stress in the ball is not the objective of this analysis, the problem can be simplified by defining applied forces using the **Remote Load/Mass** feature within SOLIDWORKS Simulation. Guidance in the application of a remote load is provided below.

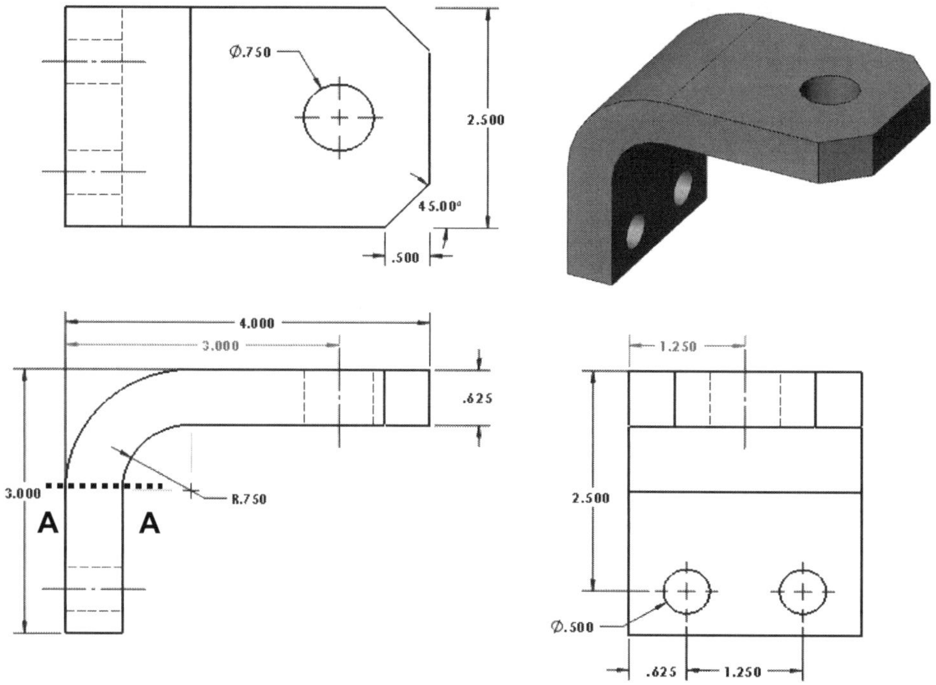

Figure E2-9 – Isolated view of the trailer hitch emphasizes its curved beam shape.

Assume the following.

- Material: **Alloy Steel** (use English units, **IPS**)
- Mesh: In the **Mesh** property manager, select ⊙ **Standard mesh** and use the default mesh size.
- Fixture: To mimic bolt fasteners, apply a **Fixed** (immovable) restraint on the inside surface of the two, ½ inch diameter bolt holes. Bolted joints are considered in Chapter 7.
- External Load: Apply force components using the **Remote Load/Mass** feature described below.
  Tongue weight **W = 200 lb** (vertical downward).
  Tow force **F_T= 550 lb** (horizontal) in the +X-direction.

Use of the **Remote Load/Mass** feature is described below. This feature permits application of remote forces, moments, and displacements. Remote masses are only used in cases of static, frequency, linear dynamic, or buckling studies. Application of a remote force is the only new topic introduced in this example. However, once the principle is understood, users should be able to apply it to other contexts. **Remote Load/Mass** is used primarily where modeling simplification can be realized. For example, application of force components to curved surfaces of the hitch ball can be accomplished using several methods. But, using the **Remote Load/Mass** option is one of the more direct approaches. Also, its introduction allows this useful feature to be applied in other situations.

Solution Guidance

It is assumed that the user has opened a Simulation file and started a Study. The following instructions are to serve as a "guide"; they are less detailed than step-by-step procedures found in example problems.

Remote Load/Mass

The **Remote Load/Mass** feature can be used to replace a more complex portion of a model (or) part of the model that is not essential to the final analysis. Because this analysis focuses on stress in the curved portion of the trailer hitch, the hitch "ball" can be replaced using a **Remote Load/Mass**. When applying force components using the **Remote Load/Mass** feature, proceed as follows.

1. If a coordinate system triad is *not* visible at the bottom of the ball attachment hole, scroll to the bottom of the SOLIDWORKS manager tree and click Coordinate System1. A "ghost" *reference coordinate system* triad is now displayed at the bottom of the "ball" hole.

2. In the Simulation manager tree right-click the **External Loads** folder and select **Remote Load/Mass…** This example deals only with remote "loads," not "mass."

3. In the **Type** dialogue box, select ⊙ **Load/Mass (Rigid connection)**. This option is used when stiffness of the part to be *replaced* is significant relative to the rest of the model (the hitch "ball" is considered very stiff). ⊙ **Load/Mass (Rigid connection)** is also selected because it can be applied to a **Face**, **Edge**, or **Vertices** of the part. NOTE: The O **Load (Direct transfer)** option could also be used; however, it is less convenient in this case because it can only be applied to **Faces** (i.e., entire surfaces) of a model.

4. Also in the **Type** dialogue box the **Faces, Edges, or Vertices, for Remote Load/Mass** field is active (highlighted light blue). Move the cursor onto the *edge* of the "ball" hole on *top* of the hitch and click to select it. **Edge<1>** appears in the active field. This action establishes the top surface of the hitch as a reference location above which the hitch "ball" forces act.

5. In the **Reference Coordinate System** dialogue box, choose ⊙ **Global** as the coordinate system *origin* from which *some* (not all) coordinates of the remote loads are defined. For example, the preceding step defined the top surface of the hitch as the position above which the horizontal "ball" force is located.

Design Insight:
The trailer *hitch* was intentionally designed with the **Global** coordinate system *origin* at the top of the ball hole. This location was chosen because it permits easy application of a **Remote Load/Mass** on the model as outlined below. Further, it is desired to apply forces **W** and **F_T** at the center of the ball.

Aided by the SOLIDWORKS **Sketch** in Fig. E2-10, it is seen that the center of the "ball" is located **1.616-in** above the ball shoulder. The ball center could also be located above the *reference coordinate system* origin at X = 0, Y = 0.625 (hitch thickness) + 1.616-in, and Z = 0. Force components **W** and **F_T** are defined in the following steps.

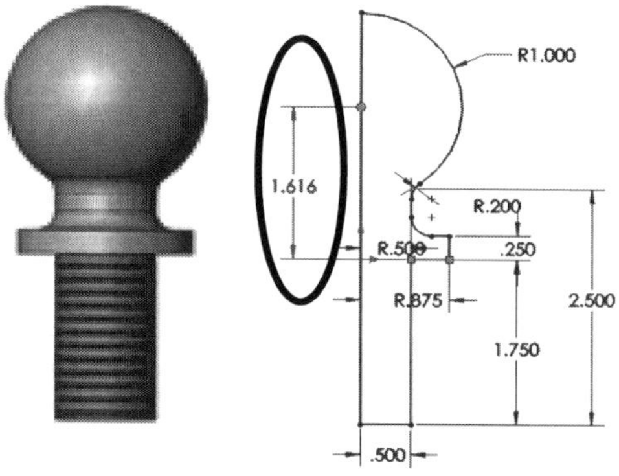

Figure E2-10 – Determination of height above the hitch surface at which forces are applied to the "ball."

Solution Guidance (continued)

6. In the **Location** dialogue box, verify that **Unit** is set to inches **in**. Then, in the **X-Location** field, accept the zero (**0**) value shown. In the **Y-Location** field, type **1.616**, which is the distance above the hole edge **Global Coordinate System** selected on the top surface of the hitch. Finally, in the **Z-Location** field, accept the default zero (**0**) value shown.

7. If necessary, check ☑ **Force** to open the **Force** dialogue box. Verify that **Unit** is set to **lbf**. Then in the **X-Direction** field type **550**. In the **Y-Direction** field, type **200** and, if the Y-force vector is directed upward, check ☑ **Reverse Direction** because tongue weight **W** is directed downward. Finally, accept the **Z-Direction** default value of zero (**0**).

8. Click ✓ **[OK]** to close the **Remote Loads/Mass** property manager.

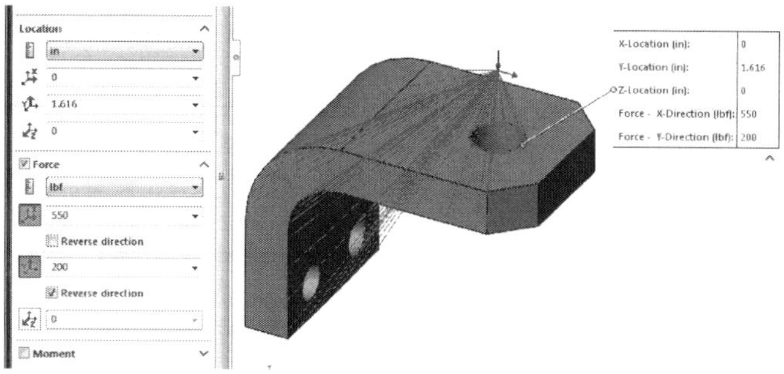

Figure E2-11 – Specifying **Location** coordinates and **Force** magnitudes in the **Remote Loads/Mass** property manager.

Determine the following:

a. Use classical equations to compute stress at the inside (concave) surface and the outside (convex) surface of the trailer hitch model at section A-A. Section A-A passes through the center of curvature and is considered to be a horizontal line in the front view of Fig. E2-9. Include a labeled free body diagram of the portion of the model above section A-A. Use definitions provided for a rectangular cross-section model shown above Fig. 24, p. 2-20 and equations [1] and [2] on p. 2-21, or use equations from your design of machine elements textbook. Clearly label each calculation.

b. Include an image of the hitch showing fixtures applied at the lower two bolt holes and the **Remote Load/Mass** applied above the "ball" hole.

c. Create a stress contour plot showing the *most appropriate stress* that should be analyzed at section A-A. The *most appropriate stress* should correspond to the stress calculated in part (a).

d. Use the **Probe** feature to determine magnitudes of the *most appropriate stress* on both the concave and convex sides of the model at section A-A. *HINT* – Display a mesh on the model. Also, to avoid edge effects, sample stress magnitudes near the middle of the model. To accurately locate the middle of the model, click the **Front** plane in the SOLIDWORKS feature manager tree or in the SOLIDWORKS flyout menu. Then rotate the model to left and right side views.

   Cut-and-paste a copy of the model that includes **Probe** information flags showing stress magnitudes at the locations sampled. See Appendix A for procedures to copy SOLIDWORKS Simulation images into a Word® document.

   After determining both classical and FEA results at section A-A, use equation [1] (repeated below) to compute the percent difference between these results at the concave and convex surfaces of the model.

$$\%\text{ difference} = \frac{(\text{FEA result - classical result})}{\text{FEA result}} * 100 = \qquad [1]$$

e. QUESTIONS: Answer the following questions on a separate page.

- Are stress magnitudes at section A-A near the middle (on front plane) of the concave and convex sides of the trailer hitch in good agreement with stresses calculated using classical curved beam equations? (Include a definition stating what you consider to be "good agreement.")

- Use the **Probe** tool to explore stress magnitude on section A-A, but at increasing distances from the model center. Does stress magnitude vary as distance from the model center increases? If stress magnitude varies, does it increase, or decrease? Is the variation of stress expected? Why?

f. Create a plot showing Safety Factor throughout the model. On this plot include a software generated label showing the minimum Safety Factor and its location on the model.

╬EXERCISE 6 – Curved Beam Stress in Bicycle Caliper Brake (Special Topic: Using a Hinge joint for Fixture)

Bicycle caliper brakes are available in many different forms. The caliper brake shown in Figs. E2-12 and E2-13 is a classic model that has been used for many years. When the brakes are operated, a pull force $\mathbf{F_P}$ acts on a cable attached to both halves of the brake assembly. Rubber pads apply nearly equal "squeezing" forces $\mathbf{F_N}$ that act normal to opposite sides of a bicycle wheel rim to stop the bike. Reaction forces $\mathbf{F_N}$ are shown in Fig. E2-12. In addition, frictional forces tangent to surfaces of the rubber pads are present, but are ignored in this exercise.

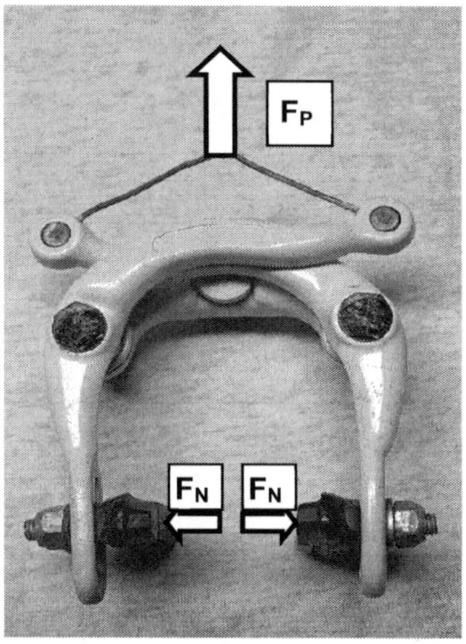

Figure E2-12 – Actual caliper brake showing applied pull force $\mathbf{F_P}$ and reaction forces $\mathbf{F_N}$.

Open file: **Bicycle Caliper Assembly**

A dimensioned view of one-half of the brake caliper model is shown in Fig. E2-13. During intense braking a maximum vertical pull force of $\mathbf{F_P}$ = 246 N is applied to the small diameter cable midway between its attachment points on each half of the caliper as shown in Fig. E2-12. The brake caliper rotates freely about a fixed pivot located at the 6 mm diameter hole at **A**.

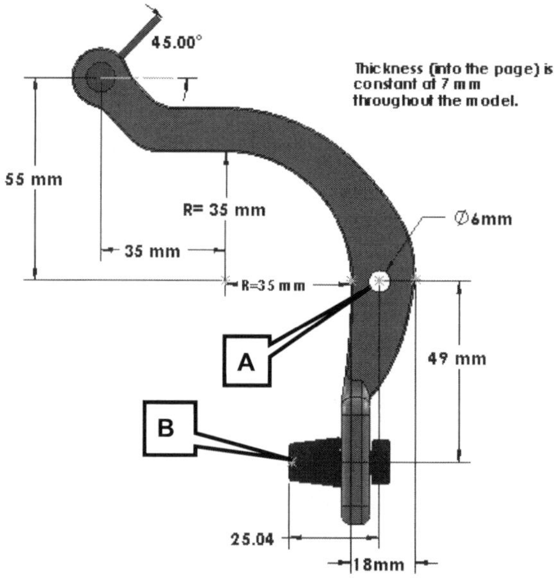

Figure E2-13 – Front view showing basic geometry of the bicycle caliper brake.

Create a finite element model of this part that includes material specification, fixtures, external loads, mesh, solution and results analysis.

- Material: Bicycle Brake Pad-1 - **Natural Rubber** (Use SI units)
  Bicycle Brake Wire-1 – **AISI 347 Annealed Stainless Steel (SS)**
  Bicycle Caliper-1 – Aluminum Alloy **2014 Alloy**

- Mesh: Use the system default size **Standard Mesh**. *Due to model complexity do NOT defeature this model prior to meshing.*

- Fixture: Apply a **Fixed Hinge** at hole **A**. Refer to the **Solution Guidance** text box in the section titled **Fixed Hinge Specification** near the bottom of page 2-44 and forward.
  Also, apply an appropriate user specified **Fixture** to the brake pad surface at **B**.

- External Load: Compute the external load applied to the right half of the caliper brake. NOTE: The horizontal radius of curvature, shown as **R=35 mm**, is dimensioned from the center of curvature to the *inside* edge of the caliper arm. The caliper arm is 18 mm wide at the location of hole **A** (see bottom dimension in Fig. E2-13).

Special Solution Note:
Due to specification of a **Fixed Hinge** on this model, it is highly likely that the following warning message will appear during the **Solution** portion of this analysis.

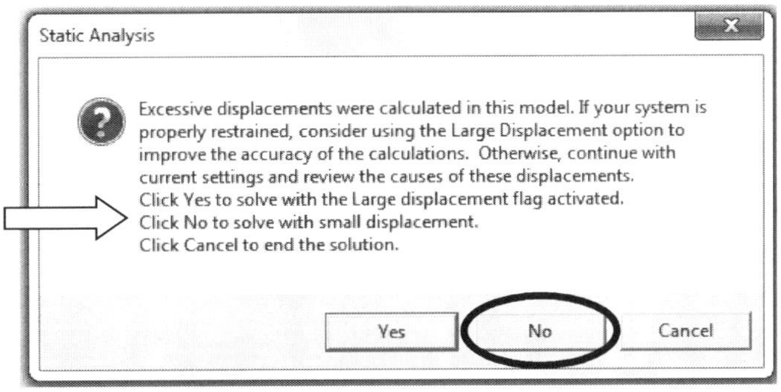

Click the **[No]** button if the above **Static Analysis** window appears and continue with the "small displacement" Solution.

> **ASIDE:**
> *Why can this large displacement be ignored?* Parts anchored by a **Fixed Hinge** are likely to rotate freely about the hinge when under load. Although these rotations may be very small, they are *relatively* large in comparison to part distortion (displacement) caused by the applied loads. Consider using a **Large displacement** solution when significant part distortion occurs due to applied loads.

Determine the following:

a. Use classical equations to compute stress at the inside and outside surfaces of the brake caliper on a horizontal section through the caliper at hole **A**. The following assumptions apply at this location: the caliper is rectangular in shape and is 7 mm thick (dimension into the page); radius of curvature to the inside (concave) surface is 35 mm and radius of curvature to the outer surface is 35 mm + 18 mm = 53 mm; these radii are considered constant for a sufficient distance above and below the hole so as not to affect calculations; the hole is to be neglected in stress calculations. Clearly label stress calculations at the inside and outside surfaces. Include a free body diagram of the upper portion of the caliper; label all forces and reactions acting on this body.

b. Use the **Probe** feature to produce a graph of the *most appropriate stress* on a horizontal section through the caliper at point **A**. Begin sampling values at the inside (concave) surface and continue to the outside (convex) surface; proceed along the straightest line possible. Use the **Stress Plot** property manager to specify the *appropriate stress* for this plot to enable comparison with manual calculations of part (a). Include a descriptive title, axis labels, and your name on this graph. Ignore the line segment connecting stresses *across* hole **A**.

   Beneath this graph, cut-and-paste a copy of the model that includes **Probe** information flags showing stress magnitudes at the locations sampled on its concave and convex sides only. See Appendix A for procedures to copy SOLIDWORKS Simulation images into a Word® document.

   After determining both classical and FEA results at section **A**, use equation [1] (repeated below) to compute the percent difference between these results at the concave and convex surfaces of the model.

$$\%\ \text{difference} = \frac{\text{(FEA result - classical result)}}{\text{FEA result}} * 100 = \qquad [1]$$

c. Create a stress contour plot of von Mises stress in the caliper. Include automatic labeling of maximum and minimum stress on this plot. Cut and paste this plot on the top half of an 8 ½ x 11 sheet.

d. Assuming the caliper is made of a ductile material, produce a plot showing regions where the safety factor < 2.0. Cut and paste this plot on the page beneath the von Mises plot of part (c) above. Also, if the safety factor is < 1.0 at any location within the caliper, produce a second plot to highlight any un-safe region(s). Manually label region(s), if any, where safety factor < 1.0 and paste the image adjacent to that showing regions where safety factor < 2.0.

e. Determine the **Result Force** acting on the flat face of the rubber brake pad. On a separate page, cut and paste a copy of the entire **Result Force** property manager;

include the **Reaction Force** table. In the same "screen shot," include the caliper assembly adjacent to the **Result Force** property manager. Adjacent to these images, draw a free body diagram of the caliper assembly. Label all known and unknown forces, and pertinent dimensions on this drawing. Then, in the remaining space manually calculate the reaction force(s) acting on the brake pad. Compare reaction force components in the X, Y, and Z directions with those determined from manual calculations. Use equation [1] to determine the percent difference between manual calculations and FEA results.

f. Beneath the "Fixture:" heading of the exercise statement, you were instructed to "*apply an appropriate user specified **Fixture** to the brake pad surface at **B**.*" In a few sentences, name the type of **Fixture** you specified at **B** and discuss the reason(s) why that **Fixture** was selected as appropriate.

g. Stress concentrations are typically associated with geometric discontinuities, such as the hole at **A**. Zoom in on hole **A** in the von Mises stress plot and examine stress magnitudes by comparing them to the color-coded stress legend. Use the **Probe** tool to search various areas around the hole and record the maximum stress at that location. Finally, discuss why or why not the hole at **A** results in higher stress.

Textbook Problems
It is highly recommended that the above exercises be supplemented by problems from a design of machine elements textbook. A great way to discover errors made in formulating a finite element analysis is to work problems for which the solution is known by independent calculation or experiment. Typical textbook problems, if well defined in advance, make an excellent source of solutions for comparison.

NOTES:

CHAPTER #3

STRESS CONCENTRATION ANALYSIS

This chapter explores stress in the vicinity of a geometric discontinuity in a part where stress concentration is known to occur. Because geometric discontinuities can assume a variety of different shapes, they often are referred to generically as "notches." Stress concentrations and their related stress concentration factors are typically studied in mechanics of materials and/or design of machine elements courses. This example focuses on the validity of Finite Element Analysis (FEA) solutions in the vicinity of these geometric discontinuities and on the effects of mesh size on solution accuracy. General principles studied in this example apply to a wide variety of finite element analysis problems. More specifically, since it is generally accepted that improved finite element solutions result when a smaller mesh size is used, this example examines convergence to a solution through the application of successive mesh refinement.

Because this is the third example problem, fewer figures and briefer step-by-step instructions are included. In fact, where you already are familiar with procedures and where *no new* procedures are introduced, special instructions encourage users to complete specific tasks on their own. The combination of these two approaches should permit users to work more at their own pace while allowing expanded discussion of new topics.

Learning Objectives

In addition to software capabilities mastered in previous chapters, upon completion of this example users should be able to:

- Recognize when, how, and why to *defeature* and *simplify* a model.
- Apply *mesh refinement* to a model and understand the influence of mesh density on stress and displacement results.
- Create *copies* of related studies quickly and easily within SOLIDWORKS Simulation.
- Check *convergence* to gauge validity of a finite element solution.
- Use multiple *viewports* to compare results of different finite element analyses.

Problem Statement

The rectangular bar illustrated in Fig. 1 is fixed at its left end and is subject to an axial, tensile load **F = 6000** lb applied to the opposite end. A rounded "notch," which causes stress concentration, is located in the center of the member.

Figure 1 – Axially loaded bar with a geometric discontinuity.

Dimensions of the notched bar, shown in Fig. 2, reveal that the member is sufficiently long so that boundary-conditions (i.e., fixtures and external loads) do not significantly affect stress near the notch. The bar is made of **AISI 1020** steel. Analysis of this model begins below.

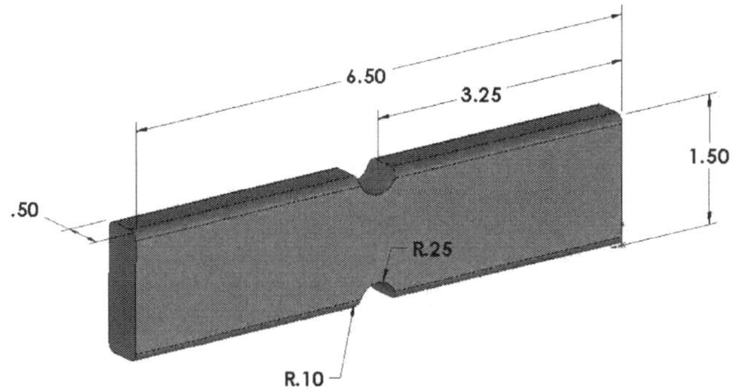

Figure 2 – Dimensioned drawing and a three-dimensional model of a notched bar. (All dimensions in "inches.")

1. Open SOLIDWORKS by making the following selections. (*Note:* ">" is used to separate successive menu selections.)

Start>All Programs>SOLIDWORKS 2026 (or) Click the **SOLIDWORKS** icon on your screen.

2. In the **Main Menu**, select **File** > **Open…** Then use procedures common to your computer environment to locate and open the file named **"Notched Bar."**

Create a Static Analysis (Study)

The new Study is to be named "**DRAFT Mesh-DEFAULT Size**." Individuals comfortable with setting up a **Static** analysis using a **Solid Mesh** are encouraged to proceed on their own. Abbreviated steps, 1 through 3 below, are provided for those desiring guidance. *NOTE: This and future chapters make use of right-clicking menu items to make selections. Users who prefer to use icons located on the Simulation tab, as demonstrated in Chapter #2, are encouraged to do so.*

1. In the main menu, select **Simulation** and from the pull-down menu select **Study…** Or, on the **Simulation** *tab* click "▼" on the **New Study** icon and in the pull-down menu, select **New Study**. The **Study** property manager opens.

2. In the **Name** dialogue box, replace the name "**Static 1**" by typing "**DRAFT Mesh-DEFAULT Size**," where the word "DRAFT" refers to the *type* of mesh (no mid-side nodes) and the word "DEFAULT" refers to the mesh *size*.

3. Verify that a **Static** study is selected and the **Use 2D Simplification** is unchecked, then click **[OK]** ✓. An outline for the study is opened in the Simulation manager tree.

Defeaturing the Model

Before beginning an analysis, it is always a good idea to examine the model to determine whether or not its geometry can be simplified without significantly impacting the results. The reason for this examination is that a simpler model results in a more computationally efficient analysis. Thus, the user must ask, "Is it necessary to include all geometric features on the model in order to obtain a valid solution?" If the answer is "no," then the model can be simplified by *suppressing* (i.e., defeaturing) unimportant features or by making use of model *symmetry*. Typical items that can be suppressed without significantly affecting results are minor geometric features, such as fillets, rounds, and chamfers. *You are cautioned, however, that defeaturing a model can have dire consequences if improper choices are made.* Begin by defeaturing the current model as described by two alternate methods outlined below. It is strongly recommended that both methods be attempted as this will provide flexibility in your approach to new problems.

Method 1:

1. Depress and *hold* the **Shift** key and move the cursor onto the graphics screen. Then click to select each of the eight rounded edges on the model. *NOTE: Release the **Shift** key when rotating the model.* Some of these surfaces are shown shaded in Fig. 3.

2. After selecting all rounds, right-click anywhere in the graphics screen and the pop-up menu shown in Fig. 3 appears. On this menu, select the **Suppress** icon circled in Fig. 3. The suppressed rounds are effectively "removed" from the model as illustrated in Fig. 4.

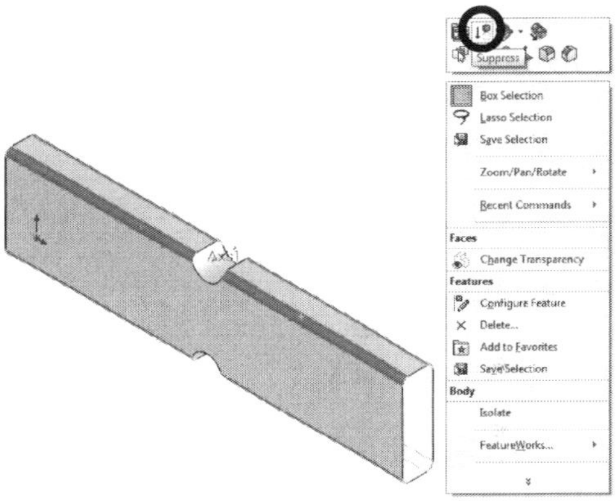

Figure 3 – Rounds selected to be suppressed on the Notched Bar model.

The above procedure works well when only a few geometries are chosen for defeaturing. However, an alternative and somewhat simpler means can be used when the goal is to suppress *all* rounded edges on this model. Next, use the alternative approach, but first the rounded edges must be returned to the model. Proceed as follows.

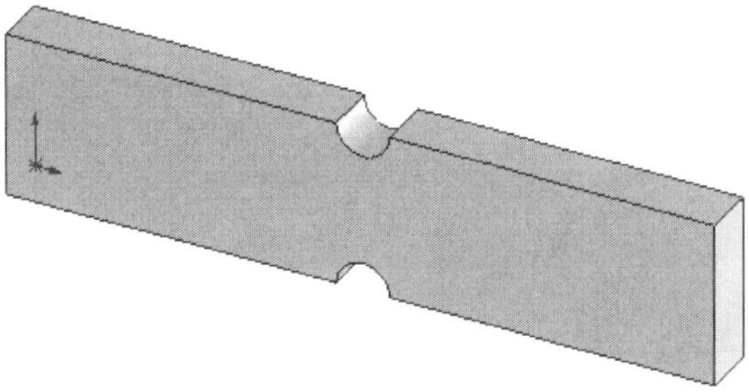

Figure 4 – Notched Bar after defeaturing.

3. In the SOLIDWORKS manager tree, located *above* the SOLIDWORKS Simulation manager at the left of the graphics screen, locate **Fillet1** and right-click this icon.

In the pop-up menu, select the **Unsuppress** icon. Fillets reappear on the model.

Method 2:

4. Once again, locate **Fillet1** in the SOLIDWORKS manager tree and right-click its label. From the box above the pop-up menu, select the **Suppress** icon. All fillets are removed from the model.

Analysis Insight:
Clearly **Method 2** is the easier of the two methods. However, its implementation requires planning ahead when the SOLIDWORKS model is created. For example, if rounds of the same size were included elsewhere on a more complex model, but if only one set of rounds were to be suppressed, then the SOLIDWORKS part should be created with two different sets of rounds, each of which is easily identified by a different name.

Aside:
SOLIDWORKS Simulation also provides a **Simplify** tool found under the **Tools** menu: **Tools>Find/Modify>Simplify**. See **Help>SOLIDWORKS Simulation>Help Topics** and type **Simplify** in the **Search** box for more information.

Assign Material Properties to the Model

If possible, specify the material for this model on your own. Choose **AISI 1020** steel and select **English (IPS)** units. An abbreviated, step-by-step procedure is provided below if guidance is desired.

1. In the SOLIDWORKS Simulation manager, right-click the model name **Notched Bar**. From the pull-down menu, select **Apply/Edit Material**.

2. In the **Material** window, select **AISI 1020** steel from the list of available steels. <u>Caution</u>: *Avoid selecting AISI 1020 Steel, Cold Rolled.*

3. On the **Properties** tab, adjacent to **Units:**, select **English (IPS)**.

4. Click **[Apply]** followed by **[Close]** to close the **Material** window. A check "✓" appears on the **Notched Bar** folder and **(-AISI 1020-)** appears next to this folder.

Apply Fixtures and External Loads

Loads and fixtures acting on this model include an **Immovable** restraint applied on its left-end and a **6000** lb axial force applied normal to its right-end. Practice applying these restraints and loads on your own. After applying restraints and loads, a partial view of the Simulation manager tree should appear as shown in Fig. 5, and the model should appear as shown in Fig. 6. A step-by-step procedure is provided if guidance is desired.

FIXTURES

1. In the SOLIDWORKS Simulation manager, right-click **Fixtures,** and from the pull-down menu select **Fixed Geometry…** The **Fixture** property manager opens.

2. In the **Standard (Fixed Geometry)** dialogue box, the **Fixed Geometry** icon should already be selected. The **Faces, Edges, Vertices for Fixture** field is highlighted (light blue) and is awaiting selection of the surface to be **Fixed**.

3. Rotate the model as necessary and select the surface on the left end of the model. **Immovable** restraints are applied to the left end of the model as seen in Fig. 6.

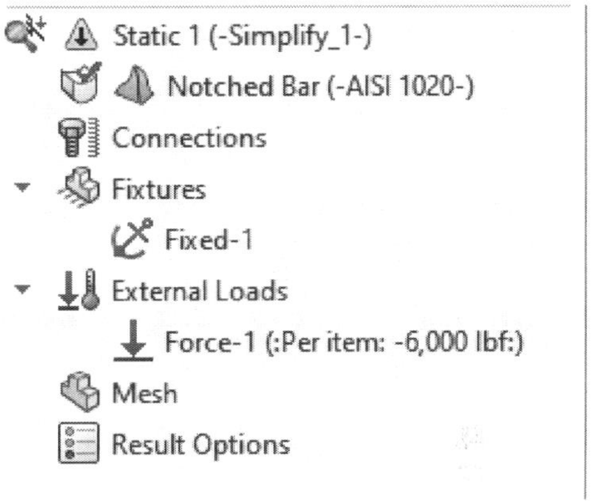

Figure 5 – SOLIDWORKS Simulation manager with **Fixtures** and **External Loads** defined.

4. Click **[OK]** ✓ to close the **Fixture** property manager. **Fixed-1** appears beneath the **Fixtures** folder as seen in Fig. 5.

EXTERNAL LOADS

1. Right-click the **External Loads** icon, and from the pop-up menu select **Force…** The **Force/Torque** property manager opens.

2. Within the **Force/Torque** dialogue box, select the **Force** icon (if not already selected) and click to select ⦿ **Normal** as the direction of the force.

3. The **Face and Shell Edges for Normal Force** field is highlighted (light blue) to indicate it is active. Rotate the model and select the right end of the part. Force vectors appear on the right-end; *ignore force direction at this time.*

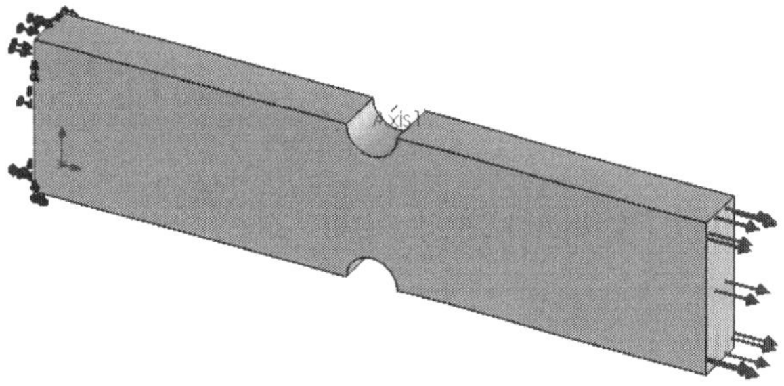

Figure 6 – Notched Bar restrained on its left end and with a **6000** lb force applied normal to its right end.

4. Verify that the Unit field is set to **English (IPS)**.

5. In the **Force Value** field, type **6000**. Note units are "lbf."
6. Because the default orientation for forces applied normal to a surface is directed *toward* the surface, it is necessary to check ☑ **Reverse direction** to apply a tensile load.

7. Click **[OK]** ✓ to close the **Force/Torque** property manager. **Force-1 (:Per item: -6000 lbf:)** is now listed beneath the **External Loads** folder in Fig. 5. The model should now appear as shown in Fig. 6.

Mesh the Model

Because a primary goal of this example is to examine differences between results obtained when a different mesh *type* or *size* of mesh is used, it is suggested that the following mesh definition steps be followed carefully. The model will be meshed five times, each time using a different size or type of mesh. This example concludes with a comparison of results obtained when using different meshes and corresponding observations about solution accuracy.

Proceed as follows to define the first mesh.

1. In the Simulation manager, right-click the **Mesh** folder and select **Create Mesh…** The **Mesh** property manager opens as shown in Fig. 7.

2. A pointer at the top of the **Mesh Density** dialogue box is located in the center of the scale between **Coarse** and **Fine** mesh sizes. This setting corresponds to the default mesh size; do *not* change it.

3. Check "✓" to open the ☑ **Mesh Parameters** dialogue box and verify that a ⦿ **Standard Mesh** is chosen and that **Unit** is set to **in**. Accept the remaining default settings.

4. Next, select the **Mesh Quality** *tab*. Click to select Notched Bar model under High: window. Press **Apply draft mesh quality** key to move the Notched Bar model to Draft: window.

5. Verify that other system default settings appear as shown in Fig. 7 and click **[OK]** "✓" to close the **Mesh** property manager and mesh the model.

6. The meshed model appears in Fig. 8.

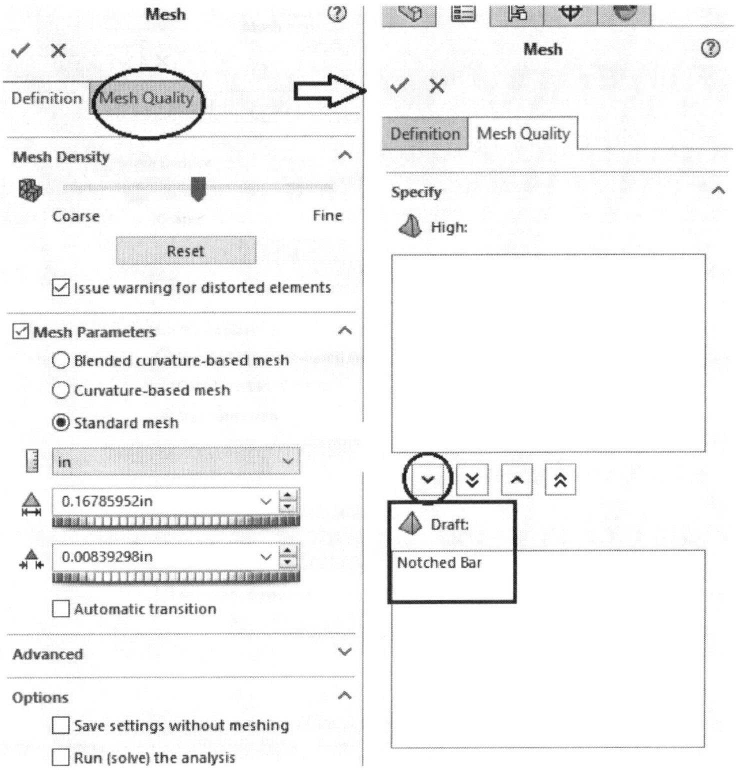

Figure 7 – Settings for mesh size in the **Mesh** property manager.

Figure 9 shows an enlarged view of a notch and the resulting straight-line approximation of the curved notch that results when a **Draft** quality mesh is used. Although rarely used for a final study, a draft quality mesh can be useful where quick results are needed for a large, complex model. Zoom-in to look at your model, then return the display to an **Isometric** or **Trimetric** view.

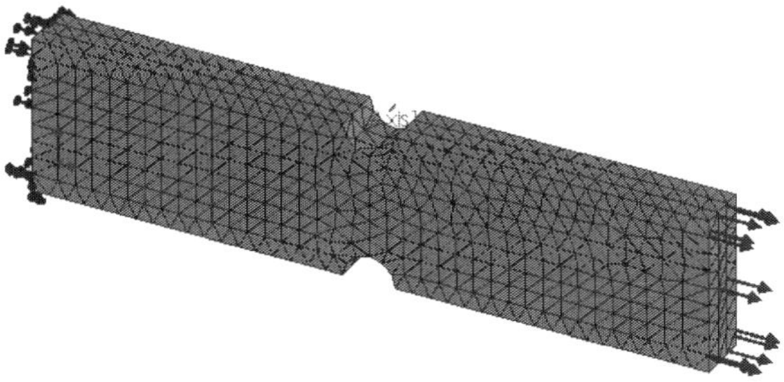

Figure 8 – Draft quality mesh shown on the Notched Bar model.

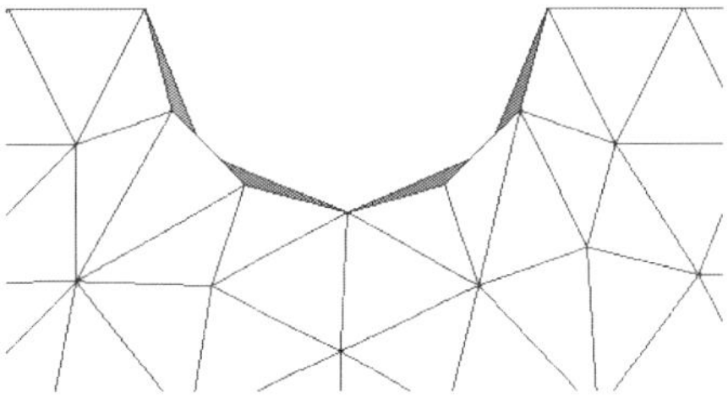

Figure 9 – Close-up view of **Draft** quality mesh reveals a straight-line approximation of the curved surface.

NOTE: Draft quality mesh specifies four corner nodes for each solid element and three corner nodes for each shell element to form elements.

Solution

Proceed directly to the solution. You are encouraged to run the **Study** on your own or follow the one-step procedure below.

1. In the Simulation manager tree, right-click the study name **DRAFT Mesh-DEFAULT Size (-Simplify_1-),** and from the pull-down menu select **Run**.

The analysis runs and, upon completion, the now familiar **Results** folders are added at the bottom of the Simulation manager tree. Next, proceed to examine the results of this analysis.

Examination of Results

Stress Plots

Recall that this example will be solved five different times, each time using a different mesh size, mesh type, or mesh control technique. Also, a second goal of this example is to introduce simple methods of creating additional studies that are identical to the first except that different mesh characteristics are used. For this reason, it is necessary to consider carefully exactly *what results* are to be examined and what plot characteristics should be defined to *display* those results. If these factors are addressed when the *first* set of results is being defined, then similar results can be produced automatically for all subsequent solutions. Proceed as follows to specify the desired plot characteristics.

1. If the **Stress1 (-von Mises-)** plot appears in the graphics area, skip this step. Otherwise, beneath the **Results** folder, double-click on **Stress1 (-vonMises-)** to display the von Mises stress contour plot and the color-coded stress legend.

The following steps are used to specify certain desired characteristics of the current plot. While some selections are arbitrary, other selections represent the author's preferences. In each case a brief justification is given. In practice, however, these selections depend upon user preference and/or standard practices within a specific company or industry. As selections below are made, the current image of the Notched Bar is altered to appear like that shown in Fig. 11.

2. Right-click **Stress1 (-vonMises-)** and from the pull-down menu, select **Edit Definition…** The **Stress plot** property manager opens. ***SHORT CUT:*** Double-click the plot title at upper left or center of your screen to open the **Stress Plot** property manager shown in Fig. 10.

3. In the **Display** dialogue box, verify **Units** are set to **psi**; if not, change them.

4. Check ☑ **Deformed Shape** to open this dialogue box (if not already open) and select ⊙**True Scale.**

5. At bottom of this property manager, click **v** to open the **Property** dialogue box. In this box check ☑ **Include title text:** and type **Stress Concentration Study using DRAFT Quality-DEFAULT Size Mesh - YOUR NAME** to provide pertinent information about this plot. *Justification:* It is important to document both the context and author of a Study so that other users of this information know who to contact if questions arise. (See top left of Fig. 11.)

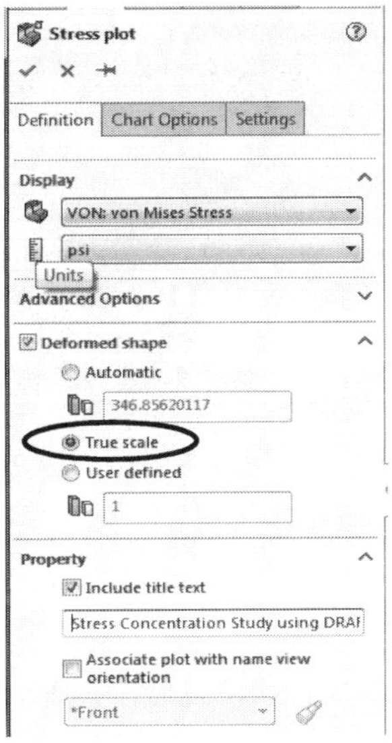

Figure 10 - **Stress Plot** property manager.

6. Next, select the **Chart Options** *tab*, and beneath **Display Options** click to check ☑ **Show max annotation**. The location of maximum stress is immediately labeled on the plot as shown near the notch in Fig. 11. *Justification:* This choice labels the location of maximum stress in the part. Rotate the model if necessary.

7. Within the **Position/Format** dialogue box slowly move the cursor over the pull-down menu, second from the bottom. Its name should appear as Number Format. If **floating** does not appear, click ⌄ and from the pull-down menu select **floating** as the desired format for numbers displayed.

8. In the **X.123** No of Decimals field (bottom field), use ⌄ to decrease the number of decimal places displayed on the stress legend to "0." *Justification:* Yield strength and other stress values are not known to the accuracy implied.

Colorblind users are encouraged to apply instructions in the 2nd bullet on page I-26.

9. Select the **Settings** *tab*, and beneath **Fringe Options** select ⌄ **Discrete.** *Justification:* This option is selected because discrete fringes reproduce better when printed in the black, white, and gray tones used in this text. Otherwise, fringe display is a user preference.

10. Beneath **Boundary Options**, select ⌄ **Mesh**. This option displays the current mesh on the model. *Justification:* Since one goal of this example is to investigate effects of mesh modification upon results, viewing the mesh provides visual feedback about mesh size.

11. Click **[OK]** "✓" to close the **Stress plot** property manager.

A completed view of the model displaying von Mises stress contours appears in Fig. 11.

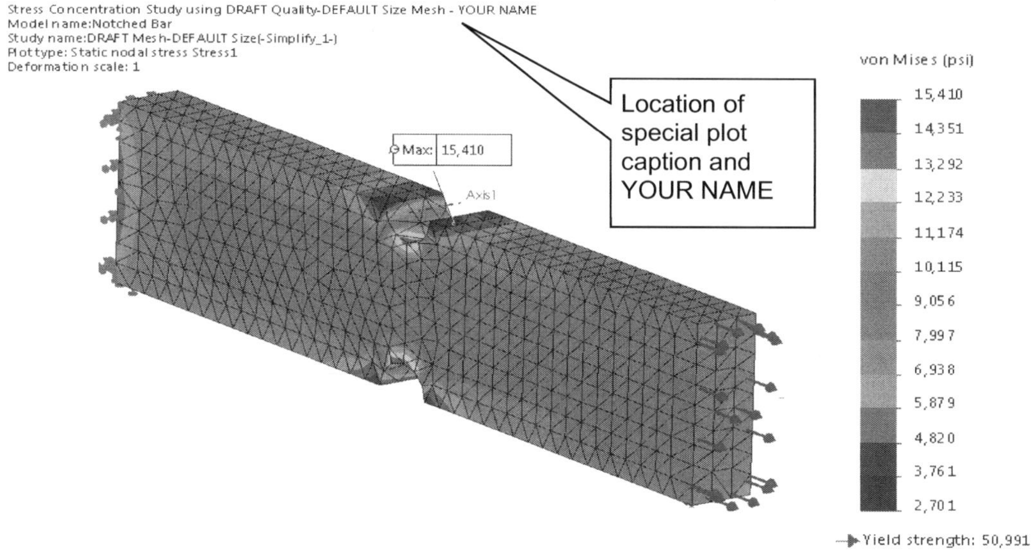

Figure 11 – Trimetric view of the Notched Bar with user specified display options.

Note the maximum magnitude of von Mises stress (15,410 psi) determined by this analysis. To more clearly understand results obtained using different meshes, you are *strongly encouraged* to enter results for maximum von Misses stress, maximum stress in the X-direction (Sigma-X), and maximum X-displacement into **Table 1**, on page 3-28. Place a scrap of paper at that page to make it easily found, and record values for these quantities as each Study is completed. ***It only takes a few seconds and the benefit to your understanding is well worth the effort.***

***[Record:** max. von Mises stress in the first row of Table 1, pg. 3-30]*

Analysis Insight

Two views of the Notched Bar showing discrete von Mises stress contours are displayed in Figs. 12 and 13. For these plots, the following observations are made.

OBSERVATIONS for Fig. 12:

- The magnitude and distribution of stress at left and right ends of the model are different due to the **Immovable** restraint applied at the left end and a uniform tensile force (**External Load**) applied normal to the right-end. These stress differences are another example of localized effects explained by St. Venant's principle. However, due to length of the model, these effects are negligible near the middle of the model (the area of primary interest).

To view items described in the bullet below, alter the model as follows.

a. Right-click **Stress1 (vonMises)** and select **Edit Definition…**
b. In the **Stress plot** property manager, open the ☑ **Deformed Shape** dialogue box and select ⦿**Automatic** to emphasize model deformation.
c. Next, click to select the **Settings** tab.
d. In the **Boundary Options** dialogue box, change **Mesh** to **Model**.
e. Click **[OK]** ✓ to close the **Stress plot** property manager.

- A comparison of deformed and *un*-deformed shapes of the model can be made by moving the cursor over the model. This action causes an outline of the *un*-deformed shape to be superimposed on the model. Zoom in on the *front view*, seen in Fig. 12, to observe a slight narrowing of the model in the Y-direction. Notice a small gap between the un-deformed model outline and the colored stress contour plot. This change of lateral dimension is due to Poisson's ratio effect. Also, on the right end of the model, note the increased length which extends from the original line of force application.

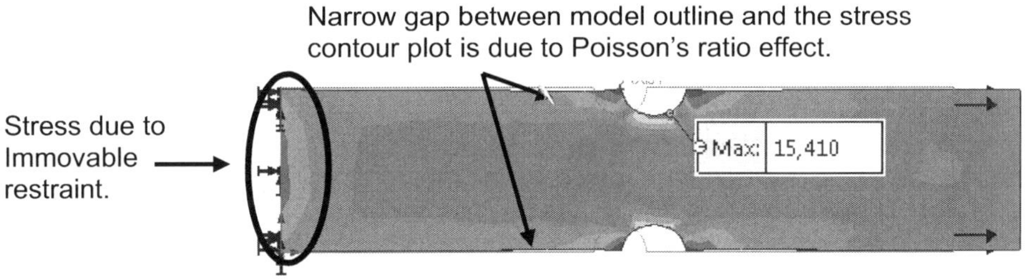

Figure 12 – von Mises stress contours and comparison of deformed and un-deformed models of the Notched Bar. The **Mesh** is not shown on this plot so that Poisson's effect is more easily seen. Deformation is exaggerated 346.856 times; see plot caption.

f. Repeat steps (a) through (f) above, except in the **Deformed Shape** dialogue box select ⦿**True Scale**, and in the **Boundary Options** dialogue box return the display to show the **Mesh**.

g. Click **[OK]** ✓ to close the **Stress plot** property manager.

Analysis Insight (continued)

OBSERVATIONS for Fig. 13:

- Superimposing the current mesh onto the model reveals slight differences between element geometry near the top and bottom notches. Carefully observe these differences on Fig. 13 or on your screen. Zoom in on the notch area.

- Stress *distribution* adjacent to notches located at the top and bottom of the bar is different. This difference is due, in part, to somewhat different mesh shapes in these two areas of the model and mathematical round-off.

NOTE: Because the meshing process is automated and because it "starts from scratch" and seeks an optimum mesh each time a part is meshed, it is possible that a user obtained mesh might differ from that shown in Fig. 13.

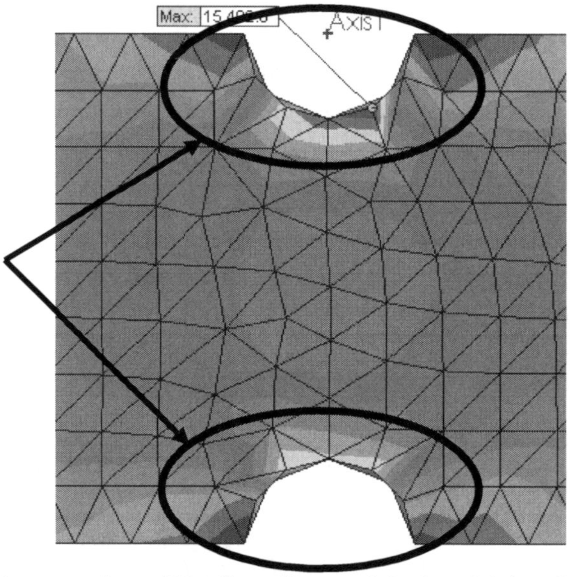

Figure 13 – Close-up view of **Draft** quality mesh in the vicinity of the two notches. Carefully observe slight differences in mesh geometry and distribution of von Mises stress.

Creating a "Copy" of a Plot

Due to the *axial* tensile force of 6000 lb applied to the Notched Bar in the X-direction, it is logical to examine stresses in the X-direction (i.e., σ_x). To do so requires definition of another **Stress plot** similar to that defined for the von Mises stress plot displayed above. However, repeating all steps necessary to produce a new plot with the *same* characteristics is somewhat tedious and time consuming. Therefore, use the following shortcut to create a *copy* of the current graph including all its display settings.

1. In the Simulation manager tree *click-and-drag* the **Stress1 (-vonMises-)** folder upward and drop it onto the **Results** folder as illustrated in Fig. 14. Then, click "▶" to re-open the ▶ **Results** folder.

   A new copy of the contents of the **Stress1 (-vonMises-)** plot appears at the bottom of the **Results** list and is labeled **Copy[1] Stress1 (-vonMises-)**, shown at the arrow in Fig. 14. This new folder contains an exact duplicate of all commands used to define the original **von Mises** plot. The following steps outline how to modify this *copied* folder to obtain a plot of σ_x.

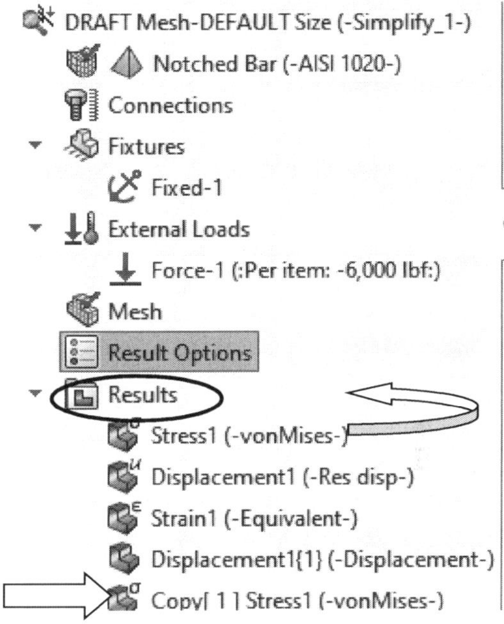

Figure 14 – Making an exact copy of a plot folder.

2. Click-*pause*-click on the name **Copy[1] Stress1 (-vonMises-)** and type a new descriptive name for the new plot. Since this new folder is to contain σ_x, type "**Sigma-X**" and press **[Enter]**.

The *changed name* now appears as **Sigma-X (-vonMises-)**. This name, of course, makes no sense because **Sigma-X** and **vonMises** represent two different stresses. The reason for this is that, although the folder *name* was changed, the copied contents (namely vonMises stress) still reside within the folder. However, this is easily corrected by the following steps.

3. Right-click **Sigma-X (-vonMises-)** and from the pull-down menu shown in Fig. 15, select **Edit Definition…** The **Stress plot** property manager opens.

4. In the dialogue box beneath **Display**, open ⌄ the **Component** pull-down menu, and from the list of possible stresses select **SX: X Normal Stress**.

5. Click **[OK]** ✓ to close the **Stress plot** property manager.

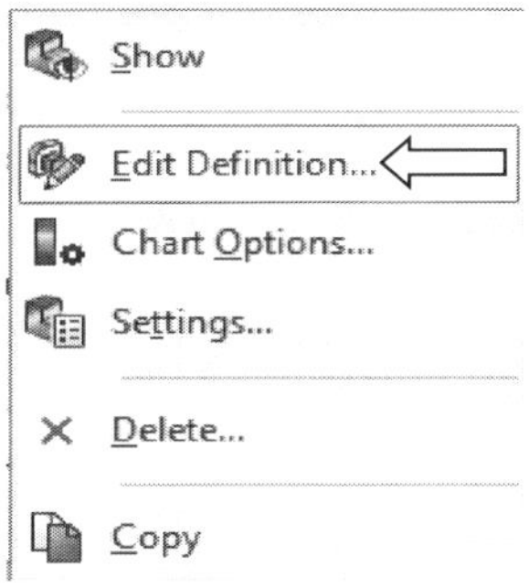

Figure 15 – Partial view of pull-down menu.

The *correct* name for the stress now appears in the Simulation manager tree as **Sigma-X (-X normal-)**. This name is a combination of the name you typed to identify the stress plus a system applied label to identify σ_x

6. To display the plot of **Sigma-X (-X normal-)**, right-click its name, and from the pop-up menu select **Show**.
   ***[Record:** max. Sigma-X in the first row of Table 1]*

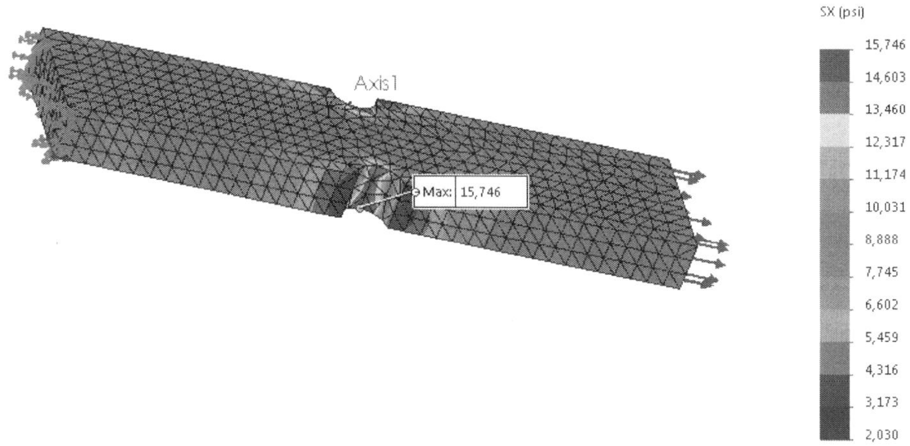

Figure 16 – Graphic display of normal stress in the X-direction (σ_x).

> **Analysis Insight**
>
> OBSERVATIONS for Fig. 16:
>
> - Maximum stress in the X-direction σ_x = 15,746 psi (values vary) is 2.2% larger than the vonMises stress σ' = 15,410 psi, and it occurs in a different location.
> - All *display settings* established for **Stress1 (-vonMises-)** are copied into the **Sigma-X (-X normal-)** plot folder, (i.e., discrete fringes are shown, your name and a brief description appear at top-left of the graphics screen, the maximum stress magnitude and its location are labeled on the plot, and the mesh is superimposed on the model). NOTE: If the description appearing next to your name in the top line is no longer valid, it can be changed; see steps 2, 5, and 11 of the previous section.

Displacement Plot

Another goal for this example is to determine when an analysis converges to a solution. Although both stress and displacement can be used to make this determination, it turns out that displacement plots typically yield better information about solution convergence than do stress contour plots. Based on your reading of the Introduction to this text, can you explain the reason for this? This question is answered later in this example. Based on this discussion, a **Displacement** plot is created next.

1. Double-click the **Displacement1 (-Res disp-)** folder to display the default displacement plot. Recall that **(-Res disp-)** is an abbreviation for "resultant displacement." If the **Displacement** plot does *not* appear beneath the **Results** folder, perform step (e) found on page 1-14, or try this on your own.

The resultant displacement image, **(-Res disp-)**, is simply a plot of the square root of the sum of the squares of the X, Y, and Z displacement components at any point within the model as given by equation [1].

$$Resultant\ Displacement = \sqrt{X^2 + Y^2 + Z^2} \qquad [1]$$

It is entirely acceptable to use **(-Res disp-)** for this analysis. However, we next select the X-displacement to be displayed for two reasons. First, the X-displacement is in the direction of the applied load and therefore it accounts for the primary displacement component (Y and Z displacements due to Poisson ratio effects are *very* small relative to X). And, second, choosing the X-displacement provides an opportunity to demonstrate selection of a different displacement component as outlined in the following steps.

2. Right-click **Displacement1 (-Res disp-)**, and from the pull-down menu select **Edit Definition…** The **Displacement plot** property manager opens as shown in Fig. 17. ***SHORT CUT:*** Double-click the plot title.

3. In the **Display** dialogue box, open ∨ the **Component** pull-down menu and select **UX: X Displacement** to display the X-component of displacement.

4. In the **Units** pull-down menu, select inches **in**.

5. In the ☑ **Deformed Shape** dialogue box, select ⊙**Automatic** to exaggerate the actual displacement.

6. Click to open the **Settings** *tab* shown in Fig. 18.

Below, two cosmetic changes are made to this plot.

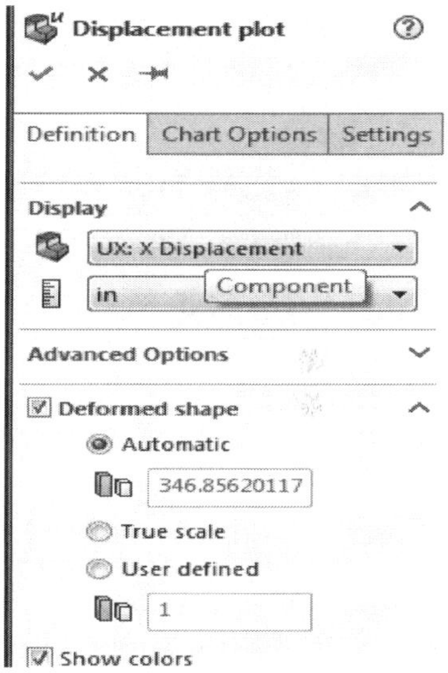

Figure 17 – Selecting the X-component of displacement.

7. Beneath **Fringe Options** select **Discrete** for the type of fringe display and beneath **Boundary Options** select **Model** (if not already selected) to turn on a black outline of the model. A mesh display is not needed here.

8. Click **[OK]** ✓ to close the **Displacement plot** property manager. A plot of **UX: X Displacement** is displayed in Fig. 19.

*[**Record:** max. Displacement1 in Table 1]*

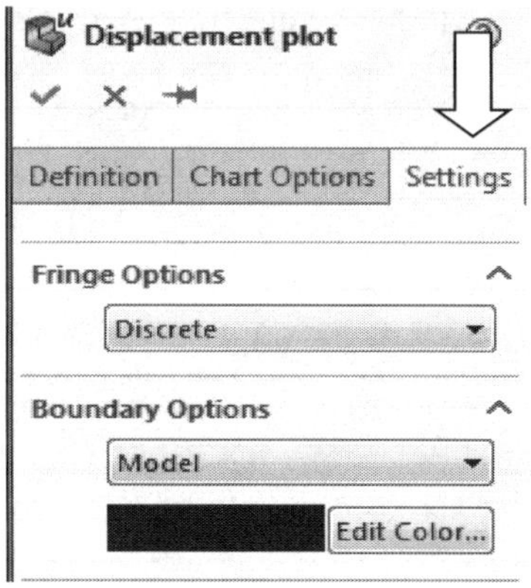

Figure 18 – Display options in the **Settings** tab.

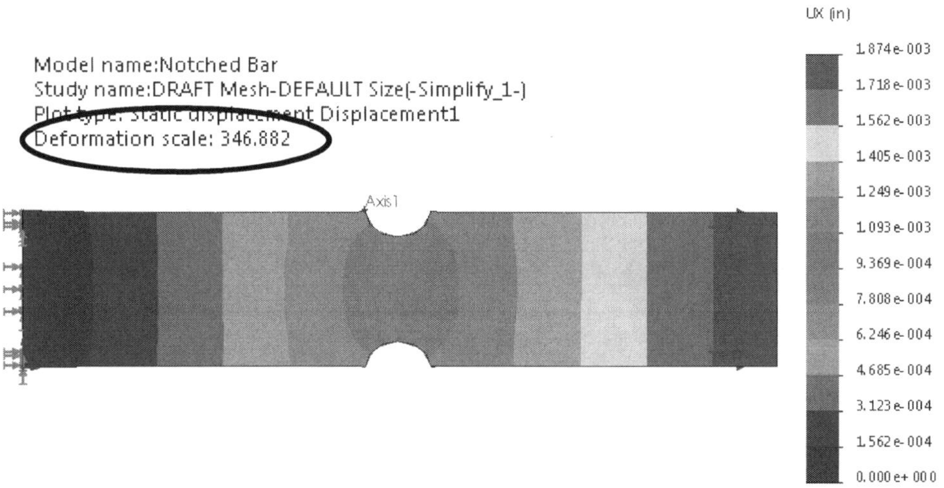

Figure 19 – Displacement plot modified to show **UX: X Displacement** using an outlined model and discrete fringes.

Recall that default plots show exaggerated displacements. The exaggeration in this case is 346.882 times larger than actual (values may vary slightly). See caption circled at top-left of the graphics screen. If it is desired to toggle quickly back-and-forth between an exaggerated view and the *true* displacement view, the short-cut of Chapter 2 can be used.

Simply click the **Deformed Result**  icon located on the **Simulation** tab toolbar.

Because both stress and displacement plots are defined above, it is possible to produce additional identical *copies* of an *entire Study*. A copy of this entire Study can be created in which everything remains the same except for mesh type and mesh size. Proceed as follows to define these new studies.

Creating New Studies

Basic Parts of the Graphical User Interface

Before outlining the method to duplicate (or copy) a Study, the names used to identify various parts of the graphical user interface are reviewed. Also, a previously unused part of the graphical user interface is introduced. Reviewing these parts of the screen image is essential because several names are quite similar. Refer to Fig. 20 while reading the descriptions below.

- SOLIDWORKS Feature Manager Tree – Users familiar with SOLIDWORKS should already be familiar with the Feature Manager tree. It is located at the top left side of the graphics screen. See label on Fig. 20. Its name derives from the fact that various features of a solid model created in SOLIDWORKS, such as sketches, holes, fillets, extrusions, mates, etc. are listed in this portion of the manager tree.
- Simulation Manager Tree (also referred to as the "Simulation manager") – The Simulation Manager tree refers to the finite element portion of a Study. It is also located at the left side of the screen just below the SOLIDWORKS Feature Manager. Both these entities are referred to as manager trees because they contain a list of items added to the model as an analysis proceeds.

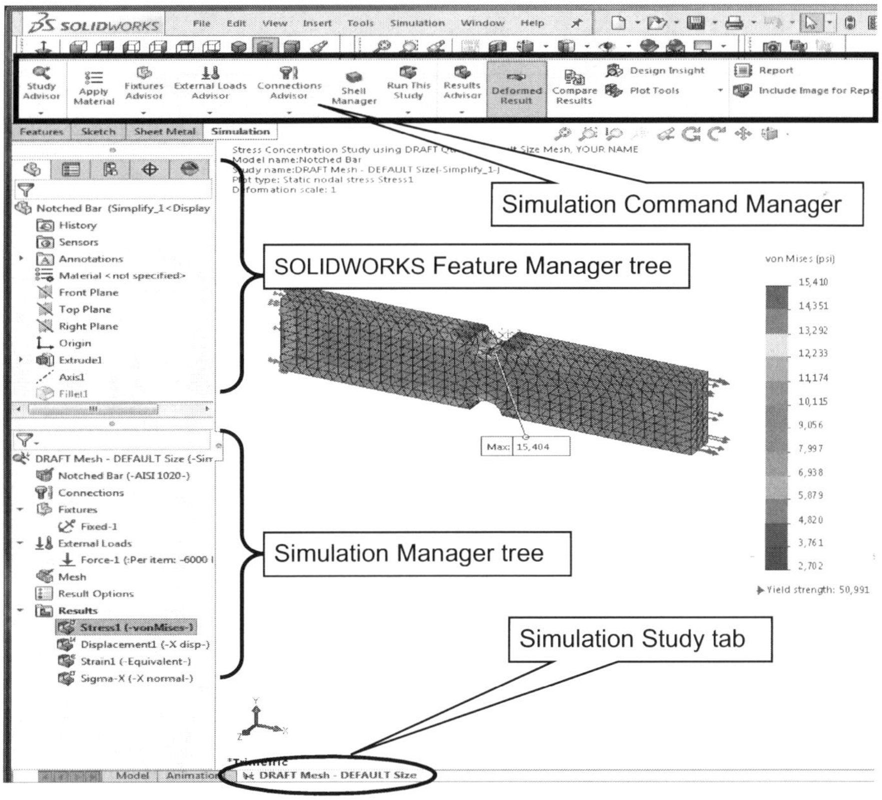

Figure 20 – Identification of various portions of the graphical user interface.

- Simulation Command Manager (also simply referred to as the **Simulation** tab) – This command manager contains icons for commands used to develop the finite element portion of a Study. Command manager icons appear "boxed" across the top of the image shown in Fig. 20. Icons located in the Simulation Command Manager were used extensively in Chapter 2.

- Simulation Study Tab – This *new* tab has always been present but is not emphasized until now. It is located beneath the graphics screen and is circled in Fig. 20. The tab is identified by the name of the current study, **DRAFT Mesh-DEFAULT Size**, and contains all information used to define the current Study. This information includes items such as **Material** specification, **Fixtures**, **External Loads**, **Mesh,** and all **Results** folders that are currently displayed in the Simulation manager tree.

The following section outlines the method for copying the contents from one Simulation Study tab to create a new Study.

Study Using High Quality Elements and COARSE Mesh Size

Copying an Entire Study

The main reason so much emphasis was placed upon refining stress and displacement plots for the draft quality mesh is that those same settings can be copied to new Studies as additional mesh types and sizes are examined. Begin by copying the current Study as outlined below.

1. At bottom of the screen, right-click to select the Simulation Study *tab* named **DRAFT Mesh-DEFAULT Size**. The pop-up menu opens as shown in Fig. 21.

2. In the pop-up menu, click to select **Copy Study**. The **Copy Study** window opens as shown in Fig. 22.

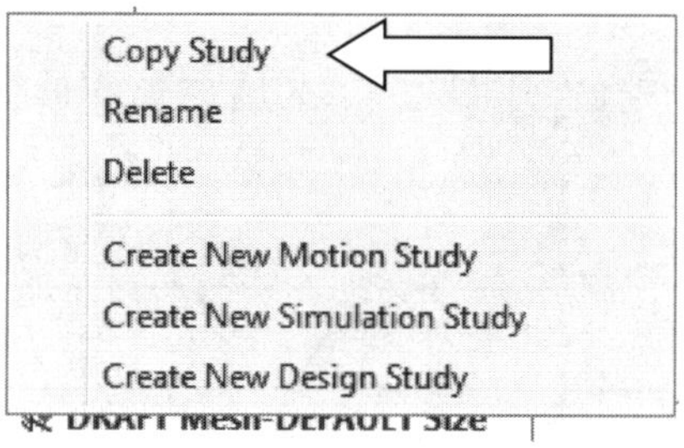

Figure 21 – Selecting the **Copy Study** command to produce an identical Study.

3. Highlight and delete the existing name in the **Study Name:** field and type **COARSE Mesh** as the name of the new Study.

4. Click **[OK]** to close the **Define Study Name** window. A tab with the new Study name "**COARSE Mesh**" is added beneath the graphics screen and an *identical copy* of the source Study appears in the Simulation manager tree.

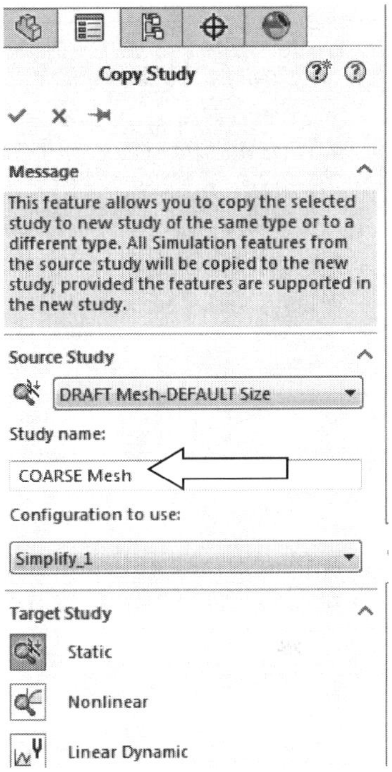

Figure 22 – Enter the new Study name "**COARSE Mesh**" in the **Study Name:** field.

The above process creates a new Study that is an *exact duplicate* of the **DRAFT Mesh – DEFAULT Size** Study that was selected in step 1 (above), *including the prior mesh specification and prior results*. However, because the new Study is to use a **COARSE** mesh, it is necessary to re-mesh the model.

5. Within Simulation manager, right-click **Mesh**, and from the pull-down menu select **Create Mesh…** to open the **Mesh** property manager.

6. Under the **Definition** *tab,* check ☑ **Mesh Parameters** to open this dialogue box. Select ⊙ **Standard mesh** and note the current mesh size is (0.16846771 in).

7. Next, within the **Mesh Density** dialogue box, Fig. 23, click-and-*drag* the **Mesh Factor** slide-control to **Coarse** at the far left-end of the scale. Mesh size is now (0.33693541 in.), which is twice as large as the default mesh size indicated when the pointer is at the middle of the scale.

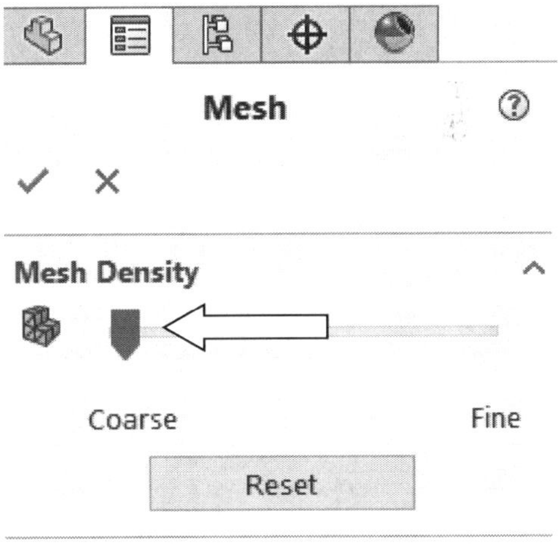

Figure 23 – Slide the **Mesh Factor** slide-control to change mesh size.

8. Next, select the **Mesh Quality** *tab.* Click to select Notched Bar under Draft: window. Press **Apply high mesh quality** key [^] to move the Notched Bar model to High: window.

9. Click to select the **Definition** *tab* again. At the bottom of the **Mesh** property manager, select ⌄ to open the **Advanced** dialogue box. **Jacobian points** are now set to **16 points**. This subtle message is not easily interpreted by new users, but it signifies that a **High** quality mesh is now active. From this point forward, *all meshes* used in this example are **High** quality meshes, i.e., meshes containing elements with mid-side nodes.

10. Click **[OK]** to close the **Mesh** property manager and the model is re-meshed with a **COARSE** mesh. Note the speed with which the model is meshed.

In the Simulation manager, Fig. 24, notice that SOLIDWORKS *warning* symbols and appear adjacent to the Study Name "**COARSE MESH (-Simplify_1-)**" and the **Results** folder. If these symbols do not appear, simply move the cursor over these two names. The meaning of these symbols is introduced below. The meaning of these SOLIDWORKS Simulation symbols is summarized below.

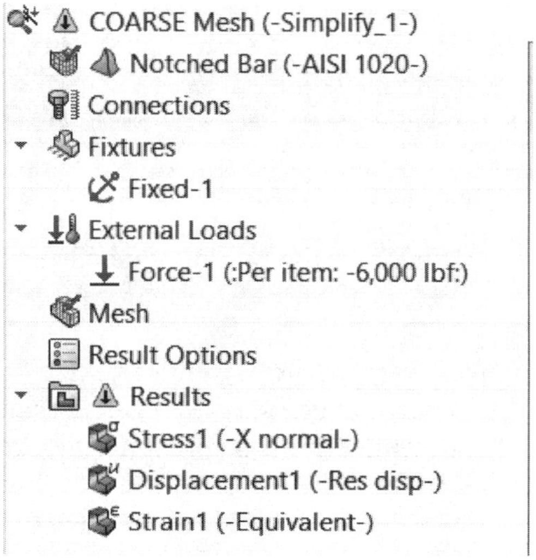

Figure 24 – SOLIDWORKS Simulation manager tree showing two warnings.

Icon	Description
	This icon indicates a warning in the Study. It appears adjacent to the Study name because previous calculations do not correspond to the revised mesh.
	This icon indicates an error with a feature in the Simulation manager tree. An error indicates a feature is invalid. No errors occur in this model.
	A warning icon appears next to the **Results** or **Mesh** folders when the plots are not up to date. In this case, **Results** of the previous analysis are not valid for the new *coarse* mesh Study.

To determine the source of these warnings, proceed as follows.

11. In the Simulation manager tree, right-click the **COARSE Mesh (-Simplify_1-)** Study name, and from the pull-down menu select **What's wrong?...** The **What's Wrong** window opens, as shown in Fig. 25 and displays two warning messages.

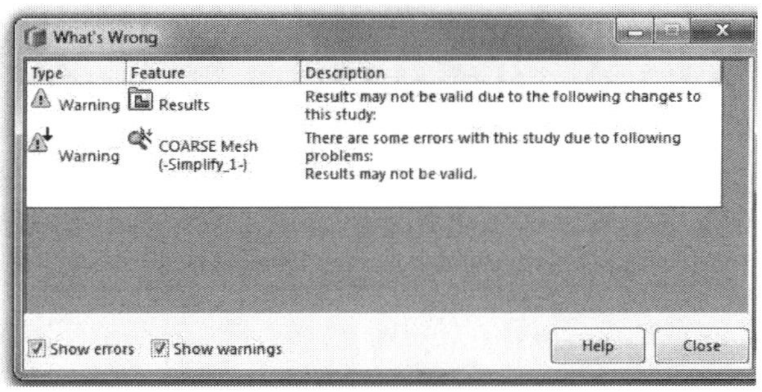

Figure 25 – Warning descriptions associated with the current Study.

Read all statements adjacent to each warning in the **What's Wrong** window. In brief, the first warning is, in effect, stating that **Results** are incorrect because they are based on a different mesh *type* (i.e., the original DRAFT quality mesh) and because the mesh *size* is different (DEFAULT size versus COARSE size). The second warning alludes to the fact that **Results** of the *new* Study are invalid because the file still contains **Results** of the former analysis. Therefore, a new Solution must be run corresponding to the new mesh.

12. Click **[Close]** to exit the **What's Wrong** window.

13. To eliminate the above warnings, simply right-click the Study name, **COARSE Mesh (-Simplify_1-)**, and from the pull-down menu select **Run**. Observe the brief time required to execute a solution.

Examine contents of the **Results** folder to observe maximum stress magnitudes shown on **Stress1 (-vonMises-)**, and **Sigma-X (-X normal-)** plots. To display each plot either double-click each plot folder (OR) right-click each and select **Show**. Also, note the maximum displacement shown on **Displacement1 (-X disp-)** plot.

*[**Record:** max. von Mises stress, max. Sigma-X, and max. Displacement1 in Table 1]*
Because the **Results** folder was *copied* from the previous study, notice that all plots are displayed using the previously selected format. Thus, no additional work is required to adjust each plot.

A plot of **Sigma-X (-X normal-)** is included in Fig. 26. This figure shows the **COARSE** size **High** quality mesh used for the current study. Compare it to the **DEFAULT** size **Draft** quality mesh shown in Fig. 16. Which has more nodes and elements? Which is more accurate? These questions are answered at the conclusion of this example.

OBSERVATIONS:

- Both the von Mises stress and normal stress in the X-direction (σ_X) are larger for the **High** quality **COARSE** mesh than predicted by the **Draft** quality default size mesh.

- The magnitude of the X-displacement is also larger for a **High** quality **COARSE** mesh than that predicted using a **Draft** quality mesh of default size. Recall an earlier statement that **High** quality elements are not as "stiff" as **Draft** quality elements. This lower mesh stiffness results in larger and more accurate deflections being modeled as is observed again later in this example.
- Greater model stiffness is another reason that a **Draft** quality mesh yields less accurate results.

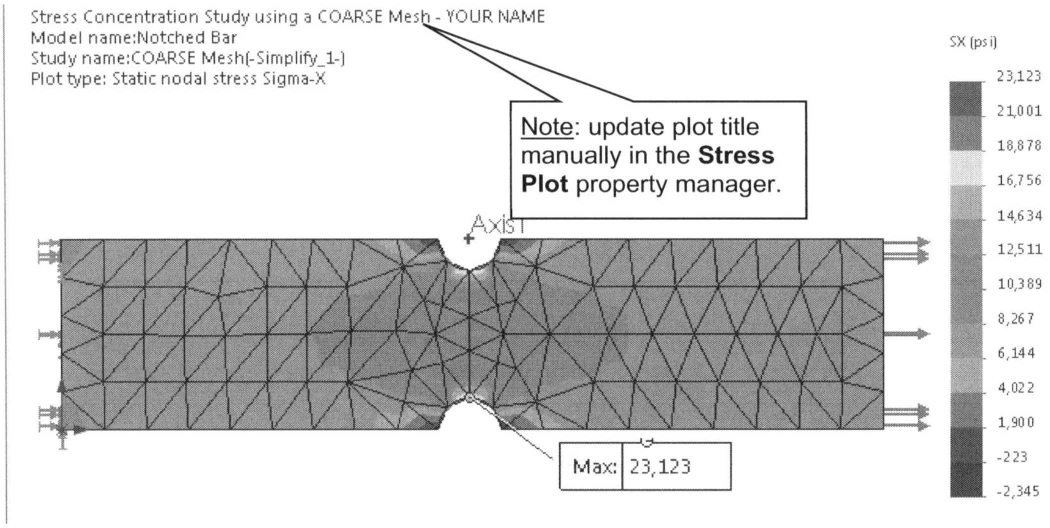

Figure 26 – A high quality, coarse mesh and stress (σ_x) displayed on the Notched Bar model.

Study Using High Quality Elements and DEFAULT Mesh Size

In this section the Notched Bar example is solved again but this time using a **High quality** mesh of **Default Size**. A default mesh is smaller than the coarse mesh of the previous section. However, the same method of *duplicating* a study can be used. To save time, individuals who are comfortable defining the Study described here are encouraged to proceed on their own. Otherwise, abbreviated versions of steps 1 through 13, of the previous section, are included below.

1. Right-click the **COARSE Mesh** Simulation Study *tab*.

2. In the pop-up menu, click to select **Copy Study**.

3. In the **Define Study Name** window of Fig. 27 change the **Study Name:** field to **DEFAULT Mesh**.

4. Click **[OK]** to close the **Define Study Name** window. A new Study tab named "**DEFAULT Mesh**" is added beneath the graphics screen.

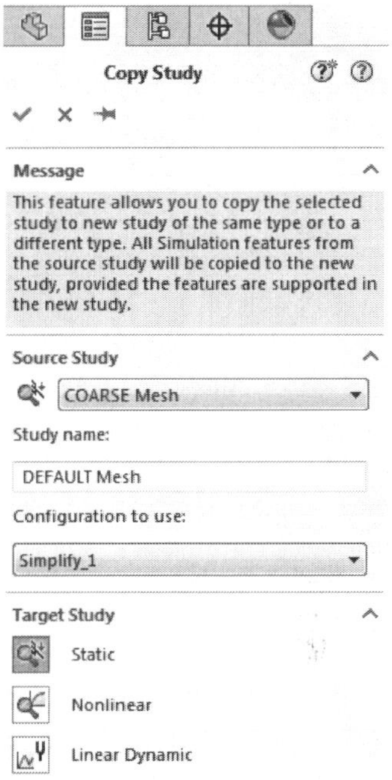

Figure 27 – Enter the new Study name "**DEFAULT Mesh**" in the **Study Name:** field.

Next, re-mesh the current model to change its **COARSE Mesh** size to a **DEFAULT Mesh** size.

5. Within Simulation manager, right-click **Mesh**, and from the pull-down menu select **Create Mesh…** to open the **Mesh** property manager.

6. In the **Mesh** property manager, check ☑ **Mesh Parameters** and verify that ⊙ **Standard mesh** is selected.

7. Next, select the **[Reset]** button, circled in Fig. 28, to return the **Mesh Factor** slider to the *exact middle* of the scale between **Coarse** and **Fine**.

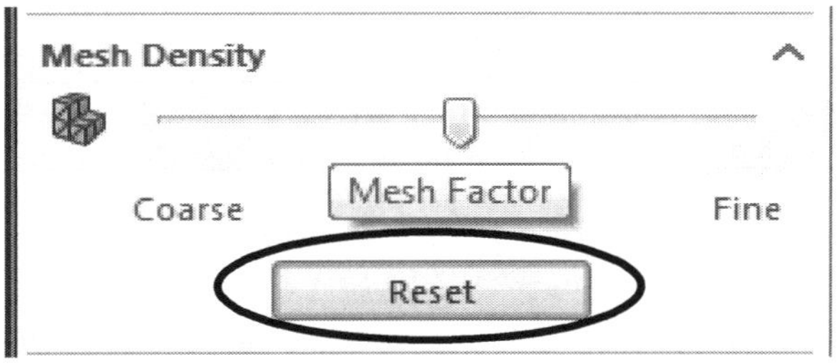

Figure 28 – Slide the **Mesh Factor** slide-control to change mesh size.

8. Click **[OK]** to close the **Mesh** property manager and the model is re-meshed with a **DEFAULT** size mesh.

9. In the Simulation manager tree, right-click the **DEFAULT Mesh (-Simplify_1-)** Study name, and from the pull-down menu select **What's wrong?...** The **What's Wrong** window opens, as shown in Fig. 25, and displays two warning messages.

10. Click **[Close]** to exit the **What's Wrong** window.

11. Eliminate any warnings by right-clicking the Study name, **DEFAULT Mesh (-Simplify_1-)**, and from the pull-down menu select **Run**. Observe the brief time required to execute a solution (1 second or less).

Examine contents of the **Results** folder to observe maximum stress magnitudes shown on **Stress1 (-vonMises-)** and **Sigma-X (-X normal-)** plots and also maximum displacement shown on **Displacement1 (-X disp-)** plot.

*[**Record:** max. von Mises stress, max. Sigma-X, and max. Displacement1 in Table 1]*

Study Using High Quality Elements and FINE Mesh Size

The Notched Bar example is solved a fourth time, but this time a **FINE Mesh** size and **High quality** mesh are used. The same method used in the preceding two sections can be used here. However, steps are not repeated, thus users are to proceed on their own (OR) refer to steps 1 to 13 of previous sections if needed.

The only differences include:

- Name the model **FINE Mesh**.
- Move the **Mesh Factor** slider all the way to the right in step 8.
- Note the increase in time required to execute the finite element solution after clicking **Run** (4 to 6 seconds).
- *Any* previous Study can be used as the starting point *(except the DRAFT Mesh)*. WHY?
- Do stress and displacement magnitudes continue to increase?

*[**Record:** max. von Mises stress, max. Sigma-X, and max. Displacement1 in Table 1]*

Study Using High Quality Elements and MESH CONTROL

Perhaps the *most important* approach to refining mesh size is that of applying *mesh control*, which is investigated in this section. By this point in the example, it is evident that a smaller mesh results in improved approximations of stress in a model. However, the "brute force" approach of using a progressively smaller mesh size results in significant computational inefficiency during the solution process. For example, when the **Fine** mesh in Fig. 29 is applied to the entire model, consider the large number of equations solved in "boxed" regions of the model where stress is nearly uniform. A fine mesh is *un*necessary in regions where stress *variation* is minimal.

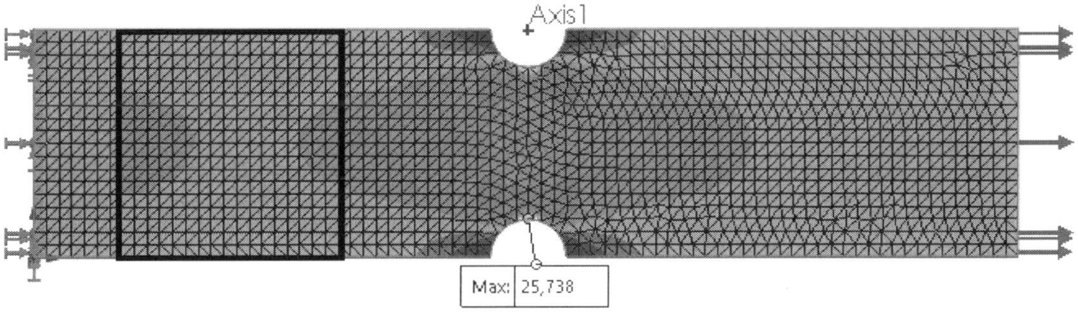

Figure 29 – "Boxed" areas denote regions where *inefficient* use is made of a **Fine** size mesh because stress is nearly uniform in these regions of the model.

Use of *mesh control* allows the user to manage element size on selected entities of the model, such as **Faces**, **Edges**, **Vertices**, or **Reference Points**. Controlling mesh size makes it possible to specify a smaller mesh only in selected regions of high stress *gradient*, such as near the notch, while simultaneously using a significantly larger mesh in regions where stress distribution is relatively uniform such as the boxed regions on the model in Fig. 29. Locating regions of high stress is easily accomplished by using a draft quality or default size mesh and performing a quick initial Study.

For the above reasons, the Notched Bar example is solved again. However, this time *mesh control* is applied only in the vicinity of the "notch." To most effectively demonstrate the true power of this method, **MESH CONTROL** is used in conjunction with a **COARSE** mesh. It is important to note that **MESH CONTROL** must be applied to the *desired "original" mesh.* Thus, in the following steps a **COARSE** mesh is selected as the starting point for this analysis. The procedure below outlines steps for applying *mesh control* to selected parts of the model.

1. At bottom of the screen, right-click *only* the Simulation Study tab named **COARSE Mesh**. In the pop-up menu choose **Copy Study**.

2. In the **Define Study Name** window, delete the old name and type: **MESH CONTROL**, then click **[OK]**.

The new Study appears in the Simulation manager tree and a new **MESH CONTROL** tab is created beneath the graphics screen.

Because everything in this new Study, except the mesh, is to remain as previously defined, the following steps introduce use of *mesh control*.

3. Right-click the **Mesh** folder, and from the pull-down menu select **Apply Mesh Control…** The **Mesh Control** property manager opens as illustrated in Fig. 30.

As noted above, an advantage of using mesh control is that it can be applied to local regions on a model. In the following steps, only portions of the model in the vicinity of the "notch" are selected due to the high stress gradient existing there.

4. In the **Selected Entities** dialogue box, the **Faces, Edges, Vertices, Reference Points, Components for Mesh Control** field is highlighted (light blue) indicating it is active.

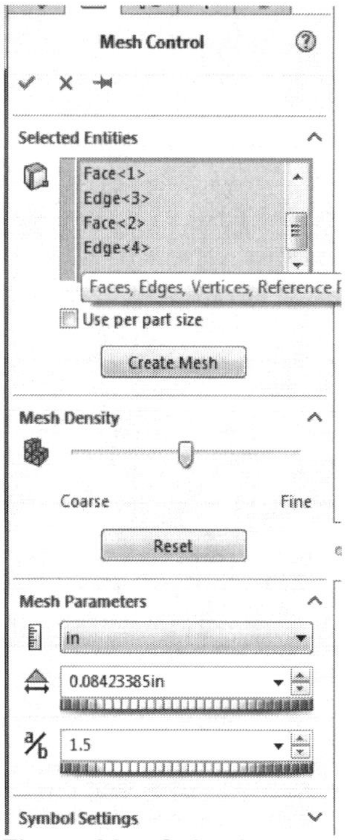

Figure 30 – Selections made in the **Mesh Control** property manager.

5. Move the cursor onto the model and *at both the top and bottom* of the model, select the two curved **Edges** and one **Face** at each notch as illustrated in Fig. 31. **Edge<1>**, **Edge<2>**, **Edge<3>**, **Edge<4>**, and **Face<1>**, **Face<2>** appear in the highlighted field of Fig. 31 in the order selected by the user.

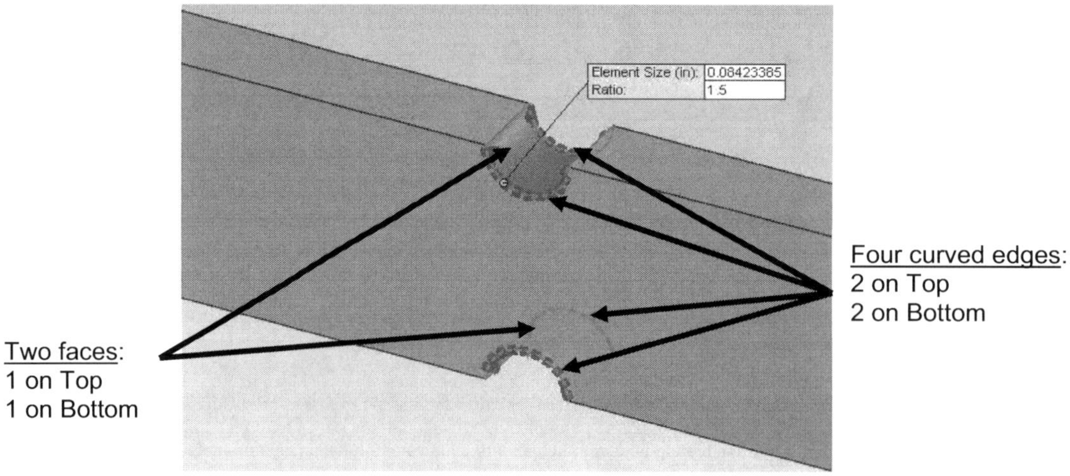

Figure 31 – Edges and faces selected for application of **mesh control** at top and bottom notches. Mesh control symbols appear on the selected entities.

At this point, no changes are made to default values in the **Mesh Parameters** dialogue box. However, the three fields in this dialogue box are explained below.

Unit: The **Unit** field should be set to **in** (if not already selected).

Element Size: Initial element size (0.08423385 in) in the **Mesh Control** region corresponds to the system default mesh size as verified by the pointer location on the **Mesh Factor** slider-scale. However, because the **COARSE** mesh study was duplicated, the software applies a **COARSE** mesh to all other regions of the model *except* where mesh control is applied. Mesh control is based on a default size mesh. *Do **not** change the slider setting.*

Ratio: **a/b** = **1.5** This value controls the increase of element size from one layer of elements to the next as elements radiate away from the selected entities. EXAMPLE: if "E" = the default element size, then subsequent layers of elements increase in size according to the progression E, E*(a/b), E*$(a/b)^2$, . . . E*$(a/b)^n$ until E $\geq$ the default element size used on the remainder of the model.

6. Click **[OK]** ✓ to close the **Mesh Control** property manager.

Unlike previous Studies, notice that a new mesh is not immediately generated on the model. Also, notice that warnings symbols appear adjacent to the Study name and on the **Mesh** and **Results** folders. Proceed as follows to update the mesh and run the solution.

7. Right-click the **Mesh** folder, and from the pull-down menu select **Mesh and Run**. Note the faster speed with which this solution is completed.

The model is re-meshed. An enlarged view of mesh and stress σ_x near the notches is shown in Fig. 32.

8. Click "►" adjacent to the **Mesh** folder and a **Mesh Controls** icon appears. Click the "►" adjacent to **Mesh Controls** and a **Control-1** icon appears in the Simulation manager tree.

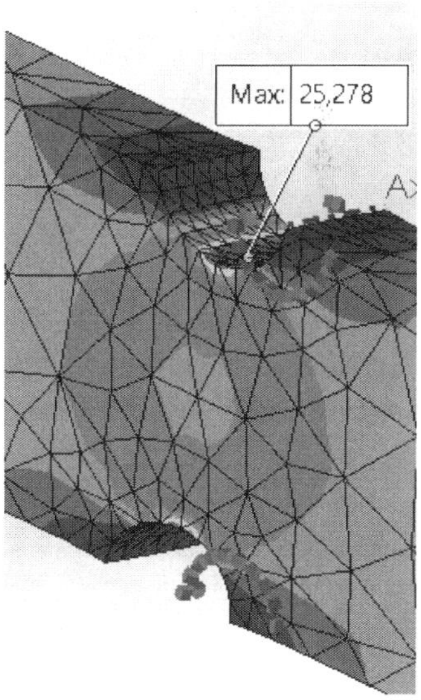

Figure 32 – View of mesh size altered by application of **Mesh Control** in the notch region.

Briefly examine plots in the **Results** folder.

***[Record:** max. von Mises stress, max. Sigma-X, and max. Displacement1 in Table 1]*

To gain greater insight into factors affecting **Mesh Control**, make the mesh changes outlined below.

9. In the Simulation manager tree, right-click the **Control-1** icon and from the pull-down menu select **Edit Definition…** The **Mesh Control** property manager opens as previously shown in Fig. 30. Notice that previously selected edges and faces remain unchanged.

10. In the **Mesh Parameters** dialogue box change the **a/b Ratio** value to **1.2**.

This action results in a smaller mesh adjacent to the notch and a decrease of size changes from one element layer to the next. Simultaneously the number of layers between the smallest and largest elements increases as is illustrated in Fig. 33.

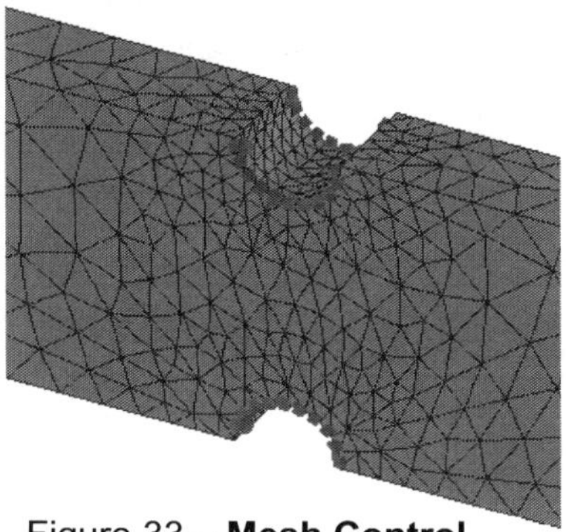

Figure 33 – **Mesh Control** using a smaller **Ratio a/b=1.2.**

11. Click **[OK]** ✓ to close the **Mesh Control** property manager.

Because the mesh is being changed again, observe the *Warning* symbols adjacent to the Study name **MESH CONTROL (-Simplify_1-)**, the **Mesh** folder, and the **Results** folder in Fig. 34. To determine the source of these warnings, proceed as follows.

12. Right-click the **MESH CONTROL (-Simplify_1-)** Study name in the Simulation manager tree, and from the pull-down menu select **What's wrong?…** The **What's Wrong** window opens, as shown in Fig. 35, and displays all three warnings.

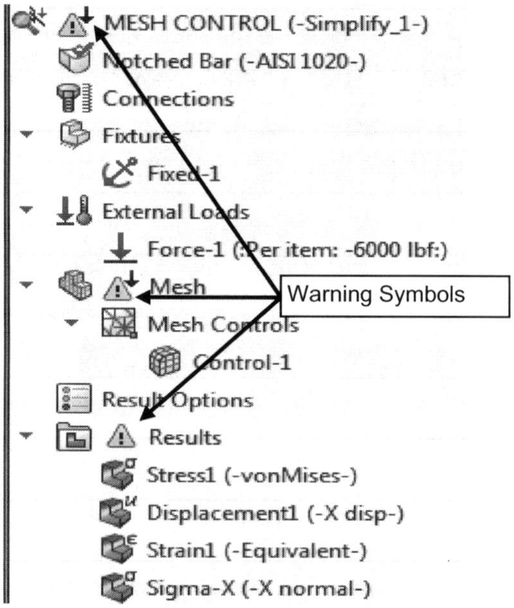

Figure 34 - SOLIDWORKS Simulation Manager tree showing two errors and a warning.

Read statements adjacent to each warning in the **What's Wrong** window. Because all warning statements are related to a change of the mesh control **Ratio** to **a/b** = **1.2**, results of the previous Solution, based on the **a/b** = **1.5** ratio, are rendered invalid and a new Solution must be run.

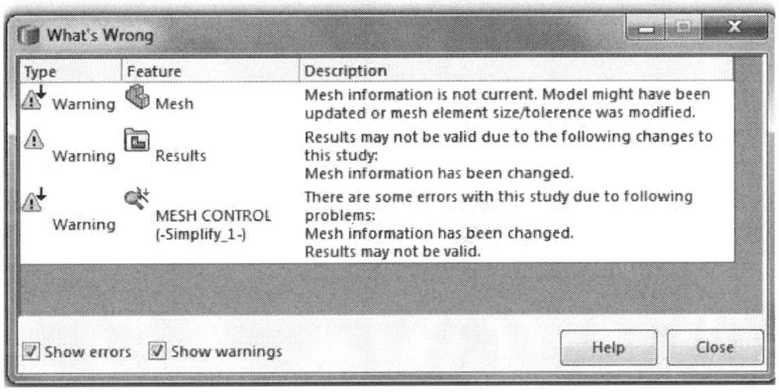

Figure 35 – Error and warning descriptions associated with the current study.

Thus, it is only necessary to run a new Solution corresponding to the revised *mesh control*. Proceed as follows.

13. Click **[Close]** to dismiss the **What's Wrong** window.

14. In the Simulation manager, right-click the **Mesh** folder, and from the pull-down menu select **Mesh and Run**. Once again notice the faster speed with which this solution is completed.

The model is re-meshed automatically and a new solution is run. This new Solution corresponds to the revised *mesh control* previously shown in Fig. 33. These values need *not* be recorded.

Summary

By using *mesh control*, a small mesh can be created in user selected areas of high stress gradient while a larger mesh is used in other regions of the model. Thus, mesh control results in efficient use of computational facilities, while simultaneously yielding good results in user specified regions. It is interesting to note that, although *mesh control* resulted in a smaller mesh near the notch for the most recent study, a larger stress was actually found for a **Ratio** of **a/b** = **1.5**.

Examine stress and displacement values recorded in Table 1. What trends are noticed for changes in stress magnitude as mesh size decreases? Are these results expected?

Table 1 – Comparison of Stress and Displacement Results for Various Meshes

Mesh Type & Size	Maximum vonMises Stress (psi)	Maximum Sigma-X (psi)	Maximum Displacement X-Direction (in)
DRAFT Mesh DEFAULT size			
HIGH Quality Mesh COARSE size			
HIGH Quality Mesh DEFAULT size			
HIGH Quality Mesh FINE size			
High Quality Mesh MESH CONTROL a/b=1.5 on COARSE size mesh			

Results Analysis

Now that the Notched Bar model has been evaluated using five different meshes, the significance of the resulting solutions is investigated below. Begin by creating a *simultaneous* display of results from the Draft quality mesh and from the three Studies for which high quality, *global* element sizes were changed. In other words, ignore *mesh control* solutions at this time. To open multiple viewports, proceed as follows. SOLIDWORKS users may be familiar with this software feature and are encouraged to proceed on their own. However, all necessary steps are outlined on the following pages.

Create Multiple Viewports

1. In the Main menu, at top of the screen, click **Window**, circled in Fig. 36. This figure also shows the pull-down menu and the options available for displaying multiple window configurations.

2. Move the cursor onto **Viewport,** and from the second-level pull-down menu select **Four View**. See Fig. 36.

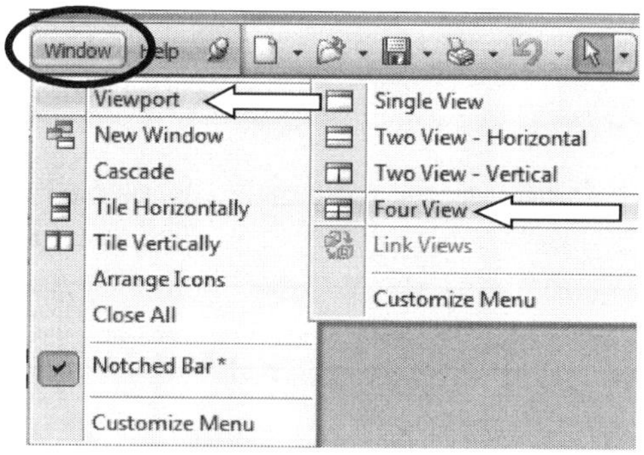

Figure 36 – Menu selections used to open multiple viewports.

The graphics area immediately displays **Front**, **Left**, **Trimetric**, and **Top** views of the current screen image, Fig. 37 (clockwise starting at the top left). This image is altered in the following steps to enable side-by-side comparisons of the four solutions.

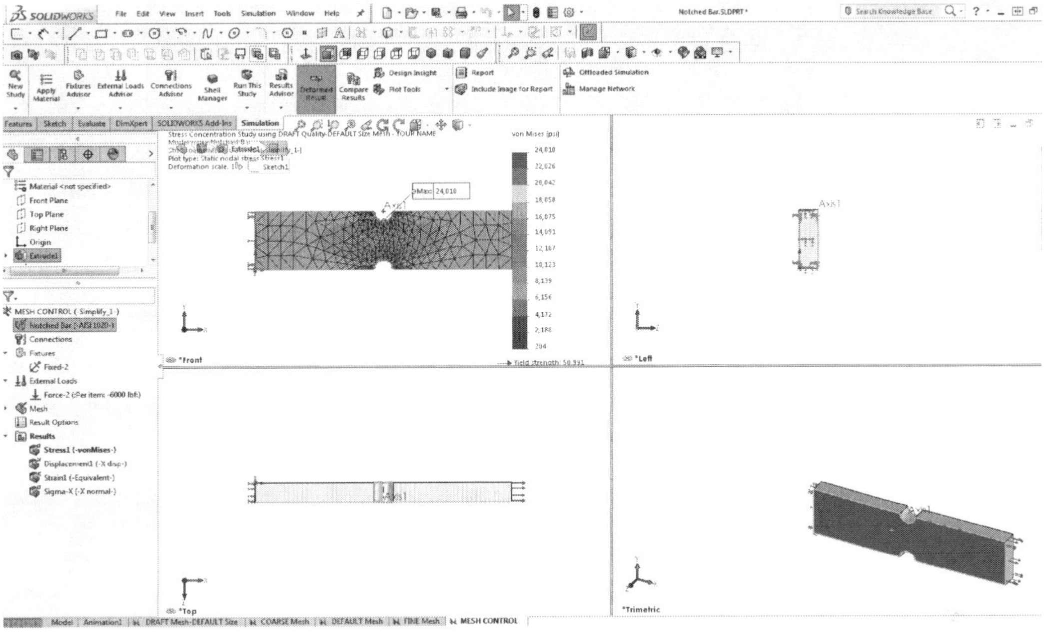

Figure 37 – The default display shows the currently active model in Front, Top, Trimetric, and Top views.

Various plots can be displayed in these viewports in keeping with user preferences. To facilitate discussion below, it is suggested that the following order be used to place images in the four viewports. Begin by placing a plot of von Mises stress found using the **DRAFT** quality mesh in the upper left-hand viewport. The following steps outline this procedure.

3. Click anywhere in the upper left-hand viewport (labeled "**A**" in Fig. 38). This action activates the viewport.

4. At the bottom of the screen, select the Simulation Study tab labeled **DRAFT Mesh-DEFAULT Size**. This action displays its contents in the Simulation manager tree.

5. Next, click "▶" adjacent to the **Results** folder to list its contents (if not already displayed).

6. Finally, double-click **Stress1 (-vonMises-)**, and the contents of that plot are displayed in viewport "**A**" as illustrated in Fig. 38. Proceed to the following steps.

7. Click in viewport **B** and repeat steps 4 to 6 except choose the von Mises stress plot found within the **COARSE Mesh** Study tab.

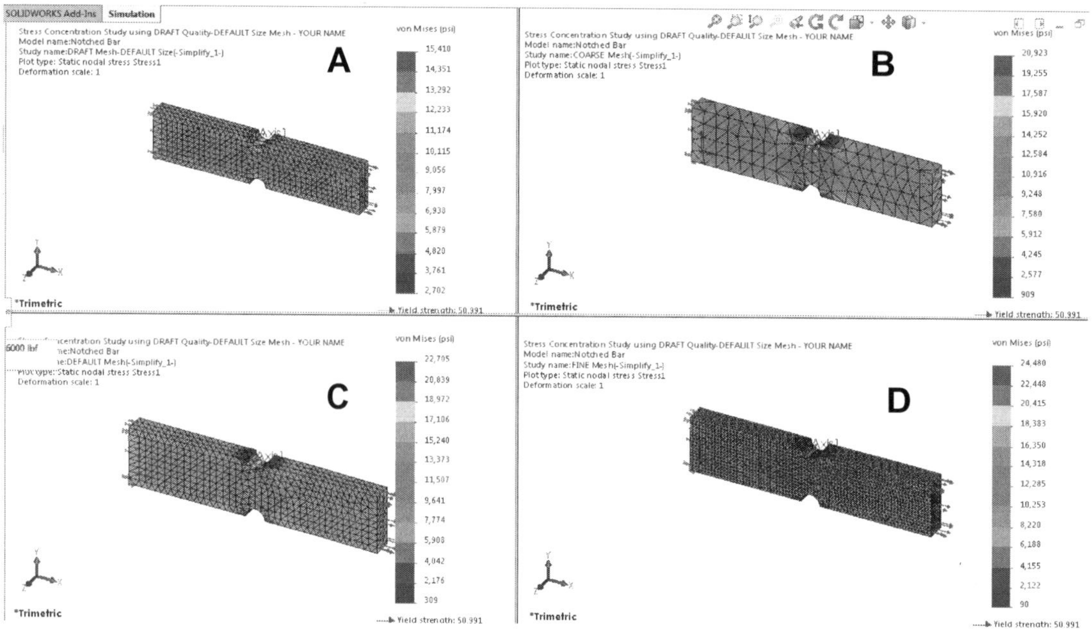

Figure 38– Multiple viewports facilitate comparison of results from multiple different studies or different aspects of a model within a single study.

8. Click in viewport **C** and repeat steps 4 to 6 except choose the von Mises stress plot found in the **DEFAULT Mesh** Study tab.

9. Finally, click in viewport **D** and repeat steps 4 to 6 except choose the von Mises stress plot found in the **FINE Mesh** Study tab. This display may take longer to appear due to more data associated with the fine mesh.

> NOTE 1: As you proceed below, do not be concerned if your *view* of the model differs from that shown. Desired views can be adjusted later based upon user preferences.

> NOTE 2: Viewport labels **A**, **B**, **C**, **D** are added to textbook Fig. 38 to facilitate discussion. These letters do not appear on the SOLIDWORKS screen image.

Now that results of the four global element size studies are displayed in individual viewports, the screen images can be adjusted according to user preferences. Typically, the choice of view depends upon those aspects that are of primary importance to a study. For example, a close-up view of the notch might be used to replace one, or all, of the views shown in Fig. 38. Viewports **A**, **B**, **C**, and **D** show trimetric views of each meshed model. To obtain these views, repeat step 10 as necessary.

10. Click inside each viewport, then select the Trimetric view  icon. Next, use the pan and zoom options to best display desired results. A trimetric view is selected because it provides a good overview of mesh size, boundary conditions, and stress magnitudes important to this analysis.

When finished, your graphics screen should look *similar* to Fig. 38.

What Can Be Learned From This Example?

Most of the primary goals of this analysis were encountered and mastered as you worked through the example itself. Those goals included (a) knowing 'when,' 'how,' and 'why' a model should be *defeatured*; (b) using the *duplicate* feature to quickly create entire new studies; (c) using multiple *viewports* to facilitate results comparisons; and, (d) most important, using *global mesh refinement* and *local mesh control* as analysis refinement tools. One final topic, the importance of *verifying convergence to a solution*, is discussed in the following "Analysis Insight" section.

Other Uses of the Copy Feature

The *copy study* feature within SOLIDWORKS Simulation is not limited to creating new studies in which mesh size change is the only analysis variable. In fact, any variable of a finite element analysis can be the central focus in a multiple solution study. For example, other variables that could be altered include, but are not limited to, material properties, loads, fixtures, part-to-part contact conditions, or modifications to model geometry.

Analysis Insight – Solution Convergence

The importance of mesh refinement and mesh control as part of a complete finite element analysis cannot be overstated! A single solution to a finite element analysis provides only one snapshot of what a possible solution to a problem might be. *One primary reason for performing multiple analyses is to determine whether or not a study converges to an acceptable solution.*

To determine *convergence*, it is possible to examine either displacement results or stress results. From the Introduction to this text, recall that displacements within the model are the primary unknowns in a finite element analysis. Next, strains are calculated from displacements, and finally, stresses are computed from strains. Because displacements are the first link in the solution chain, they are usually a better indicator than stress of convergence to a solution as element size is altered. For the sake of brevity, only von Mises stress results and X-displacement results corresponding to changes of *global* mesh size are compared when testing for convergence of this example.

To relate this discussion to the Notched Bar, **Table 2** summarizes results of all analyses developed in this example. These results should compare well with results you recorded in **Table 1**. Von Mises stress and X-displacement data in **Table 2** are obtained from Fig. 38 and various mesh plots created throughout this study.

Information about the number of nodes and elements in each mesh is obtained by right-clicking each **Mesh** folder and selecting **Details...** This procedure was first demonstrated in Chapter 1.

In **Table 2**, focus attention only on von Mises stress and X-displacement results corresponding to COARSE, DEFAULT, and FINE mesh sizes highlighted in the middle three rows of the table. These three rows show how stress magnitude increases as mesh size varies from 'coarse' to 'default' to 'fine.' Casual observation of magnitudes listed in the von Mises stress column reveals that stress increases as the number of elements increases. This result is expected due to the ability of smaller elements to better model stress magnitudes in increasingly smaller regions of high stress gradient. High stress gradients typically occur around geometric discontinuities in a part and result in stress concentrations.

This finding might lead one to expect that as element size gets smaller and smaller, the stress magnitudes will continue to grow larger and larger. However, *in a properly constructed study quite the opposite is true!* In an analysis that is *converging* to a solution, stress results should tend to *level off* and approach some limiting value. That limiting value represents the best approximation to maximum stress in the model. Thus, the reason that *multiple solutions* should be a standard part of every finite element analysis is to determine whether or not results *converge to a solution.*

Analysis Insight (Continued)

TABLE 2 – Summary of Results from the Notched-Bar Study

Mesh	No. Nodes	No. Elements	vonMises Stress (psi)	Sigma-X (psi)	Displacement X-Direction (in)
DRAFT Quality DEFAULT size	1,606	6,444	15,410	15,746	0.001874
HIGH Quality COARSE size	1,902	1,027	20,923	23,123	0.001894
HIGH Quality DEFAULT size	10,627	6,444	22,705	24,646	0.001897
HIGH Quality FINE size	80,860	54,689	24,480	25,738	0.001899
HIGH Quality MESH CONTROL	4,688	2,709	24,010	25,278	0.001898

In Figs. 39 and 40 von Mises and axial *stress* magnitudes are plotted against the number of nodes in the meshed model. These graphs reveal that as the number of nodes increases, both von Mises and the axial stress magnitudes fluctuate around an average value. The leading cause in these variations is a lack of split lines to guide mesh element/node positions, which means that the meshes that get generated are not perfectly symmetric/aligned with geometry.

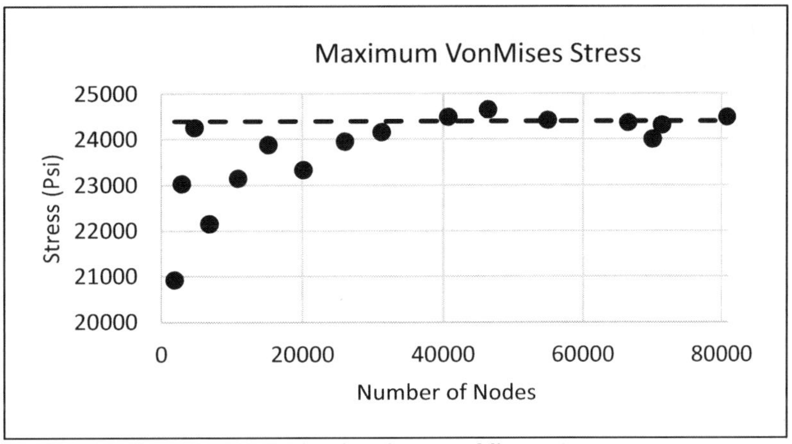

Figure 39– Convergence check using von Mises stress as a measure.

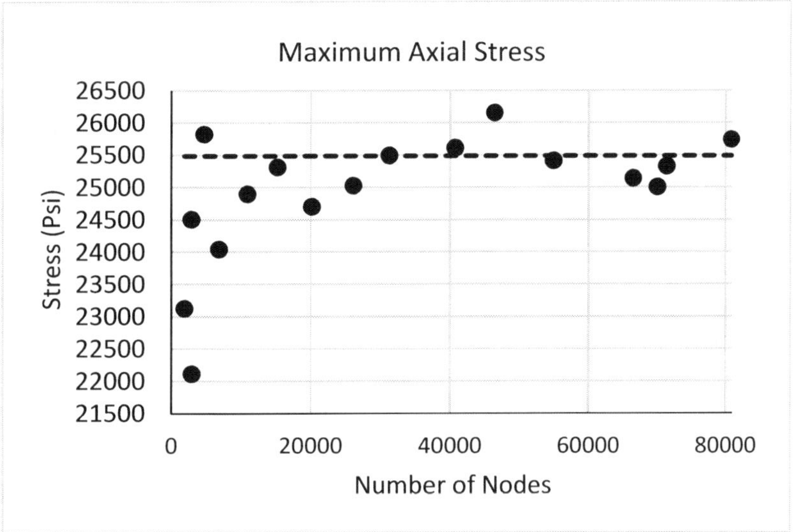

Figure 40– Convergence check using axial stress as a measure.

NOTE: *If* analysis were stopped after using only the 'default' size mesh, then maximum von Mises stress would have been underestimated by at least (24,480 – 20,923) = 3,557 psi. Do you think a higher stress would be attained with further mesh refinement?

Summary:
The *need* to conduct more than a single finite element analysis is demonstrated in this example. The *reason* for conducting more than one analysis is to determine whether or not an analysis is approaching a limiting value. This is known as a convergence check.

Aside #1:
Results of the **Draft** quality mesh are *excluded* from the above discussion because it is most revealing to compare results obtained using the same *type* of mesh while only varying mesh size. All meshes used in the above comparison used **High** quality elements, i.e., solid tetrahedral elements with mid-side nodes. *Draft quality mesh is recommended for quick evaluation and the default high quality option for final results.*

Aside #2:
Comparison of displacement results for **Draft** quality and **High** quality meshes of the *same* size (i.e., default size), shown in **Table 1** and **2**, confirm that a **Draft** quality mesh is "stiffer" than a **High** quality mesh because a smaller X-displacement results corresponding to the **Draft** quality mesh.

Aside #3:
Despite the emphasis on *global* mesh size refinement in this example (i.e., changing the size of *all* elements), perhaps the most important means for controlling mesh size is use of *mesh control*. Mesh control can be applied to a specific area or areas of interest on a *local* basis and yet provides accurate results at significantly lower computational overhead. For example, comparing values in **Table 2** reveals that *mesh control* uses approximately 9.8 times fewer elements than does a globally **Fine** mesh, yet maximum von Mises stress results differ by less than 1.5%. Consider the computational savings realized by using *mesh control* in an extremely large and complex model.

Comparison of Classical and FEA Results

The importance of checking finite element results is emphasized throughout this text. Thus, in keeping with this premise it is appropriate to conclude this example with a classical analytical check. The notched bar model of Fig. 2 is repeated below.

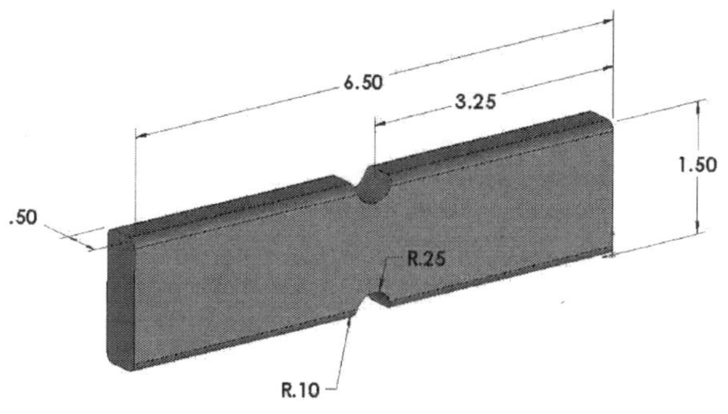

R = notch radius = 0.25 in.

h = height (top to bottom) = 1.50 in

d = h – 2*R = 1.50 – 2*0.25 = 1.00 in (dimension at the reduced cross-section)

t = bar thickness = 0.50 in

F = applied force = 6000 lb

Figure 2 (repeated) – Dimensioned image of notched bar.

Nominal stress at the reduced cross-section in the Notched Bar:

$$\sigma_x = \frac{F}{A} = \frac{F}{d*t} = \frac{6000}{1*0.5} = 12000\ psi$$

Geometric stress concentration factor: where: R/d = 0.25/1.00 = 0.25
h/d = 1.50/1.00 = 1.50

K_t = 2.1 (approximate) ← From stress concentration factor chart found in a standard machine design textbook.

Maximum stress in the Notched Bar:

$(\sigma_x)_{max} = K_t * \sigma_x = 2.1 * 12000 = 25200$ psi

Percent difference compared to the averaged results from high quality mesh (see Fig.40):

% Difference = [(SOLIDWORKS Simulation – Classic)/ (SOLIDWORKS Simulation)] * 100

% Difference = [(25500 – 25200)/(25500)] * 100 = 1.2%

Note that Sigma-X (σ_x) is used for comparison purposes since stress concentration factor charts are plotted for normal and shear stress but not for von Mises stress. The above calculations provide a good check of finite element results. Note that resultant stress $(\sigma_x)_{max}$ predicted by the *mesh control* model yields a 0.21 % difference.

Logging Out of the Current Analysis

This concludes analysis of a notched bar model where the effect of varying mesh size upon stress magnitude was investigated. It is suggested that this file *not* be saved. Proceed as follows.

1. On the **Main Menu**, click **File** followed by choosing **Close**.
2. The **SOLIDWORKS** window opens in Fig. 41 and provides the options of either saving the current analysis or not. Select **[Don't Save]**.

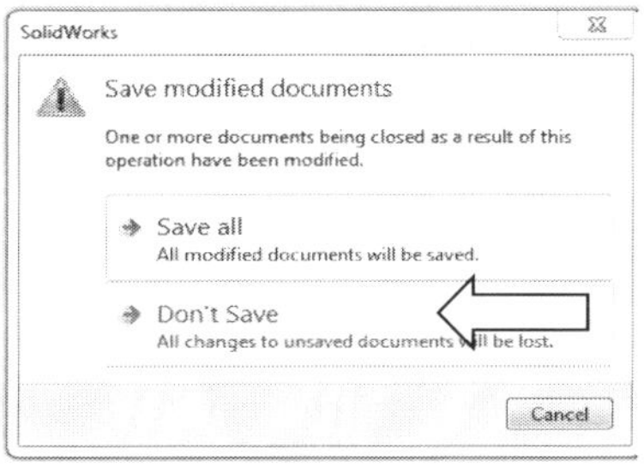

Figure 41 – **SOLIDWORKS** window prompts users to either save changes or not.

EXERCISES

End of chapter exercises are intended to provide additional practice using principles introduced in the current chapter plus capabilities mastered in preceding chapters. Most exercises include multiple parts. In an academic setting, it is likely that parts of problems will be assigned or modified to suit specific course goals.

╬ ***Designates problems that introduce new concepts. Solution guidance is provided for these problems.***

EXERCISE 1 – Effect of Mesh Size at Hole Location

A rectangular bar with a centrally drilled hole is illustrated in Fig. E3-1. The bar is supported **(Fixed/immovable)** at its left-end and subject to an axial, tensile force of 370 kN applied normal to its opposite end. The bar is made from 2018 aluminum alloy. Open the file: **Plate With Hole 3-1**.

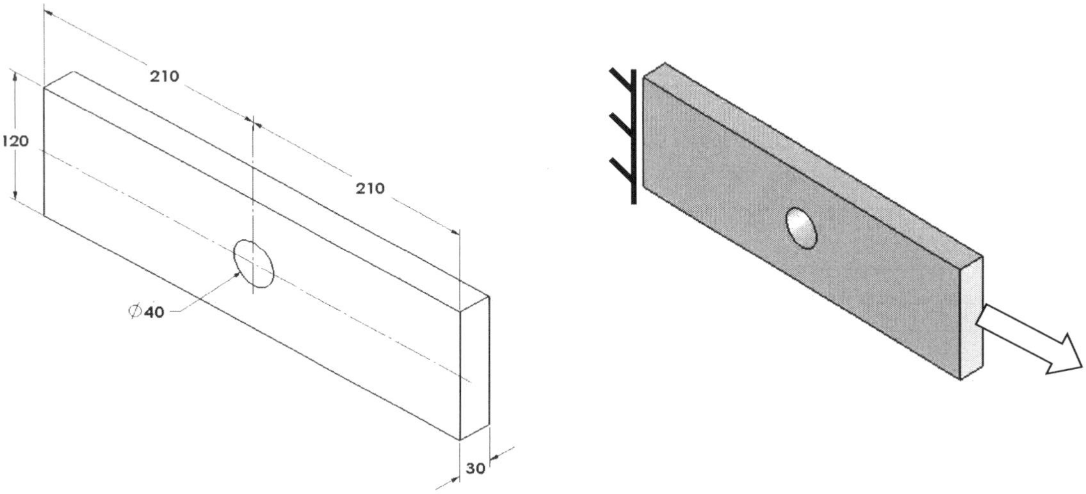

Figure E3-1 – Aluminum bar with central hole subject to an axial force. A geometric discontinuity is present in the form of the 40 mm diameter hole. **(All dimensions in mm.)**

- Material: **2018 Alloy** aluminum (Use S.I. units)
- Mesh: In the **Mesh** property manager, select a ⊙ **Standard mesh**. High quality tetrahedral elements are to be used. Use three different meshes as specified in parts (a, c, and d) below.
- Fixture: **Fixed** (Immovable) restraint applied to left end of the model.
- External Load: **370 kN** applied normal to the right-end causing tension in the bar.

Develop a finite element model that includes material specification, fixtures, external loads, mesh generation, and solution as specified below. For this analysis use high quality meshes of the sizes specified below.

Determine the following:

a. Using a *default* size mesh, create a plot of the *most appropriate stress* to permit comparison of stress magnitude adjacent to the hole with that predicted by classical equations for stress computed at the same location. See part (e) for calculation of classical results. Include fixtures, external load, the mesh and your name on this plot.

b. Use the **Probe** feature to produce a graph of the *most appropriate stress* from the top (or bottom) edge of the bar to the closest edge of the central hole. Because a straight path may not be available, choose both corner and mid-side nodes in as straight a line as possible. Include a descriptive title, axis labels, and your name on this graph.

c. Repeat part (b) after resetting the mesh size to *fine*. Use the duplicate feature to save time creating this study.

d. Repeat part (b) a third time after resetting the mesh size by applying *mesh control* around both edges and the inner surface of the hole. Use a mesh control setting: **Ratio a/b** = **1.5**. Also use the duplicate feature to save time creating this study.

e. Use classical equations and available stress concentration factor charts to manually compute maximum stress at the hole. Label all calculations.

f. Compare maximum stress results predicted using the three different meshes with that predicted by classical stress equations. Compute the percent difference for each comparison using equation [1].

$$\% \text{ difference} = \frac{(\text{FEA result - classical result})}{\text{FEA result}} * 100 = \qquad [1]$$

g. Comment upon which FEA results are in best agreement with predictions of the classical equations. Which method of mesh refinement is usually preferred and why?

h. Based upon results for the maximum *appropriate stress* in the model, is the material Yield Strength exceeded? If "yes," what does theory predict will be the outcome in a ductile material such as Aluminum used in this example? When answering this question, also consider the magnitude of nominal stress computed using classical equations applied at the hole in part (e) above but *without* applying the stress concentration factor.

EXERCISE 2 - Effect of Mesh Size at Shaft Fillet

A cylindrical rod changes diameter at the fillet shown in the Fig. E3-2. It is well known that generous fillets are beneficial in reducing stress concentration at changes of cross-section. This is particularly important because the bar in question is made from a relatively brittle material, gray cast iron, and the fillet radius is not very large. As such, the rod may be subject to significant effects of stress concentration at the geometric discontinuity. Consider the rod supported **(Immovable/Fixed)** at its left-end and subject to a 1,200 lb tensile force applied to its opposite end.

Open the file: **Shaft with Fillet 3-2**.

- Material: **Gray Cast Iron** (Use English units)
- Mesh: In the **Mesh** property manager, select a ⊙ **Standard mesh** and use three different meshes as specified below.
- Fixture: **Fixed/ Immovable** applied to left end of shaft.
- External Load: 1,200 lb applied normal to the right-end causing tension in the bar.

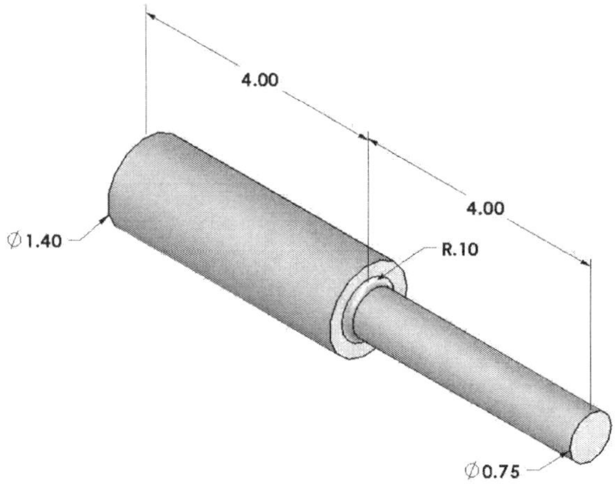

Figure E3-2 – Gray Cast Iron cylindrical rod subject to an axial tensile load of 1,200 lb. **(Dimensions shown in inches.)** The inset photo shows failure at a shoulder in a similar stepped shaft.

Determine the following:

Develop a finite element model that includes material specification, fixtures, applied external load, mesh generation (as specified below), and solution.

NOTE: This example is one where it is *not* appropriate to defeature the model because deleting the fillet radius would cause a dramatic increase of stress at the change of shaft diameter. In fact, a sharp fillet would probably result in stress values continuing to increase as the mesh size gets smaller. A sharp fillet would result in a solution where *divergence* from a solution rather than *convergence* to a solution would occur.

a. Develop a finite element model using a default size, high quality mesh. For this mesh, perform the following:

- Create a stress contour plot of the *most appropriate stress* to permit comparison of maximum stress magnitude in the vicinity of the fillet with that predicted by classical stress equations computed at the same location. Include a mesh on this plot. See part (d) for classical stress calculations.

- Use the **Probe** feature to produce a graph of the *most appropriate stress* commencing approximately ¾-in to the right of the fillet and progressing along the surface of the model, in as near a straight-line as possible, through the fillet area up to the outside diameter (large diameter) of the left segment of the shaft. Choose both corner and mid-side nodes. Include your name, a descriptive title, and axis labels on this graph.

b. Repeat part (a) after resetting the mesh size to fine. Use the duplicate feature to save time creating this study.

c. Repeat part (a) a third time beginning with the default size mesh. Use the duplicate feature to save time creating this study. Then, alter the mesh by applying mesh control on the fillet. Use a mesh control ratio setting of **Ratio a/b** = **1.15**. Zoom in on the mesh when using the **Probe** feature to select nodes.

d. Use classical equations and available stress concentration factor charts to compute maximum stress at the fillet.

e. Compare results predicted using the three different meshes with that predicted by classical stress equations; clearly label each calculation. Compute the percent difference for each comparison using equation [1] (repeated below).

$$\% \text{ difference} = \frac{(\text{FEA result - classical result})}{\text{FEA result}} * 100 = \qquad [1]$$

f. Determine the Factor of Safety, or lack thereof, at the change of cross-section (i.e., at the fillet). Create a plot showing regions (if any) of the model with a Factor of Safety less than two. NOTE: Cast iron, being a brittle material, has an ultimate strength rather than a yield strength. Account for this fact when selecting safety factor failure criteria. Name the failure criteria that was used.

g. Comment upon which FEA results are in best agreement with predictions of the classical equations. Based on your comparison, which method of mesh refinement is preferred and why?

h. For users conversant with modifying solid models in SOLIDWORKS, proceed to alter the fillet radius at the change of cross-section to a radius "r" equal to half the difference of the two shaft sizes [where: r = (D – d)/2] and repeat parts assigned by your instructor. Report the amount by which stress at the fillet is reduced.

EXERCISE 3 - Stress in a Lawn Mower Blade due to Centrifugal Force (Special Topics: Custom Material, Centrifugal Force, Soft Spring Supports)

Dimensions of a typical steel lawn mower blade are shown in Fig. E3-3. The density used for steel is 0.282 lb/in^3. For simplicity, the blade is modeled as having a uniform cross section with a centrally drilled 0.50 inch diameter hole. The goal is to determine maximum stress in the blade in the vicinity of the central hole. The blade rotates at 2800 rpm and, hence, is subject to centrifugal force. Due to the highly variable nature of "mowing forces" acting on the blade (caused by different grass heights, rocks, small branches, or other debris), mowing forces normal to cutting edges are to be neglected.

Develop a finite element model that includes material specification, applied centrifugal force, mesh generation *(use mesh control)*, and solution. Solution guidance is provided relative to the application of a *centrifugal load* and the need for *soft spring* supports.

Open the file: **Lawn Mower Blade 3-3**

- Material: Steel properties not found in the Material table (use properties below).
  *See **Custom Material Specification*** in the **Solution Guidance** section.
  Elastic Modulus: **E = 30 000 000** psi
  Poisson's Ratio: **v = 0.292**
  Mass Density: **0.282** lb/in^3
  Yield strength: S_y = **40 000** psi

- Mesh: In the **Mesh** property manager, select a ⊙ **Standard mesh**. Use a default size mesh with high quality tetrahedral elements and apply *Mesh Control* with a **Ratio a/b = 1.2.**

- Fixture: **Soft Spring** - See Solution Guidance section below for application details.

- External Load: None. Load is due to internal centrifugal forces caused by the 2800 rpm rotational speed.

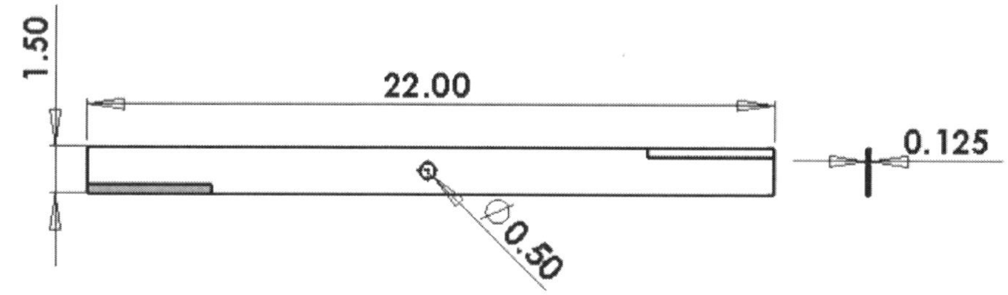

Figure E3-3 – Basic dimensions of a typical lawn mower blade.

Three aspects of the current exercise are unique. First, the blade is made from a custom material that is not available in the SOLIDWORKS material library. Second, a centrifugal force is applied to load the model. Centrifugal force is not an *external* force. Instead it is a load caused due to the mass of the blade rotating at high speed. Guidance on these two topics is provided below. Third, no **Fixtures** are applied to this model. Therefore, **Soft Springs** must be applied to maintain equilibrium.

Solution Guidance

Custom Material Specification (It is assumed that the user has started a Study in SOLIDWORKS Simulation.)

The recommended way to create a custom material definition is to begin with a *similar* existing material and then change material properties as outlined below.

- Open the **Material** window by right-clicking the part folder named **Lawn Mower Blade 3-3**, then select **Apply/Edit Material…**
- Because the steel mower blade is similar to other steels, select **Plain Carbon Steel** by *right*-clicking it in the list of available steels. Then from the pop-up menu select **Copy**.
- Continue to scroll down the materials list and *right*-click **Custom Materials**. From the pop-up menu, select **New Category**. A new file folder is opened.
- Right-click the **New Category** folder, and from the pop-up menu select **Paste**. This action opens a copy of the **Plain Carbon Steel** sub-folder beneath the **Custom Materials / New Category** folder. Click the **Plain Carbon Steel** folder to open it in the right half of the **Material** window.
- On the **Properties** tab, select **Units:** as **English (IPS)**.
- Change **Name:** to **Custom Mower Blade Steel** and ignore remaining fields in the upper portion of the window. The **Description:** and **Source:** fields also can be left blank.
- Within the **Property** column of the lower table notice that red, blue, and black colors are used to indicate different **Property** names. Red lettering indicates information *required* for a stress solution. Blue lettering indicates *desirable but unnecessary* information. And property names appearing in black *are not required* for the current solution. Replace red values with values listed beneath "Material" in the problem statement. Ignore blank fields and values listed in black type.
- Click **[Apply]** followed by **[Close]** to exit the **Material** window. A check "✓" appears on the **Lawn Mower Blade 3-3** part folder and the **Name:** assigned above appears adjacent to the part folder.

Solution Guidance (continued)

Centrifugal Force Specification

- Right-click **External Loads**, and from the pull-down menu select **Centrifugal…** The **Centrifugal** property manager opens as shown in Fig. E3-4.

- In the **Selected Reference** dialogue box the **Axis, Edge, Cylindrical Face for Direction** field is highlighted (light blue). Select the *inside cylindrical surface* of the hole.

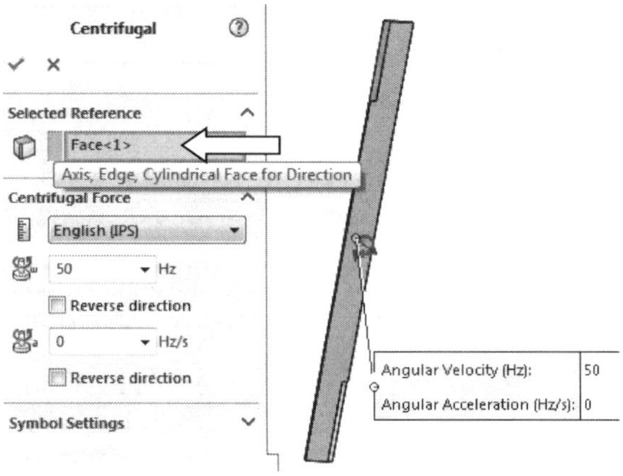

Figure E3-4 – Specifying a **Centrifugal** force on a mower blade rotating at 2800 RPM.

- Convert the constant blade rotation speed of 2800 rpm to **Hz** (i.e., cycles/second or rev/sec).

- In the **Centrifugal Force** dialogue box, verify that **Unit** is set to **English (IPS)** and in the **Angular Velocity** field, type the rotational speed calculated in the previous step *(the value shown in Fig. E3-4 is intentionally incorrect)*. After typing this value and pressing **[Enter]**, a red arrow appears at the hole to indicate the direction of rotation. If rotation is not in the direction of the cutting edges of the blade (sides with tapered edges), then check ☑ **Reverse Direction**. If rotation direction does not change, open **v** in the **Symbol Settings** dialogue box and toggle the ☑ **Show preview** check box 'on' and 'off.'

- Click **[OK]** ✓ to close the **Centrifugal** property manager. A **Centrifugal-1** symbol and label appears beneath the **External Loads** folder.

Rigid Body Motion Prevention (Soft Springs)

As noted above, **Soft Springs** must be applied to the model prior to running the solution. Therefore, a general discussion and procedures for applying **Soft Springs** begins on the following page.

Analysis Insight

The lawn mower blade model is the *first* part file encountered that does *not* have a **Fixed** or **Hinge Joint** restraint applied somewhere on the part. Recall that these restraints, when applied to tetrahedral elements, restrict translations in the X, Y, and Z directions at each node to which they are applied. Thus, equilibrium for externally applied forces in all of those directions is guaranteed due to the **Fixed** restraints. But, that is not the case for the current model where only a centrifugal force is applied, but *no* **Fixtures** are used.

It also might logically be argued that the model is in static equilibrium under the action of equal but opposite forces acting on opposing ends of the model. However, the traditional understanding of equilibrium of forces, such as are applied to a static free-body diagram, is subject to subtle differences in a finite element analysis. Those differences include possible asymmetry of the mesh, small inaccuracies in the model, and/or mathematical round-off in calculations. These factors can produce extremely small differences in what we ordinarily assume to be a body in equilibrium. Thus, in a finite element analysis, even the smallest difference from a "zero" force balance results in an *unbalanced* force acting on the body. And, according to Newton's second law of motion, any unbalanced force acting on a body results in an acceleration in the direction of that unbalanced force. Such motion is not tolerated in a *static* finite element analysis. Therefore, one way to deal with unbalanced forces is to apply *soft springs* to support the model. These springs serve to stabilize the model against any unbalanced forces. Instructions for the application of soft springs are provided in the following Solution Guidance Section.

Solution Guidance

Soft Spring Restraints

Discussion below provides guidance in the application of soft springs to the current model. This section assumes the model is already open and a finite element Study is started. Soft springs can be assigned any time before the Solution is **Run**.

- Right-click the Study name *you* entered at the top of the Simulation manager (not to be confused with the name at top of the SOLIDWORKS feature manager tree). A pull-down menu appears as shown in Fig. E3-5. From the pull-down menu, select **Properties…** The **Static** window opens as shown in Fig. E3-6.

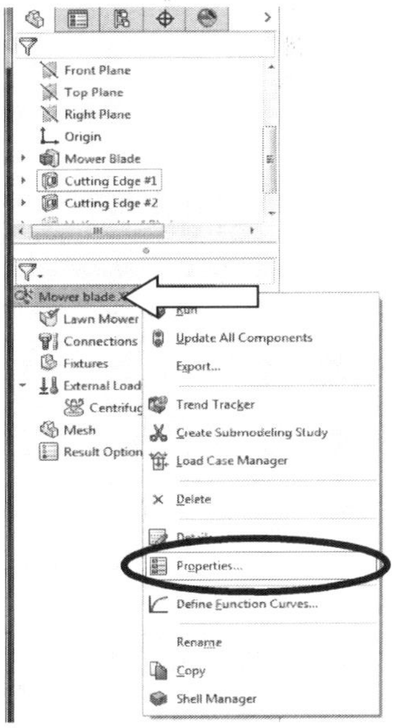

Figure E3-5 – Accessing the Study pull-down menu.

Solution Guidance (continued)

- Within the **Options** tab, make the following two selections in the **Solver** section of the window:

  a. Select ☑ **Use soft spring to stabilize model**, circled in Fig. E3-6.

  b. Select ▼ **Direct sparse solver** as the equation solver method. This solver must be used in conjunction with the soft spring option. Discussion of available solver types is included in a later chapter.

- Click **[OK]** to close the **Static** window. See Chapter #2, pg. 2-34 for discussion of "why" soft springs might be needed.

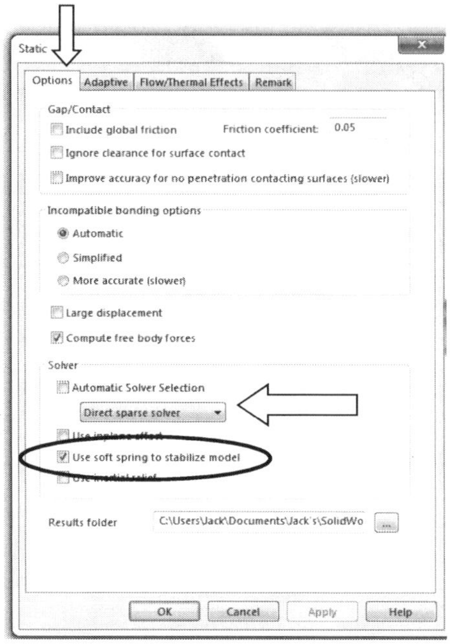

Figure E3-6 - Selecting **Soft Springs** to stabilize the model.

Springs shown in Fig. E3-7 are schematic representations only. Springs *do not appear* on a screen image of the model. However, they are mathematically present between *every* surface node and the ground. Thus, these springs effectively restrain the model in the X, Y, and Z directions.

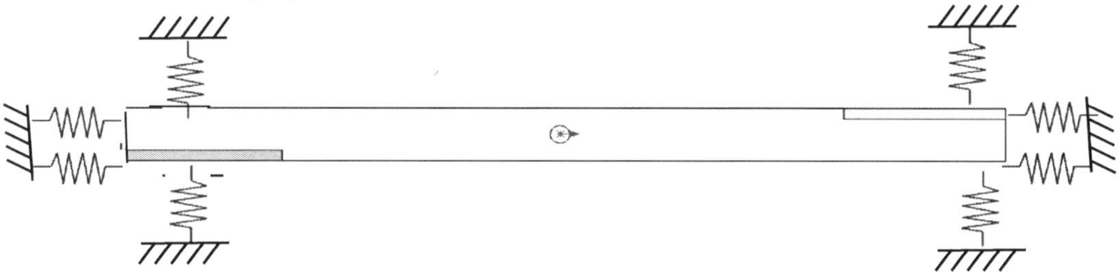

Figure E3-7 – Schematic representation of **Soft Springs** applied to stabilize a model with sufficient **Fixtures** to prevent rigid-body-motion. In actual fact, mathematical "soft springs" are attached to *all* surface nodes.

Determine the following:

Develop a finite element model that includes material specification, soft springs, applied external load (centrifugal force), mesh generation, and solution.

a. After running the solution and obtaining the **Results** folder, edit the **Stress1 (-vonMises-)** plot by doing the following. *NOTE: If a Static Analysis window warns of possible "Large Displacements," select the* ***[No]*** *option and proceed.*

- In the ☑ **Deformed Shape** dialogue box, select ⊙ **Automatic**. You will know when the deformed shape is turned off/on because the centrifugal force arrow will again appear.
- Display **Discrete** fringes on the model.
- Display the **Mesh** on the model (use *mesh control* with **Ratio a/b= 1.2**).
- Turn on ☑ **Show max annotation**.
- Next, produce a plot to display **P1: 1st Principal Stress**. Apply the same plot characteristics as applied (above) to the **Stress1 (vonMises-)** plot.
- Repeat the preceding steps, except create a plot of **SX: X Normal Stress**.

b. Orient the blade "horizontally" as shown in Fig. E3-7, then zoom in on the central hole of the mower blade that displays a plot of **P1: First Principal Stress**. Next, use the **Probe** tool to select all corner and mid-side nodes beginning at the top or bottom *inner* edge of the hole and proceeding outward to the *nearest* edge of the blade. When selecting nodes, traverse the model in the straightest line possible. Create a graph of this data. Include a descriptive title, axis labels, and your name on the graph.

c. Repeat step (b) to produce a graph showing the variation of **SX: X Normal Stress** at the same location on the model.

d. Manually calculate the nominal tensile stress at the center of the blade caused by blade rotation. Include a labeled free-body diagram used as the basis of this calculation. Also, show the calculation used to determine maximum stress at the hole location. Include a reference to the stress concentration factor chart used to make this calculation. Label each calculation. Simplify the analysis as follows. *HINT:* For the manual calculation *only*, create a free-body diagram of half of the mower blade as shown in Fig. E3-8. Assume half of the blade mass is located at the center of mass "**G**."

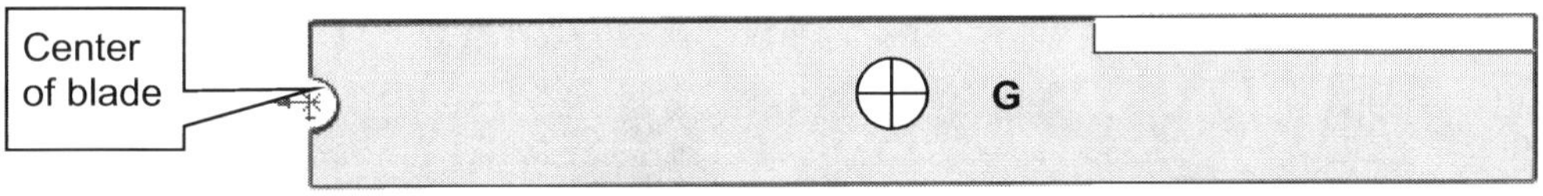

Figure E3-8 – Suggested ½ model to be used as a free-body diagram for manual calculations *only*. Do *not* use the model in this figure for finite element analysis.

e. Use equation [1], repeated below, to compare percent differences between manually calculated maximum stress value and **P1: First Principal Stress** and **SX: X Normal Stress** calculated using the finite element approach. Which of these finite element results is in best agreement with manually calculated results? *Why?*

$$\%\text{ difference} = \frac{(\text{FEA result - classical result})}{\text{FEA result}} * 100 = \qquad [1]$$

EXERCISE 4 – Stress Concentration Mitigation in Notched Bar

This exercise examines means of mitigating effects due to stress concentration. Two different models are examined. Both rectangular bars are the same overall outside dimensions and are loaded and restrained identically. The only difference is notch geometry of each. Figure E3-9 shows the model named **Deep Notched Bar – (Variation #1) 3-4**. It is **Fixed** at its left end and subject to an axial, tensile force of 640 N applied normal to its right end. Notch dimensions are shown in the accompanying drawing.

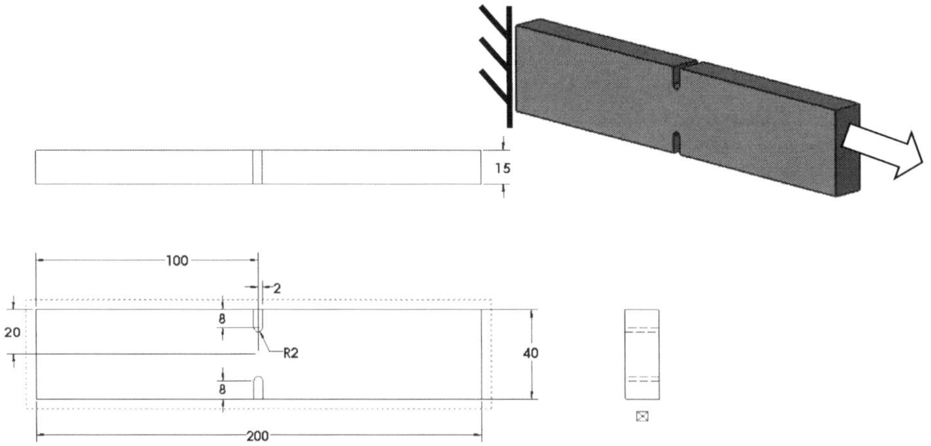

Figure E3-9 - Steel bar with centrally located, "U" shaped notch subject to an axial force. **(All dimensions in mm.)**

Conventional wisdom suggests that when a part exhibits stress concentration, a common fix is to make the part larger, and hence stronger, to reduce the effects of stress concentration. However, this exercise examines an alternate means of reducing stress concentration by careful removal of material from the model named **Deep Notched Bar – (Variation #2) 3-4** shown in Fig. E3-10. The central notch in Fig. E3-10 is identical to that in Fig. E3-9 above. However, additional notches, each one being 2 mm shorter than the adjacent notch at the model center, are removed from the model as shown.

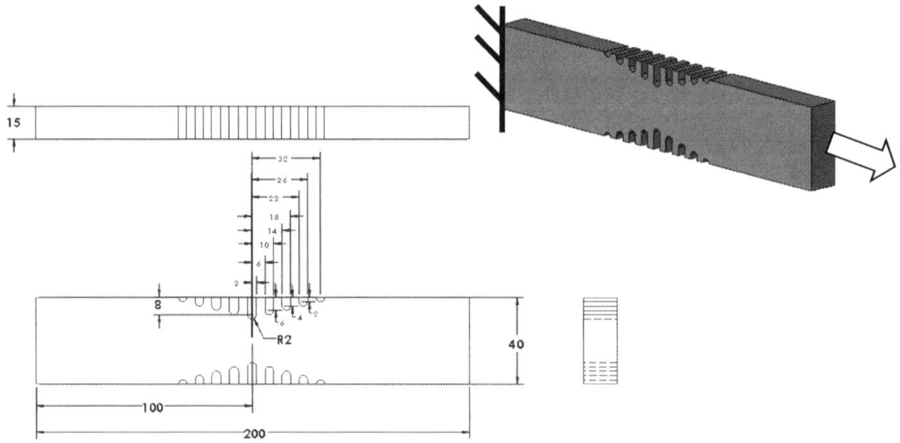

Figure E3-10 – Steel Bar with notches of graduated size on either side of a central U" notch.

- Material: **ASTM A-36 Steel** (Use S.I. units)
- Mesh: In the **Mesh** property manager, select a ⊙ **Standard mesh**. High quality tetrahedral elements are to be used. Use the mesh specified in parts (a, c, and d) below.
- Fixture: **Fixed** (Immovable) restraint applied to left end of the model.
- External Load: **640 N** applied normal to the right-end causing tension in the bar.

Develop a finite element model that includes material specification, fixtures, external loads, mesh generation, and solution as specified below.

Determine the following:

a. For the model **Deep Notched Bar - (Variation #1)**, create a plot of the *most appropriate stress* to permit comparison of stress magnitude adjacent to the "notch" with that predicted by classical equations for stress computed at the same location. Apply *Mesh Control* with a **Ratio: a/b** = **1.2** to the edges and internal surfaces of each notch. The image should include **Discrete Fringes**, the **Mesh** displayed on the model, and **Show max annotation** automatically labeled on the plot.

b. On the page with the plot of part (a), show manual calculations used to determine stress at the notch. Include the effects of stress concentration in this calculation and include figure number(s) for stress concentration factor charts from your textbook or other reference source. Use equation [1] to determine the percent difference between finite element and classical determination of stress at the notch.

$$\% \text{ difference} = \frac{(\text{FEA result - classical result})}{\text{FEA result}} * 100 = \qquad [1]$$

c. Use the **Probe** feature to produce a graph of stress from the bottom of the upper "notch" to the top of the lower notch for the model named **Deep Notched Bar – (Variation #1)**. Select both corner and mid-side nodes in the straightest path possible between these two points. Include a descriptive title, axis labels, and your name on this graph.

d. Open the file **Deep Notched Bar (Variation #2) 3-4** and create a plot of the *most appropriate stress* to permit comparison with finite element results of part (a). Follow instructions in part (a) when producing the stress plot.

e. Compare the maximum appropriate stress at the notch location determined in parts (a) and (d). Did removal of material corresponding to the geometry of **(Variation #2)** result in an increase or decrease of maximum stress? Explain the reason(s) for this change (if any) in support of your answer to the preceding question. Use equation [2] to determine the percent increase or decrease of maximum stress at the deep notch location.

$$\%\ \text{difference} = \frac{(\text{FEA result [Variation \#1]- FEA result [Variation \#2]})}{\text{FEA result [Variation \#1]}} * 100 = \quad [2]$$

<u>EXERCISE 5</u> – Stress Concentration Mitigation in a Shouldered Shaft

When mounting bearings on a shaft it is common practice to provide a shoulder that serves both to locate the bearing on the shaft and to prevent bearing movement in at least one direction on shafts subject to thrust (axial) loads. Bearing lock nuts and/or sleeves used to restrain the opposite side of a bearing are not shown in Fig. E3-11. Figure E3-11 shows an isometric and section view of a portion of a shaft with a shoulder against which a ball bearing is mounted. Also shown is a broken-out section view of a typical ball bearing. Allowable shoulder heights and maximum fillet radius at the shoulder location (transition from small diameter to large diameter region of the shaft) are listed in bearing manufacturer's literature. Because the shaft fillet radius must be small, stress concentration often results in this transition region. This exercise examines one means used to reduce stress concentration caused by small fillet radii in the shoulder transition region. Shaft support provided by the bearing is to be ignored.

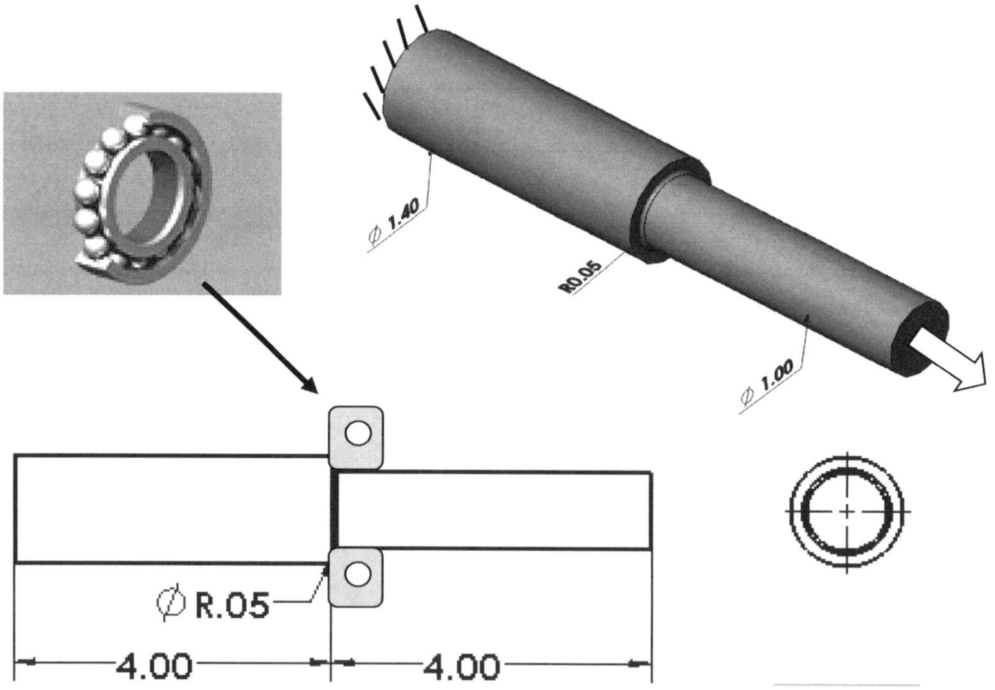

Figure E3-11 – Isometric and section views of the "original" shaft with shoulder at the location of a mounted ball bearing. **(All dimensions inches.)**

File for the above part: **Shaft With Bearing Shoulder & Fillet 3-5**

Figure E3-12 shows a revised version of the shaft with a tapered relief groove cut into the large diameter segment of the shaft to the left of the bearing shoulder. All other dimensions of the shaft are identical to those of the original shaft including the 0.05-in fillet radius in the transition region (fillet is not shown on the *revolved section* view because it was added after the revised shaft geometry was finalized).

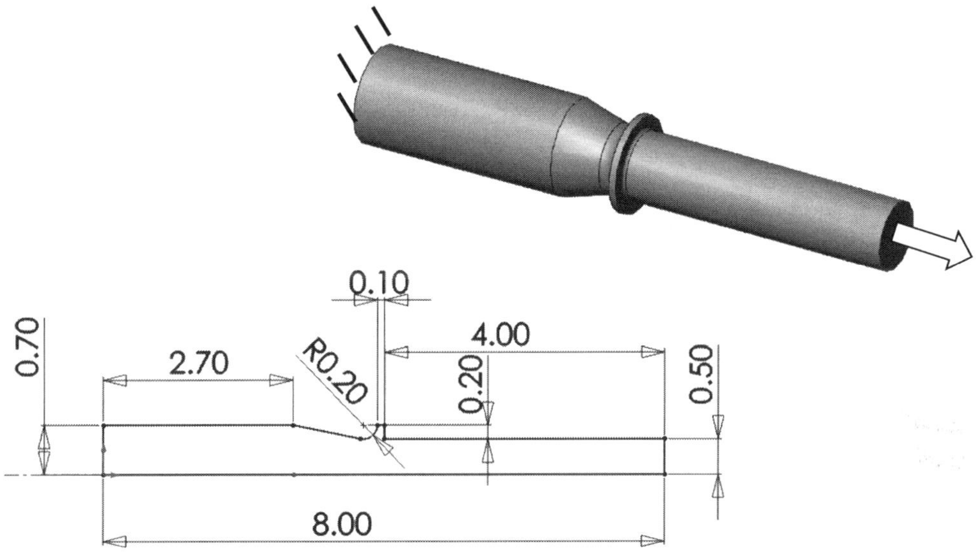

Figure E3-12 – Isometric and revolved section views of the shaft supported by a bearing at its shoulder. Shaft geometry to the left of the shoulder is modified to strategically remove material in an effort to reduce stress concentration caused by the small fillet at the bearing shoulder location. **(All dimensions inches.)**

File for above part: **Shaft With Bearing Shoulder & Relief Groove 3-5**

Create finite element models of these two parts including material specification, fixtures, external loads, mesh, solution, and results analysis as outlined below.

- Material: **AISI 1015 Steel, Cold Drawn (SS)** (use **IPS** units)
- Mesh: Use a default size **Standard mesh**.
- Fixture: **Fixed** applied to the left end (face) of the shaft segment.
- External Load: **600 lb** tensile load applied normal to the right end of the shaft.

Determine the following:

a. For the model **Shaft With Bearing Shoulder & Fillet 3-5**, create a plot of the *most appropriate stress* to permit determination of maximum stress in the vicinity of the fillet. This image should include **Discrete Fringes**, the **Mesh** displayed on the model, and **Show max annotation** automatically labeled on the plot.

b. On the same page as the plot of part (a), show manual calculations used to determine stress at the shoulder. Include the effects of stress concentration in this calculation and include the figure number(s) for stress concentration factor charts from your textbook or other reference source. Use equation [1] to determine the percent difference between finite element and classical determination of stress at this location.

$$\% \text{ difference} = \frac{(\text{FEA result - classical result})}{\text{FEA result}} * 100 = \qquad [1]$$

c. Open the file **Shaft With Bearing Shoulder & Relief Groove 3-5** and create a plot of the *most appropriate stress* to permit comparison with finite element results obtained in part (a). Follow instructions in part (a) when producing the stress plot.

d. Compare the maximum appropriate stress at the shoulder location determined for the two different shaft geometries in parts (a) and (c). For this comparison, re-mesh the parts and apply *Mesh Control* with a **Ratio: a/b** = **1.2** in the stress concentrated regions. Did removal of material corresponding to the geometry of the shaft with a relief groove result in an increase or decrease of maximum stress in the shoulder region? Provide reasons and possibly labeled sketches that support your answer to the preceding question. Use equation [2] to determine the percent increase or decrease of maximum stress at the shoulder for the model titled **Shaft With Bearing Shoulder & Relief Groove 3-5**.

$$\% \text{ difference} = \frac{(\text{FEA result [no groove]- FEA result [with groove]})}{\text{FEA result [no groove]}} * 100 = \qquad [2]$$

Textbook Problems
In addition to the above exercises, it is highly recommended that additional problems involving stress concentration and/or significant changes of part geometry be worked from a design of machine elements or mechanics of materials textbook. Textbook problems provide a great way to discover errors made in formulating a finite element analysis because they typically are well defined problems for which the solution is known. Typical textbook problems, if well defined in advance, make an excellent source of solutions for comparison.

CHAPTER #4

THIN AND THICK WALL PRESSURE VESSELS

This chapter investigates modeling of thin and thick wall pressure vessels. More importantly, however, the use of *shell* elements is introduced and guidelines are provided regarding their use as opposed to *solid* tetrahedral elements. When taken alone, thin and thick wall pressure vessel problems are solvable in a rather straightforward manner using classical stress equations. Therefore, advantages of the Finite Element Analysis approach are realized most when investigating stresses in more geometrically complex regions of a pressure vessel. These regions include, but are not limited to, nozzles, pipe connections, flanges, transition regions, and saddles or other support structures associated with pressure vessel design and installation. Many of these special situations can be handled by application of principles outlined in preceding chapters. Thus, the two examples of this chapter focus on introducing additional capabilities of the SOLIDWORKS Simulation software rather than on pressure vessels per se.

Learning Objectives

Upon completion of this example, users should be able to:

- Convert a solid model to a part modeled using *shell* elements, and use a *shell* mesh to model thin-wall parts (whether or not the part is a pressure vessel).
- Change *system default* settings to simplify analyses with common characteristics.
- Recognize load and geometry *symmetry* and use them to reduce model size, solution size, and computation time. Know when and how to apply *symmetry restraints*.
- Apply *section clipping* to enhance viewing of results.
- Apply uniform *pressure* loading.

THIN-WALL PRESSURE VESSEL (Using Shell Elements)

Thin-wall pressure vessels are found in many common applications. Included among them are carbonated beverage containers (aluminum cans and plastic bottles), aerosol cans used to dispense everything from paint to hair spray, hydraulic cylinders, SCUBA tanks, steam boilers, and water towers that provide pressure to public water systems.

Problem Statement

This example is based on a thin-wall cylindrical pressure vessel closed on both ends with hemispherical heads as illustrated in Figs.1 (a) and (b). Wall thickness t = 3 mm and inside diameter of the cylinder d_i = 144 mm. The vessel is made of **AISI 1045** cold drawn steel and is subject to internal pressure **P = 1.4 MPa**. Other dimensions are included in Fig. 1(a). Fig. 1(b) shows a typical application where a similar vessel serves as a propane gas supply tank for heating a remote building not served by natural gas.

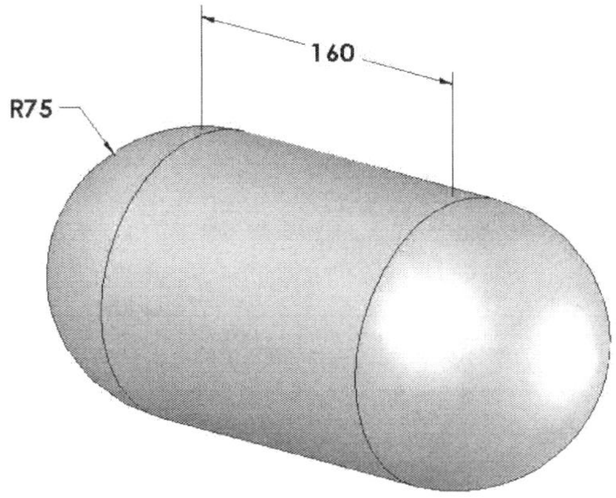

Figure 1(a) – Basic dimensions of a thin-wall pressure vessel closed with hemispherical ends.

Figure 1(b) – Pressurized cylindrical fuel tank outside a heated garage/storage building.

The dividing line between thin and thick wall pressure vessels is defined differently in various machine design[1] and mechanics of materials texts. If wall thickness "t" falls in the range where $t \le r_i/20$ to $t \le r_i/5$, (where, r_i = cylinder inside radius) then the cylinder is considered a thin-wall pressure vessel. This determination must be made at the outset of any pressure vessel problem because choice of the appropriate set of classical equations depends upon whether wall thickness is classified as "thin" or "thick." By either of the above definitions, the current model can be considered a thin-wall pressure vessel since the minimum criteria yields: $t = 3\text{ mm} \le (72\text{ mm})/20$. Another assumption applied to thin-wall pressure vessels is that the magnitude of tangential stress (σ_t), also known as "hoop" stress or "circumferential" stress is assumed *uniform* through the wall thickness.

Primary stresses in the cylindrical pressure vessel walls are given by:

Tangential stress: $$\sigma_t = \frac{p*d_i}{2*t} = \frac{(1.4e6\frac{N}{m^2})(0.144\not{m})}{2(0.003\not{m})} = 33.6e6\text{ Pa} \qquad [1]$$

Longitudinal stress: $$\sigma_\ell = \frac{p*d_i}{4*t} = \frac{1}{2}\sigma_t = \frac{1}{2}(33.6e6\text{ Pa}) = 16.8e6\text{ Pa} \qquad [2]$$
(for a closed-end cylinder)

Where: p = pressure (N/m^2) = 1.4 MPa
t = wall thickness (m) = 0.003 m
d_i = inside diameter (m) = 0.150 m – 2*0.003 m = 0.144 m

Note that $\sigma_t = 2*\sigma_\ell$.

[1] Budynas, R.G., Nisbett, J.K., Shigley's Mechanical Engineering Design, uses: $t \le r_i/20$.
Collins, J.A., Mechanical Design of Machine Elements, uses: $t \le 10\%*d = (.1)(2*r) = r_i/5$.

These two stresses are perpendicular to sides of a stress element aligned with and perpendicular to the longitudinal axis of the cylinder shown in Fig. 2. Because no shear stresses act on sides of the element shown in Fig. 2, σ_t and σ_ℓ are principal stresses. Finally, all stresses on the hemispherical ends are tangential stresses, but their magnitude is half of that in the cylindrical portion of the vessel, thus, this stress is denoted as σ'_t.

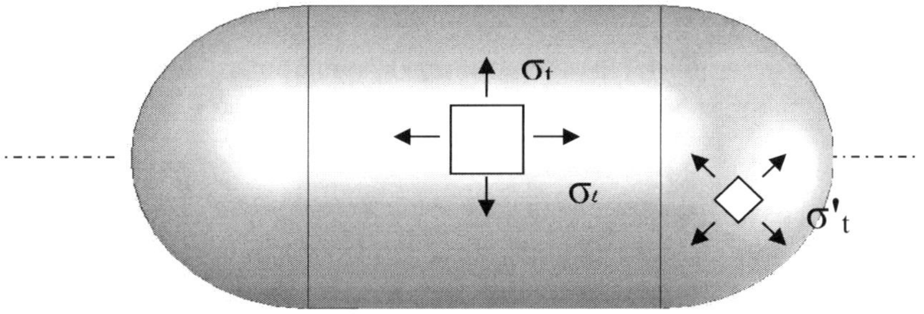

Figure 2 – Stress elements showing orientation of σ_t and σ_ℓ on the pressure vessel surface and on the hemispherical end. ($\sigma'_t = \frac{1}{2}\sigma_t$)

According to St. Venant's principle, normal stresses depicted in Fig. 2 are only valid at locations well removed from the junction between the cylindrical section and the hemispherical ends where end-conditions exist. Thus, to permit comparison with results of equations [1] and [2], the following finite element analysis focuses on stresses near the mid-section of the cylinder and on the hemispherical heads.

The next decision to be made is whether to use *solid* or *shell* elements for the finite element model. The guideline for this decision is quite different for a finite element analysis than that used to determine what set of classical equations should be used. For the current model, it is possible to use either *solid* or *shell* elements. Both would produce valid results. However, the selection of element type has a significant influence on the number of elements in a model, and hence upon solution time and memory requirements. Draft and high-quality *shell* elements are pictured in Figs. 3 (a) and (b).

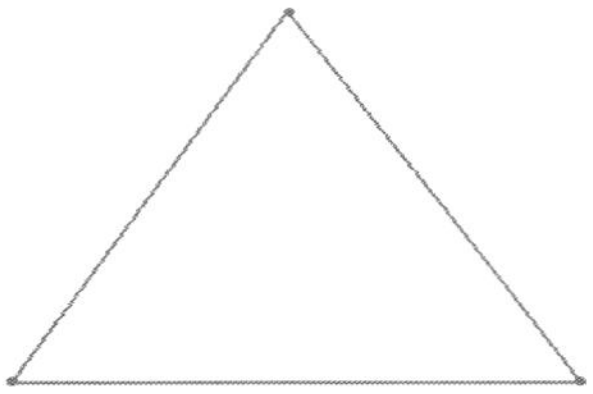

Figure 3 (a) – First-order (draft quality) triangular shell element.

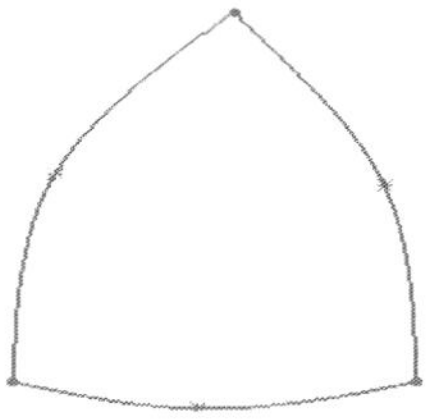

Figure 3 (b) – Second-order shell element includes three additional mid-side nodes.

Shell elements are typically used for sheet metal and other thin parts. The principle used to decide what element type to use is that *shell* elements are applied when the thickness to span ratio is less than 0.05 (i.e., when one dimension is much smaller than the other two). For the current model, if the cylinder were laid out flat, the wall thickness (3 mm) divided by the lesser of the cylinder circumference ($\pi d_i = \pi(144) = 452.4$ mm) or cylinder length (160 mm) yields: Span Ratio = 3 mm/160 mm = 0.01875 which is < 0.05.

A "rule of thumb" guideline to decide what element type to use is that *solid* elements are applied when two default size elements fit across the thickness of the part (i.e., across the part's minimum dimension). This guideline was applied to the curved beam in Chapter 2.

Shell elements look somewhat similar to solid elements except they are represented graphically as a single layer of elements, as if the mesh were drawn on a thin sheet of paper or the thin shell of an egg. Later images in this chapter will illustrate actual shell elements. However, because parts modeled using shell elements must have a finite thickness, a corresponding thickness is assigned as described later. The finite element analysis of a thin-wall pressure vessel using shell elements begins below.

1. Open SOLIDWORKS by making the following selections. (*NOTE:* ">" is used to separate successive menu selections.)

   Start>All Programs>SOLIDWORKS 2026 (or) Click the **SOLIDWORKS** icon on your screen.

2. From the main menu within SOLIDWORKS, select **File > Open...** Then browse to where your files are saved and open the SOLIDWORKS Simulation file named **Thin Wall Pressure Vessel**.

Understanding System Default Settings

This section digresses from the problem solution to investigate methods of changing system default settings. Changing system default settings at the start of a Study can be advantageous because it can save time throughout the remainder of an analysis. For example, earlier problems required frequent specification of items such as mesh quality, units, and other attributes of an analysis. However, if these attributes are specified one time at the start of an analysis, they *should* remain constant throughout the remainder of the problem. To practice altering some of these parameters, proceed as follows.

1. In the main menu, at top of screen, click **Simulation** to open a pull-down menu.

2. Near the bottom of this menu, select **Options...** The **Systems Options - General** window opens, a *portion* of which is shown in Fig. 4.

In this window, the **Systems Options** tab is initially selected as illustrated in Fig. 4. In the list at left of this window, the word **General** is highlighted to denote what settings are currently displayed. Because this Study focuses on use of a shell mesh, in the right half of this window, observe the default color scheme used to denote the bottom surface of shell elements. The text **Shell bottom face color** appears next to the system default color, orange, indicated adjacent to the arrow in Fig. 4. Before proceeding, observe other system default settings in this window. In particular, note that items such as ☑ **Show errors** and ☑ **Show warnings** are checked. These two items were introduced in the example of the previous chapter. Also, notice that ☑ **Show yield strength marker for vonMises plots** is checked, thereby establishing it as a default display item on von Mises stress plots. Recall that this feature was used in the Safety Factor analysis of Chapter 2.

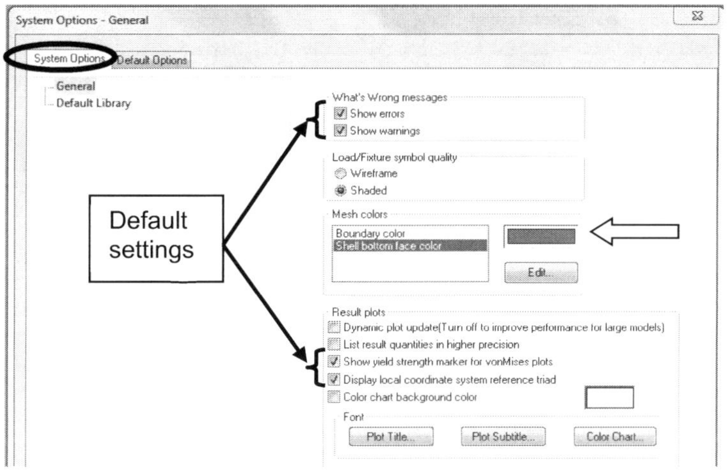

Figure 4 – Default settings beneath the **System Options** tab.
Default color of the bottom surface of a shell mesh is shown here.

3. At the top-left of this window, click the **Default Options** tab. Within this tab, **Units** is highlighted (gray) to indicate it is selected from the list of options within the window. Only the right-half of this window is illustrated in Fig. 5. Within this window, the settings should appear as listed below; if not, change to the settings shown. Note that SI units are default within SOLIDWORKS Simulation.

   - Beneath **Unit system**, set default units to ⊙ **SI [MKS]**, if not already selected.

   - Beneath **Units**, the unit of **Length/ Displacement**: should be set to **m** (meters).

   - Adjacent to **Pressure/Stress:**, default units should be set to **N/m^2**. Other units do not pertain to this analysis and can be ignored.

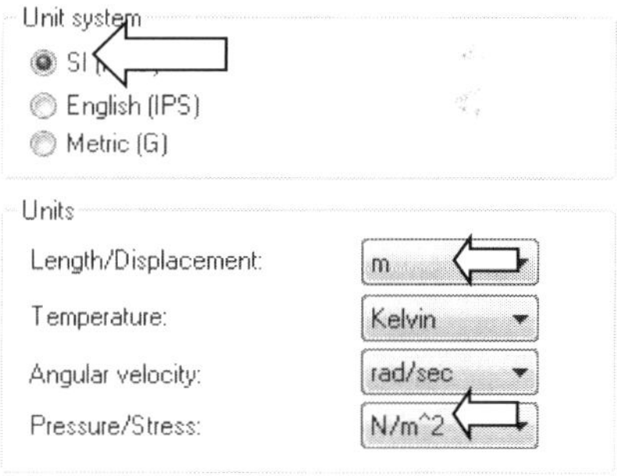

Figure 5 – Selecting units to be applied throughout the analysis.

Specifying units as outlined above establishes a common set of units for an entire analysis. If, for example, your company or future employer uses English units exclusively, it would be a time-saver to reset default units accordingly. This could have been done for English unit examples worked in Chapters 1 and 2.

4. Return to the list of **Default Options** at the left of this window and click to select **Load/Fixture**; the **Default Options – Load/Fixture** window is displayed.

Brief examination of the right-half of the window (not shown) reveals that the **Symbol size** and **Symbol colors** for various types of loads and restraints can be specified here. Although no changes are made in this window, color-blind users may find it beneficial to alter default **Symbol colors** to suit their personal preferences.

5. Next, from the list of **Default Options** at the left of the window, click to select **Mesh** and verify that the system default settings in the right half of the window appear as listed below.

Knowing the system default settings shown in this window and understanding that they remain unchanged unless altered by you, makes unnecessary many of the often repeated steps included in previous examples. For this reason, a brief explanation of each setting is included below. Reset any different settings to the default values listed below.

- **Mesh quality** set to ⊙ **High**. *Reason*: A high-quality mesh is recommended for most analyses and for models with curved surfaces. A draft quality mesh is typically used only for an initial Study where quick, approximate results are adequate.

- **Jacobian points:** set to **[16 points]**. *Reason*: This option sets the number of integration points used when checking distortion levels in tetrahedral elements. The **16 points** selection is adequate for most analyses.

- Set Mesher type to ⊙ **Curvature based**. Use 8 for the **Default number of elements on a circle**. *Reason*: Beginning in 2011, a **Curvature based** mesh became the new default mesher within SOLIDWORKS Simulation. It is somewhat slower but is more accurate than a **Standard Mesh**. A Standard Mesh has been used thus far only because a more "orderly" mesh results. A **Standard Mesh** can be selected on a case-by-case basis throughout this text.

- Beneath **Advanced Settings**, clear the check mark from ☐ **Remesh failed parts Independently**. *Reason*: This option is used where meshing difficulty occurs between bonded, solid parts by attempting to use incompatible mesh types. These instances are not encountered in this text.

6. Next, from the **Default Options** list at left of screen, select **Solver and Results**. Verify that the **Default solver** is set as ⦿ **FFEPlus**. *Reason:* **FFEPlus** is currently the fastest solver available in SOLIDWORKS Simulation.

7. Other options in this window direct analysis results to system default folders within SOLIDWORKS. Unless other guidelines for file storage exist within your organization (university or company), use the default settings and ignore other settings in this window.

8. Return to the **Default Options** tab and select **Plot**. The **Default Options - Plot** window opens. The right-half of this window is shown in Fig. 6.

9. Within this window, set **Fringe options:** to **Discrete**. This is a user preference but is typically selected as **Discrete** in this text due to enhanced image characteristics when printed in black, white, and gray tones.

10. Adjacent to **Boundary options:** select **Model** to show a black outline of the model. *Reason:* This option helps identify model boundaries when stress contour plots are viewed on complex shapes or where "clipping" is used. This selection is also a user preference.

11. Another user preference is whether or not to display results on the deformed or undeformed shape of the model. Although this text typically elects to display an undeformed model, accept the default choice ⦿ **Show results on deformed shape**. Changes will be made on a case-by-case basis.

Familiarize yourself with other settings within this window. Other settings should remain set to system defaults.

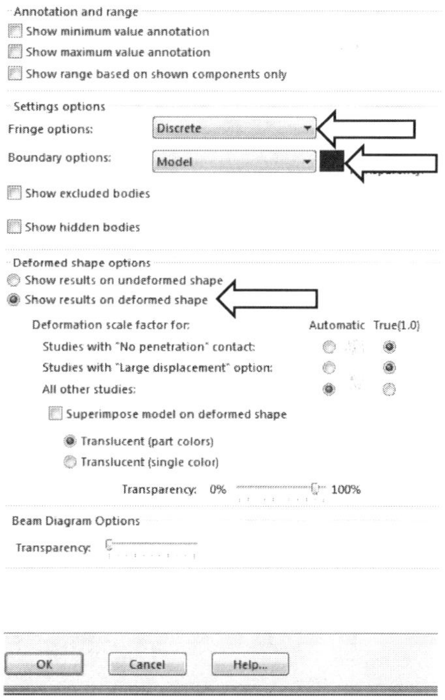

Figure 6 – The **Plot** window is used to specify display options for all plots.

12. Next, in the **Default Options** tab, click **Color Chart** and briefly observe items the user can control regarding display characteristics of the color chart including its location on the screen, its size, and the format of numbers listed adjacent to the chart. In the **Number format** box, select ⦿ **Scientific** and set **No. of decimal places:** to **3**. Make no other changes to default settings.

A nice feature about using the above capabilities is that every plot in the current and future studies can be produced with the same set of user selected settings. However, its use does not preclude altering features of a plot at any point during a Study. We next investigate default settings of all plots created during a Study.

13. Click the "+" sign adjacent to **Default Plots** (if not already selected) and a listing of system default plots appears as shown on the *left*-side of Fig. 7.

14. At the left of the screen, below the **Static Study Results** folder, click to highlight the <u>*name*</u> **Plot1**.

15. In the right-half of the window, beneath **Results type:** select **Nodal Stress** (if not already selected). This selection is chosen because it gives stress magnitudes at specific locations (i.e., at each node) on the model.

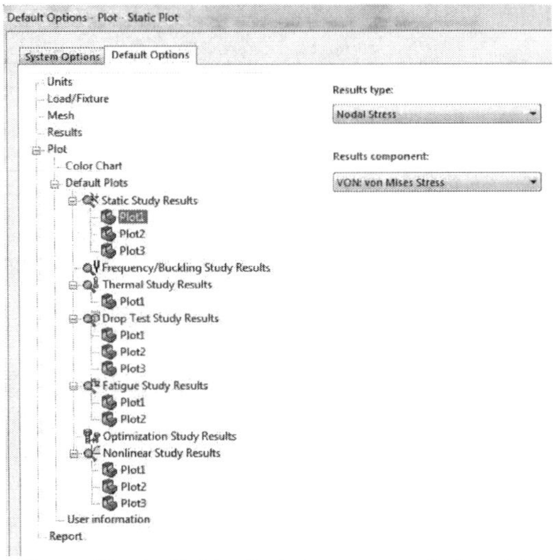

Figure 7 – Individual plots are pre-defined to indicate items and components to be plotted.

16. Observe that the default stress plot listed beneath **Results component:** is **VON: von Mises stress**. As noted in Chapter 2, von Mises stress represents the most complex state of stress as a single value. As such, its value is easily compared to material yield or ultimate strength to give an indication of the safety, or lack thereof, in a part. This reason alone justifies it as worthy of being designated a default plot.

17. Return to the list of plots at the left of the screen and click the <u>*name*</u> "**Plot2**." In the right-half of the screen observe the **Results type:** is set to **Displacement** and the **Results component:** is set to **URES: Resultant Displacement**.

18. Finally, click the <u>*name*</u> "**Plot3**" and observe the default definition for the **Results type:** is **Elemental Strain** and **ESTRN: Equivalent Strain** is listed in the **Results component:** field. Strain results might prove useful for comparison with experimentally determined strain gage readings. This plot is rarely referenced in this text.

Contents of the three default plot folders are based on the assumption that most users are interested in magnitudes of vonMises stress, model displacement, and strain in the model. Although this is a logical assumption, this text focuses primarily on stress results.

If additional default plots are desired, they can be added now or in the future. To add an additional default plot, proceed as follows.

19. Right-click **Static Study Results** and from the pop-up menu select **Add New Plot** as shown in Fig. 8. Immediately **Plot4** is added to the bottom of the current list. Define the contents of this new plot as follows.

20. In the right-side of the window, beneath **Results type:**, select **Nodal Stress** from the pull-down menu (if not already selected).

21. Beneath **Results component:**, select **P1: 1st Principal Stress.**

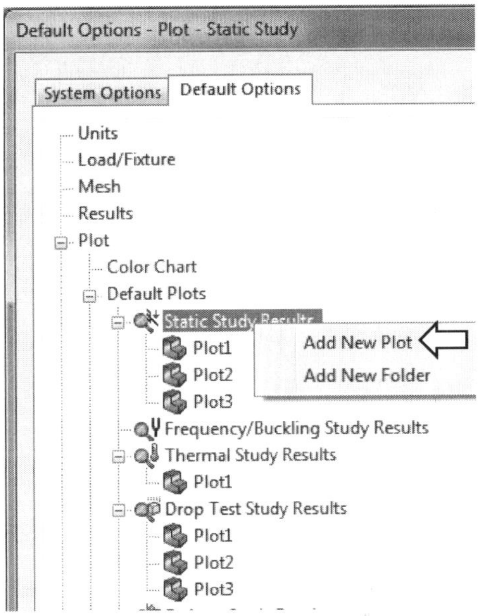

Figure 8 – Adding a new plot and including user information on all printed plots.

OBSERVATION:

Because the current Study involves analysis of stresses in the walls of a cylindrical pressure vessel, it is known in advance that tangential and longitudinal stresses will result. Further, it is well known that tangential stress (σ_t) and longitudinal stress (σ_ℓ) correspond to the first and second principal stresses (σ_1 and σ_2) respectively. Therefore, *if* a user were dealing with pressure vessel analysis on a routine basis, it would make sense to add plots of the first and second principal stresses to the *default* set of plots produced at the conclusion of every study. However, since that is not the case for future examples in this text, **Plot4** is deleted in the following step.

22. Right-click the *name* "**Plot4**" and from the pop-up menu, select **Delete**.

23. Click the **[OK]** button to close the **Default Options** window.

The above overview should provide sufficient insight so that users can access the **Default Options** window at the start of a Study to define characteristics they wish to apply.

Creating a Static Analysis Using Shell Elements

Because *shell* elements require special preparation of the model within SOLIDWORKS, this section begins with a brief overview of the basic methods of creating models to which a *shell* mesh can be applied followed by a walk-through of the actual steps.

The process begins by creating a part model within SOLIDWORKS. For the thin wall pressure vessel, a dimensioned line sketch, shown in Fig. 9, provides a starting point. This sketch is revolved about the X-axis at which time a wall thickness of 3 mm is specified. Figs. 1(a), 2 and 10 show the completed model.

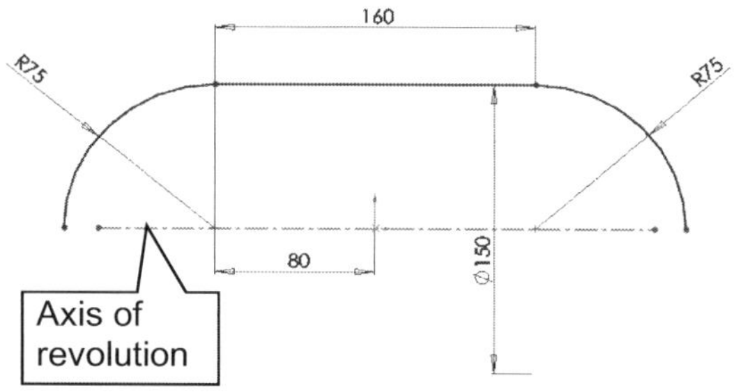

Figure 9 – Line sketch used to generate the solid model.

The three basic ways to create a *shell* model are described briefly below.

a. First, parts created as sheet metal parts are considered 'thin' by their very nature. These parts are automatically modeled as *shell* elements as demonstrated in several end-of-chapter problems.

b. Second, solid models can be converted to *shell* elements by defining a "mid-surface" located between the inner and outer surfaces of a solid model. This method is illustrated in the current example; it is the most challenging method.

c. Finally, a solid body can be converted to a sheet metal part and then to a shell model. This approach is best adapted to moderately thick parts that contain multiple bends between adjacent surfaces. This method is relatively straightforward and interested users are referred to Simulation **Help** for information.

The numerous references to "sheet metal" above do *not* imply that parts must be made of metal. Instead, "sheet metal" refers to specific capabilities within the drafting portion of SOLIDWORKS that allow bends and other metal forming operations to be incorporated into the design of sheet metal parts. However, in SOLIDWORKS *Simulation*, do not let the words "sheet metal" be misleading. In Simulation, these words refer to how the part is modeled in SOLIDWORKS rather than the material of which a part is made. Consider for example a child's plastic sand shovel or the outer surface of a remote control device. Although made of plastic, these thin-wall items can be modeled in SOLIDWORKS as sheet metal, plastic parts, thin parts, or surface parts. Each of these modeling techniques can be converted to shell elements. One caution, however, is that a shell mesh does not apply to thin models made of *composite* materials. As implied by its name, a composite material is made of multiple different materials. These materials are typically fabricated in multiple layers, and hence their properties are not uniform through their thickness.

Converting a Solid Model to a Shell Model

The model on your screen should appear similar to Fig. 10. Notice that the process for converting from a solid model to a shell model begins within SOLIDWORKS, not in the Simulation portion of the program.

However, before converting the solid model into a shell model, the model is simplified by making use of *symmetry*. The thin-wall, cylindrical pressure vessel pictured in Fig. 10 is clearly a theoretical "textbook" model. The rationale for this statement is quite obvious because no visible means of support are shown for the model as are no openings to permit fluids to enter or exit the container. However, this somewhat artificial geometry permits examination of methods to deal with *symmetry* when it occurs in a problem.

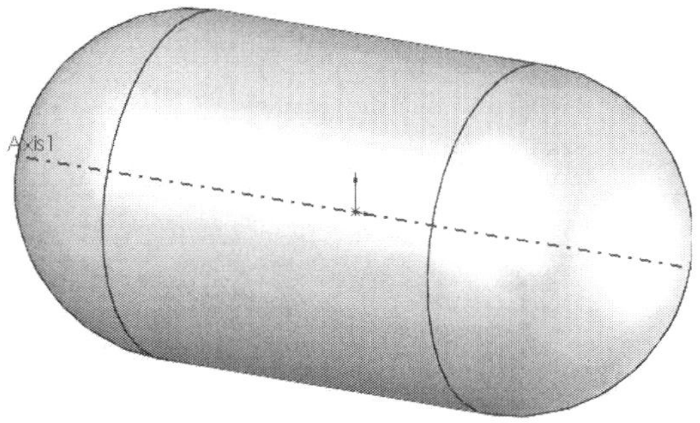

Figure 10 – Thin wall pressure vessel. Only one axis of symmetry is shown.

Because vessel shape is symmetrical (geometric symmetry) *and* because the internal pressure is uniform (symmetric loading), it is possible to analyze only a portion of the model. The sketch in Fig. 9 and solid model in Fig. 11 reveal that the current model was intentionally centered about the coordinate system origin when it was built. The front, right, and top sketch planes, included in Fig. 11, aid in visualizing that the model can be divided into eight symmetrical pieces. Model symmetry can be used to save computer memory and computation time. Because this is a rather simple model, significant savings are not realized. However, consider the computational savings realized if symmetry is used to model half of a complete aircraft fuselage (a pressure vessel when in flight). The current example demonstrates how symmetry can and should be used in other finite element solutions. Also, *symmetry* boundary conditions are introduced in this example.

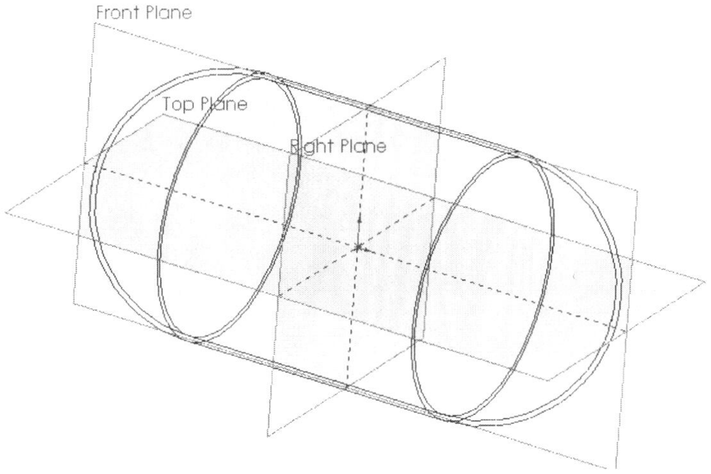

Figure 11 – Front, right, and top sketch planes introduced to show division of the model into symmetrical portions.

The following discussion outlines steps to convert a solid model into a shell model.

1. If **Axis1** does not appear on the model, from the main menu select **View**. Then, from the pull-down menu, select **Hide / Show** ► followed by Axes. **Axis1** should appear on the model as shown in Fig. 10.

2. Near the bottom of the SOLIDWORKS Feature manager tree, right-click the grayed-out **1/4 Symmetry Model**. This action causes the pop-up menu, shown in Fig.12, to open.

3. Above this menu select the **Unsuppress** icon circled in Fig. 12. Immediately ¼ of the model is displayed in the graphics area.

4. Repeat steps 2 and 3, but this time select the grayed-out **1/8 Symmetry Model** and **Unsuppress** it.

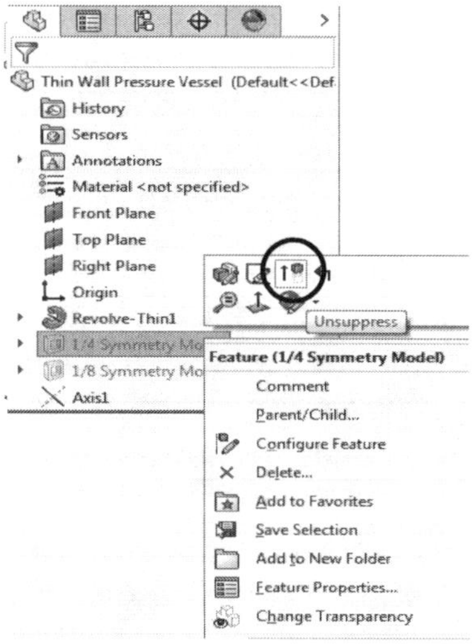

Figure 12 – **Unsuppressing portions of** the symmetrical model in the SOLIDWORKS feature manager.

The portion of the model selected for analysis should now appear as shown in Fig. 13. Note that virtually any fraction of the model could be selected, but the 1/8 model is useful for reasons described later. Observe that this is a *solid* model, i.e., it has thickness.

Also, notice how the use of descriptive names in the SOLIDWORKS feature manager facilitated identification and selection of desired model attributes in the preceding steps.

The next step is to create a mid-surface between the inner and outer faces of the solid model shown in Fig. 13. This new surface is used to create a shell mesh. It is also possible to create a surface on the inside or outside of the model.

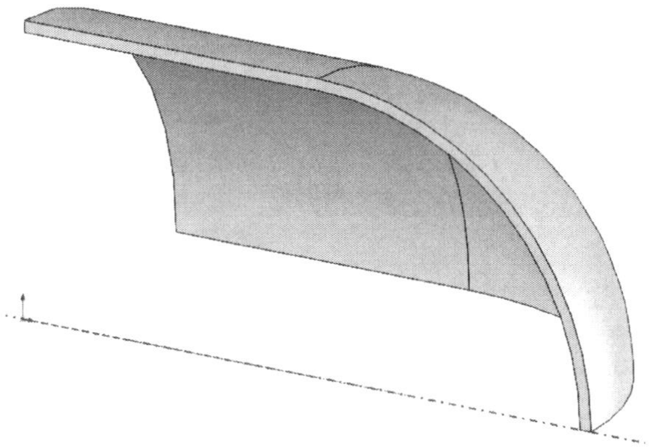

Figure 13 – A 1/8 model of the thin-wall pressure vessel. Symmetry is used to reduce analysis time and computer memory requirements.

5. From the main menu, select **Insert** and from the next two pull-down menus select **Surface** ► followed by Offset... The **Offset Surface** property manager opens as shown in Fig. 15.

6. Placing the cursor in the light blue field of the **Offset parameters** dialogue box reveals the message, **Surface or Faces to Offset**.

7. Move the cursor onto the *inner surface* of the model and *right*-click. In the pop-up menu, choose **Select Tangency** and immediately a ghost image of an offset surface appears inside the model, see Fig. 14. Also, **Face<1>** and **Face<2>** appear in the highlighted field. **Face<1>** and **Face<2>** refer to the cylindrical and hemispherical surfaces. Both surfaces are selected because they are tangent to one another and because **Select Tangency** was activated earlier in this step.

8. If the offset surface is not clearly visible, increase the **Offset Distance** by typing **10** or **15** mm in the box located at the bottom of the **Offset parameters** dialogue box.

NOTE: It is also acceptable to select outside surfaces of the model. The only difference is that the offset surface appears outside of the model and locations of the surface in the steps below will be reversed.

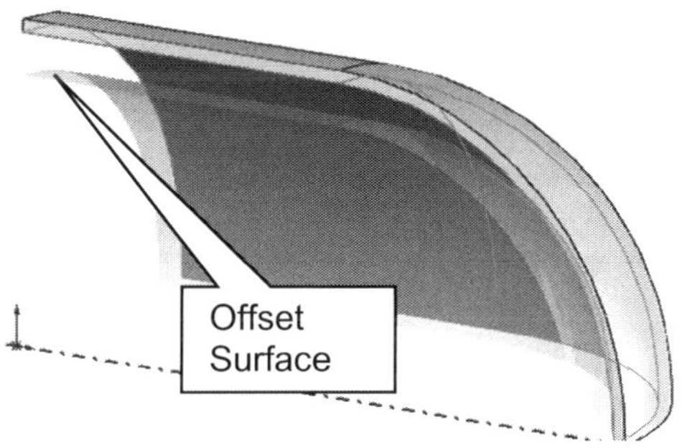

Figure 14 – An **Offset Surface** appears inside the pressure vessel model.

9. Because a shell is to be located at the mid-surface of the model, in the **Offset Distance** field, shown in Fig. 15, type **1.5** mm**,** which is half of the 3.0 mm wall thickness. Click anywhere in the graphics screen to implement the 1.5 mm offset.

10. To visualize where the offset surface is located, zoom in on any segment of the wall *edge* and toggle (i.e., multiple click) the **Flip Offset Direction** button circled in Fig. 15. When the surface appears *midway between* the inside and outside walls it is correct. NOTE: Due to its light color, the mid-surface may be *very* difficult to see when located *between* the surfaces.

11. Click **[OK]** ✓ to close the **Offset Surface** property manager. A line representing the mid-surface should appear on the model.

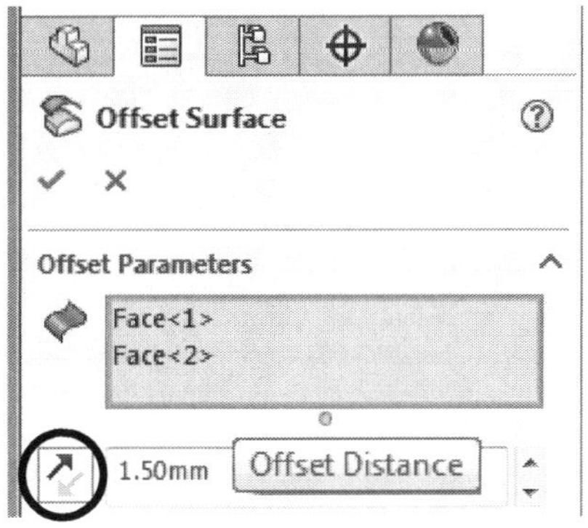

Figure 15 – Selecting offset surfaces and specifying the **Offset Distance**.

12. Near the top of the SOLIDWORKS feature manager tree, click the " ▸ " symbol adjacent to **Solid Bodies(1)**. This reveals the **1/8 Symmetry Model** as the original *solid* body.

13. Immediately below the preceding selection, click the ▸ symbol adjacent to **Surface Bodies(1)**. This action reveals **Surface-Offset1**, which was created in steps 5 to 11 above.

CAUTION: In the following step do *NOT* select the **1/8 Symmetry Model** located near the bottom of the SOLIDWORKS feature manager tree.

14. Next, return to **Solid Bodies(1)** and beneath it right-click on **1/8 Symmetry Model**. This action opens a pull-down menu. In the menu select Delete/Keep Body... .

15. The **Delete/Keep Body…** property manager opens and shows **1/8 Symmetry Model** in the **Bodies to Delete** dialogue box.

16. Click **[OK]** ✓ to close the **Delete Body** property manager and the following things occur:

   - The **Solid Bodies(1)** folder is removed from the SOLIDWORKS Feature manager tree.
   - The model appears as a thin surface (i.e., it is now a *shell*) shown in Fig. 16.
   - ☒ **Body-Delete/Keep 1** appears at the bottom of the SOLIDWORKS feature manager.

The preceding steps appear to delete the original **Solid Bodies(1)** folder and its contents from the Feature manager tree. However, **Delete/Keep Body** is simply a feature in the SOLIDWORKS manager tree, and it can be restored as follows.

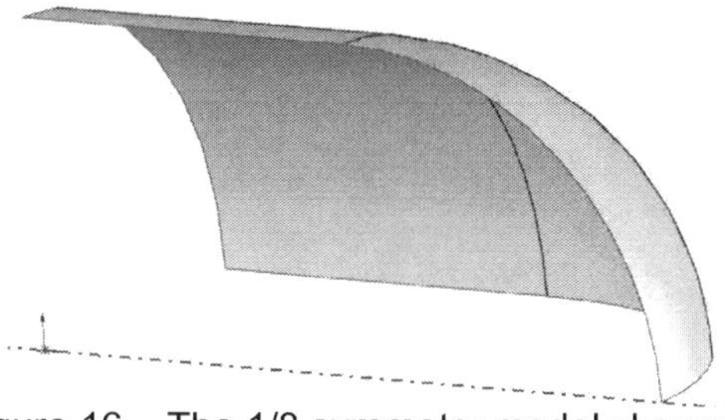

Figure 16 – The 1/8 symmetry model shown as a thin *shell*. (Compare with Fig. 13).

17. At the bottom of the SOLIDWORKS Feature manager tree, right-click ☒ **Body-Delete/Keep 1** and from the icons located just above the pull-down menu select the **Suppress** icon. The solid body model is again displayed in the graphics area and **Solid Bodies(1)** appears in the SOLIDWORKS Feature manager tree.

Because it is desired to complete this analysis using a shell model, un-do the preceding step as follows.

18. Once again right-click ☒ **Body-Delete/Keep 1** and, from the icons located just above the pull-down menu, select the **Unsuppress** icon. The shell model reappears in the graphics area.

This concludes one of the three different procedures for converting a solid model to a shell model. The next section outlines the remainder of the shell analysis process.

Open a New Simulation Study

1. In the main menu, select **Simulation** and from the pull-down menu choose **Study…** Alternatively, on the **Simulation** tab, open the ▼**New Study** and select the **New Study** icon. A partial view of the **Study** property manager is shown in Fig. 17.

2. In the **Name** dialogue box, type **Pressure Vessel-Shell Study-YOUR NAME** for the Study name.

3. Verify that the **Type** dialogue box is set to **Static** and the **Use 2D Simplification** is not selected.

4. Click **[OK]** ✓ to close the **Study** property manager. A warning appears adjacent to the Study name. On your own, check **What's wrong?...**

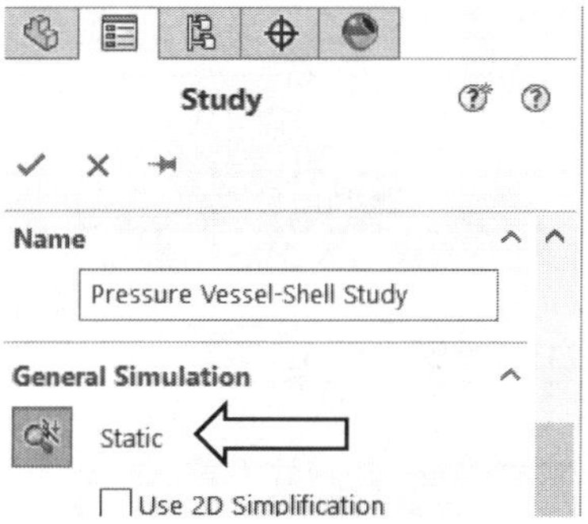

Figure 17 – **Study** property manager showing Study **Name** and Study **Type** (**Static**).

Assign Material Properties

1. In the Simulation manager tree, right-click the **Thin Wall Pressure Vessel (-Thickness: not defined-)** folder and from the pull-down menu select **Apply/Edit Material…** The **Material** window opens. Notice that the part icon appears as a thin surface rather than the original solid part.

2. Beneath **SOLIDWORKS Materials**, click the " ▸ " symbol adjacent to **Steel**, and from the list of materials, select **AISI 1045 Steel, cold drawn.** Verify that **Units:** should be set to **SI – N/m^2 (Pa)**. Recall changing default units to **SI** at the beginning of this example. *If necessary, change **Units:** to **SI**.*

3. Click **[Apply]** followed by **[Close]** to close the **Material** window. A "✓" appears on the **Thin Wall Pressure Vessel** surface icon.

Define Shell Thickness

The software recognizes that the pressure vessel is modeled as a "thin" part due to the **Revolve-Thin1** command circled in the SOLIDWORKS feature manager tree, Fig. 18. Wall thickness was specified when the original *solid* model was created in SOLIDWORKS. However, because the solid model was converted to a shell model, the software requires the user to specify its thickness again because (a) the solid part along with its thickness was "deleted," and (b) because it might be desired to specify a different thickness for analysis. Also, if you checked the meaning of the warning symbol in step 4 above, you discovered it was due to a missing thickness specification. To specify shell thickness, proceed as follows.

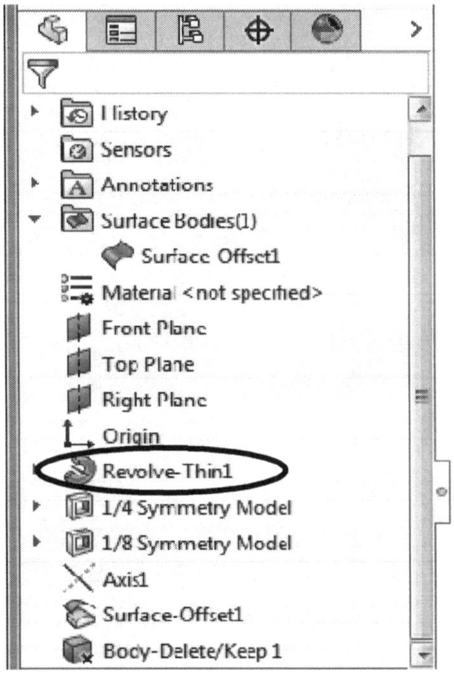

Figure 18 – SOLIDWORKS Feature manager tree.

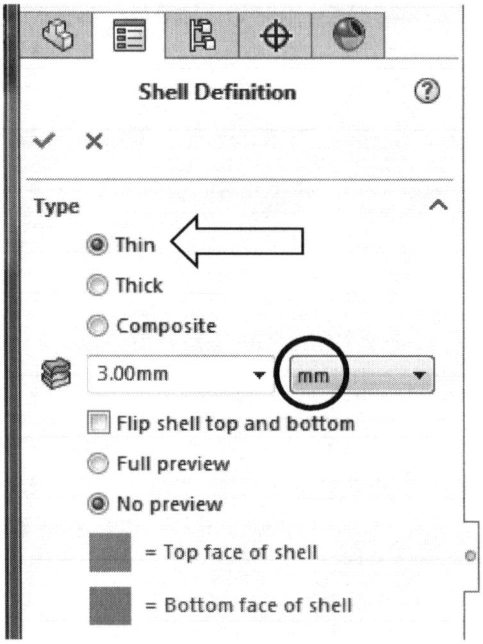

Figure 19 – Shell thickness is specified in the **Shell Definition** property manager.

1. Right-click Thin Wall Pressure Vessel (-Thickness: not defined/Material: AISI 1045 Steel, cold drawn-) in the Simulation manager. *Pass the cursor over this folder to display its entire name.* From the pop-up menu select **Edit Definition…** The **Shell Definition** property manager opens as shown in Fig. 19.

2. In the **Type** dialogue box, select ⊙ **Thin** (if not already selected).

3. Verify **Units** are set to **mm** and type **3** into the **Shell Thickness** box in Fig. 19.

4. Click **[OK]** ✓ to close the **Shell Definition** property manager. The warning symbol is removed from the Study name because shell thickness is now defined.

Assign Fixtures and External Loads

Restraints Applied Using Reference Geometry

As noted earlier, the pressure vessel is a symmetrical model as far as both geometry and loads are concerned. This section introduces symmetrical loading and fixture boundary conditions as outlined next. What is different, however, is that shell elements restrict both X, Y, Z *translations* and *rotations* about the X, Y, Z axes at all node locations. This restriction differs from that for solid tetrahedral elements where only *translations* are fixed at node locations. The next step is to define restraints along "cut" edges of the model. The method outlined here makes use of **Reference Geometry**.

1. Right-click the **Fixtures** folder and from the pull-down menu select **Advanced Fixtures…** The **Fixture** property manager opens, but initially it will *not* look like Fig. 20 until step 5 is performed.

2. Click to select **Use Reference Geometry**, circled in Fig. 20 (if not already selected).

Before proceeding to the next step, observe *possible* movement of the generic rectangular model displayed in the **Example** dialogue box. This animation illustrates that two *translations* parallel to a selected reference plane and one *translation* perpendicular to the same plane are possible. However, for a *shell* model, restricting appropriate *translation* and *rotation* edge movement is essential to define proper symmetry restraints.

> **Aside:**
> General guidance for applying restraints (fixtures) to either solid or shell models is explained here.
>
> a. **For Solid Models** – Every *face* that is coincident with a plane of symmetry should be prevented from <u>translating</u> in its *normal* direction.
>
> b. **For Shell Models** – Every *edge* that coincides with a plane of symmetry should be prevented from <u>translating</u> in the *normal* direction and from <u>rotating</u> in the other two perpendicular directions.

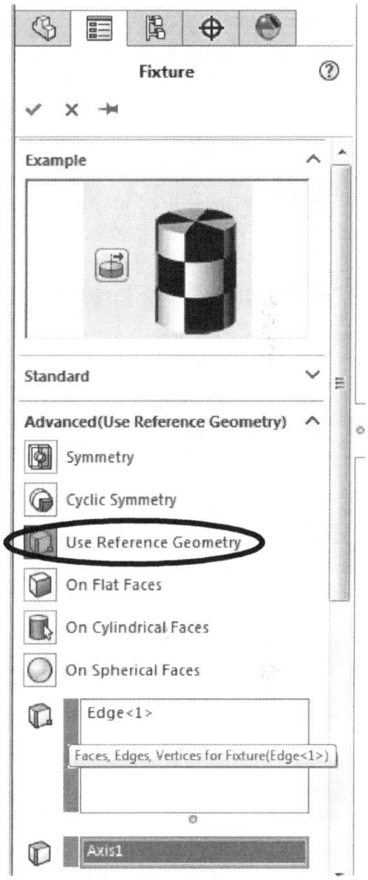

Figure 20 – The **Advanced** dialogue box is used to select edges for symmetry restraints.

Before defining restraints, it is necessary to identify those edges of the model on which restraints are to be applied.

Refer to the partial view of the **Advanced(Use Reference Geometry)** dialogue box, shown in Fig. 20, and the part model in Fig. 21 while implementing the following steps. Work carefully when selecting *edges* not *surfaces*.

3. Near the bottom of the **Advanced (Use Reference Geometry)** dialogue box the **Faces, Edges, Vertices for Fixture** field is highlighted (light blue) to indicate it is active and awaiting selection of *edges* to which restraints are to be applied. If

any item appears in this field, right-click it and in the pull-down menu select **Delete**.

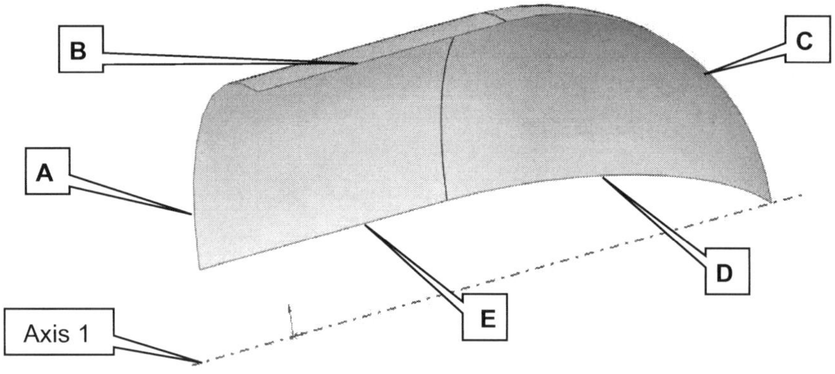

Figure 21 – Identification of shell edges to which symmetry restraints are applied.

4. Zoom-in on the model to select the ¼ circular edge, labeled **A** in Fig. 21. Do *not* select other edges, faces, or vertices. The selected edge, **Edge<1>**, appears in the **Faces, Edges, Vertices for Fixture** field in Fig. 20 and is highlighted on the model.

5. At the bottom of the **Advanced** dialogue box click to activate (light blue) the **Face, Edge, Plane, Axis for Direction** field. Then, if **Axis1** is visible on the model, click to select it. Otherwise, click to open the SOLIDWORKS flyout menu and select **Axis1** in this menu. **Axis1** now appears in the active field *and* the animated model changes to the "checker-board" cylinder shown in Fig. 20. This step establishes **Axis1** as an axis of symmetry along the length of the model.

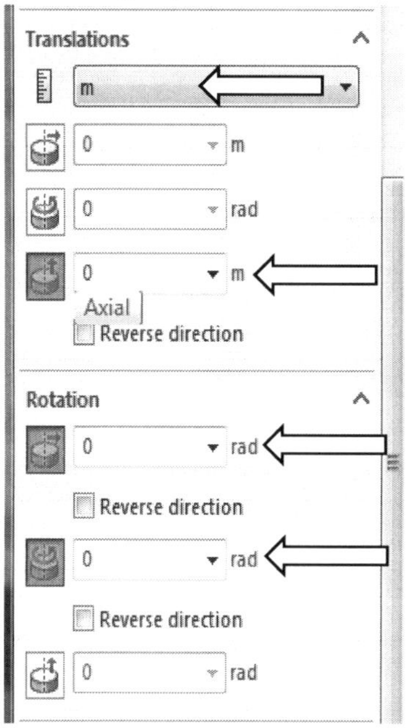

Figure 22 – Displacements set to zero on model edge.

Next, apply the principle stated in item (b) of the previous page, restated here: *"Every **edge** that coincides with a plane of symmetry should be prevented from translating in the <u>normal</u> direction and from rotating in the other two perpendicular directions."* To do this, proceed as follows.

6. In the **Fixture** property manager, scroll down to the **Translations** dialogue box shown in Fig. 22. Set **Unit** to meters **m**, then select the **Axial** icon. Ensure that **0** appears in the value box. This selection sets to zero model translation in the direction of **Axis1**, which is *normal* to edge **A**.

7. Next, scroll down to the **Rotation** dialogue box and set both **Radial** and **Circumferential** rotations to zero by clicking their icons (i.e., rotation is prevented in both of the **Radial** and **Circumferential** directions).
8. Click **[OK]** ✓ to close the **Fixture** property manager.

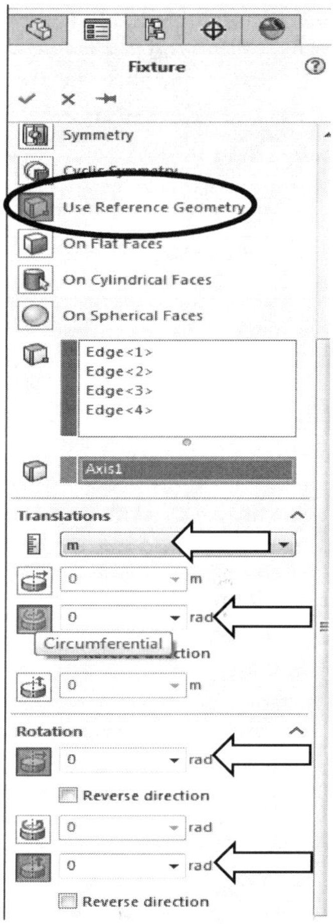

Figure 23 – **Translations** and **Rotation** settings for edges **B**, **C**. **D**. and **E.**

Next, repeat the above procedure, but select all edges **B**, **C**, **D**, and **E** of Fig. 21 and apply appropriate restraints. Try this on your own, or follow the steps outlined below.

9. Right-click the **Fixtures** folder and from the pull-down menu select **Advanced Fixtures…** The **Fixture** property manager opens.

10. In the **Advanced** dialogue box, select **Use Reference Geometry**, circled in Fig. 23. Also, the **Faces, Edges, Vertices for Fixture** field is highlighted (light blue) to indicate it is active.

11. On the model, select *edges* **B**, **C**, **D**, and **E** labeled in Fig. 21. **Edge<1>** through **Edge<4>** appear in the **Faces, Edges, Vertices for Fixture** field and are highlighted on the model. Refer to Fig. 23.

12. At the bottom of the **Advanced** dialogue box click to activate (light blue) the **Face, Edge, Plane, Axis for Direction** field. Again, either click **Axis1** in the SOLIDWORKS flyout menu or on the model. **Axis1** now appears in the active field.

13. Verify **Units** are "**m**" and set **Translations** and **Rotation** restraints to zero (**0**) as shown in Fig. 23.

14. Click **[OK]** ✓ to close the **Fixture** property manager.

The resulting symmetry restraints are shown on the model in Fig. 24.

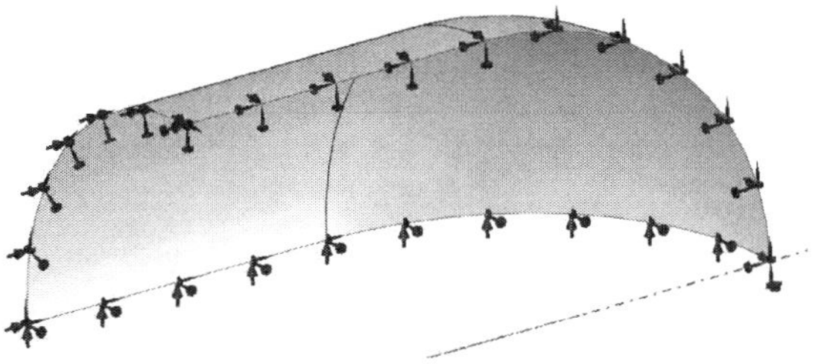

Figure 24 – An internal view of the model showing **Symmetry** restraints applied to all cut edges.

Zoom in and carefully observe the symbols used to indicate symmetry boundary conditions. All previous examples used solid tetrahedral elements for which **Immovable** restraints were appropriate. **Immovable** restraints prevent translations in the three coordinate directions X, Y, Z and are pictured in Fig. 25 (a). **Fixed** restraints are illustrated in Fig. 25 (b) where the added "disk" on the tail of each vector represents an added rotational restraint. Finally, the **Symmetry** restraint is pictured in Fig.25 (c). It prevents translation in a direction normal to the restrained face or edge (arrow shaped vector) *and* prevents rotation about the other two axes associated with the restrained edge ("thumb-tack" shaped vectors). When fully restrained, shell elements restrict three translations in X, Y, Z directions *plus* they prevent rotations specified above. Restraint symbols on edges of your model should resemble those shown in Fig. 25 (c).

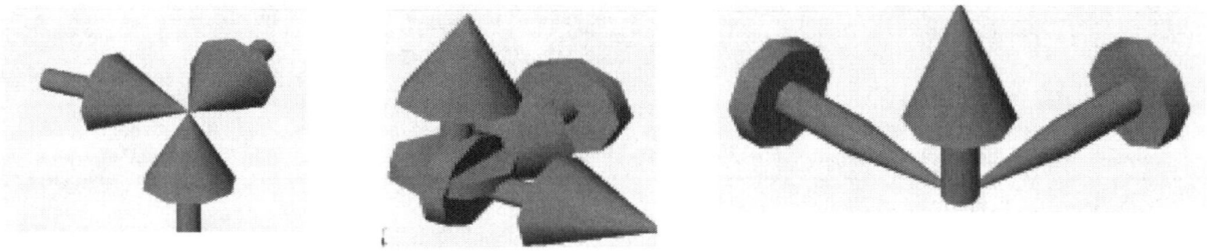

(a) (b) (c)

Figure 25 – (a) **Immovable** restraint symbol; (b) **Fixed** restraint symbol only applies to shell elements; however, it is only used where appropriate; (c) **Symmetry** restraint applied to shell elements on cut surfaces of the thin-wall pressure vessel.

Pressure Load Applied

Loading of the thin-wall cylinder is completed by the addition of an internal pressure as outlined next.

1. Right-click the **External Loads** folder and from the pull-down menu select **Pressure...** The **Pressure** property manager opens (not shown).

2. In the **Type** dialogue box, choose ⦿**Normal to selected face** (if not already selected).

3. The **Faces for Pressure** field is highlighted (light blue) to indicate it is active. Select the *inside* surfaces of both the cylindrical and hemispherical portions of the model. **Face<1>** and **Face<2>** appear in the **Faces for Pressure** field and both surfaces are highlighted to indicate their selection.

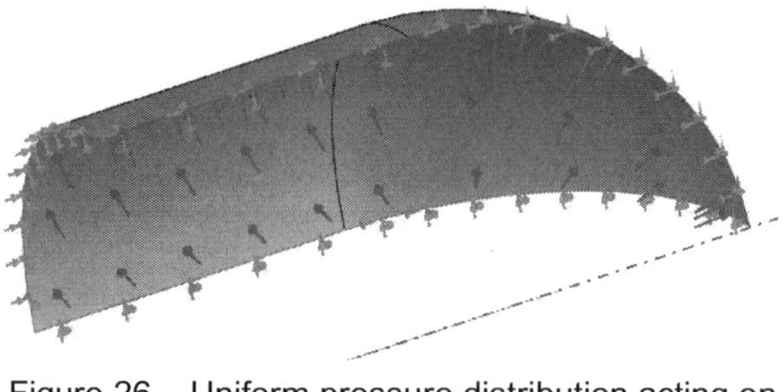

Figure 26 – Uniform pressure distribution acting on internal surfaces of the model.

4. Within the **Pressure Value** dialogue box, verify that **Unit** is set to **N/m^2**. Also, in the **Pressure Value** field, type **1.4e6** for the applied internal pressure. Units of **N/m^2** appear adjacent to this field.

Pressure vectors are displayed on interior surfaces of the model shown in Fig. 26. These arrows should be directed *toward the inner surface*; if not check **Reverse direction**.

5. Click **[OK]** ✓ to close the **Pressure** property manager.

The 1/8 model is now properly restrained using fixtures that restrict model translations and rotations in the appropriate directions. No additional restraints are needed. However, if the model were not fully restrained, a warning would appear during the Solution and additional restraints to prevent "rigid body motion" would be required. The need for rigid body restraint is demonstrated in the second half of this chapter.

Mesh the Model

The meshing process outlined below is considerably shortened because the system default mesh is used.

1. In the Simulation manager tree, right-click the **Mesh** folder and from the pull-down menu select **Create Mesh…** The **Mesh** property manager opens.

2. Check "✓" to open the ☑ **Mesh Parameters** dialogue box and select ⊙**Curvature based mesh** (if not already selected).

This is the first time the system default mesh is used. However, be aware that a curvature based mesh is *not* being used because a shell model is to be meshed. Rather it is used to acquaint users with this alternate mesh type and to show differences between it and the **Standard mesh** used in earlier examples.

3. Accept the default mesh size and click **[OK]** ✓ to close the **Mesh** property manager.

Meshing proceeds automatically and Fig. 27(a) shows an image of the thin-wall pressure vessel displayed with a **Curvature based** *shell* mesh. Also shown are all applied loads and fixtures. Recall that a curvature based mesh is more accurate, hence the reason it is the default mesh applied within SOLIDWORKS Simulation. Also, notice that the model appears as a "paper-thin" shell.

Figure 27(b), on the other hand, shows the thin-wall pressure vessel with a **Standard mesh** displayed on its surface. Although solutions that accompany a standard mesh execute slightly faster than the curvature based mesh, the resulting solutions are not quite as accurate. The primary reason a standard mesh has been specified for problems up to this point is that a *more orderly* mesh results. Such a mesh is advantageous when selecting nodes in a straight line across an area of interest on a model. Carefully examine the shape of each mesh in Figs. 27(a) and (b). You should only have the mesh shown in Fig. 27(a) on your model. The "bottom" (orange) surface is also labeled in Fig. 27(a).

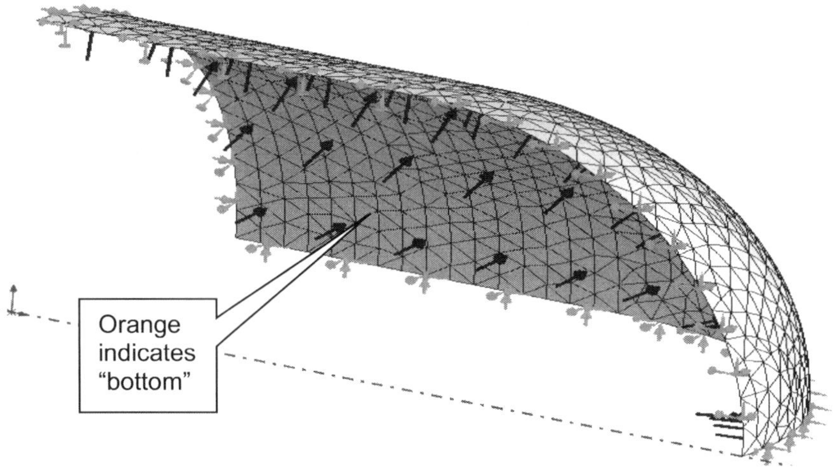

Figure 27 (a) – **Curvature based mesh** displayed on a shell model of the thin-wall pressure vessel.

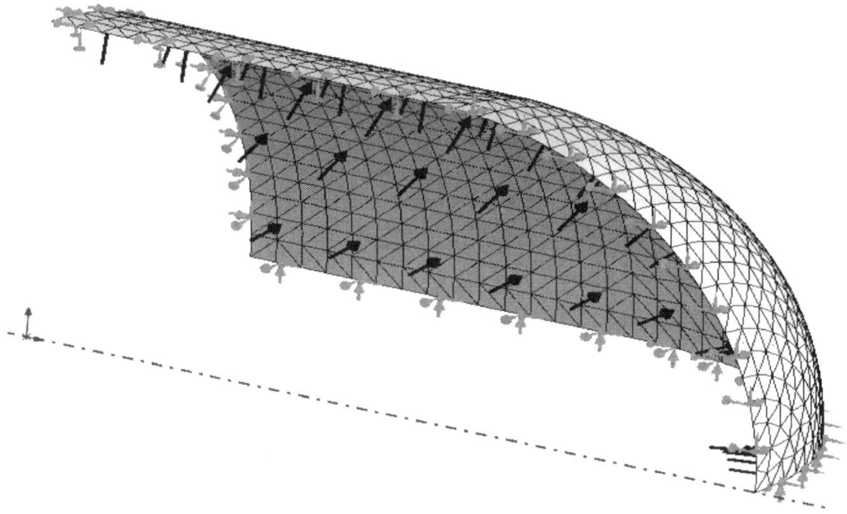

Figure 27 (b) – **Standard mesh** displayed on a shell model of the thin-wall pressure vessel. Notice that a **Standard mesh** is more orderly than the **Curvature based mesh**.

Recall the system default conventions adopted near the beginning of this example where the color orange denotes the "bottom" surface of shell elements. Assuming the inner surface of the model is considered as the "bottom," then this surface should appear orange. If it is not orange, then model surfaces must be reversed (i.e., "flipped").

4. Click to select the cylindrical surface on either the inside or outside of the model. Then, while pressing the **[Shift]** key, select the adjacent hemispherical surface.

5. Right-click the **Mesh** icon and from the pull-down menu select **Flip Shell Elements**. This action should reverse locations of the top and bottom surfaces.

6. As an alternate method, right-click the model name "**Thin Wall Pressure Vessel**" in the Simulation manager and select **Edit Definition…** The **Shell Definition** property manager opens.

7. In the **Type** dialogue box, select ⊙ **Full Preview**. Three colors appear on the model. Orange on the bottom (inside) surface, blue on the mid-surface, and light green on the top (outside) surface. It is also possible to "Flip" shell elements by checking ☑ **Flip shell top and bottom** in the **Type** dialogue box. Make sure the orange surface appears on the bottom (inside) before proceeding.

8. Click **[OK]** to close the **Shell Definition** property manager.

Solution

1. Right-click **Pressure Vessel-Shell Study (-Default-)** and from the pull-down menu select **Run**, or click the **Run This Study** (Run This Study) icon on the **Simulation** tab.

After the Solution is complete, three default plots, **Stress1 (-vonMises-)**, **Displacement1 (-Res disp-)**, and **Strain1 (-Equivalent-)** are listed below the **Results** folder.

Results Analysis

Because the emphasis of this example is on mastering basic techniques for working with shell elements, only stress results are examined below.

1. Right-click the **Results** folder and from the pull-down menu select **Define Stress Plot…** The **Stress Plot** property manager opens as seen in Fig. 28.

2. In the **Display** dialogue box, click to open the ▼ **Component** pull-down menu and select **P1: 1st Principal Stress**. Also verify that **Units** appear as **N/m^2**.

3. Also, in the **Display** dialogue box notice that the **Shell face** field indicates the stress plot is pre-set to display stresses on the **Top** (outside) surface of the model.

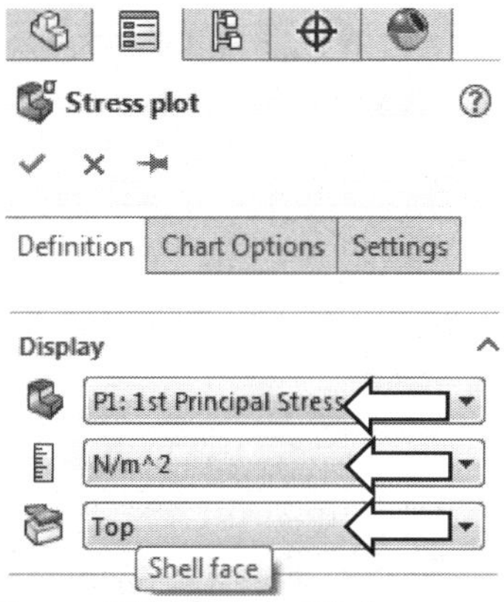

Figure 28 – **Stress Plot** property manager.

4. Click **[OK]** ✓ to close the **Stress Plot** property manager. A plot of first principal stress, like that shown in Fig. 29, appears in the graphics area. Also, **Stress2 (-1st principal-)** is listed beneath the **Results** folder.

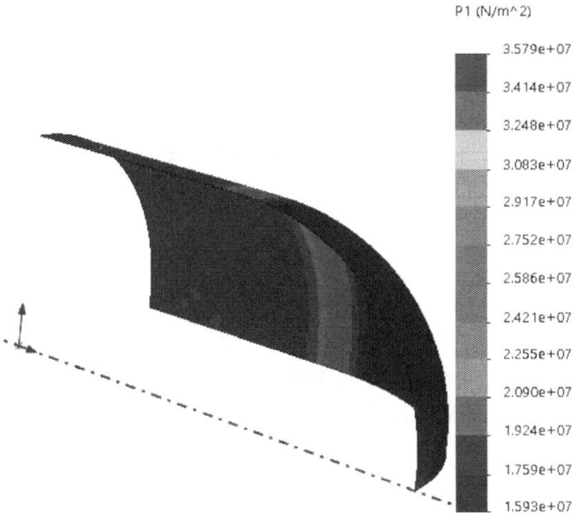

Figure 29 – First principal stress distribution over the TOP surface of the thin-wall pressure vessel. **Fixtures** and **External Loads** are hidden.

To easily identify these results as occurring on the top surface of the model, change the name of the **Stress2 (-1st principal-)** folder as follows.

5. At the bottom of the Simulation manager tree, click-*pause*-click on the name **Stress2 (-1st principal-)** and type **1st Principal Stress-TOP** and press **[Enter]**. This new name, shown in Fig. 30, identifies the current plot that appears in Fig. 29 above.

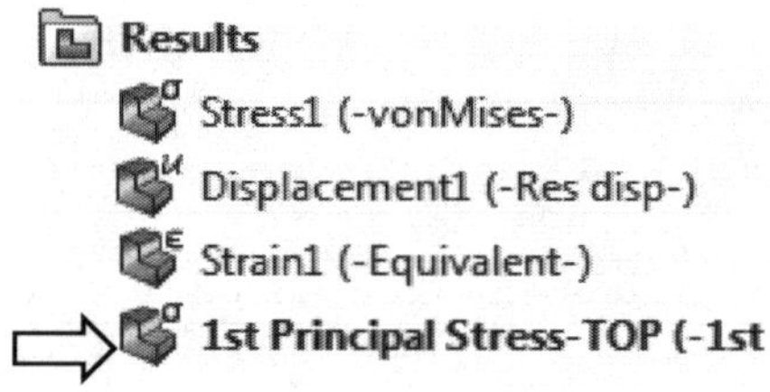

Figure 30 – Re-naming the stress plot using a descriptive name.

For convenience viewing results, turn off the **External Loads** and **Fixture** symbols. Try this on your own or use the following steps.

6. Right-click the **Fixtures** folder and from the pop-up menu select **Hide All**. Repeat this step for the **External Loads** folder.

7. If the model appears deformed, click the  **Deformed Result** icon located on the **Simulation** tab at top of screen. The model should now look like Fig. 29.

Unlike solid, tetrahedral elements for which stress variation is shown *through* the model, results plotted for *shell* elements correspond to stress on either the *top*, *membrane*, or the *bottom* surface. We next investigate the magnitude of σ_1 on the *bottom* model surface.

8. Repeat steps 1 to 7 above, except:
   - In step 3, select the **Bottom** shell surface to display σ_1.
   - In step 5, change the plot name to indicate **1st Principal Stress-BOTTOM**.

- Next, alternately double-click on **1st Principal Stress-TOP** and then **1st Principal Stress-BOTTOM** to display the plots. Compare the two *different* values of σ_1 on each surface. Note value changes in the stress legend.

Finally, a third option to view stress, displacement, and strain results on both surfaces of a 3D representation of a shell model is available. To use this option, proceed as follows.

9. Right-click the **Results** folder, and from the pull-down menu, select **Define Stress Plot…** The **Stress Plot** property manager opens.

10. In the **Display** dialogue box pull-down menu, select **P1: 1st Principal Stress**.

11. In the **Advanced Options** dialogue box, check ☑**Render shell thickness in 3D (slower)**. Note the **Shell Face** field is grayed out to indicate it is inactive.

12. Click **[OK]** ✓ to close the **Stress Plot** property.

13. Finally, right-click the **Stress4(-1st principal-)** and from the pull-down menu, select **Probe**. Clicking anywhere on the model yields an information "flag" that indicates stress values on both top *and* bottom surfaces. These two values also appear in the **Results** dialogue box of the **Probe Result** property manager.

14. Click **[OK]** ✓ to close the **Probe Result** property manager.

The user is free to select the most advantageous / meaningful display method.

Results Comparison (Tangential Stress = σ_1 on Cylindrical Surface)

To obtain a representative value of first principal stress, σ_1, on the cylindrical pressure vessel, an area well removed from restrained model edges and from the cylindrical to hemispherical head transition region is selected. Proceed as follows.

1. Double-click **1st Principal Stress-TOP (-1st principal-)** to display this plot.

2. Right-click **1st Principal Stress-TOP**, and from the pull-down menu, select **Probe**. The **Probe Result** property manager opens.

3. In the **Options** dialogue box, select ⊙**At location** and proceed to select three or four points removed from the transition region on the model as depicted in Fig. 31.

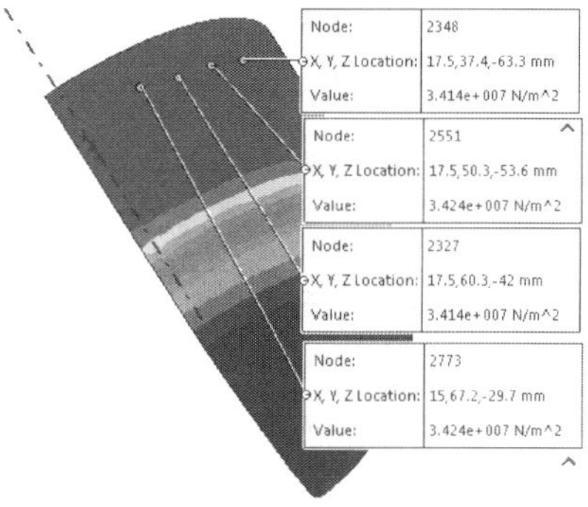

Figure 31 – Stress **Probe** on **Top** surface of cylindrical area.

4. Values will vary at points selected. For the three points selected in Fig. 31, the **Avg** value of stress is listed in the **Summary** dialogue box as σ_1 = 3.419e+007 N/m^2 (numbers will vary). Using this average value yields the following percent difference (rounded values used).

$$\%\ \text{difference} = \left[\frac{\text{FEA result} - \text{classical reesult}}{\text{FEA result}}\right]100 = \left[\frac{3.419\text{e}7 - 3.36\text{e}7}{3.419\text{e}7}\right]100 = 1.7\% \quad [3]$$

Equation [3] yields good agreement between classical and FEA results. Notice that it would *not* be appropriate to compare classical values with the maximum stress displayed on the model. Maximum stress is ignored because it typically occurs on a cylindrical edge where effects attributed to St. Venant's principle occur. You can quickly verify this statement by displaying ☑ **Show max annotation** on the **Chart Options** tab of the **Stress plot** property manager.

To further explore comparison of stress results, consider comparing the magnitude of tangential stress, $\sigma_1 = \sigma_t$, on the entire cylindrical *top and bottom surfaces*. Proceed as follows.

5. Right-click the **Stress4(-1st principal-)** and from the pull-down menu, select **Probe**. In the **Options** dialogue box of the **Probe Result** property manager, choose ⊙ **On selected entities**. This action clears all values from the model and from the property manager.

6. In the **Results** dialogue box the **Faces, Edges or Vertices** field is highlighted (light blue). Move the cursor onto the *cylindrical* section of the model and click to select it. **Face<1>** appears in the **Faces, Edges or Vertices** field.

7. Click to select both **Shell top face results** and **Shell bottom face results**.

8. Near the middle of the **Results** dialogue box, click the **[Update]** button, circled in Fig. 32. The table is automatically populated with stress magnitudes at all nodes on the cylindrical surface.

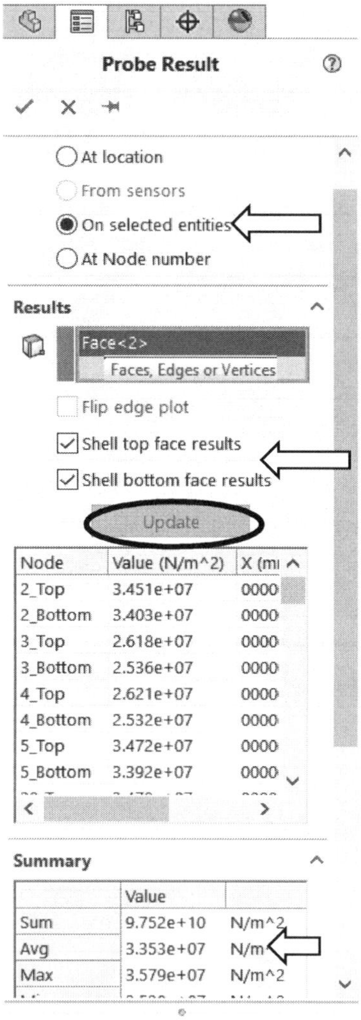

Figure 32 – **Probe Results** on the *entire* cylindrical surface of the pressure vessel.

9. In the **Summary** dialogue box, near bottom of the property manager, observe the average (**Avg**) value of stress $\sigma_1 = \sigma_t$ on this surface is 3.353e+007 N/m^2, in Fig. 32 (numbers may vary). Be aware that this value includes a portion of both higher (dark red) and lower (orange, yellow, and light green) stresses near the hemispherical to cylindrical transition region.

When compared to the same classical result used above, the following percent difference is obtained (rounded values used).

$$\%\ \text{difference} = \left[\frac{\text{FEA result} - \text{classical result}}{\text{FEA result}}\right]100 = \left[\frac{3.353e7 - 3.36e7}{3.353e7}\right]100 = 0.2\% \quad [4]$$

This result is also in good agreement with classical results but is more affected by stress values in the transition region.

10. Click **[OK]** ✓ to close the **Probe Result** property manager.

Other Meaningful Results Comparisons

Two additional comparisons would be useful to verify stress results for the thin wall pressure vessel analyzed using shell elements. Those comparisons include FEA results for longitudinal stress σ_ℓ in the cylindrical segment of the vessel and tangential stress in the hemispherical head, where -

$$\sigma'_{t(Hemispherical)} = \frac{1}{2}\sigma_{t(Tangential)} = \frac{1}{2}\sigma_1 \qquad [5]$$

Either of these stresses can be investigated using steps similar to those outlined above.

If, however, stress magnitudes on the hemispherical head are to be investigated, the following additional guidance is essential. Briefly zoom in on the hemispherical head and notice the more "blotchy" medium-blue and dark-blue appearance of this region. Because greater stress variation is observed on this surface, a larger number of **Probe** points should be selected when used to determine an *average* stress magnitude in this region.

Guidance for Determining Symmetry Fixtures

The key to determining **Fixtures** for *shell* or *solid* models that exhibit some symmetry is to begin by identifying edges of the model that satisfy the previously stated guideline, which is paraphrased below:

> "Every *surface* or *edge* that coincides with a plane of symmetry should be prevented from translating in the *normal direction* . . . "
> Note emphasis on the word "translating."

The following discussion attempts to clarify the meaning of the above statement. Once the *normal direction* is identified on a symmetrical model, then its **Translation** fixture can be selected and set equal to zero (0). Next, **Rotation** fixtures are selected by choosing the *other two* remaining **Fixtures** listed in the **Rotation** fixture dialogue box.

Because symmetry and its associated **Fixtures** can be puzzling to first time users, the following example is provided. Hopefully the example will clarify, using words and images, what might be confusing in the preceding paragraph.

EXAMPLE:
Figure 33 (a) shows a symmetrical vessel subject to zero internal pressure. Similarly, Fig. 33 (b) shows a deformed view of the same vessel when subject to an internal pressure (model deformation is exagerated). The dashed vertical line represents one plane of symmetry that divides the vessel into equal left and right halves. Also shown are three infinitesimally small stress elements of the type encountered in a basic mechanics of materials course (not to be confused with *finite elements*). Figure 33 (a) shows these elements located at a distance x to the left and right of a central element, which is located on the axis of symmetry represented by a dashed line.

Begin by considering the question: *"Why is <u>translation = 0</u> on a symmetrical surface or edge?"*

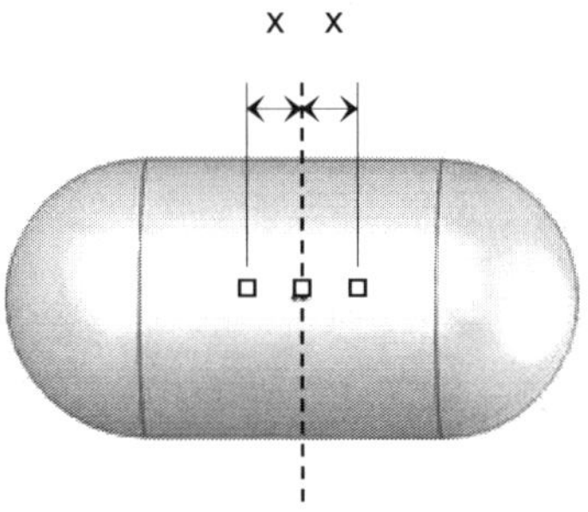

Figure 33 (a) – Undeformed pressure vessel.

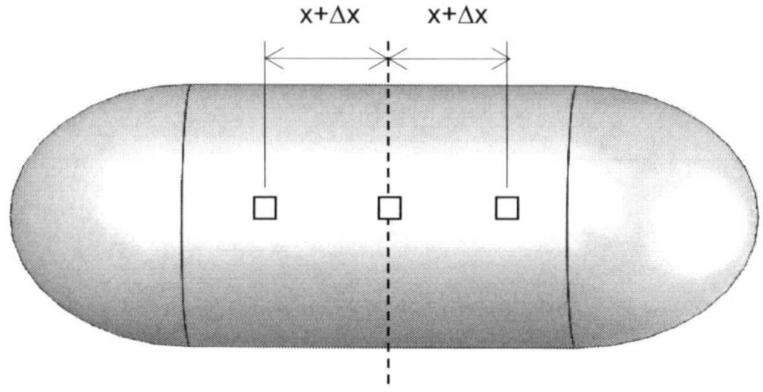

Figure 33 (b) – Deformed pressure vessel showing stress element *deformation* and *translation*.

After the vessel is pressurized, two things happen. First, *all elements change size* due to strain and the resulting stress. Second, stress elements to the left and right of the symmetry plane also undergo *translation* (Δx) due to deformation (elongation) of the pressure vessel. However, although the center element also deforms due to strain, it does *not* undergo translation because it is located *on* an axis of symmetry. This then is the reason why *translation* **Fixtures** are set equal to zero *normal* to a plane of symmetry.

The next question is: *"After the **Translation Fixture** is defined, how are **Rotation Fixtures*** defined?"

Refer to Figs. 21 and 22 repeated on the following page. The answer to the above question is quite simple. In Fig. 22 notice that **Radial**, **Circumferential**, and **Axial** fields appear in the same order from top to bottom in both the **Translations** and the **Rotation** dialogue boxes (see labels added to Fig. 22 repeated). Thus, whatever **Fixture** is set equal to zero in the **Translations** dialogue box (bottom field), the *other two* **Fixtures** are set equal to zero in the **Rotation** dialogue box (top two fields).

The above discussion focused only on **Fixtures** applied to edge **A** of the symmetrical model in Fig. 21 below. But, similar logic applies to edges **B**, **C**, **D**, and **E**.

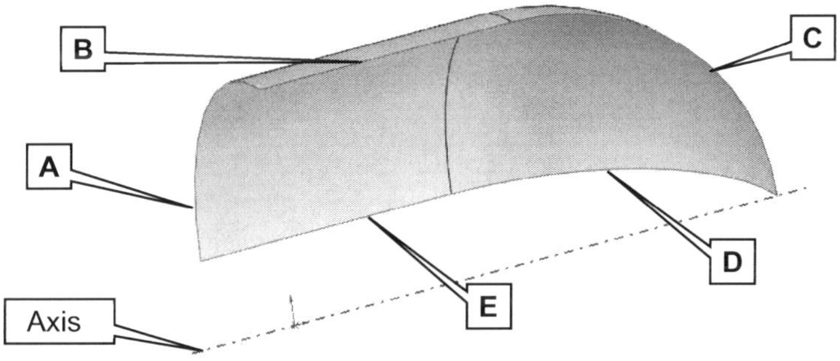

Figure 21 (repeated) - Identification of shell edges to which symmetry restraints are applied.

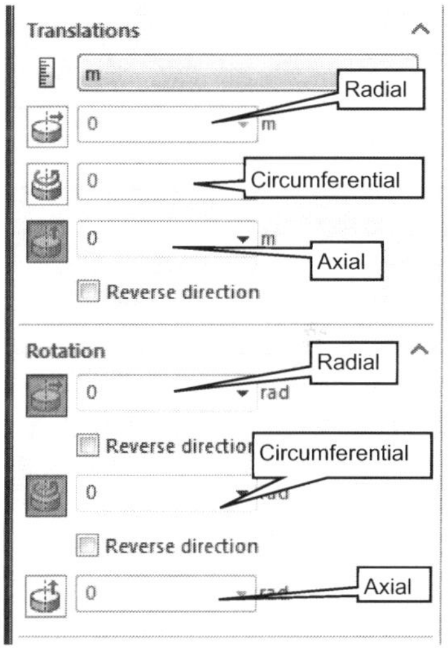

Figure 22 (repeated) - Displacements set to zero on model edge.

Although slightly more confusing for *translations* along symmetry edges **B**, **C**, **D**, and **E**, where circumferential **Fixtures** are set equal to zero in the **Translations** dialogue box, you will notice that the *other two* **Fixtures** are set equal to zero in the **Rotation** dialogue box as shown in Fig. 23 (not repeated here). Using concepts outlined above, think through the set of **Fixtures** applied to edges **B**, **C**, **D**, and **E**. HINT: Make sketches like Figs. 33 (a) and (b) corresponding to these edges to better understand how **Fixtures** were determined.

Application of Symmetry Fixtures

The curious user might have noticed the **Symmetry** option in the **Fixture** property manager and wondered why this **Fixture** was not applied to the Thin Wall Pressure Vessel example. Because this model demonstrates the presence of both geometric and load symmetry, it affords an excellent opportunity to examine the ease with which **Symmetry** fixtures can be applied. The use of **Symmetry** fixtures for this example is outlined next. Proceed as follows.

1. In the Simulation manager beneath the **Fixtures** folder, right-click **Reference Geometry-1 (:variable:)**, and in the pull-down menu click Delete... . In the pop-up **Simulation** window, select **[Yes]** to complete the deletion process.

2. Repeat step 1 for **Reference Geometry-2(:variable:)**. Observe that two warnings and are displayed in the Simulation manager tree because all **Fixtures** were removed from the model.

3. Right-click the **Fixtures** folder, and from the pull-down menu, select **Advanced Fixtures…** The **Fixture** property manager opens.

4. In the **Advanced(Use Reference Geometry)** dialogue box, click to select the **Symmetry** icon. The dialogue box name changes to **Advanced (Symmetry)** shown in Fig. 34.

5. Next, successively click to select *all five of the cut edges* on the model in any order and observe that "ghost images" of the model's symmetrical parts are displayed in the graphics area.

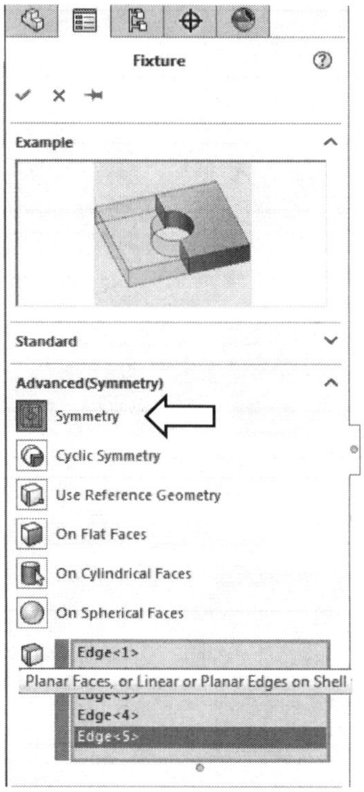

Figure 34 – Application of **Symmetry Fixture** to the 1/8 model.

6. Click **[OK]** ✓ to close the **Fixture** property manager.

7. Click either the **Run This Study** icon on the **Simulation** tab or right-click the study name, **Pressure Vessel Shell Study (-Default-)**, and from the pull-down menu, select **Run**.

Results of this analysis differ slightly from those found using the **Use Reference Geometry** approach. Differences of approximately 0.0023% result at random points selected on the cylindrical surface.

Closing Observations

1. SOLIDWORKS Simulation applies a linear interpolation across the model thickness when determining results (stress, displacement, or strain) on the **Top**, **Membrane** (middle), and **Bottom** surfaces of shell models.

2. Maximum stress magnitudes may occur on the **Bottom** (inside) or **Top** (outside) surface of shell elements depending upon part loading. This observation is valid for all thin *shell* models, not just for pressure vessels.

3. It is also possible to display shell stresses on the **Membrane** which is located between the **Top** and **Bottom** surfaces of the shell thickness. This option is available in the **Display** property manager of the **Stress Plot** property manager; its use was not demonstrated.

4. If geometric, restraint, material properties, and load symmetry exist for a model, then the **Symmetry Fixture** option can be used. More technically stated, the **Symmetry** restraint is intended for use *only in cases* where *true orthogonal symmetry* can be achieved by cutting the model using one, two, or three orthogonal (perpendicular) planes, resulting in 1/2, 1/4, or 1/8 of the whole model.

5. Either the simpler to use **Symmetry** fixture or the **Reference Geometry** fixture can be used for the symmetric example of this example. The more arduous **Reference Geometry** approach was introduced to enhance user competency for those cases where complete model symmetry might be lacking.

Log Out of the Current Analysis

This concludes analysis of a thin wall pressure vessel using *shell* elements. It is suggested that this file *not* be saved. Proceed as follows.

1. On the **Main Menu**, click **File** followed by choosing **Close**.

2. The **SOLIDWORKS** window in Fig. 34 opens and provides the options of either saving the current analysis or not. Select **[Don't Save]**.

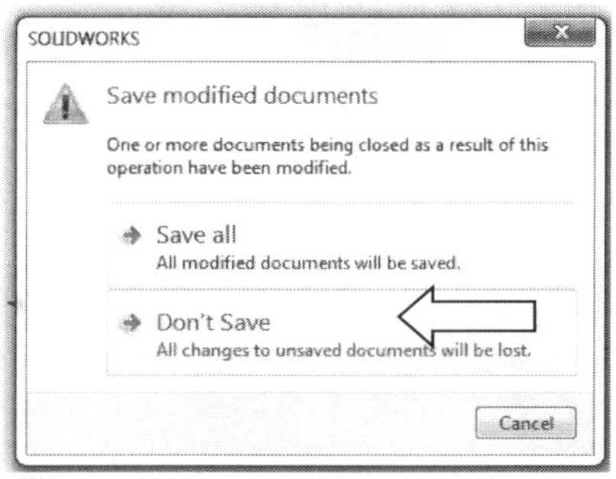

Figure 35 – **SOLIDWORKS** window prompts users to either save changes or not.

THICK WALL PRESSURE VESSEL

The second-half of this chapter explores analysis of a thick-wall pressure vessel. Thick-wall pressure vessels are found in many applications including high pressure piping, gun and cannon barrels, some hydraulic cylinders, and related uses. Thick-wall pressure vessels are classified as such in applications where wall thickness "t" exceeds $t > r_i/20$, where r_i = vessel inside radius. For these applications, assumptions related to thin-wall pressure vessels are no longer valid. Primary among these differences are (a) radial stress, which is neglected in thin-wall formulations, is known to vary through the wall thickness; and (b) tangential (a.k.a., hoop or circumferential) stress may vary significantly through the wall thickness. Much of thick-wall cylinder theory is also relevant to analysis of press and shrink fits, which are investigated in the next chapter.

Problem Statement

Thick-Wall Pressure Vessel

This example is based on a thick-wall cylindrical pressure vessel that is closed on one end, but attached to a rigid pipe connection at the opposite end as illustrated in Fig. 36. This vessel is made of Alloy Steel and is subject to an internal pressure P_i = 16.0 MPa and an external pressure that approximates standard atmospheric pressure P_o = 0.101 MPa. Cylinder dimensions necessary to apply classical stress equations are included in a partial view in Fig. 36. The goal is to determine tangential and radial stress variation through the cylindrical wall of this pressure vessel.

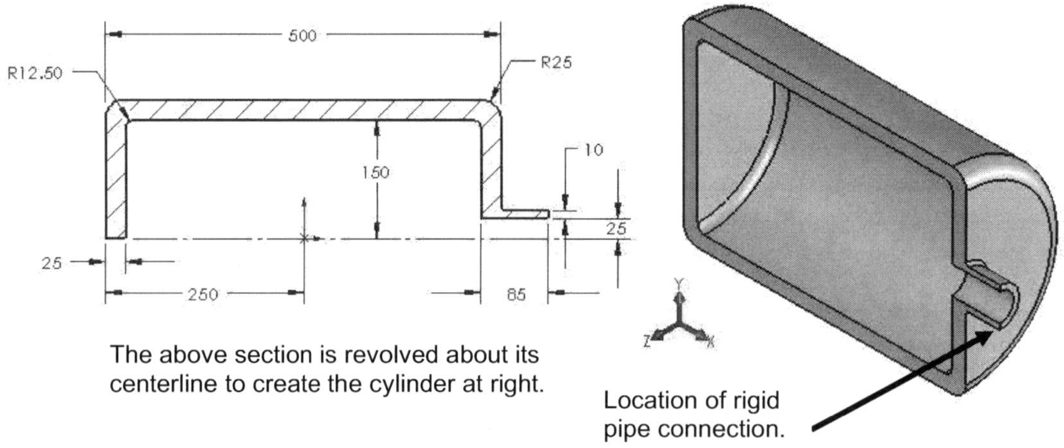

Figure 36 – Basic dimensions and geometry of a thick-wall pressure vessel.

1. *Skip to step 2 if SOLIDWORKS is already open.* Otherwise, open SOLIDWORKS by making the following selections. **Start>All Programs>SOLIDWORKS 2026** (or) Click the **SOLIDWORKS** icon on your screen.

2. In the SOLIDWORKS main menu, select **File > Open...** Then, open the file named **Thick Wall Pressure Vessel**.

Defining the Study

Because tetrahedral elements are used to create a solid model of the pressure vessel, the majority of procedural steps employed to create this study are familiar to users who have worked examples in the preceding chapters. However, all necessary steps are included below. This study again uses symmetry restraints, but of a different type, and also introduces new methods for viewing results.

1. On the **Simulation** tab click ▼ on the **New Study** icon and from the pull-down menu select **New Study**. Or, in the main menu, click **Simulation** and from the pull-down menu, select **Study...** The **Study** property manager opens.

2. In the **Name** field, type: **Thick Wall Pressure Vessel-YOUR NAME**.

3. Select a **Static** study and make sure the **Use 2D Simplification** is unchecked. We will review the **Use 2D Simplification** later this chapter.

4. Click **[OK]** ✓ to close the **Study** property manager.

Due to geometry differences (left and right ends of the model differ) and to introduce the concept of *rigid body* motion, a ½ model, rather than a $^1/_8$ model, is selected for the thick-wall example. Prior to commencing a finite element analysis, the model is defeatured; also, half of the model is suppressed. To demonstrate defeaturing, the small fillet at the pipe connection is selected to be removed. Proceed as follows. NOTE: It may be necessary to drag down the bottom of the SOLIDWORKS Feature manager tree to view the **Pipe Connector Fillet** and **Half-Model of Cylinder** referenced in steps 4 and 5.

5. At the bottom of the SOLIDWORKS Feature manager, right-click **Pipe Connector Fillet** and select the **Suppress** icon. This action removes the fillet at the junction between the cylinder and pipe joint in Fig. 37. Is this really necessary? On this simple model, probably not. Also, deleting it could *introduce* a significant stress concentration at this location. The fillet is only removed to remind users to defeature a model when appropriate.

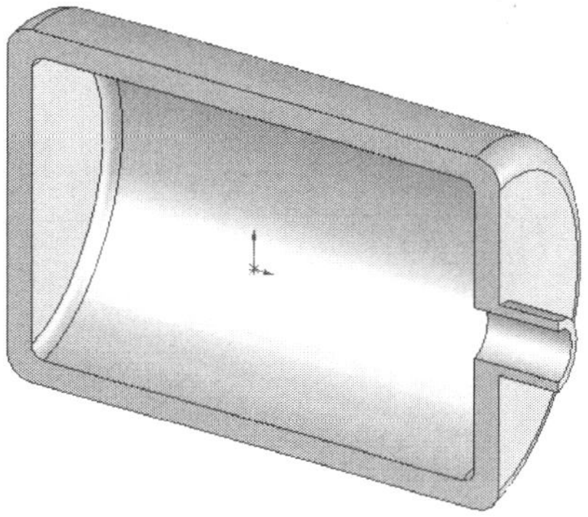

Figure 37 – Half-section of the thick-wall pressure vessel after defeaturing.

6. Also near the bottom of the SOLIDWORKS Feature manager, right-click **Half-Model of Cylinder**, and from the pop-up menu select the **Unsuppress** icon.

The model changes to a half-cylinder representation shown in Fig. 37. Notice how assigning descriptive names to folders facilitates identifying their function. Prior to renaming the **Half-Model of Cylinder** folder, its generic name was "Cut-Extrude2."

Assign Material Properties

1. Right-click the **Thick Wall Pressure Vessel** folder *(not the Study name)*, and from the pull-down menu, select **Apply/Edit Material…** The **Material** window opens.

2. Because users should be familiar with this window, on your own select **Alloy Steel (SS)**. Verify that units are set to **SI-N/m^2 (Pa)**, then click **[Apply]** followed by **[Close]**. A check "✓" appears on the **Thick Wall Pressure Vessel** folder and the material designation is listed adjacent to the part name.

Define Fixtures and External Loads

1. Right-click **Fixtures** and from the pull-down menu choose **Advanced Fixtures…** The **Fixture** property manager opens.

2. In the **Advanced Fixtures** dialog box, select the **Symmetry** icon. Next, select the cut surface highlighted in Fig. 38. **Face<1>** is listed in the **Planar Faces for Fixture** field and **Fixtures** *normal to the plane of symmetry* appear. As a reminder that symmetry is specified, a ghost image of the other half of the model also appears.

3. Click **[OK]** ✓ to close the **Fixture** property manager.

Restraint symbols appear on the model *normal* to the cut face. Restraints act in the Z-direction. Physically this means that these symmetry restraints permit axial displacements (along the length of the cylinder) and radial displacements (change of cylinder diameter) when the cylinder is subject to internal or external pressure. These displacements are consistent with the half-model selected. At present, however, both X and Y *rigid body* displacements of the model are still possible because the model currently is not restrained in the X, Y directions.

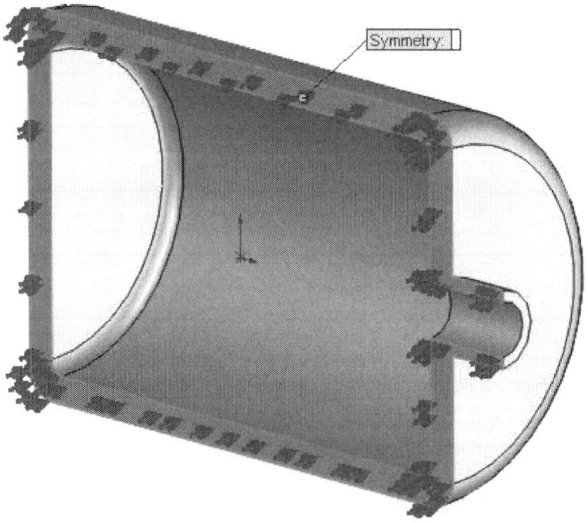

Figure 38 – Half-model of pressure vessel with symmetry restraints applied in the Z-direction.

Because symmetry fixtures only restrain this solid model in the Z-direction, it is necessary to apply additional fixtures in the X and Y directions to prevent what is called "rigid body" motion (Chapter 2, p 2-33). The type of restraints selected depends heavily upon the nature of actual operating conditions. Because the pipe connection on right end of the cylinder is considered attached to a rigid (i.e., immovable) pipe, not shown, the remaining restraints are applied at that location. Fortunately, this immovable restraint does not interfere with finite element results in the thick-wall portion of the cylinder.

Analysis Insight

Although not part of this example, consider the following two scenarios:

Scenario #1 - A different set of fixtures results if, in addition to being attached to a rigid pipe at its right end, the left end of the cylinder is mounted against a fixed surface (e.g., an immovable wall or support bracket). That additional restraint would alter stress distribution within the cylinder because longitudinal deformation of the model would then be prevented at both ends.

Scenario #2 - Consider an additional analysis scenario in which the model, restrained as described in the preceding paragraph, is subsequently subjected to a significant temperature change. This condition would add temperature induced deformation (expansion or contraction) associated with the coefficient of thermal expansion for the model material. This scenario would require a separate thermal analysis to determine deformations and stresses caused by temperature change.

Continue to define remaining restraints and loads in the following steps.

4. Right click the **Fixtures** folder and from the pull-down menu select **Fixed Geometry…** The **Fixture** property manager opens.

5. Within the **Standard (Fixed Geometry)** dialogue box, select **Fixed Geometry** (if not already selected).

6. Zoom in on the right-end of the pipe extension, shown in Fig. 39, and click to select the cut surface. Immovable restraint symbols (shown dark) in the X, Y, and Z directions are added to the model and **Face<1>** appears in the **Faces, Edges, Vertices for Fixture** dialogue box.

7. Click **[OK]** ✓ to close the **Fixture** property manager. The model is now restrained in all directions.

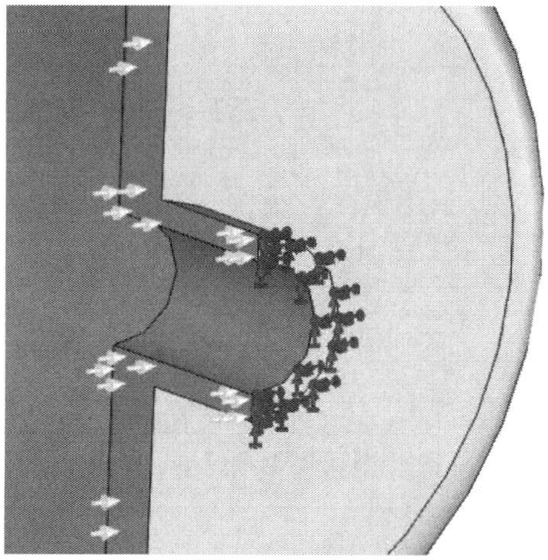

Figure 39 – A **Fixed/Immovable** restraint is added to the attachment surface associated with a rigid pipe connection.

The next step is to apply an internal pressure P_i = 16.0 MPa to all internal surfaces of the pressure vessel. Proceed as follows.

8. Right-click **External Loads** and from the pull-down menu select **Pressure...** The **Pressure** property manager opens.

9. In the **Type** dialogue box, verify that ⦿**Normal to selected face** is chosen.

10. The **Faces for Pressure** field is highlighted (light blue) to indicate it is active and awaiting user input.

11. Move the cursor onto the model and click to select *all interior* surfaces (both cylinder ends, both internal fillets, the cylindrical surface of the cylinder, and inside the pipe extension). A total of six faces **(Face<1>, Face <2>, ... Face<6>)** should be listed in the **Faces for Pressure** field.

12. Beneath **Pressure Value**, verify that **Units** are set to **N/m^2** and type **16.0e6** in the **Pressure Value** field.

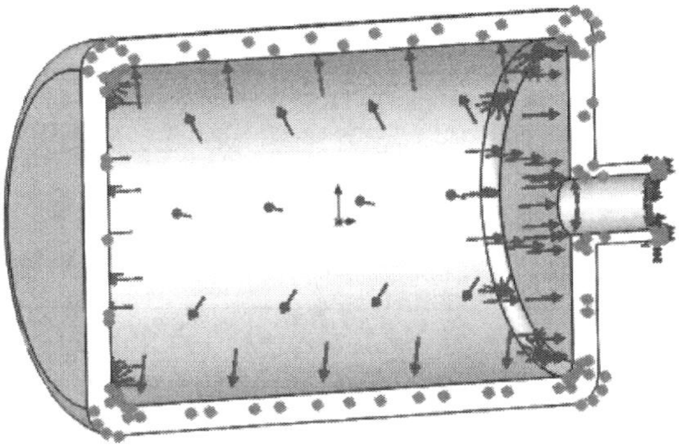

Figure 40 – Internal pressure applied to six faces within the thick-wall pressure vessel.

13. Click **[OK]** ✓ to close the **Pressure** property manager. The model should appear as shown in Fig. 40.

Next apply atmospheric pressure P_o = 0.101 MPa to all external surfaces of the model. Try this on your own or follow steps below.

14. Repeat steps 8 through 13 with the following two exceptions.

    a. In step 11, select *all exterior* surfaces. Once again, a total of six faces should be chosen.

    b. In step 12, type **0.101e6** N/m^2 in the **Pressure Value** field.

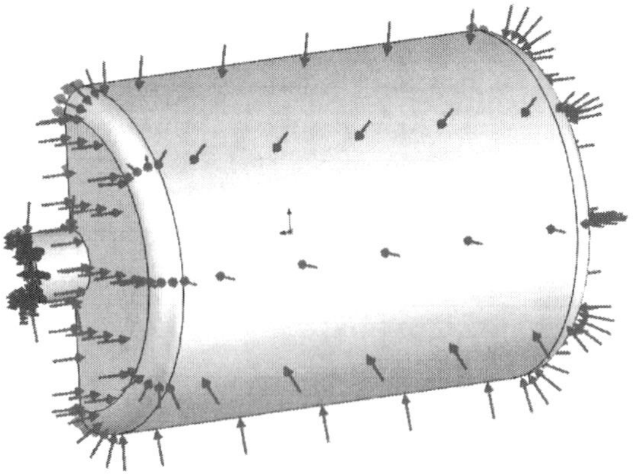

Figure 41 – Atmospheric pressure applied to exterior of the thick-wall pressure vessel.

The exterior pressure vessel surface should now appear as shown in Fig. 41.

Create a Duplicate Study

Because it is desired to model the thick-wall pressure vessel with two different meshes, a duplicate study is created *before* the model is meshed. Either duplicate the study on your own or follow steps 1 through 3 outlined below.

1. Beneath the graphics area, right-click the **Thick Wall Pressure Vessel-YOUR NAME** Study *tab*, and from the pop-up menu, select **Copy Study**. The **Copy Study** window opens.

2. In the **Study name:** field, replace the existing name by typing **Thick Wall Pressure Vessel-FINE Mesh**.

3. Click **[OK]** ✓ to close the **Copy Study** window.

Mesh the Model – Default Size Standard Mesh

1. Beneath the graphics area of the screen, select the *tab* labeled **Thick Wall Pressure Vessel-YOUR NAME** to return to the original Study.

2. Right-click the **Mesh** folder and from the pull-down menu select **Create Mesh…** The **Mesh** property manager opens.

Because an *orderly* mesh is desired for this analysis, a **Standard Mesh,** rather than the system default **Curvature based mesh**, is used. Proceed as follows.

3. In the **Mesh Density** dialogue box accept the default mesh size (pointer located at the middle of the **Coarse** to **Fine** slider-scale).

4. Open the ☑ **Mesh Parameters** dialogue box and select ⊙ **Standard Mesh**. Also verify that **Units** are set to **mm**.
   This selection results in creation of an orderly mesh on the model.

5. Click **[OK]** ✓ to close the **Mesh** property manager.

The meshed model along with its boundary conditions is shown in Fig. 42.

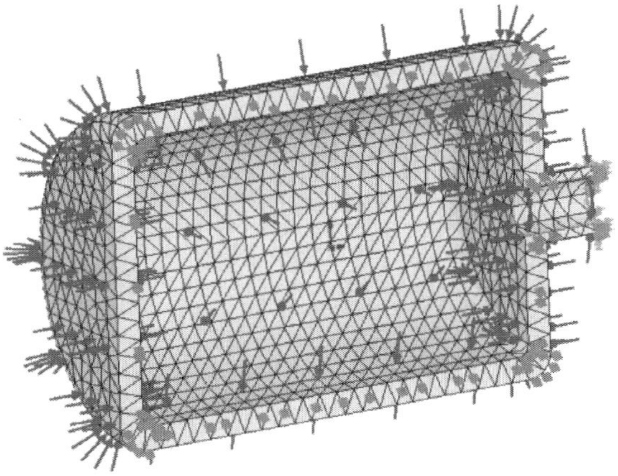

Figure 42 – Default size **Standard Mesh** applied to the thick-wall pressure vessel.

Analysis Insight

Examination of mesh size on the *cut surface* of the pressure vessel in Fig. 42 reveals that a *single* element spans the entire wall thickness. However, near the beginning of this chapter, a general guideline for determining when *solid* elements can be used stated that, "…the minimum number of elements recommended across the thickness of a part (i.e., across the part's minimum dimension) should be *at least two elements.*"

Mesh the Model – Fine Size Standard Mesh

Given the guideline in the **Analysis Insight** above, it is appropriate to reduce element size so that at least two elements span the pressure vessel wall thickness. This change is easily made as follows.

1. Beneath the graphics area of the screen, click to select the **Thick Wall Pressure Vessel-FINE Mesh** Study *tab.* This action switches to the duplicate Study.

2. Right-click the **Mesh** folder and from the pull-down menu select **Create Mesh…** The **Mesh** property manager opens

3. Check ✓ to open the ☑ **Mesh Parameters** dialogue box and select a ⊙ **Standard Mesh**. Also verify that **Units** are set to **mm**.

4. In the **Mesh Density** dialogue box, click-and-*drag* the pointer, on the **Mesh Factor** slider-scale, from its default mid-range position to the **Fine** position.

5. Click **[OK]** ✓ to close the **Mesh** property manager and initiate re-meshing the model. Note the increased time required to mesh the model. The model now appears as shown in Fig. 43 with two elements across the cylinder wall thickness. NOTE: Exterior pressure symbols are hidden to reduce clutter on Fig. 43.

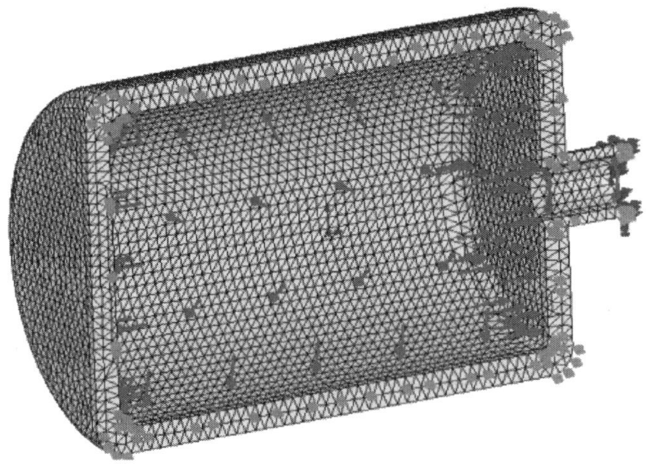

Figure 43 – Pressure vessel showing mesh size reduced to half of the default mesh size so at least two elements span the cylinder wall thickness.

Analysis Insight

Based on the stress concentration example of Chapter 3, where variation of mesh size was investigated, it was found that moving the pointer on the **Mesh Factor** slider-scale to either the left or right extreme position had the effect of doubling or halving the default mesh size.

The default mesh size for the model shown in Fig. 42 is **20.06035261 mm**. Thus, changing element size to **Fine** reduces its nominal size to **10.0301763 mm**, or exactly half the previous size. As a consequence, two elements now span the thick-wall portion of the pressure vessel as illustrated in Fig. 43 and on your screen.

Although two elements span the thick-wall portion of the model, only one element spans the thickness in the pipe connector neck. Zoom in to examine the neck area. This outcome is considered acceptable because tangential and radial stresses in the thick-wall portion of the pressure vessel are of primary importance in this study.

When compared to the original model, however, a dramatic increase in the number of nodes and elements is observed for the fine mesh model. These changes are summarized in Table 1.

Aside:

The default mesh size would yield adequate results for this model. However, because stress through the cylindrical wall thickness is to be examined in greater detail, the additional nodes and elements will prove helpful.

Table 1 – Comparison of Finite Element Model Size

	Original Model (Default Mesh Size)	Revised Model (Fine Mesh Size)	Increase in Model Complexity
No. of Nodes	16,132	88,246	Approx. 5.5 times larger
No. of Elements	9,399	56,002	Approx. 6 times larger

In this instance, following the general guideline, which suggests at least two solid elements across a part's minimum thickness, results in a significant increase in mesh density with a corresponding increase in solution time. This is a logical cause-and-effect consequence of changing global mesh size.

Solution

After defining material properties, fixtures, loads, and a mesh, the thick-wall model Study is ready to be solved as outlined below.

1. Click the **Run This Study** Run This Study icon on the **Simulation** toolbar. Solution time for the **Fine** mesh is only slightly longer. To view actual "run time" at the end of the Solution, right-click the **Results** folder and from the pop-up menu select **Solver Messages…** In the **Solver Message** window, the **Total solution time** is listed as **00:00:15** seconds (more or less). Click **[OK]** to close the **Solver Message** window.

2. Computed results, in the form of plots, are listed beneath the **Results** folder. Notice that plots contained in these folders revert to the system default plots.

Results Analysis

Displacement Analysis

To gain some insight into deformation of the thick-wall pressure vessel subject to internal and external pressures, attention is first directed to the **Displacement1 (-Res disp-)** plot.

1. Right-click the **Displacement1 (-Res disp-)** folder, and from the pull-down menu select **Show**. A displacement plot of the model is shown in Fig. 44.

2. *If* the pressure vessel does not appear deformed, click the **Deformed Result** icon in the Simulation toolbar.

3. In the Simulation manager tree, right-click **Fixtures**, and from the pull-down menu select **Hide All**. This action hides all restraints acting on the model.

4. Repeat step 4 for the **External Loads** folder.

5. Orient the model in a front view.

6. To compare the deformed and undeformed model shapes, right-click **Displacement1 (Res-disp)** and from the pull-down menu select **Settings…** The **Displacement Plot** property manager opens and the **Settings** tab is selected.

7. In the **Deformed Plot Options** dialogue box, check ☑ **Superimpose model on the deformed shape** and drag the **Transparency:** slider to the left to "**0**." If the un-deformed shape is not shown in *gray*, click **[OK]** ✓ to close **Displacement Plot** property manager and then toggle (i.e., alternately click) the **Deformed Result** icon located on the **Simulation** toolbar.

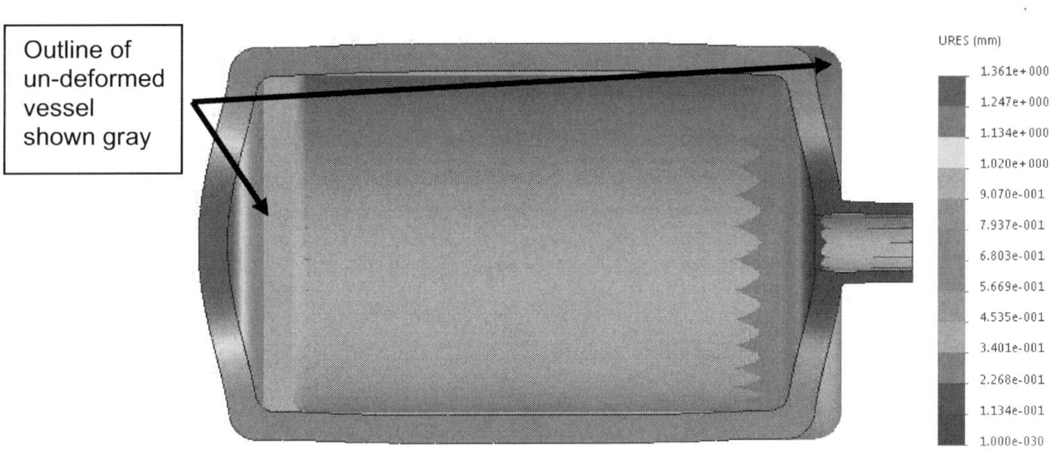

Figure 44 – Image of the model with symmetry and pressure boundary conditions "hidden." **Fixtures** are also hidden. The un-deformed model shape is superimposed on the image.

A comparison of the displacement plot (color image) with the un-deformed shape (gray image) of the pressure vessel reveals the following, common sense, observations.

a. All axial displacements are *away* from the immovable pipe-end.

b. Bulging of both the left and right ends of the model contributes to longitudinal (axial) deformation *away* from the immovable end.

c. Longitudinal deformation (axial stretch) of the cylindrical section also contributes to overall axial deformation.

d. Slight radial deformation (bulging) of cylindrical walls is observed.

e. Virtually zero displacement occurs in the pipe connection.

8. Return to the **Displacement Plot** property manager and clear the check mark from ☐ **Superimpose model on the deformed shape**; then Click **[OK]** ✓.

Analysis Insight

Taking into account the fact that displacements depicted in Figs. 44 and 45 are greatly exaggerated, approximately 41.16 times larger than actual (see bottom line of text on the plot title), briefly consider how different boundary conditions (such as supports or a fixed wall at the left-end of the pressure vessel) described in an earlier **Analysis Insight** section, would impact results of the current example.

The importance of correct boundary conditions (i.e., loads and fixtures) on finite element analysis results cannot be overemphasized!

Von Mises Stress Analysis

The next topic for investigation is interpretation of stresses occurring within the model.

1. Double-click the **Stress1 (-vonMises-)** folder to display the plot shown in Fig. 45.

Figure 45 – Regions of high vonMises stress on the thick-wall pressure vessel model.

Regions of high vonMises stress at fillet radii on both ends of the cylinder and in the vicinity of the pipe-to-cylinder connection are circled on Fig. 45. All von Mises stress magnitudes are less than the yield strength listed beneath the color-coded stress chart.

Tangential Stress Analysis

The next focus of this study is on tangential and radial stress distributions typically associated with analysis of pressurized thick-wall cylinders. However, before examining stress plots, it is helpful to have some expectation of magnitudes associated with these two stresses. Therefore, solutions based on Lame's equations for values of tangential and radial stresses at both the inside and outside surfaces of a thick-wall cylinder are included below.

Tangential stress at outside surface:

$$(\sigma_t)_o = \frac{p_i r_i^2 - p_o r_o^2 - r_i^2 \cancel{r_o^2}(p_o - p_i)/\cancel{r_o^2}}{r_o^2 - r_i^2}$$

$$= \frac{16.0e6(0.15)^2 - 0.101e6(0.175)^2 - (0.15)^2(0.101e6 - 16.0e6)}{(0.175)^2 - (0.15)^2} = 87.9 \text{ Mpa} \qquad [6]$$

Tangential stress at inside surface:

$$(\sigma_t)_i = \frac{p_i r_i^2 - p_o r_o^2 - \cancel{r_i^2} r_0^2 (p_o - p_i)/\cancel{r_i^2}}{r_o^2 - r_i^2}$$

$$= \frac{16.0e6(0.15)^2 - 0.101e6(0.175)^2 - (0.175)^2(0.101e6 - 16.0e6)}{(0.175)^2 - (0.15)^2} = 103.8 \text{ Mpa} \qquad [7]$$

Radial stress at inside surface:

$$(\sigma_r)_i = \frac{p_i r_i^2 - p_o r_o^2 + \cancel{r_i^2} r_0^2 (p_o - p_i)/\cancel{r_i^2}}{r_o^2 - r_i^2} = \frac{p_i r_i^2 - \cancel{p_o r_o^2} + \cancel{p_o r_o^2} - p_i r_o^2}{r_o^2 - r_i^2}$$

$$= \frac{-p_i \cancel{(r_o^2 - r_i^2)}}{\cancel{(r_o^2 - r_i^2)}} = -p_i = -16.0 \text{ Mpa} = \text{ (internal pressure)} \qquad [8]$$

Radial stress at outside surface:

$$(\sigma_r)_o = \frac{p_i r_i^2 - p_o r_o^2 + r_i^2 \cancel{r_0^2} (p_o - p_i)/\cancel{r_o^2}}{r_o^2 - r_i^2} = \frac{\cancel{p_i r_i^2} - p_o r_o^2 + p_o r_i^2 - \cancel{p_i r_i^2}}{r_o^2 - r_i^2}$$

$$= \frac{-p_o \cancel{(r_o^2 - r_i^2)}}{\cancel{(r_o^2 - r_i^2)}} = -p_o = -0.101 \text{ MPa} = \text{ (external pressure)} \qquad [9]$$

So that we can learn more about how to use the software to our advantage, two alternative ways of viewing these results in SOLIDWORKS Simulation are investigated on the following pages. We begin with what might be considered the most intuitive method of viewing stress results and then proceed to a second method that makes use of the *Section Clipping* capability of the software. Begin by adding a plot of first principal stress within the **Results** folder. Try this on your own or follow the steps outlined below.

NOTE: If a plot of ***Stress2 (-1st principal-)*** *already appears beneath the* ***Results*** *folder, then verify that* ***Units*** *are displayed as* ***N/m^2*** *and resume reading at the paragraph after step 4 on the next page.* Otherwise create a plot of **1st principal stress** as outlined in steps 1 through 4 below.

1. Right-click the **Results** folder, and from the pull-down menu, select  **Define Stress Plot…** The **Stress Plot** property manager opens.

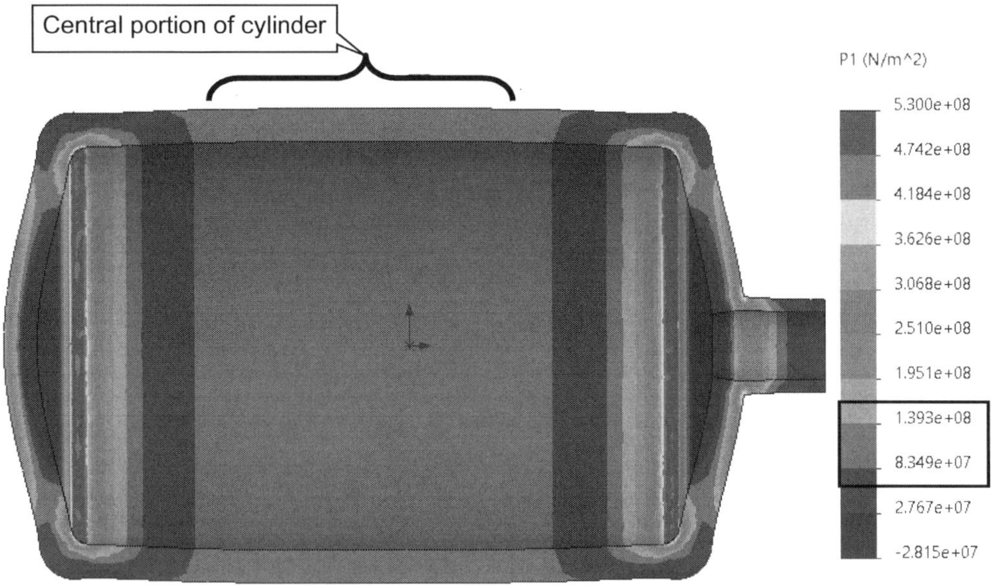

Figure 46 – Plot of 1st principal stress distribution throughout the thick-wall pressure vessel.

2. In the **Display** dialogue box, click ▼ to open the **Component** pull-down menu and from the list of available stresses select **P1: 1st Principal Stress**.

3. Verify that **Units** are set to **N/m^2**.

4. Click **[OK]** ✓ to close the **Stress plot** property manager.

Figure 46 shows a front view of 1st principal stress distribution (σ_1) throughout the model. Once again observe regions of high stress at both end fillets where the cylinder and flat ends join. Unfortunately, the figure above does not provide good delineation of stress variation through the central, thick-wall portion of the cylinder labeled in Fig. 46. That is to say, the mid-section of the cylinder is a fairly uniform shade of medium blue.

Analysis Insight

Regions of high principal stress and maximum vonMises stress are typically most important to a designer whose focus is on product safety. However, because a primary objective of this example is to investigate stresses associated with thick-wall pressure vessel theory and to investigate different ways to display those results in SOLIDWORKS Simulation, the following section describes how better to examine these stresses while simultaneously discovering additional software plotting capabilities.

Adjusting Stress Magnitude Display Parameters

A quick review of previous calculations for tangential stress variation from the inside to the outside cylindrical surfaces of the model, equations [6] and [7] above, reveals:

Tangential stress at inside: $(\sigma_t)_i = 103.8$ MPa
Tangential stress at outside: $(\sigma_t)_o = 87.9$ MPa

Comparing the above values with the range of 1st principal stress magnitudes displayed in the color-coded stress legend (currently displayed on your screen) reveals that these stresses occupy only a small portion of the full range of stress values displayed on the model; refer to the boxed portion of the stress legend in Fig. 46. Thus, if it is desired to verify values of 1st principal stress between 87.9 MPa to 103.8 MPa, in the cylinder wall, then the stress display can be adjusted to bracket these stress values. The following steps outline one procedure to accomplish this.

1. In the Simulation manager, right-click the **Stress2 (-1st principal-)** and from the pull-down menu select **Chart Options…** The **Stress plot** property manager opens to the **Chart Options** tab which is partially shown in Fig. 47.

2. Within the **Display Options** dialogue box, clear the "✓" from both ☐ **Automatically defined maximum value** and ☐ **Automatically defined minimum value.** This provides a means of setting user defined minimum and maximum bounds for stress magnitudes to be displayed.

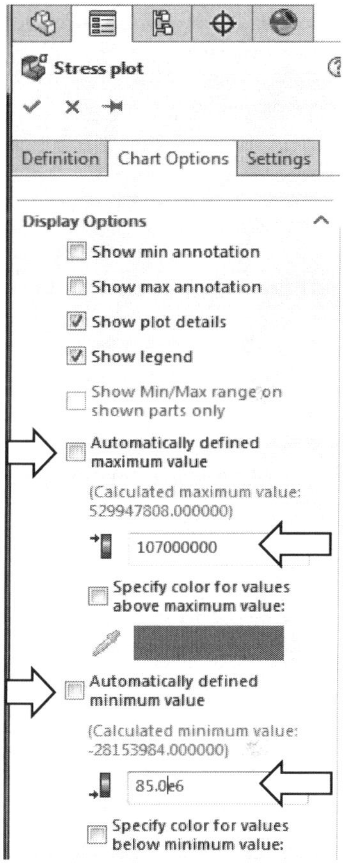

Figure 47 – Controlling the range of stresses displayed using the **Defined** option.

3. In the upper **[Max]** stress field, shown in Fig. 47, type **107.0e6**, which is slightly higher than the *maximum* 1st principal stress value of $(\sigma_t)_i = 103.8$ MPa expected at the inside surface of the cylinder.

4. Similarly, in the bottom **[Min]** stress field, type **85.0e6**, which is slightly lower than the *minimum* 1st principal stress value of $(\sigma_t)_o = 87.9$ MPa expected at the outside surface.

5. Click **[OK]** ✓ to close the **Stress plot** property manager. Figure 48 (a) displays 1st principal stress magnitudes throughout the model using values cited above.

6. Next, zoom-in on the boxed region, shown in Fig. 48 (a), to obtain a close-up view of stress variation through the cylinder wall as illustrated by the multiple color fringes in Fig. 48 (b). Notice that the mid-section of the cylinder is well removed from effects of end-conditions cau … cylinder.

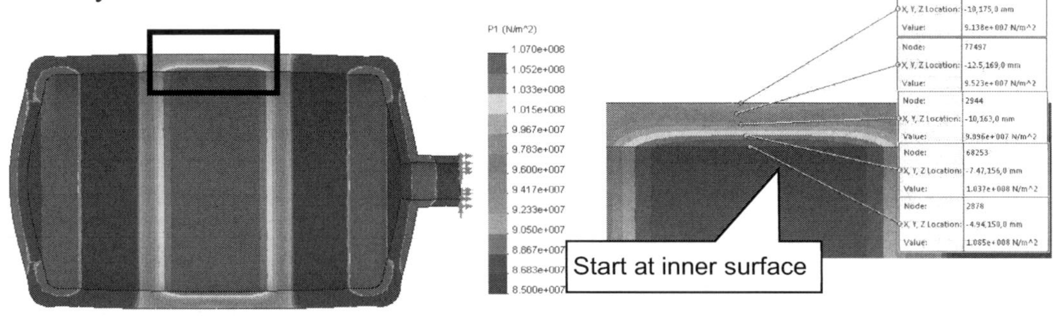

(a) (b)

Figure 48 – (a) 1st principal stress plot after magnitudes are restricted to the range: 85.0 MPa < σ_1 < 107.0 MPa; (b) close-up of tangential stress distribution (σ_1) through the thick-wall.

Next, the **Probe** feature is used to determine actual values of 1st principal stress at various nodes across the wall thickness.

7. Right-click **Stress2 (-1st principal-)** and from the pull-down menu select **Probe**. The **Probe Result** property manager opens as shown in Fig. 49 (a). *Initially no values appear in the table.*

8. Begin at the inside of the cylinder wall, as near as possible to the mid-section of the cylinder; see "**START**" label on Fig. 48 (b). Then successively click and move the cursor slightly upward (moving in as straight a line as possible) and repeat until five node points are selected across the wall thickness. Stress values at each node point are simultaneously displayed on the model [also shown in Fig. 48 (b)] and in the **Results** dialogue box, Fig. 49 (a). *If difficulty selecting nodes is experienced, see the **Aside** section below.*

Aside:

If difficulty is experienced selecting the *unseen* nodes, temporarily close the **Probe Result** property manager by clicking ✖ and turn "on" the mesh display as follows.

a. Right-click **Stress2 (-1st principal-)** and from the pull-down menu select **Settings…**

b. Within the **Settings** tab, click ▼ to open the pull-down menu in the **Boundary Options** dialogue box and select **Mesh**. Click **[OK]** ✓.

A mesh displayed on the model should facilitate selecting corner *and* mid-side nodes on each element across the wall thickness. Repeat steps 7 and 8 with the mesh shown.

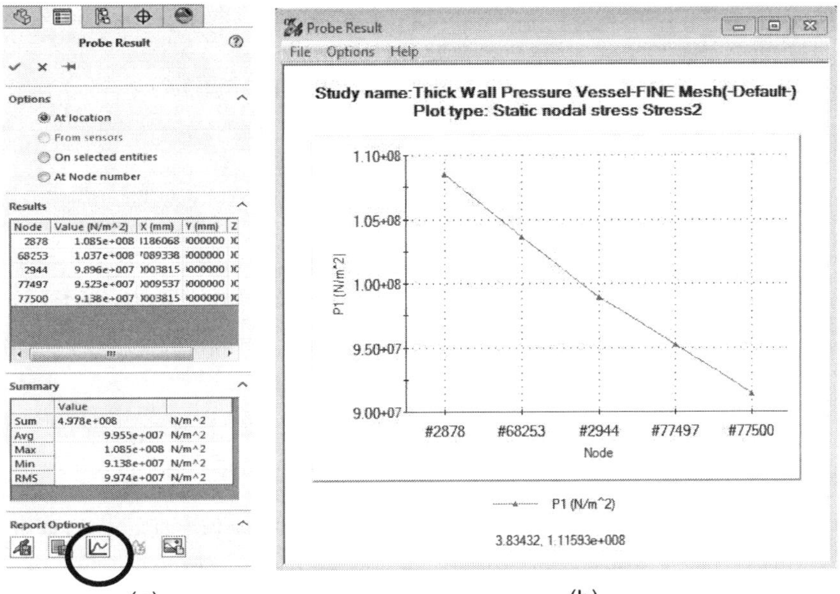

(a) (b)

Figure 49– (a) **Probe** window displays values of $\sigma_1 = \sigma_t$ at node locations across the cylinder thick-wall; (b) the **Probe Result** window shows a graph of tangential stress variation from the inside surface (high stress) to the outside surface (lower stress) of the thick-wall pressure vessel.

9. After using the **Probe** feature to select nodes, click the **[Plot]** button (circled in Fig. 49 (a) at bottom of the **Probe Result** property manager) to display a graph of tangential stress variation through the wall thickness as shown in Fig. 49 (b). Note the addition of a descriptive title, including your name, and axis labels.

10. After examining the graph, click ☒ to close the **Probe Result** graph.

11. Click **[OK]** ✓ to close the **Probe Result** property manager.

12. If the mesh is still displayed on the model, right-click **Stress2 (-1st principal-)** and from the pull-down menu select **Settings…** In the **Boundary Options** dialogue box, open the pull-down menu and select **Model.**

13. Click **[OK]** ✓ to close the **Settings** property manager.

A quick comparison of classical results found using Lame's equations, [6] and [7] above, and finite element results for tangential stress magnitudes at the inside and outside wall surfaces yields the following.

For tangential stress at the inside surface; see Fig.48 (a):

$$\% \text{ difference} = \left[\frac{\text{FEA result} - \text{classical result}}{\text{FEA result}}\right] 100 = \left[\frac{108.5e6 - 103.8e6}{108.5e6}\right] 100 = 4.3\% \quad [10]$$

Tangential stress at the outside wall surface (see Fig.48 (a)):

$$\% \text{ difference} = \left[\frac{\text{FEA result} - \text{classical result}}{\text{FEA result}}\right] 100 = \left[\frac{91.38e6 - 87.9e6}{91.38e6}\right] 100 = 3.8\% \quad [11]$$

Both these percent difference values are low enough that the analyst should have confidence in the finite element analysis results.

This concludes examination of tangential stress variation through the cylinder wall by conventional methods. The next section examines an alternate means of viewing these same results by using **Section Clipping** plots.

Using Section Clipping to Observe Stress Results

Use of *Section Clipping* is introduced in this section. Section plots are used where it is desirable to view stresses at locations *interior* to a solid model. Possible uses include stress in a complex assembly or at locations otherwise obscured from view. Steps below outline use of *Section Clipping* at various sections within the pressure vessel.

1. If the previous close-up view of the pressure vessel wall, appearing in Fig. 48 (b) remains on the screen, use the **Zoom to Fit** icon 🔍 to restore the graphic display to a full image of the model. Then click the **Trimetric** view icon to orient the model in a view like that shown in Fig. 50.

2. Activate *Section Clipping* by right-clicking **Stress2 (-1st principal-)** and from the pull-down menu select **Section Clipping…** The **Section** property manager opens as shown in Fig. 51.

3. In the **Section1** dialogue box, notice that **Front Plane** is selected as the default viewing plane. Also, the **Distance** field, located immediately below **Front Plane** in Fig. 51, is set at **0.00 mm**, thereby indicating that the section view is currently displayed *on* the front surface of the model.

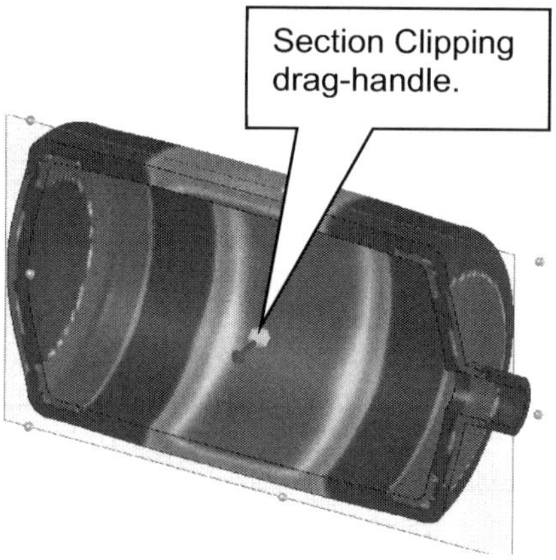

Figure 50 – Trimetric view of model showing 1st principal stress and the **Section Clipping** drag-handle.

4. In the **Options** dialogue box, clear the "✓" from ☐ **Show contour on the uncut portion of the model**. Immediately the interior and exterior surfaces of the model are shaded the default model color (typically gray). This makes for easier viewing stress contours on cut sections.

5. Next, click-and-drag the *Section Clipping* drag-handle shown in Fig. 50. This action permits dynamic viewing of stresses within the model at any depth from the **Front Plane**.

6. Undo step 4 by checking ☑ **Show contour on the uncut portion of the model**, and again move the *Section Clipping* drag-handle.

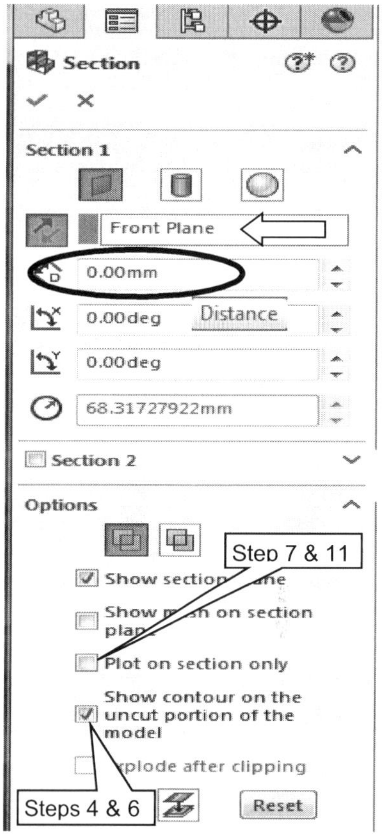

Figure 51 – The **Section** property manager is used to control display of stress contours *within* a model.

A similar effect to that created in step 4 can be obtained as outlined next.

7. In the **Options** dialogue box, check to select ☑ **Plot on section only**. This action restricts plotted stresses to the **Front Plane** *at its current location*. Once again, move the *Section Clipping* drag-handle and observe the resulting display.

8. To display stress distribution on a mid-plane through the model, type **0** in the **Distance** field of the **Section 1** dialogue box shown circled in Fig. 51, and press **[Enter]**. This action creates the display shown in Fig. 52.

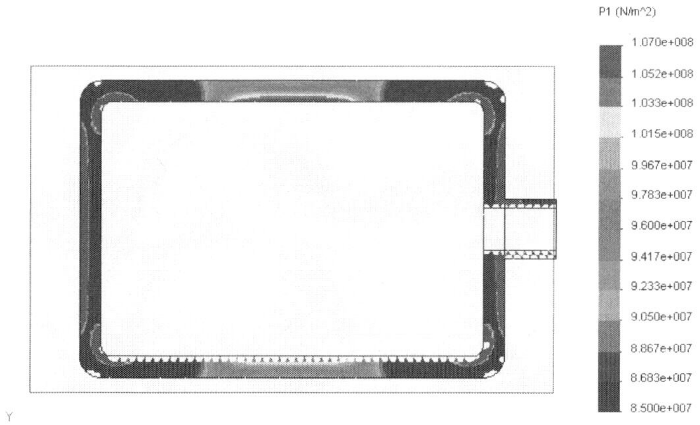

Figure 52 – Image of tangential stresses in the cylinder wall with the ☑ **Plot on section only** option active.

Section Clipping options demonstrated in steps 4 through 8 are convenient for masking stress contours which otherwise might make it difficult to differentiate between desired stress contours and other nearby colored fringes.

9. Within the **Section1** dialogue box, experiment by clicking the down arrow ▼adjacent to **0.00mm** in the **Distance** spin box. The down arrow moves the section away from the front plane in the negative z-direction and into the model. Conversely, the up arrow ▲ moves the section viewing plane away from the model (+ z-direction). For values greater than **0.00mm**, the section plane is located *in front* of the model, thus the model is not sectioned and no stresses are

visible. It is also possible to examine stress at a particular depth within the model by typing any desired location into the **Distance** spin-box.

10. Also experiment by clicking ▲ and ▼ arrows in the **Rotation X** and **Rotation Y** spin boxes located in the **Section 1** dialogue box and observe the display.

11. Reset **Distance** to **0.00** mm and clear the check-mark "✓" from ☐ **Plot on section only**.

As a final demonstration of the *Section Clipping* feature, tangential stress variation through the cylinder wall is viewed by sectioning the cylinder perpendicular to its length as outlined below.

12. Either rotate the model to display its right-side view or, from the SOLIDWORKS toolbar, select the right-side view icon. A right-side view, looking down the axis of the cylinder from the pipe connection-end, appears in Fig. 53.

13. In the **Section 1** dialogue box, click to activate (highlight light blue) the **Reference entity** field (top field that currently shows the words "**Front Plane**").

14. Next, click ▸ to open the **SOLIDWORKS** flyout menu, at top-left of the graphics screen. Then select the **Right Plane**.

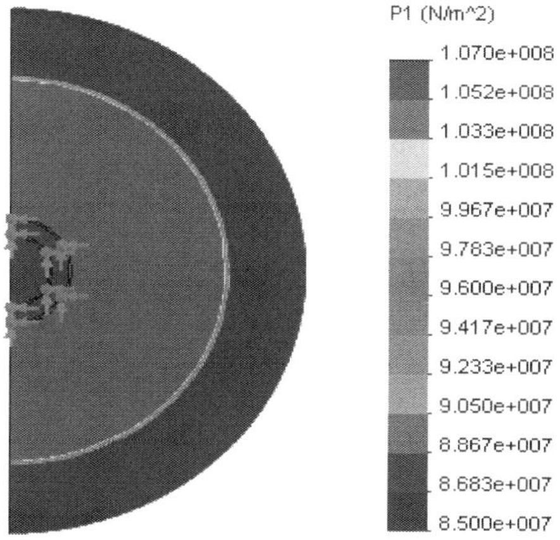

Figure 53 – Right-side view of model prior to taking a section view.

15. Notice that **Right Plane** now appears in the highlighted **Reference entity** field and, because the origin of the Cartesian coordinate system is located at the mid-section of the model, the right plane bisects the model at its mid-section. As a result, tangential stress variation through the wall thickness is shown as illustrated in Fig. 54. Rotate the model to verify this view.

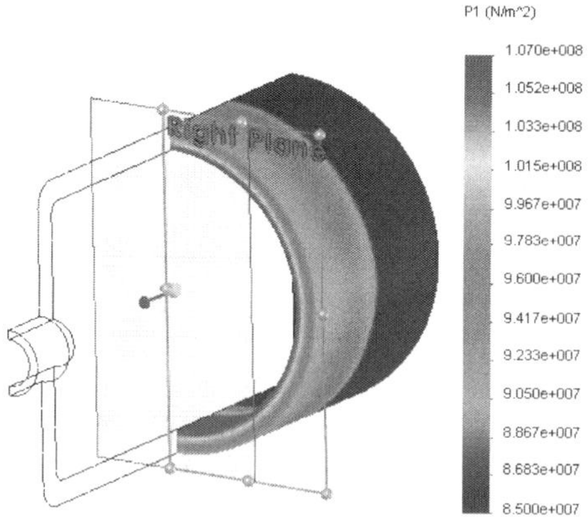

Figure 54 – Section view taken at the right plane.

16. Once again, to aid in examining stresses in the wall only, in the **Options** dialogue box, click to check ☑ **Plot on section only**. The resulting display is shown in Fig. 55.

Figure 55 shows stresses on the cut section only. The section clipping drag-handle is also visible and the model is rotated to reveal the current section location on an outline of the model. This view clearly shows tangential stress variation through the cylinder wall.

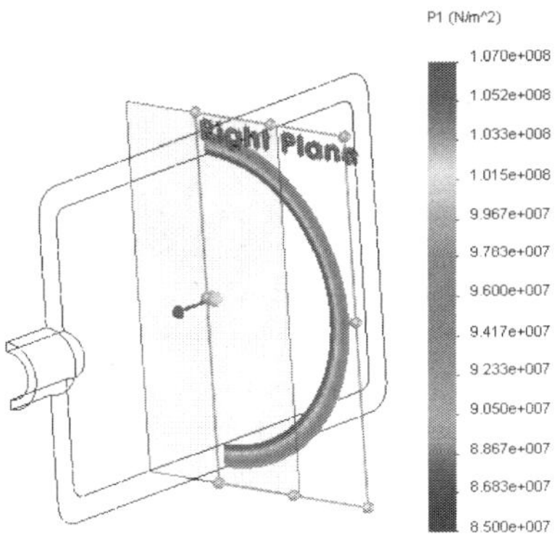

Figure 55 – Tangential stress display on mid-section of the model.

17. In the **Section 1** dialogue box, experiment by clicking the up ▲ or down ▼ arrows on the **Distance** spin box to observe the effect on stresses displayed in the model. Also experiment using the **Rotation X** and **Rotation Y** spin boxes.

18. Click **[OK]** ✓ to close the **Section** property manager.

Analysis Insight

Section Clipping is most advantageous for heat transfer and fluid flow problems where temperature or pressure variation throughout a model is of primary importance. It finds less use for stress analysis problems because maximum stresses always occurs on part surfaces. It is also possible to use the **Probe** feature in combination with any of the *Section Clipping* plots to investigate stress at specific locations *within* a model.

This concludes the analysis of thin and thick-wall pressure vessels using both *shell* and *solid* elements, respectively. In continuation of this chapter we look at using the **2D Simplification** for the analysis of the thick-wall pressure vessel.

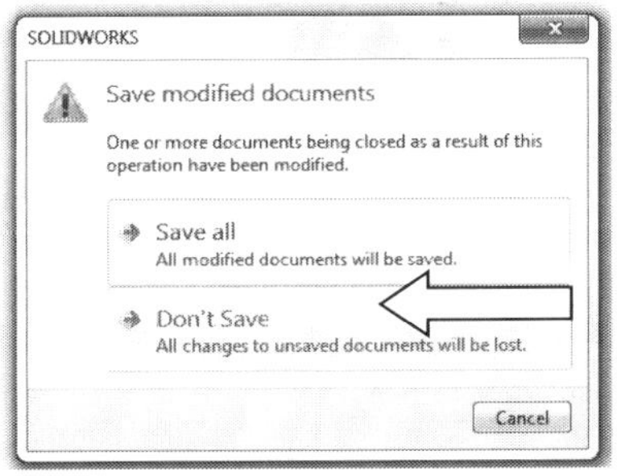

19. Close the model without saving results.

Design Insight

When engaged in the design of any sort of pressure vessel, ASME Boiler and Pressure Vessel Codes[2] or other international codes must be consulted. The Premium version of SOLIDWORKS Simulation contains a Study type aligned with ASME codes. See the 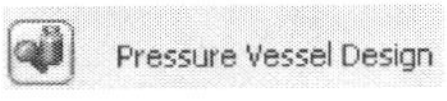

icon in the **Type** dialogue box of the **Study** property manager.

[2] The ASME Boiler and Pressure Vessel Code, B31.3-1013 American Society of Mechanical Engineers, New York, NY, 2013.

THICK WALL PRESSURE VESSEL (AXISYMMETRIC APPROACH)

In an axisymmetric finite element problem, the model of interest is rotationally symmetric about an axis. Examples of axisymmetric models are round pins, pressure vessels, shafts, disks, etc. Axisymmetric features allow us to analyze a 3-dimensional (3D) model by using only 2-dimensional (2D) elements. This is highly accurate for axisymmetric loads and deflections, while computationally is less expensive. As an example, in Fig. 56, only 20 shell elements are needed in the cross section of an axisymmetric hub to perform FEA analysis without needing to mesh the whole geometry.

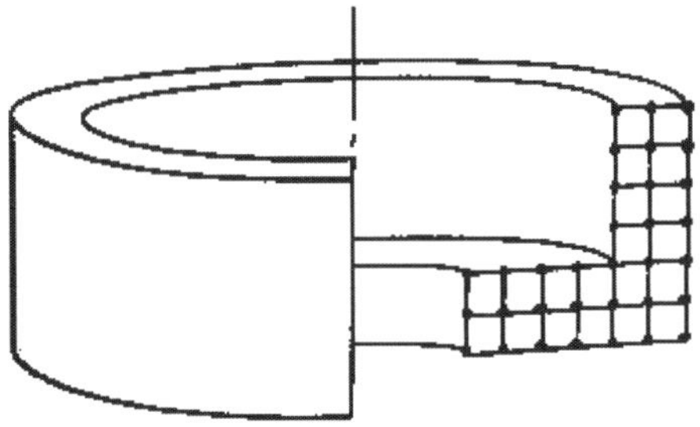

Figure 56 – An Axisymmetric 3D hub with a 2D mesh.

In this section, we repeat the analysis of the thick-pressure vessel wall using the axisymmetric feature of the vessel and its boundary conditions.

Problem Statement

Thick-Wall Pressure Vessel

This example is based on the same thick-wall cylindrical pressure vessel used in the previous section (see Fig.36). The vessel is made of alloy steel and is subject to an internal pressure, $P_i = 16.0$ MPa, and an external pressure that approximates standard atmospheric pressure, $P_o = 0.101$ MPa. The goal is to determine the tangential and radial stress variation through the cylindrical wall of this pressure vessel using the **2D Simplification** option in SOLIDWORKS.

1. *Skip to step 2 if SOLIDWORKS is already open.* Otherwise, open SOLIDWORKS by making the following selections: **Start>All Programs>SOLIDWORKS 2026** or click the **SOLIDWORKS** icon on your screen.

2. In the SOLIDWORKS main menu, select **File > Open…** Then, open the file named **Thick Wall Pressure Vessel**.

3. In the SOLIDWORKS Feature manager tree, right-click on **Revolve1** icon 

and from the pull-down menu select **Delete.** (see Fig. 57). Select **Yes** to confirm the deleting of the Revolve feature in the pop-up window.

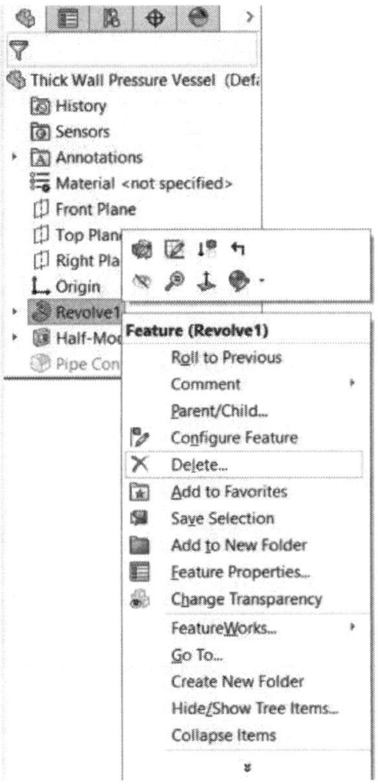

Figure 57 – Removing the Revolve feature in the model.

4. Repeat the previous step to delete **(-) Sketch4** in the SOLIDWORKS Feature manager. Now, the Feature manager should only contain **Sketch1**, which is the cross section of the thick-wall vessel (see Fig. 58).

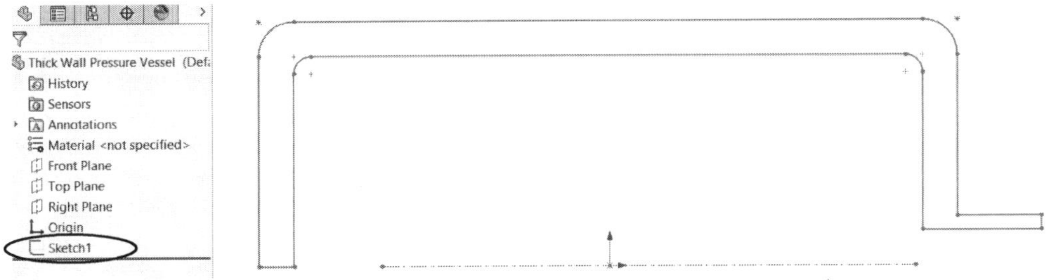

Figure 58 – Cross section of the thick-wall vessel

5. Select **File** from the main menu and click on **Save as...** from the pull-down menu. This opens a pop-up window. In this window change the **File name:** to **Thick Wall Pressure Vessel Cross Section.SLDPRT** and press **Save** to save the SOLIDWORKS model in your project folder.

Create a Static Analysis (Study)

6. On the **Simulation** tab click ▼ on the **New Study** icon and from the pull-down menu select **New Study**. Or in the main menu click **Simulation** and from the pull-down menu select **Study…** The **Study** property manager opens.

7. In the **Name** field type: **2D Thick Wall Pressure Vessel-YOUR NAME**.

8. Select a **Static** study and you can see the **Use 2D Simplification** is automatically selected since we have a 2-dimensional sketch.

9. Click **[OK]** ✓ to confirm your selection and to open the Feature manager for **2D Thick Wall Pressure Vessel** (see Fig. 59).

10. In this window, select the **Axi-symmetric** icon 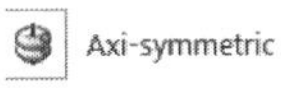 for the **Study Type**. Since the **Sketch1** is drawn in the **Front Plane**, select this plane (from the Flyout menu) for the **Section Plane:**, and finally choose the dash-dotted line in the sketch for **Axis of symmetry:**. **Line11@Sketch1** which now appears in this field. Click **[OK]** ✓ to confirm your selection.

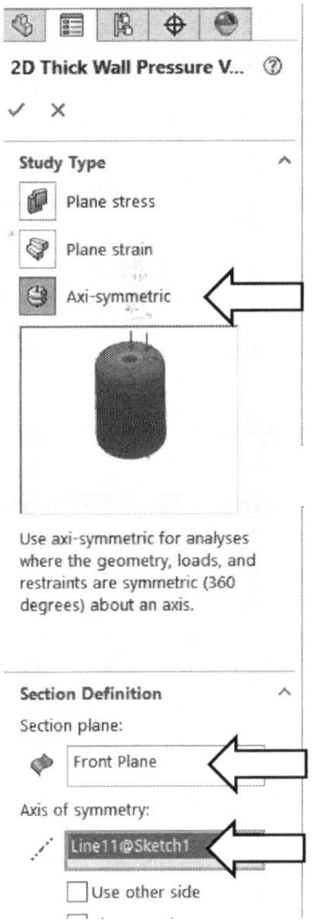

Figure 59 – 2D Static Analysis Feature Manager.

Assign Material Properties

11. Right-click the **Thick Wall Pressure Vessel Cross Section** folder and from the pull-down menu select **Apply/Edit Material…** The **Material** window opens.

12. Select **Alloy Steel (SS)**. Verify that the units are set to **SI-N/m^2 (Pa)** then click **[Apply]** followed by **[Close]**.

Define Fixtures and External Loads

13. Right-click the **Fixtures** folder and from the pull-down menu select **Fixed Geometry…** The **Fixture** property manager opens.

14. Within the **Standard (Fixed Geometry)** dialogue box, select **Fixed Geometry** (if not already selected).

15. Zoom in on the right-end of the pipe extension, shown in Fig. 60, and click to select the line associated with the pipe inlet. Immovable restraint symbols (shown dark) in the X and Y directions are added to the model and **Edge<1>** appears in the **Faces, Edges, Vertices for Fixture** dialogue box.

16. Click **[OK]** ✓ to close the **Fixture** property manager.

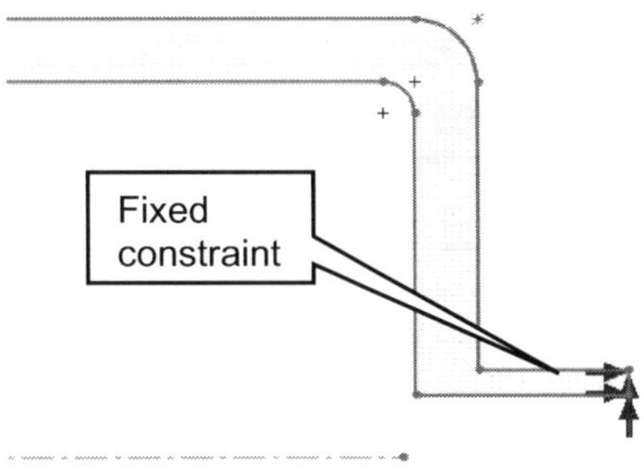

Figure 60 – Fixed Geometry constraint for the vessel.

The next step is to apply an internal pressure, P_i = 16.0 MPa, to all internal lines of the pressure vessel. Proceed as follows.

17. Right-click **External Loads** from the pull-down menu and select **Pressure…** The **Pressure** property manager opens.

18. In the **Type** dialogue box verify that ⦿**Normal to selected face** is chosen.

19. The **Faces for Pressure** field is highlighted (light blue) to indicate it is active and awaiting user input.

20. Move the cursor onto the model and click to select *all interior* lines (see Fig. 61). A total of six faces **(Edge<1>, Edge<2>, … Edge<6>)** should be listed in the **Faces for Pressure** field.

21. Beneath **Pressure Value**, verify that **Units** are set to **N/m^2** and type **16.0e6** in the **Pressure Value** field.

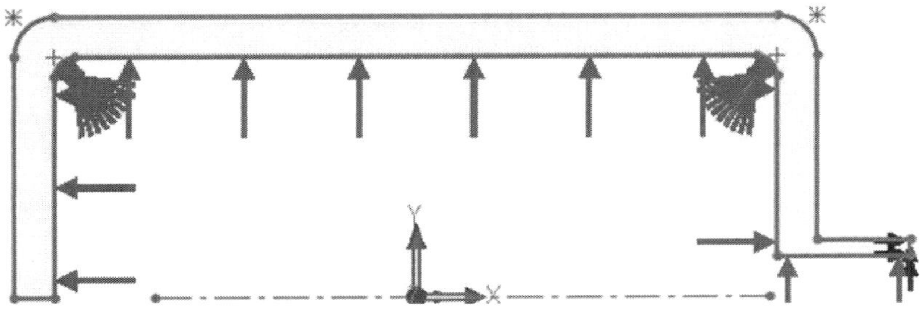

Figure 61– Internal pressure applied to six lines within the thick-wall pressure vessel.

22. Click **[OK]** ✓ to close the **Pressure** property manager. The model should appear as shown in Fig. 61.

Next, apply an atmospheric pressure, $P_o = 0.101$ MPa, to all external surfaces of the model. Try this on your own or follow the steps below.

23. Repeat steps 17 through 22 with the following two exceptions.

    a. In step 20 select *all exterior* lines. Once again, a total of six lines should be chosen.

    b. In step 21 type **0.101e6** N/m^2 in the **Pressure Value** field.

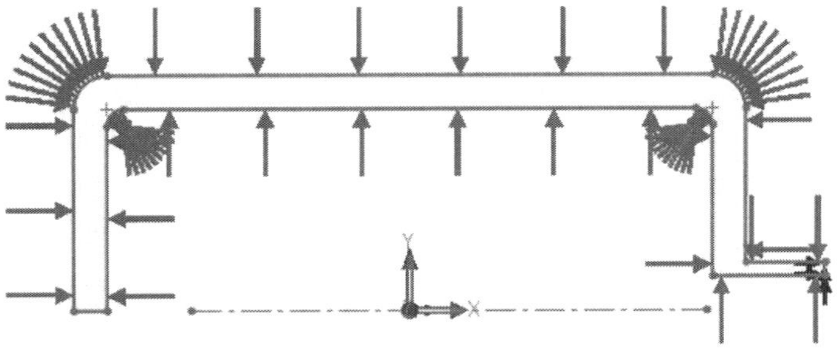

Figure 62 – Atmospheric pressure applied to exterior of the thick-wall pressure vessel.

The interior and exterior pressure vessel lines should now appear as shown in Fig. 62.

Mesh the Model – Standard Size Standard Mesh

24. In the Simulation manager, right-click the **Mesh** folder and from the pull-down menu select **Create Mesh…** The **Mesh** property manager opens.

25. Check ✓ to open the ☑ **Mesh Parameters** dialogue box and select a ⊙ **Standard Mesh**. Also verify that **Units** are set to **mm**.

26. In the **Mesh Density** dialogue box, use the default value by pressing the **Reset** button.

27. Click **[OK]** ✓ to close the **Mesh** property manager and initiate meshing the model.

Solution

After defining the material properties, fixtures, loads, and a mesh, the thick-wall model study is ready to be solved as outlined below.

28. Click the **Run This Study** icon on the **Simulation** toolbar. The Solution time is less than 1.0 second for this study.

29. Computed results, in the form of plots, are listed beneath the **Results** folder. Notice that the plots contained in these folders revert to the system default plots.

Results Analysis

To compare the current (2D) simulation results with the 3D simulation results of the thick-wall vessel we only look at the 1st principal stress.

30. Right-click the **Results** folder and from the pull-down menu select **Define Stress Plot…** The **Stress Plot** property manager opens.

31. In the **Display** dialogue box, click ▼ to open the **Component** pull-down menu and from the list of available stresses select **P1: 1st Principal Stress**.

32. Verify that **Units** are set to **N/m^2**.

33. Click **[OK]** ✓ to close the **Stress plot** property manager.

Figure 63 shows a front view of the 1st principal stress distribution (σ_1) throughout the model. Once again observe regions of high stress at both end fillets where the cylinder and flat ends join.

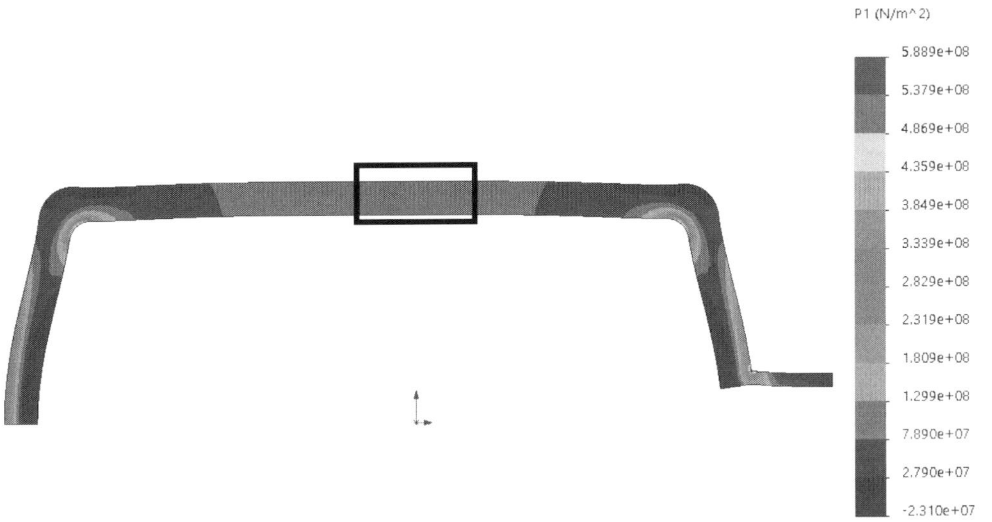

Figure 63 – Plot of 1st principal stress distribution throughout the thick-wall pressure vessel.

Next, zoom-in on the boxed region and use the **Probe** feature to determine the actual values of 1st principal stress at various nodes across the wall thickness.

34. Right-click **Stress2 (-1st principal-)** and from the pull-down menu select **Probe**. The **Probe Result** property manager opens.

35. Begin at the inside of the cylinder wall, as near as possible to the mid-section of the cylinder, and successively click and move the cursor slightly upward (moving in as straight a line as possible). Repeat until five node points are selected across the wall thickness. Stress values at each node point are simultaneously displayed on the model and in the **Results** dialogue box (see Fig. 64).

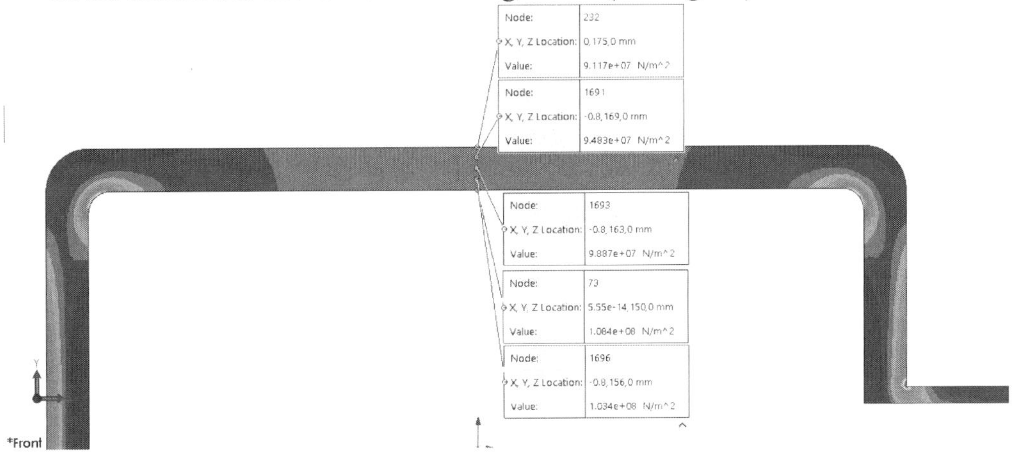

Figure 64– Tangential stress distribution through the thick-wall.

The probe results show the tangential stress magnitudes at the inside and outside wall surfaces are 108.4 MPa and 91.17 MPa, respectively.

A quick comparison of classical results found using Lame's equations and finite element results for tangential stress magnitudes at the inside and outside wall surfaces yields the following.

For tangential stress at the inside surface:

$$\% \text{ difference} = \left[\frac{\text{FEA result} - \text{classical result}}{\text{FEA result}}\right]100 = \left[\frac{108.4e6 - 103.8e6}{108.4e6}\right]100 = 4.2\% \quad [12]$$

Tangential stress at the outside wall surface:

$$\% \text{ difference} = \left[\frac{\text{FEA result} - \text{classical result}}{\text{FEA result}}\right]100 = \left[\frac{91.17e6 - 87.9e6}{91.17e6}\right]100 = 3.6\% \quad [13]$$

Both these percent difference values are low enough that the analyst should have confidence in the finite element analysis results.

To conclude this section, we compare these results with the 3D simulation results for the thick-wall vessel shown earlier in this chapter. Table-2 has the summary of comparison

Table 2 – Comparison of the 3D and 2D simulation results

	3D Model (Fine Mesh Size)	**2D Model (Standard Mesh Size)**
No. of Nodes	88,246	2636
No. of Elements	56,002	1165
Simulation Time (sec)	~10	<1.0
% Simulation error in tangential stress (inside surface)	4.3%	4.2%
% Simulation error in tangential stress (outside surface)	3.8%	3.6%

This concludes examination of 2D Simulation for axisymmetric models and boundary conditions. As the results in Table-2 confirm, the 2D simulation for axisymmetric models is highly accurate while is computationally less expensive.

36. Close the model without saving the results.

EXERCISES

EXERCISE 1 – Thick Wall Pressure Vessel

The vessel in Fig. E4-1 allows three separate pipe connections. The top connection on the cylinder is considered **Fixed** due to its rigid external attachment (not shown). However, both pipes on the flat, right-end are connected to flexible pipe segments (also not shown) that permit movement in the X (axial) and Y (vertical) directions. Movement in these directions is permitted to accommodate axial and circumferential expansion when the tank is pressurized. In other words, movement is only restricted in the Z-direction at these pipe connections. Perform a finite element analysis of this cylinder subject to the following guidelines. Open the file: **Pressure Vessel 4-1**. (Use SI units)

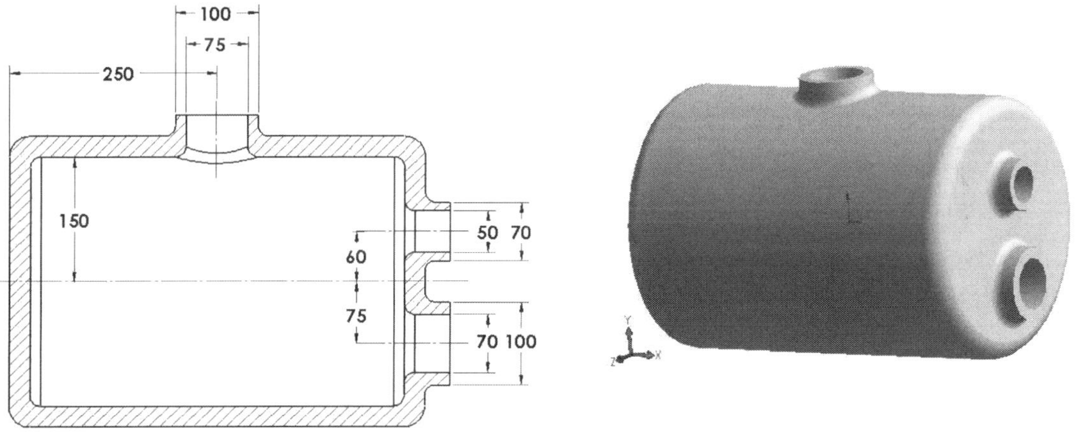

Figure E4-1 – Cylindrical pressure vessel with three pipe attachments. Wall thickness t = 25 mm.

- Material: **AISI Type 316L stainless steel** (Use S.I. units)
- Mesh: In the Mesh property manager, select a ⊙ **Standard Mesh**. (NOTE: Determine whether $t \leq r_i/20$ to ascertain if thin or thick wall classical stress equations should be used to calculate stress in the cylinder walls.)
- External Loads: Internal pressure **P = 950 kN/m^2**; external pressure is negligible.
- Fixtures: The pipe connection on top of the cylinder is **Fixed/Immovable**.

  Pipes on the right end of the tank restrain movement in the **Z**-direction only. This restraint and its direction are somewhat arbitrary but are included to illustrate how alternative restraints might be applied.

  *Assistance dealing with these pipe restraints is included in the **Solution Guidance** box below.*

  Apply appropriate symmetry restraints on cut cylindrical surfaces.

Solution Guidance

It is assumed that a Simulation Study has been started. Begin by reducing the model to half of the tank geometry.

- In the SOLIDWORKS Feature manager locate **Half-Model of Cylinder** and **Unsuppress** it.
- Do *not* remove fillets at each pipe connection since their removal will cause a significant increase in stress, due to stress concentration, at these locations.

To apply restraints in the Z-direction on end surfaces of the horizontal pipe connections, proceed as follows.

i. Right-click **Fixtures** and from the pull-down menu select **Fixed Geometry…**

ii. In the **Advanced** dialogue box, select **Use Reference Geometry** (if not already selected).

iii. Click the *end faces* of both pipe extensions located on the right-side of the cylinder. **Face<1>** and **Face<2>** appear in the **Faces, Edges, Vertices for Fixture** field.

iv. Activate (highlight) the **Face, Edge, Plane Axis for Direction** field. Then, in the SOLIDWORKS flyout menu, select **Right Plane** (it is oriented in the Z-direction).

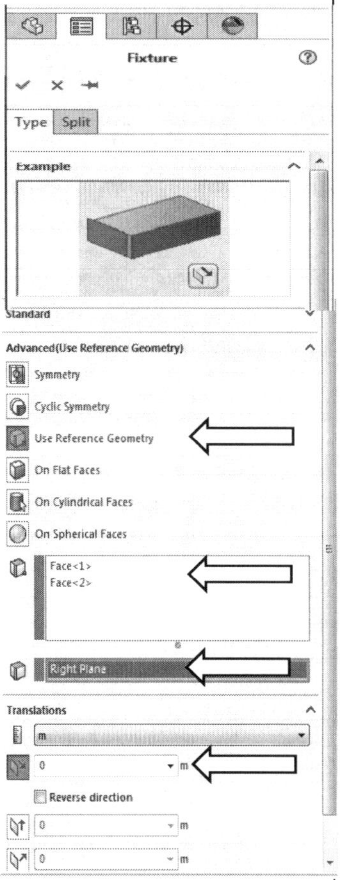

Figure E4-2 -Restraints applied to prevent motion in the Z-direction.

v. In the **Translations** dialogue box, select the **Along Plane Dir 1** icon. The field is highlighted (white) and "**0**" appears. This value indicates zero translation is allowed in the selected Z-direction. See Fig. E4-3

vi. Click **[OK]** ✓ to close the **Fixture** property manager.

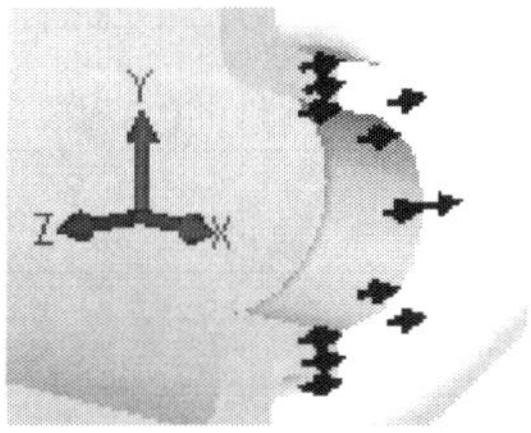

Figure E4-3 – Restraint symbols in Z-direction.

Vectors displayed on the horizontal pipe ends should be oriented in the Z-direction; see Fig. E4-3. Either the $\pm$ Z-direction is acceptable since displacement = 0.

Develop a finite element model that includes material selection, fixtures, external loads, mesh the model (two elements are required across the cylinder wall thickness; one element thickness is permitted on pipe extensions), and a solution.
Determine the following:

a. Create a stress contour plot of von Mises stress in the model. Display this stress on a **Deformed** view looking from the front of the model. Hide all fixtures and external loads, but include automatic labeling of maximum von Mises stress on this plot. Does the maximum von Mises stress exceed material yield strength?

b. Use classical equations to calculate magnitudes of tangential and radial stresses at both the inside and outside surfaces of the cylinder. Label calculations. Assume these calculations are made in a region well removed from the cylinder ends and pipe connections.

c. Use finite element analysis to determine tangential stress in the cylinder wall *opposite* the top pipe connection. When determining this stress, reduce the range of stress values plotted to magnitudes slightly above and slightly below tangential stress magnitudes anticipated on the inside and outside surfaces. Plot the *appropriate stress* contour to show tangential stress distribution through the cylinder wall.

d. Use the **Probe** feature to produce a graph of tangential stress variation through the cylinder wall from inside to outside; choose both corner and mid-side nodes. Explore this stress at the mid-section of the cylinder (i.e., midway between its left and right ends.) Add a descriptive title, axis labels, and your name to this graph.

e. Repeat step (c), but replace "tangential" stress with "radial" stress.

f. Repeat step (d), but replace "tangential" stress with "radial" stress.

g. Compare the percent difference between FEA results and results obtained using classical pressure vessel calculations determined in part (b). Results to be compared include the tangential stresses at inside and outside surfaces of the cylinder and also radial stresses at inside and outside surfaces. Use the following equation to compute the percent difference between results.

$$\%\ \text{difference} = \frac{(\text{FEA result - classical result})}{\text{FEA result}} * 100 = \qquad [1]$$

h. Comment upon the "goodness" of agreement between results of part (g). If classical and FEA results differ by more than 5%, explain why.

EXERCISE 2 – Analysis of a Sheet Metal Bracket Using Shell Elements

The bracket shown in Fig. E4-4 is one of two brackets used to attach a cargo case to the rear of a motorcycle frame. **Chrome Stainless Steel** is used for the bracket to enhance appearance and to provide corrosion resistance. Bolts attach the bracket to the frame through three holes on the vertical (left) leg shown in Fig. E4-4. A downward design load of 14 lb is applied at the hole on tab **A**. This load represents a design load carried by tab **A** in a fully loaded cargo case. Perform a finite element analysis of this part using *shell* elements applied at the mid-surface of the part.

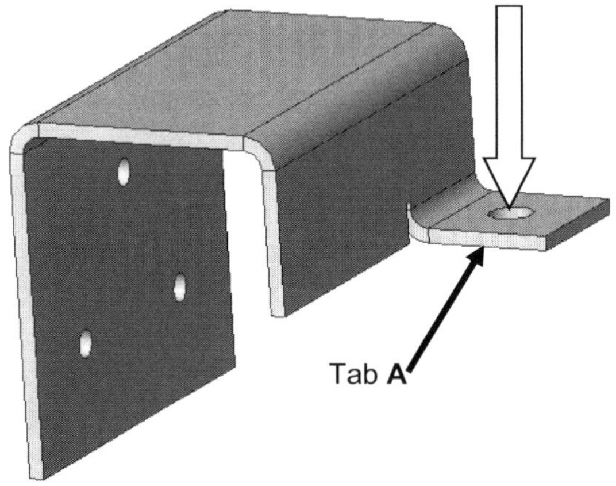

Figure E4-4 – Bracket used to attach a cargo case to a motorcycle frame.

Open the file: **Bracket 4-2**.

- Material: **Chrome Stainless Steel** (Use English units)
- Mesh: Use the default ⊙ **Curvature based mesh** and default mesh size. Mesh using *shell* elements defined on the mid-surface. NOTE: When using the **Shell mesh using mid-surface** option, thickness of the elements is automatically extracted from the SOLIDWORKS model geometry.
- Fixtures: Apply a **Fixed** restraint to the three bolt holes. This fixture can be applied to either the hole edge or to its inner surface.
- External Load: **14-lb** vertical load applied to the hole edge or inner surface of the hole on Tab **A**. This force is directed downward on the tab as shown in Fig. E4-4.

This exercise is used to demonstrate application of shell elements to a sheet metal part. Recall from the chapter introduction that sheet metal parts are automatically treated as shell elements by the software. As such, this exercise provides insight into a second way of creating a shell model. Guidance used to create a shell model of the bracket using this second method is provided below.

How is it known that the current model is a sheet metal part? To answer this question, open the part file and examine the SOLIDWORKS Feature manager tree. In the tree, **Sheet-Metal1** is listed along with several SOLIDWORKS features that pertain exclusively to sheet metal parts. Also, in the Simulation manager tree observe that **Bracket 4-2** is represented by a "thin sheet" icon Bracket 4-2 rather than by the solid body icon Bracket 4-2.

Solution Guidance

1. Apply **Fixtures** to the three holes. **Fixed** restraints can be applied to either the hole edge or to surfaces within each hole. Restraints are automatically transferred to edges of a shell element model.

2. Applying a downward force on tab **A** is similar to that of applying a directed force. The 14-lb downward force can be applied to either an *edge* or the *inner surface* of the hole in tab **A**.

Method #2 for Defining a Shell Model

1. Right-click **Bracket 4-2 (-Chrome Stainless Steel-)** (or) choose whatever filename was specified by you. From the pull-down menu, select **Edit Definition…** The **Shell Definition** property manager opens; see Fig. E4-5.

2. In the **Type** dialogue box, choose ⊙ **Thin** and set **Unit** to **in**. The grayed-out number appearing in the **Shell thickness** field **0.1046** corresponds to the sheet metal thickness specified when the part was created in SOLIDWORKS.

3. Also in the **Type** dialogue box, select ⊙ **Full Preview** to show color coded Top, Middle, and Bottom surfaces of the bracket. Consider the 14 lb load as applied to the Top surface. If needed, check ☑ **Flip shell top and bottom**.

4. Open ˅ the **Offset** dialogue box. This box shows the default plane location is at the **Middle surface** of the model. Place the cursor on the icon circled in Fig. E4-5.

5. Click **[OK]** ✓ to close the **Shell Definition** property manager.

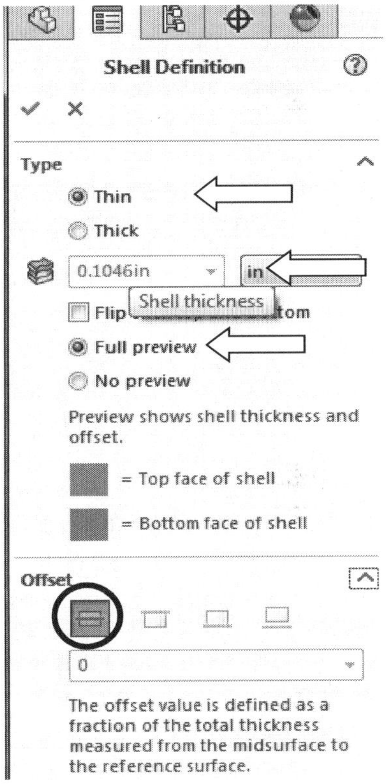

Figure E4-5 – Checking shell thickness as specified in the original SOLIDWORKS drawing.

Note the small number of steps required to create a shell mesh on this sheet metal bracket [steps (1) to (4) above] as compared to approximately twenty steps required to define the shell mid-surface in the thin wall pressure vessel example. This streamlined procedure is realized because the original model was defined as a sheet metal part and the software automatically recognizes this fact. Models classified as “surface parts” are equally simple to convert to a shell mesh.

Develop a finite element model that includes material specification, fixtures, external loads, mesh generation, and solution.

Determine the following:

a. Plot von Mises stress on the top surface of the shell face; include the applied load and fixtures on this plot. Consider the top surface to be that shown facing upward in Fig. E4-4 (i.e., the top side of the model is the side to which the external 14-lb load is applied). Include automatic labeling of maximum and minimum von Mises stress on this plot.

   NOTE: If the "top" surface, as defined in (a) above, appears orange in color (recall orange denotes the "bottom" surface), then **Flip Shell Elements** as outlined in the chapter example problem. However, remember to hold the **[Shift]** key while selecting *all* surfaces on one side of the model.

b. Repeat part (a) for the "bottom" surface of the bracket. By what percent do the maximum von Mises stresses on the top and bottom surfaces differ? On what surface does the maximum von Mises stress occur? (top or bottom)

c. Questions: Where on the model does maximum stress occur? Does this stress exceed the material yield strength? Describe factors, such as part geometry, location of the applied load, and other factors that cause the maximum stress to occur where it does on the model.

EXERCISE 3 – Stress Distribution in the Yoshida Buckling Model

The part shown in Fig. E4-6 is commonly referred to as the "Yoshida Buckling" model by individuals familiar with experimental stress analysis techniques. It is often used as an experimental model in an academic setting due to the interesting stress distributions that exist within the part. In an experimental course, strain gages and/or photoelastic techniques are used to determine strains, and from them stresses in the part are determined. This exercise investigates the model using finite element analysis.

Open the file: **Yoshida Buckling Model 4-3**.

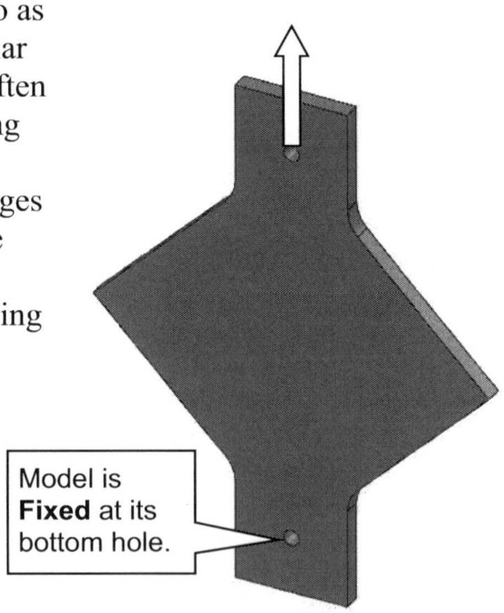

Figure E4-6 – A Yoshida buckling model subject to an upward acting force at its upper end and a **Fixed** restraint at its bottom hole.

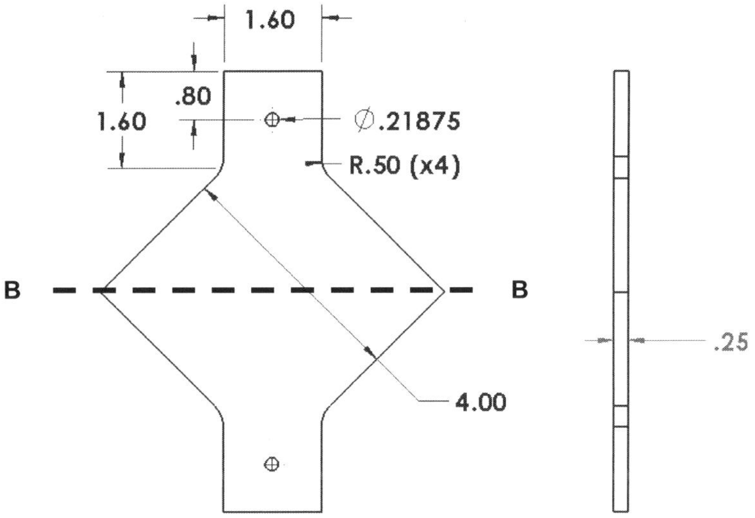

Figure E4-7 – A typical Yoshida Buckling Model. Model dimensions may differ provided proper proportions are retained. (Units: inches).

Create a finite element model of the above part subject to the following conditions.

- Material: **1060 Alloy** Aluminum (Use English customary units)
- Mesh: In the **Mesh** property manager, select a **Standard mesh**. Tetrahedral elements are the (system default) high quality elements.
- External Load: Assign the applied tensile **Force** of **F** = **530** lb to the *edge* of the upper hole on the model.
- Fixture: Apply a **Fixed** restraint to the *edge* of the bottom hole.
- Convert the solid model to a *Shell* model using methods outlined in Chapter #4. Locate the offset surface at the mid-section of the model and base stress results below as occurring on the mid-surface.

Determine the following:

a. Create a plot of von Mises stress throughout the model. Also, have the software automatically label **Show max annotation**.

b. Create a plot of stress in the **Y**-direction on the model. Display a standard mesh on this model.

c. Use the **Probe** tool to create a graph of stress in the **Y**-direction across the middle of the model. Select nodes *from right to left* across the model approximating imaginary line **B-B**, shown in Fig. E4-7. Select only corner nodes in as straight a line as possible across the face of the model. Provide a descriptive graph title, include your name, and descriptive labels for both the X and Y axes.

d. Like part (b), except plot stress in the X- direction. Include a standard mesh on this image.

e. Use the plot of part (d) to create a graph of stress in the X-direction by selecting corner nodes along a vertical center-line extending between edges of the two holes that are closest to the center of the model.

f. Beneath images of the two graphs created for part (c) and for part (e) discuss general observations regarding changes of magnitude of σ_x and σ_y within the part. Consider questions such as whether or not the distribution of stress magnitude makes sense and explain "why" or "why not?" Why might this part be referred to as a buckling model?

g. Create a plot that shows areas of the model where the Factor of Safety < 1.6.

EXERCISE 4 – Joist Hanger Analysis Using Shell Elements

"Joist" is the name commonly applied to beams used to support floors in residential and commercial construction. So called "joist hangers" are often used to connect the ends of joists to a "header beam." For individuals unfamiliar with floor joists, header beams, and joist hangers, these items are labeled in Fig. E 4-8. Common nails are used to fasten joist hangers, beams, and joists. However, this exercise is simplified to examine only loads transferred to a joist hanger by a single floor joist. Also, nails used to fasten a joist to the joist hanger are not explicitly modeled. The joist hanger to be analyzed is shown in Figs. E4-9 (a) and (b).

Open the File: **Joist Hanger**

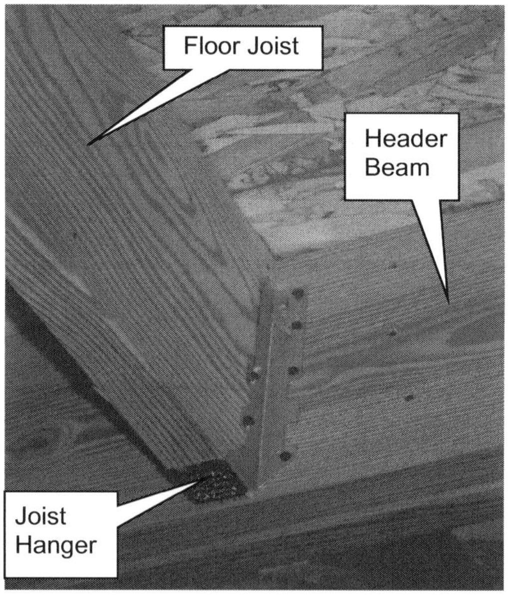

Figure E4-8 – A joist hanger and related beams are identified in the image above. View looking up at a joist hanger from below.

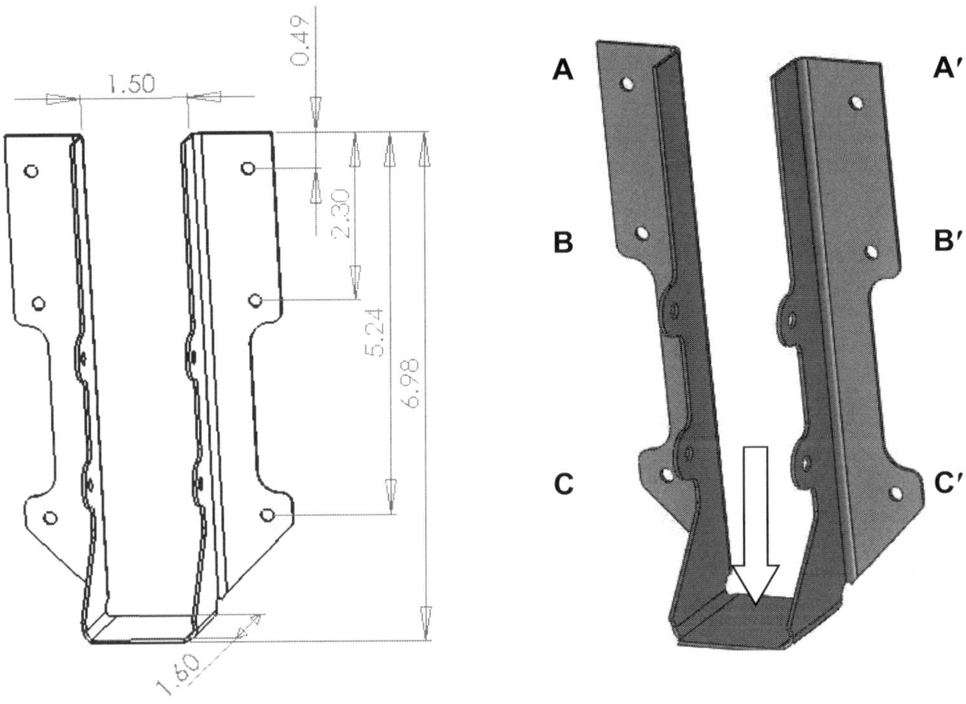

(a) (b)

Figure E4-9 – Typical joist hanger used to support 2"x10" floor joists. A load of 95 lb is distributed over the bottom surface indicated by the arrow in the figure.

- Material: **Galvanized Steel** (Use English units) Galvanized steel is used because joist hangers are also used under porches, decks, and in other exposed exterior environments.

- Mesh: **Shell Mesh** – Traditionally used to model sheet metal parts. Use a default **Curvature based mesh** and default mesh size.

- Fixture: **Fixed** restraints are applied *only* to nail holes at locations **A**, **A′**, **B**, **B′**, and **C**, **C′** in Fig. E4-9(b). Nails passing through these holes connect the joist hanger to a header beam like that labeled in Fig. E4-8.

- External Load: A **95** lb downward load is applied normal to the bottom surface of the joist hanger. This load accounts for lumber weight plus the weight of furnishings, appliances, and people on the floor above. It is *uniformly distributed* over the bottom of the joist hanger.

Develop a finite element model that includes material specification, fixtures, external load, mesh generation, and solution as specified below. See Solution Guidance for Exercise 2 to determine thickness of the joist hanger.

Determine the following:

a. Before creating any plots, ensure that the "top" side of the meshed model corresponds to the inside of the "U" shaped joist hanger. Recall that *all* surfaces that share the same *side* of the model must be specified as the same surface (i.e., top and bottom surfaces cannot be mixed together on the same surface). It may be necessary to imagine the part flattened out to help identify surfaces common to one side of the model. Next, create a von Mises stress plot showing the stress distribution on the top surface of the joist hanger. For this plot, turn on the **Show max annotation** feature. Adjacent to this image, show a manual calculation of the uniform load (pressure) applied to the bottom of the joist hanger.

b. On the plot created in part (a), identify all regions of high stress by circling them. Also, on the plot, answer the question: "Is the material yield strength exceeded at any of these high stress locations?" If "yes" label these locations as "FS < 1."

c. Repeat parts (a) and (b), but create a plot of von Mises stress on the bottom surface of the joist hanger. On this plot, state whether the largest von Mises stresses occur on the top or bottom surface of the shell model.

d. Assume that lack of attention to detail, carelessness, rushing to finish the job, or just plain laziness, results in fewer than all nails being driven through holes **Fixed** to the header beam at locations **A**, **A′**, **B**, **B′**, and **C**, **C′**. On your own create two additional scenarios. In scenario 1, omit one nail from *each side* of the joist hanger where it is attached to the header beam. In scenario 2, omit two nails from *each side* of the joist hanger. Do this by editing the **Fixtures** folder as follows.

   - In the Simulation manager tree, select **Fixture-1** and from the pull-down menu, select **Edit Definition…**
   - In the **Standard (Fixed Geometry)** dialogue box right-click the nail fixtures to be eliminated and then from the pull-down menu, select **Delete**.
   - Click **[OK]** ✓ to close the **Fixture** property manager.

e. For both scenarios 1 and 2, repeat parts (a) and (b) of this problem. Does the joist hanger become unsafe for either of these two scenarios? If "yes" identify the unsafe scenario(s) and label areas where the safety factor is "FS < 1."

╬ EXERCISE 5 – Stress Analysis of a Bulk Material Handling Chute (Special Topics: Split Lines, Non-Uniform Pressure)

Figure E-10 shows a truck dumping system used to quickly and efficiently unload fresh potatoes received by truck from regional farming operations. The truck dumper is capable of lifting semi-trailers up to 70 feet long and weighing up to 120,000 lb fully loaded. Flow of potatoes is controlled by a discharge metering gate visible in both Figs. E4-10 and labeled in E4-11. Potatoes are off-loaded into a receiving chute of the type shown in Fig. E4-11 where they are assumed to produce *non*-uniform loading on the chute *sides* but not on its right end.

Figure E4-10 – Truck dumper capable of raising semi-tractor trailers to quickly discharge produce at food processing facilities. Photo courtesy of Heat and Control, Hayward, CA, www.heatandcontrol.com.

Figure E4-11 shows the discharge metering gate and the V-shaped chute that channels potatoes onto a conveyor belt for transport into a food processing plant. The focus of this exercise is to analyze stresses in the V-shaped chute subject to *non*-uniform loading caused by potatoes that fill the chute.

The chute is made of stainless steel due to the need for routine cleaning associated with food handling equipment. As shown in Fig. E4-12, the chute is easily removable by lifting it off of its side supports. Carefully note how the chute is supported because a proper understanding is necessary to assign fixtures to this model.

Open the File:

V-Chute with Flanges 4-5

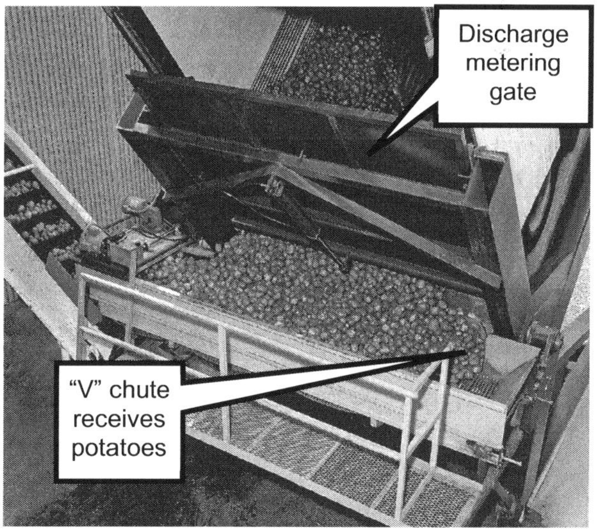

Figure E4-11 – Potatoes are shown entering the V-shaped chute and being carried by conveyor into a food processing plant. Photo courtesy of Heat and Control, Hayward, CA, www.heatandcontrol.com.

The chute base is supported on two bottom flanges that rest in parallel grooves located on either side of the conveyor system. These grooves run the full length of the flanges on the chute bottom and are intended to prevent lateral (outward) movement of chute sides at the bottom. A *clearance fit* exists between flanges and the grooves. Similarly, upper flanges on both sides of the chute rest on steel plates shown schematically in Fig. E4-12. The chute is easily removed for cleaning by lifting it off of the upper supports and out of the lower grooves. Support plates and grooved slots are *not* provided with the model. Instead, **Fixtures** will be applied in their place.

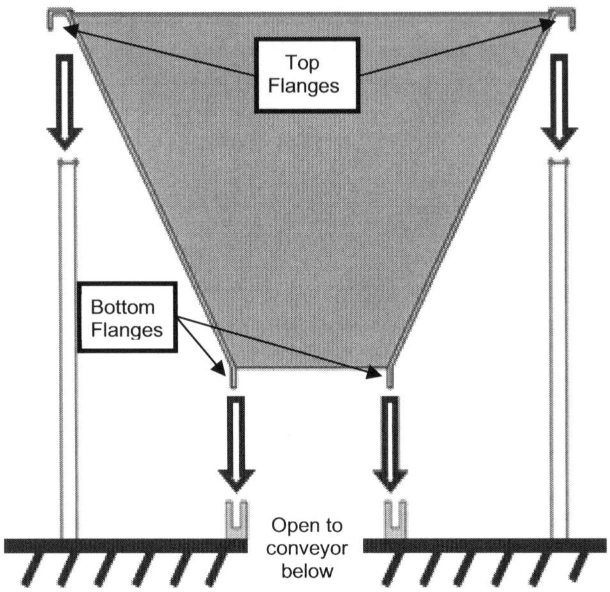

Figure E4-12 – End view showing how the chute is lowered onto side support plates (at its top flanges) and into grooves along its bottom flanges. All contact in these regions is considered *clearance fits*, (i.e., these supports do *not* provide **Fixed** restraints).

Figure E4-13 shows basic dimensions of the chute. The chute length of 112 in. exceeds the standard semi-trailer width of 102 in by 10 inches to ensure that all off-loaded items are captured in the chute. In Fig. E4-11, notice that potatoes do *not* fill the right end of the chute. Therefore, locate a *Split Line* on chute sides at 105 in. from the open end; see dashed line in Fig. E4-13.

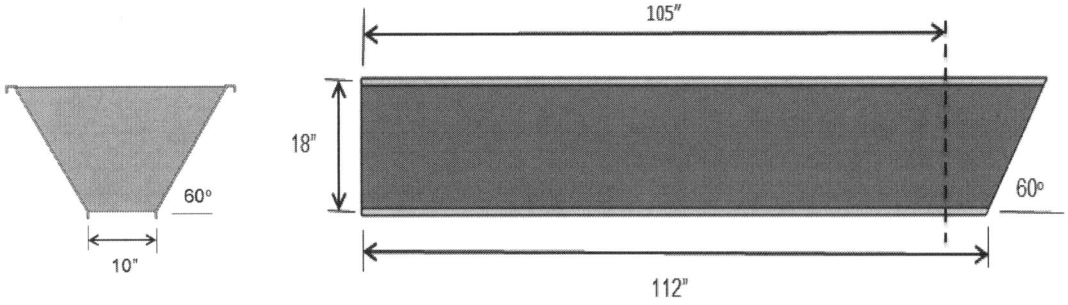

Figure E4-13 – Front and left-side views showing overall dimensions of the V-shaped chute.

Create a finite element model of the above part subject to the following conditions.

- Material: **AISI 321 Annealed Stainless Steel (SS)** (Use English Units). Material is 3 gage stainless (0.250in./6.36 mm) thick.

- Mesh: Use a default size **Standard mesh**. Mesh the model using *shell* elements located at the model mid-surface. *HINT #1*: Be sure to select all surfaces on the model when defining shell elements at the mid-surface. All surfaces should lie on the same "side" of the model (i.e., either the inside or outside). *HINT#2*: Because the chute is a solid model, convert to a shell model using the procedure outlined beginning on page 4-12, step #5, and foreword to page 4-16 step #4.

- Fixtures: Apply *appropriate* **Fixtures** to flanges located at top and bottom of the chute. *If* selected restraints do not restrain the model in the X, Y, and Z directions, then apply one **Fixed** restraint to a single vertex on the bottom right end of the model. Consider the bottom right end to be located at the extreme right of Fig. E-13.

- External Load: External load is due to potatoes within the chute. Apply a uniform pressure only to the 105 inch segment of the *long sides* of the chute.

If, when the Study is run, the ***Static Analysis*** *window opens and warns "Excessive displacements were calculated in this model...," etc. (see Fig. E-14). Select* ***[No]*** *and continue to run the small displacement solution.*

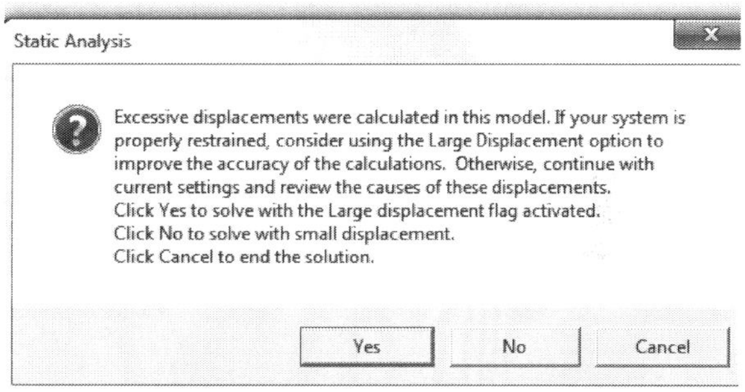

Figure E4-14 – Warning gives the option of running either a small or large displacement analysis. Choose **[No]** and run the small displacement analysis.

Solution Guidance
(It is assumed that a Study has been started in SOLIDWORKS Simulation and that **Material** and **Fixtures** have been defined).

Split Line Specification

- The **Right Plane** for this model is located at the open end of the chute.
- Therefore, create a **Reference Plane** at 105 in. from the **Right Plane**.
- Create *Split Lines* on both sides by using the **Reference plane** to **Intersect** the model. (See **Inserting Split Lines** on p. 2-9 for further guidance.)

Specify *Non*-Uniform Pressure

Steps below provide guidance to define a non-uniform pressure distribution on inclined sides of the chute.

- Right-click **External Loads** and from the pull-down menu select **Pressure…** The **Pressure** property manager opens as seen in Fig. E4-15.
- In the **Type** dialogue box select **⊙Normal to selected face**. Then activate (light blue) the **Faces for Pressure** field and proceed to select the sloped inside surface on the *back of the chute when the open end of the chute faces the left of the screen.* Select the surface between the chute open-end and *Split Lines* located at 105 inches.
- In the **Pressure Value** dialogue box set **Units** to **psi** and in the **Pressure Value** field type **0.75** psi.
- Check to open the ☑ **Nonuniform Distribution** dialogue box. Also open the SOLIDWORKS flyout menu at top left of the graphics area.

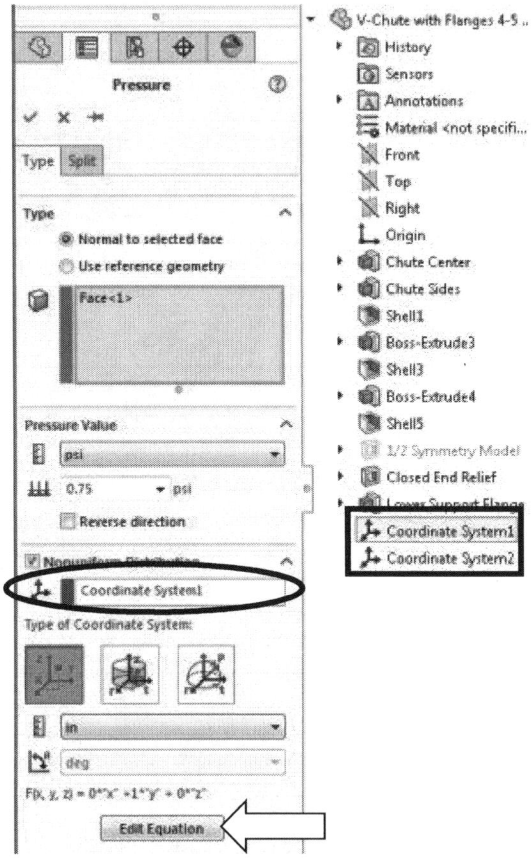

Figure E4-15 – **Pressure** property manager used to define non-uniform pressure distribution on sides of the chute.

- Click to highlight (light blue) the **Select a Coordinate System** field circled in Fig. E4-15. Next, at bottom of the SOLIDWORKS flyout menu, select **Coordinate System1** boxed in Fig. E4-15. A coordinate system appears at the top (rear) corner at the *open end* of the V-Chute. *NOTE: Observe that the +Y axis is directed downward along the sloped side of the chute.*
- In the **Nonuniform Distribution** dialogue box, once again set **Units** to **in**. Then click the **[Edit Equation]** button shown at arrow in Fig. E4-15. The **Edit Equation (Cartesian)** window opens as shown in Fig. E4-16. The "original" equation in this window appears as **F(x,y,z) = "x" + "y" + "z"**. This equation expresses the pressure distribution in the general form **p(x,y,z) = P*F(x,y,z)**. In other words, pressure **P** is a mathematical function of **x** and **y** and **z**. Pressure **P** was defined as **0.75** psi in a previous step.

Solution Guidance (continued)

- To represent a linearly increasing pressure on the side of the chute, we need only express that as Y increases toward the bottom of the chute, the pressure acting on the side wall also increases. Pressure is independent of the X coordinate along the length of the chute and likewise is independent of the Z coordinate normal to the walls.

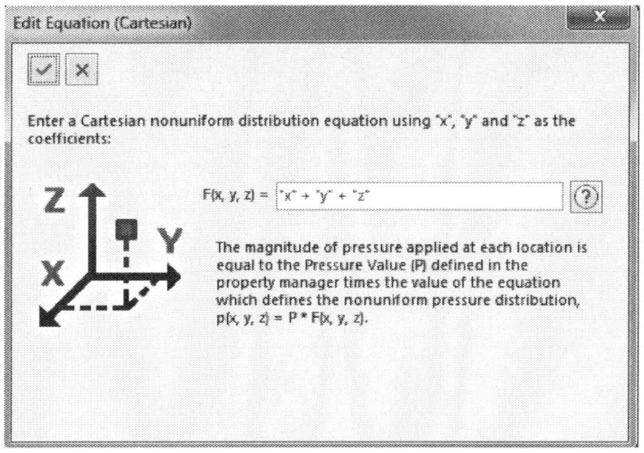

Figure E4-16 – The equation expressing non-uniform pressure distribution on chute walls is defined within the **Edit Equation** window.

- In the equation box type either **1.0*"y"** or **0*"x" + 1.0*"y" + 0*"z"**.
  Thus, in general terms: pressure **p(x,y,z) = P*F(x,y,z)**
  or
  more specifically: pressure **p(x,y,z) = 0.75*(1.0*"y")**
  Which is to say that pressure is a linear function of "y" only.

- Click the green check mark to close the **Edit Equation** window. Then click again to close the **Pressure** property manager. A non-uniform pressure distribution appears on one side of the chute.

- Repeat the above procedure for the other side of the chute. The only difference is that **Coordinate System2** is selected. It appears at the bottom of the SOLIDWORKS flyout menu.

Determine the following:

a. Create a plot containing one or two views of the model that show all fixtures and external loads applied to the model. Include the SOLIDWORKS Simulation manager tree with this plot. Do not show a mesh on this model. This/these plots should fill one-half to three quarters of an 8 ½ x 11 inch page. In the space beneath the plot(s), clearly describe the **Fixtures** selected and applied to the top flanges and, in a separate paragraph, describe **Fixtures** applied to the bottom flanges. In addition to *naming* the type of fixture, as found in the **Fixture** property manager, also describe your reasons for selecting the fixtures used.

b. Plot **Displacement1 (-Res disp-)** and print a plot of the deformed model. On this plot, **Hide** the **External Loads**, include the mesh, and apply automatic labeling of the maximum displacement. Adjacent to the deformed model, record the value of the **Deformation scale** appearing on that plot.

c. Alter the plot of part (b) to display **Displacement1 (-Res disp-)** using the ⦿**True scale** option. Then use the **Probe** feature to create a graph of **Displacement1 (-Res disp-)** along as straight a line as possible from top to bottom of the V-chute and passing through the point labeled **Max** displacement. Include a descriptive title, axis labels, and your name on this graph. In one sentence, compare the actual magnitude of maximum displacement with the visual impression of this same displacement observed in the deformed plot of part (b). Describe the relevance of the **Deformed Result** plot.

d. Answer the following questions for the plot of part (b). Given that the V-chute model is symmetrical about its long axis and its vertical axis and that external loads are also symmetrical, were the displacements plotted for both sides of the chute identical or nearly so? If not, provide a logical explanation for differences.

e. If your explanation of differences (if any) observed in part (d) focuses on the possibility that a **Fixed** restraint applied at only one vertex caused this inconsistency, then delete the questionable fixture and replace it with **Fixed** restraint at a different vertex and re-run the analysis. Plot your results and circle the revised Fixed restraint. Beneath this plot answer the following questions. Do symmetrical displacements result for the revised fixture, or do they remain the same/similar? Explain why or why not?

f. Create a plot showing von Mises stress distribution on the model. Choose a view that shows stress distribution in both "legs" of the chute. On this plot do not show **Fixtures**, **External Loads**, or the **Mesh**. Place this plot on one-half of an 8 ½ x 11 inch page. Beneath this plot state whether or not the material yield strength is exceeded and, if not, perform a simple Factor of Safety calculation using equation [1].

$$n = \frac{\text{Yield Strength}}{\text{Max von Mises Stress}} \qquad [1]$$

On the lower half of the same page, include the following plot. Based on the value of Factor of Safety determined by equation [1], create a **Factor of Safety** plot based on ⦿**Yield Strength** on the *top* shell surface. In **Step 3 of 3** of the **Factor of Safety** plot procedure, choose ⦿**Factor of safety distribution** as the type of plot and specify an integer value of safety factor "n" that is two digits greater than the rounded-up value of "n" calculated using equation [1]. (EXAMPLE: If manual calculation of n = 2.372, round-up to 3, then set the **Minimum factor of safety:** field to 5). Rotate the model to best show areas where Factor of Safety is less than "n+2."

CHAPTER #5

INTERFERENCE FIT ANALYSIS

This chapter examines modeling of an interference fit between two mating parts. For purposes of discussion the generic term "interference fit" is considered synonymous with the terminology "force fit" or "shrink fit." In SOLIDWORKS Simulation, however, all these fit types are referred to as "shrink fits." Interference fits are often used to join two members together without the need for other fastening devices such as pins, set-screws, or keys, key seats, and keyways. Interference fit analysis is often considered together with thick wall pressure vessel analysis since the internal member exerts the equivalent of an outward pressure on the part into which it is force fit. And, conversely, the external member exerts the equivalent of an external pressure onto the part it surrounds.

Although this example solves an interference fit problem for a single set of part dimensions, it is important to recognize that, in practice, maximum and minimum stress levels occur due to dimensional variations of mating parts. For example, a minimum level of interference must be ensured in order to transfer a desired torque between mating components. Minimum interference results when the smallest shaft is inserted into the largest hole. Conversely, when tolerances are such that the largest shaft is inserted into the smallest hole maximum, interference results. Stress levels correspond directly to the amount of interference. Another factor to consider occurs when different materials are used for mating parts. In these instances, the effects of differential dimension changes due to thermal expansion or contraction may also have to be considered. The above scenarios are cited to alert the user to some additional factors that affect interference fits. However, because the emphasis of this text is on mastering use of SOLIDWORKS Simulation, these additional factors are not considered in this example.

Learning Objectives

Upon completion of this example, users should be able to:

- Set-up and analyze an *interference fit* in an assembly.
- Specify and use a *cylindrical* coordinate system.
- Examine results in a *local (cylindrical)* coordinate system.
- Generate a *report* summarizing Study results.
- Apply alternative means of *controlling rigid body motion.*

Problem Statement

A partially dimensioned section view of a wheel and its axle is shown in Fig. 1. The wheel is part of an overhead traveling crane used to transport heavy materials from point-to-point on a factory floor. The 2.5041 inch diameter shaft is shrink fit into a wheel-hub with inside diameter of 2.5000 inches resulting in a 0.0041 inch diametral interference.

This example is the first to include analysis of an *assembly* involving more than one part. Analysis of this model begins below.

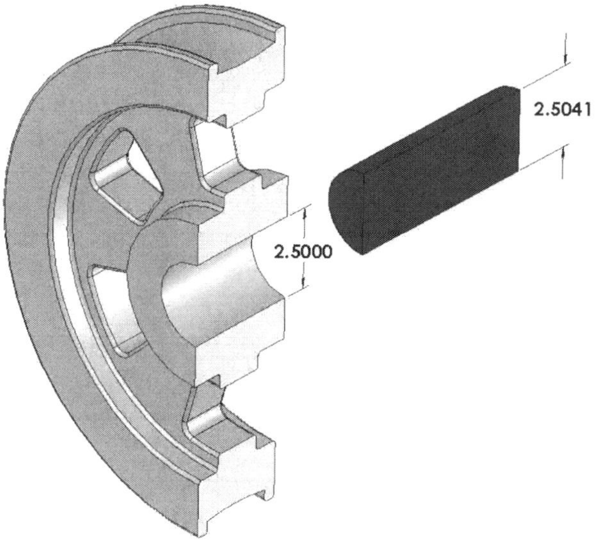

Figure 1 – Maximum shaft size and minimum hole size (minimum bore) for an interference fit between a shaft and crane wheel.

1. Open SOLIDWORKS by making the following selections. (*NOTE:* ">" is used to separate successive menu selections.)

Start>All Programs>SOLIDWORKS 2026 (or) Click the **SOLIDWORKS** icon on your screen.

2. When SOLIDWORKS is open, select **File > Open...** and open the file named **Wheel Shaft Assembly**. The model opens, and the **Assembly** tab appears at the top left of your screen. *(If the **Assembly** menu is to be opened, simply click its tab.)*

Interference Check

Before beginning an analysis of this assembly, confirm that interference does indeed exist between the shaft and wheel. Check for interference as follows.

1. In the Main menu, click **Tools > Evaluate** and from the pull-down menu select Interference Detection... A partial view of the **Interference Detection** property manager is shown in Fig. 2.

2. In the **Selected Components** dialogue box observe that the **Wheel Shaft Assembly.SLDASM** is pre-selected as the assembly to be checked for interference. Also notice that the **Results** dialogue box currently indicates that interference is **Not calculated**.

3. In the **Selected Components** dialogue box, click the **[Calculate]** button. Immediately the *volume* of interference between the shaft and wheel is calculated and listed in the **Results** dialogue box as **0.06 in^3**. Also, the interference region between the shaft and wheel is highlighted as seen in Fig. 2. Interference is thus verified.

4. Click **[OK]** ✓ to close the **Interference Detection** property manager.

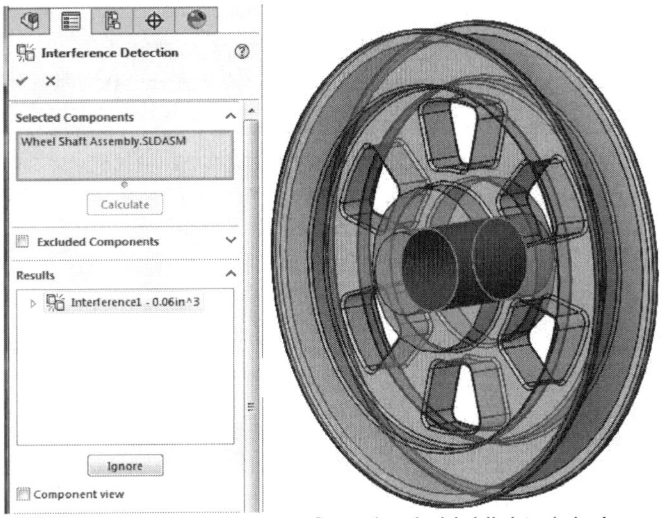

Figure 2 – The interference fit region is highlighted during an Interference Check of parts in the shaft and wheel assembly.

Create a Static Analysis (Study)

1. Click the **Simulation** *tab* to activate it. Next, on the **New Study** icon, open ▼ the pull-down menu and select **New Study**. A partial view of the **Study** property manager is shown in Fig. 3.

2. In the **Name** dialogue box type "**Force Fit Analysis-YOUR NAME**" as a descriptive name for this Study.

3. In the **Type** dialogue box select **Static** as the analysis **Type** (if not already selected). Leave the **Use 2D Simplification** and **Import Study Features …** unchecked.

4. Click **[OK]** ✓ to close the **Study** property manager.

5. The Simulation manager tree opens at left of the graphics area.

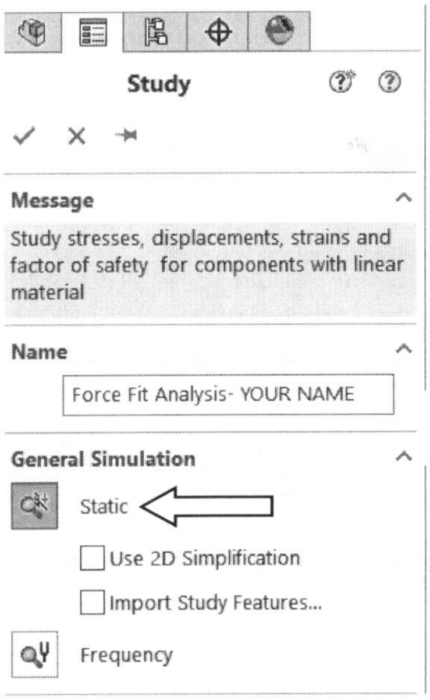

Figure 3 – Initial steps to create a Study in SOLIDWORKS Simulation.

Assign Material Properties to the Model

Unlike previous examples, materials for the **Shaft** and **Wheel** were *pre-assigned* when the model was built in SOLIDWORKS.

1. Click the " ▸ " symbol adjacent to the **Parts** folder. This action reveals that material for **Shaft-1** is listed as **(-[SW]Alloy Steel-)** and for **wheel-1** material is listed as **(-[SW]Cast Alloy Steel-)** shown circled in Fig. 4. The **[SW]** designation indicates material properties were assigned in SOLIDWORKS and are automatically transferred into Simulation.

Before proceeding, verify material properties are specified using English units as outlined below.

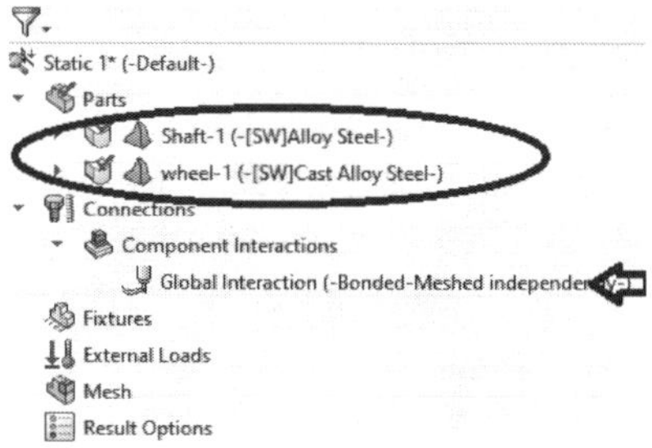

Figure 4 – Simulation manager tree showing that materials for the Shaft and Wheel assembly are pre-selected in SOLIDWORKS.

2. Right-click **Shaft-1(-[SW]Alloy Steel-)** and select **Apply/Edit Material…** In the **Materials** window set **Units:** to **English (IPS)**; then select **[Apply]** and **[Close]**.

3. Repeat step 2 for **wheel1(-[SW]Cast Alloy Steel-)**.

SOLIDWORKS Default Connection Definition

Before proceeding, examine the **Connections** defined between the wheel and shaft.

1. Click the " ▸ " symbol to open the **Connections** folder. Then, within this folder click the " ▸ " symbol to open the **Component Interactions** sub-folder.

2. Observe that **Global Interaction (-Bonded-Meshed independently-)** is initially defined between the shaft and wheel. A **Bonded** contact indicates that parts act as if they are permanently "glued" together, which is *not* the case in this example.

Analysis Insight

- It is possible to *change* the material specified within SOLIDWORKS at any time. Simply follow the steps listed below Fig. 4 before a Solution is run.
- The **Global Interaction (-Bonded-Meshed independently-)** which appears beneath the **Component Interactions** sub-folder, is the software default setting for parts in direct contact. Because the intent is to investigate a "Force Fit" between the wheel and shaft, this contact interaction setting is changed later in this example.

Defeature and Simplify the Model

An enlarged view of the shaft and wheel assembly is shown in Fig. 5. Careful observation reveals numerous small fillets and rounds on various edges of the model. Knowing in advance that the current assembly is to be analyzed using finite element methods, the original SOLIDWORKS model was created to facilitate the defeaturing process by creating all small fillets and rounds in a single step. Therefore, the defeaturing steps outlined below are very efficient.

NOTE: Larger fillets at the four "corners" of the spoke cut-outs are *not* removed from the model because, if removed, they might be a source of significant stress concentration. This insight is based upon engineering judgment. Proceed as follows to defeature the model.

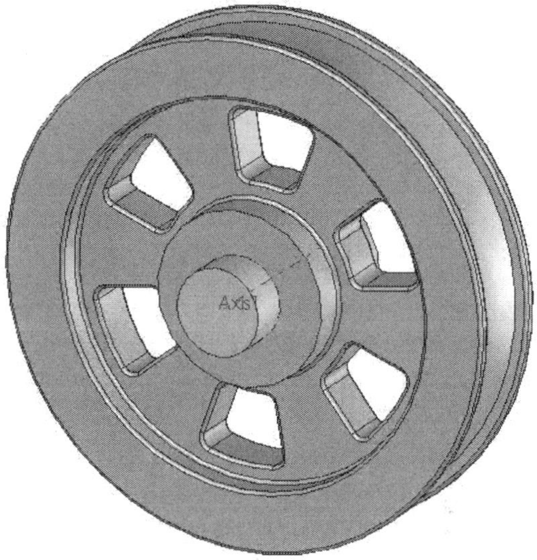

Figure 5 – Observe multiple fillets and rounds on various edges of the model.

1. In the SOLIDWORKS manager, click the " ‣ " symbol adjacent to the **wheel<1>** folder, circled in Fig. 6, to display steps used to create the wheel model.

2. If necessary, click-and-drag the lower boundary of the SOLIDWORKS feature manager tree downward to reveal its full contents. See arrow at bottom of Fig. 6.

3. Right-click "**0.10 inch Fillets & Rounds**" highlighted near the bottom of the feature manager in Fig. 6. A pop-up menu also appears to the right of the feature manager tree in Fig. 6.

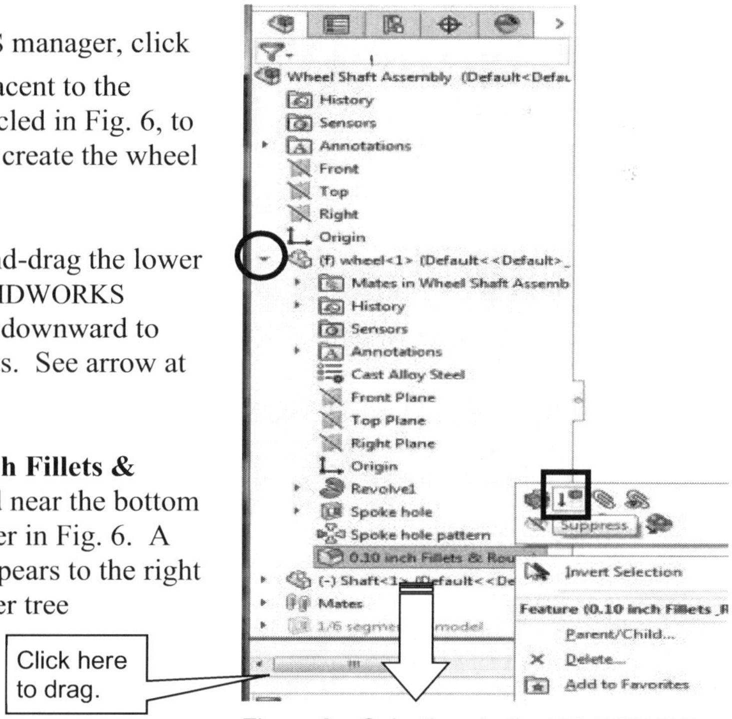

Figure 6 – Selections in the SOLIDWORKS feature manager tree to simplify wheel geometry (i.e., to defeature it).

4. Within the pop-up menu, select the **Suppress** icon boxed in Fig. 6. This action removes all small fillets and rounds from the wheel as shown in Fig. 7. The model should be simplified (defeatured) prior to meshing.

The model is further simplified by making use of model symmetry as outlined below.

Apply Fixtures

Reduce Model Size Using Symmetry

Examination of the defeatured model in Fig. 7 reveals symmetry in the repeated pattern of spokes and holes on the wheel. Once again, it is possible to reduce model size and speed up the solution process if model symmetry is used to our advantage. Because there are six spokes and six openings, it is obvious that 1/6th of the model (or a 360°/6 = 60° "slice" or "wedge") is the smallest symmetrical segment that can be used. It is possible to select other fractions of the assembly provided geometric symmetry is preserved. Other convenient model segments would be 1/3 (a 120° slice),1/2 (a 180° slice), or 2/3 (a 240° slice). Proceed as follows.

Figure 7 – Observing symmetry of the defeatured shaft and wheel assembly.

1. At the very bottom of the SOLIDWORKS manager tree, right-click the grayed-out "**1/6 segment of model**" beneath the arrow in Fig. 8.

2. From the pop-up menu, select the **Unsuppress** icon shown boxed in Fig. 8.

The result of steps 1 and 2 produces a 1/6th segment of the shaft and wheel assembly shown in Fig. 9.

3. Click-and-drag the upper boundary of the Simulation manager tree *upward* to provide more room to view its contents. CAUTION: Do *not* use the "rollback" bar pictured here as it is associated with the SOLIDWORKS manager tree.

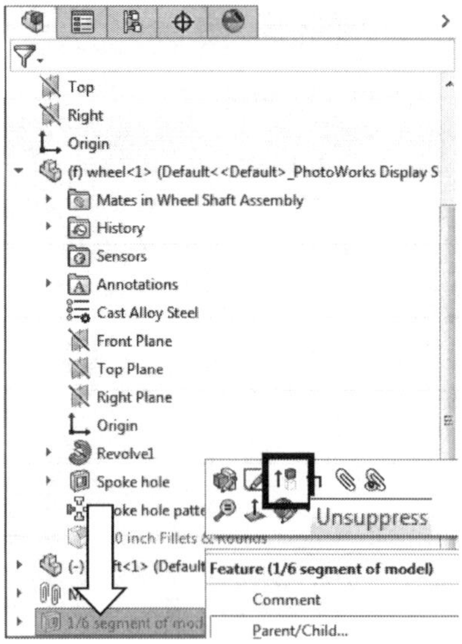

Figure 8 – Unsuppressing the 1/6th model of the shaft and wheel assembly.

Analysis Insight

Due to model symmetry, it is possible to select a "slice" of the model that either intersects openings between wheel spokes (as illustrated in Fig. 9) or one that intersects spokes on both sides of an opening.

The decision to model using the segment shown in Fig. 9 is based on an understanding that a full picture of stresses in a single spoke is more revealing than a split image of stress distribution in a half-spoke on either side of an opening. While this is the preferred selection, FEA results are *not* affected by this choice.

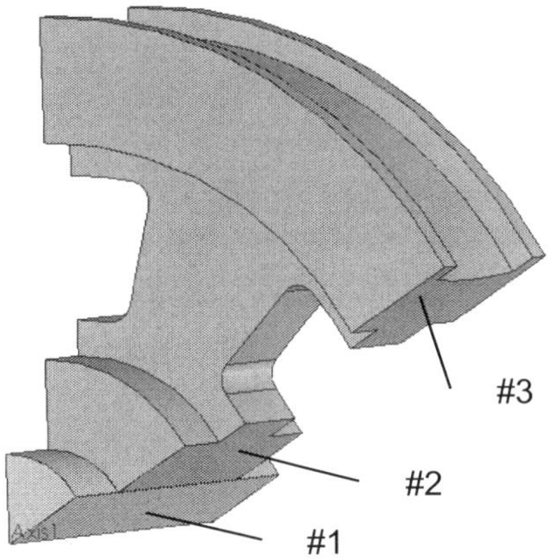

Figure 9 – Symmetry applied to yield a 1/6th segment of the shaft and wheel assembly.

Define Symmetry Restraints (Fixtures)

Symmetry restraints were first introduced in the previous chapter where segments of thin and thick-wall pressure vessels were considered. Symmetry restraints serve the purpose of making the cut portion of a symmetrical model behave *as if* the entire model were still present. Therefore, symmetry restraints must be applied to all surfaces created when the model is cut. Figure 9 shows one surface (#1) on the shaft and two surfaces (#2 and #3) on the hub and outer rim of the wheel, respectively. Of course, three duplicate surfaces exist on the opposite side of the "slice." Therefore, symmetry restraints must be applied to a total of six surfaces. Proceed as follows to apply symmetry restraints.

1. In the Simulation manager tree, right-click Fixtures **Fixtures** and from the pull-down menu select **Roller/Slider...** The **Fixture** property manager opens.

2. Observe motion of the "generic" model in the **Example** dialogue box. In essence this image shows that the block is able to move (translate) left or right and up or down on the plane, but it cannot translate in a direction normal to the plane.

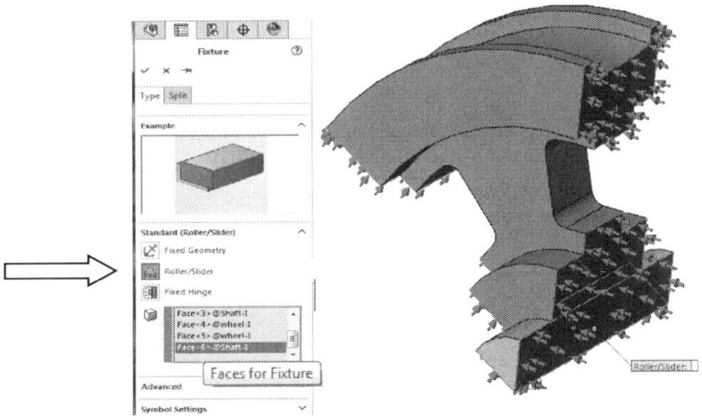

Figure 10 – **Roller/Slider** Fixture applied to all cut surfaces of the shaft and wheel assembly.

3. The **Faces for Fixture** field is active (highlighted light blue) and awaits selection of surfaces to which symmetry restraints are to be applied. Move the cursor over the model and, in any order, select the three numbered surfaces shown in Fig. 9. Also, select their counterparts on the opposite side of the model. Rotate the assembly as necessary to select all cut faces.

With each selection, a new surface is highlighted and is listed as **Face<1>@wheel-1** (or **@Shaft-1** etc.), **Face<2>@...**, up to … **Face<6>@...** in the **Faces for Fixture** field. Also, restraint symbols appear *normal* to model surfaces as illustrated in Fig. 10.

4. Click **[OK]** ✓ to close the **Fixture** property manager. **Roller/Slider-1** appears beneath the **Fixtures** folder in the Simulation manager tree.

Analysis Insight

Prior versions of SOLIDWORKS Simulation permitted application of the **Symmetry** fixture to restrain the current model. However, commencing in 2013 the **Symmetry** fixture was redefined to apply only to1/2, 1/4, or 1/8 models or models having *true orthogonal symmetry*. Recall application of the **Symmetry** fixture to the 1/8th model of a thin wall pressure vessel (see Fig. 34 in Chapter 4). This same fixture was also applied to the ½ model of a thick wall pressure vessel (Fig. 38, Chapter 4). But, because the 1/6 "slice" of the wheel-shaft assembly does not exhibit the required true orthogonal symmetry, different fixtures must be used. NOTE: If, however, ½ of the wheel-shaft assembly were used, then the **Symmetry** fixture could be applied.

Be aware that there remain at least three different **Fixtures** that can be applied to a symmetrical model that is reduced in size by cutting it into *non*-orthogonal "slices" or "wedges." Those three **Fixtures** types are described below.

Roller/Slider – Roller/Slider...
This restraint is a good option because it allows translation in two directions along a plane, but restricts motion *normal* to the plane. A **Roller/Slider** restraint is demonstrated in this example.

On Flat Faces – On Flat Faces
Cut faces of the wheel-shaft assembly "slice" are *not* orthogonal, they are *flat*. Therefore, like the **Roller/Slider** restraint, the **On Flat Faces** fixture allows translations in two directions along a cut face, but no translation *normal* to the face. Thus, this restraint could also be applied to the current example.

Use Reference Geometry – Use Reference Geometry
This option requires the user to specify which of three translations (two along the plane and one normal to the plane) are set to zero. Based on previous discussion, translation *normal* to the plane *must be set equal to zero* on a plane of symmetry if this option is used. When both solid and shell elements occur in the same model, separate **Use Reference Geometry** fixtures must be specified for each element type.

Analysis Insight (continued)

Circular Symmetry – Cyclic Symmetry
If given a choice, many users might choose the **Circular Symmetry** fixture for the wheel-shaft assembly based simply on its icon shape. The icon depicts a slice of a generic circular model. However, this is one **Fixture** that *absolutely cannot* be applied to the current model. *Why?* Use of this restraint is limited to cases where loads or displacements are present only in the *circumferential* direction. Examples of a circumferential load might be caused by *forces acting tangent to the circumference* of a circular model such as a belt pulley, a chain sprocket, a circular saw blade, or a gear.

Rigid Body Motion -
As noted in the thick-wall pressure vessel example, while assignment of symmetry boundary conditions applies proper restraints to account for missing portions of a model, those same boundary conditions may not provide sufficient restraint to prevent "rigid body motion" of the model.

For this example, note the following two facts: (a) All restraints shown in Fig. 10 are applied normal to cut surfaces of the $1/6^{th}$ model; and (b) *If* each restraint vector were broken into components, then each vector could be replaced by its X and Y force components. Rotate the model to a front view to convince yourself of the above two facts. Therefore, an obvious conclusion is that model translations are restrained in the X and Y directions, but *no restraint* exists in the Z-direction (i.e., the axial direction). Thus, rigid body motion of the model currently is *not* restrained in the axial direction.

Because rigid body motion is not allowed in finite element studies, additional restraints must be added to this, or similarly supported models, as outlined next.

Apply Fixtures to Eliminate Rigid Body Motion

Because the assembly consists of two parts, the shaft and the wheel, both parts must be restrained properly. The need to restrain both parts may seem counter-intuitive since a shrink fit is defined between the shaft and wheel and a shrink fit is considered to be a semi-permanent connection. However, this seeming contradiction provides an opportunity to note that shrink fit contact is considered frictionless by default within SOLIDWORKS Simulation. Therefore, proceed as follows to apply restraints to prevent rigid body motion.

1. Right-click Fixtures **Fixtures** and from the pull-down menu select **Fixed Geometry…** The **Fixture** property manager opens as shown on the left side of Fig. 11. The property manager initially appears different than shown in Fig. 11.

2. Open the **Advanced** dialogue box and select **Use Reference Geometry**. The reason for selecting **Reference Geometry** will be apparent in a future step.

3. In the **Advanced** dialogue box the **Faces, Edges, Vertices for Fixture** field is active (light blue). Proceed to select two *vertices* on the model (one on the shaft center-line and the other on the wheel). Selected vertices are shown circled on Fig. 11. After selecting these vertices, **Vertex<1>@Shaft-1** and **Vertex<2>@ wheel-1** appear in the active field. The actual number within **Vertex< >** depends on the order of selection. *Any other vertices could have been selected.*

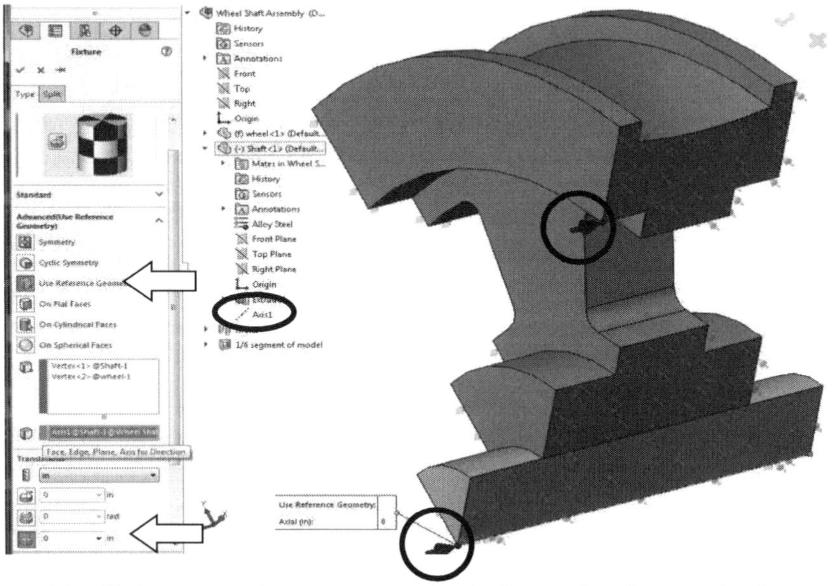

Figure 11 – **Fixture** property manager and selections of vertices and reference geometry needed to prevent rigid body motion of the shaft and wheel assembly.

4. Next, click to activate (light blue) the second field from the top in the **Advanced** dialogue box. The identifier **Face, Edge, Plane, Axis for Direction** appears when the cursor is passed over this field as illustrated in Fig. 11.

5. Select **Axis1** either on the model (shaft center-line) or near the bottom of the SOLIDWORKS flyout menu (circled in Fig. 11). **Axis1** is selected because it is oriented in the Z-direction, the direction in which rigid body translation is to be prevented. After making this selection, **Axis1@Shaft-1@Wheel Shaft Assembly** appears in the highlighted field.

6. Open the **Translations** dialogue box (if not already open) and set **Unit** to **in**. Then, at the bottom of this dialogue box (see bottom arrow in Fig. 11), select the **Axial** icon and accept the zero value shown. This value indicates that *no* translation is permitted in the **Axial** (Z) direction.

7. Click **[OK]** ✓ to close the **Fixture** property manager. **Reference Geometry-1 (:0 in:)** appears beneath the **Fixtures** folder in the Simulation manager tree. Also, restraint symbols appear on the model at the two locations circled in Fig. 11.

8. Right-click **Fixtures** and from the pull-down menu select **Hide All**. This action temporarily hides restraint symbols to reduce clutter on the model.

The preceding steps ensure that the assembly is restrained against rigid body translation in the axial Z-direction.

> **Aside:**
>
> The focus of this example is on modeling and analyzing an interference fit. Therefore, no *external* loads or *reactions* are applied to the model. In real life, external loads and reactions would be due to wheel-to-rail contact and shaft support reactions.
>
> As a consequence, only forces due to an interference fit are included in this analysis. These forces are equal and opposite between contacting surfaces. In brief, forces caused by interference fits are internally balanced.

Use Contact Interactions to Define a Shrink Fit

Because the wheel hub inside diameter is smaller than the shaft outside diameter, an interference fit exists. When analyzing shrink fits in SOLIDWORKS Simulation you are cautioned that the amount of interference should be greater than 0.1% of the larger diameter at the interface between mating parts (in this case: 0.0041 > 0.001*2.5041 = 0.0025041). Because the 0.0041-in interference is greater than 0.1% of the larger shaft size, the above restriction is satisfied, thus a valid solution is expected. This restriction is imposed because the amount of overlap between mating parts must be sufficiently large to overcome approximations introduced during meshing and mathematical round-off. If the amount of interference is too small, inaccurate solutions may result.

To establish a shrink fit between the shaft and wheel, it is necessary to specify the surfaces where interference occurs. To facilitate selecting these surfaces, components of the assembly are separated by creating an exploded view as follows.

1. From the Main menu select **Insert**. Then from the pull-down menu select **Exploded View…** A portion of the **Explode** property manager is seen in Fig. 12.

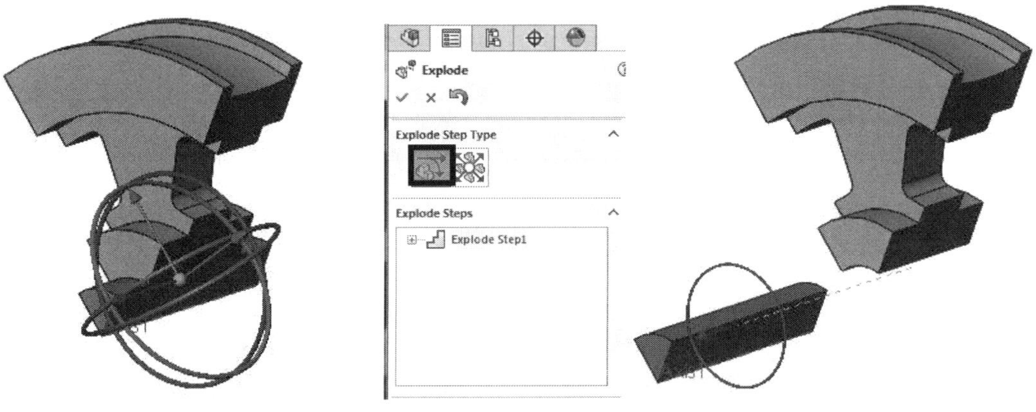

(a) (b)

Figure 12 – Manually creating an exploded view of the shaft and wheel assembly.

2. In the **Explode Step Type** dialogue box, select the **Regular step (translate and rotate)** icon, shown boxed in the middle of Fig. 12 (if not already selected).

3. For this example, move the cursor onto the graphics screen and click to select the *shaft*. Immediately, an X, Y, Z coordinate triad and three rings appear to "float" on the shaft Fig. 12(a). Click-and-drag the vector aligned with the direction of the shaft axis and drag the shaft away from the wheel as illustrated in Fig. 12(b). This action is recorded in the **Explode Steps** dialogue box as **Explode Step1**.

4. Click **[OK]** ✓ to close the **Explode** property manager. NOTE: Either component could be moved in any direction to create an acceptable exploded view.

5. Within the Simulation manager, right-click the **Connections** folder. A pull-down menu appears. *NOTE: This is the first time the* **Connections** *folder is used.*

6. From the pull-down menu select **Local Interaction…** The **Local Interaction** property manager opens, but it initially appears different than illustrated in Fig. 13.

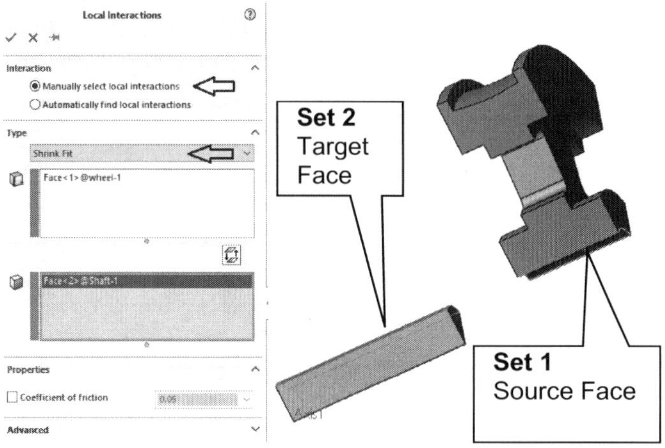

Figure 13 – Defining faces where a shrink fit occurs between the shaft and wheel. For this example the **Target** and **Source** faces can be interchanged without consequence.

7. In the **Local Interaction** dialogue box, choose ⊙ **Manually select local interactions**.

8. At top of the **Type** dialogue box, click ▼ to open the pull-down menu and select **Shrink Fit** as the type of contact to be modeled between the shaft and wheel.

9. The **Faces, Edges, Vertices for Set 1** field is activated (light blue) and awaits input. Rotate the model as necessary and select the *inside surface* of the hole as the **Set 1**. **Face<1>@wheel-1** appears in the top field of Fig. 13. **Set 1** entities are also referred to as the "source."

10. Next, click to activate the second field in the **Type** dialogue box. This is the **Faces for Set 2** field. Move the cursor over the model and select the *cylindrical*

surface of the shaft as the **Set 2** surface, also shown in Fig. 13. **Face<2>@Shaft-1** appears in the active field. **Set 2** is also referred to as the "target." NOTE: In this example either surface can be designated as **Set 1** or **Set 2**. However, this observation is not valid in all cases. See item (c) in the Analysis Insight section below for important details about "source" and "target" designations.

Analysis Insight:

a) Refer to the **Local Interaction** property manager, in Fig. 13 and on your screen, and examine the **Properties** dialogue box at the bottom of this manager. As noted earlier, interference fits are considered frictionless by default. However, if our goal were to investigate torque transmitted by an interference fit joint, then friction between mating surfaces would be defined here. Note that the friction value is "grayed out" (inactive). This example does not examine **Friction** effects.

b) Also, before closing the **Local Interaction** property manager, briefly revisit the pull-down menu that lists the various types of connections available. Understanding these criteria and a built-in hierarchy that accompanies them is essential to proper modeling a variety of design and analysis situations. For example, in *assemblies* of multiple parts, SOLIDWORKS Simulation applies a system default assumption that all contacting surfaces are **Bonded** together. This assumption treats all contacting faces of different components in an assembly as if they are permanently "glued" together. As such, the **Bonded** condition is applied *Globally* to all contacting parts. This assumption is applied unless one of the other contact conditions, such as the **Shrink Fit** used in this example, is specified *locally* (i.e., limited to contact between specific contacting entities in an assembly). Contact conditions defined in the **Local Interaction** property manager have higher priority than do Global or component contact definitions.

To pursue this topic further, the interested reader is referred to **Help** located on the main menu. From the **Help** pull-down menu, select **SOLIDWORKS Simulation** followed by **Help Topics**. Next, in the SOLIDWORKS Help window, type "source and target" in the Search Web Help field and scroll down the list to review discussion under the **Types of Contact** link. Virtually all types of contact interactions found there are excellently described and illustrated by animated examples.

c) The use of "source" or "target" is interchangeable in this example since both contacting surfaces are *faces*. However, the true definition of **Set 1** "source" entities refers to faces, edges, vertices, points, or beam joints. Whereas the definition of a **Set 2** "target" refers *only* to a face. Thus, in terms of the shrink fit modeled here, contacting faces satisfy the criteria for both a "source" and a "target." On the other hand, if a specific contact were to be defined between the surface of the shaft and the *edge* of the wheel hub, then the shaft *face* must be **Set 2**, the "target," while an *edge* of the wheel hub must be **Set 1**, the "source."

11. Finally, click **[OK]** ✓ to close the **Local Interaction** property manager. **Local Interaction-1 (-Shrink Fit<wheel-1, Shaft-1>-)** appears beneath " ▸ " **Local Interactions**.

Mesh the Model and Run the Solution

Although a correct solution is obtained with the model in either the exploded or unexploded state, return it to its *un*exploded state before meshing. This is done to permit observation of node alignment, or lack thereof, between nodes on the shaft and wheel after meshing. One way to *un*explode the model is outlined below.

1. Click the **Configuration Manager** icon shown circled at top of the SOLIDWORKS Feature manager in Fig. 14.

2. Next, click the " ▸ " symbols adjacent to **Wheel Shaft Assembly Configuration(s)** (if not already selected) and also adjacent to **Default [Wheel Shaft Assembly]**.

3. Next, right-click **ExplView1**. Then, from the pull-down menu shown in Fig. 14, select **Collapse** to return the model to its assembled view.

4. Toggle back to the **SOLIDWORKS Feature Manager** icon shown boxed in Fig. 14.

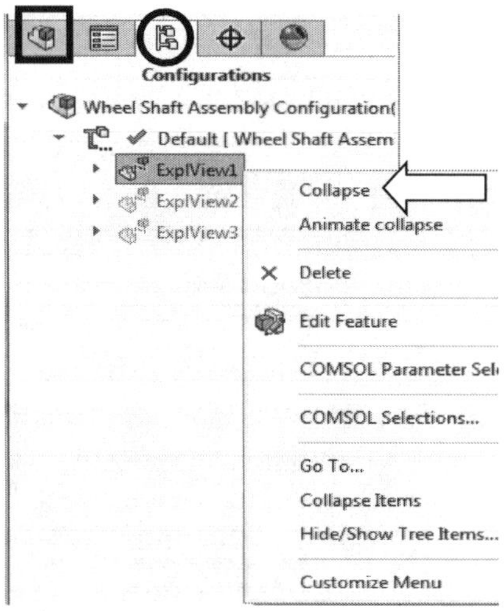

Figure 14 – Accessing the **Configuration Manager** tree to "collapse" (*un*explode) the shaft and wheel assembly.

5. In the Simulation manager tree, right-click the **Mesh** icon and from the pop-up menu select **Create Mesh…** The **Mesh** property manager opens.

6. Check ☑ **Mesh Parameters** to open this dialogue box. In this box verify that **⊙Curvature based mesh** is selected and **Unit** is set to inches (**in**).

7. The default mesh size is considered acceptable for this analysis. However, before meshing, click ˅ to open the **Options** dialogue box. One of the options listed there is ☐ **Run (solve) the analysis**. *If* this option is selected, the software proceeds directly to the Solution after meshing the model. While this action eliminates one step in the solution process, it is typically *not* recommended. *Why?* Because, if an error occurs, the user does not know if it is due to a failure to mesh the model or due to an error in the solution process. Therefore, click **[OK]** ✓ to close the **Mesh** property manager and mesh the model.

8. Finally, click the **Run This Study** icon on the Simulation tab. Alternately, right-click the Study name, **Force Fit Analysis-YOUR NAME (-Default-),** and from the pull-down menu select **Run**. The solution process takes slightly longer when solving for an interference fit (typically <10 seconds).

9. If the mesh is not displayed after the solution, right-click the **Mesh** icon, and from the pull-down menu select **Show Mesh**.

The meshed model appears in Fig. 15. NOTE: The system default **Curvature based mesh** was used in this example for the simple reason that it provides a more accurate solution. Also, an orderly mesh is not needed in subsequent steps.

Zoom in to examine nodes on the edge between the contacting surfaces circled in this figure. Notice that nodes on the shaft and wheel are not necessarily aligned with one another. This is called an "incompatible mesh."

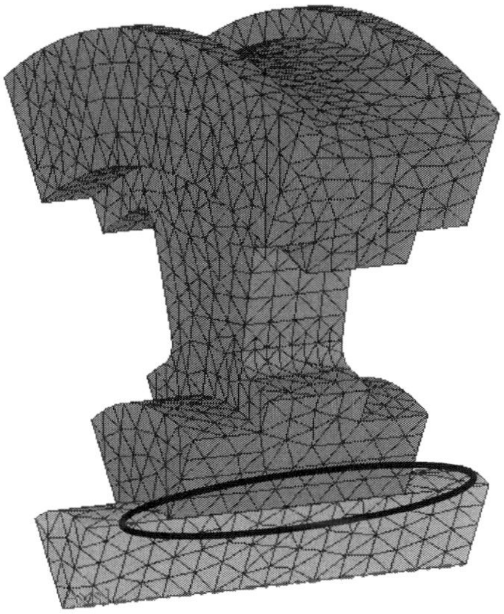

Figure 15 – Meshed model of the shaft and wheel assembly. Approximately nine corner nodes exist along the contacting surfaces.

Examination of Results

Default Stress Plot

Begin by examining the vonMises stress plot to gain an overview of results. Desired appearance attributes for this plot are defined below so that they can be copied when producing additional plots.

1. If necessary, click the " ‣ " symbol adjacent to the **Results** folder to display a list of the three default plots, **Stress1**, **Displacement1**, and **Strain1**.

2. If necessary, double-click the **Stress1 (-vonMises-)** *icon* to display this plot. Zoom-in on the model to observe deformation between the shaft and wheel hub in the interference fit region. If the deformed model does *not* appear or if units on the stress legend are *not* psi, follow steps 3 to 5. Otherwise skip to step 6.

3. Right-click **Stress1 (-vonMises-)**, and from the pop-up menu select **Edit Definition…** The **Stress Plot** property manager opens.

4. In the **Display** dialogue box, change **Units** to **psi**.

5. Check "✓" to open the ☑ **Deformed Shape** dialogue box (if not already open). Within this dialogue box, select ⊙ **Automatic**. Then click **[OK]** ✓ to close the **Stress Plot** property manager. The system default, exaggerated deformation scale, is applied to an exploded view of the model.

After examining the deformed model, return it to its un-deformed shape as follows.

6. On the **Simulation** tab, located above the graphics area, click the **Deformed Result** icon.

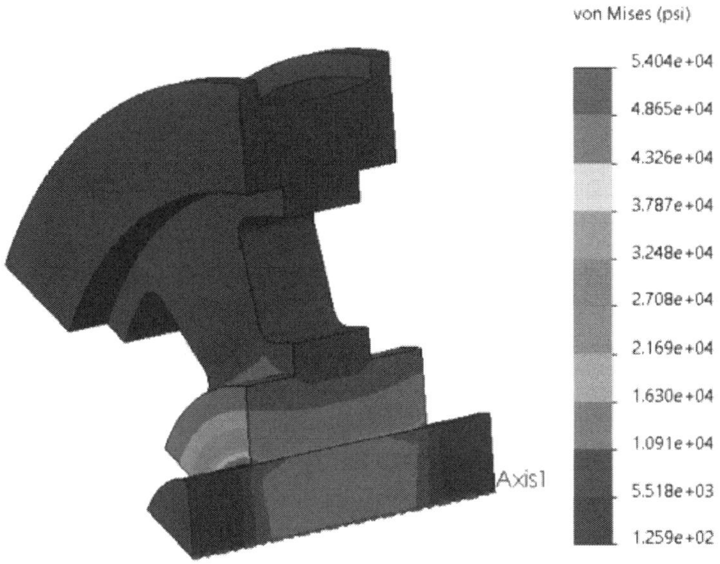

Figure 16 – vonMises stress plot incorporating modified display characteristics outlined in this section.

Next, adjust appearance of the von Mises plot so that, at the conclusion of this process, the plot appears as shown in Fig. 16. Proceed as follows.

7. Right-click **Stress1 (-vonMises-)**, and from the pop-up menu select **Edit Definition…** The **Stress Plot** property manager opens.

8. Click ˅ to open the **Advanced Options** dialogue box. Then, click to *clear* the check from ☐ **Average results across boundary for parts**. This action is important because parts of this assembly are made of two *different materials*. Also, the shaft is loaded in radial and circumferential compression while the inside of the wheel is subject to radial compression and circumferential tension. Therefore, it is not appropriate to average stress results across these two different parts. The resulting values would be meaningless.

9. Also, within the **Stress Plot** property manager, click ˅ to open the **Property** dialogue box. In this dialogue box, click to "check" ☑ **Include title text** and in the empty field, type your name followed by a descriptive title for the plot.

10. Next, within the **Stress Plot** property manager, select the **Settings** tab.

11. In the **Fringe Options** dialogue box, click ▼ to open the pull-down menu and select **Discrete** as the display mode for fringes.

12. Within the **Boundary Options** dialogue box, open the pull-down menu ▼ and select **Model** to display a black outline on the model (if not already selected).

13. Click **[OK]** ✓ to close the **Stress Plot** property manager.

Observation of Fig. 16 reveals that maximum stress levels in the vicinity of the shrink fit (54,040 psi, rounded value) *exceed* Yield Strength of the wheel material, which is 35000 psi. Figure 17 shows a summary of properties for the wheel in the **Material Details** window. Material yield strength, 241.28 MPa ≈ 35000 psi, is listed adjacent to the arrow. Another way to examine this fact is explored in the "Aside" section below.

Aside:

Recall that material information is available at any time by clicking the " ▸ " symbol adjacent to the **Parts** folder to reveal **Shaft-1** and **wheel-1**. Next, right-click **wheel-1 (-Cast Alloy Steel-)** and in the pull-down menu, shown in Fig. 17, select **Details...** This action opens the **Material Details** window located at the right side of Fig. 17.

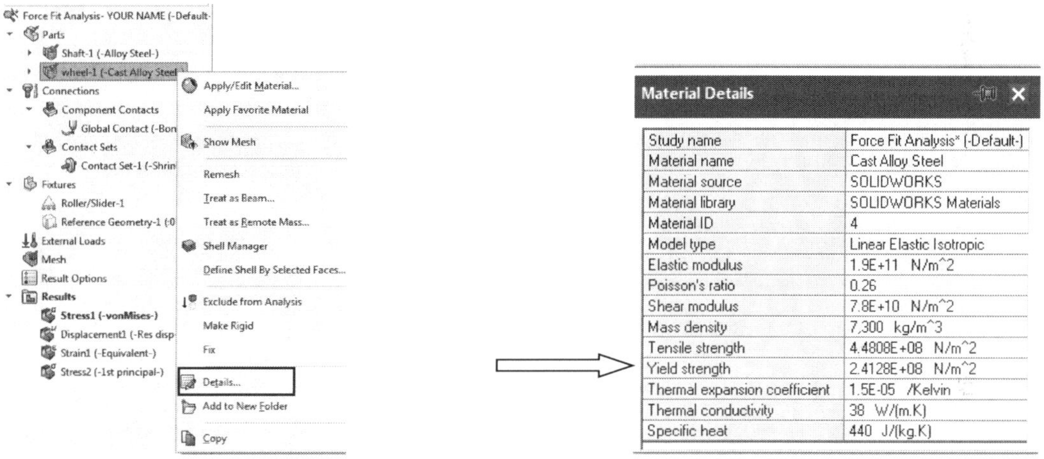

Figure 17 – Accessing material property details for the wheel to permit comparison of material Yield Strength with resulting stress in the component.

Notice that material yield strength does not appear on the vonMises stress plot as occurred in earlier examples. The reason for this is that assemblies involve multiple parts, which are often made of different materials. Therefore, the potential for different material properties prohibits the display of a single yield strength value. For this reason an alternative procedure to that of using the *Safety Factor* check can be applied to display regions where yield strength is exceeded. To apply this method, begin by making a *temporary* change in the **Stress Plot** property manager outlined below.

a) If **Stress1 (-vonMises-)** plot is not displayed, double-click its icon to display it.

b) Right-click **Stress1 (-vonMises-)** and from the pull-down menu select **Chart Options...** The **Stress Plot** property manager opens.

c) Near the bottom of the **Display Options** dialogue box uncheck □**Automatically defined maximum value**. Then, in the box corresponding to maximum stress, type a value such as **38000** (or **3.8e4**). This value is greater than yield strength for the wheel by approximately 3,000 psi.

d) Do *not* change the **Automatically defined minimum** value determined on the von Mises stress plot. Click **[OK]** ✓ to close the **Stress Plot** property manager.

A new plot of vonMises stress within the shaft and wheel assembly is shown in Fig. 18. However, this plot highlights (in red) the entire region where stress due to the interference fit exceeds the yield strength. Examination of the colored stress chart reveals that stresses in red range from approximately 34,840 psi to 38,000 psi. Therefore, the stress region above the yield strength (35,000 psi) is easily identified. Next, reset the plot to its original settings as follows.

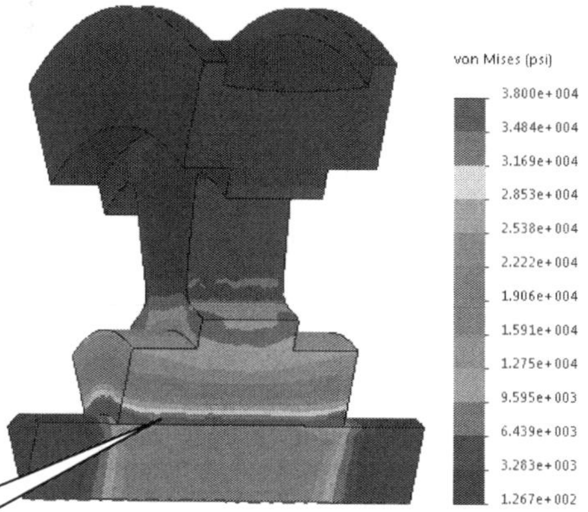

Note enlarged region shown in red

Figure 18 – Locating regions where yield strength is exceeded by re-defining chart **Display Options**.

e) Return to the **Display Options** dialogue box and check ☑ **Automatically defined maximum value**, which restores previous Max. and Min. stress values. The smaller red region now depicts stresses near the true maximum values.

f) Click **[OK]** ✓ to close the **Stress Plot** property manager. The image is reset to display the full-range of von Mises stress throughout the assembly.

The fact that yield strength of the wheel is exceeded is cause for redesign of the interference fit and/or selection of an alternative wheel material. However, since the goal of this example is to focus on defining interference fits and interpreting results related to those fits, a re-design of the shaft and wheel assembly is not pursued here. We now return to investigate other more meaningful ways to display results.

Stress Plots in a Cylindrical Coordinate System

Tangential (Circumferential or Hoop) Stress

Tangential stress is one of two stresses easily calculated using classical stress equations for a shrink fit. However, because traditional stresses like σ_x, σ_y, σ_z, σ_1, σ_2, σ_3, τ_{xy}, τ_{yz}, τ_{zx}, etc., in a Cartesian (X, Y, Z) coordinate system are not conducive for representing tangential stress in cylindrical parts, a cylindrical coordinate system is introduced below to facilitate the examination of results.

When establishing a cylindrical coordinate system, *any* axis can be used to define the axis of a local cylindrical coordinate system. However, this axis must be chosen wisely because once an axis is selected, stresses usually associated with SX = σ_x, SY = σ_y, and SZ = σ_z take on new meanings as summarized in Table 1.

In the following discussion, "reference axis" refers to an axis aligned with the centerline of a cylindrical coordinate system.

Table 1 – Correspondence between stresses in a Cartesian coordinate system and their equivalents in a cylindrical coordinate system.

Original Meaning of Stress	New Meaning in the Cylindrical Coordinate System
SX = stress in X-direction σ_x.	SX = now denotes stress in the *radial* direction (σ_r) relative to the selected reference axis.
SY = stress in Y-direction σ_y.	SY = denotes stress in the *circumferential* or *tangential* direction (σ_t) relative to the selected reference axis.
SZ = stress in Z-direction σ_z.	SZ = denotes stress in the *axial* direction (σ_a) relative to the selected reference axis.

In brief, no matter what axis is chosen to be the reference axis[1] of a cylindrical coordinate system, the correspondence between radial, circumferential, and axial stresses defined in Table 1 remains valid. Thus, a reference axis is selected consistent with the above criteria.

Before selecting an axis to define a cylindrical coordinate system, a *copy* of the existing vonMises stress plot is made. The primary reason for making a copy of this plot is to save the time it would take to recreate all of the graphic settings defined earlier. Copy the plot as follows.

1. Right-click **Stress1 (-vonMises-)** and from the pop-up menu select **Copy**.
2. Right-click the **Results** folder and from the pop-up menu select **Paste**. A plot named **Copy[1] Stress1 (-vonMises-)** is added to the list of plots beneath the **Results** folder.
3. Double-click **Copy[1] Stress1 (-vonMises-)** to display an *identical* plot of the vonMises stress that includes all previously defined display options.

Next, a cylindrical coordinate system is defined. **Axis1**, aligned with the shaft centerline, is the *only logical choice* for the axis of a cylindrical coordinate system. However, since the goal is to display tangential stress in the cylindrical coordinate system, two changes must be made to the *copied* plot. First, **SY** must be specified as the stress to be viewed in this plot because, according to Table 1, **SY** = *tangential* stress in a cylindrical coordinate system. And second, **Axis1** must be defined as the axis of a cylindrical coordinate system. Proceed as follows to alter the copied plot.

4. Right-click **Copy[1] Stress1 (-vonMises-)** and from the pop-up menu select **Edit Definition…** The **Stress Plot** property manager opens as shown in Fig. 19.

---

[1] Reference axis refers to an axis aligned with the centerline of the cylindrical coordinate system.

5. In the **Display** dialogue box, click ▼ to open the stress **Component** pull-down menu and change it to **SY: Y Normal Stress**. This action also opens the **Advanced Options** dialogue box shown in Fig. 19. Recall that according to Table 1, stress **SY** represents *tangential* stress in a cylindrical coordinate system.
6. Move the cursor over the top field in the **Advanced Options** dialogue box to identify it as the **Plane, Axis, or Coordinate System**. Click to highlight this field (light blue) to indicate it is active and awaiting user input (if not already selected).
7. In the graphics screen, either click to select the center-line of the shaft axis (or) click to select **Axis1** in the SOLIDWORKS flyout menu shown circled in Fig. 19. Either selection establishes **Axis1** as the reference axis of a cylindrical coordinate system, and the name **Axis1@ Shaft-1@Wheel Shaft Assembly** appears in the currently active field.
8. Verify that ⊙ **Node Values** is selected and click **[OK]** ✓ to close the **Stress Plot** property manager.

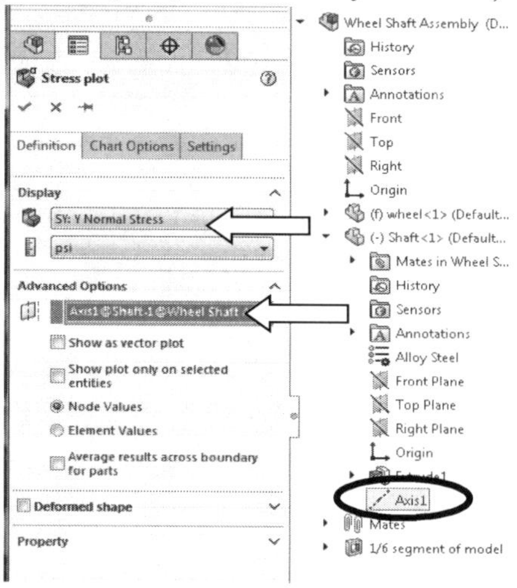

Figure 19 – Selections to define a cylindrical coordinate system and circumferential stress.

The tangential stress distribution, as it appears in a cylindrical coordinate system, is shown in Fig. 20. Most of the model is green except in the contact region.

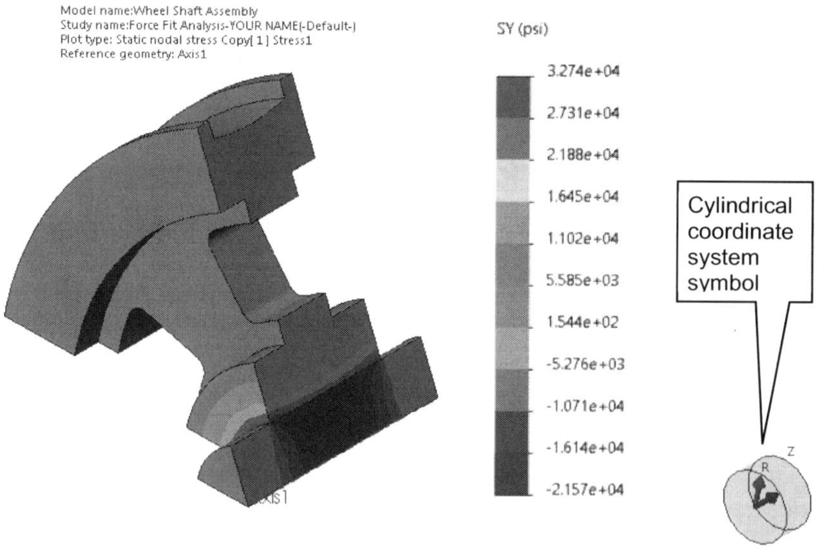

Figure 20 – Illustration showing tangential stress distribution in the shaft and wheel in a cylindrical coordinate system.

9. Once again move the cursor onto **Copy[1] Stress1 (-Y normal-)** and click-*pause* to select this 'name.' Then within the name field, type "**Tangential Stress**" and press **[Enter]**. The plot name is changed to **Tangential Stress (-Y normal-)**.

Observations:

Figure 20 displays the tangential stress distribution in a cylindrical coordinate system. Tangential stress in the wheel hub is analogous to tangential (circumferential or hoop) stress induced in a thick-wall cylinder subject to internal pressure. In this example, however, an interference fit is the cause of internal pressure acting on the external wheel hub. In Fig. 20, and on your screen, notice that the Global X, Y, Z coordinate system triad is supplemented by a cylindrical coordinate system symbol.

Also, observation of stress magnitude reveals that maximum tangential stress is approximately 2,150 psi below the wheel material yield strength. However, recall that von Mises stress in Fig. 16 and given by equation [1] is made up of *all* components of principal stress at a point. For simplicity, consider only a two-dimensional state of stress within the wheel hub, then both tangential *and* radial stress components contribute to von Mises stress (σ') as follows.

$$\sigma' = \sqrt{\sigma_t^2 - \sigma_t \sigma_r + \sigma_r^2} \qquad [1]$$

where - σ_t = tangential stress (circumferential or hoop stress)
σ_r = radial stress
σ' = von Mises stress

This brief digression emphasizes the need to consider the *appropriate* stress when reaching conclusions about part safety. Von Mises stress magnitude still governs!

Radial Stress

The above observation leads to the conclusion that *radial* stress should also be examined in order to obtain a complete picture of stress due to the interference fit. Proceed as follows to produce a plot of radial stress.

1. Make a copy of the **Tangential Stress (-Y normal-)** plot by clicking and dragging it onto the **Results** folder. A new copy, listed as **Copy[1] Tangential Stress (-Y normal-)** appears beneath the **Results** folder.

2. Double-click **Copy[1] Tangential Stress (-Y normal-)** to open this plot and make it active. The plot appears unchanged because it is an exact copy of the previous display.

3. Right-click the new **Copy[1] Tangential Stress (-Y normal-)** and from the pull-down menu select **Edit Definition…** The **Stress Plot** property manager opens as shown in Fig. 21. Next, click  to open the **Advanced Options** dialogue box.

Because the preceding steps copied a plot that already includes a cylindrical coordinate system, there is no need to repeat steps required to define that coordinate system. Verify this by observing that **Axis1@Shaft-1@Wheel Shaft Assembly** appears in the top field of the **Advanced Options** dialogue box shown at the arrow in Fig. 21.

4. In the **Display** dialogue box, click ▼ to open the **Component** pull-down menu and from the stresses listed select **SX: X Normal Stress** which, according to Table 1, represents the *radial* stress in a cylindrical coordinate system.

5. Click **[OK]** ✓ to close the **Stress Plot** property manager.

Before proceeding, change the name of the plot currently named **Copy[1] Tangential Stress (-X normal-)** to reflect that it now contains a plot of *radial* stress. Try this on your own or use the following step.

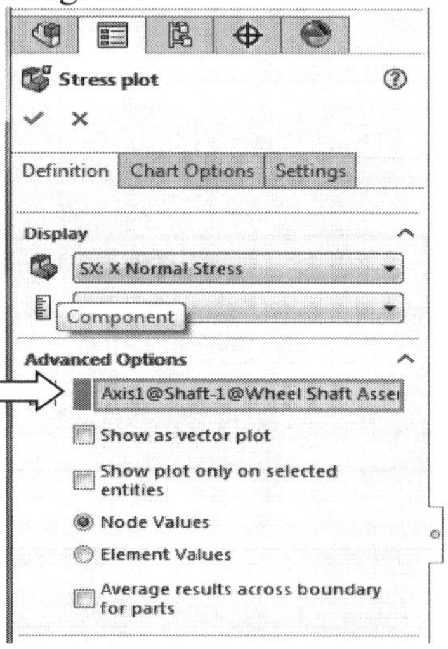

Figure 21 – Selecting SX: X Normal to display *radial* stress in the cylindrical coordinate system.

6. Click-*pause*-click the current folder and type **Radial Stress**. Then press **[Enter]**. The revised plot name should appear as **Radial Stress (-X normal-)**.

The resulting plot of radial stress is shown in Fig. 22. Radial stress represents stress normal to the two contacting surfaces. As such, radial stress represents the contact pressure between the shaft and wheel bore. Also observe the + and - signs of radial stress magnitudes shown in the color-coded stress scale. Virtually all radial stress magnitudes are negative within the model. Negative signs indicate compressive stresses acting on the outer surface of the shaft and on the inner surface of the wheel hub in the vicinity of the interference fit. This result is consistent with a general understanding of what happens in a shrink fit.

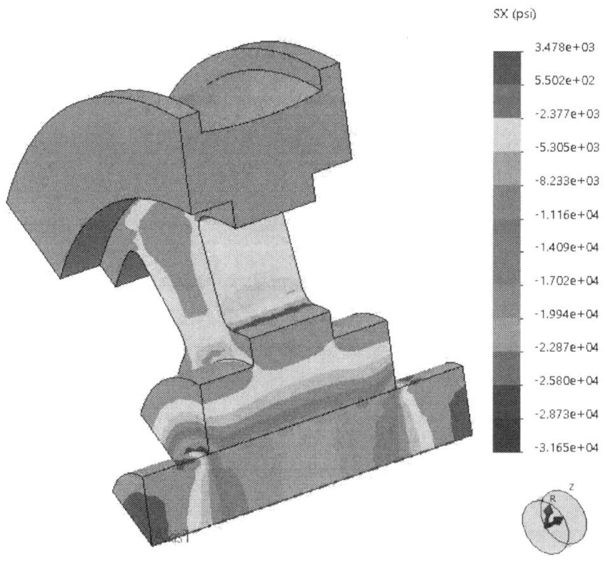

Figure 22 – Plot of *radial* stress distribution throughout the shaft and wheel assembly caused by an interference fit.

Verification of Results

Stress Predicted by Classical Interference Fit Equations

Consistent with previous examples, a check is made to determine the validity of results in the current analysis. However, classical equations for interference fits between mating parts are based on two assumptions. Those assumptions are that (a) both components are of equal length, and (b) components are uniform thickness throughout their contact length. Both of these assumptions are violated in the current example; therefore, some differences between classical and FEA results are anticipated. The next paragraph describes two reasons for the expected differences.

First, the fact that both inner and outer members are not of equal length gives rise to higher stresses near both ends of the wheel hub at locations indicated in Fig. 23. These regions of high stress are caused by stress concentration effects due to pressure induced by the shrink fit combined with the geometric discontinuity where the shaft meets the wheel hub. Higher tensile stress in this region of the hub was previously observed in Fig. 16. Second, a stiffening effect occurs in the central region of the hub, circled in Fig. 23, where the hub is thicker due to spokes and a built-up section located near its center. Stiffening in this region has the effect of altering magnitudes of all stresses examined thus far (tangential stress, vonMises stress, and radial stress).

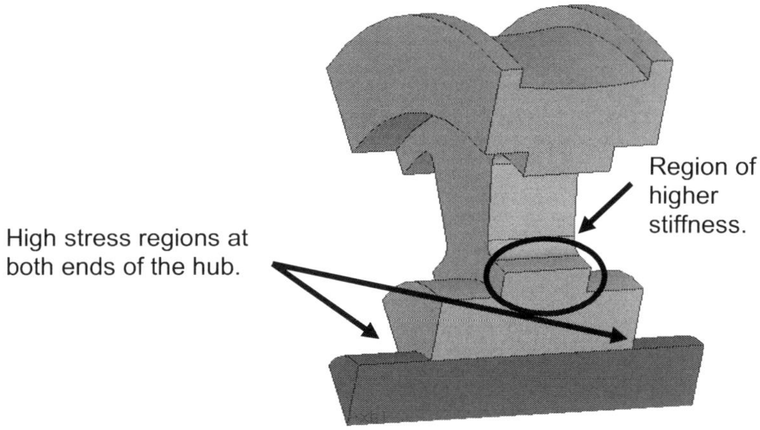

Figure 23 – Geometric differences between the actual model and assumptions of classical interference fit equations.

Classical interference fit equations are applied below to determine tangential and radial stresses at the contact surface. Nominal part dimensions, given in Fig. 1, combined with SOLIDWORKS material properties for the shaft and wheel, are used in equation [2] to determine the common contact pressure "p" between mating parts.

Solution for common contact pressure between force fit parts.

$$\delta = \frac{pR}{E_o}\left(\frac{r_o^2 + R^2}{r_o^2 - R^2} + \nu_o\right) + \frac{pR}{E_i}\left(\frac{R^2 + r_i^2}{R^2 - r_i^2} - \nu_i\right) \qquad [2]$$

$$0.00205 = \frac{p(1.25)}{27.6e6}\left(\frac{(2.5)^2 + (1.25)^2}{(2.5)^2 - (1.25)^2} + 0.26\right) + \frac{p(1.25)}{30.5e6}\left(\frac{(1.25)^2 + 0^2}{(1.25)^2 - 0^2} - 0.28\right)$$

Solving equation [2] for contact pressure "p" between the wheel and shaft yields p = 17,530 psi = radial stress at the contact surface = σ_r.

Where: δ = radial interference = 0.0041/2 = 0.00205 in.
- p = the *unknown* contact pressure between mating parts
- R = common radius at contacting surfaces = 1.25 in.
- r_i = inside radius of inner member (r_i = 0 for a solid shaft)
- r_o = outside radius of external member (wheel hub radius, r_o = 2.5000 in.) [not to be confused with shaft diameter = 2.50 in. shown on Fig. 1]
- E_i = modulus of elasticity for inner member (shaft)
- E_o = modulus of elasticity for outer member (wheel)
- ν_i = Poisson's ratio for inner member (shaft)
- ν_o = Poisson's ratio for external member (wheel)

Next, using the contact pressure "p" that exists between the shaft and wheel hub, radial stress at the inner surface of the outer member (i.e., on the inner surface of the wheel hub) is computed in equation [3]. Logically, this value should equal the contact pressure.

$$(\sigma_r)_o = -p\frac{r_o^2 - R^2}{r_o^2 - R^2} = -17530\left(\frac{(2.50)^2 - (1.25)^2}{(2.50)^2 - (1.25)^2}\right) = -17{,}530\,psi \qquad [3]$$

Finally, the tangential stress at the inner surface of the outer member (i.e., tangential stress on inner surface of the wheel hub) is given by equation [4].

$$(\sigma_t)_o = p\frac{r_o^2 + R^2}{r_o^2 - R^2} = 17530\left(\frac{(2.5)^2 + (1.25)^2}{(2.5)^2 - (1.25)^2}\right) = 29{,}200\,psi \qquad [4]$$

Stress Predicted by Finite Element Analysis

Radial Stress Comparison

Given the prior observations about obvious differences between classical equation assumptions and the actual model, it is logical to expect differences between results predicted by classical equations and a finite element analysis (FEA). This section focuses on comparing results at contact locations predicted by classical equations [2] through [4].

Proceed as follows to determine radial stress (i.e., the contact pressure) between the shaft and wheel. Begin by reproducing the exploded view as follows.

*As of this writing, second time access to the **Explode** feature of SOLIDWORKS is not working properly. Thus, follow steps 1 through 4 below to turn exploded views "on" or "off."*

1. Click the **Configuration Manager** icon at top of the SOLIDWORKS Feature manager tree. Click successive " ▸ " symbols until ExplView1 appears.

2. Right-click **ExplView1**, and from the pull-down menu select **Explode**. (NOTE: Although **Axis1** may move away from the model, the explode action is not executed until step 4 below.)

3. Return to the **Radial Stress (-X normal-)** and double click its name. The **Stress Plot** property manager opens.

4. Click **[OK]** ✓ to close the **Stress Plot** property manager and the model appears as an exploded view.

Now back to our investigation of radial stress on the contacting surfaces.

5. In the Simulation manager, right-click **Radial Stress (-X normal-)** and from the pull-down menu choose **List Selected**. The **Probe Result** window opens as shown in Fig. 24.

6. In the **Options** dialogue box, choose ⊙ **On selected entities** (if not already selected).

7. In the **Results** dialogue box the **Faces, Edges, or Vertices** field is highlighted (light blue) and awaits selection of the item for which results are to be displayed. On the graphics screen, rotate and zoom-in on the inner surface of the wheel hub shown "boxed" in Fig. 24, then click to select it. **Face<1>@wheel-1** appears in the active field.

8. Next, in the **Results** dialogue box, click the **[Update]** button.

Immediately the table is populated with data occurring at every node on the selected surface. The **Value (psi)** column contains values of *radial* stress at all nodes on the inside surface of the wheel hub. Also included are node numbers and X, Y, Z coordinates of each data point on the selected surface, and a column identifying the **Components**, in this case **wheel-1**, to which the data applies. NOTE: To accurately view tabulated data it may be necessary to click-and-drag the right margin of the Simulation manager tree as well as column-edges within the table to increase their width.

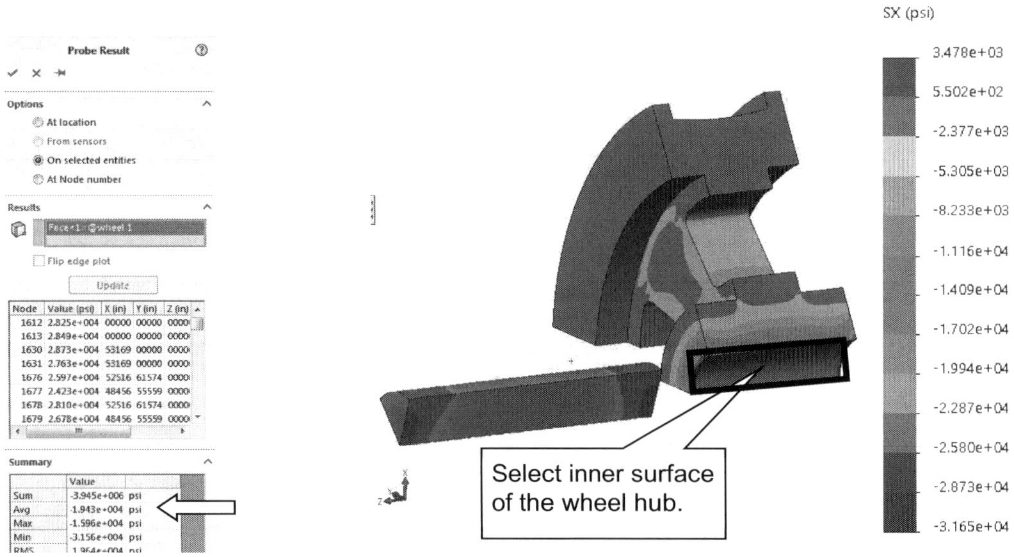

Figure 24 – Inside of the wheel surface is selected to examine results of all radial stresses acting on that surface. Results are summarized in the **Probe Result** table.

In the **Summary** dialogue box, located near the bottom of the **Probe Result** property manager, observe that radial stress values on the selected surface are summarized in several different forms (**Sum**, **Avg**, **Max**, **Min**, and **RMS**). For this example, consider only the **Avg** value listed as **-1.943e+4 psi** for the radial stress (values may vary). Using this value, a comparison with the result of classical equation [2] above yields

$$\%\text{difference} = \frac{\text{FEA result} - \text{classical result}}{\text{FEA result}} = \frac{-19430 - (-17530)}{-19430} = 9.9\% \quad [5]$$

Although the percent difference found in equation [5] exceeds desired expectations, it is a reasonable value given the differences between assumptions associated with use of classical equations and the actual model geometry. This larger than desired difference is another case where St. Venant's principle influences results due to a discontinuity.

9. Select the **[OK]** ✓ to close the **Probe Result** property manager.

Tangential Stress Comparison

Next return to the **Tangential Stress (-Y normal-)** plot and repeat the above procedure, except this time determine the *tangential* stress on the inner surface of the wheel hub. Try this on your own. If needed, follow the steps outlined below.

1. Right-click **Tangential Stress (-Y normal-)**, then from the pull-down menu select **Show**.
2. Right-click **Tangential Stress (-Y normal-)** and from the pull-down menu choose **List Selected**. The **Probe Result** property manager opens.

3. In the **Options** dialogue box, choose ⊙ **On selected entities** (if not already selected).

4. On the graphics screen, select the inner surface of the wheel hub shown "boxed" in Fig. 24.

5. In the **Results** dialogue box, click the **[Update]** button.

Compare the **Avg** value (**2.880e+4 psi**) for the tangential stress from the finite element analysis with that predicted by equation [4] above. The comparison is shown in equation [6] below.

$$\%\text{difference} = \frac{\text{FEA result} - \text{classical result}}{\text{FEA result}} = \frac{28800 - 29200}{28800} = 1.4\% \quad [6]$$

6. Click **[OK]** ✓ to close the **Probe Result** property manager.

These findings represent much better agreement between Finite Element Analysis stress prediction and classical equation results. It might appear that the next logical step would be to compare finite element results for tangential and radial stresses on the outer surface of the *shaft* with results predicted by equation [3]. However, because the process outlined above selects data at *all* nodes on the cylindrical shaft surface, poor agreement is expected. *Why?* Because considerable area, on both ends of the shaft surface, lies outside of the contact area, results on this surface would be unduly influenced by stress in those regions. For this reason, these results are not compared here. However, if desired, *Split Lines* could be added to the shaft to limit comparison to the contact region only.

Quantifying Radial Displacements

Through additional application of the **List Selected** feature, SOLIDWORKS Simulation provides a convenient means to verify the interference fit imposed on the mating parts. NOTE: Because the shaft and wheel hub are of different lengths, results obtained from the following analysis are expected to differ from those predicted by classical equations, which assume inner and outer members are equal in length. However, in instances where inner and outer members are of the same length, as in most end-of chapter exercises, excellent agreement of results is obtained (often < 1% difference). Our goal here is to learn how to make this comparison. Proceed as follows to determine part deformation.

1. In the Simulation manager, right-click **Displacement1 (-Res disp-),** and from the pull-down menu select **Show**. The **Displacement** plot is displayed.

2. Again, right-click **Displacement1 (-Res disp-)**, and from the pull-down menu select **Edit Definition…** The **Displacement Plot** property manager opens as shown in Fig. 25.

3. In the **Component** field of the **Display** dialogue box, select **UX: X Displacement**. According to Table 1, **UX: X Displacement** corresponds to *radial* displacement in a cylindrical coordinate system.

4. Also in the **Display** dialogue box, verify that **Units** are set to **in** and that ⊙ **True scale** is selected in the ☑ **Deformed Shape** dialogue box.

5. Click ˅ to open the **Advanced Options** dialogue box. Click to activate (light blue) the **Plane, Axis or Coordinate System** field. It now awaits selection of an axis to define a cylindrical coordinate system.

6. On the model, select **Axis1** on the shaft centerline as the reference axis for a cylindrical coordinate system. Alternately, near the bottom of the SOLIDWORKS flyout menu, select **Axis1**. **Axis1@Shaft-1@Wheel Shaft Assembly** should appear in the highlighted field.

7. Click **[OK]** ✓ to close the **Displacement plot** property manager.

8. If the plot produced in the preceding step does not appear on the graphics screen, double-click **Displacement1 (-X disp-)** to display the plot.

9. Right-click **Displacement1 (-X disp-)** and from the pull-down menu choose **List Selected**. The **Probe Result** property manager opens.

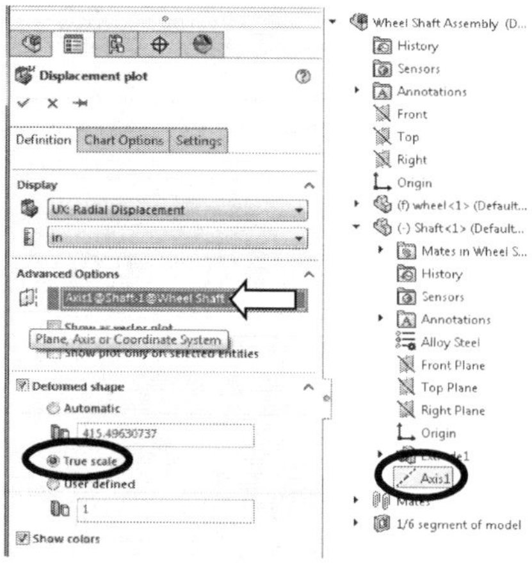

Figure 25 – Set-up of the **Displacement Plot** property manager to produce a plot of radial displacement.

10. In the graphics area, click the inner surface of the wheel hub shown "boxed" in Fig. 24. Then in the **Results** dialogue box, click the **[Update]** button.

The preceding step causes radial displacements at every node on the inner surface of the hub to be listed in the table of the **Results** dialogue box. Once again it may be necessary to click-and-drag to adjust column widths so that complete numerical values of displacement can be observed.

Of primary importance to this analysis is the **Avg** value of displacement listed in the **Summary** dialogue box. The value shown there corresponds to *radial* displacement of the inner surface of the wheel hub for the interference fit defined at the start of this example. The **Avg** value of radial deformation on the inside surface of the wheel is listed as **1.510e-3 in** (values may vary).

Without exiting the **Probe Result** property manager, proceed to examine deformation on the shaft surface as follows.

11. In the **Options** dialogue box, once again click ⊙ **On selected entities**. This action clears all values in the **Results** dialogue box.

12. Next, rotate the model so that the *cylindrical* surface on top of the shaft is visible and click to select it. **Face<2>@Shaft-1** appears in the active field.

13. Once again, click the **[Update]** button in the **Results** dialogue box. The table is now populated with values of the *radial* displacement on the outer surface of **Shaft-1**.

14. The **Avg** value of radial displacement listed in the **Summary** table is **-3.184e-4 in**. This value of radial deformation is smaller than expected because both ends of the shaft extend outside the wheel hub where little or positive (swelling) deformation occurs due to the force fit.

15. Exit from the **Probe Result** property manager by clicking **[OK]**✓.

To determine total radial interference between the shaft and wheel, the absolute values of the above two **Avg** radial displacements are added together in equation [7]. The sum of these two values provides a reasonable (but smaller) approximation of the original radial interference specified in the opening statement of this example.

Total radial interference = |1.510e-3 | + |-3.184e-4| = 1.8284e-3 in [7]

Thus, diametral interference based on displacement plots is given by:

Total diametral interference = 2 * 1.8284e-3 = 3.6568e-3 in [8]

When compared to the given diametral interference specified between the shaft and the wheel hub on page 5-2 of this example (0.0041 in), the difference is

Difference = 4.1e-3 – 3.6568e-3 = 4.43e-4 in (rounded values) [9]

The difference should, of course, be zero (i.e., the specified interference should equal the FEA interference). However, knowing that the *entire* shaft surface is selected, but only that portion of the shaft surface within the contact region *should* be considered, the above difference is not investigated further. The important lesson to be learned is the *process* used to determine whether or not the final interference equals that specified for the shrink fit.

This concludes the analysis portion of the current example. The closing section describes a semi-automated method of generating a **Report** within SOLIDWORKS Simulation. *Do not close SOLIDWORKS Simulation at this time.*

Generating a Report

SOLIDWORKS Simulation provides a pre-defined **Report** format for quickly generating and sharing information related to any Study. The **Report** folder contains a list of items that a user can choose either to include or to exclude from a report. The report also provides a means for sharing information with others either via the internet (as an HTML file) or in print (as a Word® file). The process for including or excluding items from a report is outlined below.

1. Before generating a report, adjust the model size and orientation on the screen to best display graphical characteristics of interest to the user. This is done because the orientation of *all* plots produced within the report are identical to the current screen image. Thus, choose a view that reveals significant aspects of your model.

2. On the **Simulation** *tab*, select the **Report** Report icon. Or, in the main menu, click **Simulation**. Then, from the pull-down menu select **Report...** Either action opens the **Report Options** window shown in Fig. 26.

At the top-center of this window the **Current report format:** is set to **Static Study Format**.

Immediately below the **Report sections:** caption is a listing of sections that the user can either check ☑ to include in a report or clear the check mark ☐ to exclude that section from a report. By default, all sections are checked ✓.

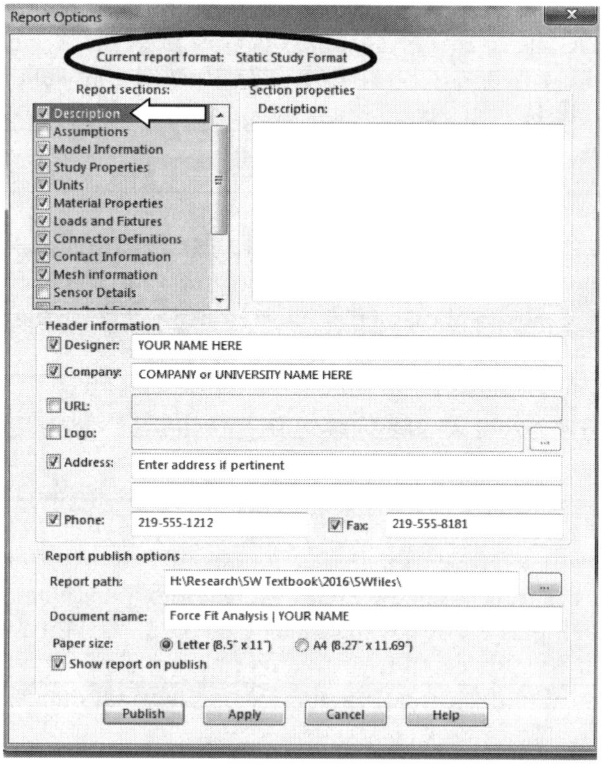

Figure 26 – Initial window of the **Report** folder showing a list of possible items that can be included or removed from a sample report.

When each section name is highlighted in the left-hand column of Fig. 26 (see arrow), the user has the option of entering explanatory text into a comments box on the right-hand side of the window.

In the report generated below, several items are omitted for the sake of brevity.

3. Begin by clicking to highlight ☑ **Description** at top of the **Report sections:** column. Then, in the upper right side of the window, enter a brief description of the current "Force Fit" example problem in your own words.

4. Clear the check mark adjacent to ☐ **Assumptions**, thereby omitting this section.

5. Proceed down the list leaving virtually all sections of the report checked ☑. However, clear check marks from ☐ **Sensor Details**, ☐ **Resultant Forces**, and ☐**Beams** because these items were *not* included in this study.

6. Begin at the top of the **Report sections:** column, and click the *name* **Model Information**. Then beneath **Model Information** on the right side of the window, check the ☑ **Comments:** box and type a brief description in the accompanying text box. NOTE: By typing in the **Section name:** field, located just above the **Comments:** field, it is possible to change the name of any section to that which you would like included in the report. Repeat the above for two or three other sections. It is not necessary to provide **Comments** for all report sections.

7. Near the middle of the window, beneath **Header information** check ☑ **Designer** and enter your name in the adjacent field. Do likewise for the ☑ **Company** name and enter either your company or university name. If you wish to experiment, check other boxes ☑ and enter information about yourself (e.g., **Address** or **Phone** number, etc.). This information is placed at the top of each page of the report.

8. At the bottom of this window check ☑ **Show report on publish** and then press the **[Publish]** button. These settings automatically generate a Word® version of the report.

When the automatic report generation is complete, a Word® document opens on the screen. Take several minutes to scroll through the report and review the information you entered and the information automatically recorded within the report folder. Notice the variety of details relevant to the current example that are saved. Items such as the mesh type, mesh quality, and mesh size, are included along with data about the FEA solver used, material specifications, fixtures, and full color plots, etc. are *summarized* in the **Report**. While this file contains much useful data, it cannot replace the engineering insight that goes into evaluating results of a Study.

This concludes the present example. Unless instructed to save results of this example, proceed as follows to exit SOLIDWORKS Simulation without saving the solution.

1. From the main menu select **File** and from the pull-down menu select **Close**.

2. A **SOLIDWORKS** window opens and prompts "**Save documents before closing.**" Select **[Don't Save]**.

EXERCISES

╬ ***Designates problems that introduce new concepts. Solution guidance is provided for these problems.***

EXERCISE 1 – Interference Fit Between a Bushing and Machine Frame

A bronze bushing is to be force fit into a hole in the cast iron wall of a machine frame. A bushing of this type serves as a bearing in a journal bearing set. The journal (i.e., the shaft) and bearing are separated by a thin film of lubricant, typically oil. Only the bushing and a small, square *portion* of the machine frame are shown in Fig. E5-1; the shaft is not shown and is *not* part of this analysis. Important dimensions of the bushing and machine frame are included. The machine frame thickness and bushing length are equal. It is assumed that a sufficiently large segment of the machine frame is included in the model below so that boundary effects, due to influences of St. Venant's principle, are insignificant. Create a finite element analysis of the interference fit between these two mating parts.

Open the file: **Bushing and Frame 5-1**.

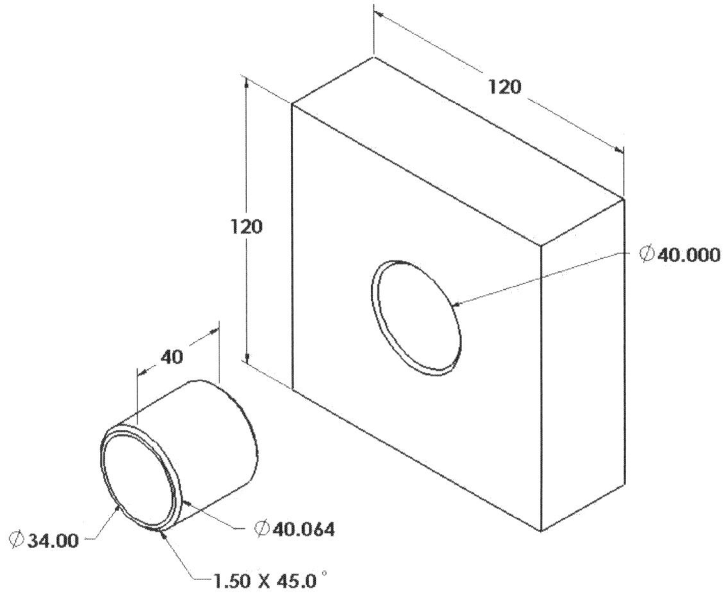

Figure E5-1 – Bushing and a portion of a machine frame wall. A comparison of the bushing outside diameter (o.d. = 40.064 mm) and the hole inside diameter (i.d. = 40.000 mm) in the machine frame reveals an interference fit exists between these mating parts.

- Material: Machine frame – **Gray Cast Iron** (Use S.I. units)
  Bushing – **Tin Bearing Bronze** (listed beneath "**Copper Alloys**")
- Mesh: Use system default size **Curvature based mesh**, tetrahedral elements
- Fixture: Set **Connections > Component Interaction** to **Shrink Fit** between the bushing and machine frame. If necessary, add restraints to prevent rigid body motion.

Solution Guidance

Discussion below provides general guidance (i.e., hints and reminders) for the solution to this problem. In particular instances where this solution differs from the example problem of this chapter, specific steps are provided.

Early in the solution process, defeature the model by removing chamfers from both the bushing and frame.

- Expand the SOLIDWORKS Feature manager tree if necessary to view its contents.
- Click " ▸ " to open the **Frame <1> (Default<<Default>_Display State 1>)** folder at the upper arrow in Fig. E5-2.
- Locate and **Suppress** the **Frame Chamfer** circled in Fig. E5-2.
- Similarly, beneath ▸ **Bushing<2> (Default<<Default>_Display State 1>)**, locate and **Suppress** the **Bushing Chamfer** (not shown in Fig. E5-2).

Also, use load and geometric symmetry to reduce the model to ¼ of the given assembly. (See lower arrow in Fig. E5-2.)

- In the SOLIDWORKS Feature manager tree, right-click **Quarter Model – Assembly** and from the pop-up menu select the **Unsuppress** icon.

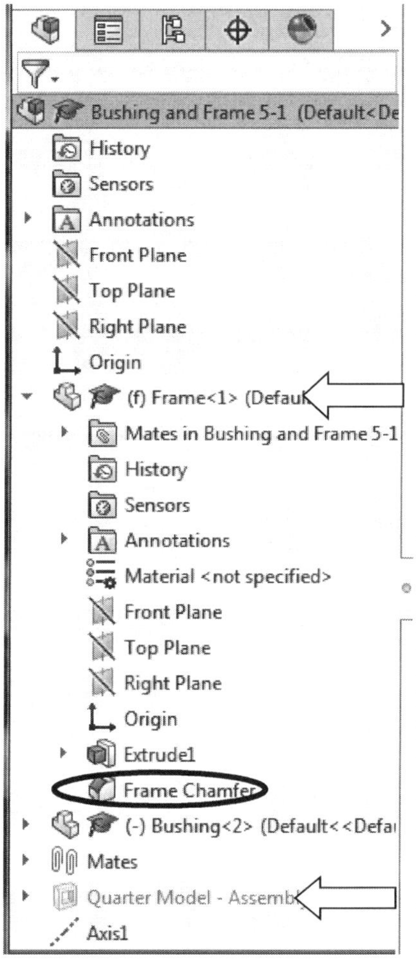

Figure E5-2 – Menu selections used to defeature the Frame and unsuppress the **Quarter Model-Assembly**.

<u>HINT</u>:
When applying restraints to the model, consider carefully what restraint(s), if any, must be specified to prevent rigid-body-motion.

Develop a finite element model that includes material specification, fixtures, a meshed model, and a solution. Defeature the model prior to analysis.

Determine the following:

a. Perform an interference check between the bushing and machine frame. Plot the resulting image.

b. In a separate image, show the ¼ model with symmetry and rigid body restraints (only if additional restraints are needed). This image is to show the defeatured model.

c. Use classical equations to compute tangential and radial stresses at the inner surface of the machine frame and the outer surface of the bushing. It is common practice to use the *radius* of a circle tangent to the inside of the block that represents the machine frame as the outside "radius" of the outer member. Also determine the common contact pressure between the bushing and machine frame surfaces. Label each calculation.

d. In a cylindrical coordinate system, plot and compare tangential stress at the inner surface of the machine frame with results calculated using classical equations determined in part (c). The value to be used for the finite element stress on the frame is the **Avg.** value of tangential stress determined by using the **List Selected** feature applied to the inner surface of the hole in the frame. If necessary, click-and-drag to adjust column widths to show all digits of tabulated data. Compute the percent difference between classical and finite element analysis results using equation [1].

$$\%\ \text{difference} = \frac{(\text{FEA result - classical result})}{\text{FEA result}} * 100 = \qquad [1]$$

e. Repeat part (d) for tangential stress at the outer surface of the bushing.

f. In a cylindrical coordinate system, plot and determine the average value of radial stress (contact pressure) between mating surfaces. Apply the **List Selected** feature to the inner surface of the hole and outer surface of the bushing. Although, theoretically, these values should be the same, some differences may occur. Therefore, determine the average of these two values and compare it with the classical result predicted for contact pressure determined in part (c). Then determine the percent difference by again using equation [1].

g. Because length of inner and outer members is equal, determine the *radial* displacement of the bushing (inner member) and machine frame (outer member) corresponding to the average **(Avg.)** value determined using the **List Selected** option. Determine the total radial interference and compare it with the given interference. Determine the percent difference using equation [1] above. If these values do not agree within 2% or less, determine the source(s) of error and correct it/them. Comment upon whether or not the results agree, and if not, explain why.

╬ EXERCISE 2 – Force Fit Between a Bushing and Belt Sander Drive-Roll (Special Topic: Soft Spring supports)

A bronze bushing is force fit into a hole on the left end of a drive-roll for the industrial belt sander shown in Fig. E5-3. The drive-roll is supported by a stub shaft, not shown, inserted into the bushing from the left side and by a drive shaft on its right end as seen in Fig. E5-4. Only the force fit between the bushing and drive-roll, circled at the left end of the model in Fig. E5-4, is to be analyzed. Therefore, the affected parts can be modeled as a circular disk and bushing shown in Fig. E5-5. This model assumes that effects, due to St. Venant's principle caused by the hollow portion of the drive-roll, are insignificant and can be ignored. Important dimensions of the bushing and disk are shown in the figure below. The disk thickness and drive-roll hole outside diameter are equal (0.6250-in). Create a finite element analysis of the interference fit between these two mating parts.

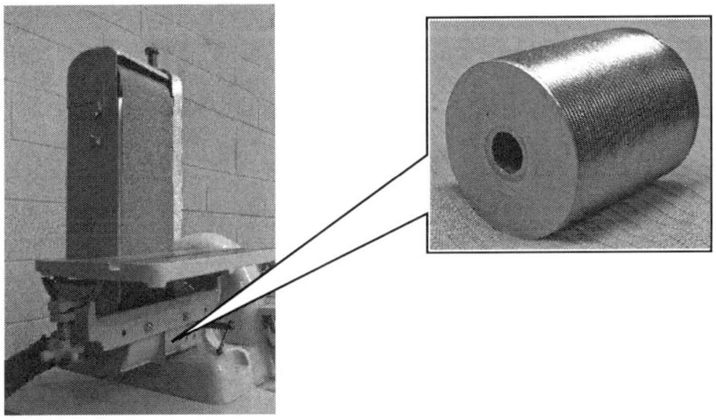

Figure E5-3 – Industrial belt sander and drive-roll showing force fit bushing at left end.

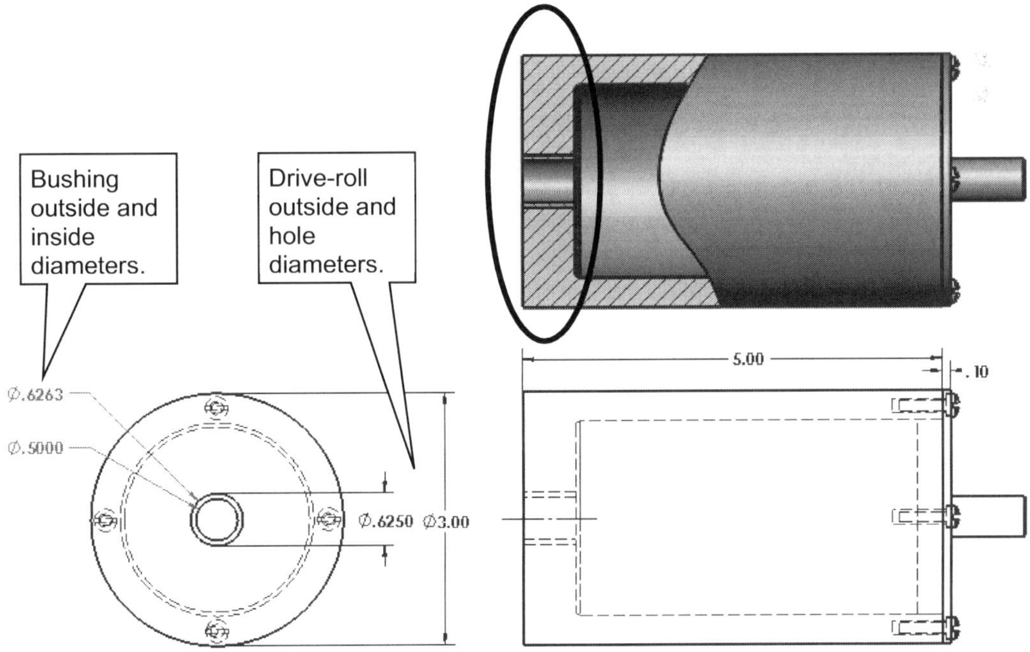

Figure E5-4 – Geometry of belt sander drive-roll assembly.

- Material: Sander Disk - **2014-T4 Aluminum**
  (Use English units)
  Bushing – **Tin Bearing Bronze**
  (listed beneath "**Copper Alloys**")

- Mesh: Use system default size **Curvature based mesh**, tetrahedral elements.

Figure E5-5 – Simplified model of *left end* of the belt sander drive- roll and its bushing.

- Fixture: Set **Connections > Component Interaction** to **Shrink Fit** between the bushing and belt sander disk. If necessary, add **Soft-Spring** restraints (see page 3-44 and forward) to prevent rigid body motion.

Open the file: **Belt Sander Disk and Bushing 5-2**

Develop a finite element model that includes material specification, fixtures, a meshed model, and a solution.

Determine the following:

a. Perform an interference check between the bushing and belt sander disk. Plot the resulting image and report the volume of interference value.

b. Use classical equations to compute tangential and radial stresses at the inner surface of the belt sander disk and the outer surface of the bushing. Also determine the common contact pressure between these surfaces. Label each calculation.

c. In a cylindrical coordinate system, plot and compare the finite element value of tangential stress at the inner surface of the belt sander disk with results calculated using classical equations determined in part (b). For this comparison use the **Avg.** value of tangential stress determined using the **List Selected** feature applied to the appropriate surface of the model. If necessary, click-and-drag to adjust column widths to show all digits of tabulated data. Compute the percent difference between classical and finite element analysis results using equation [1].

$$\% \text{ difference} = \frac{(\text{FEA result - classical result})}{\text{FEA result}} * 100 = \qquad [1]$$

d. Repeat part (c) for tangential stress at the outer surface of the bushing.

e. In a cylindrical coordinate system, plot and determine the average value of radial stress (contact pressure) between mating surfaces. Apply the **List Selected** feature to the inner surface of the hole and outer surface of the bushing. Although, theoretically, these values should be the same, some differences may occur. Therefore, determine the average of these two values and compare it with the classical result predicted for contact pressure determined in part (b). Then determine the percent difference by again using equation [1].

f. Because length of inner and outer members is equal, determine the *radial* displacement of the bushing (inner member) and belt sander disk (outer member) corresponding to the average **(Avg.)** value of displacement determined using the **List Selected** option. Then, determine the total diametral interference and compare it with the given interference. Determine the percent difference using equation [1] above. If these values do not agree within 2% or less, determine the source(s) of error and correct it/them. Comment upon whether or not the results agree, and if not, explain why.

<u>EXERCISE 3</u> – Interference Fit Between a Gear and Shaft

To realize greater economy in manufacturing and assembly, the means of attaching a spur gear to its shaft is to be simplified. Originally, the gear was mounted to a hub by two screws at **A** shown in Figs. E5-6 (a) and (b). The hub, in turn, was keyed to a shaft to prevent relative rotation between itself, the gear, and the shaft. An initial analysis revealed that a shrink fit between the gear and its shaft would be adequate to transmit the required torque, thereby eliminating the need for four parts (hub + two screws + key). Also eliminated are the operations of drilling two holes in the gear, drilling and tapping two holes in the hub, and broaching and milling the keyway and keyseat in the hub and shaft respectively. Finally, additional costs associated with producing the hub and associated machining operations, material, and inventory/handling are also eliminated.

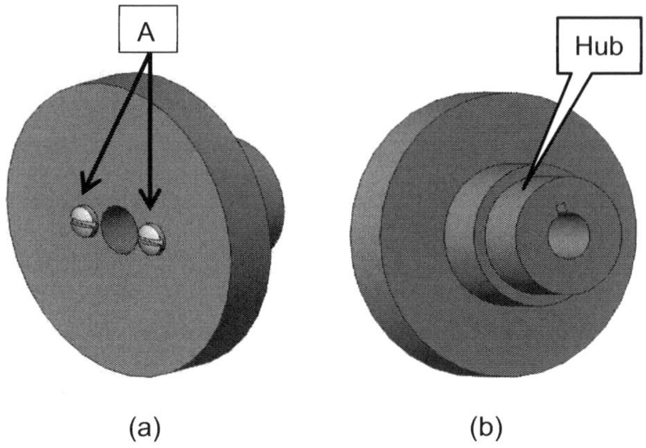

(a) (b)

Figure E5-6 - Schematic representation of gear and hub assembly before simplification

Figure E5-7 - Simplified geometry of spur gear and shaft using force fit.

The 96 tooth spur gear in Fig. E5-7 is to be shrink fit onto an **Alloy Steel** shaft. As noted above, contact pressure between the shaft and gear was determined to be sufficient to transmit the desired power including over-torque during start-up and shut-down. However, a finite element study is proposed to determine tangential and radial stress in both the shaft and gear due to the shrink fit. Also, stress due to stress concentration is known to occur where the shaft exits the gear due to the change of geometry at that location. A simplified model of the gear and shaft is shown in Fig. E5-8 along with dimensions of the gear hole inside diameter and shaft outside diameter.

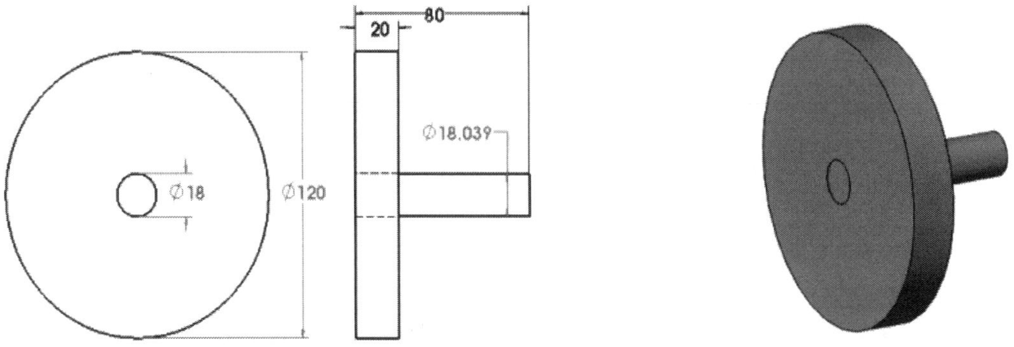

Figure E5-8 – Dimensions necessary to perform analyses. (All dimensions in mm.)

Open the file: **Spur Gear and Shaft Assembly 5-3**

- Material: Shaft – **Alloy Steel** (Use SI units)
  Spur Gear – **1046 Steel, cold drawn**

- Mesh: a. Use system default size **Curvature based mesh**, tetrahedral elements when determining tangential and radial stresses in the shaft and gear.

  b. Refine *mesh size* and/or use *mesh control* in the contact region to better determine stress due to stress concentration where the shaft exits the gear.

- Fixture: Set **Connections > Component Interaction** to **Shrink Fit** between the gear and shaft. If necessary, add restraints to the right (free) end of the shaft to prevent rigid body motion.

Develop a finite element model that includes material specification, fixtures, a meshed model, and a solution. Defeature the model, if necessary, prior to analysis.

Determine the following:

a. Perform an interference check between the gear and shaft. Plot the resulting image and report the volume of material interference.

b. Use classical equations to compute tangential and radial stresses at the inner surface of the gear blank and the outer surface of the shaft. Also determine the common contact pressure between these surfaces. Label each calculation. Gear outside diameter = 120 mm.

c. In a cylindrical coordinate system, plot and compare tangential stress at the inner surface of the gear with results calculated using classical equations determined in part (b). The value to be used for the finite element stress in the gear is the **Avg.** value of tangential stress determined by using the **List Selected** feature applied to the inner surface of the gear hole. If necessary, click-and-drag to adjust column widths to show all digits of tabulated data. Compute the percent difference between classical and finite element analysis results using equation [1].

$$\% \text{ difference} = \frac{(\text{FEA result - classical result})}{\text{FEA result}} * 100 = \qquad [1]$$

d. Repeat part (c) for tangential stress at the outer surface of the shaft.

e. In a cylindrical coordinate system, plot and determine the average value of radial stress (contact pressure) between mating surfaces. Apply the **List Selected** feature to the inner surface of the gear hole and outer surface of the shaft. Although, theoretically, these values should be the same, differences may occur. Compare the separate values determined for the gear and shaft with the classical result predicted for contact pressure determined in part (b). Which of these values, for the gear or the shaft, is in best agreement with the classical result? State the reason for differences, if any, between results in best agreement and the reason why results differ more for those in worst agreement. Determine the percent difference for each by again using equation [1]. Label calculations.

f. Next, pay particular attention to the region where the shaft exits the gear. And, using a method of your own choosing, refine the mesh size to obtain a more accurate determination of stress in this region. For the model using a refined mesh, apply *Section Clipping* to cut both the gear and shaft in half, along the shaft centerline, and to examine stress in this region. Produce a section clipping plot of half of the entire model *and* a zoomed-in plot of stress in the contact region. Manually label which part is the gear and which is the shaft.

g. Questions: What stress did you choose to display on the model plotted for part (f) above? State reason(s) why you choose the particular stress displayed on the model for part (f). Can the stress magnitude plotted in part (f) be compared with a manual calculation for stress at the juncture between the gear and shaft? If the answer to the previous question is "yes," include a manual calculation of stress beneath the plot and reference the stress concentration factor chart used to make your calculation. If the answer is "no," then explain why a comparison cannot be made. Finally, if classical and finite element results are compared, compute the percent difference between stress magnitudes determined using these two methods; label this calculation.

EXERCISE 4 – Stress Variation in a Saw Blade due to Centrifugal Force (Special Topics: Centrifugal Force, Soft Spring Supports)

A saw blade of the type used on table saws, miter saws, and portable power saws is shown in Fig. E5-9. This part is considered to be a thin rotating disk provided (a) its thickness is constant, (b) its outside radius is large compared to its thickness, and (c) stresses are constant through its thickness. Blades of this type are labeled with a maximum rotational speed limit, which in this case is 5500 rpm. Additional external loads, due to cutting forces between the saw blade and work-piece, are not considered in this exercise. Despite the hole at the center of the saw blade, both stress concentration and interference fits are *ignored* in this exercise.

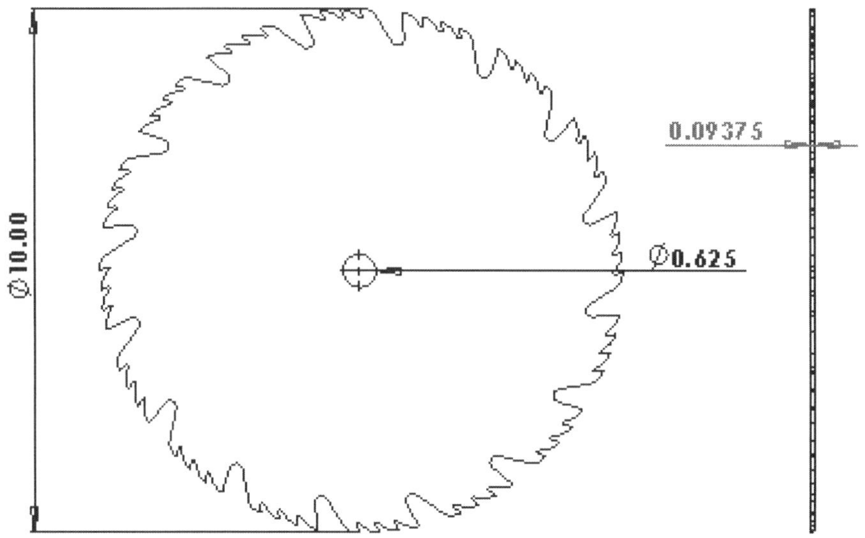

Figure E5-9 – Front and side views of a typical circular saw blade used in wood cutting applications. (All dimensions in inches.)

Develop a finite element model that includes material specification, applied centrifugal force, mesh generation, and solution. Because *centrifugal loading* and use of *soft springs* to support the part are not topics of the current chapter, guidance is provided to deal with these two aspects of the solution.

Open the file: **Circular Saw Blade 5-4**

- Material: **Chrome Stainless Steel** (English units) density $\rho = 0.282$ lb/in^3
- Mesh: Specify a default size **Standard mesh**
- Fixture: **Soft Springs**. See Solution Guidance section below.
- External Load: None. Load is due to centrifugal force caused by rotational speed of 5500 rpm.

Solution Guidance

Guidance is provided below regarding (a) the use of soft springs to restrain the model, and (b) the application of a centrifugal force to load the model. Steps below presume that the **Circular Saw Blade** file is open and a Simulation Study has been initiated.

Rigid Body Motion Prevention (Soft Springs)

As noted above, **Soft Springs** must be applied to stabilize the model. Model stabilization is necessary because (a) **Fixed** or other common restraints are not appropriate for a part that is considered to be rotating, and (b) the centrifugal force applied to the blade does not provide restraints in the X, Y, or Z directions. Simply stated, static restraints are not consistent with assumed rotation of the saw blade.

For additional discussion about soft springs see Chapter 2, p. 2-34 and Chapter 3 p. 3-45 (bottom) to 3-47 (bottom). Soft springs can be assigned any time before the solution is run.

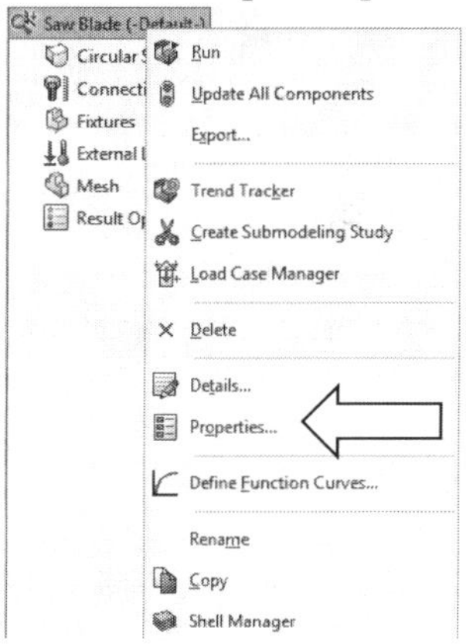

Figure E5-10 – Accessing the Study level pull-down menu to assign **Soft Spring** support to the model.

- Right-click the Study name at top of the Simulation manager tree (not to be confused with the name at top of the SOLIDWORKS Feature manager tree). A pull-down menu appears as shown in Fig. E5-10. From the pull-down menu, select **Properties...** The **Static** window opens as shown in Fig. E5-11.

- In **Solver** section of the **Options** tab, check ✓ to select ☑ **Use soft spring to stabilize model**.

- Also in the **Solver** section, open the pull-down menu adjacent to **FFEPlus ▼**and select **Direct sparse solver** as the equation solving method. This solver must be used in conjunction with the soft spring option.

- Click **[OK]** to close the **Static** window.

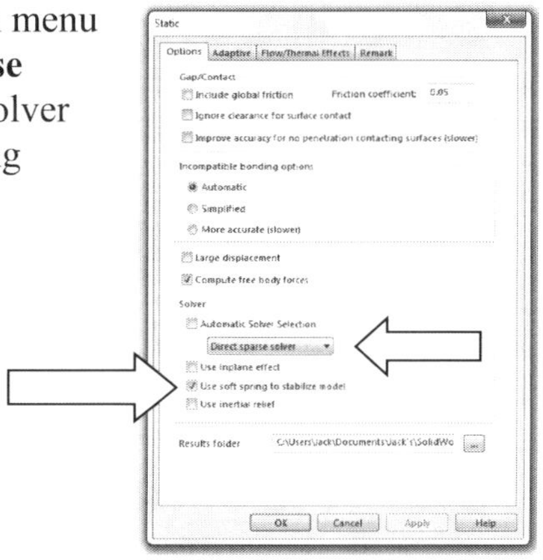

Figure E5-11 – Selecting **Soft Spring** support in the **Static** window.

Solution Guidance (continued)

Centrifugal Force Specification

- Right-click **External Loads** and from the pull-down menu select **Centrifugal...** The **Centrifugal** property manager opens. See Fig. E5-12.
- In the **Selected Reference** dialogue box the **Axis, Edge, Cylindrical Face for Direction** field is highlighted (light blue). Select the *inside* cylindrical *surface* of the hole.

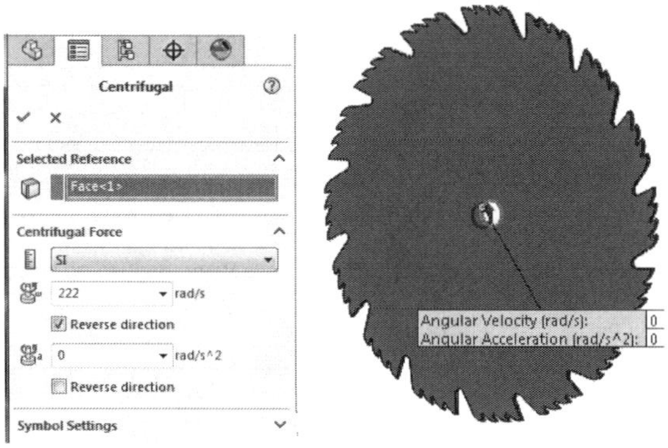

Figure E5-12 – Specifying a **Centrifugal** force on a saw blade rotating at 5500 RPM.

- In the **Centrifugal Force** dialogue box, type the rotational speed into the **Angular Velocity** field. Convert 5500 rpm to **Hz** (i.e., cycles/second = rev/sec). After typing this value, click in the graphics area and a red arrow appears at the hole to indicate the direction of rotation. If the arrow is opposite the direction in which the saw teeth are "leaning," then select ☑ **Reverse Direction** and click **[OK]** ✓ to close the **Centrifugal** property manager. *NOTE: Value shown in Fig. E5-12 above for Hz is not correct.*
- The notation **Centrifugal-1** appears beneath the **External Loads** folder.

Determine the following:

Develop a finite element model that includes material specification, soft springs, applied load (due to centrifugal force), mesh generation, and solution.

a. After running the solution and obtaining the **Results** folder, edit the **Stress1 (-vonMises-)** plot by doing the following.
   - Turn off the ☐ **Deformed Shape**. You will know when the deformed shape is turned off because the centrifugal force arrow will again appear at the central hole.
   - Display **Discrete** fringes on the model.
   - Display the **Mesh** on the model.
   - Turn on ☑ **Show max annotation**.

- Next, *copy* the **Stress1 (-vonMises-)** plot. Then change the copied plot to display **P1: 1st Principal Stress**. Also, re-name this plot to reflect its true identity. HINT: Does the 1st principal stress represent *tangential* or *radial* stresses caused by rotation?

- Repeat the preceding step, except create a plot of **P2: 2nd Principal Stress**. HINT: Does the 2nd principal stress represent *tangential* or *radial* stresses caused by rotation?

b. Zoom in on the saw blade that displays a plot of **P1: 1st Principal Stress**. Then, use the **Probe** tool to select all corner and mid-side nodes beginning at the edge of the center hole and proceeding outward to as near as possible to the tip of any tooth. When selecting nodes, traverse the model in the straightest line possible. Create a graph of this data. Alter the graph title and axes labels to better describe information contained on the graph. Include your name in the graph title.

c. Repeat step (b) to produce a graph showing the variation of **P2: 2nd Principal Stress** at the same location on the model.

d. Either write a computer program or set up a spreadsheet to calculate both the tangential and radial stress variation from the central hole outward to the blade tip. Calculate the two stress magnitudes at 0.20 inch increments beginning at the hole inside radius and proceeding outward to the 5.00 inch outside blade radius. Also, within this computer program or spreadsheet, plot and label graphs of stress variation for both stress types. Use the following classical equations to compute tangential and radial stresses. (Alternately – Use equations from the design of machine elements textbook with which you are familiar.)

Tangential stress in a rotating disk.

$$\sigma_t = \rho\omega^2\left(\frac{3+\nu}{8}\right)\left(r_i^2 + r_o^2 + \frac{r_i^2 r_o^2}{r^2} - \frac{1+3\nu}{3+\nu}r^2\right) \qquad [2]$$

Radial stress in a rotating disk.

$$\sigma_r = \rho\omega^2\left(\frac{3+\nu}{8}\right)\left(r_i^2 + r_o^2 - \frac{r_i^2 r_o^2}{r^2} - r^2\right) \qquad [3]$$

Where,

ρ = mass density of the saw blade = density/(386 in/sec^2)
ν = Poisson's ratio
r_i = inside radius (inches)
r_o = outside radius (inches)
r = radius to the point of interest, a variable value (inches)
ω = angular velocity in cycles/sec = rev/sec

e. Use equation [1], repeated below, to compare percent differences between maximum stresses calculated using equations [2] and [3] with the corresponding maximum stress values **P1: 1st Principal Stress** and **P2: 2nd Principal Stress** calculated using the finite element approach. Based on comparisons of calculated values and graphs, identify which finite element stress (**P1** or **P2**) corresponds to the tangential stress in the saw blade. Does the other finite element stress correspond to the radial stress in the saw blade? If "yes," state the basis for this conclusion. If "no," state why not.

$$\% \text{ difference} = \frac{(\text{FEA result - classical result})}{\text{FEA result}} * 100 = \qquad [1]$$

╬ EXERCISE 5 – Stress Variation in Solar Furnace Window (Special Topics: Custom Material Specification)

When in operation, the Solar Furnace, shown in Fig. E5-9, is located at the focal point of a parabolic mirror called a "concentrator." Sunlight is reflected onto the concentrator by a 6.2-m x 6.2-m (20-ft x 20-ft) heliostat that tracks the sun across the sky. Ultimately the sunlight is focused into a small "window" in the solar furnace. Dashed lines trace typical sun rays from the sky to the heliostat, to the concentrator, and finally focused into the solar furnace window. The solar furnace circular window is shown in Fig. E5-10 (a).

A window is needed to contain a pressurized inert gas atmosphere within the solar furnace where high temperature chemical reactions take place. Due to temperatures in excess of 3,000 °F, the furnace "window" is made of quartz crystal. This exercise explores a preliminary stress analysis of the quartz crystal window to determine its feasibility for this application.

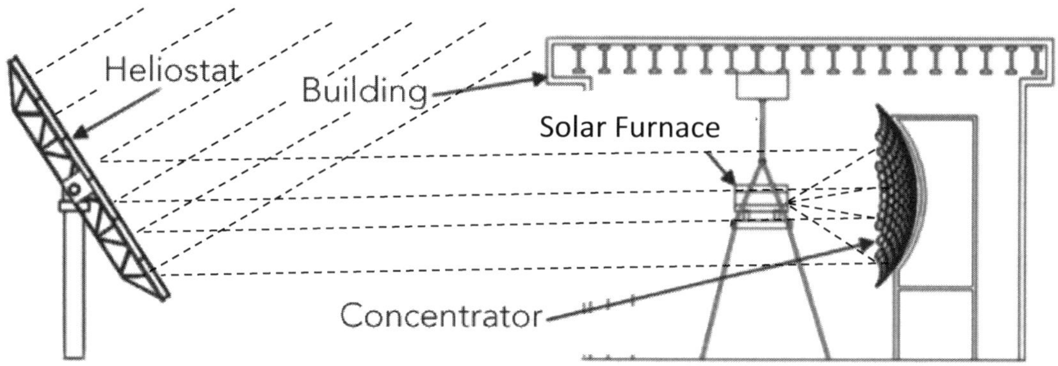

Figure E5-13 - Overview of solar facility and location of the solar furnace at focal point of the concentrator mirror.

Open the file: **Solar Furnace Quartz Window 5-5**

Figure E5-14 – (a) Close-up view of solar furnace quartz window held in place by a spring loaded steel ring.

(b) Solar furnace located at focal point of the concentrator mirror array.

- Material: Quartz Crystal window (aka: Fused Quartz), a custom material whose properties are listed in Fig. E5-15. (Use S.I. units.) See **Solution Guidance** section for assistance.

- Mesh: Use a **Standard Mesh**, solid tetrahedral elements. A shell mesh is optional at the discretion of the user or course instructor. *However, if a shell mesh is used, Split Lines which are defined <u>only</u> on the solid model will need to be defined again by the user.*

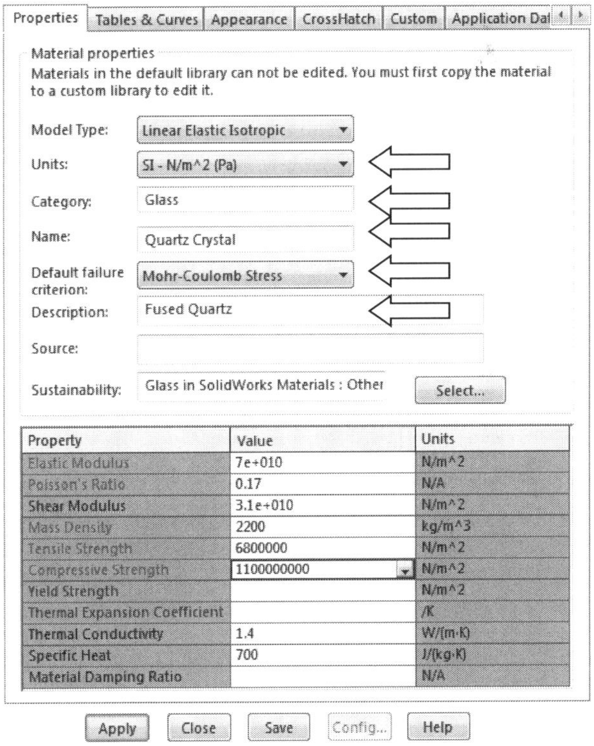

Figure E5-15 – Mechanical properties of Quartz Crystal (also known as fused quartz).

- Fixture: Apply **Fixed** restraints between the *Split Lines* and the outside diameter of the window on *both sides*. Also apply **Fixed** restraints to the outside circular *edge* of the window. In actual practice the window is clamped in place by spring loaded bolts and a steel ring to ensure a tight seal.

- External Load: Apply a uniform pressure of 18,000 N/m^2 acting in the negative (-Z) direction on one side of the window. Pressure should act inside the circle formed by the *Split Lines*.

Determine the following:

Develop a finite element model that includes *custom* material specification, fixtures, external loads, a meshed model, and solution. It is assumed the custom material is defined within **SOLIDWORKS** *prior to beginning a* Simulation study.

Solution Guidance

Custom Material Specification

To create a **Custom Material**, start with an existing material similar to the material you want to create.

- In the SOLIDWORKS manager tree, right-click Material <not specified> and from the pull-down menu select **Edit Material**. The **Material** window opens.
- In the **Material** window click the "◢" symbol to close the **Steel** category and, from the list of **SOLIDWORKS Materials**, select " ▸ " to open the **Other Non-metals** category.
- Within this category, right-click **Glass**, and from the pull-down menu select **Copy**. Glass is *not* a good match for quartz crystal properties, but it provides a better starting point than most other possibilities listed.
- Scroll to the very bottom of the material tree, right-click **Custom Materials** and from the pull-down menu select **New Category**. Immediately, right-click the **New Category** *folder* and from the pop-up menu select **Paste**. The **Glass** category is pasted beneath the **New Category** heading.
- Next, left click the **Glass** category and the **Properties** tab on the right side of the **Material** window is populated with properties of common glass.
- Finally, make certain **Units:** are set to **SI-N/mm^2 (MPa)** then type values shown in Fig. E5-15 into the **Property** table. Also include other information typed into the upper fields of this window.
- Finish by clicking **[Apply]** followed by **[Close]**.

Determine the following:

a. In a cylindrical coordinate system, plot a graph of tangential stress variation on the inner (concave) surface of the window. Use the **Probe** feature and in the **Options** dialogue box, select ⊙**At location**. Start this graph at the split line and proceed across the model to the opposite split line. Choose as straight a line of nodes as possible across the model and select only corner nodes. Include your name and a descriptive title and axis labels on this graph.

b. Repeat part (a) on the convex side of the window.

c. Allowing for minor differences of values due to modeling inaccuracies, mesh irregularities, and mathematical round off, write at least two technical statements regarding your observations about the graphs of parts (a) and (b).

d. In a cylindrical coordinate system, plot a graph of radial stress variation on the inner (concave) surface of the window. Use the **Probe** feature and in the **Options** dialogue box, select ⊙**At location**. Start this graph at the split line and proceed across the model to the opposite split line. Choose as straight a line of nodes as possible across the model and select only corner nodes. Include your name and a descriptive title and axis labels on this graph.

e. Repeat part (d) on the convex side of the window.

f. Repeat part (c), except observations and statements should refer to the graphs of parts (d) and (e).

g. In your judgment is the quartz crystal window likely to fail? Why or why not? Also, what is static pressure internal to the solar furnace in psig?

Exercise 6 – Shear Stress in a Shaft (Special Topic: Shear Stress due to Torsion)

A cylindrical shaft supplies torque between a constant rpm electric motor and a smooth running circulation pump in a commercial cold water chilling system. The central portion of the shaft, analyzed below, is considered sufficiently well removed from its connection points between driving and driven equipment so that any "end-effects" due to St. Venant's principle can be neglected. The shaft rotates at 1,800 rpm and delivers 14.92 kW (20 HP) to the pump. Shaft diameter is 44.45 mm (1.75 in.) and its length is 254.0 mm (10.00 in.) and is made of Alloy steel. Create a finite element analysis to determine requested stresses within this shaft.

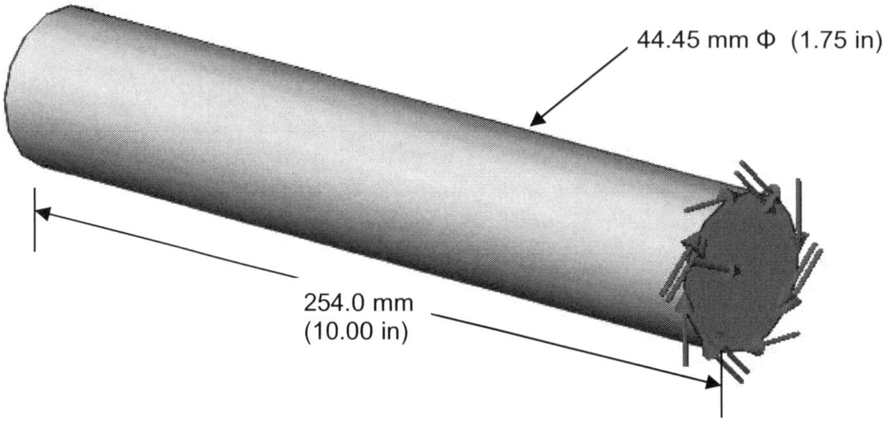

Figure E5-16 – Basic geometry and **Torque** applied to the pump shaft.

Open the file: **Pump Shaft 5-6**

- Material: Shaft – **Alloy Steel** (Use SI or English units as assigned).
- Mesh: Use a system default **Curvature based mesh**, tetrahedral elements.
- External Load: Because both the electric motor and pump are smooth running, a steadily applied (static) torque is used to model the load applied to the rotating shaft. Torque is to be applied to right end (surface) of the shaft as shown in Fig. E5-16.
  *Assistance applying a torque to the shaft is included in the **Solution Guidance** section.*
- Fixtures: Due to the assumption of a statically applied torque, the left end of the shaft is considered **Fixed/Immovable**.

Solution Guidance

Adding Torque as an External Load

It is presumed that the pump shaft model is open and a Simulation Study has been started. Guidance below provides insight into adding a **Torque** to the right end of the shaft. Other restraints are added by the user.

1. Right-click **External Loads**, and from the pull-down menu select **Torque**. The **Force/Torque** property manager opens as shown in Fig. E5-17.

Solution Guidance (Continued)

2. Click to select the *surface* on the right end of the Pump Shaft. **Face<1>** appears in the **Faces for Torque** field.

3. Click to activate (light blue) the **Axis, Cylindrical Face for Direction** field and select *either* the shaft cylindrical surface *or* select **Axis1** in the SOLIDWORKS flyout menu.

4. Enter torque magnitude into the **Torque Value** field using appropriate units. *The torque value shown in Fig. E5-17 is intentionally NOT correct.*

5. If torque direction differs from that shown in Fig. E5-16, check ☑ **Reverse direction**.

6. Click **[OK]** to close the **Force/Torque** property manager.

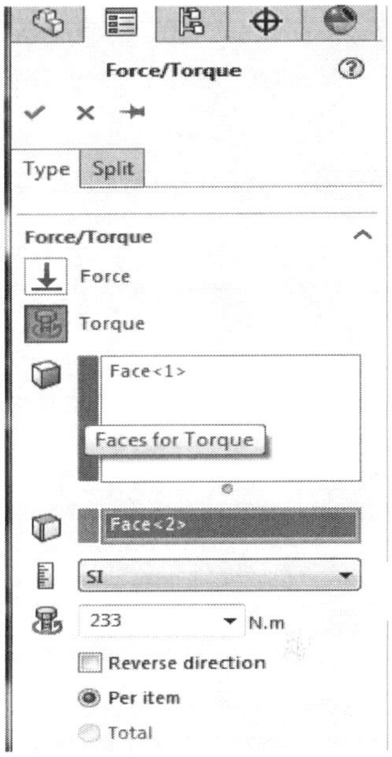

Figure E5-17 – **Force/ Torque** property manager showing **Torque** definition.

Shear Stress Determination

Because the example problem in the current chapter dealt only with tangential and radial stresses, which are both *normal* stresses, Fig. E5-18 is included to show the orientation of *shear* stresses acting on the axial, radial, and tangential faces of a stress element in a cylindrical coordinate system. Study this figure to understand stress directions and locations related to the pump shaft.

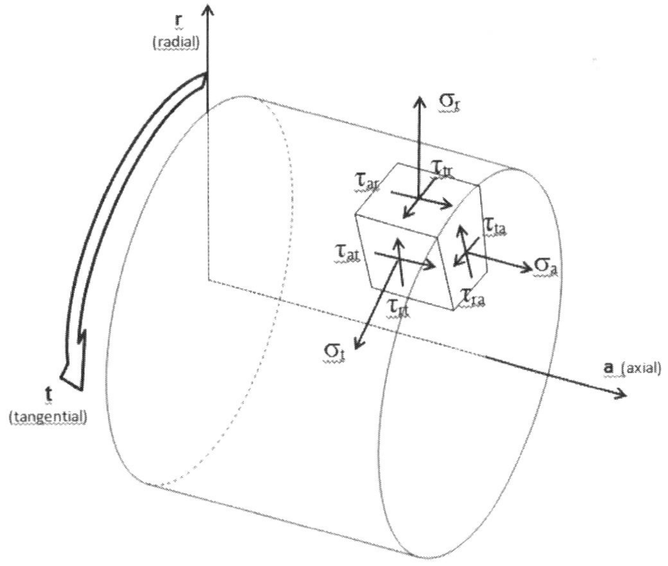

Figure E5-18 – Orientation of shear and normal stresses in the axial, radial, and tangential directions on a stress element in a cylindrical coordinate system.

Table 2 below tabulates the correspondence between shear stresses shown in Fig. E5-18 and shear stress relative to a Cartesian coordinate system. Table 2 is needed because stresses listed in the **Stress Plot** property manager relate only to a Cartesian coordinate system.

Table 2 – Correspondence between shear stresses in a Cartesian coordinate system and their equivalents in a cylindrical coordinate system.

Original Meaning in a Cartesian Coordinate System	**New Meaning in a Cylindrical Coordinate System**
TXY = $\tau_{xy} = \tau_{yx}$ = Shear in Y direction on the X face (or) shear in the X direction on the Y face	TXY = $\tau_{tr} = \tau_{rt}$ = Shear in the tangential direction on the radial face (or) shear in the radial direction on the tangential face
TYZ = $\tau_{yz} = \tau_{zy}$ = Shear in Y direction on the Z face (or) shear in the Z direction on the Y face	TYZ = $\tau_{ta} = \tau_{at}$ = Shear in the tangential direction on the axial face (or) shear in the axial direction on the tangential face
TXZ = $\tau_{xz} = \tau_{zx}$ = Shear in the X direction on the Z face (or) shear in the Z direction on the X face	TXZ = $\tau_{ra} = \tau_{ar}$ = Shear in the radial direction on the axial face (or) shear in the axial direction on the radial face

Develop a finite element model that includes material specification, fixtures, a meshed model and solution. **Use either SI or English units as assigned for this exercise.**

Determine the following:

a. Use classical equations to determine shear stress on the shaft surface. Below this calculation, draw an isometric sketch of the shaft, similar to that in Fig. E5-12. On this sketch, show the fixed end and the torque applied to the right end of the shaft. Label torque magnitude and direction on this figure. Also, sketch and label a two-dimensional stress element on the visible, cylindrical surface of the shaft. On this sketch include *appropriate* stress vectors on each edge of the stress element and label the stress magnitude. Finally, on the shaft right end, sketch vectors representing shear stress variation on a vertical line drawn across the shaft diameter.

b. Use SOLIDWORKS Simulation, in conjunction with Table 2, to create a plot of shear stress on the shaft surface in a cylindrical coordinate system. This plot should correspond to the shear stress calculated in part (a) above. Next, use the **Probe** tool and select no more than six locations on the shaft surface to determine the shear stress using the ⦿ **At location** option in the **Probe Result** property manager. In the **Annotations** dialogue box check to select ☑ **Show Node/Element Number**, ☑ **Show X,Y,Z Location**, and ☑ **Show Value** to show values on the plot. Finally, cut and paste the shaft image, including the **Probe Result** property manager, onto an 8 ½" x 11" sheet. On this sheet, compute the percent difference between the classical result from part (a) with that of the **Avg** value of shear stress found in the **Summary** dialogue box. Use equation [1].

$$\% \text{ difference} = \frac{(\text{FEA result - classical result})}{\text{FEA result}} * 100 = \qquad [1]$$

c. Begin with the shear stress model created in part (b) and use **Section Clipping...** to simultaneously section the shaft using a **Front** plane in the **Section 1** dialogue box and using a **Right** plane located at the shaft mid-length **(5.00 in** or **127 mm**). Then, use the **Probe** tool and the ⊙ **At Location** option to create a graph of shear stress magnitude across the diameter of the shaft. Select approximately ten equally spaced locations across the shaft diameter. Include a title, axis labels and your name.

d. Make multiple *copies* of the plot developed in part (c). From these plots create individual plots of σ_x , σ_y, σ_z, and the other two shear stresses *not plotted* for part (c). Then, construct a table like that shown in Fig. E5-19, and using the **Probe** tool and the ⊙ **At Location** option, click at least five locations on the shaft surface of each plot and record the **Avg** stress magnitude in a table like that of Fig. E5-19. The **Avg.** stress is found in the **Summary** dialogue box of the **Probe Result** property manager. Cut and paste two of these plots on the same page with the table. Beneath this table discuss what you observe about stresses *other than* the shear stress investigated in parts (b & c) of this exercise. Does this observation make sense in terms of your understanding of shear due to torsion? When answering this question, recall that all these stress values assume a different meaning when plotted in a cylindrical coordinate system.

Stress Component	**Avg** Stress Magnitude
σ_x	
σ_y	
σ_z	
τ_{xy}	
τ_{xz}	
τ_{yz}	
σ_1	

Figure E5-19 – Create a table like that above and enter **Avg** values of other stresses found on the shaft surface.

e. Finally, create a plot of **P1: 1st Principal Stress** (σ_1) using the following. On the **Definition** tab of the **Stress Plot** property manager, open the **Advanced Options** dialogue box and select ☑ **Show as vector plot**. Then, print a front view of the model displayed in the graphics portion of the screen. Use the **Probe** tool to select at least five points on the shaft surface and record the **Avg** value of σ_1 in a table like that of Fig. E5-19. Beneath the vector plot calculate the first principal stress (σ_1) using classical stress equations and compare its magnitude with the **Avg** value of σ_1 from the FEA analysis. Determine the percent difference using equation [1]. Also, beneath the vector plot, sketch and label a Mohr circle diagram depicting both the shear and principal stress σ_1 acting on the shaft surface.

f. Questions: Beneath a plot of part (c) what is the meaning of the fact that shear stresses on both shaft surfaces are negative? Beneath the plot of σ_1, what is the reason for the directions of σ_1?

Textbook Problems

In addition to the above exercise, it is highly recommended that additional problems involving interference fits between mating parts be worked from a design of machine elements textbook. Textbook problems provide a great way to discover errors made in formulating a finite element analysis because they typically are well defined problems for which the solution is known. Typical textbook problems, if well defined in advance, make an excellent source of solutions for comparison.

CHAPTER #6

CONTACT ANALYSIS

Examples up to this point have included models for which various preliminary steps, such as suppressing or un-suppressing certain model features, were pre-planned so that examples could proceed quickly to introduce new finite element principles and techniques. However, a real analysis is not often delivered in such a "ready to go" condition unless the user, or a CAD technician, plans ahead to prepare a model in the desired format. Thus, to better prepare FEA users for a more realistic scenario, this example includes many of the necessary preparatory steps thereby creating a more realistic example from beginning to end. In addition, contact conditions existing between mating parts under load and iso clipping are also explored.

Learning Objectives

Upon completion of this example, users should be able to:

- Assign loads to a *non-flat surface* in *specified direction*(s)
- Define *Contact/Gap* conditions with *no penetration*
- Use *Animation* to understand deformation and stress development as load(s) are applied
- Apply *Iso Clipping* to view model stresses
- Display *Contact Pressure* plots

Problem Statement

A trunion mount, of the type used to attach hydraulic or pneumatic cylinders to a fixed surface, is shown in Fig. 1. Both the trunion and pin are made of **Alloy Steel**. The pin is subject to an 800 lb force acting upward to the right at 60° from the horizontal as shown in a right-side view in Fig. 2. The goal of this analysis is to determine maximum von Mises stress and its location on the trunion mount and to determine contact pressure distribution between the pin and holes in the trunion.

Figure 1 – Typical trunion mount.

Contacting surfaces occur where the pin passes through holes in the side-plates of the trunion and where the mid-portion of the pin is acted upon by a cylinder. For this reason, it is necessary to create separately identifiable contacting surfaces on the pin; *Split Lines* are used for this purpose. Figure 31, pg. 6-23 shows an assembled view of a trunion mount and cylinder base.

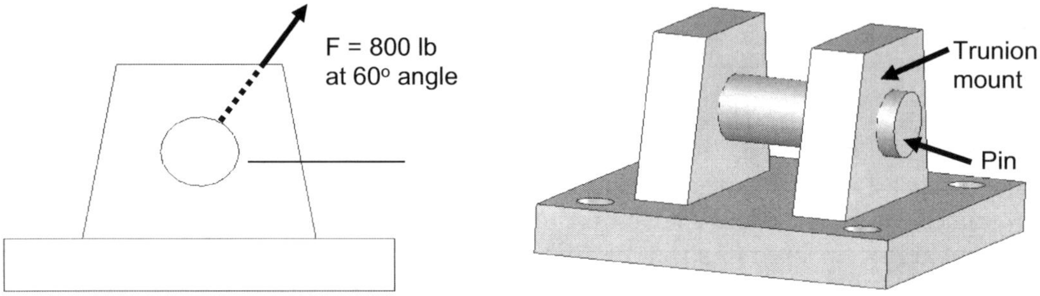

Figure 2 – Right-side view of trunion mount and pin showing direction of applied force.

The procedure outlined below is not the only way to apply *Split Lines* to the pin. It is, however, deemed simpler to demonstrate this aspect of model preparation on the pin alone before joining it with the trunion base to form an assembly. Proceed as follows. *(Because a personal goal should be to develop independent competence using SOLIDWORKS Simulation, some steps below are abbreviated where prior experience should be sufficient.)*

Preparing the Model for Analysis

1. Open **SOLIDWORKS 2026**.

2. Select **Files** > **Open…** and open the part file named "**Trunion Pin**."

All steps related to locating and creating *Split Lines* occur within SOLIDWORKS; therefore, a new Study is not started at this time. Two *Split Lines* are to be added to the trunion pin at locations indicated in Fig. 3. It is important to know that the origin of the coordinate system is located at the center of the pin and that the pin is centered in the trunion mount. Given this information, those who are comfortable in their ability to locate the necessary reference planes and *Split Lines* are encouraged to proceed on their own. These individuals can skip the next two sections titled "Add Reference Planes" and "Insert Split Lines." However, all necessary steps are provided below if guidance or review is desired.

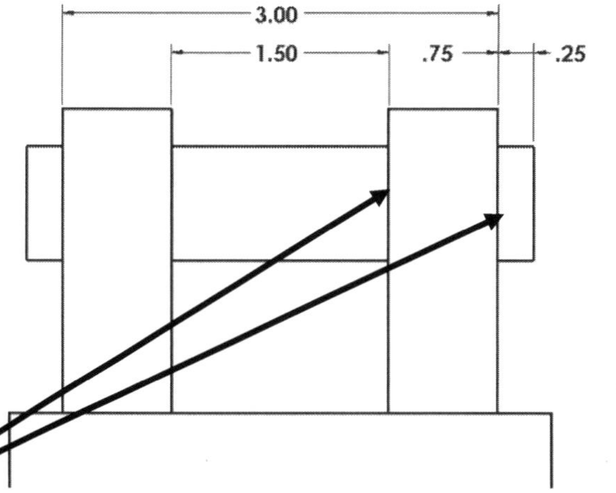

Figure 3 – Location of *Split Lines* at the intersection of the pin and side supports of the trunion mount.

Add Reference Planes

1. From the main menu select **Insert**.

2. In the pull-down menu, highlight **Reference Geometry ▶** and from the subsequent pop-up menu select **Plane...** The **Plane** property manager opens.

3. To open the SOLIDWORKS flyout menu, click either the **Feature Manager icon** or "▶" circled in Fig. 4.

4. In the **First Reference** dialogue box the field is active (light blue). In the SOLIDWORKS flyout menu, select **Right Plane**. See arrow **#1** in Fig. 4. The **Right Plane** appears at the center of the model with a shaded *reference plane* offset from it a short distance.

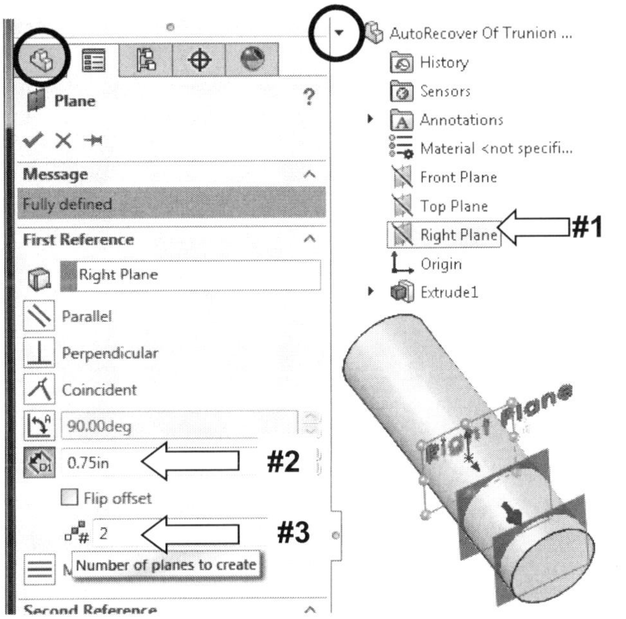

Figure 4 – Selecting the **Right Plane** as a starting point, the first and second **Reference Planes** are successively located 0.75-in and 1.5-in to its right.

5. In the **Offset Distance** spin box, at arrow **#2**, type **0.75** as the distance from the **Right Plane** to the location of the first **Reference Plane**. Left-click in the graphics area and the shaded image of the **Reference Plane** moves to its proper location. *Do NOT right-click to accept this plane because the property manager will close.*

By coincidence, a second reference plane is located 0.75 in. to the right of the first. This is due to the fact that each vertical side of the trunion support is 0.75 inches thick (confirm this by examining dimensions on Fig. 3). Because the second reference plane is to be located the *same* distance from the first, proceed as follows to locate it.

6. In the **Number of planes to create** field, at arrow **#3**, click the up arrow on the spin box to increase the number of planes to **2**. Left-click in the graphics area and a second shaded reference plane appears as shown in Fig. 4.

7. Click **[OK]** ✓ to close the **Plane** property manager to accept these two reference planes. **Plane1** and **Plane2** are labeled on the pin and added to the bottom of the SOLIDWORKS feature manager tree.

A model of the pin and its two **Reference Planes** is shown in Fig. 5.

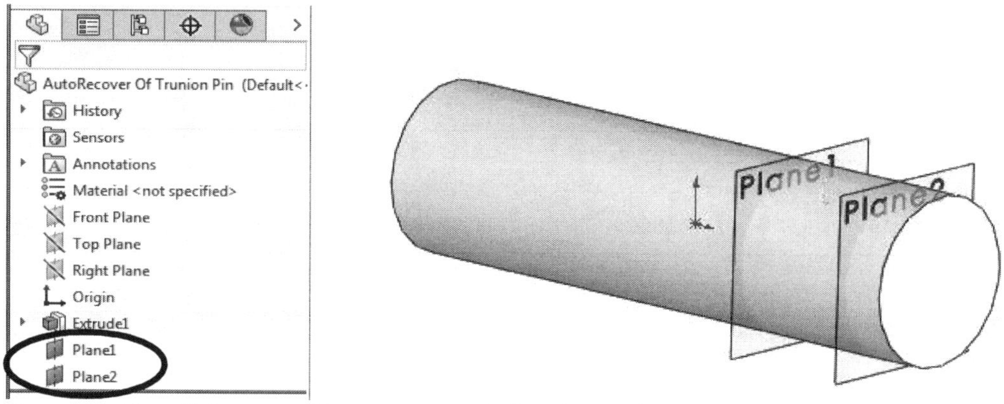

Figure 5 – Two **Reference Planes** are created to denote locations where *Split Lines* are to be added to the pin.

Insert Split Lines

Intersections of **Plane1** and **Plane2** with the pin are used to locate *Split Lines* on the model as outlined below.

1. In the Main menu select **Insert** and from the pull-down menu highlight **Curve ►**. Then from the pop-up menu, select **Split Line...** The **Split Line** property manager opens as shown in Fig. 6.

2. Because **Split Lines** are to be located where each plane intersects the pin, in the **Type of Split** dialogue box choose ⦿ **Intersection**.

3. Click to activate the upper field of the **Selections** dialogue box. The **Splitting Bodies/Faces/Planes** field is highlighted. Either select each of the planes appearing on the pin or click **Plane1** and **Plane2** in the SOLIDWORKS flyout menu. Names of the two planes are listed in the upper field in the order selected.

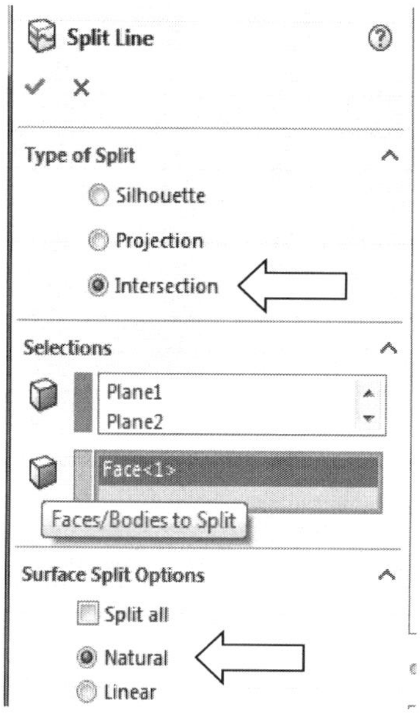

Figure 6– The **Split Line** property manager is used to determine locations of *Split Lines* on the model.

4. Move the cursor onto the second field; its name appears as **Faces/Bodies to Split.** Click to activate this field (light blue). Then, move the cursor into the graphics area and select anywhere on the *cylindrical* surface of the pin. **Face<1>** appears in the active field.

5. In the **Surface Split Options** dialogue box, the setting should appear as ⦿ **Natural**. If not, select it.

6. Click **[OK]** ✓ to close the **Split Line** property manager and two *Split Lines* appear on the pin as shown in Fig. 7. Also, **Split Line1** is listed at the bottom of the SOLIDWORKS feature manager.

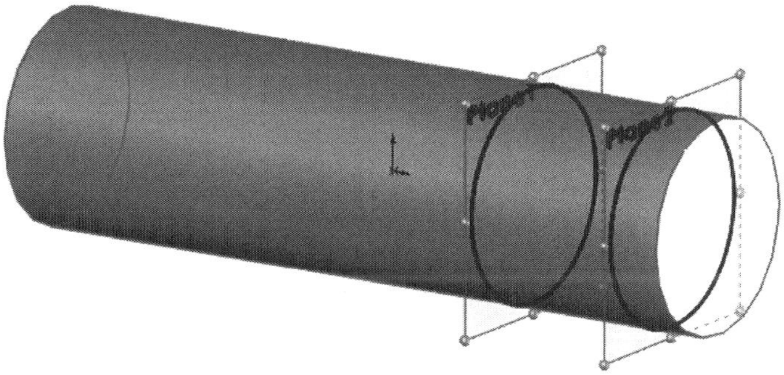

Figure 7 – *Split Lines* located on the trunion pin surface at intersections with the two **Reference Planes**.

Because symmetry exists between left and right halves of the trunion and pin assembly, only the right-half of the pin is used for analysis. Therefore, no additional *Split Lines* need be added to the other half of the model. Save this file as outlined below.

7. From the main menu, select **File** followed by **Save As…**

8. In the **Save As** window, name the part "**Pin with Split Lines**" and **[Save]**. Save the file to the same location as other SOLIDWORKS files. It is *not* recommended to save the file to a temporary storage device such as a USB drive for reasons described in the Introduction.

9. Close the file by selecting **File > Close**. *(Do not close SOLIDWORKS.)*

Create the Assembly Model

It is assumed that most SOLIDWORKS Simulation users are familiar with the SOLIDWORKS work environment and the process of creating an *assembly* composed of two or more *parts*. Those individuals can proceed on their own to join the **Trunion Base** and the **Pin with Split Lines** to form an assembly and proceed to the section titled **Create a Finite Element Analysis (Study)**. The pin should be centered between sides of the trunion base. However, for users who are new to both SOLIDWORKS and SOLIDWORKS Simulation, a step-by-step procedure to create the assembly follows.

In the assembly the pin is located concentric with holes in the trunion base and extends ¼ inch outside of the two side supports as shown in Fig. 3. This location will be replicated in the assembly created in the following steps.

1. In the main menu, click **File > New...** The **New SOLIDWORKS Document** window opens.

2. Click the **Assembly**  icon and then click **[OK]**. The **Begin Assembly** property manager opens as shown in Fig. 8.

3. Click to activate the **Keep Visible** push-pin circled at top-center of the property manager. This action keeps the property manager open during several steps. Also read the upper sentence in the yellow **Message** dialogue box.

4. At the bottom of the **Part/Assembly to Insert** dialogue box, select the **[Browse...]** button. The SOLIDWORKS **Open** window appears. Scroll down the list of files to the location where the **Trunion Base** file is stored. If not found, browse to the file location you set up.

5. From the list of files, select **Trunion Base** and click **[Open]**.

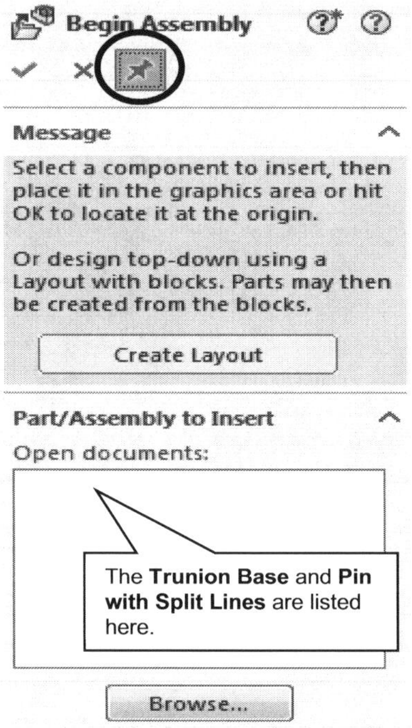

Figure 8 – The **Begin Assembly** property manager used to bring *parts* into an *assembly*.

6. The cursor and part appear and move together in the graphics area. Move the cursor to the top of the **Begin Assembly** property manager and click **[OK]** ✓. The trunion base automatically moves to the coordinate system origin. If the cursor is moved back into the graphics area, a second trunion base appears on the screen. ***Do not click again!***

Ignore the second trunion base that appears and proceed directly to the next step.

7. Move the cursor into the **Part/Assembly to Insert** dialogue box and again select the **[Browse...]** button. The SOLIDWORKS **Open** window appears.

8. In the **Open** window, select the **Pin with Split Lines** and click **[Open]**. The cursor and pin appear and move together on the graphics screen.

9. Move the pin to a position above and to the left of the trunion base as illustrated in Fig. 9 and click to place it there. NOTE: *It may be necessary to roll the middle mouse button to down-size the screen image.* A small image of a mouse should appear with a green checkmark "✓" on the right mouse button; click the right mouse button to accept this position and simultaneously close the **Begin Assembly** property manager. *(The actual pin location is arbitrary, but first-time users will gain greater insight into the assembly process if the pin and base do not initially intersect.)*

The next task is to assemble the pin into holes on the trunion base. This requires use of a **Mate** definition between the parts to be joined. Because we are currently working in the *assembly* mode, the **Assembly** tab and its tool bar, shown in Fig. 10, should be displayed near the top of the screen.

10. If the **Assembly** tab does not appear, apply steps 11 and 12 below. Otherwise skip to step 13.

11. Right-click *any* ***tab*** at top-left of the graphics area, shown boxed in Fig. 10.

12. From the pull-down menu, check "✓" to select ✓ **Assembly** and the **Assembly** *tab*, like that shown in Fig. 10, appears.

13. Open the **Assembly** toolbar by clicking its *tab* shown at the arrow in Fig. 10.

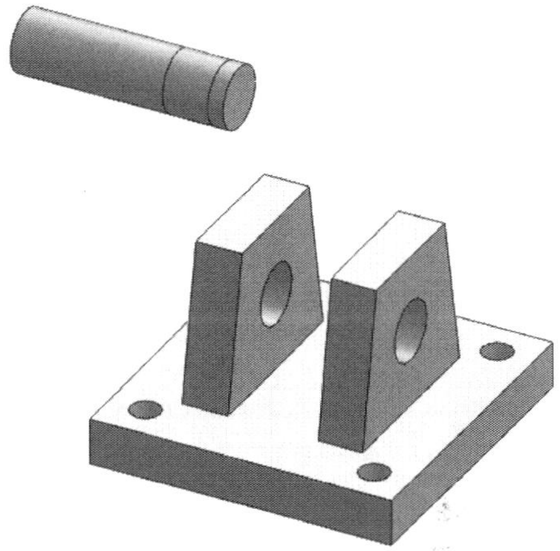

Figure 9 – Trunion base and pin (in an arbitrary position) prior to assembly.

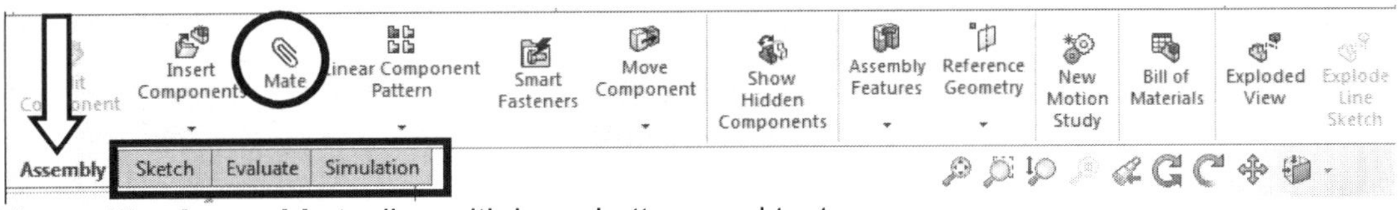

Figure 10 – **Assembly** toolbar with large buttons and text.

<u>CAUTION #1</u>: In the steps that follow, the **Mate** icon is a single paper clip. It is *not* to be confused with the two paper clips labeled **Mates** located at the bottom of the SOLIDWORKS feature manager.

<u>CAUTION #2</u>: Make sure system units are set to **IPS (inch, pound, second)** before proceeding. Make the following menu selections: **Tools** > **Options...** >, then select the **Document Properties** tab > and in the left column select **Units** >. On the right side of the window select ⊙ **IPS (inch, pound, second)**, and click **[OK]** to close the window.

The **Mate** icon circled is circled in Fig. 10. The **Mate** property manager is used to define geometric relationships (i.e., locations) of one part relative to another.

14. On the **Assembly** tab click the **Mate** icon. A portion of the **Mate** property manager opens as seen in Fig. 11.

15. The **Mate Selections** dialogue box is active (highlighted light blue). Passing the cursor over this field indicates it is to be filled with the **Entities to Mate**.

The first step in creating a mate is to position the pin so that it is concentric (aligned) with holes in the trunion base. To accomplish this, the two parts are selected as described next. NOTE: Because *Split Lines* are defined on the pin, its surface is effectively subdivided into segments at each *Split Line*. However, as described in the next step it is necessary to select *only one* cylindrical segment on the pin.

16. Click to select *any cylindrical surface* on the pin and the *cylindrical* surface *inside* either hole as highlighted in Fig. 12. The Pin moves to align its cylindrical surface with that of a hole in the Trunion Base. Names of the two selected faces appear in the **Mate Selections** dialogue box. The software is “smart” enough to guess that a concentric mate is probably desired, but this is not confirmed until the next step.

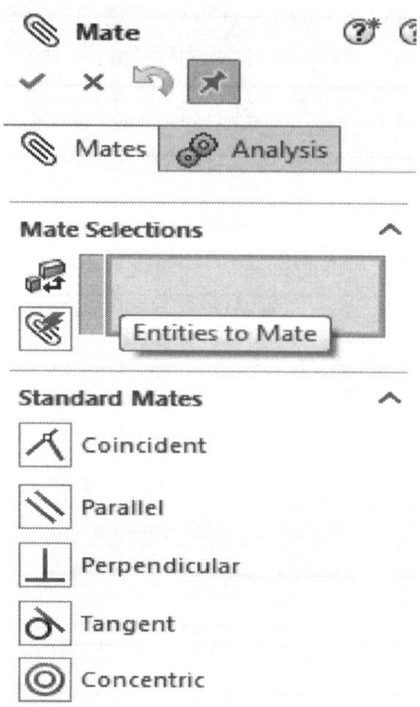

Figure 11 – Initial selection of surfaces to be specified as concentric is made in the **Mate** property manager.

A small pop-up icon bar appears in the graphics area as shown in Fig. 12. It shows icons of several possible mates that might be defined between the two cylindrical surfaces. The **Concentric** icon is circled in Fig. 12.

17. New users may also choose to select the **Concentric** icon in the **Standard Mates** dialogue box, shown boxed in Fig. 12; its name is listed adjacent to its icon. However, either icon (boxed or circled) in Fig. 12 can be selected.

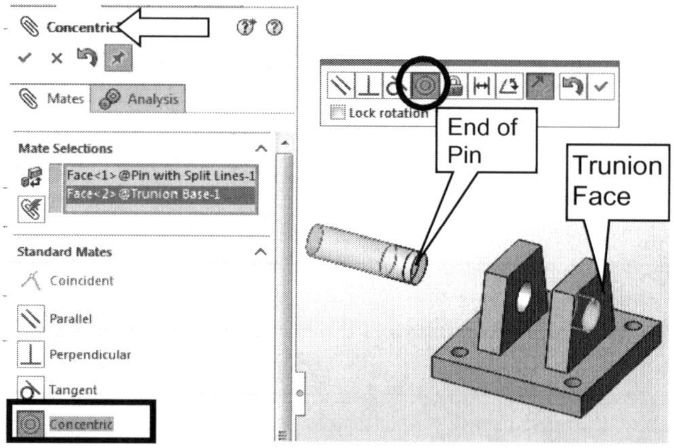

Figure 12 – Defining a **Concentric** mate between the pin and trunion base holes results in alignment between the two parts.

After selecting **Concentric**, the name **Concentric1** appears at the top of the property manager (see arrow in Fig. 12) and names of the two selected faces are listed in the **Mate Selections** dialogue box.

18. Click **[OK]**✓ to close the **Concentric1** property manager. *(Do NOT click **[OK]** twice; see next step.)*

The property manager remains open, but its name changes back to **Mate**. Proceed as follows to further define pin location within the holes

19. Click the right *end* of the pin *and* the right-face of the trunion support shown in Fig. 12. The pin-end aligns flush with the inner trunion face.

However, because the 3.5 inch long pin is to be centered between the two supports (whose outside dimension is 3.00 in, see Fig. 3), final pin location is altered as follows.

20. At arrow **#1** in Fig. 13, click the **Distance** icon and type **0.25** into the **Distance** spin box. Next click anywhere in the graphics screen, then verify units appear as **in**. This value ensures that the pin is offset 0.25 inch from the two selected surfaces. *See next step.*

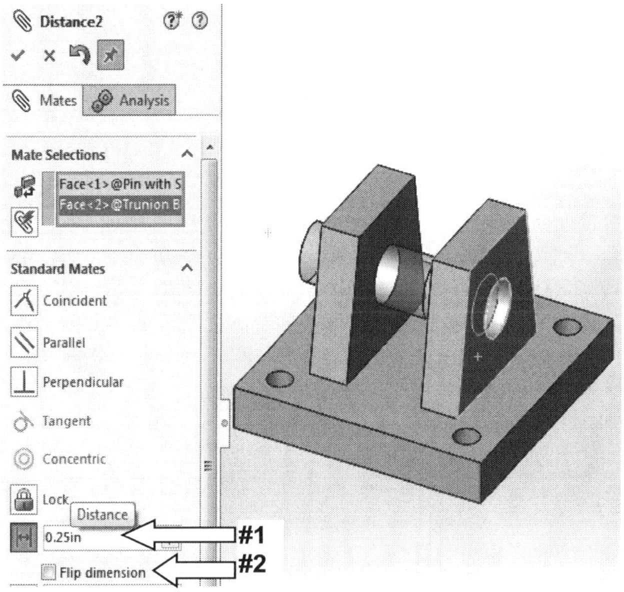

Figure 13 – Two faces are selected so that the appropriate **Distance** between them can be defined to center the pin between holes on the trunion base.

21. If the pin appears recessed within the right-side hole, it is necessary to check ☑ **Flip dimension** located at arrow **#2** below the **Distance** spin box. The assembly should now appear as shown in Fig. 2, repeated below.

22. Click **[OK]** ✓ *twice* to close the **Distance1** and then the **Mate** property managers.

23. To protect the work invested in this example thus far, from the main menu select **File > Save As…** and in the **Save As** window, name the assembly "**Trunion and Pin Assembly**" then click **[Save]** to save the file.

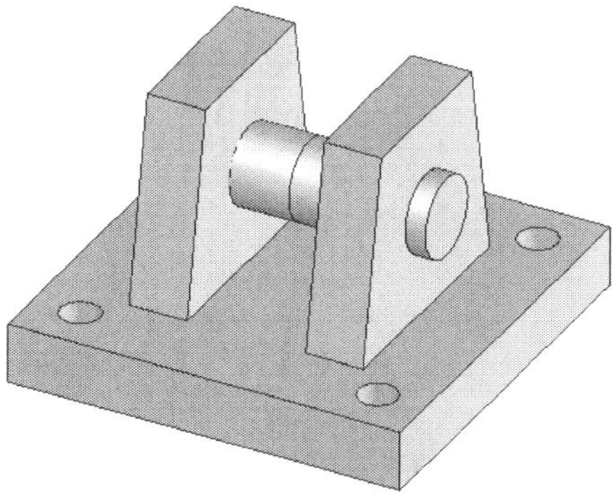

Figure 2 – (Repeated) Shows the pin centered between two trunion sides.

Cut Model on Symmetry Plane

This example makes use of model symmetry to realize computational efficiencies associated with a smaller assembly and to provide additional practice using this powerful software feature. Steps below lead the user through one of several possible procedures to create a symmetrical half-model.

1. Rotate a front view of the model into the plane of the screen by clicking ▼on the **View Orientation** icon. Then select the **Front** view icon. See Fig. 14.

2. Next, in the SOLIDWORKS Feature manager, click to select **Front Plane**; see arrow in Fig. 14. A **Front Plane** is shown on an image of the model in Fig. 14.

NOTE: Additional top, front, and right planes exist for both the trunion base and for the pin. Although consistency of plane location was carefully coordinated for this example, it is important to realize that individual parts are created in their own *local* coordinate system. These individual local coordinate systems may be oriented differently once parts are brought together into the *global* coordinate system of an assembly.

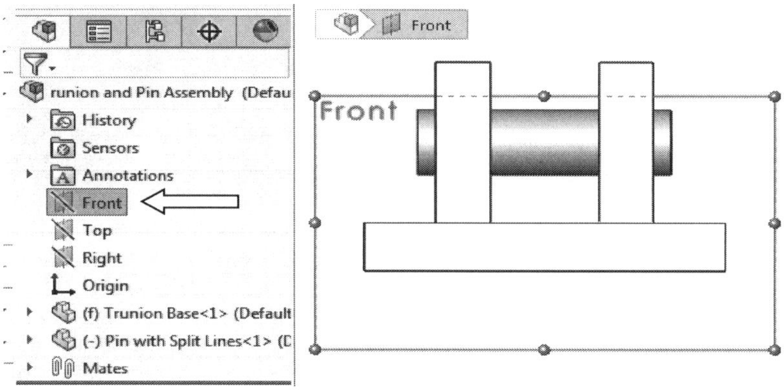

Figure 14 – The **Front Plane** is selected as the plane to sketch on as part of the process of cutting the model in half.

3. Switch to sketch mode by clicking the **Sketch** *tab* near the top of the graphics screen; the **Sketch** toolbar opens. Within the **Sketch** toolbar select the **Sketch** icon to open a sketch on the front plane. If the **Sketch** tab is not available, follow steps 11 and 12 of the previous section to add it, but replace the word **Assembly** with **Sketch.**

4. In the **Sketch** toolbar, select the **Line** icon and move the cursor onto the graphics screen. The cursor changes to a + symbol with a line adjacent to it.

5. Move the cursor above (or below) the *middle* of the assembly and a vertical dashed line appears to indicate alignment with the coordinate system origin. Click at this location and move the mouse to create a vertical line that extends

completely through the model and beyond its opposite border, then click again to end the line. Press **[Esc]** to terminate line drawing and click the close sketch icon if it appears at top right of the graphics screen.

A screen image of the assembly should now appear as shown in Fig. 15.

6. At left of screen in the **Features** toolbar, select the **Extrude Cut** icon and the **Cut-Extrude** property manager opens. NOTE: If the **Features** toolbar is not visible, right-click the main menu, and from the pull-down menu select the **Features** icon. Part of the **Cut Extrude** property manager is shown in Fig. 16.

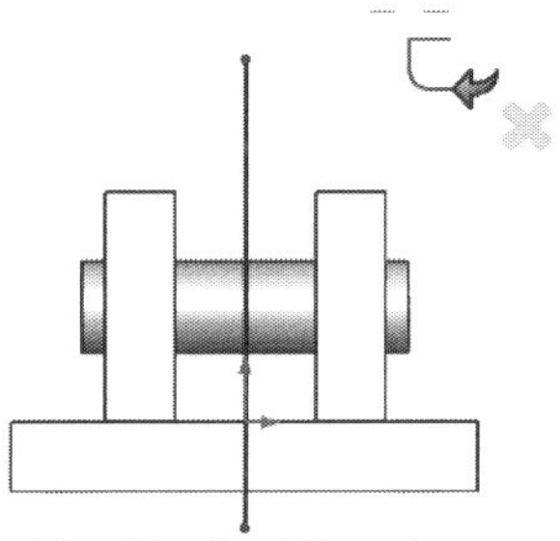

Figure 15 – Vertical line drawn on the **Front Plane** at center of the trunion and pin assembly. Also shown is the warning window that appears when closing a sketch.

7. The **From** dialogue box should indicate **Sketch Plane** and the **Direction1** dialogue box should indicate **Through All**. If not, change it.

8. If necessary, rotate the model so the surface created by extending the vertical line into a cutting plane is visible slicing through the model as shown in Fig. 17.

Three arrows appear on the cutting plane. They point in directions in which the model is cut and material is removed. Carefully observe the direction of the arrow *normal* to the plane. It should point *away* from the right-half of the model. Recall that the right-half of the pin was modified by the addition of *Split Lines*. Thus, the right-half of the model is to be saved.

9. *Only if* the normal arrow is directed toward the right half of the model, click to change its direction by selecting ☑ **Flip side to cut**. When the normal arrow is directed toward the left-side of the assembly (see Fig. 16) proceed to the next step.

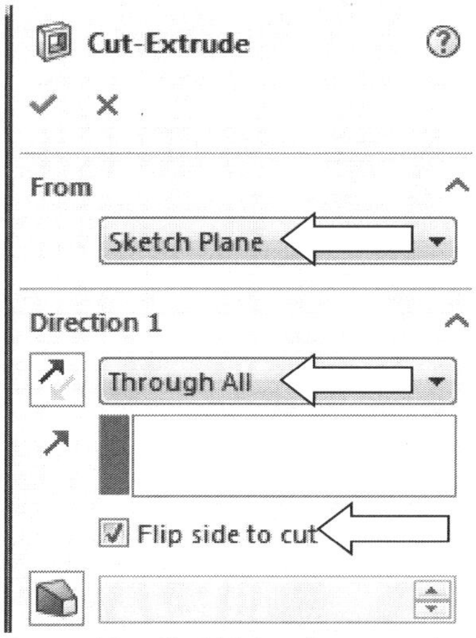

Figure 16 – **Cut-Extrude** property manager used to define direction for the portion of the assembly that is removed by the sketch plane.

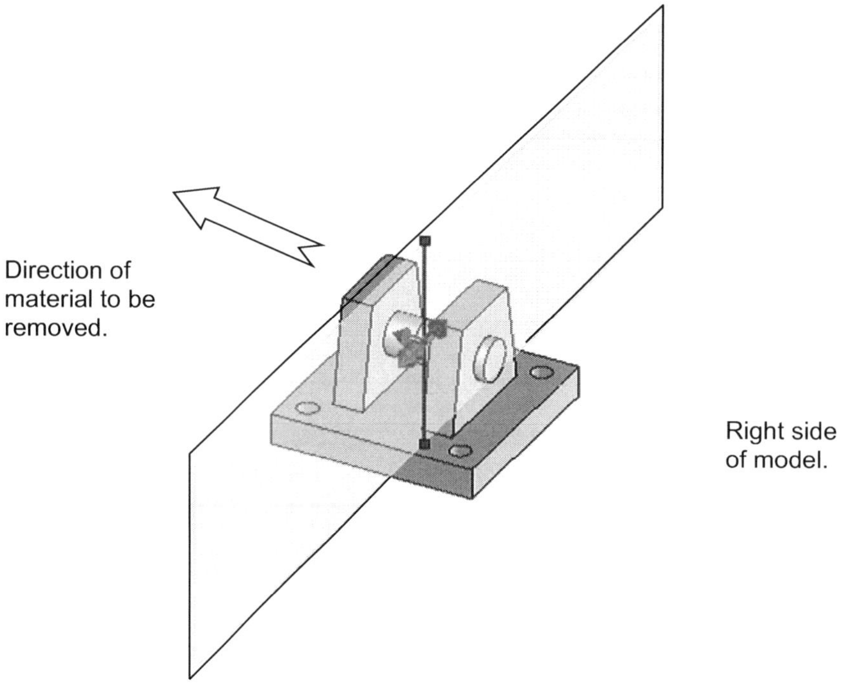

Figure 17 – The cutting plane created by extending the vertical line into a plane is shown along with arrows indicating the direction in which material is to be removed.

10. Click **[OK]** ✓ to close the **Cut-Extrude** property manager. After cutting, the assembly should appear as shown in Fig. 18.

This concludes the somewhat lengthy process of preparing a model for finite element analysis. Although these, or similar steps, were done for you in previous problems, one goal of the current example is to develop a comprehensive picture of typical tasks involved in formulating a complete analysis. The following sections define and solve the finite element model.

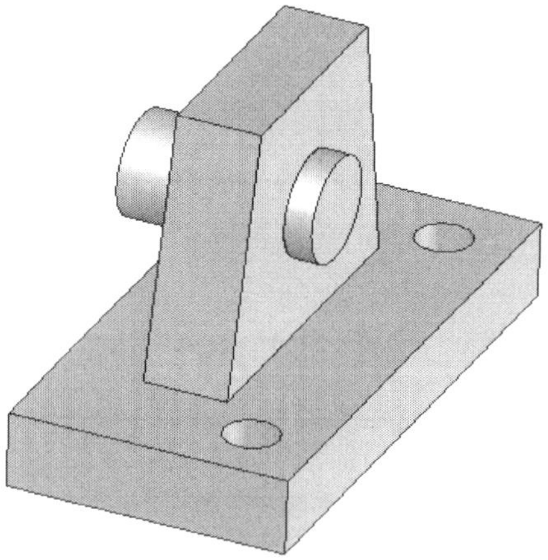

Figure 18 – Assembly after cutting it in half to make use of geometric symmetry.

Create a Finite Element Analysis (Study)

1. In the main menu, click **Simulation**, and from the pull-down menu select **Study…** The **Study** property manager opens.

2. In the **Name** field, type **Trunion and Pin Contact Analysis – Your Name** to identify this study.

3. Verify that a **Static** analysis is selected then click **[OK]** ✓ to close the **Study** property manager. The Simulation manager appears on the left of the screen.

4. In the main menu, click **Simulation** and from the pull-down menu select **Options…** The **Systems Options - General** window opens.

5. Under the **Default Options** tab, select **Units** and set the following options:
   - In the right-half of the window under **Unit system**, select ⊙ **English (IPS)**
   - Under **Units**, set **Length/Displacement:** to **in** and **Pressure/Stress:** to **psi** (if not already selected). Ignore remaining options.

6. Click **[OK]** to close the **Default Options - Units** window.

Assign Material Properties

1. In the Simulation manager tree, right-click the **Parts** folder and select **Apply Material to All…**

2. In the left half of the **Material** window, beneath **SOLIDWORKS Materials**, open the ▶ **Steel** folder. And, from the list of materials, select **Cast Alloy Steel**.

3. In the right-half of the **Material** window, **Units:** *should* appear as **English (IPS)** as defined above. If not, change units at this time.

4. Click **[Apply]** followed by **[Close]** to exit the **Material** window.

Assign Fixtures and External Loads

The following section includes subtitles to identify specific restraint types applied to the model. Individuals are encouraged to use subtitles to guide their application of restraints on their own. However, complete instructions are provided if desired.

Symmetry and Immovable Restraints

In the following steps, **Fixed** (immovable) and **Symmetry** restraints are applied at bolt holes on the trunion base and at cut (symmetrical) surfaces respectively.

1. Right-click the **Fixtures** folder, and from the pull-down menu select **Fixed Geometry…**

2. In the **Standard (Fixed Geometry)** dialogue box, ensure the **Fixed Geometry** icon is selected (gray highlight) and the **Faces, Edges, Vertices for Fixture** field is active (highlighted light blue).

3. Move the cursor over the model and zoom in, as necessary, to select the *inside surface* of each bolt hole on the trunion base. Restraint symbols appear inside each hole as illustrated in Fig. 19.

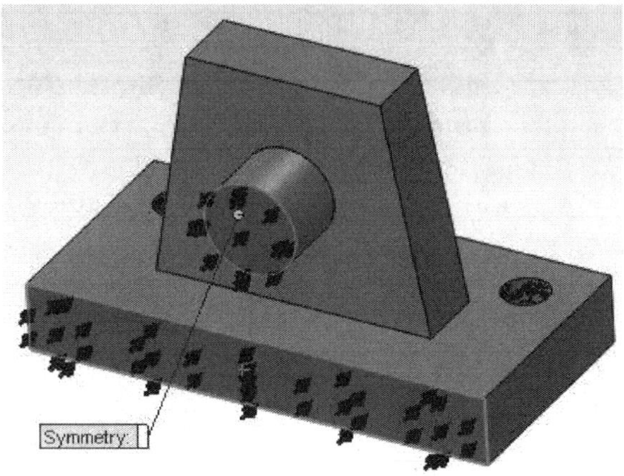

Figure 19 – **Fixed** restraints are applied to bolt holes and **Symmetry** restraints are applied to cut surfaces of the pin and trunion base.

4. Click **[OK]**✓ to close the **Fixture** property manager.

5. Again, right-click the **Fixtures** folder and from the pull-down menu select **Advanced Fixtures…** The **Fixture** property manager opens.

6. Click to select the **Symmetry** icon from the list of available fixture types.

7. Apply this restraint by selecting both *cut surfaces* on the pin and trunion base highlighted in Fig. 19. An outline of the left-half of the model appears to visually confirm that symmetry modeling is active. **Symmetry** restraints appear normal to the cut surface, thereby preventing displacement in the model's X-direction.

8. Click **[OK]** ✓ to close the **Fixture** property manager.

Connections Define Contact Conditions

In the Simulation manager tree in Fig. 20, open the **Connections** folder and all its sub-folders by selecting the "▸" symbol adjacent to each folder. This folder is always present, but it only becomes important when an *assembly* is analyzed so that interactions (i.e., contact conditions) between mating parts can be defined. The **Connections** folder was also encountered in Chapter 5, where a Shrink Fit was analyzed. The following steps outline how **Connections** are used to define a local contact condition between the pin and inner surface of the hole in the trunion base. Notice the default condition assumes all surfaces are bonded.

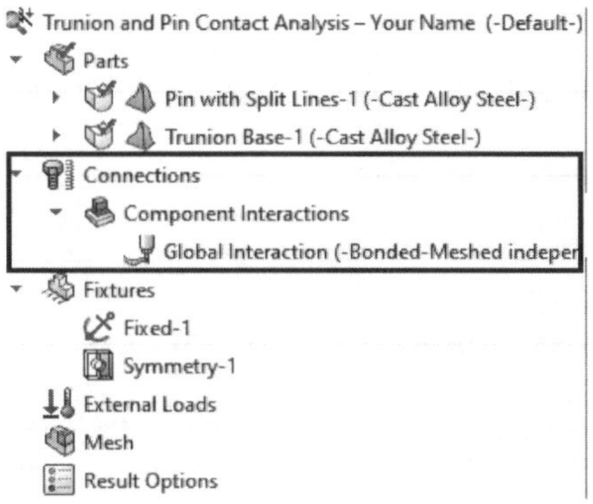

Figure 20 – **Connectors** folder in the Simulation manager tree.

To facilitate selection of the contacting surfaces, begin by creating an exploded view of the assembly. Try this on your own or apply steps below.

1. In the main menu click **Insert** and from the pull-down menu select **Exploded View…** This opens the **Explode** property manager.

2. In the **Explode Step Type** dialogue box select the **Regular step** icon .

3. On the model, click to select the pin. Then *drag* the manipulator arrow in the direction of the +X-axis (this direction corresponds to the pin axis) to move the pin away from the model as shown in Fig. 21.

4. Click **[OK]** ✓ to close the **Explode** property manager.

Figure 21 – Explode the assembly to facilitate selection of contacting surfaces.

5. In the Simulation manager tree, right-click the **Connections** folder, and from the pop-up menu select **Local Interactions.** The **Local Interactions** property manager opens as shown in Fig. 22.

6. In the **Local Interactions** dialogue box, select ⊙ **Manually select local interactions**.

7. In the **Type** dialogue box, select **Contact** from the pull-down menu. This action defines the type of contact between the pin and hole surfaces that has no penetration.

8. The upper field of the **Type:** dialogue box should be active (light blue). Select the *inner surface* of the hole, highlighted in Fig. 22, and **Face<1>@ Trunion Base-1** is listed in the **Faces, Edges, Vertices for Set 1** field.

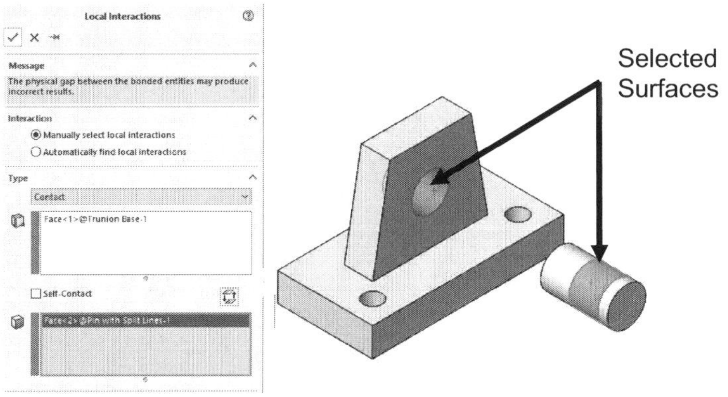

Figure 22 – Selecting surfaces between which the **Contact/Gaps** restraint is applied.

9. Next, click inside the **Faces for Set 2** field (second field from top) to activate it. Then, on the pin, select the corresponding surface, also highlighted in Fig. 22. **Face<2> @Pin with Split Lines-1** appears in the **Faces for Set 2** field.
10. Click **[OK]** ✓ to close the **Contact Sets** property manager. Beneath the **Connections** folder appears an icon labeled ▸ **Local Interactions**. Click the "▶" symbol to reveal **Local Interaction-1 (-Contact<Trunion Base-1, Pin with Split Lines-1>-)**." Place the cursor over this text to reveal its entire name.

Apply a Directional Load

This section outlines steps to apply a directional load to the round pin. In previous examples, force components in the X, Y, or Z directions were applied to parts with flat surfaces. Using that approach, the 800 lb force applied to the pin at a 60° angle from the horizontal in Fig. 1 should be represented by its Y and Z force components. However, this example demonstrates application of these force components in a way not used in earlier problems. Further, because only half of the model is being analyzed, only half of the 800 lb force is applied to the pin. First, however, the model is re-assembled (i.e., un-exploded) as follows.

1. Select the **Configuration manager** icon located at top of the SOLIDWORKS feature manager tree.

2. At top of the **Configurations** manager, click the "▶" symbol adjacent to **Default [Trunion and Pin Assembly]** to display an additional sub-folder.

3. Next, right-click ▶ ExplView1, and from the pull-down menu select **Collapse**.

After the model is re-assembled, proceed as follows to apply the load.

4. In the Simulation manager, right-click the **External Loads** folder, and from the pull-down menu select **Force…** The **Force/ Torque** property manager opens; see Fig. 23.

5. In the **Force/Torque** dialogue box, select the **Force** icon circled in Fig. 23.

6. Also in the **Force/Torque** dialogue box, choose ⊙ **Selected direction**. The property manager changes to look like that shown in Fig. 23.

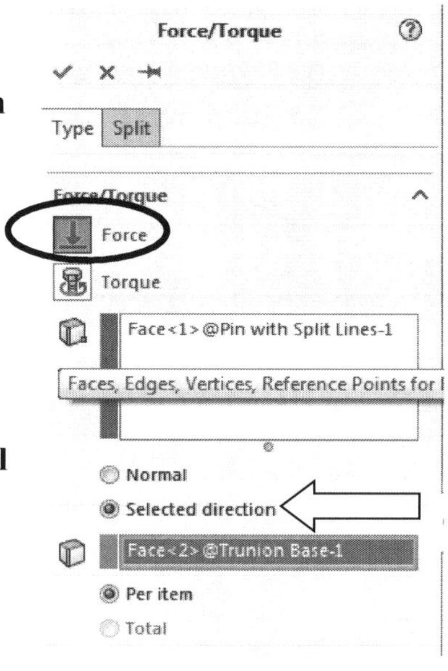

Figure 23 – Selecting faces to define force component direction in the **Force/Torque** property manager.

7. Click to highlight the **Faces, Edges, Vertices, Reference Points for Force** field. Rotate the model as necessary and click the cylindrical pin surface indicated in Fig. 24. **<Face1>@Pin with Split Lines-1** is listed in the upper field.

8. Also in the **Force/Torque** dialogue box, click to activate the **Face, Edge, Plane, for Direction** field (second field from top) and proceed to select the trunion support face also indicated in Fig. 24. **Face<2>@Trunion Base-1** appears in the active field.

Aside: It is also possible to select any other face, edge, plane or axis that is aligned with the direction of the applied force components. Other *surfaces* that could be selected include the cut-end of the pin; the cut-face of the trunion base; or the **Right Plane** in the SOLIDWORKS flyout menu (the plane selected *must* be at the assembly level, *not* at the component level). Also, edges in the Z-direction can be used.

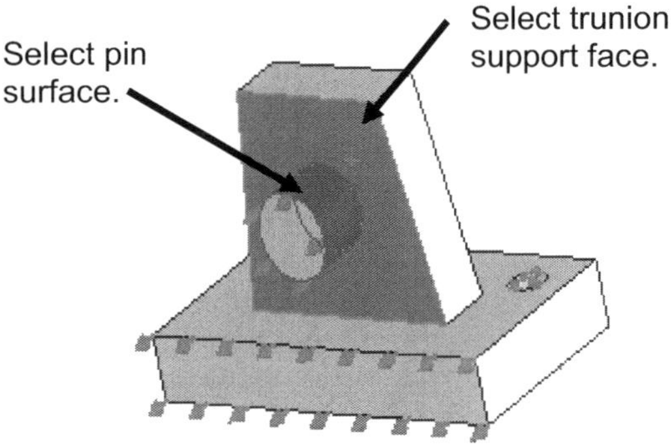

Figure 24 – Selecting the surface for force application and a face to define its direction.

The bottom portion of the **Force/Torque** property manager is shown in Fig. 25. In the **Force** dialogue box, three choices are available for defining magnitude and direction of a force. Icons adjacent to the top two fields *show two different directions for applying forces parallel to the* selected face while the bottom field indicates a force applied perpendicular to the selected face.

9. In the **Force** dialogue box, move the cursor over the top field. Its name appears as **Along Plane Dir 1**. Click the icon adjacent to this field to activate it. Immediately, force vectors are displayed on the center segment of the pin. *(Ignore their direction for now.)*

10. These vectors are parallel to the trunion face selected in step 8 above. Use the coordinate system triad to verify that these vectors lie in the Z-direction. This direction corresponds to the horizontal component of the 400 lb force[1]. Therefore, the force component entered in the top field is **200** lb, which is determined from:

$$F_Z = 400*\cos 60^o = 200 \text{ lb}$$

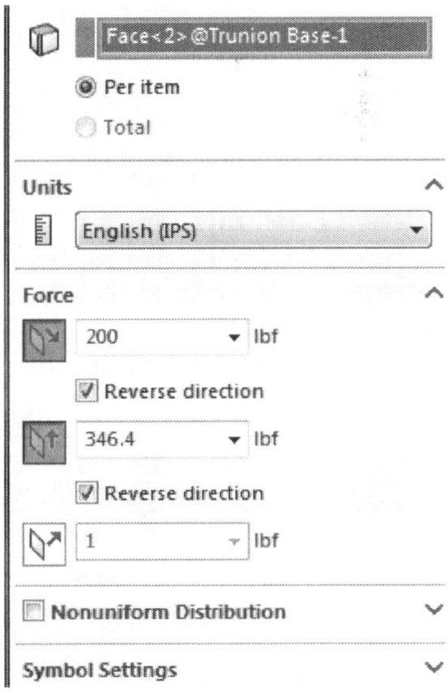

Figure 25 – Specifying magnitude and direction of force components.

[1] Recall, only half the total force of 800 pounds, or 400 pounds, is applied to the half-model.

Figure 1 (repeated below) shows geometry related to the above calculation. Also observe an on-screen "flag" that displays direction, units, and magnitude of the force component.

11. If force vectors are oriented in the incorrect direction, check ☑ **Reverse direction**. Refer to Fig. 26 for proper directions of force components.

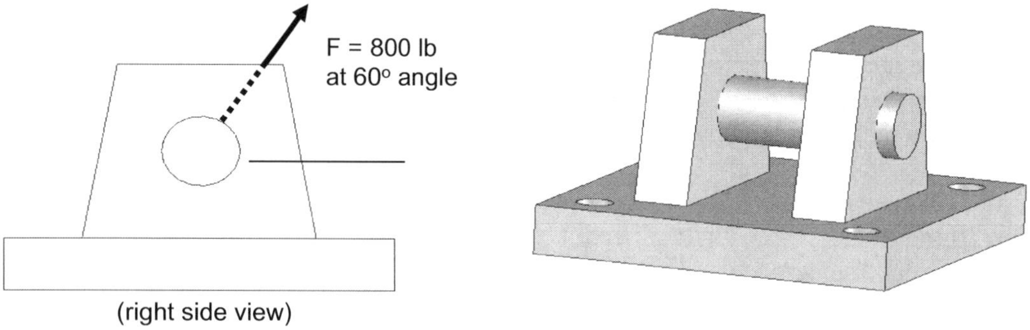

Figure 1 (repeated) – Right-side view of trunion mount and pin showing direction of applied force.

12. Enter the Y-component of force on your own and verify that its direction is upward as shown on Fig. 26. Use a force magnitude of:

$$F_Y = 400*\sin 60^\circ = 346.4 \text{ lb}$$

13. Make certain the force **Normal to plane** is deselected (i.e., the bottom field in the **Force** dialogue box should be "grayed" out).

14. Click **[OK]** ✓ to close the **Force/Torque** property manager.

Y and Z force components applied to the pin should now appear as shown in Fig. 26. If force component directions differ from those shown, right-click the **Force-1** and select **Edit Definition…**; then select ☑ **Reverse direction**. **Symmetry** and **Fixed** restraints are temporarily hidden to reduce clutter in Fig. 26.

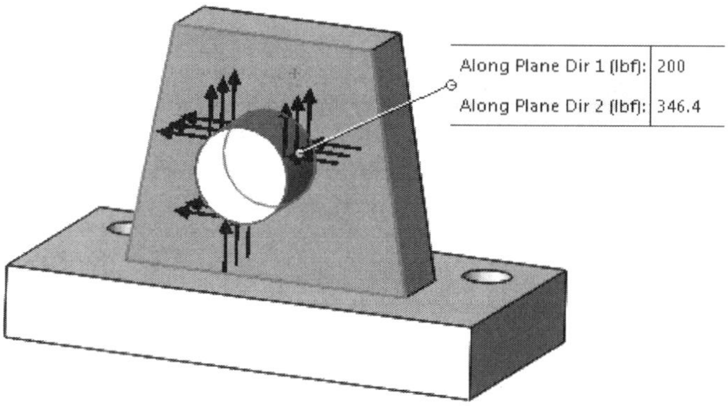

Figure 26 – To improve visibility, the Y and Z components of force applied to the pin are illustrated to a somewhat enlarged scale. (Left-side view.)

Mesh the Model and Run the Solution

1. Right-click the **Mesh** folder, and from the pull-down menu select **Create Mesh…**

2. Check "✓" to open ☑ **Mesh Parameters** and accept the default mesh size. Also, select ⊙**Standard Mesh**. Click **[OK]** ✓ to close the **Mesh** property manager and mesh the model.

3. On the Simulation tab, click the **Run This Study** icon. ***If the analysis fails in an error, click [OK] to close error windows and repeat step 3.***

Notice the longer time required for this solution (approx. 5 seconds). Extra time is due to the **Solving contact constraints:** portion of the analysis. NOTE: Meshing the model must occur *after* **Contact** (i.e., **No Penetration)** is specified as the contact mode between mating parts.

Results Analysis

A primary goal of this example is to introduce tools used to observe contact pressure (stress) between mating components. Also, because the resulting state of stress is rather complex to model using simple classical stress equations, little attention is focused on other stress results in the current model. However, because von Mises stress is widely used to compare stress magnitude against material Yield Strength, its results are examined briefly below.

Von Mises Stress

1. If von Mises stress is not displayed on the model, double-click **Stress1 (-vonMises-)** located beneath the **Results** folder. An image of von Mises stress distribution in the model is displayed in Fig. 27 and on your screen.

2. If the model does not appear as a deformed view, right-click **Stress1 (-vonMises-)** and select **Edit Definition…** Within the **Stress plot** property manager, verify that a check appears adjacent to ☑ **Deformed Shape** and select ⊙ **Automatic** as the scaling method.

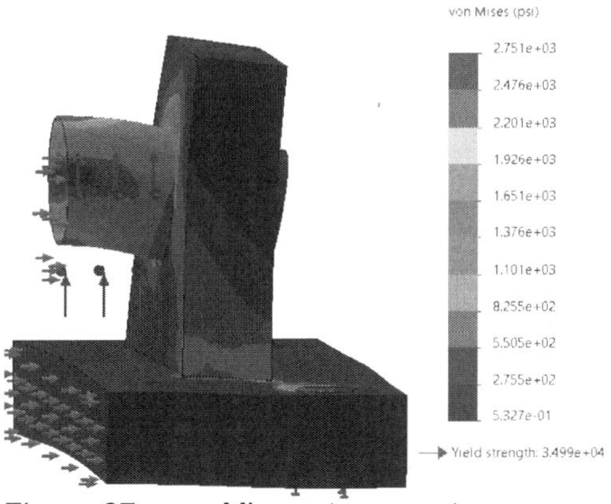

Figure 27– von Mises stress contours displayed on the deformed shape of the trunion and pin assembly.

3. Click **[OK]** ✓ to close the **Stress plot** property manager. The image should appear similar to that shown in Fig. 27; if not, double click **Stress1 (-vonMises-)**.

Observe the maximum von Mises stress of 2751 psi (values may vary) is well below the material Yield Strength (34,994 psi). Yield Strength is *not* typically displayed on assembly plots because dissimilar materials might be used for different components. However, in this example all materials are the same, thus Yield Strength is shown.

Iso Clipping

Unlike **Section Clipping** that permits stepping through a model at user specified increments of *distance* to view stresses on different "slices" of the model, **Iso Clipping** aids interpretation of results by permitting a variety of display options *based on stress magnitude.* These options are investigated below.

1. Right-click **Stress1 (-vonMises-)** and from the pull-down menu select **Iso Clipping...** An initial view of the **Iso Clipping** property manager is illustrated in Fig. 28.

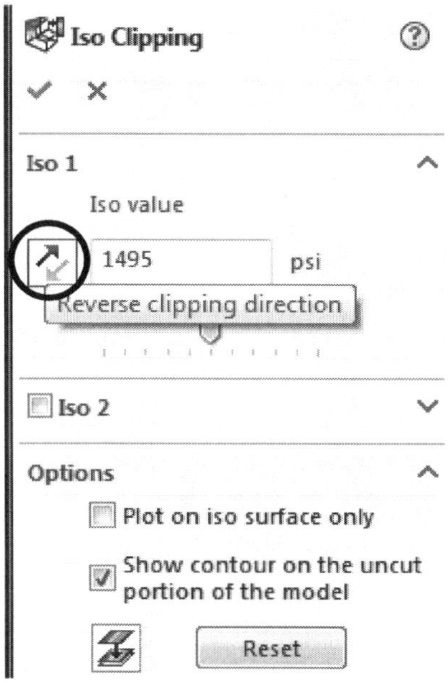

Figure 28 – Sliding stress scale in the **Iso Clipping** property manager.

The **Iso 1** dialogue box contains a sliding scale whose two extreme values correspond to the minimum and maximum values of the quantity displayed on the color-coded stress scale appearing on the graphics screen. In the present case, von Mises stress magnitudes are displayed at the mid-range value.

2. In the **Iso 1** box, click-and-*drag* the sliding scale pointer and observe stress *levels* change on the model. Simultaneously, a moving arrow, adjacent to the color-coded stress scale, indicates the magnitude of stresses currently being displayed. Sliding the pointer from left-to-right results in lower stress levels being peeled away such that only areas of high stress remain. The *current value* of stress magnitude also appears in the **Iso value** box in the **Iso 1** dialogue box.

3. By clicking the **Reverse clipping direction** icon, circled in Fig. 28, and then moving the sliding scale pointer from left-to-right, increasing levels of stress are displayed on the model.

4. Next, in the **Options** dialogue box, located at bottom of the **Iso Clipping** property manager in Fig. 28, check ☑ **Plot on iso surface only** and once again move the sliding scale pointer. This time observe that *only* stress of a certain magnitude is plotted. This result is *not* pictured on the model in Fig. 29. Return **Iso Clipping** to its original setting by again clicking the **Reverse clipping direction** icon

The option demonstrated in step 4 permits easy identification of regions where stress is *at* a certain magnitude.

5. Before proceeding, clear the check mark from ☐ **Plot on iso surface only**.

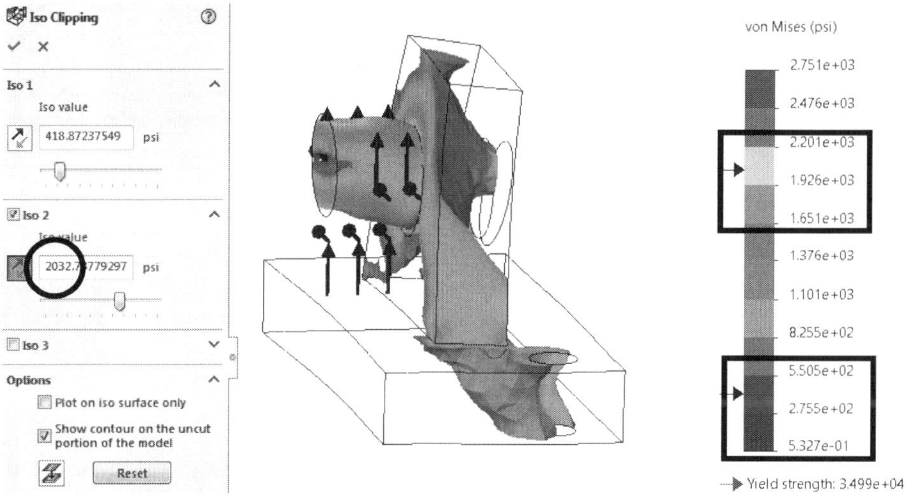

Figure 29 – **Iso Clipping** is set to display stresses *between* values set in the **Iso 1** and **Iso 2** dialogue boxes.

6. Next, check ☑ **Iso 2** to open a second dialogue box in the **Iso Clipping** property manager and click the **Reverse clipping direction** icon for **Iso 2**. See Fig. 29.

7. Use the sliding scale in each dialogue box to set a lower bound and an upper bound for stress magnitudes to be displayed. In Fig. 29 **Iso 1** is set at **418.87** psi and **Iso 2** is set at **2032.73** psi. *Any approximations of these values are acceptable.*

The corresponding plot, shown at the right side of Fig. 29, displays stress values *between* approximately 418 psi to 2032 psi. Also observe two arrows adjacent to the color-coded stress scale. These arrows mark the lower and upper bounds of stress magnitudes currently displayed. NOTE: If an error was made in the steps above, it may be necessary to click the **Reverse clipping direction** icons to properly set upper and lower bounds.

Analysis Insight

Iso Clipping permits easy identification of regions where stress levels are *above or below* a given value.

Iso Clipping also permits isolating and displaying stresses *at* a specific level or *between* specified lower and upper limits.

Before proceeding, return the full display of von Mises stress contours to the model as follows.

8. Clear the checkmark "✓" from the ☐ **Iso 2** dialogue box.

9. In the **Iso 1** dialogue box, slide the scale pointer to the extreme left position to display the full range of stress contours on the model. If they do not appear, click the **Reverse clipping direction** icon.

10. Click **[OK]** ✓ to close the **Iso Clipping** property manager.

Animating Stress Results

SOLIDWORKS Simulation **Animation** capability permits dynamic viewing of a model due to applied loads provided ☑ **Deformed Shape** and ⊙ **Automatic** were selected, as specified in steps 2 and 3 of the "**von Mises Stress**" section. During animation the model is cycled from no load to maximum load while stress, displacement, or strain is displayed. Insight gained by viewing these variations can be valuable in determining whether or not the model is behaving as expected based on applied loads and restraints. Proceed as follows to animate the von Mises stress results.

1. Right-click **Stress1 (-vonMises-)** and from the pull-down menu select **►Animate…** The **Animation** property manager opens as shown in Fig. 30.

2. If the model is animated, click the **Stop** button near top of the **Basics** dialogue box.

3. Within the **Basics** dialogue box, the upper field controls the number of **Frames** (i.e., the number of still images that are played back in sequence to simulate continuous motion). Set the **Frames** spin-box value to **10**. This value is a user preference. Higher values create smoother, but slower, animations.

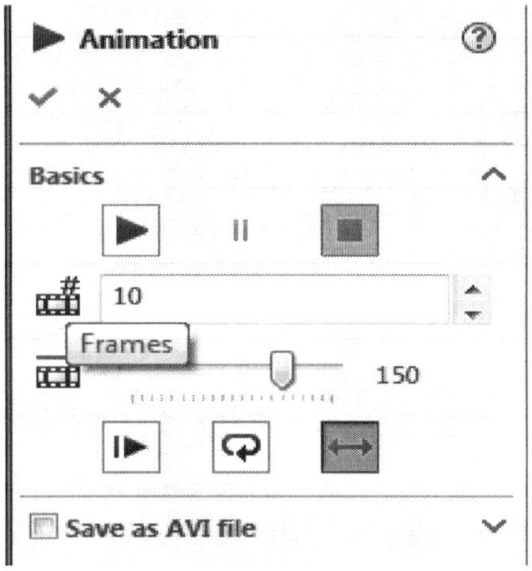

Figure 30 – A portion of the **Animation** property manager showing the **Frames** and **Speed** controls.

4. The slide-scale, located at the bottom of the **Basics** dialogue box, controls the **Speed** of animation. Moving the slide to the left slows the animation and, conversely, movement to the right increases animation speed.

Experiment with these capabilities on your own. The model can be rotated to view it from different angles while animation is proceeding. Observe the model in a front view and note that planes of symmetry do *not move* in the X-direction. Use the **Start**, **Pause**, and **Stop** buttons, located from left to right across the top of the **Basics** dialogue box, to control animation. If desired, an animated sequence can be saved as an AVI file.

5. After experimenting with this capability, click **[OK]** ✓ to close the **Animation** property manager.

Animation of stress variation in the trunion mount corresponds to each power stroke of a cylinder. Although not studied here, cycling of stress from minimum to maximum should emphasize the need to conduct a fatigue analysis of a machine component.

Displacement Results

Displacement or **Strain** results can be displayed and examined in like manner to that described above for the von Mises stress plot. Users are encouraged to examine the displacement display and animate it on their own.

Analysis Insight

For those familiar with the actual hardware used in a trunion mounted pneumatic or hydraulic cylinder, the deformed model should raise questions about the validity of loads applied to the pin. A photograph of a complete trunion mount, shown in Fig. 31, reveals that the central portion of the pin passes through a *close-fitting* hole on the cylinder base. As such, it is highly unlikely that the pin deforms (bends) like images in Figs. 27 or 29. A better model of the trunion mount and pin assembly should include a more rigid **Contact Set** definition applied on the center portion of the pin.

Figure 31 – Close-up view of a trunion mount attached to the base of a pneumatic cylinder.

This insight is introduced to emphasize, once again, the significant influence of using *proper boundary conditions* to obtain accurate and meaningful finite element results. On your own, consider whether or not the accuracy of boundary conditions (i.e., **Loads** and **Fixtures**) applied to this model could be further improved. For example, knowing that the trunion mount is to be bolted down, should another restraint be applied to the bottom surface of the trunion mount to prevent deflection (i.e., penetration) *into* a rigid surface beneath it? Also consider how additional restraints applied to the bottom surface of the trunion depend on the stiffness of the surface to which it is fastened.

Proper finite element analysis requires its users to carefully consider numerous factors that directly influence the validity of results. The ability to easily create and model these alternate design scenarios is clearly one of the strengths of the finite element approach.

Contact Pressure / Stress

The final section of this example explores the **Contact Pressure** plot. This plot displays, in a unique graphical format, the contact pressure developed between mating parts for which **Contact Interaction** conditions are specified. Proceed as follows to display this plot.

1. Begin by turning off the display of loads and restraints on the model. Right-click the **Fixtures** folder and from the pull-down menu, select **Hide All**. Do the same for the **External Loads** folder.

2. Next, right-click the **Results** folder, and from the pull-down menu select **Define Stress Plot...** The **Stress plot** property manager opens.

3. Within the **Display** dialogue box, click ▼ to open the stress **Component** pull-down menu and from the list of options select **CP: Contact Pressure**.

4. Open **v** the **Advanced Options** dialogue box and check ☑ **Show as vector plot**.

5. Click **[OK]** ✓ to close the **Stress plot** property manager. A new plot named **Stress2 (-Contact pressure-)** is displayed and listed beneath the **Results** folder.

6. If the contact pressure plot is not displayed, right-click **Stress2 (-Contact pressure-)**, and from the pop-up menu select **Show**. *Rotate the model and examine the results.* The *default display* of contact pressure is relatively small.

The following steps outline how to adjust the contact pressure plot to appear as shown in Figs. 32 (a) and (b).

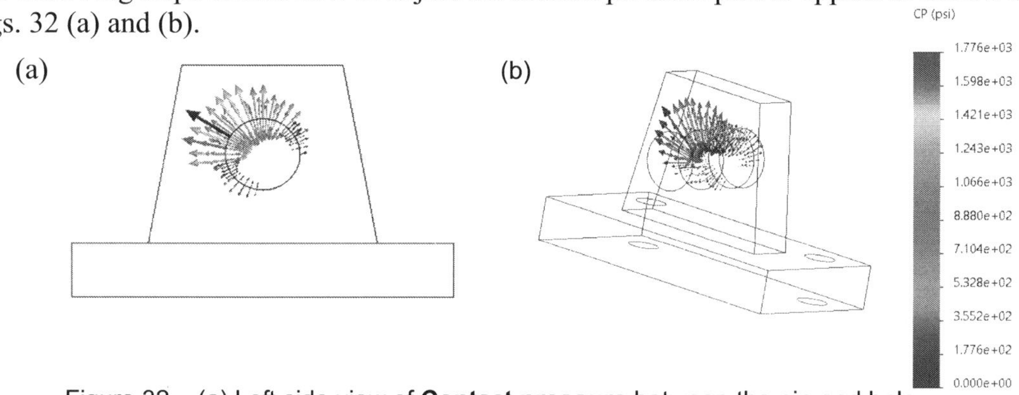

Figure 32 – (a) Left-side view of **Contact pressure** between the pin and hole in the trunion mount; (b) view showing the three-dimensional nature of **Contact pressure** between mating surfaces.

7. Right-click **Stress2 (-Contact pressure-)** and from the pull-down menu select **Vector Plot Options...** The **Vector plot options** property manager opens as shown in Fig. 33.

8. In the **Options** dialogue box, type **600** in the **Size** field to enlarge the contact pressure vectors currently displayed. The **Size** value is a user preference and should be selected to create a meaningful display. (Maximum **Size** = 1000 %.)
9. Make certain that ⦿ **Match color chart** is selected. This option adds color to the vector plot such that, in addition to vectors indicating the direction of contact pressure, vector color also corresponds to magnitude displayed in the color-coded stress legend.
10. Click **[OK]** ✓ to close the **Vector plot options** property manager. Your display should now appear similar to that shown in Figs. 32 (a) or (b).

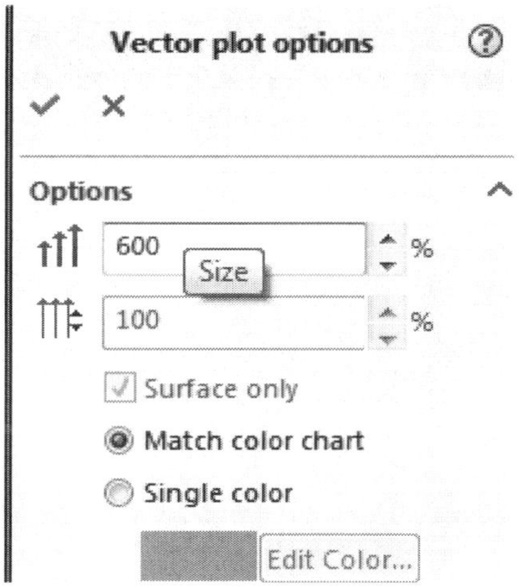

Figure 33 – Magnitude of the vector display is controlled within the **Vector plot options** property manager.

11. Rotate and zoom-in on the model to gain a better appreciation of the three-dimensional nature of contact pressure variation between the pin and hole in the trunion mount. Observe that higher contact pressure exists toward the loaded side of the pin and in the direction of the applied force.

A **Contact Pressure** plot is somewhat unique because it displays both magnitude and direction of pressure between the contacting surfaces. Existence of this plot is dependent on the *Contact* **Contact Interaction** condition defined earlier in this example.

This concludes analysis of contact pressure developed between the trunion base and a pin subject to an external load. This example file can be closed without saving. If file space is at a premium, delete the file.

12. In the main menu, select **File > Close**. Then in the SOLIDWORKS window select **Don't Save**.

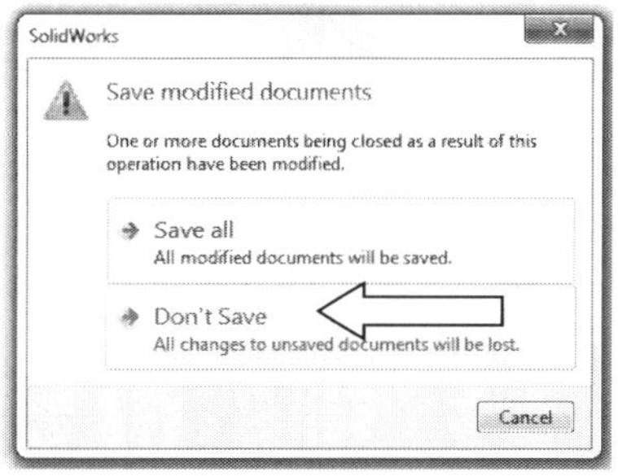

Analysis Insight – How Contact Pressure relates to previous examples.

In closing, consider how methods of this chapter could have been applied to the pin used to attach a roller to the cam follower in the example of Chapter #1 or to determine contact stress in the vicinity of the pin hole in the curved beam model of Chapter #2. Likewise, it could have been used to reveal a plot of contact pressure caused by the interference fit between the wheel and shaft assembly of Chapter #5.

EXERCISES

EXERCISE 1 – Contact Pressure Between a Clevis and Pin

At the push-rod end of a hydraulic or pneumatic cylinder (opposite end from the trunion mount) is a part that connects the cylinder push-rod to a driven component. This connector, commonly called a "clevis," takes many different forms, one of which is illustrated in Fig. E6-1. A clevis is typically threaded onto the end of a cylinder push-rod. It then is connected to a driven device by means of a pin joint. The figure below shows the geometry of a typical clevis with a reaction force, F = 8600 N, applied to its clevis pin. As in the example problem of this chapter, open the part files **Clevis 6-1** and **Clevis Pin 6-1** to create an appropriate assembly **Mate** *after* defining *Split lines* on the pin. Then perform a finite element analysis to determine the items requested below.

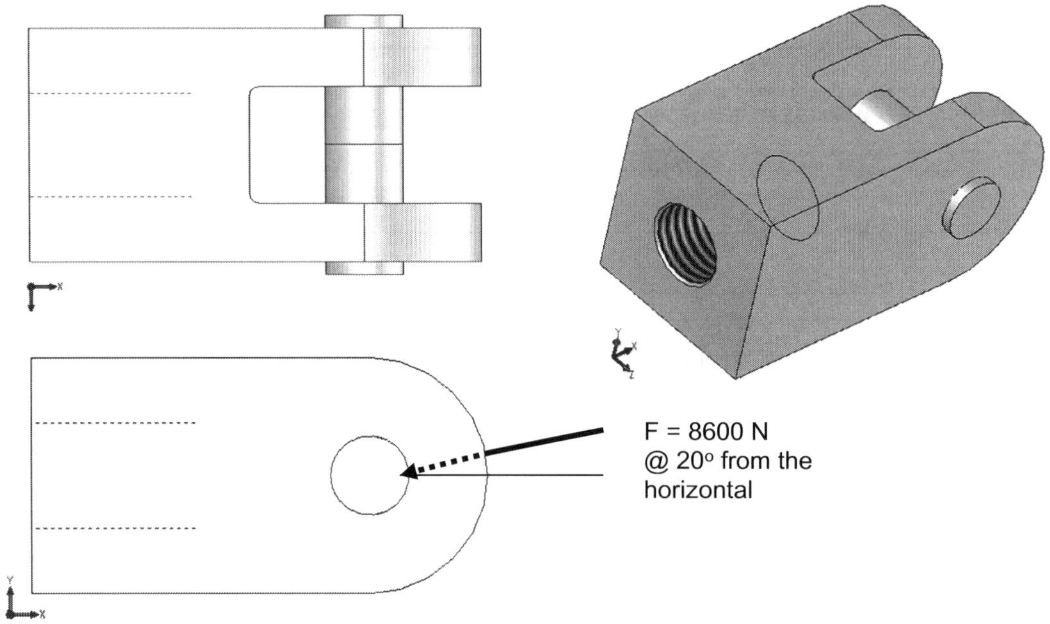

Figure E6-1 – Top, front, and isometric views of a clevis and pin assembly. A force of 8600 N is applied to the pin as shown in the front view. (Use SI units.)

- Material: **1045 Steel, cold drawn** for both the clevis and pin. (Use S.I. units), consider steel to be ductile.
- Mesh: Use system default size **Curvature based mesh**, tetrahedral elements.
- Fixtures: **Fixed (immovable)** -Appropriate for a push-rod threaded into the hole.
  Symmetry - as instructed below.
  Contact Interaction - Specify **Contact** between the clevis pin surface and the clevis hole.
- External Load: Apply appropriate force components to model the load applied to the pin.

Assumptions:

- The pin (40 mm long) is centered between sides of the clevis (clevis height = clevis width = 36 mm, square). Clevis length is not important.
- Use symmetry to model half of the clevis and pin assembly.

Determine the following:

Develop a finite element model that includes material specification, fixtures, external load(s), mesh, and a solution. Defeature the model if needed and delete the "cosmetic threads" as outlined below. *Reminder: Assuming the example of the current chapter was worked, recall that system default units were changed to English at the outset of that example. Refer to section* "**Create a Finite Element Analysis (Study)**," *page 6-13 (steps 4 to 6) to define SI units for the current exercise.*

Cosmetic Threads

So called "cosmetic threads" are included on the Clevis model to provide insight into its means of attachment to a cylinder push-rod end. Cosmetic threads are a symbolic representation of screw threads rather than actual geometric shapes cut into the model. As such, they serve their intended purpose of conveying information but do not affect results. For example, they do not cause stress concentration due to thread profiles cut into the model. It is often desirable to **Delete** cosmetic threads because, if not deleted, they cause a circle and/or dashed lines to appear on various views of the model as shown in top, front, and isometric views in Fig. E6-1. Although this remnant of the thread profile does not affect results, it may be found bothersome by some individuals. *At the start of this exercise*, delete cosmetic threads as follows.

1. Open the file **Clevis 6-1**.

2. Contents of the SOLIDWORKS feature manager are shown in Fig. E6-2.

3. Near the bottom of the SOLIDWORKS feature manager, click the "►" symbol adjacent to **Threaded Hole Cut-Extrude2**.

Beneath this icon, right-click **Cosmetic Thread 4** and from the pull-down menu select **Delete**.

4. Return to the problem solution.

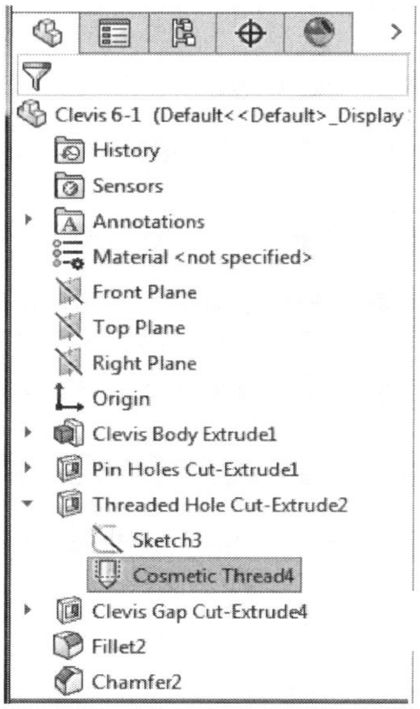

Figure E6-2 – **SOLIDWORKS** feature manager used to **Delete** the **Cosmetic Threads**.

a. Create a plot showing all restraints and loads applied to half of the assembly model. This image might be thought of as the finite element equivalent of a free-body diagram. Do not show stresses or a mesh on this plot. Adjacent to the image, hand write calculations used to determine the X and Y force components acting on the pin. Also, on a small sketch oriented the same as the model, draw and label magnitudes of the X and Y force components applied to the model.

b. Create a plot showing **Contact Pressure** between the pin and clevis. Enlarge the vector size to make them easily visible but in reasonable proportion to the overall image. Select a view that clearly shows the three-dimensional nature of contact pressure variation within the clevis.

c. Create a plot of von Mises stress contours displayed on a deformed image of the pin and clevis assembly. Show the deformed model by checking ☑ **Deformed Shape** and select ⊙ **Automatic** as the scaling method. Also, incorporate automatic labeling of the maximum von Mises stress.

d. Create a safety factor plot based on von Mises stress. Identify region(s) of the assembly that have a safety factor less than 2.0 (if any) based on the material yield strength.

e. Use **Iso Clipping** to create a plot that shows regions of the model where von Mises stress exceeds the material yield strength (if any such regions exist). Include automatic labeling of the maximum von Mises stress on this plot.

f. Discuss **Fixtures** you applied to the clevis and pin model. Provide sound reasoning and justification for restraints applied at the threaded clevis attachment location. If you believe the suggested restraints are incorrect or can be improved, provide a detailed discussion that justifies your opinion.

g. Briefly describe the procedure used to plot stress magnitudes for part (e) of this exercise and discuss the correspondence, or lack thereof, between the safety factor plot of part (d) and the Iso Clipping plot of part (e).

EXERCISE 2 – Contact Pressure in a Hip Prosthesis

Hip replacement joints are frequently used for individuals who suffer from severe arthritis or hip bone fractures. Fig. E6-3 illustrates the stem and cup for a typical hip prosthesis. The femur (upper leg bone) is prepared by removing its upper portion and by reaming an appropriate size cavity into which the prosthesis stem is cemented. To further distribute upper body weight to the femur and relieve shear forces in the bone cement between the stem and femur, a lip, labeled in Fig. E6-3 (b), transfers a compressive load to the upper end of the femur. Similarly, the cup is fixed into the hip bone by bone adhesive and projections that protrude into receiving holes drilled into the hip bone. These protrusions stabilize the cup and prevent cup rotation relative to bone tissue. A screw connector is also used. Specific surface areas of the stem and cup are porous (not illustrated below). Re-growth of natural bone tissue into these porous areas promotes development of a stronger bond between the prosthesis and bone. A cup liner provides a low friction wear surface between the ball and cup.

Open File: **Stem and Cup Assembly 6-2**

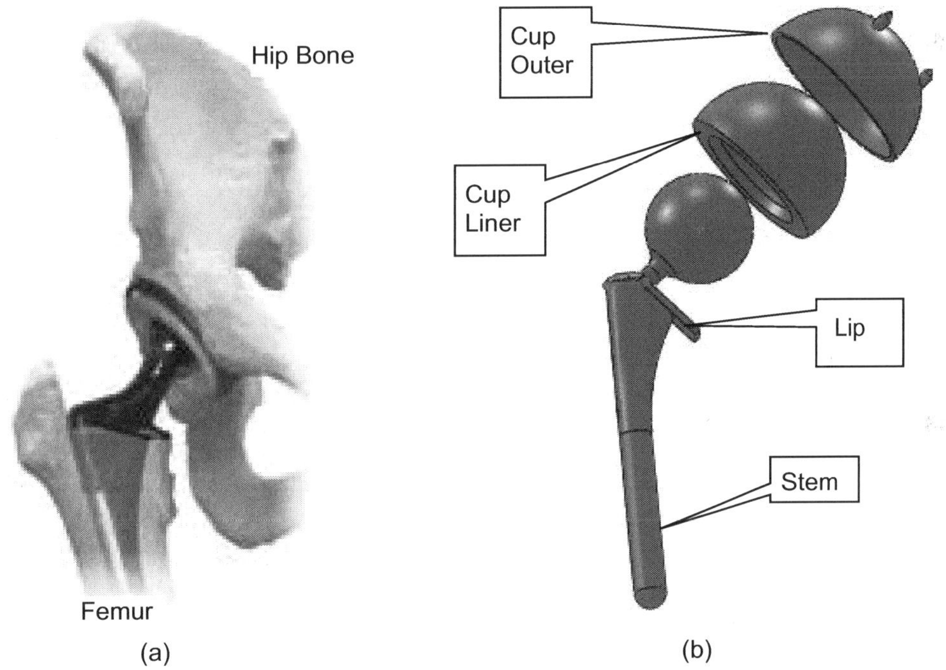

Figure E6-3 – Figure (a) shows a hip prosthesis as it would appear implanted in the human body.[2] Figure (b) is an exploded view showing the three main components of the **Stem and Cup Assembly**.

> **Disclaimer**
> Actual part dimensions and materials are considered proprietary information. Therefore, dimensions and part materials used in this exercise are *not* representative of actual data.

[2] Photo [Fig. E6-3 (a)] courtesy of Zimmer Inc., Warsaw, Indiana

- Material[3]:
  - **Cup Liner** - Locate under **Plastics**, then choose **PA Type 6**
  - **Stem** - Locate under **Titanium Alloys** then choose **Commercially Pure CP-Ti UNS R50700 Grade4 (SS)**
  - **Cup Outer** - Same material as **Stem**
- Mesh: Use system default size **Curvature based mesh**, tetrahedral elements.
- Fixture: To be specified by the user based on experience gained in previous exercises and an understanding of the hip replacement process described above. Carefully consider how and where restraints are applied to the model relative to how and where external loads are applied.
- External Load: Person's weight = **145** lb. You may decide to use a different external load. If so, include the reason for your decision in part (a) of the exercise listed below.

Determine the following:

Develop a finite element model that includes material specification, realistic fixtures, Realistic external load(s), mesh generation, and solution.

a. On the upper half of one page, create a plot showing all fixtures and loads applied to the stem and to the cup assembly. Manually label vectors representing **Fixtures** to differentiate them from vectors representing **External Loads**. This image represents the finite element equivalent of a free-body diagram. Do not show stresses or a mesh on this plot. On the lower half of the page, provide:

   - good reason(s) and justification for fixtures and/or external load(s) applied to the cup outer. Discuss items such as magnitude(s), direction(s), and point(s) of application.
   - good reason(s) and justification for fixtures and/or external load(s) applied to the stem. Discuss items such as magnitude(s), direction(s), and point(s) of application.
   - If an external load other than the person's given weight is used, provide insight into the reasoning used to determine and recommend an alternate load.

b. Create a plot of von Mises stress contours displayed on a deformed image of the stem and cup assembly. Show the deformed model by checking ☑ **Deformed Shape** and select ⦿ **Automatic** as the scaling method. Also, incorporate automatic labeling of the maximum von Mises stress.

c. Create a plot showing **Contact Pressure** between the "ball" (located at top of the Stem) and the Cup Liner (located between the ball and Cup Outer). Enlarge contact vector size to make vectors easily visible, but in reasonable proportion to

---

[3] Materials and their associated properties shown here *do not* reflect actual manufacturer's specifications.

the overall image. Select a view that clearly shows the three-dimensional nature of contact pressure variation.

d. Question: Based on your understanding of fatigue in metals, does the maximum von Mises stress determined in part (b) place this Stem and Cup Assembly in danger of fatigue failure? Discuss practical reasons for your answer in terms of stress repetitions expected for the assembly. Also discuss the engineering reasons for your answer. Consider topics such as stress magnitude, type of stress (tensile versus compressive), and material characteristics of the general class of titanium steels.

EXERCISE 3 – Stress Concentration Analysis using Part Symmetry

Exercise No. 1 of Chapter 3 is repeated here. However, make use of model symmetry discussed in the **Analysis Insight** section on pages 5-8 and 5-9 of Chapter 5 and techniques mastered in the current chapter to reduce the size of the **Plate With Hole** model. For your convenience, all necessary parts of the previous exercise are repeated here. NOTE: The previous exercise need *not* have been worked.

Open the file: **Plate With Hole 3-1**.

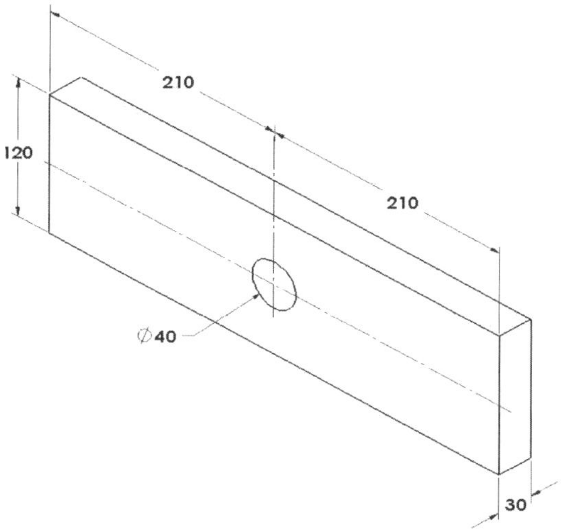

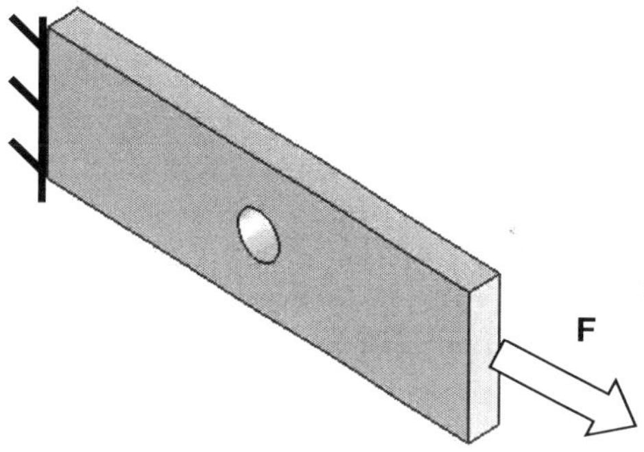

Figure E6-4 (Figure E3-1 repeated) – Aluminum bar with central hole subject to an axial force **F**. A geometric discontinuity is present in the form of the 40 mm diameter hole.

- Material: **2018 Alloy** aluminum (Use S.I. units)
- Mesh: In the **Mesh** property manager, select a ⊙ **Standard mesh**; high quality tetrahedral elements are used. Use three different meshes as specified in parts (a, c, and d) below.
- Fixtures: Determined by user.
- External Load: **F = 370 kN** acts normal to right-end causing tension in the bar.

Develop a finite element model that includes material specification, symmetry restraints, external load, mesh generation, and solution as specified below. For this analysis use high quality meshes of the sizes specified below and perform the following.

Solution Guidance

To simplify application of model symmetry, refer to the SOLIDWORKS Simulation manager tree. Two partial models (½ **Symmetry Model** and ¼ **Symmetry Model**) are provided. Choose the most appropriate model to reduce computation model time for this exercise. Apply **Symmetry** 

Fixtures only if appropriate.

Determine the following:

a. Using a *default* size mesh, create a plot of the *most appropriate stress* to permit comparison of its magnitude adjacent to the hole with that predicted by classical equations for stress computed at the same location; see part (e) for calculation of classical stress results. Include fixtures, symmetry restraints (if any), external load(s), and mesh on this plot. On the plot, specify the magnitude of the applied load. Also on this plot answer the question: Is it necessary to apply any additional restraints on the symmetry model? If "yes," include them on this plot and specify its/their direction.

b. Use the **Probe** feature to produce a graph of the *most appropriate stress* from the top edge of the bar to the upper edge of the central hole. Note that a straight path should be available for this model because nodes must lie on a cut edge; select both corner and mid-side nodes. On this graph, include a descriptive title, axis labels, and your name.

c. Repeat part (b) after resetting the mesh size to *fine*. Use the duplicate feature to save time creating this study.

d. Repeat part (b) a third time after resetting the mesh size by applying *mesh control* around both edges and the inner surface of the hole. Use a mesh control setting of **Ratio a/b** = **1.2**. Also, use the duplicate feature to save time creating this study.

e. Use classical equations and available stress concentration factor charts to manually compute maximum stress at the hole. Label calculations.

f. Compare results predicted using the three different meshes with that predicted by classical stress equations. Compute the percent difference for each comparison using equation [1].

$$\% \text{ difference} = \frac{(\text{FEA result - classical result})}{\text{FEA result}} * 100 = \qquad [1]$$

g. For the three different meshes, comment upon which FEA results are in best agreement with predictions of the classical equations. Which method of mesh refinement is usually preferred and why?

h. If Exercise 1 of Chapter 3 was worked, compare magnitudes of the maximum *appropriate stress* at the hole location. Compare magnitudes *only* for the case when *Mesh Control* is used. Then answer the question, Which FEA model (i.e., the *complete* model or the *symmetrical* model) is in best agreement with calculation of stress at the hole location determined using classical equations and stress concentration factor charts? If differences exceeding 4% are obtained, explain the reason(s) for this difference.

i. Symmetry is used to reduce model size and computation time, especially for large, complex models. For this exercise two partial symmetric models of the **Plate With Hole 3-1** were provided in the SOLIDWORKS feature manager tree. You were asked to make a decision regarding what you believe to be the smallest symmetric model segment that could be used to solve this problem. In retrospect, do you think it is possible to further reduce model size through the application of symmetry principles? If "yes," *sketch* the reduced model and show all restraints (symmetry included) acting on that model. Apply **Fixture** vectors to the model showing their correct direction and label them using "**S**" to denote *symmetry* restraints (if any) and "**RB**" to denote *rigid body* restraints (if any). Also show and label magnitude(s) of any **External Loads**.

Textbook Problems
In addition to the above exercises, it is highly recommended that additional problems involving contact between mating parts be worked from a design of machine elements textbook. Textbook problems provide a great way to discover errors made in formulating a finite element analysis because they typically are well defined problems for which the solution is known. Textbook problems, if well defined in advance, make an excellent source of solutions for comparison.

NOTES:

CHAPTER #7

BOLTED JOINT ANALYSIS

Machine screws, bolts, and/or nuts and bolts in combination, are some of the most frequently used means of joining mechanical components. Bolted joints are commonly used in non-permanent connections where access to components for repair or replacement is essential. This example examines steps involved to successfully model bolted connections. Bolted connections are but one of many connection types available in SOLIDWORKS Simulation. Other connector types contained within the software, but not examined here, include springs, rigid, pins, links, spot welds, edge welds, and bearing connections between components.

Learning Objectives

Upon completion of this example, users should be able to:

- Specify *bolt connectors.*
- Define *custom material properties* for bolt connectors.
- Identify when mesh refinement is necessary based on a *high stress gradient.*
- Define *local interactions* between parts without the use of Split Lines (see Exercise 1).

Problem Statement

An angle bracket is attached to a long, rigid support plate as illustrated in Fig. 1. Both the support plate and angle bracket are made of **ANSI 1020 Steel**. For purposes of this example, the support plate is shortened by arbitrarily cutting it in the vicinity of the two dashed lines on either side of the angle bracket. Four **M 12 x 1.75** bolts with nuts (i.e., 12 mm diameter metric bolts with a thread pitch = 1.75 mm) fasten the two parts together through the four holes shown. Bolts and nuts are not shown in the accompanying figure. All bolts are tightened to a preload of **24000** N. The goal is to determine bolt loads when the joint is loaded by a force of **5000** N, which acts normal to the top surface of the tab at the right end of the angle bracket. Force **F** can act either toward or away from the tab surface shown on Fig. 1 but is not a cyclic load.

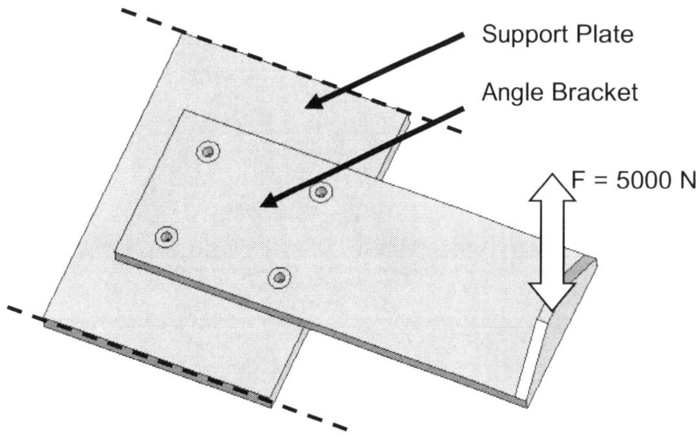

Figure 1 – Basic geometry of the angle bracket and support plate, showing bolt hole locations.

1. Open SOLIDWORKS by making the following selections. (*NOTE:* ">" is used to separate successive menu selections.)

Start>All Programs>SOLIDWORKS 2026 (or) Click the **SOLIDWORKS** icon on your screen.

2. When SOLIDWORKS is open, select **File** > **Open...** Then use procedures common to your computer environment to open the file named "**Support Plate and Angle Bracket**." The screen image should look similar to Fig. 1.

Create a Static Analysis (Study)

1. Select **New Study** found beneath the ▼ **New Study** icon on the **Simulation** tab. Alternatively, in the main menu, select **Simulation**. Then from the pull-down menu select **Study...** Either action opens the **Study** property manager.

2. In the **Name** dialogue box, type "**Bolted Joint-DOWNWARD Load-YOUR NAME**."

3. Verify that a **Static** analysis is selected and click **[OK]** ✓ to close the **Study** property manager. A Study outline appears in the Simulation manager.

Assign Material Properties to the Model

Material properties of the support plate and angle bracket are assigned in this section. Because both components are the same material, this procedure is quite straightforward. Try it on your own using **AISI 1020** steel and select **SI – N/m^2 (Pa)** units. Steps are provided below if guidance is desired.

1. Right-click the **Parts** folder and from the pull-down menu select **Apply Material to All...** The **Material** window opens.

2. In the **Material** window, open the + **Steel** folder (if not already open) and from the list of materials choose **AISI 1020**.

3. In the right-half of the **Material** window, verify that **Units:** are set to **SI – N/m^2 (Pa)** and verify the material Yield Strength is **351571000** N/m^2.

4. Click **[Apply]** followed by **[Close]** to close the **Material** window.

Notice that bolt material is *not* specified at this time. Bolt material is specified independently when other bolt characteristics are defined.

Apply External Load and Fixtures

Traditional Loads and Fixtures

This section outlines the application of restraints and an external load using procedures similar to those encountered throughout this user manual. Those wishing to apply fixed/immovable restraints to top and bottom cut edges of the support plate and a 5000 N load normal to the tab on the right end of the angle bracket are encouraged to proceed on their own. However, steps are provided below if guidance is desired.

1. In the Simulation manager, right-click the **Fixtures** folder and from the pull-down menu, select **Fixed Geometry…** The **Fixture** property manager opens.

2. In the **Standard (Fixed Geometry)** dialogue box, select the **Fixed Geometry** icon (if not already selected).

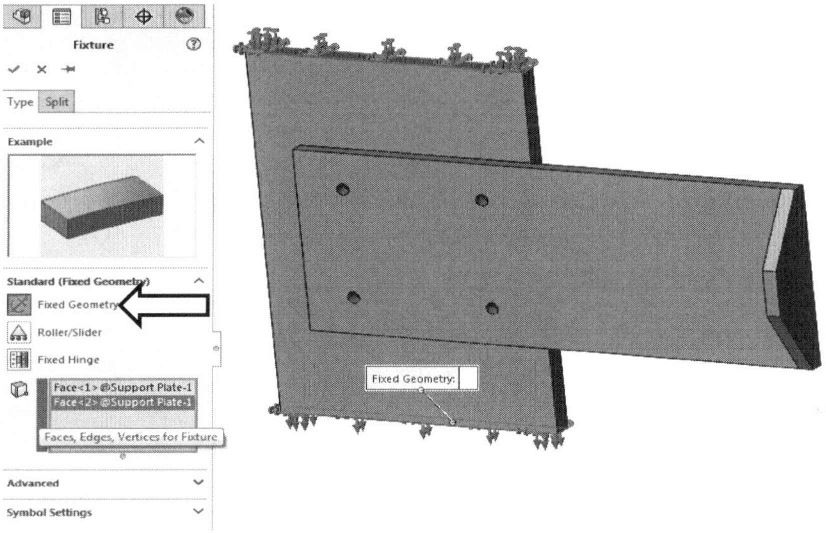

Figure 2 – Application of restraints to cut-surfaces at top and bottom of the support plate.

3. The **Faces, Edges, Vertices for Fixture** field is active (highlighted light blue). Move the cursor into the graphics screen and rotate and zoom-in on the model as necessary to select the two cut surfaces of the support plate shown in Fig. 2. **Face<1>** and **Face<2>@Support Plate-1** appear in the highlighted field.

4. Click **[OK]** ✓ to close the **Fixture** property manager. **Fixed-1** appears beneath the **Fixtures** folder.

Next apply a downward force on top of the tab at the right-end of the angle bracket.

5. Right-click the **External loads** folder and from the pull-down menu, select **Force…** The **Force/Torque** property manager opens as illustrated in Fig. 3.

6. In the **Force/Torque** dialogue box, verify that the **Force** icon is selected (gray highlight) and that force direction is selected as ⦿ **Normal**.

7. The **Faces and Shell Edges for Normal Force** field is highlighted (light blue) and awaits input. Select the top surface of the angle bracket shown in Fig. 3.

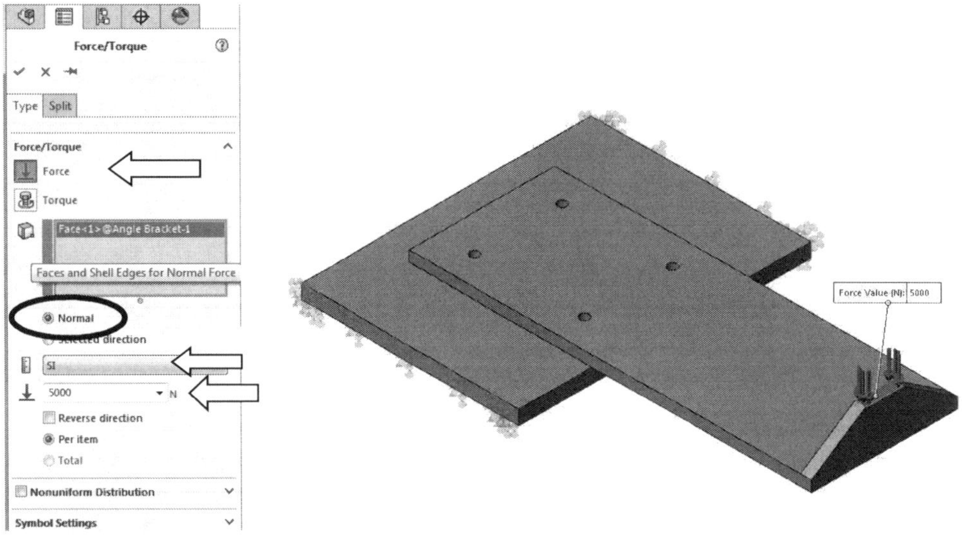

Figure 3 – Application of a downward force normal to top surface of the tab located at the right-end of the angle bracket.

8. From the **Unit** pull-down menu, select **SI** as the desired units.

9. In the **Force Value** field, type **5000** N and select ⦿ **Per item**. The force should act downward, if not check ☑ **Reverse Direction**.

10. Click **[OK]** ✓ to close the **Force/Torque** property manager. **Force-1 (:Per item: 5000 N:)** appears in the Simulation manager tree.

Define Bolted Joint Restraints

Individual bolted fasteners used to join the angle bracket and support plate are defined next. Discussion below assumes the bolt head is located on top of the angle bracket while the nut is located against the bottom surface of the support plate as identified in Fig. 4. Definition of bolted joints takes place within the **Connections** folder located in the Simulation manager tree.

Carefully and sequentially work through the following steps to define *one bolt at a time.* NOTE: If all bolt clamping surfaces are selected in a single step, software ability to isolate *individual* bolt reactions is lost. Also, while proceeding through the following steps, place the cursor onto each field or icon to reveal its name. This approach enhances insight into understanding the function of each option.

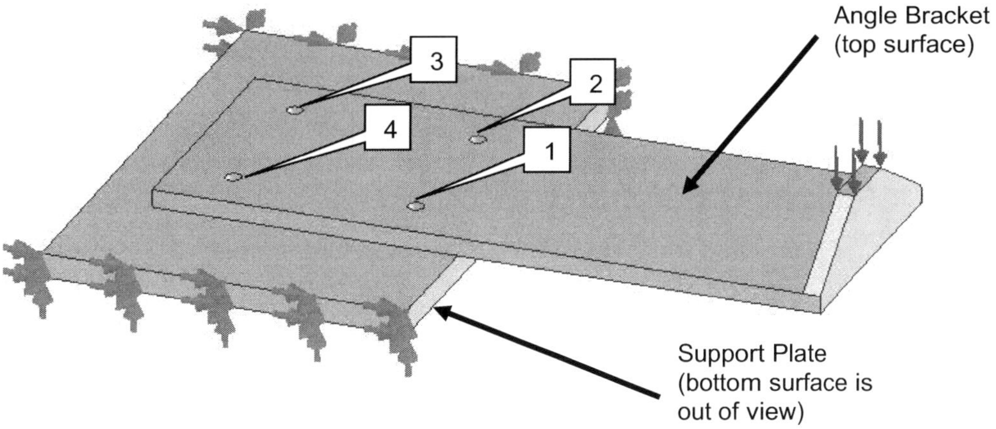

Figure 4 – Angle bracket and support plate showing bolt holes numbered from 1 to 4 in counterclockwise order.

1. In the Simulation manager tree, right-click **Connections** and from the pull-down menu select **Bolt…** The **Connectors** property manager opens; a partial view is shown in Fig. 5. Carefully note the **Message** highlighted in yellow.

2. To avoid having to re-open the **Connectors** property manager for every bolt, click the **Keep Visible** "push-pin" circled in Fig. 5.

3. At top of the **Type** dialogue box, click ▼ to open the pull-down menu and examine the various connector types listed. Then, from the list of possible connectors, select **Bolt** (if not already selected).

4. Select the **Standard or Counterbore with Nut** fastener shown boxed in Fig. 5. Move the cursor over the remaining icons to get an overview of other connector types available within the **Bolt** connector sub-group.

Within SOLIDWORKS Simulation there exist multiple ways to define bolted connectors. The most direct method is outlined below. In order to define a nut and bolt, the parameters listed in Table 1, on the next page, are needed. Table 1 shows values applicable to metric grade 5.8, **M 12 x 1.75** bolts and nuts used in this example. Information shown in Table 1 is readily available in most design of machine elements texts.

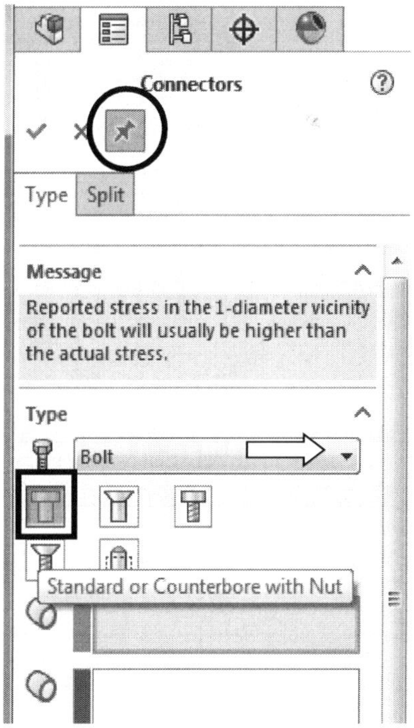

Figure 5 – Partial view of the **Connectors** property manager with the **Keep Visible** push-pin and connector type selected.

Table 1 – Data required to define nut and bolt characteristics.

PARAMETER	VALUE
Bolt shank diameter	12 mm
Bolt head diameter	18 mm
Nut diameter	18 mm
Bolt Elastic Modulus	207e9 N/m^2
Bolt Poisson's Ratio	0.292
Bolt Pre-load	24000 N

The following steps proceed from top to bottom of the **Connectors** property manager. To ensure selection of the correct field, move the cursor over each field to reveal its name. Also, recall that the bolt head is located on the angle bracket, considered to be the top of the model, and the nut is located in contact with the support plate (bottom side of the model) in Fig. 8.

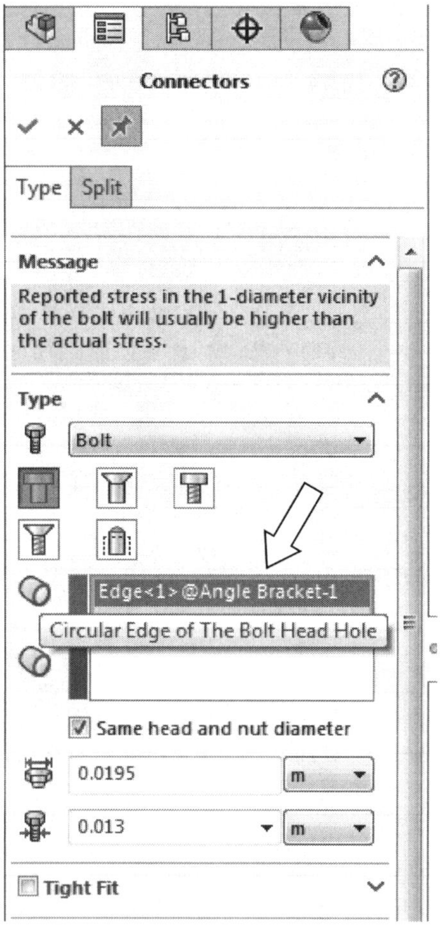

Figure 6 – The **Connectors** property manager after selecting **Bolt** as the connector type.

5. Click to activate (light blue) the **Circular Edge of The Bolt Head Hole** field (if not already selected). Then zoom-in on the *top* of the angle bracket and click to select the *top edge* of bolt hole #1; see Fig. 8. **Edge<1>@Angle Bracket-1** is listed in the active field as shown in Fig. 6 and symbols surround the selected edge in Fig. 8. An information "flag" should also appear attached to the selected bolt hole. This flag summarizes all bolt parameters as they are defined. Neglect initial values shown in the flag. Click and drag the information flag to a convenient location on the screen.

6. Next, in the **Type** dialogue box, click to activate (highlight) the **Circular Edge of The Bolt Nut Hole** field labeled in Fig. 7. *CAUTION: This step is easily missed in the repetitive process outlined below.*

7. Rotate the model and zoom-in on the *bottom* of the support plate to select the corresponding bottom *edge* of bolt hole #1. **Edge<2>@ Support Plate-1** is listed in the active field.

8. Immediately beneath this field, check ☑ **Same head and nut diameter**. This step matches the nut and bolt head diameters, which is common practice for standard bolt connections.

9. To the right of the **Bolt Head** diameter field, click to open the **Unit** pull-down menu and select **mm**. *Units must be specified prior to entering the bolt head diameter.*

10. To the left of the **Unit** field, type **18** mm in the **Head Diameter** field.

11. Next, adjacent to the **Nominal Shank Diameter** field, click to change **Unit** to **mm**.

12. In the **Bolt Shank Diameter** field, type **12** mm.

13. Select **Rigid** for **Connection Type**. **Rigid** coupling doesn't allow the faces attached to nut and bolt connectors to deform.

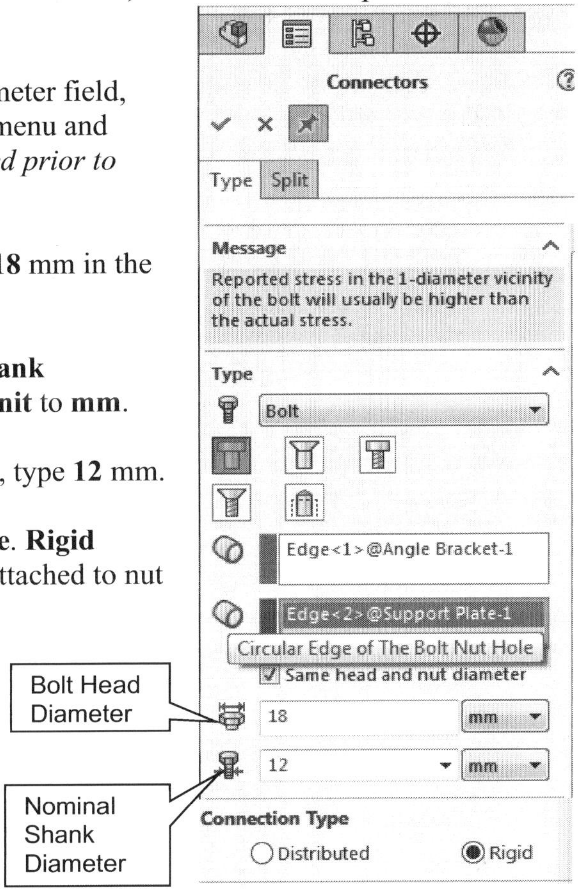

Figure 7 – Top portion of the **Connectors** property manager showing selections used to define bolts and nut contact faces.

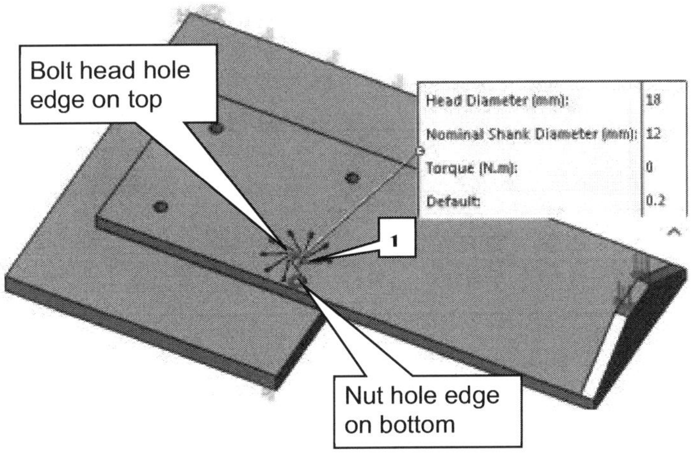

Figure 8 – Model showing selection of hole edges for the bolt head and nut contact faces for bolt #1.

Next, direct your attention to the **Material** dialogue box. In this dialogue box it is possible to select bolt material from the **Material** window, as has been done in all previous examples, or to specify custom material properties as outlined below.

14. Scroll down to the **Material** dialogue box shown in Fig. 9, select ⦿ **Custom**. The bolt information "flag" expands to display additional information to be specified by the user.

15. In the **Unit** dialogue box, verify that **SI** is selected.

16. Adjacent to the **Young's Modulus** Ex field, type **207e9** N/m^2 to identify the bolt modulus of elasticity.

17. In the **Poisson's Ratio** field, type **0.292**.

18. Ignore the **Thermal expansion coefficient** α field. Temperature is not a factor in this bolt joint. *(If the **Select Parameter** window opens, select **[Cancel]**.)*

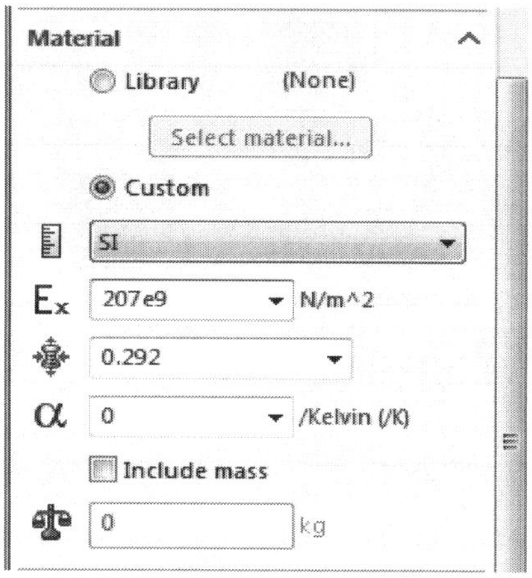

Figure 9 – Specifying custom material properties for bolts in the **Material** dialogue box.

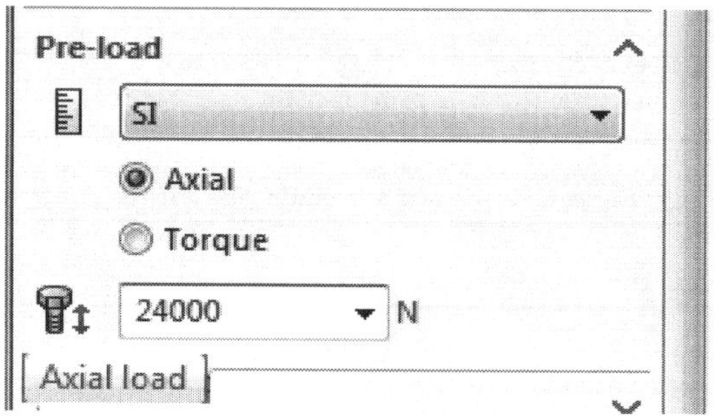

Figure 10 – Bolt preload specified as an axial (tensile) force in the bolt.

19. Scroll to the bottom of the **Connectors** property manager where the **Pre-load** dialogue box appears as shown in Fig. 10. Open the **Unit** pull-down menu and from the list, again select **SI** (if not already selected).

20. Next, select ⦿ **Axial**. This selection indicates that the bolt preload is expressed by an axial (tensile) load in the bolt caused when the nut is tightened.

21. In the **Axial load** field, type **24000** N.

22. Return to the top of the **Connectors** property manager and click **[OK]** ✓ (green check mark). This action applies all of the above settings to bolt #1.

As specifications are entered for each remaining bolt and nut, symbols representing bolt connectors appear at each hole location as illustrated in Fig. 11.

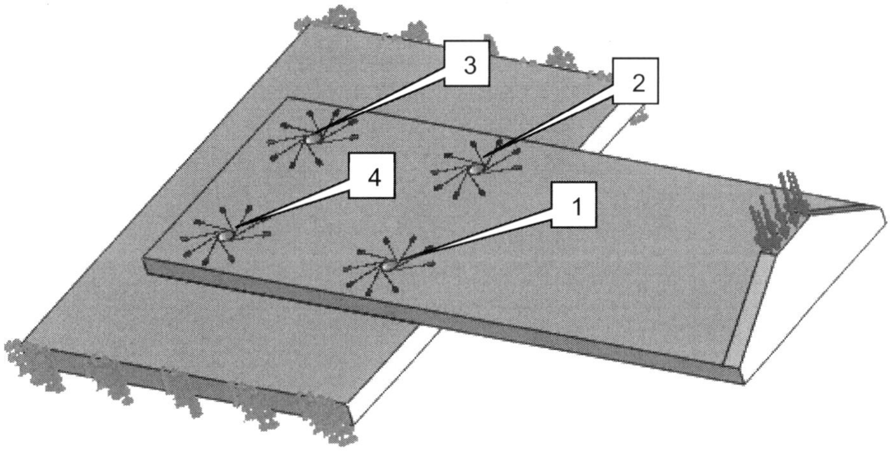

Figure 11 – Bolt connector symbols appear at locations of the Head and Nut Contact Faces. Rotate the model to view symbols on bottom of the support plate.

Because the **Keep visible** push-pin was selected, the **Connectors** property manager remains open and all values entered to describe the first bolt are retained. Unless changed by the user, the software assumes that additional identical bolts are used. Thus, it only remains to select the top and bottom hole-edges for the remaining bolts and nuts. Define additional bolts in the counterclockwise order shown numbered in Fig. 11. *NOTE: Keeping track of the order in which bolts are specified is only necessary to identify bolt locations during the analysis portion of a solution.* Proceed as follows.

23. Return to the top of the **Type** dialogue box and click to select the **Circular Edge of the Bolt Head Hole** field to highlight it. On the *top* surface of the angle bracket, select the *edge* of hole #2. The hole edge is highlighted.

24. Beneath the above field, click to activate the **Circular Edge of the Bolt Nut Hole** field. Rotate the model and zoom-in on the *corresponding* hole on the *bottom* of the support plate. Click to select the edge of this hole and bolt connector symbols appear on the model. In the property manager, scroll down and notice that all other data entries remain as previously defined.

25. Return to the top of the **Connectors** property manager, and again click **[OK]** ✓. This action applies the previous settings to the bolt at location 2.

Repeat steps 23 through 25 for *each* remaining bolt. Follow the numerical order shown in Fig. 11. ***See step 26 after defining bolt #4.***

26. After defining bolt #4 (and clicking **[OK]** ✓ in step 25), select **Cancel** ✖ to close the **Connectors** property manager. Schematic images of bolts and nuts appear on the model.

27. In the Simulation manager tree, click (as necessary) the " ▸ " symbol adjacent to ▸ **Connections**, next choose ▸ **Connectors** followed by ▸ **Bolt Group-1** to reveal **Counterbore with Nut-1** through **Counterbore with Nut-4** listed beneath these folders as illustrated in Fig. 12.

NOTE: If all bolts had been specified using the **Hole Series** feature in SOLIDWORKS, then Simulation would have asked **"Do you want to add bolt connectors to all holes in the Hole Series?"** Selecting **Yes** would have automatically applied the selected bolt to all holes in the same series.

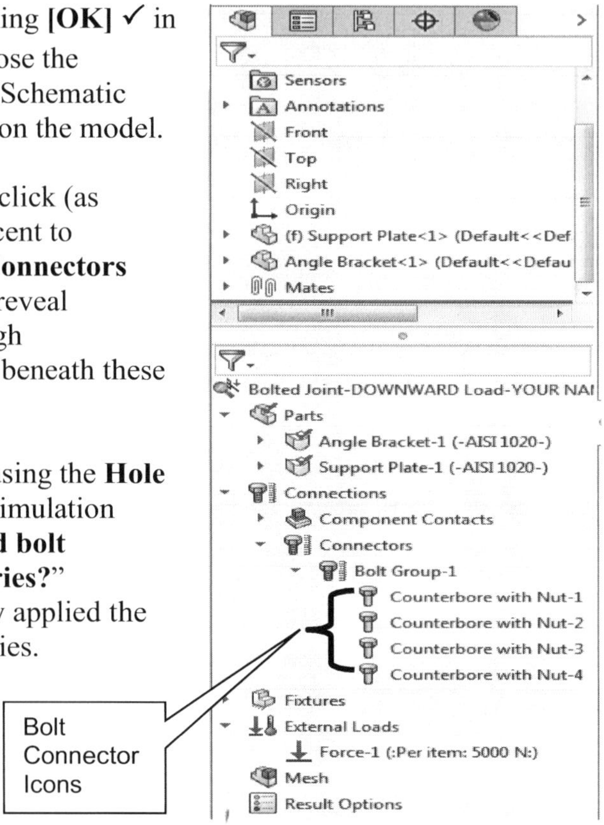

Figure 12 – Individually defined bolt connectors listed beneath the **Load/ Restraint** folder.

Analysis Insight

Instead of specifying bolt preload as an **Axial** force, in the **Pre-load** dialogue box, it is also possible to specify bolt preload in terms of torque applied to tighten the nut as shown in the **Pre-load** dialogue box of Fig. 13.

When bolt ⊙**Torque** is specified, the software uses a re-arranged form of equation [1], see next page, to compute the axial preload $\mathbf{F_i}$. Notice that the torque coefficient **K**, listed as "**Friction Factor (K)**" at the bottom of the **Pre-load** dialogue box, can be changed to account for specific joint conditions.

Friction Factor (K) is affected by a variety of joint and bolt characteristics, such as surface finish (painted, plated, clean, etc.); alignment (parallelism of surfaces and/or flatness under the bolt head and nut); and thread condition (dry, lubricated, or coated, etc.).

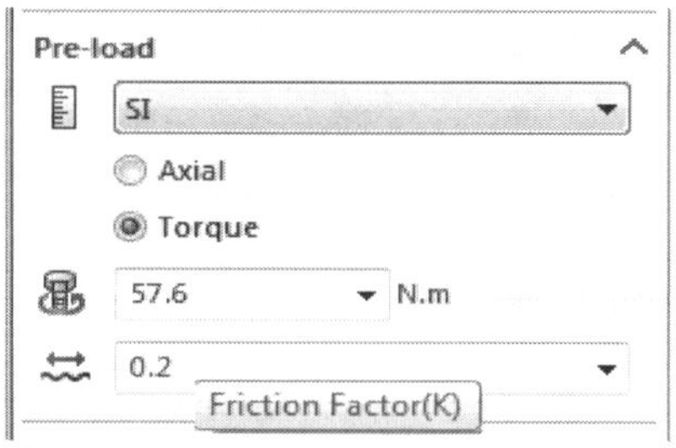

Figure 13 – **Preload** dialogue box showing specification of bolt **Torque** rather than an axial preload value.

The relationship between bolt preload and bolt torque is typically defined in design of machine elements texts by the following equation.

$$\mathbf{T = K^*F_i^*d}$$

[1]

Where: $\mathbf{F_i}$ = desired bolt preload (the initial axial tensile force in the bolt)
$\mathbf{T}$ = applied torque required to develop a desired preload $\mathbf{F_i}$
$\mathbf{K}$ = torque coefficient (K = 0.20 is a generally accepted value)
$\mathbf{d}$ = nominal bolt diameter

For this example, if ⦿ **Torque** were selected rather than ○ **Axial** preload, then the torque used to tighten the bolt is given by:

$$\mathbf{T = K^*F_i^*d} = (0.20)(24\ \text{kN})(0.012\ \text{m}) = 57.6\ \text{N-m}$$

See the entry typed into the **Torque** field in Fig. 13.

This completes the definition of individual bolt connectors. However, because we are dealing with an assembly, it is also necessary to define contact conditions between the two members that are bolted together. This task is addressed in the next section.

Define Local Contact Conditions

Contact between the angle bracket and support plate must also be defined. Because there are only two components in this assembly, it would be possible to define contact between mating surfaces by applying a *Global* contact. Specifying *Global* contact applies the same contact condition to all contacting surfaces in an assembly. However, it is more instructive to define contact in a *Local* sense (i.e., specific to the two contacting surfaces). This approach provides the user with greater control when defining contact between two specific parts and prepares the user to deal with more unique situations should they be encountered in other modeling applications. Begin by switching to an exploded view.

1. In the main menu, select **Insert** and from the pull-down menu choose **Exploded View…** The **Explode** property manager opens.

2. Click to select the angle bracket (top part) in Fig. 14. A coordinate system triad appears on the part. Drag the Y-axis of the triad upward. Release the mouse button when the figure looks similar to Fig. 14. (Alternatively, drag the support plate downward.)

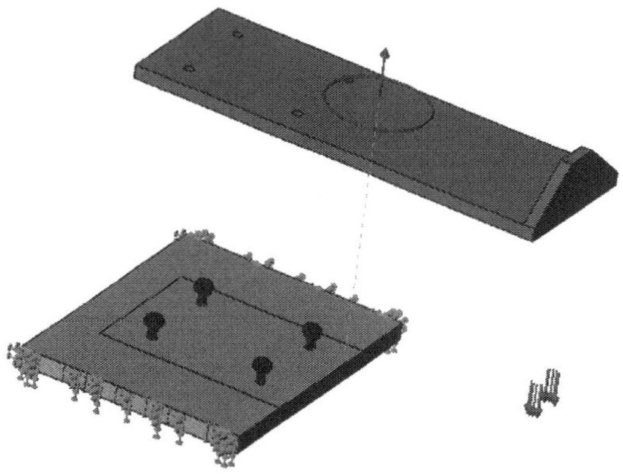

Figure 14 – Exploded view prior to defining contact conditions.

3. Click **[OK]** ✓ to close the **Explode** property manager.

4. In the Simulation manager tree, right-click the **Connections** folder and from the pull-down menu select **Local Interaction.** The **Local Interaction** property manager opens as shown in the middle of Fig. 15.

5. In the **Contact** dialogue box, choose ⊙ **Manually select local interactions**.

6. In the pull-down menu at top of the **Type** dialogue box, select **Contact**.

7. The **Faces, Edges, Vertices for Set 1** field is highlighted (light blue) and awaits input. Move the cursor into the graphics screen and rotate the model to select the bottom, left-end of the angle bracket shown with dark highlight in Fig. 15 (a). A *Split Line* is provided to facilitate selecting only the contact surface. **Face<1>@Angle Bracket-1** is listed in the active field.

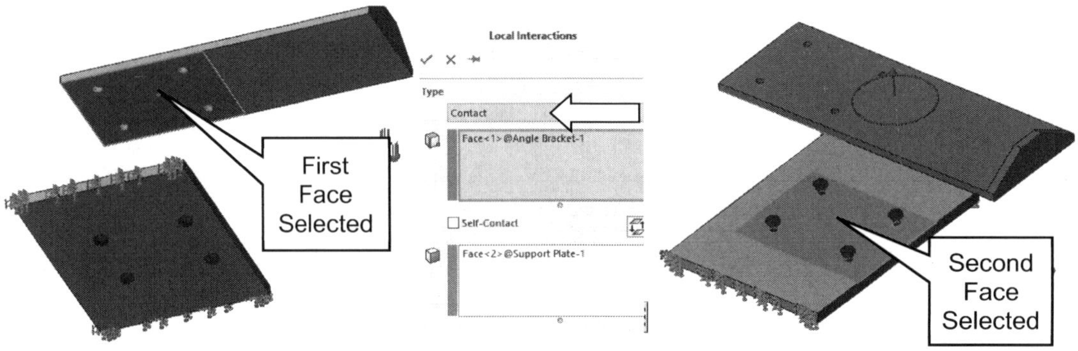

(a) Select bottom of Angle Bracket. (b) Select top of Support Plate.

Figure 15 – Selection of equal and opposite faces defined to be in contact with no penetration.

8. Click to highlight (light blue) the **Faces for Set 2** field, located at the bottom of the **Type** dialogue box. Then, proceed to select the contact face in the vicinity of bolt holes on top of the support plate. See highlighted face in Fig. 15 (b). **Face<2>@Support Plate-1** is listed in the active field. Once again *Split Lines* are provided to permit selection of only the contact surface. NOTE: Exercise 1, at end of this chapter, outlines steps to *automatically* find contact interactions *without* use of Split lines.

Analysis Insight:

In the **Properties** dialogue box, notice that it is possible to define **Friction** between the contacting surfaces. This option is typically applied when the potential for movement is investigated between mating parts. Since friction is not pertinent to this example, clear the ☐ **Friction** check-box (if necessary) before proceeding. Also, in our model the **Gap range** can be set close to 0.0% since the two surfaces are completely touching.

9. Click **[OK]** ✓ to close the **Local Interaction** property manager. Highlighting disappears from the model and beneath the **Connections** folder appears an icon labeled **Local Interaction**. Click the "▸" symbol to reveal the full name: "**Local Interaction -1 (-Contact<Angle Bracket-1, Support Plate-1>-)**."

Before proceeding, return the model to its original, un-exploded state as follows.

10. Toggle to the **Configuration Manager** by clicking its icon at top of the SOLIDWORKS manager tree.

11. Click the "▸" symbol adjacent to **Default [Support Plate and Angle Bracket]**.

12. Right-click ▸ ExplView1 and from the pull-down menu select **Collapse**.

13. Toggle back to SOLIDWORKS by clicking the **SOLIDWORKS** icon.

Mesh the Model and Run Solution

1. In the Simulation manager, right-click the **Mesh** folder and from the pull-down menu select **Create Mesh…** The **Mesh** property manager opens.

2. Check "✓" to open the ☑ **Mesh Parameters** dialogue box, set **Unit** to **mm**, accept the default mesh size, and select ⊙ **Curvature based mesh**.

3. Click ⌄ to open the **Advanced** dialogue box and verify that **Jacobian points** is set to **[16 Points]**, the default setting. This setting indicates a high-quality mesh.

4. Click **[OK]** ✓ to close the **Mesh** property manager and mesh the model. WARNING: Do *not* select ☐ **Run (solve) the analysis**.

The above warning is included because there is a reasonable likelihood that the current solution might fail. Recall an earlier warning that indicated it is *not* recommended to use the "☐ **Run (solve) the analysis**" option available in the **Options** dialogue box of the **Mesh** property manager. The reason for this recommendation is that, if a solution fails, the user does not know whether the model failed to mesh properly or whether the solver failed to run the analysis. By keeping these two steps separate, the user is better able to pin point the source of a solution failure. And, knowing the source of a failure facilitates correcting the problem as outlined below.

Before proceeding to the next step be forewarned that, *although unlikely,* the solution might fail. *The solution below* ***assumes failure occurs*** *in the equation solver. Thus, whether or not the solver fails, proceed as if it does fail to learn more about software capabilities. Therefore, after starting to* ***Run*** *the solution in step #5, proceed immediately to step #6 and the following steps up to and including step #10.* ***It is suggested to pre-read these steps.*** ***Continue reading to top of page 7-16.***

5. On the Simulation tab, select **Run This Study**. *NOTE: If a **Simulation** window opens and warns: "Contact pair is not defined for bolt connectors. Do you wish to continue?" Select **[Yes]**.*

6. Immediately after starting the solution, the **Bolted Joint-DOWNWARD Load-YOUR NAME** solution window opens. This window tracks the percent of the solution completed as a bar-graph shown in Fig. 16.

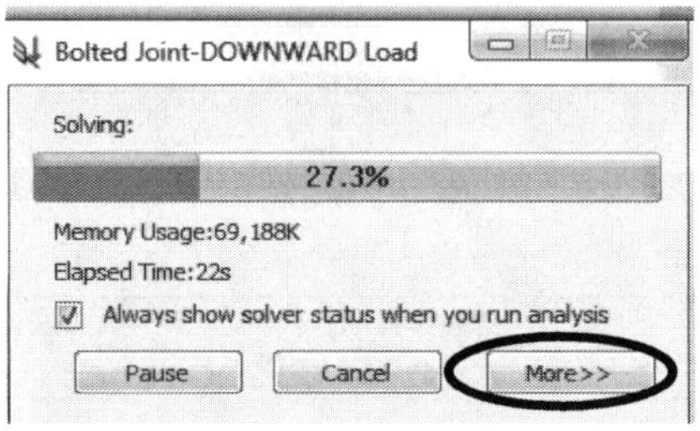

Figure 16 – Window used to track progress toward a Solution.

7. Within this window select the **[More>>]** button, circled in Fig. 16. This action expands window size to that shown in Fig. 17.

Figure 17 shows a second bar-graph. This graph tracks progress of individual parts of the overall solution. Observe the **Current Task:** caption circled in Fig. 17, which changes from:

a. **Establishing stiffness matrix** – The first step sets-up equations based on material stiffness, and corresponding displacements caused by loads applied to the model.

b. **Decomposition of stiffness matrix** – Iterates equations of part (a) multiple times seeking convergence to a solution that satisfies *consistent* displacements throughout the model.

c. **Solving contact constraints** – Because **No Penetration** is specified between the two *different* parts, it is more difficult to establish consistent displacements at nodes in contacting areas of the model. Gaps also might occur between mating parts. Most solution time is devoted to solving contact constraints. The Solution then alternates between steps (b) and (c).

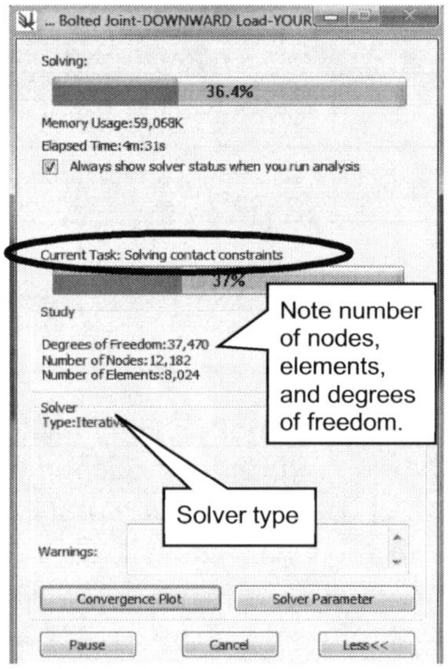

Figure 17 – The expanded solution window permits viewing computation time devoted to different aspects of the Solution.

8. After about 45 seconds, depending on computer speed, the solution *may* stop in a state of error. In that case, the **Linear Static** window shown in Fig. 18 (a) tells that "**The Iterative Solver stopped. Status code: 8 FILE ERROR No result saved.**" *NOTE: Successful solutions may require more than 2 minutes to solve.*

9. Click **[OK]** to close the **Linear Static** window. A second window, Fig. 18 (b) may open and direct the user to "**Use the Direct Sparse solver**" as an alternate solution method. Click **[OK]** to close the second **Linear Static** window.

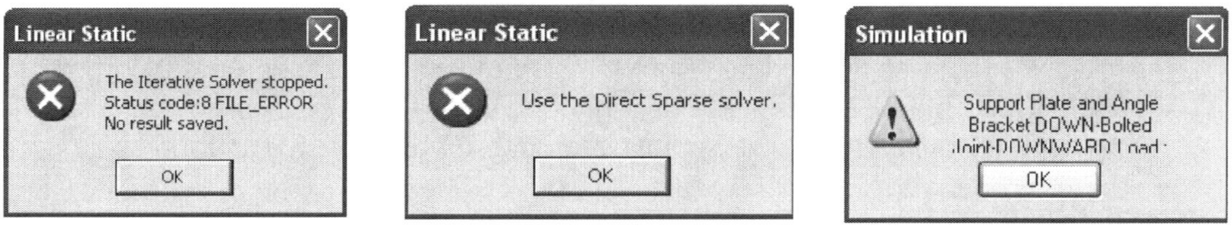

(a) (b) (c)

Figure 18 – Error and warning windows displayed upon termination of a failed analysis.

10. Next, the **Simulation** window shown in Fig. 18 (c) opens. This window informs the user that the current Study **Failed**. However, due to the long File and Study names used for this example, the last part of the message, which indicates the Study **Failed**, is not visible. Click **[OK]** to close the **Simulation** window.

Analysis Insight

Notice the increase in time required to solve this problem. The primary time increase occurs during multiple iterations required to solve the contact constraints portion of the solution. This is where contact conditions between nodes on mating parts are determined. The following paragraph provides a non-technical description of the solution process.

To help understand the reason for this time increase, consider that deformation of one part (the angle bracket) causes or transfers its deformation to the mating part (the support plate) where the surfaces are in contact but cannot penetrate one another. Also, imagine the parts starting from an un-deformed state and gradually transitioning to a fully deformed state. Throughout this incremental deformation process, the governing equations between mating parts must be satisfied at all times. Or, stated another way, consistent deformations must exist throughout the model *and* across the contact area. Thus, each small change of deformation is accompanied by new calculations that begin where the previous deformation (displacement) ended. Therefore, the governing equations are solved and satisfied multiple times as the deformation "grows" step-by-step to its final maximum displaced condition.

Solving contact constraints is further complicated by the fact that very small separations, or gaps, may occur between the originally contacting surfaces. Hence the solver must also deal with discontinuities (i.e., gaps) in the displacement field that initially was consistent (i.e., no gaps). This, in part, explains why so much computation time is devoted to the **Solving contact constraints** portion of the solution. Can you guess where these gaps might occur in the current model? What display technique, introduced in an earlier chapter, might be used to reveal such gaps?

Whether or not your solution failed, proceed as follows.

The error shown in Fig. 18 (b) prompts the user to apply the **Direct Sparse** Solver to the solution of this problem. Details about this solver are beyond the scope of this text. However, problems involving **No Penetration** tend to result in longer solutions for reasons cited in the preceding **Analysis Insight** section. Techniques incorporated into the **Direct Sparse** solver are better suited to solve this type of problem. Thus, *the solution is repeated below* using this alternate solver. Proceed as follows.

11. Right-click to select the Study name, **Bolted Joint-DOWNWARD Load-YOUR NAME (-Default-)**, listed at top of the Simulation manager. From the pull-down menu select **Properties…** The **Static** window opens.

12. In the **Solver** area, near bottom of the **Options** tab, click ▼ to open the pull-down menu and select the **Intel Direct sparse**. The previous solver was **FFEPlus**.

13. Click **[OK]** to close the **Static** window.

14. On the Simulation tab, select **Run This Study**.

15. As the solution runs, it is suggested that the **[More>>]** button in the Solution window be selected again. Note the **Solver Type:** is now listed as **Sparse**.

Observations: As the solution proceeds, again click the **[More]** button (see step 7 above).

- The solution time decreases significantly.
- Most of the solution time, 65%, is still devoted to **Solving contact constraints** while 27% is devoted to **Decomposition of stiffness matrix** operations. Only 8% of solution time is devoted to **Forming stiffness matrix**.

After a successful solution is complete, proceed as follows.

Results Analysis for the Downward External Load

Von Mises Stress

Briefly examine a plot of von Mises stress to gain an understanding of the magnitude and distribution of this stress throughout the assembly.

1. Click the "▸" symbol adjacent to the **Results** folder (if not already selected).

2. If the von Mises stress plot is not already displayed, right-click **Stress1 (-vonMises-)**, and from the pull-down menu select **Show**.

3. Right-click **Stress1 (-vonMises-)** and from the pull-down menu select **Edit Definition...** The **Stress Plot** property manager opens.

4. In the **Display** dialogue box change **Units** to **N/m^2**, if necessary.

5. In the **Advance Options** dialogue box, clear the check mark from ☐ **Average results across boundary for parts** and verify that ⊙ **Node Values** is selected.

6. Check "✓" to open the ☑ **Deformed Shape** dialogue box, and within this box select ⊙ **Automatic** to apply the system default exaggerated deformation to the model display.

7. Click to open the **Chart Options** tab. If this tab is not visible, click-and-drag the right edge of the Simulation manager tree and proceed to widen the column.

8. In the **Display Options** dialogue box, check both ☑ **Show min annotation** and ☑ **Show max annotation**.

9. In the **Position/Format** dialogue box, select **scientific** as the **Number Format** and select **3** as the **No of Decimals** to be displayed.

10. If fringes on the model are not discrete, select the **Settings** tab and change **Fringe Options** to **Discrete**.

11. Click **[OK]** ✓ to close the **Stress Plot** property manager.

A plot of von Mises stress is displayed on a deformed model in Fig. 19. The maximum von Mises stress, indicated on the model and in the color-coded legend as 2.068e+008 N/m^2 is considerably less than the material Yield Strength of 3.516e+008 N/m^2. (Stress values may vary.)

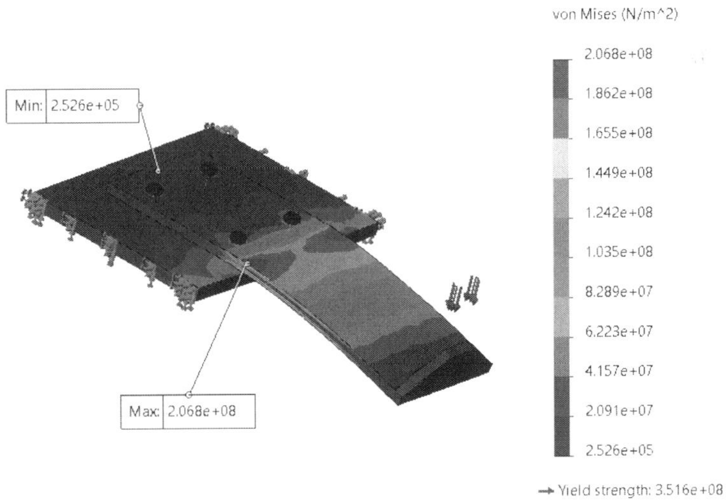

Figure 19 – von Mises stress distribution as seen in a top view of the assembly corresponding to a downward acting load on the model.

Did you notice that the *same* numerical results were obtained using the **FFEPlus** and **Direct sparse** solvers?

Bolt Forces (for Downward Load)

A primary feature of a bolt analysis is the ability to determine forces acting at each bolt. In the assembly analyzed in this example, it is reasonable to expect similar bolt forces in bolts #1 and #2, which are equidistant from the applied load. Similarly, for bolts #3 and #4, which are located further, but at equal distance, from the applied load. Axial force in each bolt is the algebraic sum of its preload, due to tightening the nut, plus effects due to external load(s) acting on the joint. Bolt forces are examined as follows.

1. Right-click the **Results** folder and from the pull-down menu select **List Connector Force...** The **Result Force** property manager opens. *The image on your screen will not initially look like Fig. 20.*

2. In the **Options** dialogue box, verify that ⊙ **Connector force** is selected.

3. In the **Selection** dialogue box verify that **Units** are set to **SI** and the **Connector** field is set to either **All connectors** or **All bolts**. Either choice yields the same results since, in this example, all connectors are bolts.

4. Click-and-drag ↔ the right boundary of the **Result Force** property manager to widen it to display all columns within the **Connector Force** dialogue box.

The **Connector Force** dialogue box lists **Shear Force**, **Axial Force**, **Bending Moment**, and **Torque** for each bolt labeled "**Counterbore with Nut-1**" through "**Counterbore with Nut-4**."

For the present case, focus your attention exclusively on the **Axial Force (N)** *rows* and the **Resultant** force *column* for each bolt listed in the **Connector Force** table.

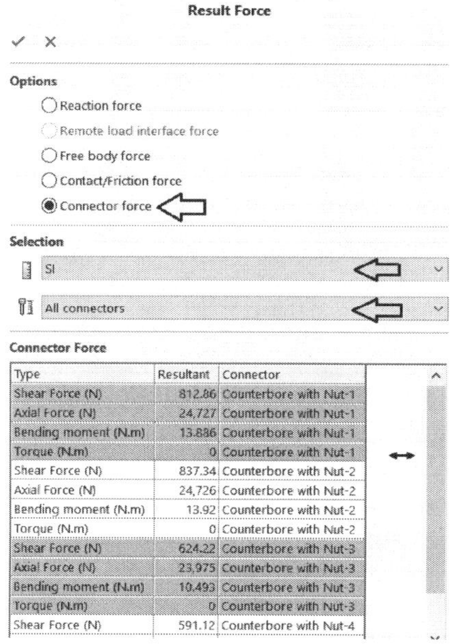

Figure 20 – The **Result Force** property manager summarizes all Shear Force, Axial Force, Bending moments, and Torques that act on each bolt in the joint.

5. For the **Axial Force** in **Counterbore with Nut-1** (bolt #1), observe its value of **24727** (N) in the **Resultant** column. *(Values may vary.)*

6. Further down in the table find the value of **Axial Force** for **Counterbore with Nut-2** (bolt #2) of **24726** (N) in the **Resultant** column. This bolt is positioned adjacent to bolt #1 on the model. Note the similarity of these force magnitudes.

7. Next, examine **Axial Force** results for **Counterbore with Nut-3** and **Counterbore with Nut-4**. The value for bolt #3 in the **Resultant** column is **Axial Force** = **23975** N and for bolt #4 **Axial Force** = **23959** N.

8. Click **[OK]** ✓ to close the **Result Force** property manager.

Observations:

a. Axial forces at both bolts in the same row differ by only 0.11% in bolts closest to the applied load and by 0.02% in the row furthest from the applied load.

b. Forces at bolts #1 and #2 differ at most by 3.3% from the specified bolt preload (24000 N) and both loads are slightly *higher* than the given preload.

c. Forces in bolts #3 and #4, located furthest from the applied load, differ by at most 0.60% from the specified bolt preload of 24000 N and are slightly *lower*.

d. The bolted joint is well designed because most of the load is carried by the material clamped between the bolt head and nut.

e. Symmetry of results between bolts in the two different rows lends credence to the fact that the problem is formulated correctly.

Define a New Study with the Applied Force Acting Upward

Because the above analysis does not reveal significantly different bolt loads at the two rows of bolts, the example is next re-worked with an upward force applied to the angle bracket as shown in Fig. 22. To efficiently run a new analysis, a *copy* of the existing study is created; this topic was introduced in Chapter 3. That Copy Study will then be altered to reflect application of an upward load. Notice how easy it is to complete this new study! Try this on your own or follow steps outlined below.

1. Beneath the graphics area of the screen, right-click the Simulation Study *tab* labeled **Bolted Joint-DOWNWARD Load** and from the pop-up menu select **Copy Study** as shown in Fig. 21. This opens the **Copy Study** manager.

2. In the **Study Name:** field, type **Bolted Joint-UPWARD Load** and click **[OK]**. This action creates an exact duplicate of the former study and opens a new Simulation Study tab beneath the graphics screen. The new tab is now active.

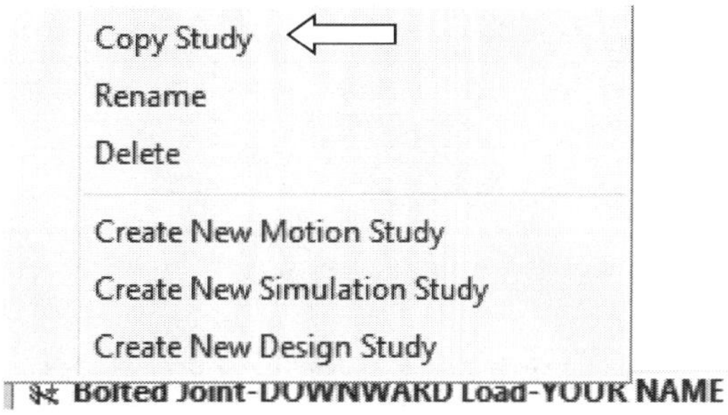

Figure 21 – Create a *copy* of the existing study.

To differentiate this study from its predecessor, it is only necessary to reverse the load applied to the angle bracket using the three quick steps below.

3. If necessary, click the "▸" symbol adjacent to **External Loads** in the Simulation manager to reveal **Force-1 (:Per item: 5000 N:)** defined during the previous Study.

4. Next, right-click **Force-1 (:Per item: 5000 N:)** and from the pull-down menu select **Edit Definition…** The **Force/Torque** property manager opens.

5. Just below the **Force Value** of **5000** N, click to check "✓" ☑ **Reverse direction**. Force vectors applied at the end of the angle bracket should now be directed upward as shown in Fig. 22.

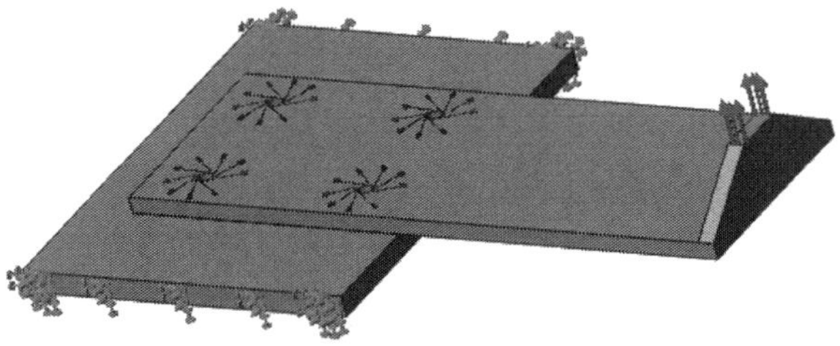

Figure 22 – Bolted joint model with the applied force reversed so that it acts upward.

6. Click **[OK]** ✓ to close the **Force/Torque** property manager.

Because all aspects of the previous study were copied, nothing else need be done except to re-run the solution corresponding to the altered loading condition. Re-running the solution eliminates the warning symbols ⚠ and ⚠ adjacent to the **Results** folder and adjacent to the Study name **Bolted Joint-UPWARD Load (-Default-)**, respectively. Why do these warning symbols appear? HINT: What was changed in step 5?

7. On the **Simulation** tab, click the **Run This Study** icon.

NOTE: Because the duplicated Study already contains the **Direct Sparse solver** this solution should run without an error.

Results for the bolted assembly subject to an upward acting load are examined next.

Results Analysis for the Upward External Load

Von Mises Stress

Begin by examining von Mises stress.

1. If the von Mises stress plot is not displayed, click the "▸" symbol adjacent to the **Results** folder to reveal a list of available plots. Then right-click **Stress1 (-vonMises-)** and from the pull-down menu, select **Show**.

The von Mises stress plot corresponding to an upward acting load is shown in Fig. 23. Zoom in on the small circled area and note the *small area* of high stress near the **Max.** stress flag.

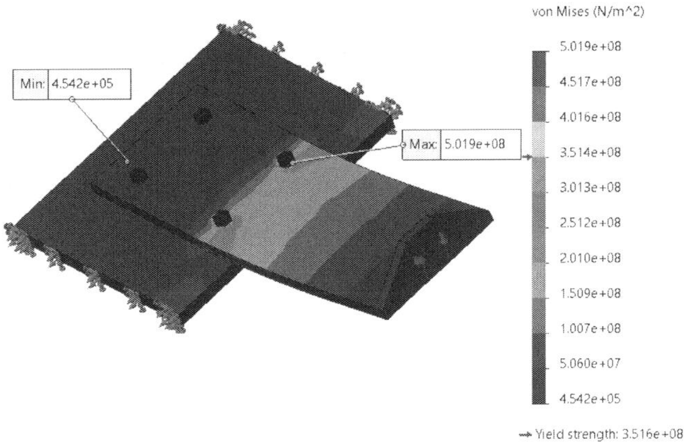

Figure 23 – von Mises stress distribution throughout the model corresponding to an *upward* acting load of 5000 N.

To obtain a good overview of stress distribution throughout the model, rotate the model to view all surfaces. Notice that, corresponding to an upward load, a maximum stress within the model of 5.019e+008 N/m^2 (*values may vary*) is observed. Also, note that material yield strength is exceeded. Close examination reveals the region of maximum stress is located adjacent to bolt hole #2 with a similar high stress region near bolt #1. The region of maximum stress is very small, and some important implications of this finding are discussed in the **Analysis Insight** section below. Begin by zooming in to observe the small area of high stress adjacent to bolt #2, circled in Fig. 23.

Analysis Insight

If the load is statically applied and the material is ductile, it can be argued that localized yielding will occur in regions of maximum stress if the material yield strength is exceeded (which is true in this example). A further argument is that localized yielding in a highly stressed area results in a lowering of that stress (due to local yielding) and increased strength. This increased strength is due to the phenomenon commonly referred to as "cold-working" of the material. On the other hand, if the material is brittle or if loads are repeatedly applied and released (or reversed), failure by fracture or fatigue will likely occur.

Also, SOLIDWORKS Simulation literature warns that stress in the vicinity of bolts is often overestimated by the software.

The most instructive way to investigate any high stress region is with the mesh displayed on the model. The reason for this is that the rate of change of stress magnitude, also known as "stress gradient," can be observed in relation to element size. Therefore, we next examine the region of high stress gradient on the *surface* of the angle bracket, circled in Fig. 23, to demonstrate its significance relative to mesh size.

2. Begin by hiding the "simulated" bolt connectors appearing at each bolt hole. In the Simulation manager click the "▸" symbol to open the ▸**Connections** and then the ▸**Connectors** folders (if not already open). Next, right-click **Bolt Group-1** and from the pull-down menu select **Hide All**.

To further emphasize the stress gradient in this region, Fig. 24 shows an enlarged view of the area adjacent to bolt #2 with the default curvature based mesh superimposed on the model. On your own, create a view like that shown in Fig. 24. The following steps are provided in the event that guidance is desired.

3. In the **Results** folder, right-click **Stress1 (-von Mises-)**. From the pull-down menu, select **Settings…** The **Stress Plot** property manager opens.

4. Verify that the **Fringe Options** dialogue box is set to **Discrete**; if not, change it. This action further emphasizes the boundary of the high stress (red area) relative to mesh size.

5. Next, from the pull-down menu in the **Boundary Options** dialogue box, select **Mesh**. The current mesh is superimposed on the model.

6. Click **[OK]** ✓ to close the **Stress plot** property manager.

7. Select a **Top View** and zoom-in on the high stress area circled on Fig. 23. The high stress (red) area is outlined in black for emphasis in Fig. 24. Similar high stress occurs near bolt #1.

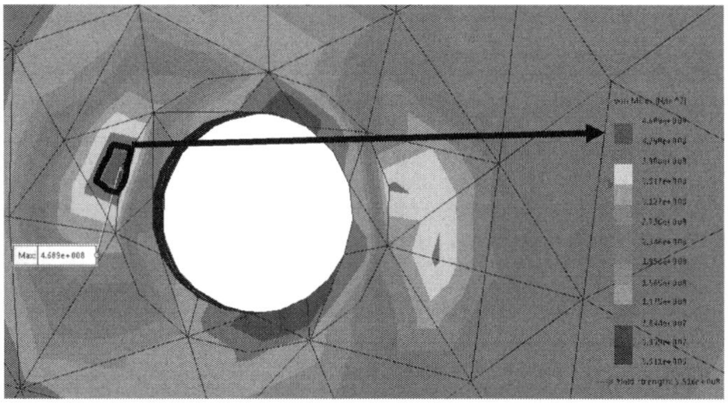

Figure 24 – Enlarged view showing the maximum stress region lies within a *portion* of an element shown in the figure. Stress magnitude is correlated to the color-coded stress scale.

Conclusion: Because the high stress region is *smaller than any individual element* (i.e., in Fig. 24 the [boxed] red area occupies only a small portion of three adjacent elements), *a smaller mesh should be used in this region. Why?* Page I-9 and Fig. 15 of the Introduction noted that stress is calculated at Gauss points within each element. Thus, if high stress occurs *within a small region of any element*, that stress magnitude will be sorely *underestimated* in that element due to averaging it with much lower stress magnitudes at remaining Gauss points within the element. Also, recall that a finer mesh typically reveals stress levels more accurately. Because this small area occurs adjacent to a geometric discontinuity (the bolt hole), use of *Mesh Control* outlined in Chapter 3 should be considered.

The above observation is of paramount importance in any analysis where a high stress gradient occurs. However, because determination of bolt forces is the primary goal of this example, and because mesh refinement was investigated previously in Chapter 3, we return to analyze the bolted joint results without applying mesh refinement at this time.

Bolt Forces (for Upward Load)

The effect of altering direction of the applied load upon bolt forces is examined next.

1. Right-click the **Results** folder, and from the pull-down menu, select **List Connector Force…** The **Result Force** property manager opens; *only* its lower portion is shown in Fig. 25. *The initial figure will be altered to look like Fig.25.*

2. In the **Selection** dialogue box set **Unit** to **SI**. Also, open ▼ the **Connector** pull-down menu and select **Counterbore with Nut-1**. (Alternatively, select **All bolts** from the pull-down menu, and scroll through the results). *[Not shown.]*

3. In the **Report Options** dialogue box, check "✓" to select ☑ **List X,Y,Z components** circled in Fig. 25. Your screen should now look like Fig. 25. It may be necessary to click-and-drag ⟷ the right boundary to reveal all values.

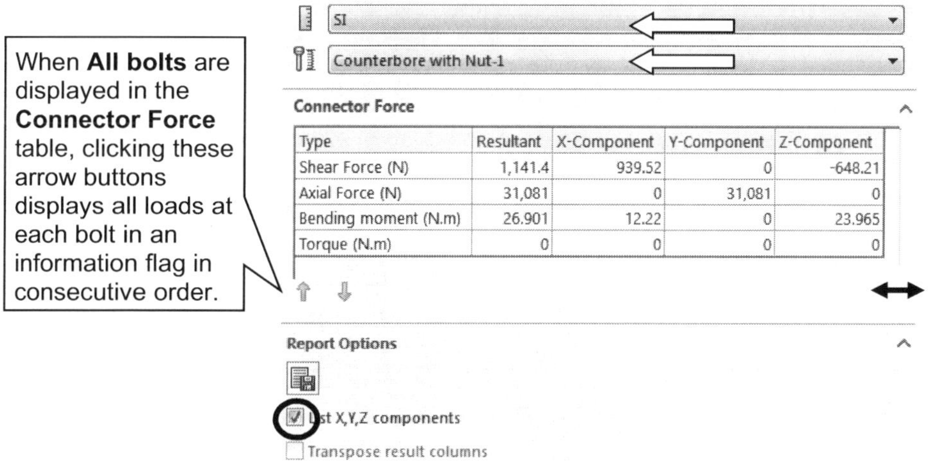

Type	Resultant	X-Component	Y-Component	Z-Component
Shear Force (N)	1,141.4	939.52	0	-648.21
Axial Force (N)	31,081	0	31,081	0
Bending moment (N.m)	26.901	12.22	0	23.965
Torque (N.m)	0	0	0	0

Figure 25 – All forces and components at **Counterbore with Nut-1** corresponding to an upward load applied to the angle bracket.

4. For bolt #1 the **Axial Force (N)**, in the **Resultant** column at the left of the table, is **31081** N (values may differ). This value represents an increased axial (tensile) bolt load of 7181 N above the initial bolt pre-load of 24000 N.

5. Next, open ▼ the **Connector** pull-down menu and from the list of connectors, select **Counterbore with Nut-2**. In the **Axial Force** row, the **Resultant** force in this bolt is now **31066** N, which is within 15 N of the value obtained at bolt #1 in the previous step. (Resultant axial loads at bolts #1 and #2 differ by only 0.06%.)

Recall that bolts #1 and #2 are located adjacent to one another at the same distance from the applied load. Theoretically, identical bolt loads are expected at these two locations.

6. Repeat steps 4 and 5 for **Counterbore with Nut-3** and **Counterbore with Nut-4**. Axial bolt forces at these two locations are **24003** N and **24023** N respectively. (Resultant axial loads at bolts #3 and #4 differ by only 0.01 %.)

A side view of the model in Fig. 26 supports the finding of larger bolt tensile forces at bolts nearest to the applied load due to the additional upward "pull" resisted by bolts #1 and #2. In this instance, only a slight increase above the bolt preload of 24000 N occurs at bolts #3 and #4, which are farthest from the applied load. Check these values on your own.

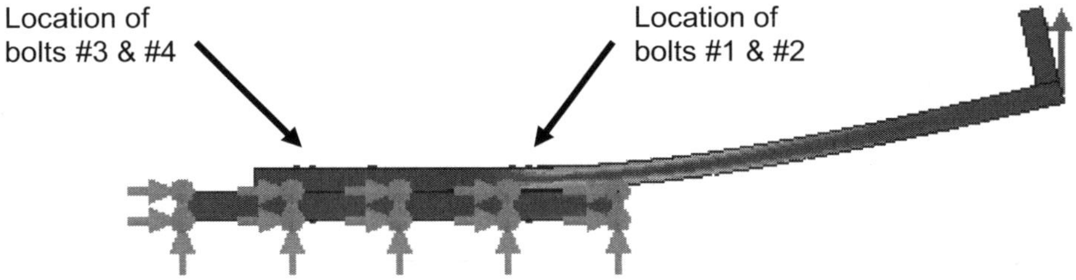

Figure 26 – Side view of the bolted joint with the angle bracket subject to an upward load at its right end.

Analysis Insight

Before closing the **Result Force** property manager, observe magnitudes of the **Shear Force** and the **Bending moment**. **Bending moment** is defined to act under the head of a bolt. Although **Bending *moment*** values appear quite small, bending *stress* in the bolts combines with axial stress and is quite high; it should be checked. The magnitude of Resultant **Shear Force** varies from a high of 1116.6 N at bolt #1 to a low of 913.01 N at bolts #3 and #4 respectively. Resultant **Shear Forces** are small compared to axial forces acting on the bolts. More importantly, however, shear stress in the bolt subject to the maximum shear force is small relative to bolt shear strength. The following calculation examines shear stress in the most heavily loaded bolt #1.

$$\tau = F_s/A_s = (1116.6 \text{ N}) / (0.0763 \text{ m}^2) = 14.55 \text{ k N/m}^2 = 0.01463 \text{ MPa} \quad [2]$$

where:

F_s = maximum shear force at a bolt (see calculation of F_s below)
A_s = minor area of bolt thread (at root of thread profile) NOTE: For structural bolts, the nominal bolt diameter should be used.
τ = shear stress in bolt caused by maximum shear force

When compared to a conservative value of shear strength (S_{sy} = 234 MPa) for a Grade 5.8 metric bolt, the shear stress is only 0.006 % of bolt shear strength. For this reason, shear stress is not considered significant in this example.

However, for many structural applications, shear in bolts is the *primary* mode of loading. In those instances, shear load on bolts is of prime importance. An end-of-chapter exercise examines a bolted joint where shear in the joint is the governing factor.

NOTE: The shear force F_s in equation [2] is determined as follows from the maximum X and Z shear force components occurring at bolt #1 and shown in Fig. 28.

$$F_S = \sqrt{(917.1)^2 + (-636.93)^2} = 1116.6 \text{ N} \quad [3]$$

It may be possible to gain some insight into the origins of the X and Z components of shear force, by animating the model. Do this on your own, or proceed as follows.

7. Select **[OK]** ✓ to exit the **Result Force** property manager.

8. If the von Mises stress plot is not displayed, double-click **Stress1 (-vonMises-)**.

9. Right-click **Stress1 (-vonMises-)**, and from the pull-down menu select **Edit Definition…** The **Stress Plot** property manager opens.

10. Check "✓" to open the ☑ **Deformed Shape** dialogue box and verify that ⊙ **Automatic** is selected. The distortion scale factor is **7.9476** (values may differ). This value is altered below.

11. Click **[OK]** ✓ to close the **Stress Plot** property manager.

12. Right-click **Stress1 (-vonMises-)**, and from the pull-down menu select ▶**Animate…** If the model is animated, select the **Stop** ■ icon.

13. In the **Basics** dialogue box, increase the **Frames** to **10** and move the **Speed** control slide to the left. These actions smooth-out and slow the animation.

14. Click the **Start** ▶ icon.

15. Slowly rotate the model to examine its deformation due to the applied load. Pay particular attention to deformations in the region below bolts #1 and #2 where the angle bracket and support plate intersect. Does a "gap" appear between parts?

16. Click **[OK]** ✓ to close the **Animation** property manager.

Because it may be difficult to observe deformations that cause shear forces in bolt #1 and bolt #2, repeat steps 9 through 15 above, except replace step 10 with the following.

17. In the ☑ **Deformed Shape** dialogue box, select ⊙ **User defined**. In the adjacent field, type **30** as the **Scale Factor**. Then continue at steps 11 to 15. This action artificially increases the magnitude of deformation displayed in Fig. 27. Rotate the model and observe the exaggerated separation (gap) that occurs between the plate and angle bracket in the boxed region.

Figure 27 – Using animation to visualize origins of shear forces in the X and Z directions at bolts #1 and #2.

The deformed model should appear similar to that illustrated in Fig. 27. In the following discussion, particular attention is focused on deformations between mating parts in the vicinity of the bolts.

18. **Stop** ■ the animation and click **[OK]** ✓ to close the **Animation** property manager.

Figure 28 is a top view of the bolted joint where bolt connectors are represented by circles. Shear force components, directed according to their ± signs listed in the **Result Force** property manager, are shown at each location. Using a combination of Fig. 28 and deformations viewed when animating the model, directions of the shear force components should begin to "make sense."

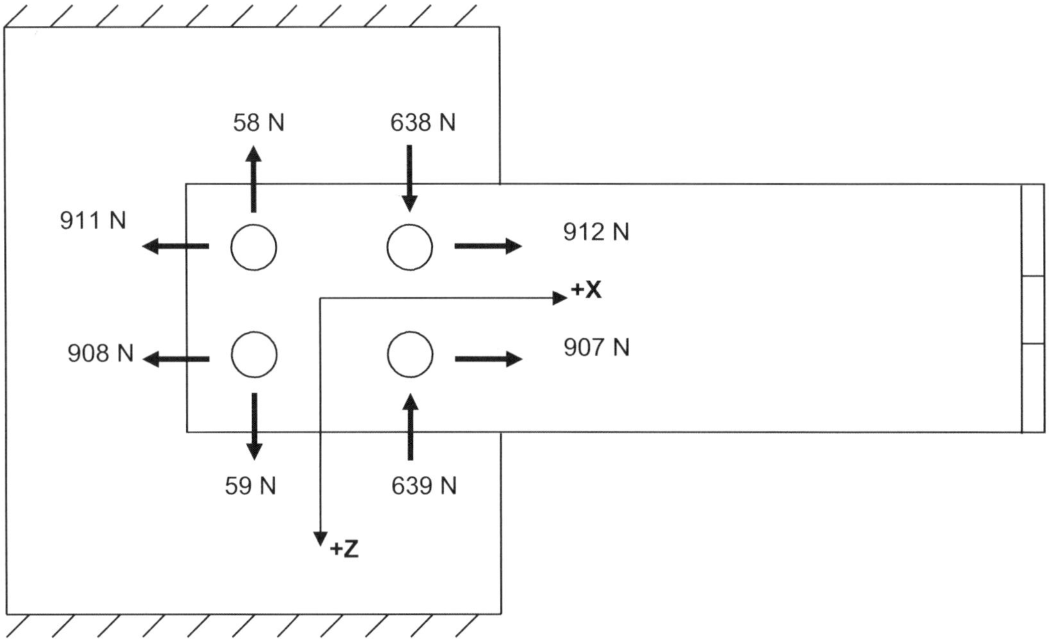

Figure 28 – Shear force components in the X and Z-directions developed in each bolt.

Bolt Clamping Pressure

Bolt preload is known to apply an equal and opposite clamping force on the joined members. Using software capabilities introduced in Chapter 6, contact pressure is investigated next. This analysis provides further insight into the intent of the bolted joint analysis capability within SOLIDWORKS Simulation.

1. Right-click the **Results** folder, and from the pull-down menu select **Define Stress Plot…** The **Stress Plot** property manager opens.

2. In the **Display** dialogue box, click ▼ to open the pull-down menu adjacent to **VON: von Mises Stress** and from the pull-down menu select **CP: Contact Pressure**.

3. Verify that **Units** are set to **N/m^2**.

4. Next, in the **Advanced Options** dialogue box, check ☑ **Show as vector plot** and clear the checkmark from ☐ **Average results across boundary for parts**.

5. Select the **Settings** tab and verify that **Fringe Options** is set to either **Discrete** (preferred) or **Continuous**. Also, within the **Boundary Options** dialogue box, open the pull-down menu and from it select **Model** (if not already selected).

6. Click **[OK]** ✓ to close the **Stress Plot** property manager. A new plot, labeled **Stress2 (-Contact pressure-)**, is listed beneath the **Results** folder.

7. If not already displayed on the graphics screen, double-click **Stress2 (-Contact pressure-)** to display a contact pressure plot like that shown in Fig. 29.

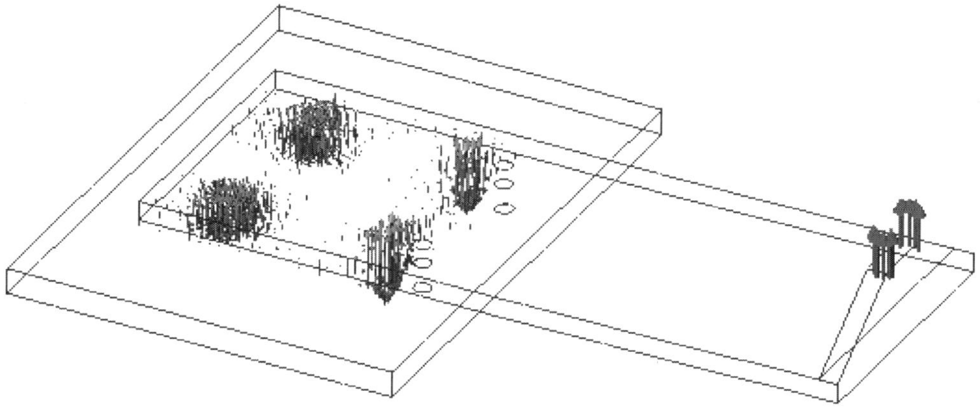

Figure 29 – Contact pressure plot showing interaction between the angle bracket and the support plate when subject to the upward load.

Users are encouraged to alter the graphic display to appear like Fig. 29. Necessary steps are provided below if guidance is desired.

8. *If visible*, bolt restraint symbols might obscure other pertinent graphical information. Temporarily remove them by right-clicking the **Connectors** folder and from the pull-down menu select **Hide All**.

9. Repeat step 8 to temporarily hide **Fixtures**.

If the contact pressure vectors initially appear too small, which is often the case, increase their size as follows. Try this on your own or apply the steps listed below.

10. *If necessary*, double-click **Stress2 (-Contact pressure-)** to again display the contact pressure.

11. Right-click **Stress2 (-Contact pressure-)** and from the pull-down menu select **Vector Plot Options…** The **Vector plot options** property manager opens.

12. In the **Options** dialogue box, type **600** in the **Size** field (upper spin-box) to enlarge the size of contact pressure vectors displayed. Vector **Size** is a user preference.

13. Accept other default settings in this property manager and click **[OK]** ✓ to close it. Your display should now appear similar to Figs. 29 and 30.

14. Rotate and zoom-in on the model to gain better insight into what is actually plotted.

Figure 30 shows three different views of contact pressure vectors in the vicinity of the bolt holes and throughout the assembly.

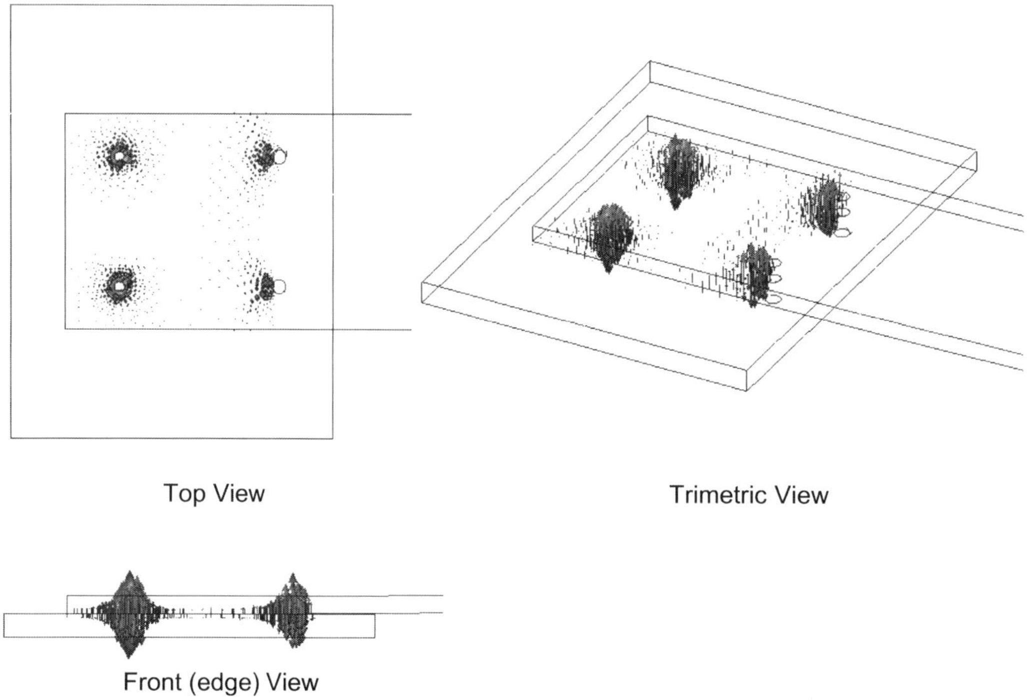

Figure 30 – Various views showing distribution of contact pressure between mating parts in the bolted joint subject to an upward load.

Analysis Insight

Do graphical results in Fig. 30 (currently displayed on your screen) correspond with what you expected to see? The answer might surprise many users. However, it is valuable to understand what these plots reveal in order to ensure that results are interpreted correctly. These are some additional questions that might be asked:

a. Is the contact pressure shown in Fig. 30 applied by the bolts onto the plates?

or

b. Is the contact pressure shown in Fig. 30 the pressure that exists between the plates themselves?

or

c. Do the plots represent the superposition of contact pressure due to bolt clamping forces (i.e., forces beneath the head of the bolt and nut) and due to plate contact?

The answer to question (a) is that, although bolt preload "grips" the parts together, a **Connections** condition was not specified between contacting faces of the bolt or nut and corresponding top and bottom surfaces on the parts. For this reason, contact pressure between the bolt or nut and the plate surface is *not* illustrated.

Based on the preceding observation, it should be clear that the answer to question (b) is that contact pressure between the mating parts (i.e., between the plates) *is shown* in Fig. 30. Verify this by observing the direction of pressure vectors shown in a front view of the contacting surfaces. All vectors originate at the contacting surface between the parts and point away from the surface on which pressure acts. Also, in all views, notice that no contact pressure is shown to the right of bolts #1 and #2. This is consistent with Fig. 26, repeated below, which indicates a location where separation (i.e., a gap) between the plates occurs. This gap reduces or eliminates contact pressure between the structural members.

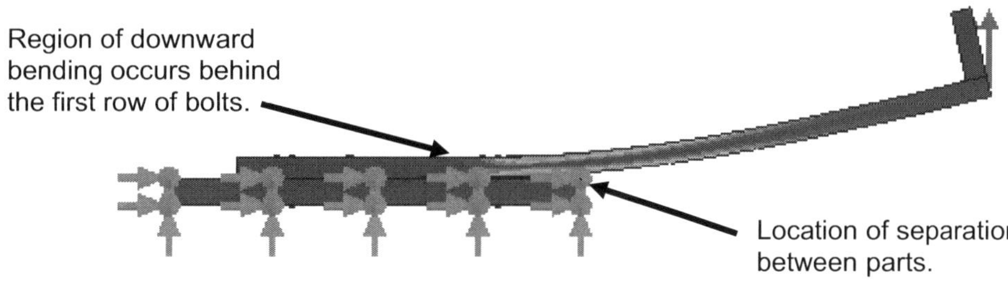

Figure 26 – (repeated) Probable location for a **Gap** to develop between parts.

Fig. 30 also reveals a "footprint" of pressure to the left of and between bolts #1 and #2. This pressure distribution is due to the downward bending of the bracket to the left of bolts #1 and #2 caused by the upward deformation of the part to the right of these bolts.

Analysis Insight (continued)

Question (c) is already answered in response (a) above. However, it is worthy to note that even if no external load were applied to the angle bracket, contact pressure would still result in both plates in the vicinity of all four bolt connectors. In other words, the images reveal that bolt preload causes contact pressure between the parts that are gripped rather than between the bolt connectors themselves and the gripped members.

Bolts #3 and #4 are relatively unaffected by the upward load applied at the right end of the bracket. Therefore, notice the fairly uniform shape of contact pressure distribution both in terms of magnitude (front view) and geometry ("circular" shapes in the top view) around these bolt holes.

Summary

Based on this example, it is evident that bolt force determination is one of the primary outcomes of a bolted joint analysis. This capability is useful for predicting and verifying design or analysis of bolt connections under load. Also, application of the **Contact Pressure** capability permits an analyst to determine the contact pressure distribution between mating parts in the vicinity of connectors, such as bolts. This knowledge enhances understanding of factors such as bolt spacing when used to create "pressure tight" connections.

Exercises on the following pages outline a different method for defining contact between mating parts that does not require the use of Split Lines.

This concludes the study of bolted joints, their definition, resulting contact pressure(s), and bolt reaction forces.

It is suggested that this example file not be saved. Proceed as follows.

1. From the main menu, select **File > Close** (suggested) and select **Don't Save**.

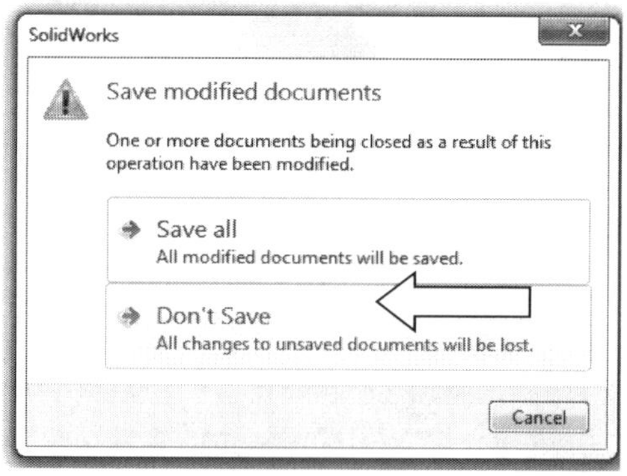

Figure 31 – Close the current example file without saving results.

EXERCISES

╬ EXERCISE 1 - Eccentrically Loaded Bolt Joint (Special Topic: Automatically Find Contact interactions)

A steel plate is connected to a vertical column by means of four **M 16 x 2, Grade 8.8** steel bolts. Bolt material properties are **E = 207 GPa** and **Poisson's Ratio** = **0.292**. The column is a 254 mm x 76 mm structural steel channel. Both the column and plate are made of **ASTM A36 Steel**. The channel can be considered rigidly fixed (**immovable**) on cut surfaces above and below the connection location. Only a segment of the channel is shown in the figures below. The plate is subject to a vertical load of **16** kN applied to its top-right *edge* as shown in Fig. E7-1. Figure E7-1 shows the basic geometry of parts in this assembly. For simplicity, detailed images of the bolts are not shown. Open files **Column 7-1** and **Plate 7-1** and perform a finite element analysis to determine items requested below.

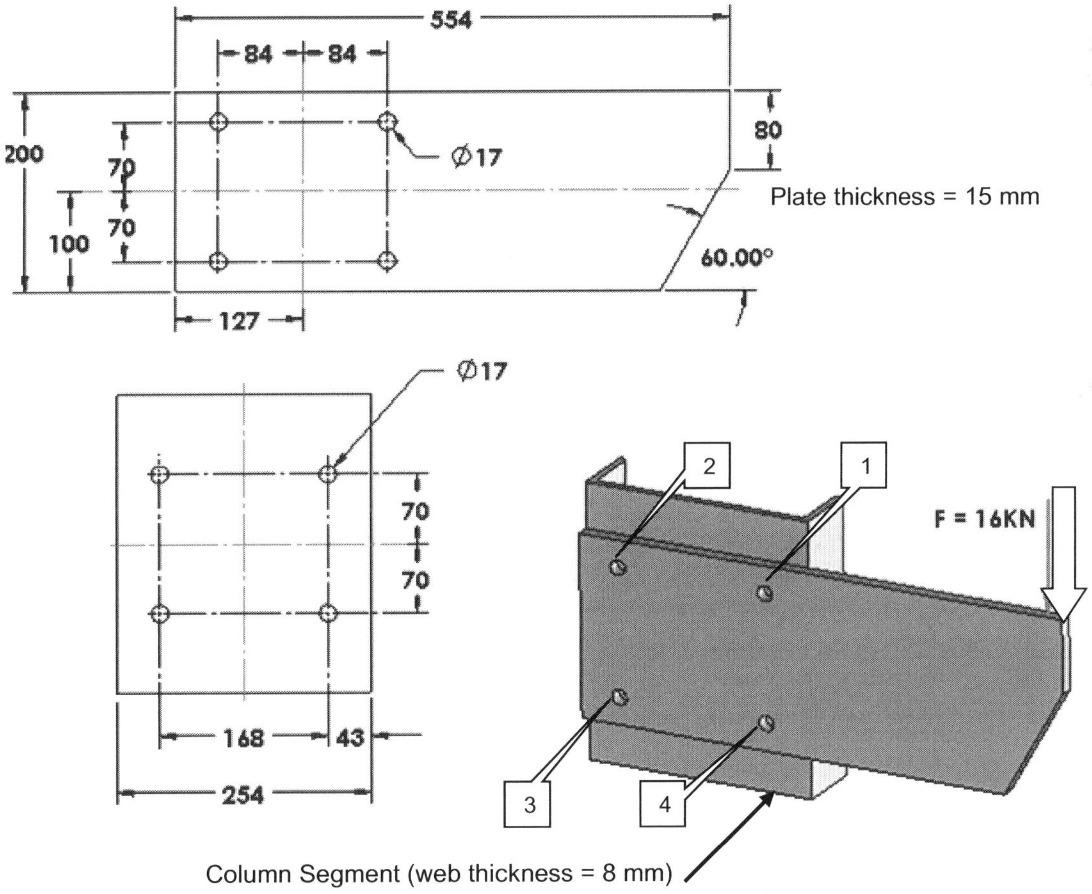

Figure E7-1 – Basic geometry of the column and plate. A 16 kN load is applied on the upper-right *edge* of the plate. Bolt numbers are shown in "call out" boxes.

- Material: **ASTM A36 Steel** (column and plate material properties)
  E = 207e9 Pa, and Poisson's ratio **ν = 0.292** (bolt properties)

- Mesh: Use system default size **Curvature based mesh**, tetrahedral elements.

- Fixtures: **Fixed** as necessary on top and bottom cut surfaces of the column.

  Connections with **No Penetration** between the column and plate. A simplified method for defining contact between these two parts is outlined in the **Solution Guidance** section below.

  Bolt connector with **Nut**; use a contact diameter = 30 mm under the bolt head and nut.

- External Load: **16 kN** downward at top-right *edge* of the plate.

- Assumptions: Bolts fit in clearance holes where D_{Hole} = 17 mm
  Bolts are field tightened to a torque T = 226 N-m
  Bolt torque coefficient K = 0.20

Determine the Following:

Begin by creating an assembly of the **Column 7-1** and **Plate 7-1** parts. If assistance creating the assembly is desired, see **Create the Assembly Model** on pg. 6-5 and foreword. Then develop a finite element model that includes material specification, fixtures, external load(s), contact specification, bolt connectors, mesh, and solution.

Solution Guidance

This section outlines a simplified means for defining contact between mating parts *without* the need for *Split Lines, after* creating an assembly of the **Column** and **Plate** and after defining **Mates**. (HINT: define **Coincidence** between at least two holes. Why?) The model should appear as shown in Fig. E7-2 prior to defining part contact.

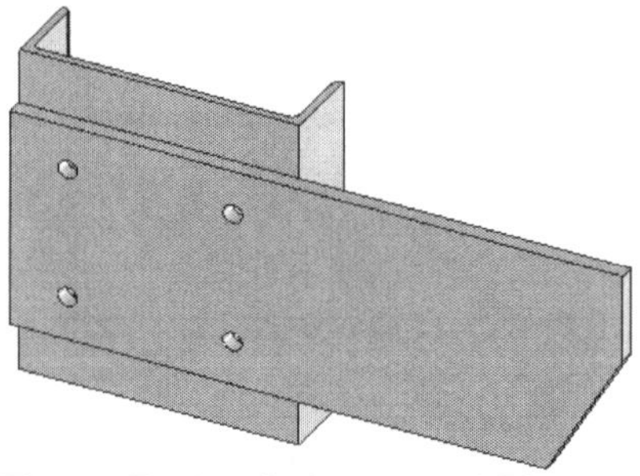

Figure E7-2 – **Column** and **Plate** assembly prior to definition of contact conditions.

The following steps outline use of the **Automatically Find Local Interactions** software option when defining contact between mating parts. Despite the power of this option, it should be used with care because, in complex assemblies, it may find extra contact interactions that are not intended, or it may not find a contact interaction that the user wants. As a case in point, the **Automatically Find Local Interactions** option is applied *prior* to defining bolted connectors. This sequence is used because bolted connectors add the potential

Solution Guidance (continued)

for contact under the bolt head and nut and between the bolt shank and inside surfaces of the bolt holes. This sequence of steps minimizes the possibility of unwanted contact interactions being defined. Proceed as follows to apply the simplified contact interaction capability. Steps below assume a Simulation Study has been started *and* proper **Mates** between the column and plate have been defined.

- In the Simulation manager, right-click the **Connections**, and from the pull-down menu select **Local Interaction…** The **Local Interaction** property manager opens as shown in Fig. E7-3.
- In the **Contact** dialogue box, select ⊙ **Automatically find local interactions**. The property manager changes to look like Fig. E7-3.
- In the **Options** dialogue box, select ⊙**Find faces** (if not already selected). The Maximum clearance can be set to 0 mm for the gap.
- In the **Components** dialogue box, the **Select Components or Bodies** field is active (highlighted light blue). Move the cursor into the graphics screen and click to select *both* the **Column** and the **Plate**. Select parts in any order. Names of the selected parts, **Extrude1@Plate 7-1-1@Assem1** and **Cut-Extrude1@Column 7-1-1@Assem1**, are listed in the active field.
- Next click the **[Find local interactions]** button and the software automatically identifies *any* contacting faces on these two parts. Within the **Results** dialogue box, names of the contacting faces are listed as **Contact interaction-1 (-Plate 7-1-1, Column 7-1-1-)**. Word order may be reversed.
- Also, within the **Results** dialogue box, open the pull-down menu adjacent to **Type:** and select **Contact** to define the type of contact between the column and plate.
- Click **[OK]** ✓ to close the **Contact interactions** property manager.
- Click **[Yes]** in the pop-up **Simulation** window.

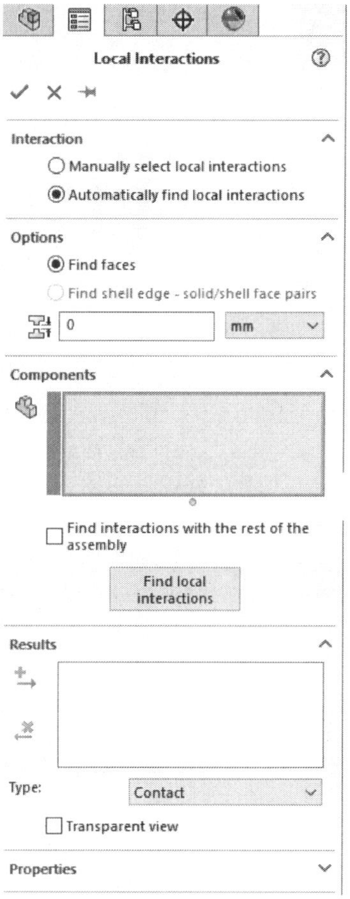

Figure E7-3 – The **Contact interactions** property manager facilitates definition of contact between mating parts.

Although a number of selections were involved in defining contact between the column and plate, use of the single **Local Interaction** property manager is much simpler than creating an exploded view; outlining contact areas using *Split Lines;* and then defining contact using the **Local Interaction** icon. At this point, complete the definition of the finite element model and perform the analysis outlined below.

a. Create an isometric or trimetric plot showing all fixtures and external loads, including bolt connectors, applied to the model. This image is the finite element equivalent of a free-body-diagram. Do not show a mesh or stresses on this plot. This plot should fill at least half of an 8 ½ x 11 inch page. [See also item (c) below.] Manually label bolt numbers 1 through 4 on this figure. Bolt numbers should correspond to those shown on Fig. E7-1.

b. Due to loading on this model, shear forces create the primary load on each bolt. Using SOLIDWORKS Simulation, determine the shear force components at each bolt location. Then, plot a front view of the model. This plot should be large enough to sketch and label the magnitude and direction of each shear force component and the resultant shear force at each bolt.

c. Create a plot of contact pressure between the column and plate. Exaggerate the scale of contact pressure to best depict pressure distribution on the mating parts. Choose the best view or views to show the contact pressure plot(s).

d. Check the solution by manually calculating the shear force(s) at each bolt. Compare manually calculated results with finite element results and compute the percent difference between resultant shear forces at each bolt using equation [1]. Label calculations to correspond to the appropriate bolt number. Cut-and-paste copy(ies) of the **Result Force** table from the finite element solution onto a page accompanying the manual solution. Be sure to correlate finite element results with the corresponding manual calculations of bolt shear force. Expect differences on the order of 12 to 15% between finite element and manual calculations. These differences may seem high, but there is a fundamental difference between assumptions applied to the manual calculations and to the finite element results. Questions: (1) State the assumptions applied to manual calculations of bolt shear force. (2) Based on your understanding of how FEA solutions are obtained, what is the difference in assumptions applied by these two methods of analysis?

$$\% \text{ difference} = \frac{(\text{FEA result - classical result})}{\text{FEA result}} * 100 = \qquad [1]$$

e. Question: Do directions of shear force components appearing in the **Result Force** table correspond to shear forces acting on the bolt, or do they represent directions of shear forces exerted by the bolt on the members? Justify your answer in terms of sketches made in part (b).

<u>EXERCISE 2</u> – Bolted Cylinder Head

A **Ductile Iron** "pipe-end" on a pressurized tank is sealed by an **Alloy Steel** cylinder head as shown in Fig. E7-4. The cylinder head is held in place by eight **5/8 inch-11 UNC, SAE Grade 8.2** steel bolts for which the modulus of elasticity, **E = 30e6 psi**, and Poisson's ratio, **μ = 0.30**. The pipe-end is subject to an internal static pressure of 900 psi. A confined gasket seal (not shown) is located in the flange groove. Because the gasket is located in a confined groove rather than "sandwiched" between the cylinder head and the flange, its low stiffness relative to other components can be ignored. Figure E7-5 shows the basic geometry of parts in this assembly. Open files **Cylinder Head 7-2** and **Pipe End & Flange 7-2** and perform a finite element analysis to determine items requested below.

Figure E7-4 – Bolted joint closing a "stub-end" on a pressurized tank.

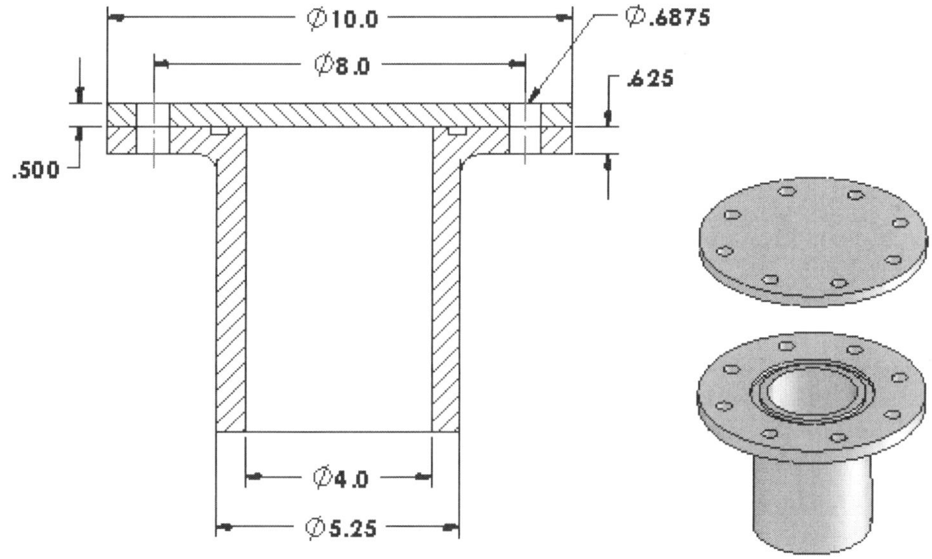

Figure E7-5 – Basic geometry of the cylinder head and flanged pipe end. Assume the pipe segment is sufficiently long to minimize the effect of fixtures applied to its bottom end.

- Material: **Alloy Steel** (cylinder head)
  Ductile Iron (pipe-end and flange)
  E = 30e6 psi, and Poisson's ratio **ν = 0.30** (bolt material)

- Mesh: Use system default size **Curvature based mesh**, tetrahedral elements.

- Fixtures: Define as appropriate on the cut (bottom) pipe-end.

  Local Interaction between cylinder head and pipe flange is to be specified as **Contact**. See **Solution Guidance** in Exercise 1 of this chapter for a simplified method of defining contact between the cylinder head and pipe flange.

  Bolt connector with **Nut**: Assume the outside diameter under the bolt head and nut is 15/16 inch (0.9375 in).

- External Load: Pressure = **900 psi** acts on all internal surfaces

- Assumptions: Bolts fit in clearance holes where D_{Hole} = 0.6875 in
  Bolts are field tightened to a torque T = 2540 lb*in
  Bolt torque coefficient K = 0.20

Determine the Following:

Begin by creating an assembly of the **Cylinder Head** and **Pipe End & Flange**. If assistance creating the assembly is desired, see **Create the Assembly Model** on pg. 6-5 and foreword. Next, use the simplified **Automatically Find Local Interactions** procedure outlined in the **Solution Guidance** section of Exercise 1 in this chapter as you develop the finite element model. The complete model should include material specification, contact specification, fixtures, external load(s), bolt connectors, mesh, and solution.

a. Create a plot showing all restraints and loads applied to the model. This image is the finite element equivalent of a free-body-diagram. Do not show a mesh or stresses on this plot. This plot should fill at least half of an 8 ½ x 11 inch page. On this plot, write a brief statement that clearly identifies the type of fixture(s) applied to the cut-end of the pipe segment shown in Fig. E7-5.

b. Create a plot of contact pressure between the cylinder head and the pipe flange. Exaggerate the scale of contact pressure to best depict pressure distribution on the mating parts. What can be stated about the uniformity of contact pressure between the mating surfaces (i.e., between the cylinder head and pipe flange)? In your answer pay particular attention to pressure distribution in spaces *between* bolts on the bolt circle that joins these two parts together. Why is this pressure distribution important?

c. Due to loading on this model, each bolt is subject to its initial pre-load plus a portion of the load due to internal pressure. Use SOLIDWORKS Simulation to determine the load in a representative number of bolts (at least four) by accessing results in the **Result Force** property manager. Cut-and-paste screen images of four **Result Force** tables onto an 8 ½ x 11 inch page. See also item (d) below.

d. Develop a set of manual calculations, based on bolt theory, to determine the resultant tensile load in a typical bolt. This bolt load should include both the bolt preload and the portion of external load carried by each bolt. Place these calculations on a page following the page created for item (c). Compare manually calculated results for total axial bolt load with finite element results and compute the percent difference between resultant bolt tensile forces using equation [1].

$$\% \text{ difference} = \frac{(\text{FEA result - classical result})}{\text{FEA result}} * 100 = \qquad [1]$$

EXERCISE 3 – Bolted Trailer Hitch
(Special Topics: Application of Remote Loads, Automatically Find Local Interactions)

The trailer-hitch assembly shown in Fig. E7-6 is subject to both vertical and horizontal force components when towing a trailer. The vertical force component, or "tongue weight," (**W**) is defined as the downward force due to a *portion* of the trailer weight including its cargo that acts on the hitch. Towing force (**F_T**) is the force required to pull the trailer; its reaction on the hitch "ball" is shown in Fig. E7-6. **F_T** is zero when the trailer is at rest; is reasonably steady when pulling a trailer at constant speed; and is maximum during acceleration or deceleration. NOTE: Hitch geometry shown in Fig. E7-6 is different than that in Exercise 5 of Chapter 2; therefore, *do not use* results or the model from that problem.

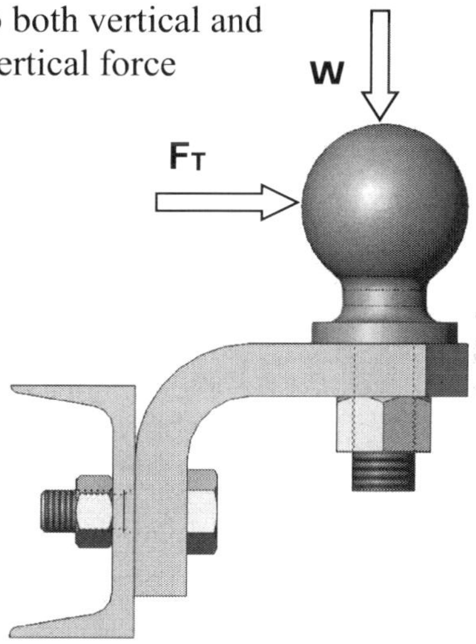

Figure E7-6 – Trailer hitch, ball, and channel assembly.

The goal of this exercise is to determine bolt forces and contact pressure between a 20-in long, 3x5 steel channel and the trailer hitch assembly shown in Fig. E7-7, (where channel height = 3-in and weight = 5 lb/ft). Left and right *ends* of the **ASTM A36 Steel** channel are considered rigidly fixed (**immovable**) where it is welded to a truck frame (not shown). Two **1/2–13 UNC, SAE Grade 7** steel bolts attach the hitch to the channel through holes 1 and 2 labeled below. Because application of forces to the hitch "ball" is not the objective of this analysis, the problem can be simplified by defining applied forces using the **Remote Load/Mass** feature available in SOLIDWORKS Simulation. Open file **Hitch-Channel Assembly 7-3**.

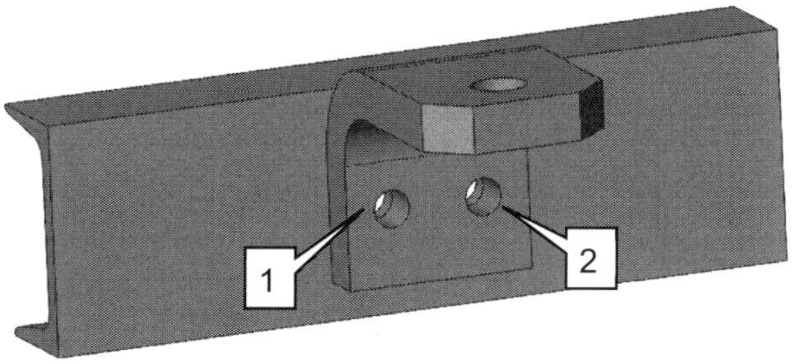

Figure E7-7 – Trailer hitch and channel assembly showing bolt hole locations.

Assume the following:

- Material: **ASTM A36 Steel** (structural steel channel), English units: **IPS**
  Alloy Steel (trailer hitch)
  E = 30e6 psi, and Poisson's ratio **ν** = **0.30** (bolt material)

- Mesh: In the **Mesh** property manager, select ⊙ **Curvature based mesh** and use the default mesh size.

- Fixture: Apply **Fixed** (immovable) restraints on both left and right ends of the 3x5 steel channel.

  The **Local Interaction** between the channel and hitch is to be specified as **Contact**. See **Solution Guidance** text box in Exercise #1 of this chapter (middle of pg. 7-32 and forward), for a simplified method of defining contact between the channel and trailer hitch.

  Bolt connector with **Nut**: Assume the outside diameter under the bolt head and nut is 3/4 inch (0.750 in) and bolt diameter = ½ in.

- External Load: Apply force components using the **Remote Load/Mass** feature.
  Tongue weight **W = 220 lb** (vertical downward).
  Tow force **F_T = 440 lb** (horizontal) in the -X direction. This towing force component corresponds to maximum acceleration.

- Assumptions: Bolts are a "tight fit" in holes where D_{Hole} = 0.5 in
  Bolts are tightened to a torque T = 1340 lb*in
  Bolt torque coefficient K = 0.20

Analysis Insight

Use of the **Remote Load/Mass** feature permits application of forces[1] at locations remote from a model. The **Remote Load/Mass** feature is used primarily where modeling simplification is desired. In this example, application of force components to curved surfaces of the hitch ball can be accomplished by several methods. However, using the **Remote Load/Mass** option is one of the more direct approaches. Also, understanding this software capability enables you to use this feature in other situations.

To begin, a brief review of SOLIDWORKS coordinate systems is in order. Each *part* created within SOLIDWORKS has its own *local* coordinate system. The channel origin is located half-way between its upper and lower surfaces and midway between its left and right ends shown circled in Fig. E7-8(a). The hitch origin is located at the bottom of the ball-hole illustrated and circled in Fig. E7-8(b). These origin locations were specified when dimensioning the original parts in SOLIDWORKS **Sketch** mode.

---

[1] Additionally, moments, displacements, and (in the case of static, frequency, linear dynamic, or buckling studies) model mass can be defined at locations remote from the model.

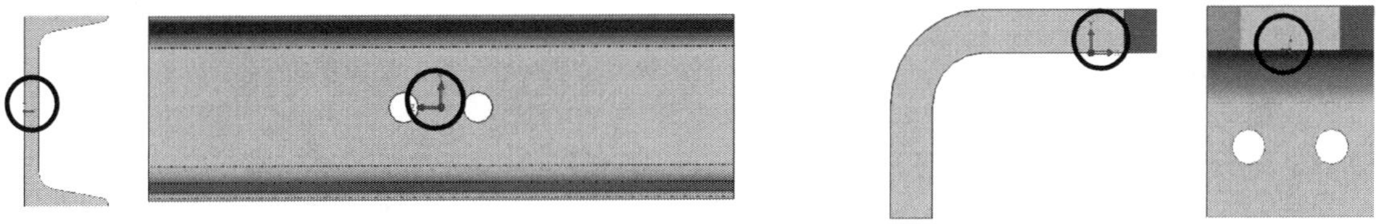

Figure E7-8 – Local coordinate system origin locations for the Channel and Hitch as defined within SOLIDWORKS sketch mode.

However, when the channel and hitch are joined to form an *assembly*, the first part brought into the assembly is considered to be the *base component* and its origin becomes the default origin of the assembly[2]. In this example the channel is the base component. Thus, a **Global** coordinate system corresponds to that of the channel.

Furthermore, defining coordinates for force application at a **Remote Load/Mass** location (presumed to be at center of the hitch-ball) relative to the **Global** coordinate system (located on the channel) is somewhat tedious. However, Fig. E7-9 reveals that the center of the hitch-ball is located **1.616-in** above the ball shoulder (see circled dimension). Thus, a **User defined** coordinate system will be defined at the base of the hitch-ball. Use of **Global** versus **User defined** coordinate systems will be clarified as this example proceeds.

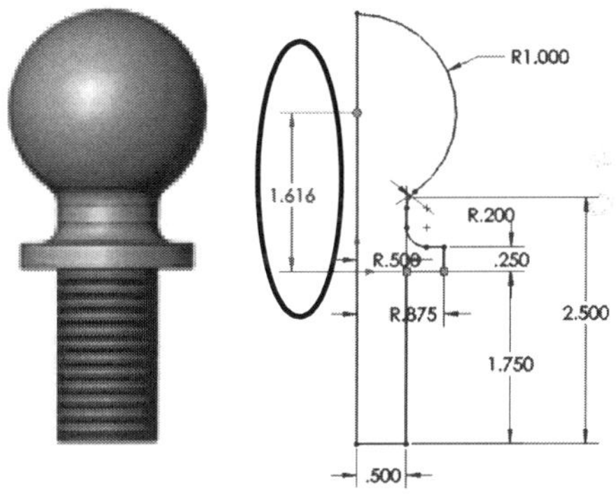

Figure E7-9 – The original **Sketch** shows height of the ball center above the base of the hitch shoulder. Force components **W** and $\mathbf{F_T}$ are applied at the ball center.

Solution Guidance

It is assumed that the user has opened a Simulation file and started a Study. The following instructions serve as a guide; they are less detailed than step-by-step procedures found in example problems.

<u>Application of a Remote Load/Mass</u>

Because coordinate systems play an integral role in simplifying application of remote loads, begin by displaying the original *origins* on the model.

a. In the **Main Menu** select **View > Hide/Show** followed by **Origins**. Origins of the Channel and Hitch are displayed on the model.

[2] The *base component* can be changed and along with it the assembly origin. However, that topic is best considered within SOLIDWORKS and is not pursued here.

Solution Guidance (continued)

b. On the **Main Menu**, choose **Insert > Reference Geometry > Point**. The **Point** property manager opens. In the **Selections** dialogue box, choose **Arc Center** and move the cursor onto the *top edge* of the ball-hole and click to select it. Click **[OK]** ✓ to close the **Point** property manager. *Point 1* appears.

c. In the **Main Menu** select **Insert > Reference Geometry > Coordinate System**. A new origin appears at *Point 1* specified in the preceding step. Observe directions of the X, Y, Z coordinate axes. Specifically, the +X axis is directed toward the front of the towing vehicle and +Y, and +Z directions are determined using the right-hand rule. Click **[OK]** ✓ to close the **Coordinate System** property manager. An image of the new coordinate system remains on the model.

Aside: Directions of the X, Y, Z axes can be changed while the **Coordinate System** property manager is open in step (c) above. Alternatively, directions of force components can be changed when they are defined in the **Remote Load/Mass** property manager. In this example the latter option is used.

When ready to apply **External Loads**, proceed as follows.

d. In the Simulation manager tree right-click the **External Loads** folder, then select **Remote Load/Mass...**

e. In the **Type** dialogue box, select ⊙ **Load/Mass (Rigid connection)**. This option is used when stiffness of the part to be *replaced* by a remote load is significant relative to the rest of the model. It is also selected because it can be applied to **Faces**, **Edges**, or **Vertices** on the model as executed in the next step.

Aside: The O **Load (Direct transfer)** option could also be used; however, it is less accurate in this case because it can only be applied to **Faces** (i.e., entire surfaces) of a model. Doing so results in a less accurate depiction of actual forces on the hitch.

f. Next, in the **Type** dialogue box the **Faces, Edges, or Vertices, for Remote Load/Mass** field is active (highlighted light blue). Move the cursor onto the *top edge* of the ball-hole and click to select it.

g. In the **Reference Coordinate System** dialogue box, select ⊙ **User defined**. If **Coordinate System1** does *not* appear at center of the top hole, then go to the main menu and select **View**, then from the pull-down select **Hide/Show > Coordinate Systems**. **Coordinate System1** appears at the top center of the hitch. Also, click to activate the **Select a Coordinate System** field and then select **Coordinate System1** on the model. The coordinate system should now appear at top of the ball hole.

Solution Guidance (continued)

h. In the **Location** dialogue box, verify that **Unit** is set to **in**. Then in the **Y-Location** field, type **1.616** and leave the **X** and **Z** coordinates equal to zero (**0**).

i. In the **Force** dialogue box, verify **Unit** is set to **lbf** and specify the **X-Direction** force as **440** lbf acting in the –**X** direction and specify the **Y-Direction** force component as **220** lbf acting downward. Select ☑ **Reverse direction** as necessary so that your model appears as shown in Fig. E7-10.

j. Click ✓ **[OK]** to close the **Remote Loads/Mass** property manager.

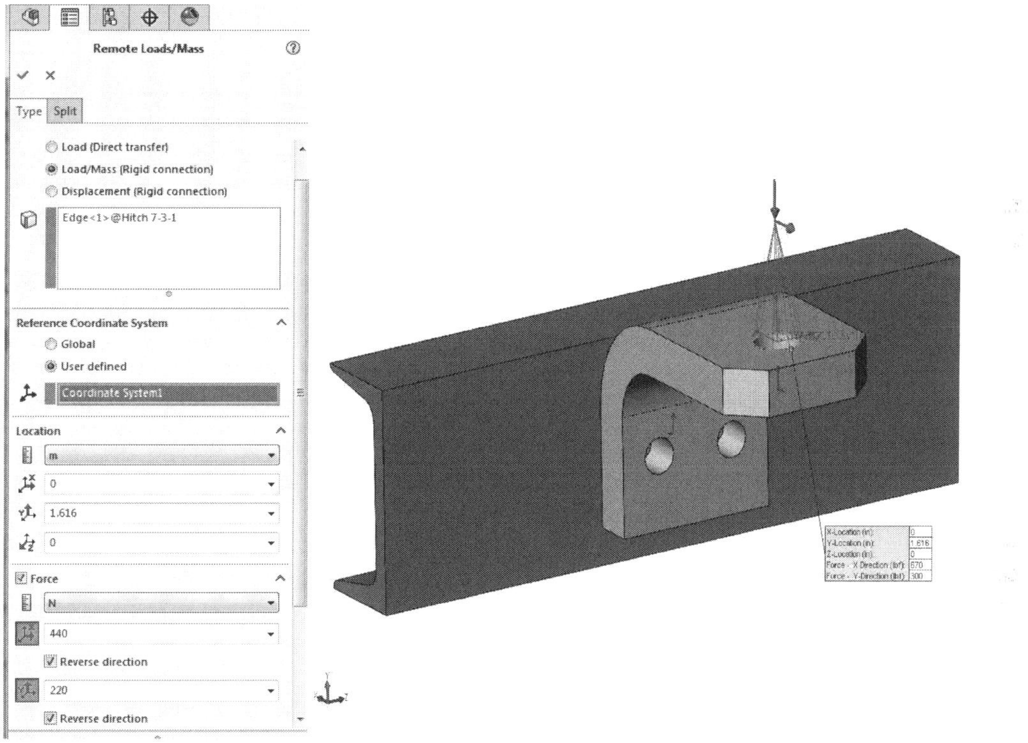

Figure E7-10 – Specifying **Location** coordinates and **Force** magnitudes in the **Remote Loads/Mass** property manager.

HINT: If a solution is not obtained within a few minutes, it will probably end in a *Failure Error* as shown in the **Static Analysis** window of Fig. E7-11. Click **[OK]** to close this window. Next, click **[OK]** to close the **Simulation** alert window.

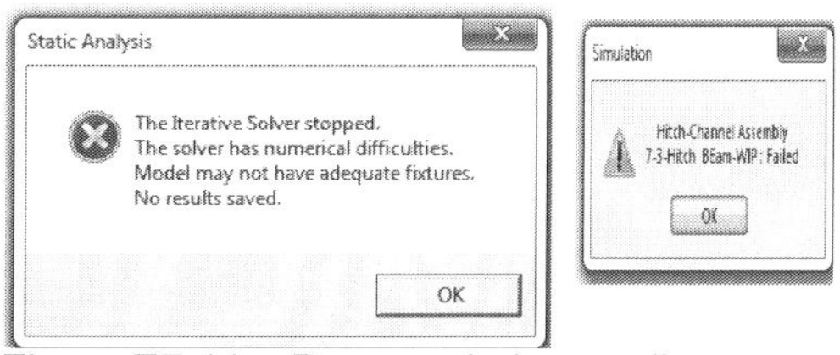

Figure E7-11 – Pop up windows call attention to a failed solution.

To re-start a successful solution, *read the procedure* beginning at step #8, pg. 7-14, and begin by *performing the procedure* beginning at step #11, pg. 7-16. When using the **Direct Sparse** solver approach, solution time will run between 1.5 to 2 minutes on most 64 Bit computers.

Determine the following:

Begin by creating the SOLIDWORKS Simulation model. If not already done, use the simplified procedure to **Automatically Find Contact Interactions** between the hitch and channel. Steps to accomplish this task are outlined in the **Solution Guidance** section of Exercise 1 in this chapter. The complete model should include material specification, contact specification, fixtures, remote external load(s), bolt connectors, mesh, and solution.

a. Create an isometric or trimetric plot showing all fixtures and remote external loads, including bolt connectors, applied to the model. This image is the finite element equivalent of a free-body-diagram. Do not show a mesh or stresses on this plot. This plot should fill at least half of an 8 ½ x 11 inch page. Manually label bolt numbers 1 and 2 on this figure to correspond to those in Fig. E7-7.

b. Create a plot of contact pressure between the channel and trailer hitch. Exaggerate the scale of contact pressure to best depict pressure distribution on the mating parts. Choose a *rear view* and a *left-side view* to show the contact pressure plot(s). Place the images on the lower half of the page containing the figure from part (a) of this exercise.

c. Due to loading on this model, each bolt is subject to its initial pre-load plus a portion of the load due to force components acting on the hitch ball. Use SOLIDWORKS Simulation to determine the load in bolts #1 and #2 by accessing results in the **Result Force** window. In the **Connector:** field of this window, select **[All bolts]**. Cut-and-paste a screen image of the **Result Force** window onto an 8 ½ x 11 inch page. See also item (d) below.

d. Develop and label a set of manual calculations, based on bolt theory, to determine the resultant tensile load in a typical bolt. This bolt load should include both the bolt preload and the portion of external load carried by each bolt. Place these calculations beneath the **Result Force** window on the page created for item (c). Compare manually calculated results for the total axial bolt load with finite element results and compute the percent difference between resultant bolt tensile forces using equation [1].

$$\%\ \text{difference} = \frac{(\text{FEA result - classical result})}{\text{FEA result}} * 100 = \qquad [1]$$

e. Questions:
   - Do directions of shear force components appearing in the **Result Force** table correspond to shear forces acting on the bolt, or do they represent

directions of shear forces exerted by the bolt on the hitch? Justify your answer by producing a sketch showing external loads acting on the hitch and shear forces acting at bolt holes 1 and 2.

- Is the hitch in equilibrium when considering shear forces? Show calculations to support your answer.

- Discuss reasons for any moderate to large percent differences between FEA predicted bolt forces and bolt forces calculated using manual calculations. Describe shortcomings (if any) of manual calculations used to predict actual bolt forces.

Textbook Problems

In addition to the above exercise, it is highly recommended that additional problems involving bolted connections be worked from a design of machine elements or a structural analysis textbook. Bolted assemblies can be loaded by axial loads, bending loads, shear loads, or a combination of all three. Textbook problems provide a great way to discover errors made in formulating a finite element analysis because they typically are well defined problems for which the solution is known. Typical textbook problems, if well defined, make an excellent source of solutions for comparison.

NOTES:

CHAPTER #8

DESIGN OPTIMIZATION

In keeping with demands for faster, lighter, more sustainable, and efficient designs, the Optimization Design feature within SOLIDWORKS Simulation[1] should be a standard tool applied to all designs. Although the Optimization Design process performs much of the grunt work by iteratively seeking an optimum solution, control of the design process remains in the engineer's hands. This means that the designer still makes decisions regarding what *variables* of a machine part are allowed to be altered, what *constraints* are to be applied to the design, and what overall *goals* the design is to satisfy. Each of these aspects of the optimization design process is explored in the following example.

Learning Objectives

Upon completion of this example, users should be able to:

- Select and define *variables* to be optimized during the design process.
- Specify and limit *constraints* (sensors) applied to the optimization process.
- Define desired *goals* (sensors) for the optimization process.
- *Set-up*, *run*, and *interpret results* of the optimization design process.
- Plot and interpret *Local Trend Graphs.*

Problem Statement

An **Alloy Steel** part is comprised of a 180 mm long cylindrical rod joined perpendicular to a rectangular bar of length 100 mm. Except for a 2 mm fillet between the cylinder and rectangle, additional dimensions of this part are shown in Fig. 1. This part might be viewed as an "L" shaped cantilever beam fixed at its right end. The goal of this example is to minimize weight of the part while subject to restraints and loads shown in Fig. 2.

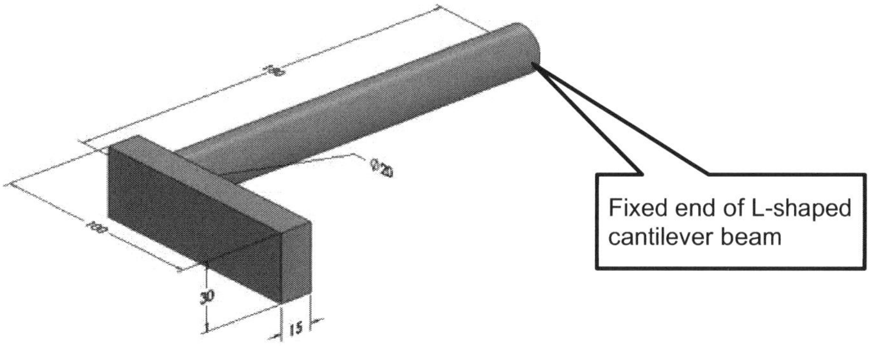

Figure 1 – Dimensioned view of the machine component named **L-Part**.

[1] The Optimization Design capability is available only in SOLIDWORKS Simulation Professional and SOLIDWORKS Simulation Premium. It is not included in basic SOLIDWORKS Simulation.

A SOLIDWORKS Simulation model of the **L-Part** and a portion of its Simulation Study are shown in Fig. 2. This example begins with a partially completed finite element model for two reasons. First, an *Initial Study* is *required* prior to initiating the optimization design process. And, second, beginning with a partially completed model allows us to focus attention on new topics rather than repeating topics mastered in previous chapters. Figure 2 shows a **Fixed** restraint applied on end **A** of cylindrical rod **AB** and a downward force of **775** N acting on the surface at end **C** of rectangular segment **BC**. Other information to be satisfied by the optimization design is that stress in the part must not exceed one-half of the material yield strength (S_y = 620.422e+6 N/m^2) and the maximum allowable part deflection must not exceed 2.50 mm.

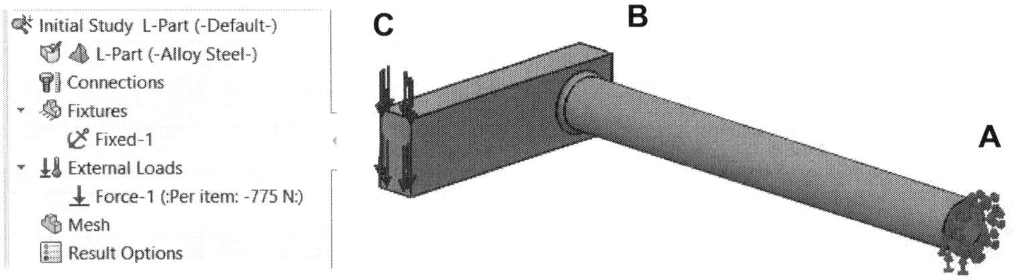

Figure 2 – Finite element model of the **L-Part** showing **Fixtures**, **External Loads** and the Simulation manager tree.

1. Open SOLIDWORKS by making the following selections. *(NOTE:* ">" is used to separate successive menu selections.)

   Start>All Programs>SOLIDWORKS 2026 (or) Click the **SOLIDWORKS** icon on your screen.

2. Within SOLIDWORKS, select **File > Open…** Then use procedures common to your computer environment to open the file named "**L-Part**," (***not:*** "L-Part 1-3").

Complete and Run the Initial Study

Begin by completing the *Initial Study*. An initial study serves as the basis, or starting point, for a subsequent design optimization study. It does this by calculating finite element results for the current part "as is" before any changes are made. Open the initial Simulation Study as follows.

1. On the Simulation Study *tab,* located *beneath* the graphics area, click the *tab* labeled **Initial Study L-Part**. This opens the partially completed Simulation Study. The model and Simulation manager tree should look similar to Fig. 2.

2. In the Simulation manager tree, verify that (a) the L-Part **Material** is specified as L-Part (-Alloy Steel-), (b) the **Fixtures** folder shows Fixed-1 and corresponding restraints appear on end **A** of the cylinder; and (c) the **External Loads** folder

shows ⊥ Force-1 (:Per item: -775 N:) and downward vectors appear at end **C** of the rectangular beam.

Design Insight

The 775 N **External Load** is *intentionally distributed* on the rectangular beam *face* at location **C**. A concentrated load applied to the top or bottom edge or to a split line on this face would cause a localized high stress region. If that stress exceeds one-half of the material yield strength, it might cause the design optimization solver to focus on it as a "false" upper stress value in the model. A possible consequence might result in design optimization at that location rather than optimize part dimensions to limit maximum stress throughout the entire model when the L-Part is taken as a whole.

3. On the **Simulation** tab near top of the screen, click the **Run This Study** Run This Study icon.

Upon completion of the run, the **Results** folder should list the three default plots [**Stress1 (-vonMises-)**, **Displacement1 (-Res disp-)**, and **Strain1 (-Equivalent-)**]. Before proceeding, a few alterations are made to the stress and displacement plots to set units and other display settings desired for these and future plots. Proceed on your own to incorporate SI units, discrete fringes, un-deformed model plots, label maximum stress, maximum displacement, and display legend values in scientific notation with three digits. If you make these changes on your own, skip to the **Observations- Design Optimization Considerations** text box (on page 8-5), otherwise follow the abbreviated steps below.

4. Right-click **Stress1 (-vonMises-)**, and from the pull-down menu select **Edit Definition…** The **Stress plot** property manager opens.

5. In the **Display** dialogue box change **Units** to **N/m^2** and remove the check "✓" from the ☐ **Deformed Shape** dialogue box.

6. Click to open the **Chart Options** tab.

7. In the **Display Options** dialogue box, check ☑ **Show max annotation**.

8. In the **Position/Format** dialogue box, click to open the ▼ **Number Format** XXX.XX X.Xe2 box and select XXX.XX X.Xe2 scientific **scientific** notation as the desired number format.

9. Immediately beneath the **Number Format** box, set the **No of Decimals** to **3**.

10. Click to open the **Settings** tab.

11. Change the **Fringe Options** dialogue box to **Discrete** (if not already selected).

12. Click **[OK]** ✓ to close the **Stress plot** property manager.

The von Mises stress plot should now look like that shown in Fig. 3.

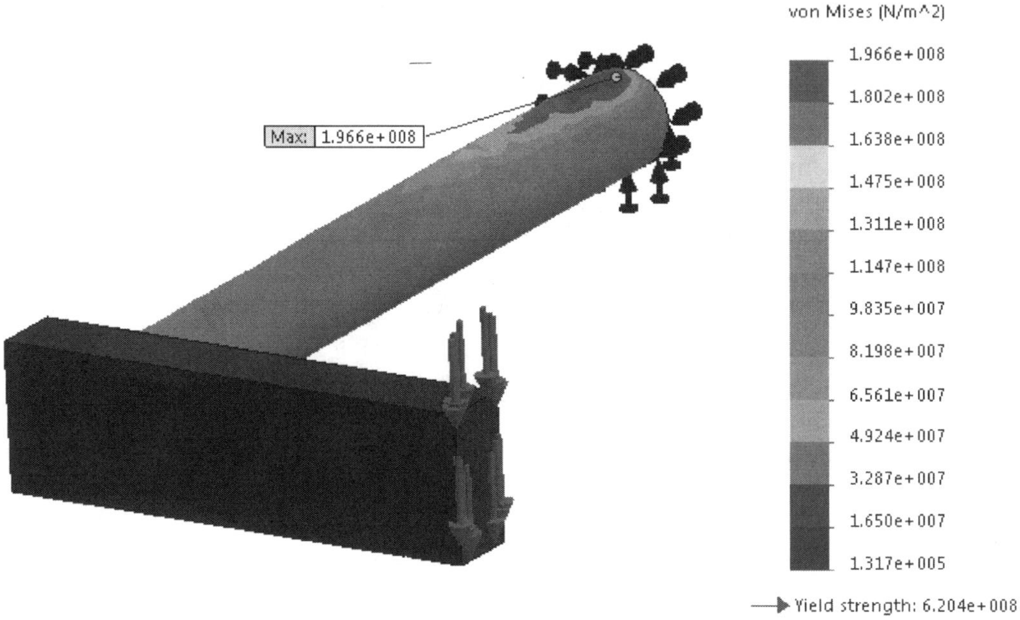

Figure 3 – Von Mises stress plot showing maximum stress occurs on the top surface near the fixed end. Results from the Initial Study.

The following steps are used to alter display of the displacement plot.

13. In the Simulation manager tree, right-click **Displacement1 (-Res disp-)**, and from the pull-down menu select **Show**.

14. Right-click **Displacement1 (-Res disp-)** again, and from the pull-down menu select **Edit Definition…** The **Displacement plot** property manager opens.

15. In the **Display** dialogue box change **Units** to **mm** and clear the check "✓" to turn off ☐ **Deformed Shape**.

16. Click to open the **Chart Options** tab.

17. In the **Display Options** dialogue box, check ☑ **Show max annotation**. Also, in the **Position/Format** dialogue box, verify that **scientific** notation with **No of Decimals** is set to **3**; if not, change them.

18. Click to open the **Settings** tab.

19. Change the **Fringe Options** dialogue box to **Discrete** (if not already selected).

20. Click **[OK]** ✓ to close the **Displacement plot** property manager. The displacement plot should now appear as shown in Fig. 4.

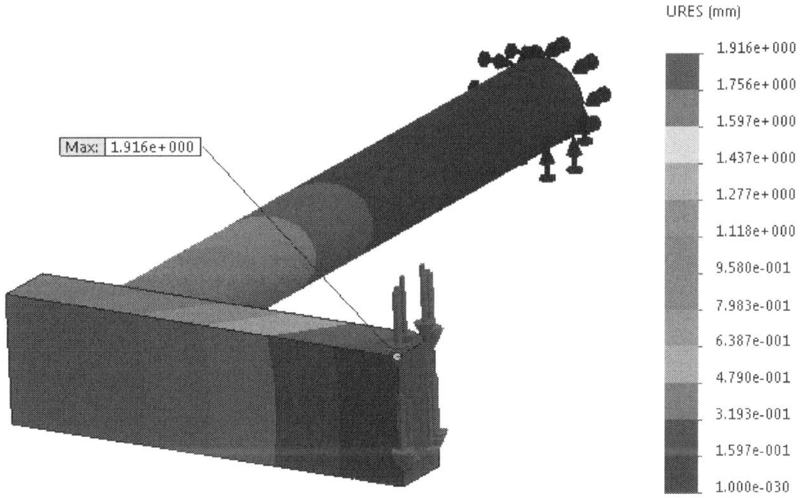

Figure 4 – Displacement plot results for the Initial Study of the L-Part.

Observations – Design Optimization Considerations

1. Figure 3 reveals a maximum von Mises stress in the part of 196.6 MPa. This stress value is only about 31.7% of the material yield strength. This magnitude indicates that the part may be overdesigned relative to stress magnitude.

2. The maximum displacement shown in Fig. 4 is 1.916 mm. Although this displacement might be excessive in some situations, the problem statement indicates that a 2.50 mm maximum displacement is permissible in this case. This observation also leads to the conclusion that part size may be reduced, thereby resulting in an increased deflection (displacement).

3. For simplicity, this example examines only the magnitude of **URES** (the maximum *resultant* displacement). However, in an actual machine application, specific displacements in the **X**, **Y**, and/or **Z** directions would probably be more meaningful to examine.

As stated earlier, an Initial Study serves as the basis for an Optimization Design Study by providing a starting point (i.e., an estimate of initial values) for the iterative design process. Because magnitudes of both stress and displacement are found in the Study completed above, it is the only Initial Study needed. However, if thermal and vibration effects also influence the outcome of this part design, then two additional Initial Studies are needed. One study would be needed to establish *initial* thermal effects on the part (because expansion or contraction influence part displacement) and a second *Initial Study* is needed to determine a baseline natural frequency (f_n) for the part (because f_n would affect part displacement), and hence part dimensions and mass may also change.

Because neither thermal nor vibration aspects are investigated in this text, they are not included in the current example. However, be aware that depending upon optimization goals, additional initial studies might be required.

After the Initial Study has been run, the next step is to set up an optimization Study. The following section introduces steps unique to the Optimization Design process.

Creating an Optimization Design Study

Because of its importance when determining the Variables, Constraints, and Goals needed to set up this problem, the optimization design goal is restated here.

DESIGN GOAL: To ***minimize weight*** of the **L-Part**.

1. Beneath the graphics area, right-click the Simulation Study *tab* labeled **Initial Study L-Part**, and from the pop-up menu select **Create New Design Study**. The lower portion of the graphics area changes to that shown in Fig. 5.

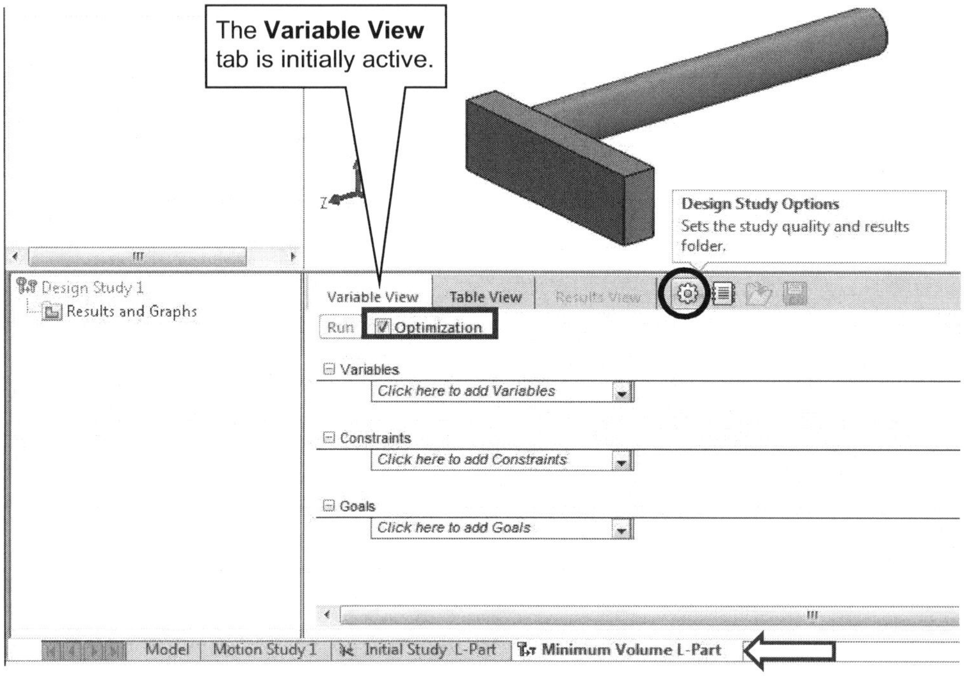

Figure 5 – Appearance of bottom of the screen upon launch of an Optimization Design Study. The current figure shows contents of the **Variable View** tab.

2. Just below the **Variable View** tab, click to select the ☑ **Optimization** check box (if not already selected) shown boxed in Fig. 5. NOTE: Only the **Variable View** optimization tab is demonstrated in this example because it is the most commonly used approach for optimization design studies.

3. At the bottom of the screen, see arrow on Fig. 5, right-click the **Design Study 1** tab, and from the pop-up menu select **Rename**. Then type **Minimum Volume L-Part** and press **[Enter]**. This action creates a more descriptive Study name.

4. Next, click the **Design Study Options** icon circled in Fig. 5. The **Design Study Properties** manager opens as shown in Fig. 6.

5. Within the **Design Study Quality** dialogue box, select ⊙ **High quality (slower)**. This approach selects a more refined iterative solver that takes more time to solve but yields better results.

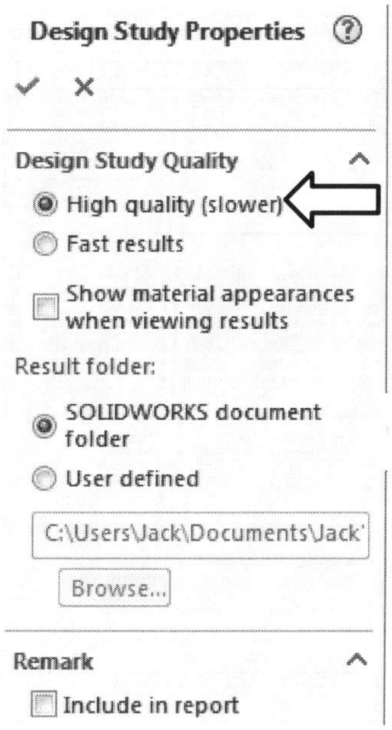

Figure 6 – Specifying **quality** of the optimization scheme.

Solution time depends on:

- Quality of the design study (selected in step 5).
- Complexity of model geometry.
- The number of variables, constraints, and goals to be optimized.
- The number of Simulation Studies to be run for each iteration. Each *initial* study requires its own optimization design study.
- The mesh size used in the Simulation Study.

6. Make no other changes in this property manager and click **[OK]** ✓ to close it.

Understanding Optimization Design Terminology

Before setting up the Optimization Design it is helpful to develop an understanding of terminology associated with this type of Study. The terms to be defined include **Variables**, **Constraints**, **Goals**, and **sensors**. All of these terms, except **sensors**, are listed in the design study area located at the bottom left of your screen and repeated in Fig. 7. A definition of terms and an overview telling how they apply to this example follows.

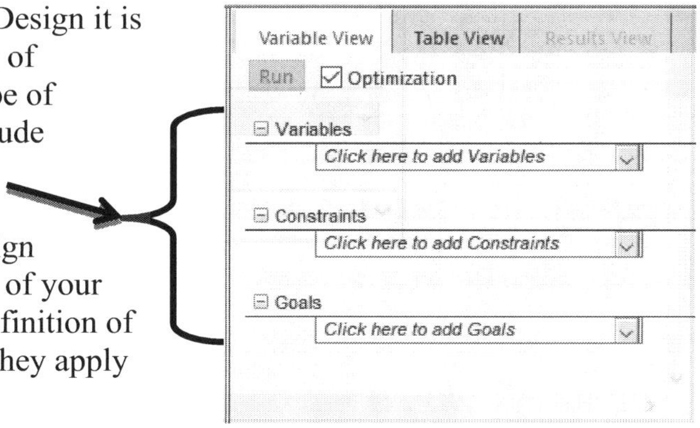

Figure 7 – Area of the optimization design table where variables, constraints, goals and sensors are defined.

- **Variables** – As implied by the name, variables are items that are allowed to change within the software as it attempts to find an optimal solution to a problem.
  EXAMPLE – **Variables** identified
  For the current example it is assumed that lengths of the cylindrical rod **AB** and the rectangular member **BC** (see Fig. 8), as well as the fillet radius and location of attachment between the cylindrical rod and the rectangular segment, *cannot* be changed. Thus, the only remaining dimensions that can be varied during the optimization process are **width** = 15 mm and **height** = 30 mm of rectangular member **BC** and the **diameter** = 20 mm of cylindrical rod **AB** labeled in Fig. 8.

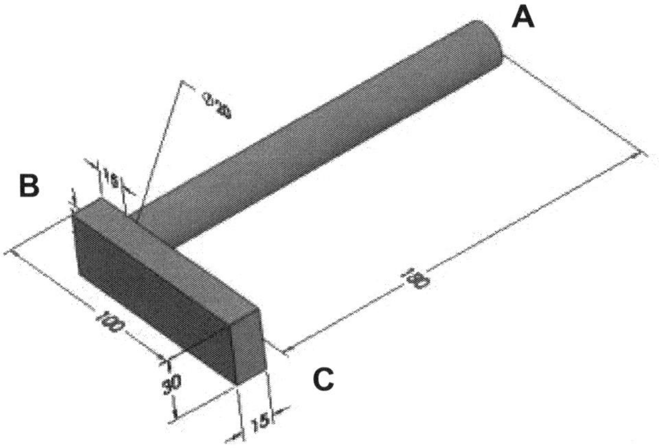

Figure 8 – Basic dimensions applied to the **L-Part**.

- **Constraints** – Constraints are used to specify conditions that the final design must satisfy. As such, constraints are measurable quantities that are monitored during the optimization process. Each **Constraint** whose magnitude is monitored is assigned a **sensor** to track that item's value. (**Sensors** are defined last.)

  EXAMPLE – **Constraints** identified
  The original problem statement included two constraints that are re-stated here. They are (1) stress in the part must not exceed one-half of the material yield strength (S_y = 620.422e+6 N/m^2), and (2) the maximum allowable part deflection must not exceed 2.50 mm. The final design must satisfy these two constraints.

- **Goals** – Goals are used to specify the objective(s) of an Optimization Design Study. As such, goals are also measurable quantities and therefore **sensors** are needed to monitor values specified for each goal.

  EXAMPLE – **Goals** identified
  The goal of the current example is to minimize weight of the part. Note, however, that because the entire part is made of the same material, minimizing part weight is analogous to minimizing part volume.

- **Sensors** – Sensors are *quantifiable* items, such as **Constraints** and **Goals**, that are calculated and assigned numerical values during each iteration of the optimization process. As such, **sensors** are applied to monitor these values to ensure that they remain within the limits defined for **Constraints** and **Goals**. **Sensors** described in the following paragraph must be applied to the current model.

EXAMPLE – **Sensors** identified

- A **sensor** is required to monitor magnitude of von Mises stress so that it does not exceed one-half of the material yield strength.
- A **sensor** is required to monitor part displacement (deflection) so that it does not exceed the maximum specified deflection of 2.50 mm.
- A **sensor** is required to monitor part volume during each step of the optimization process to ensure that a minimum value is achieved.

Given an understanding of these definitions, the optimization design Study begins below.

Selecting and Specifying Design Parameters (Variables)

As previously noted, the goal of this optimization design study is to minimize weight of the L-Part. This goal intuitively leads to determination of the variables that are to be altered during the optimization process. Because the entire part is made from the same material (Alloy Steel), it is reasonable to assume that part weight is proportional to part volume. Hence, *dimensions* of the part are selected as **Variables** to be minimized in this example.

The preceding statement would not be true if, for example, the part were made from two different materials (say steel and aluminum) where mass densities of the two different materials would play a role in minimizing overall part weight. In that case mass density rather than volume would be selected for minimization.

We begin by defining the **Variables** to be used in the optimization design process.

1. On the currently active **Variable View** *tab*, beneath **Variables**, open the pull-down menu labeled ***Click here to add Variables*** ▼ shown at the arrow in Fig. 9.

2. From the pull-down menu, select ***Add Parameter…*** This action opens the **Parameters** window shown in Fig. 10.

   Also notice that dimensions appear on the model after this selection is made. In the graphics area, click-and-drag to re-position either the **Parameters** window or the **L-Part** so that both can be seen.

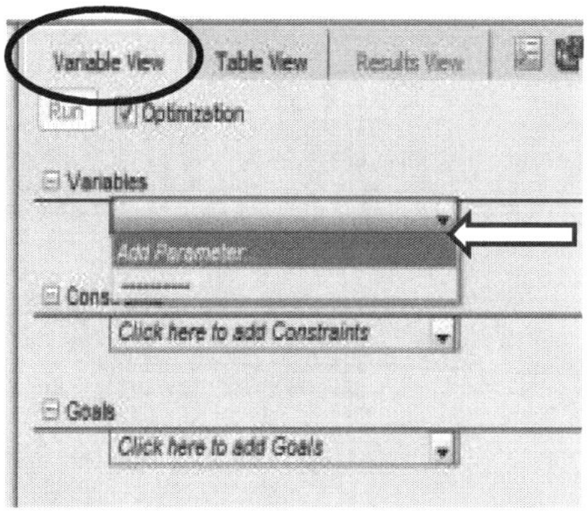

Figure 9 – Access to pull-down menus for adding **Variables**, **Constraints**, and **Goals**.

3. Within the **Parameters** window, click in the field beneath **Name** and type **Width**.

4. Also in the **Parameters** window, beneath **Category**, verify that **Model Dimension** appears. If not, open the pull-down menu ▼ and select it.

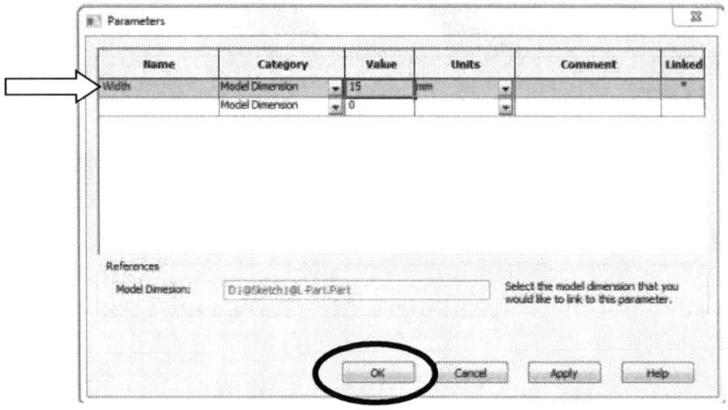

Figure 10 – Specifying a dimension as a **Variable** during the Optimization Design process.

5. Next, in the graphics area, rotate and zoom-in on the model to select the **15** mm *Width* dimension of the rectangular cross section shown at **#1** in Fig. 11. Immediately the **15** mm dimension is entered in the **Value** column and **(mm)** appear beneath the **Units** heading.

*The **Dimension** property manager may also open on your screen. If so, ignore it until later.*

6. Click **[OK]** at bottom of the **Parameters** window to close it. The *Width* **Variable** now appears in the design table as circled and indicated by the arrow in Fig. 11.

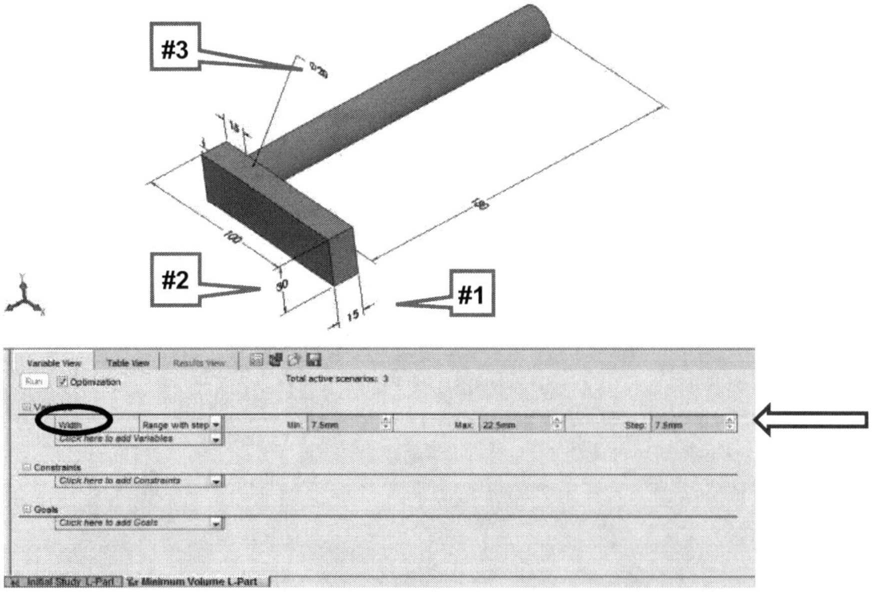

Figure 11 – Selection of part dimensions as **Variables** and listing of the **Width** variable in the Optimization Design field.

7. Repeat steps 1 through 6, except in step 3 type **Height** into the *second row* beneath the **Name** column of the **Parameters** window. Then proceed to select the **30** mm dimension labeled **#2** on the model in Fig. 11. Immediately its **Value** and **Units** are entered in the table. Click **[OK]** to close the **Parameters** window.

8. Repeat steps 1 through 6 a third time, except in step 3 type **Diameter** into the *third row* beneath the **Name** column. Then proceed to select the **Φ20** mm dimension on the model labeled **#3** in Fig. 11. Again its **Value** and **Units** appear in the table. Click **[OK]** to close the **Parameters** window.

At this point all three design **Variables** have been selected.

9. *If the **Dimension** property manager opened between steps 5 and 6, notice it is not used during the **Variable** definition process.* Thus, click **[OK]** to close it at this time.

The Optimization Design table should now appear as shown in Fig. 12. *If it does not*, a variation of the above procedure might have been used.[2] In that case, open the pull-down menu labeled **Click here to add Variables ▼**, and select the items listed there (**Height**, and **Diameter**) to display them in the design table.

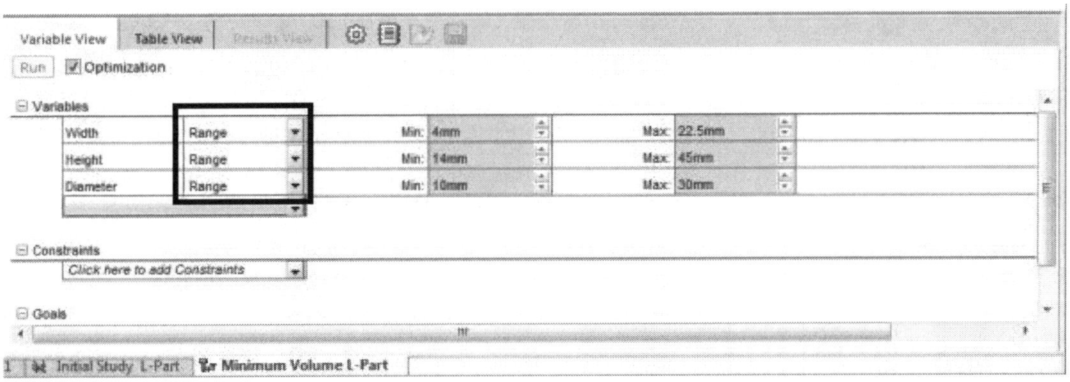

Figure 12 – The **Width**, **Height**, and **Diameter Variables** as they originally appear in the Optimization Design field.

Several observations about the **Variables** section of the optimization design table are made on the following page. Refer to the image on your screen while reviewing these observations.

---

[2] It is also possible to enter all variables (**Width**, **Height**, and **Diameter**) one line at a time without exiting the **Parameters** window. If that approach is used, it is necessary to execute the step in the sentence following footnote number 2 located just above Fig. 12. However, to maintain correspondence with remaining steps outlined in this chapter, it is suggested that **Width**, **Height**, and **Diameter** be selected in the order listed.

Observations

Begin by opening ▼ any of the drop down menus shown boxed in Fig. 12. The drop down menu is repeated in the figure at right. This menu reveals that three different approaches can be used to search for an optimum design. Of these, the **Range with Step** and **Discrete Values** approaches are described below along with examples of their use. The **Range** approach is later applied to the current Study and its use becomes apparent there.

Range with Step -

- All variables are originally listed as **Range with Step**. The **Range with Step** approach is useful when seeking minimum, maximum, and mid-range values over a specified optimization range. The software automatically suggests **Min:**, **Max:**, and **Step:** values according to the following equations.

$$\text{Step} = \frac{\text{(original dimension)}}{2}$$

$$\text{Min.} = \text{(original dimension) - Step}$$

$$\text{Max.} = \text{(original dimension)} + \text{Step}$$

However, the user is free to substitute other values for **Min:**, **Max:**, and **Step:** by typing new values into the appropriate fields shown in Fig. 12. (See current values for **Width** listed in the **Variables** section of the table on your screen.) For **Width** = 15mm, the default optimization study would be run for values of **Min:** = 7.5mm, **Max:** = 22.5mm, and **Step:** size = 7.5mm yielding optimization results corresponding to widths of 7.5mm, 15.0mm, and 22.5mm. *Only these three values would be evaluated.* Units must be included with all values. The designer is free to alter the **Step** size to investigate other discrete increments

Discrete Values

- A second option in the drop-down menu is **Discrete Values**; select it now to view the resulting field. If this option were selected, the user would type each value and its units separated by a comma. For example, the following values might be entered as possible rod diameters to be investigated: 0.1875in, 0.250in, 0.3125in, 0.375in, etc. This approach is useful where a *standard size* steel bar is sought. NOTE: The above values each differ by 1/16 inch increments.

Why might a user choose the **Discrete Values** option? Because steel bars are available in standard *discrete* sizes such as 1/16 inch increments for sizes from 3/16 inch diameter up to 5/8 inch diameter, at which point standard bar diameters increase by 1/8 inch increments for rod sizes up to 1¼ inches in diameter. Thus, conducting a design optimization using **Discrete Values** is a useful approach in situations like that described here where standard part sizes are available.

For the current example we apply use of the **Range** option as outlined next.

10. Open ▼ the pull-down menu adjacent to **Width** and from the pull-down menu select **Range**. The **Range** option allows *continuous* variable values (i.e., any value) between a specified minimum and maximum. It is not limited to a specific step size nor is it limited to discrete values as described in the **Observations** text-box on the previous page.

When using the **Range** option, observe that the software-selected **Min:** and **Max:** values are initially the same as previously specified for the **Range with Step** approach. However, **Min:** and **Max:** values can be changed according to the designer's preference. Proceed as follows. Changing the **Min:** value is demonstrated in the next step.

11. Adjacent to **Width**, type **4.0mm** as the new **Min:** value and leave the **Max:** value as specified at **22.5mm**. *Be sure to include units.*

Design Insight

Why might a designer choose a lower value for **Width** of the rectangular segment of the L-Part? Recall the equation below for moment of inertia **I** for a rectangular cross-section subject to bending such as occurs in segment **BC** of the L-Part.

$$I = \frac{bh^3}{12}$$

Where: **Height** (**h^3**) has a greater effect on **I** than does **Width** (**b**) of a rectangle.

Because the goal of this optimization is to minimize weight (volume) of the part, and because a larger moment of inertia is associated with the **Height** dimension *(cubed)* relative to the 775 N downward force, it follows that less resistance to bending in the vertical plane is realized due to part **Width**. Therefore, a lower limit is selected for the **Min: Width** dimension with the hope that that part volume can be minimized smaller than would result corresponding to the software selected **Min:** value of 7.5mm.

12. Adjacent to the **Height** variable, select **Range** from the ▼ pull-down menu.

13. Next, change the **Min:** value to **14mm** and leave the **Max:** value as specified at **45mm**.

Why make this small change from 15mm to 14mm? Looking ahead to the **Diameter** variable, its **Min:** value is currently listed as 10mm. Therefore, *if* the optimization design process determines that cylinder diameter can be reduced to 10mm, then the smallest **Height** dimension should not be less than 14 mm based on the following calculation.

Min: Height = (10mm cylinder diameter) + (2mm fillet radius x 2) = 14mm

Thus, 14mm would correspond to the minimum **Height** allowable to permit a full 2mm fillet radius around the entire 10mm cylinder where it joins rectangular segment **BC**. Recall, the fillet radius is *not* selected as a design **Variable**.

14. For the **Diameter** variable, select **Range** from the ▼ pull-down menu. However, make no changes to either **Min:** or **Max:** values. The **Variable** table should now look like Fig. 13.

⊟ Variables					
Width	Range	Min:	4mm	Max:	22.5mm
Height	Range	Min:	14mm	Max:	45mm
Diameter	Range	Min:	10mm	Max:	30mm
Click here to add Variables					

Figure 13 – Completed **Variable** table for the **L-Part** Optimization Design example.

Define Constraints and their Sensors

Although it is probably unnecessary, it is worth emphasizing that **Constraints** are *not* the same as Restraints. Restraints refer to **Fixtures** used to anchor or attach parts and assemblies to other segments of a machine, structure, hinge joint, or base, etc. Whereas **Constraints** are measurable quantities used to specify conditions that the final, optimized design must satisfy. The two constraints identified for the current example are (1) the maximum von Mises stress must not exceed one-half of the material yield strength, and (2) the maximum resultant displacement of any point on the model must not exceed 2.5mm. Next proceed to define these constraints and their sensors.

Define the Stress Constraint and Sensor

1. On the **Variable View** *tab* in the optimization table, beneath **Constraints,** click ▼ to open the pull-down menu labeled ***Click here to add Constraints*** ▼. From the pull-down menu, select ***Add Sensor…*** The **Sensor** property manager opens as shown in Fig. 14 but does not initially look like Fig. 14.

2. In the **Sensor Type** dialogue box, select **Simulation Data** from the pull-down menu.

3. Within the **Data Quantity** dialogue box, in the **Results** field, select **Stress** as the item to be monitored (if not already selected), and in the **Component** field select **VON: von Mises Stress** as the specific stress to be monitored (if not already selected).

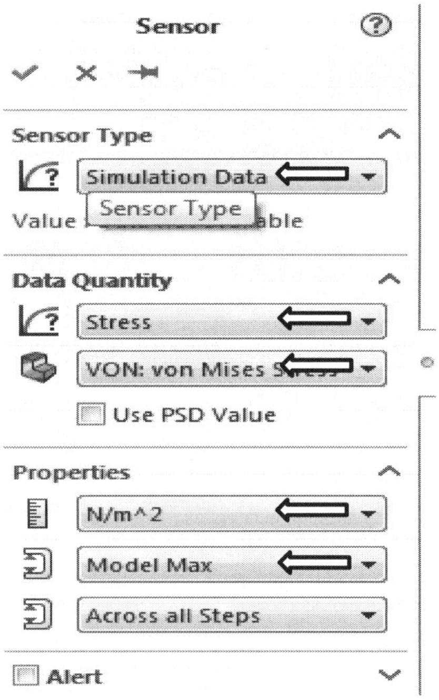

Figure 14 – Defining the stress **Constraint** applied to the optimization design process.

4. In the **Properties** dialogue box under **Units**, select **N/m^2** and for the **Criterion** field choose **Model Max** (if not already selected).

5. Click **[OK]** ✓ to close the **Sensor** property manager. **Stress1** is listed beneath the **Constraints** section in the design optimization table.

Design Insight

You might be asking, *"Why is **Simulation Data** selected as the **Sensor Type**?"*

Because stress magnitude is to be no more than half of the material yield strength and because stress is calculated in a Simulation Study, **Simulation Data** is monitored as the source for this stress magnitude during the optimization process. Model displacement is also a result calculated in SOLIDWORKS Simulation; thus, **Simulation Data** is also specified to monitor displacement as outlined next.

Define the Displacement Constraint and Sensor

1. Beneath **Constraints**, again click ▼ to open the pull-down menu labeled ***Click here to add Constraints*** ▼. From the pull-down menu, select ***Add Sensor…*** The **Sensor** property manager opens.

2. In the **Sensor Type** dialogue box, once again select **Simulation Data** from the pull-down menu.

3. In the **Data Quantity** dialogue box, open ▼ the **Results** pull-down menu and select **Displacement** as the item to be monitored. Also, from the **Component** pull-down menu select **URES: Resultant Displacement** as the specific item to be monitored.

Aside: If, for example, only the vertical (Y-displacement) were important, then it could have been selected in the previous step.

4. In the **Properties** dialogue box under **Units**, select **mm**, and for the **Criterion** field choose **Model Max** (if not already selected).

5. Click **[OK]** ✓ to close the **Sensor** property manager and **Displacement1** is listed beneath the **Constraints** section in the optimization table shown in Fig. 15.

Stress and displacement are the only two constraints stated for the L-Part model. Thus, turn your attention to the right half of the optimization table to define limiting values for these **Constraints**.

6. In the drop down menu ▼ adjacent to **Stress1**, shown boxed in Fig. 15, select "**Is less than**." And, adjacent to **Max:** type *half* the value of the material yield strength. That value is[3]:

$$\tfrac{1}{2} * S_y = \tfrac{1}{2} * 620422000 = 310211000 \text{ N/m\^{}2} = 3.10213\text{e+8 N/m\^{}2}$$

7. In the drop down menu adjacent to **Displacement1**, select "**Is less than**." And, adjacent to **Max:** type **2.5mm**. The **Constraints** portion of the optimization table should now look like Fig. 15.

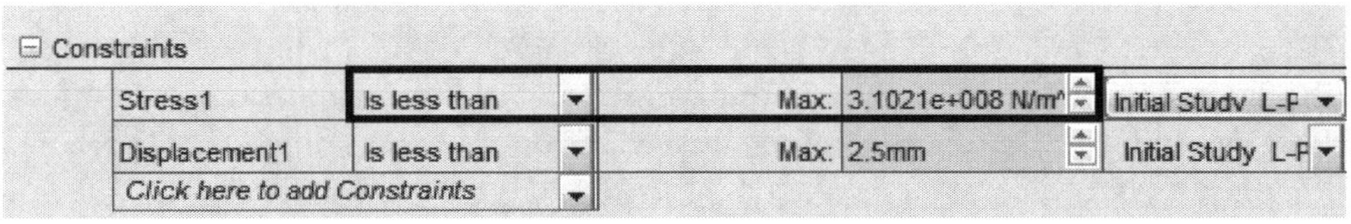

Figure 15 – Completed **Constraint** table for the **L-Part** Optimum Design example.

8. Near the top of the SOLIDWORKS feature manager tree, click the "▶" symbol adjacent to **Sensors**. In Fig. 16 and on your screen, note the values listed adjacent to the **Sensors** for **Stress1** and **Displacement1**. These values were computed during the *Initial Study*. (Values may vary slightly.)

   In the event these values do not appear and an information symbol ⓘ appears instead, "*not to* worry." This is due to an occasional glitch observed when this information is accessed for the *first* time. These values will be revisited later in this example when they appear elsewhere in the display.

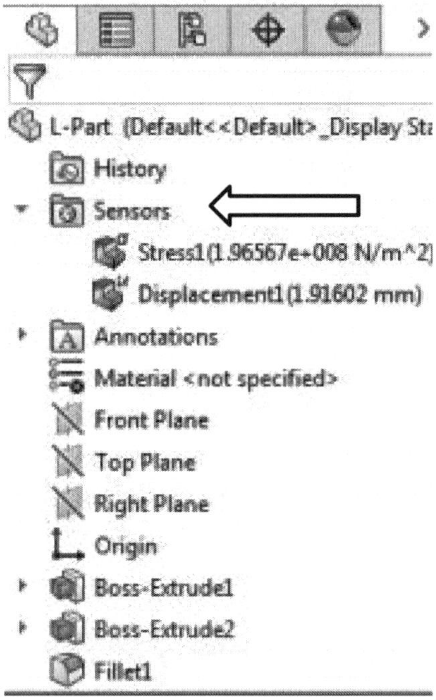

Figure 16 – **Sensors** and their original values calculated during the Initial Study.

Recall that values from the *Initial Study* form the starting point from which to run and track sensor values during subsequent optimization design studies.

---

[3] Yield Strength shown is that for **Alloy Steel** as listed in the **Material** window when the *Initial Study* was defined.

Define a Goal and its Sensor

Although only a single **Goal** is specified in this example, it is important to note that multiple goals can be specified. When multiple goals are used, it is also possible to apply "weights" for each goal, where a higher weight assigns more importance to that goal during the optimization process.

The optimization design goal, namely to *minimize part volume*, has been stated several times throughout this example. Implementation of this step is outlined next.

1. Scroll down to the **Goals** section at bottom of the design optimization table, and select ***Click here to add Goals*** ▼ and from the pull-down menu select ***Add Sensor…*** The **Sensor** property manager opens as shown in Fig. 17.

2. In the **Sensor Type** dialogue box, select **Mass Properties** from the pull-down menu (if not already selected).

3. Next, within the **Properties** dialogue box, select **Volume** from the pull-down menu. In this example, part *volume* is synonymous with its weight.

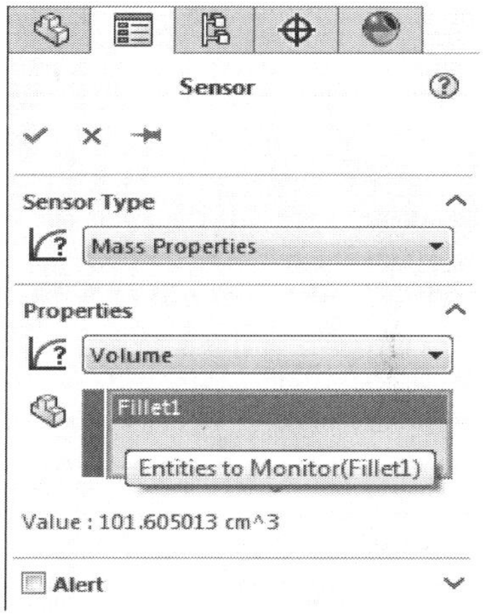

Figure 17 – Defining the design optimization Goal and its sensor.

4. Finally, observe the **Entities to Monitor** field (highlighted light blue). *If* **Fillet1** does not appear there, then move the cursor *anywhere* on the **L-Part** model and click to select it as the item to be monitored for minimum volume.

It may seem ridiculous that **Fillet1** appears in the **Entities to Monitor** field. But, in this case, **Fillet1** is selected by the software because it was the last feature added when the model was built in SOLIDWORKS. Verify this by referring to the bottom of the SOLIDWORKS feature manager tree, or flyout menu, where **Fillet1** is listed. *This entry does not imply that only volume of the fillet will be monitored and/or minimized.*

5. Click **[OK]** ✓ to close the **Sensor** property manager and **Volume1** is listed beneath the **Goals** section of the design optimization table.

6. Also beneath the **Goals** section, verify that **Minimize** appears next to **Volume1**. If not, click ▼ to open the pull-down menu and select **Minimize**. Briefly examine other optimization criteria available in this drop down menu.

7. Within the SOLIDWORKS feature manager, observe that the total volume of the original (initial) **L-Part** appearing as 101.605013 cm^3 is now listed beneath the **Sensors** folder. Clearly this is the entire part volume, not just the fillet volume.

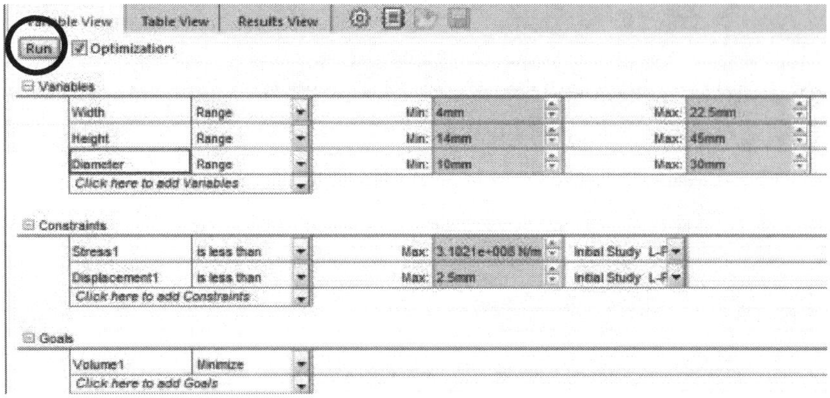

Figure 18 – Select the **[Run]** button to begin the Optimization Design study.

The Optimization Design Study is completely defined and ready to execute. The **[Run]** button, located just beneath the **Variable View** tab, is now active (no longer grayed-out).

8. Click to select the **[Run]** button circled in Fig. 18.

As the Design Optimization process executes, direct your attention to model images displayed on the screen. Then, continue reading below.

The optimization process steps through 13 iterations (15 iterations if the Initial Study and the final **Optimal** design scenario are included). The number of iterations is proportional to the number of design **Variables**. As the optimization proceeds, **Iteration** columns are added to tabulated results beneath the graphics screen while images of each model are briefly displayed in the graphics area. Notice that part geometry associated with some iterations is undesirable or invalid based on the practical desire to have a complete fillet between mating parts; see circled area in Fig. 19.

Figure 19 – Undesirable results due to mis-match of sizes. (Iteration 2)

Results are reviewed below to gain further insight into the findings.

Overview of Results

We begin by making some general observations applicable to all results displayed on the final screen and in the Optimization Design table (located beneath the graphics area). First, notice that results are displayed in the **Results View** tab rather than the **Variable View** tab where this study was defined. Also, it is assumed that most monitors are not wide enough to display all 13 iterations simultaneously. Therefore, results only up to **Iteration 6** are shown in Fig. 20 (more are displayed on wide screen monitors). To see additional iterations, click-and-drag the horizontal scroll bar located beneath the table.

General Observations

1. To display results of a particular iteration, click the **Iteration** *name* located at the top of each column. Example: **Iteration 1**, **Iteration 2**, **...** etc. The image shown in Fig. 20 is that of the **Optimal** solution. Its name is circled in Fig. 20. The **Optimal** solution column is highlighted light green.

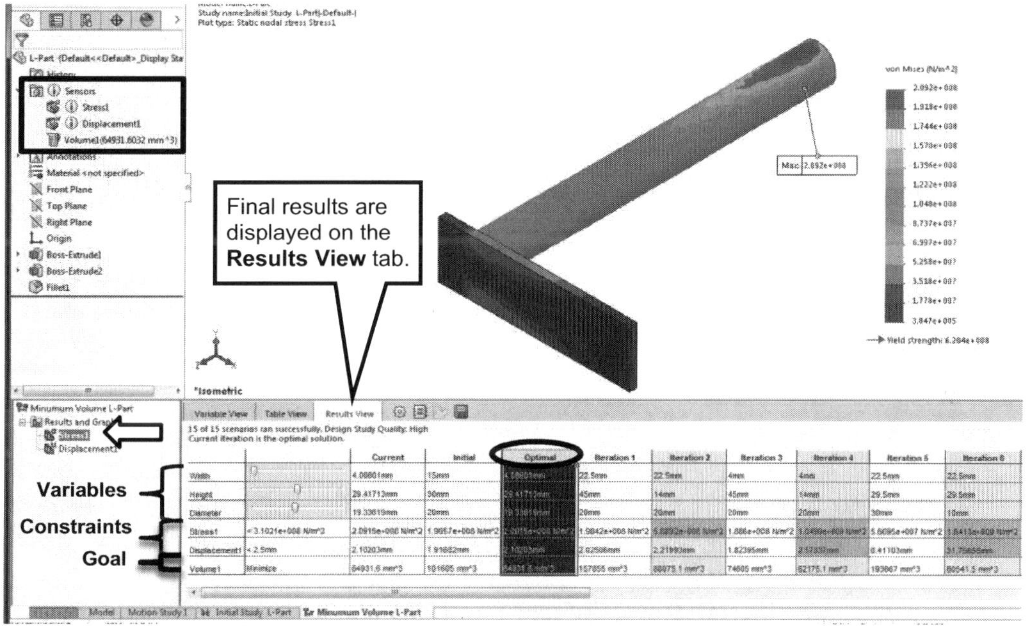

Figure 20 - Table summarizing results of the first six iterations of the optimization design process for the **L-Part**.

2. To the left of the **Optimal** column are listed results of the **Initial Study** and the **Current** column. As implied by its name, the **Current** column contains the same results as those in the currently selected column.

3. At the far left of the optimization table part dimensions (**Width**, **Height**, and **Diameter**) are displayed as sliders showing current sizes relative to the design **Range**. These sliders can be moved to update the model (*not recommended until you become proficient using optimization studies*). Also shown are the original **Constraints (Stress1** and **Displacement1**) and the optimization **Goal (Volume1**).

4. Design constraint plots for **Stress1** and **Displacement1** can be displayed in the graphics area by clicking "▶" to open the **Results and Graphs** folder (see arrow at lower left of Fig. 20). Then, double click the desired plot name. For example: Fig. 20 shows the **von Mises** stress plot corresponding to the **Optimal** solution.

5. **Sensors**, shown boxed in the SOLIDWORKS feature manager at the top left of Fig. 20, are updated to show the currently displayed **Volume1**. Note that **Stress1** and **Displacement1 Sensors** are indicated by an information ⓘ symbol only. Refer to the optimization table for current values of these two **Variables**.

6. All columns highlighted in light-red (or "pink") indicate cases where one or both of the design **Constraints** is violated. The darker red cells in these columns indicate the specific **Constraint(s)** violated. For example, in **Iteration 2** the **Stress1 Constraint** is violated (because actual **Stress1** > ½*Yield Strength). The maximum stress is also exceeded in several other iterations. However, in **Iterations 4**, **6**, **8**, **10**, and **12** both the **Stress1** and **Displacement1 Constraints** are violated because actual **Stress1** > ½*Yield Strength > (3.102e+008 N/m^2) and **Displacement1** > 2.50 mm. Scroll to the right in the optimization table and examine **Iterations** that violate one or both **Constraints.**

7. Click the **Iteration** *name* at top of any of the red columns to display the model and corresponding **Stress1** or **Displacement1** plots.

8. **Iteration** columns highlighted in light gray satisfy all **Constraints**. However, those solutions do not satisfy the design **Goal** which results in *minimum volume* for the L-Part.

Local Trend Graphs

A series of Trend Graphs can be plotted at the conclusion of an Optimization Design Study. A trend graph displays either the **Goal** or a **Constraint** with respect to a design **Variable**. Alternatively, a trend graph can display variation of a **Constraint** relative to a selected design **Variable**. Examples of each are illustrated on the following pages. NOTE: **Local Trend Graphs** are not available when *discrete* variables and a **High Quality** study are selected.

Local Trend Graph of the Design Goal versus a Design Variable

Begin by examining a typical graph showing the relationship between a design **Variable**, in this case cylindrical rod diameter, and the design **Goal** (the "Objective") which is to minimize part volume. Proceed as follows.

1. To the left of the tabulated results, right-click **Results and Graphs**, and from the pull-down menu select **Define Local Trend Graph…** The **Local Trend Graph** property manager opens as shown in Fig. 21(a).

2. In the **Design variables (X-Axis)** dialogue box, select **Diameter** from the pull-down menu as the variable to be displayed on the graph X-axis.

3. In the **Y-Axis** dialogue box, select ⊙ **Objective**, then from the pull-down menu select **Volume1**.

Notice that **Volume1** is the *only* choice available. This is because, in SOLIDWORKS Simulation jargon, the design **Goal** (in this case minimum volume) is also named the "**Objective**" of the design optimization process. The **Local trend at** dialogue box should show the **Optimal** solution as currently selected; if not, change it.

4. Click **[OK]** ✓ to close the **Local Trend Graph** property manager and the graph shown in Fig. 21(b) appears.

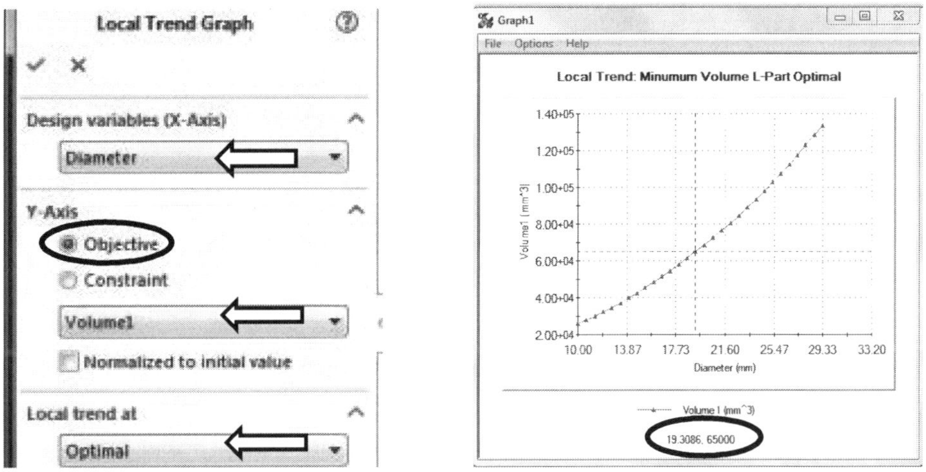

(a) (b)

Figure 21 – Definition of a **Local Trend Graph** showing the relationship between cylinder diameter (a **Variable**) and part volume (the **Objective** or **Goal**) of this optimization study.

Observations

a. Figure 21(b) reveals the full **Range** of possible rod diameters [10mm ≤ **Range** ≤ 30mm (approx.)]. In Fig. 21(b), the cursor was moved into the graph and intersecting horizontal and vertical dashed lines automatically appear.

b. At the intersection point, *approximate* values of the *optimum* cylinder **Diameter** (19.31 mm, rounded value) and *minimum* part **Volume** (65500 mm^3, also a rounded value) occur. See circled values beneath the graph.

c. Similar graphs of **Height** vs **Volume** or **Width** vs **Volume** can be made.

d. Software default captions appear for the graph title and axis labels in Fig. 21(b). Titles can be altered as outlined in Chapter 1.

5. Click ☒ to close the current graph. Notice that **Graph1** is now listed beneath the **Results and Graphs** folder in the Simulation manager tree.

Local Trend Graph of a Constraint versus a Design Variable

Next examine a typical graph showing the relationship between a design **Variable** and a design **Constraint**. The design **Variables** remain the same as above (**Height**, **Width**, and **Diameter**). However, the **Constraints** applied to the model include a maximum **Stress1** value and a maximum **Displacement1** value. Proceed as follows to examine one of these graphs.

1. Right-click **Results and Graphs**, and from the pull-down menu select **Define Local Trend Graph…** The **Local Trend Graph** property manager opens as shown in Fig. 22(a).

2. In the **Design variables (X-Axis)** dialogue box, select **Height** from the pull-down menu. Note that either of the remaining two variables (**Width**, or **Diameter**) also could be selected.

3. In the **Y-Axis** dialogue box, select ⊙ **Constraint**, then from the pull-down menu select **Displacement1**. It is also possible to select **Stress1** if it is of primary interest.

4. The **Local Trend at** dialogue box should show the **Optimal** solution as currently selected; if not, change it.

5. Click **[OK]** ✓ to close the property manager and the graph shown in Fig. 22(b) appears.

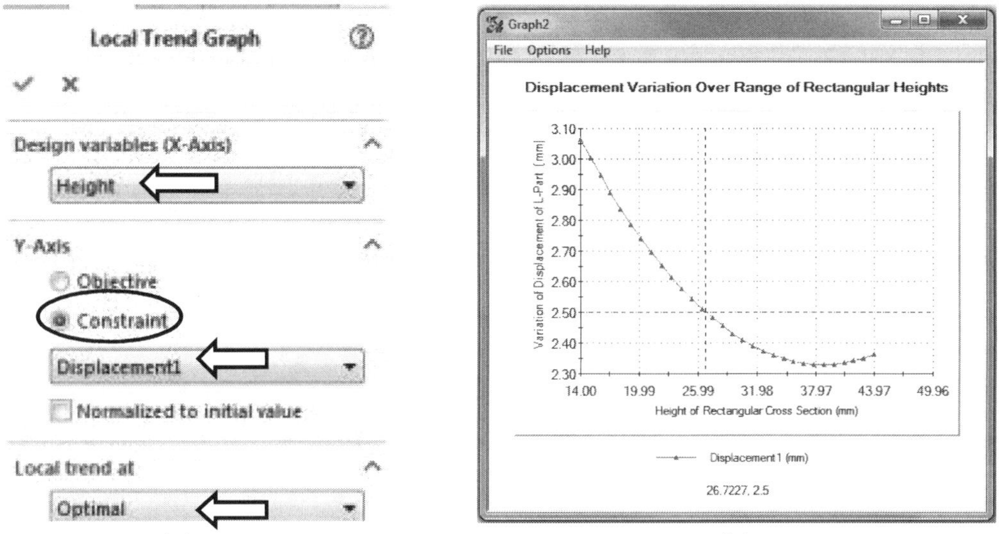

(a) (b)

Figure 22 - Definition of a **Local Trend Graph** showing the relationship between **Height** of the rectangle (a **Variable**) and **Displacement1** (a **Constraint**) applied to the part. Values are plotted for all iterations necessary to find an optimum design.

The **Local Trend Graph** plots variation of **Displacement1** with respect to **Height** of the rectangular beam section. In general, the graph in Fig. 22 (b) reveals that as beam height increases, the maximum displacement decreases up to approximately **Height** = 37.97 mm. Above this value, displacement components, due to twisting of the model, may contribute to increasing the *resultant* displacement.

Observations

a. Intersecting dashed lines are located at the approximate intersection of the *maximum* **Displacement** (2.50 mm, rounded value) and the *corresponding* part **Height** value (26.7 mm, rounded value). (Values may vary.) Because maximum displacement occurs at a height less than the **Optimal** height, it is evident that other design constraints limit optimization of this design.

b. All displacement values to the left of or above the dashed lines correspond to displacement magnitudes that exceed the **Constraint** which is limited to **Displacement1** < 2.50 mm.

c. The **Local Trend Graph** of Fig. 22(b) plots the variation of **Displacement** with respect to **Height** of the rectangular member. **Local Trend Graphs** assume the other two design variables (**Width**, and **Diameter**) are set to their optimum values as shown in the **Optimal** design scenario column.

d. A custom title and axis labels are added to Fig. 22(b) using procedures outlined in Chapter 1.

e. Although not investigated here, if *discrete* rather than *continuous* variables are investigated, then either the **Variable View** tab or the **Table View** tab in the optimization study table can be used. Also, for *discrete* variables, a **Design History Graph** is used rather than the **Local Trend Graph** described here.

6. Click ☒ to close the current graph. **Graph2** appears beneath the **Results and Graphs** folder.

Next, proceed to close the current file without saving results.

7. From the main menu, select **File > Close** followed by selecting **Don't Save** as shown in Fig. 23.

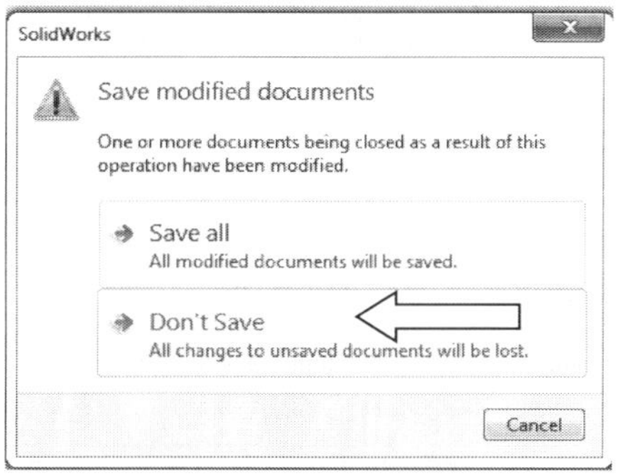

Figure 23 – Close the Study without saving results.

Closing Observations

The above Optimization Design Study introduces only some of the more important and frequently used capabilities available within the design optimization module of SOLIDWORKS Simulation Premium. This capability is not available in the Standard version of SOLIDWORKS Simulation and is available to a more limited extent within the

Simulation Professional version. Beyond this basic example, it is possible to optimize designs based on other parameters such as shape, safety factor, mass, weight, and others. The optimization search scheme is based on the "design of experiments" approach to find an optimum solution using a minimum number of iterations.

When should the optimization process be applied? It is highly recommended to run a design optimization *near the beginning of the design process*. This approach allows the designer to benefit from software recommended changes to model geometry early in the design process when the influence of those changes can be factored into the design of related components, sub-components, and assemblies.

Also, the user should *not* consider completion of a single design optimization study to be the "best" solution. For example, in the current example a value of 4.0 mm was arbitrarily specified for the lower range of **Width** for the rectangular beam cross-section. However, the **Optimal** solution converged to a value just slightly greater than 4.0 mm (4.04037 mm to be exact). This observation, combined with the fact that both the optimal **Stress** and optimal **Displacement** are lower than the maximums specified for these **Constraints**, leads one to believe that a more optimal design might be possible. Thus, further investigations are warranted. The interested reader should also access the available SOLIDWORKS Simulation Design Optimization tutorials found under **Help** > **SOLIDWORKS Simulation** > **Tutorials** > **Design Studies**.

CAUTION:
Use caution when specifying and/or accepting software suggested estimates for **Min:** and **Max:** values specified in the **Range** fields. Incorrect values, that is out-of-bound values or values that cause segments of the model to "self-intersect," may cause the design optimization process to fail. In these cases, the error message shown in Fig. 24 results. Therefore, use caution when applying values to **Variables**, **Constraints**, and **Goals** to ensure selected values are realistic.

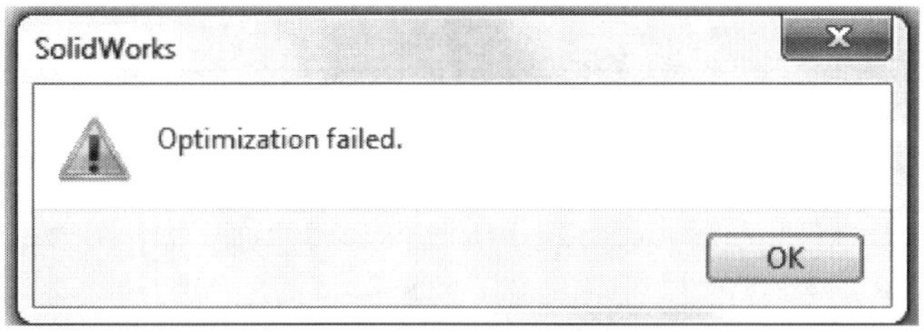

Figure 24 –Error received when "incorrect" estimates for **Range** values are used or if software suggested **Min:** and **Max:** values cause unrealistic events such as segments of a model "self-intersecting" with one another.

This concludes discussion for the current chapter.

EXERCISES

EXERCISE 1 – Design Optimization of a Milling Support

A milling support is being designed. It is to be bolted to the horizontal table of a CNC milling machine in the orientation pictured in Fig. E8-1. Bolts are inserted into "T" slots in the milling machine table (not shown) and pass through slots at the bottom left and right ends of the milling support base. The part is being designed to carry a maximum horizontal force F = 450 lb that acts as a *uniform pressure* over the area between the top end of the support and Split Line 1, which is also shown in Fig. E8-1. Material used for this part is **Cast Carbon Steel**. The part is manufactured as a casting to minimize final machining operations and thereby minimize production costs. As a consequence, the only machined surfaces are the bottom of the base, a 'finish cut' in the two bolt slots, and the surface to which the *uniform* pressure is applied. Also, because the support is in the early stages of design and because it is to be manufactured as a casting, it is desired to minimize the amount of material used in the part. However, to provide a minimum clamping area in the vicinity of force **F**, thickness of the vertical triangular portion of the model cannot be reduced below its original ¾ in thickness. Material reduction is to be accomplished without exceeding a maximum deflection (**URES** displacement) of 0.003 inch and without exceeding ¼ of the material Yield Strength. NOTE: Although this part is a casting, fillets and rounds are not shown on *all* external edges to simplify and, therefore, shorten optimization calculations within the software. Open the file **Milling Support 8-1** and perform a finite element analysis to optimize this design according to items requested below.

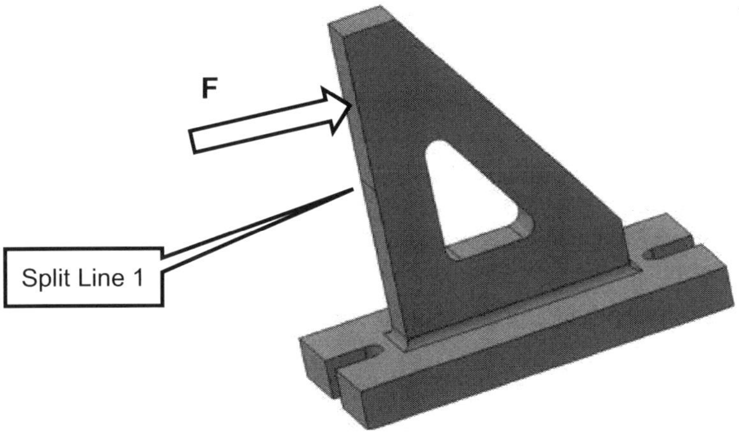

Figure E8-1 – The **Milling Support** base showing force **F** applied to the area above Split Line 1.

- Material: **Cast Carbon Steel**, round-off yield strength to nearest 1000 psi.
- Mesh: System default **Curvature based mesh**.

- Fixtures: **Fixed (immovable)** restraints applied to all inner surfaces of each bolt slot.
- External Load: Apply **450** lb **Force** uniformly to the area above Split Line 1. Dimensions of this area are Height = 3 in, Thickness = ¾ in.
- Limitations: Maximum **von Mises** stress ≤ (¼)*Yield Strength. Maximum part deflection (**URES**) ≤ 0.003 in.

Determine the following:

Develop a finite element analysis that includes material specification, fixtures, external load(s), mesh, and initial and optimized solutions. Do *not* defeature the model.

a. Create a plot showing all restraints and external loads applied to the model. This image is the finite element equivalent of a free-body diagram. Do not show stress or a mesh on this plot. Then, set-up and run an *Initial Study* to form the basis for an Optimization Design Study which is to follow. **IMPORTANT:** SAVE results of this *initial analysis* for possible re-use. (**Save As…** "Milling Support - Initial Study" *also* **Save** the **Results Files.**)

b. Based on the *Initial Study*, create a new design study to minimize the amount of material needed to cast the upper (triangular shaped) portion of the milling support *and* its rectangular base. In the optimization design study, select **High quality (slower)** as the quality level to be used. Also select **Range** as the optimization scheme and accept default **Min:** and **Max:** values for variables. Dimension changes are limited to those shown on the upper triangular segment *and* base of the model labeled in Fig. E8-2.

Initial dimensions are:

- **Rectangular Base** thickness = 0.75 in (this thickness cannot be reduced smaller than 0.30 inches due to minimum casting thickness limitations).
- **Vertical Leg** width = 1.00 in
- **Horizontal Leg** width = 1.25 in
- **Hypotenuse Leg** width = 1.00 in

Use descriptive names suggested above.

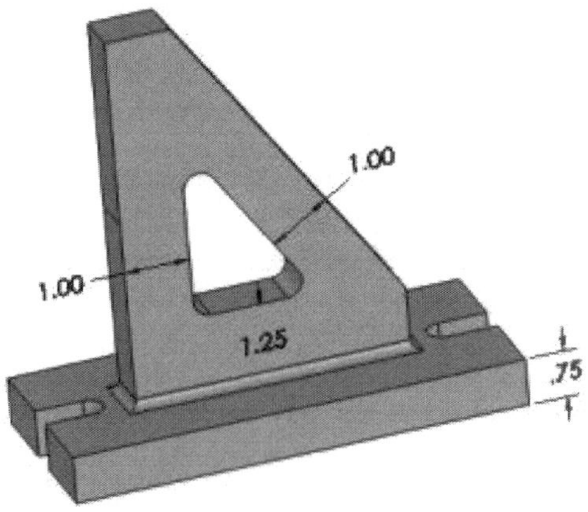

Figure E8-2 – Dimensions that can be altered on the upper triangular section and base.

c. After completely filling in all fields within the **Variables**, **Constraints**, and **Goals** sections on the **Variable View** tab, use techniques outlined in Appendix A to copy, paste and crop a readable image of the design table onto an 8 ½″ x 11″ sheet of paper. It may be necessary to click-and-drag the upper boundary of the table to reveal all values.

d. Before running the Optimization Study, write down the initial volume of the milling support base. It may be necessary to return to the SOLIDWORKS Manager tree in the *Initial Study* to find this value. Then run the optimization design study.

SOLUTION GUIDANCE - How to Proceed if the Optimization Fails

1. If your design optimization terminates with the warning shown in Fig. E8-3, then review the **CAUTION** section found on pg. 8-24.

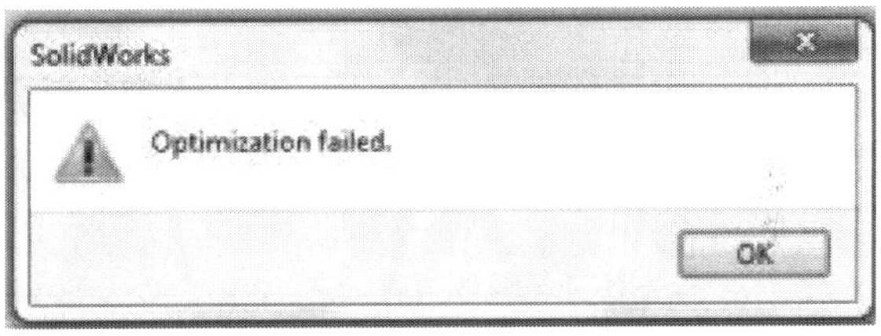

Figure E8-3 – Warning received if the optimization process fails. Such failures are typically due to bad data entered for **Variables**, **Constraints**, or **Goals**.

2. To identify the cause of this failure, click the name at the top of each iteration column (**Iteration 1**, **Iteration 2**, etc. *including the first grayed out column*) until the errant model is displayed. *See HINT below.*

<u>*HINT*</u>: As each iteration is selected, observe sliders at the left of the **Results View** iteration table. The location of each slider provides a quick, visual indication of whether the **Min:**, **Max:**, or some intermediate value of each variable is applied to a particular iteration. Also read content of the **What's Wrong** window when the first errant iteration is found.

Carefully observe geometry of the failed model and ask yourself, "Does the model intersect itself?" (i.e., Has the **Max:** value of one or more variables become so large that the model is "closed" [intersects itself] at some location, thereby indicating that **Max:** limits of variable size(s) may be too large?) Note **Max:** values of the variables that caused the self-intersection.

3. Delete the entire Optimization Design Study by right-clicking its Study *tab* and from the pop-up menu select **Delete**.

Do NOT attempt to edit values in the Variable View tab of the just completed Optimization Study. WHY? Because values of previous part dimensions, stress, and displacement are replaced by values from the "failed" Study. Those values differ from the Initial Study and subsequent designs will only fail again.

Solution Guidance (continued)

4. Deleting the failed Optimization Design Study returns you to the *Initial Study*. However, notice that original part dimensions, stress, and displacement of the *Initial Study* have also changed based on the recently run, but "failed," Optimization Design Study.

Next, retrieve the Initial Study that was to be named "Milling Support - Initial Study" and **Saved** as instructed in step "a." If the Study was not saved, it is necessary to re-create it from the beginning. However, if the Study was saved, proceed as follows.

5. From the **Main Menu** select **File** > **Close** > **Don't Save** and the current file and its results are discarded.

6. Next, from the **Main Menu** select **File** > **Open** > and select the filed named "**Milling Support – Initial Study**" or whatever name was used. The original *Initial Study* opens.

7. At the bottom of the graphics screen, select the *Initial Study* filename and the *original Initial Study* is opened along with all its saved **Results** files. *IMPORTANT*: The *Initial Study* must be **Run** again to re-establish its original results. Observe the warning symbols ⚠ adjacent to the filename and Mesh folders.

8. Open a *new* Design Optimization Study and populate the **Variable View** tab with **Variables**, **Constraints**, and **Goals** as before, except this time enter new, lower values for the **Horizontal Leg** as follows **Min: = 0.5in** and **Max: = 1.0** values.

9. ***Carefully*** check all other values in the table as values may have changed.

10. **[Run]** a new solution.

e. Create a graph of each **Constraint** versus variation of the hypotenuse leg width. Move the cursor to place horizontal and vertical dashed lines at the intersection of each limiting **Constraint** value and the curve on the graph. Beneath each graph, write a brief statement indicating the significance of this point relative to the optimal solution for width of the hypotenuse leg. Modify the graph title and axis labels to best describe what is shown on each graph; include your name. Copy and paste each graph onto the upper and lower half of an 8 ½" x 11" sheet of paper.

f. Copy and paste all values shown on the **Results View** tab from the left side of that table up to the third or fourth iteration. Beneath this table show a calculation of the total annual weight savings of cast steel to be expected when comparing the initial part to the optimized design. For this calculation assume the density of steel = 0.282 lb/in^3 and that 2,500 parts are made per year.

g. Questions: (1) Which **Constraint** appears to be the "limiting factor" for this design optimization and what result(s) lead you to this conclusion? (2) If **Min:** and **Max: Range** values were changed again, might a better solution be found? Give sound reasons for your answer by referring to values listed in the **Optimal** solution.

EXERCISE 2 – Design Optimization of Slotted Rectangular Block

The initial design of a slotted rectangular block, used to measure lateral (sideways) loads on an outdoor structure, is shown in Fig. E8-4. In its final configuration, not shown, strain gages are to be mounted on its left and right vertical legs to measure bending stress and correlate those stresses to loads applied to the structure. When in service, the part is fixed on its bottom surface and subject to a maximum horizontal force of 200 lb applied to its upper left edge as illustrated in Fig. E8-4 (a). To obtain larger strain magnitudes at the gage locations, if it is desired, reduce the width and thickness (depth into the page) of both vertical legs. The approach proposed is to minimize volume of the slotted block by reducing the width of the two vertical legs and thickness of the block. Common sense dictates that doing so will result in larger deflections with resulting higher strains measured by the strain gages. Practical limitations, however, restrict displacements to 0.05 inch or less and limit stress in the part to 32,000 psi or less. Open file: **Slotted Rectangular Block 8-2**.

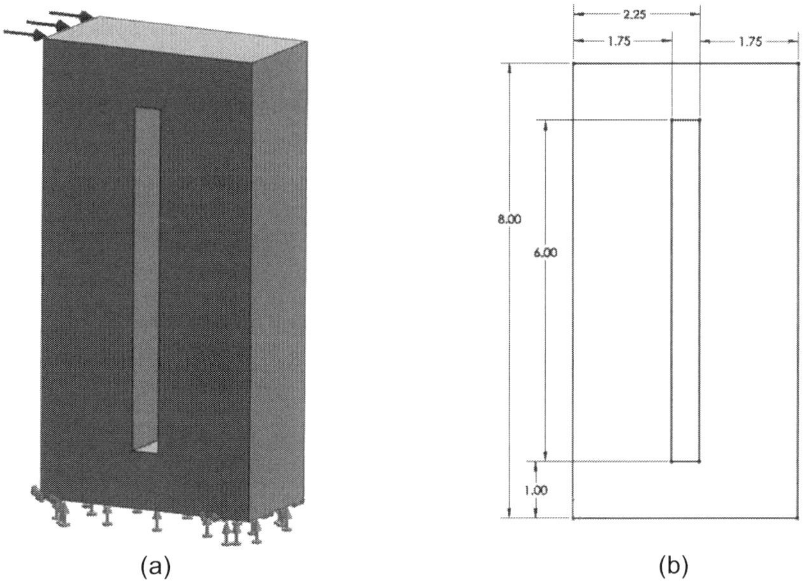

Figure E8-4 – Loading and geometry of the **Slotted Rectangular Block**.

- Material: **AISI 1020** steel

- Mesh: System default **Curvature based mesh**.
- Fixtures: **Fixed (immovable)** restraints applied to bottom surface.
- External Load: Apply a **200** lb horizontal force to the top left edge of the model.
- Limitations: Maximum **von Mises** stress ≤ 32000 psi.
  Maximum part deflection ≤ 0.05 in.

Determine the following:

Develop a finite element analysis that includes material specification, fixtures, external load(s), mesh, and initial and optimized solutions.

a. Run an *Initial Study* for the original part to form the basis for an Optimization Design Study which is to follow. Create a plot showing the restraints and external loads applied to the model along with the initial von Mises stress distribution. IMPORTANT: **SAVE** the results of this *initial analysis* for possible re-use.

b. Based on the *Initial Study*, create a new Optimization Design Study that results in reduction of the width of the two vertical legs and thickness of the entire part. Dimension changes are limited to the dimensions labeled in Fig. E8-5. See step (c) for items to be done prior to running the optimization study. These are the initial dimensions:

   - **Left vertical leg** initial width = 1.75 in
   - **Right vertical leg** initial width = 1.75 in
   - **Thickness** (depth into the page) = 2.00 in

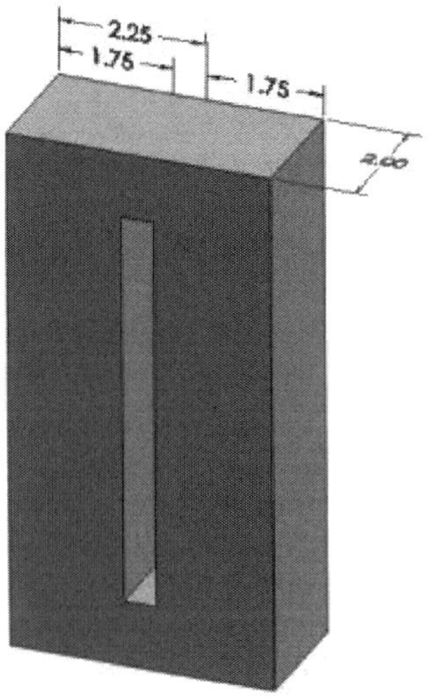

Figure E8-5 – Dimensions that are to be reduced on the slotted rectangular block.

c. After completely filling in all boxes within the **Variables**, **Constraints**, and **Goals** sections on the **Variable View** tab, use techniques outlined in Appendix A to copy, paste, and crop a readable image of the design table onto an 8 ½″ x 11″ sheet of paper. It may be necessary to click-and-drag the upper boundary of the table to show all values in the table. Then, run the optimization design study. NOTE: *If* your design optimization terminates with the warning shown in Fig. E8-3, then review the **CAUTION** section found on pg. 8-24. Also, follow guidelines outlined in the **SOLUTION GUIDANCE** section of pg. 8-27 and carefully re-define **Min** and **Max:** values.

d. Upon completion of the optimization study, examine contents of the **Results View** tab. In particular, based on results displayed in the **Optimal** solution column, state whether or not a *more* optimal solution can be found. State specific reasons for your answer and include reference to values listed in the **Optimal** study column.

e. Create a graph of each **Constraint** versus the variation of leg width. On each graph, show horizontal and vertical dashed lines at the intersection of the limiting **Constraint** value and the curve on the graph. Modify the graph title and axis labels to best describe what is shown on each graph; include your name. Copy and paste each graph onto the upper and lower half of an 8 ½" x 11" sheet of paper. Beneath each graph, write a brief statement indicating the significance of the intersection point relative to the optimal solution for width of the rectangle legs.

<u>EXERCISE 3</u> – Design Optimization of Solar Furnace Triangular Support

A current undergraduate research project uses energy from concentrated sunlight to reduce metal oxide particles to extract metal in a high temperature rotary reactor.[4] Reactor weight is carried by the cantilevered triangular support pictured in Fig. E8-6. The support is designed to withstand a maximum vertical force of 1250 lb_f that acts uniformly on top of a rectangular 9 in. x 10 in. plate beneath an adjustable table that carries the reactor. The plate is located at the free end of the support shown in Fig. E8-7.

The original support, shown in Fig. E8-6, was designed using traditional engineering design principles. However, it is proposed that further weight reduction may be achieved by altering geometry and size of the cut-out areas by using optimization software. To this end, cut-out triangle geometry is altered and sides **A**, **B**, and **C** of triangles, labeled in Fig. E8-7, may be varied in a search for optimized geometry. The design goal is to reduce weight of the existing support while maintaining or improving its current load and deflection characteristics. To simplify manufacture of the support, the radii of all corners on each triangular cut-out must remain constant at 0.25 in. Also, to avoid interference issues[5] between the triangular cut-outs, Side **A** is allowed to vary between 3 and 10 inches in length and sides **B** and **C** can vary within a range of 3 to 8 inches. *Investigate*

[4] Research performed in the James S. Markiewicz Solar Research Facility at Valparaiso University.

[5] "Interference" refers to self-intersection (i.e., overlapping dimensions) that could occur during an improperly defined optimization process.

the entire range of these values. After optimization, the support cannot experience a stress greater than 80 percent of the Yield Strength of **2024-T4** Aluminum. Also due to the small reactor aperture into which sunlight is focused, support deflection is limited to no more than 0.015 in. at any point on the support.

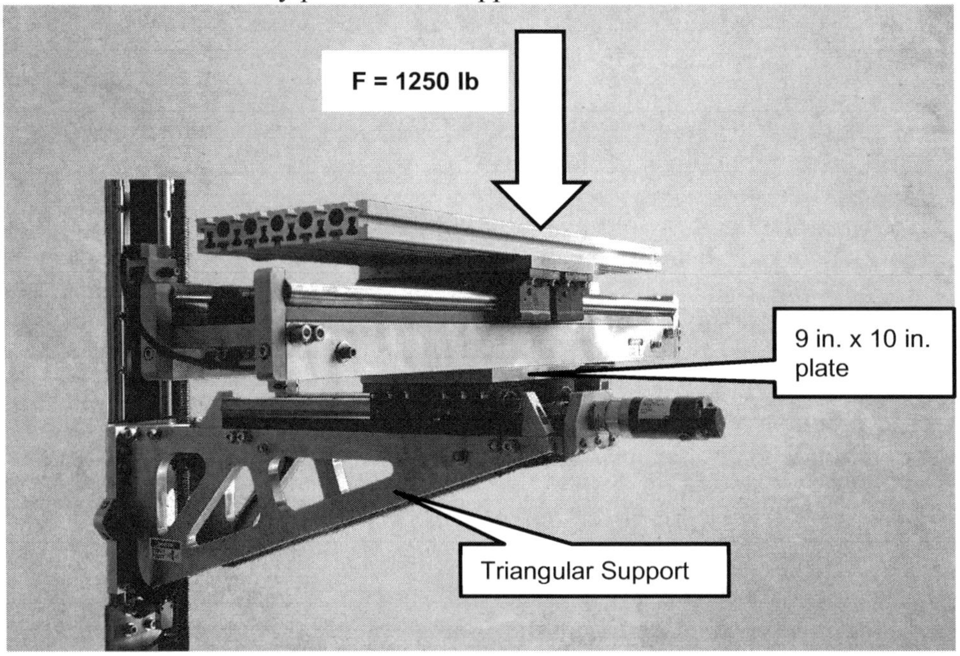

Figure E8-6 - Triangular support arm is pictured with an adjustable table that locates and supports the rotary reactor. The reactor is not shown.

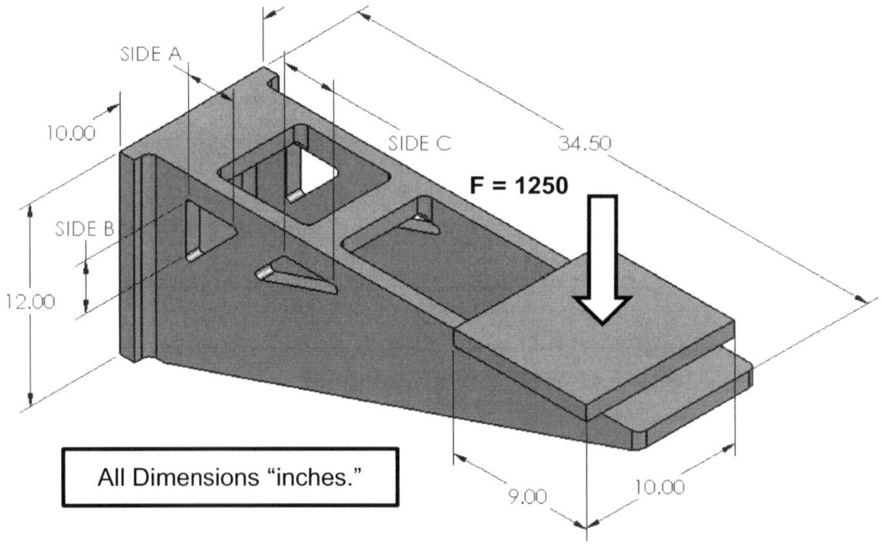

Figure E8-7 - Loading and dimensioned view of the solar furnace triangular support. Note that length of triangle sides is dimensioned to their end (*corner*) points, not to radii centers at each corner.

Open File: **Triangular Support - Solar Furnace**

- Material: Aluminum **2024-T4** (use English units).
- Mesh: System default **Curvature based mesh**.
- Fixture: **Fixed (immovable)** restraints applied to the 10 in. x 12 in. vertical left-face of the triangular support.
- External Loads: Apply a uniformly distributed downward force **F=1250 lb**$_f$ on the 9 in. x 10 in. rectangular plate located near its free end.
- Limitations: Maximum **von Mises** stress ≤ 0.80* material yield strength. Maximum Deflection **(URES)** ≤ 0.015 (inches)

Determine the following:

Develop a finite element analysis that includes material specification, fixtures, external load(s), mesh, and initial and optimized solutions. Do *not* defeature the model.

a. Create and run an *Initial Study* for the model of Fig. E8-8 to form a basis for an Optimization Design Study. Create a plot showing all restraints and external loads applied to the model along with the initial von Mises stress distribution. Create a second plot showing the resultant displacement distribution **(-Res disp-)**. These plots should show un-deformed model images, include discrete fringes, and include automatically labeled values of maximum stress and displacement on the triangular support. Copy and paste each plot onto the upper and lower half of an 8 ½" x 11" sheet of paper. <u>IMPORTANT:</u> **SAVE** results of this *Initial Study*.

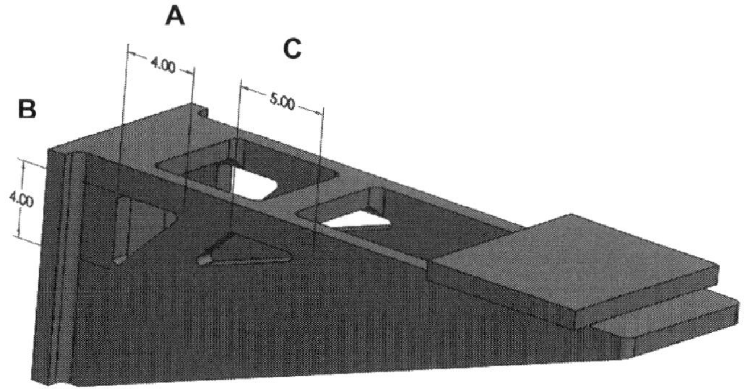

NOTE: When defining variables the part initially appears with *all* dimensions shown. Because of the large number of dimensions on this model, it is suggested that a **Front View** be used to simplify the selection of dimensions **A**, **B**, and **C**.

Figure E8-8 - Dimensions that may be altered during an optimization design study of the solar furnace triangular support.

b. After completely defining all **Variables, Constraints,** and **Goals** in the **Variable View** tab, use the techniques outlined in Appendix A to copy, paste, and crop a readable image of the design optimization Table onto an 8 ½" x 11" sheet of paper. It may be necessary to click-and-drag the upper boundary of the table to reveal all values. Then run the optimization design study. NOTE: *If* your design optimization terminates with the warning shown in Fig. E8-3, then review the **CAUTION** section found on pg. 8-24.

c. On a separate page, copy and paste a plot showing von Mises stress distribution on the optimized triangular support. This plot should display units in psi, show discrete fringes on an un-deformed model, and include automatic labeling of maximum von Mises stress.

d. Beneath the plot of von Mises stress created for part (c) determine the percent reduction in volume between the triangular support used for the *Initial Study*, and the optimized triangular support. On this same page also compare the maximum von Mises stress from the *Initial Study* to yield strength of **2024-T4** Aluminum by calculating the percent of the yield strength that the maximum von Mises stress constitutes. Repeat the calculation to determine the percent of yield strength constituted by von Mises stress for the optimized solution. Label each calculation.

e. Examine contents of the **Results View** tab. Based on calculations of part (d) and on results displayed in the **Optimal** solution column, state whether or not a more *optimal* solution can be found. Include specific reasons that support your answer by referring to values listed in the **Optimal** study column and elsewhere in the table. Also answer the question, what design variable(s) should be chosen to further optimize the design (if applicable)? Include reason(s) for your answer. (In other words, *WHY* did you choose a particular design variable(s) for the preceding question?)

f. Create a graph of each **Constraint** versus the length variation of Side B. Modify the graph title and axis labels to best describe what is shown on each graph; include your name in the title. Copy and paste each graph onto the upper and lower half of an 8 ½" x 11" sheet of paper.

CHAPTER #9

Elastic Buckling

Designing to avoid buckling of an axially loaded component (or *column*) is very significant in the design process. A column can buckle before it yields or it can yield before it buckles. Determining when a column buckles using finite element software is challenging due to the inherent nonlinearity in buckling. In this chapter, *elastic (linear) buckling* theory is used to find the factor of safety for an axial loaded cylindrical rod supported by a variety of end conditions. The effect of an eccentric loading on the cylindrical rod's factor of safety is studied as well. The main goal of this chapter is to introduce elastic buckling and to identify the limitations when using SOLIDWORKS Simulation to perform buckling analysis.

Learning Objectives

Upon completion of this example, users should be able to:

- Perform buckling analysis using SOLIDWORKS Simulation package.
- Apply different boundary or end conditions (fixed-free, fixed-fixed, pinned-fixed, and pinned-pinned) to a buckling analysis.
- Perform buckling analysis for eccentrically loaded columns.
- Understand the limitations of buckling analysis in SOLIDWORKS Simulation.

Problem Statement

A small diameter **Alloy Steel** cylindrical rod, (hereafter referred to as a "pin" due to its very small diameter) with a diameter of 0.052in and a length of 1.9in, is subject to an axial compressive load (see Fig.1). The goal of this example is to find the maximum axial load that can be applied to the pin before the pin buckles or yields. The pin will be analyzed for a variety of different end conditions: fixed-free, fixed-fixed, pinned-fixed, and pinned-pinned.

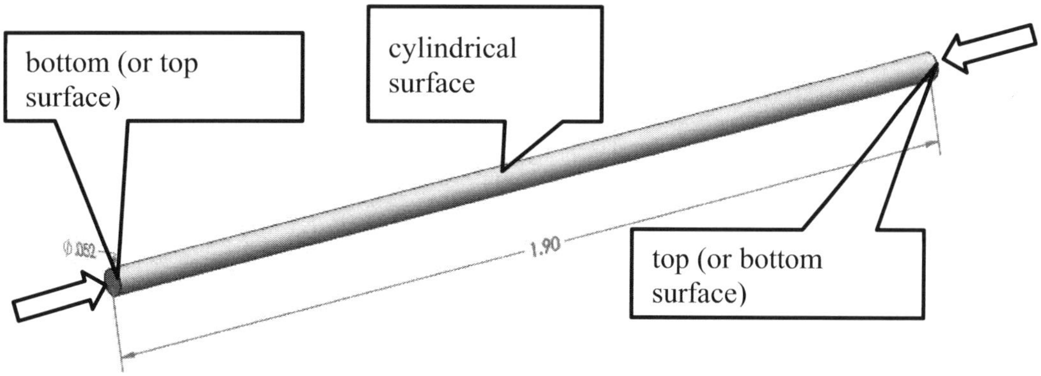

Figure 1 – Dimensioned view of the pin (all dimensions in "inches").

Opening SOLIDWORKS

1. Skip to step 2 if **SOLIDWORKS** is already open. Otherwise, open **SOLIDWORKS** by making the following selections. **Start>All Programs>SOLIDWORKS 2026** (or) Click the **SOLIDWORKS** icon on your screen.

2. In the SOLIDWORKS main menu, select **File>Open...** Then, open the file named **Round Pin**.

Create a Buckling Analysis (Fixed-Free End Conditions)

1. In the **SOLIDWORKS Add-ins** *tab,* located *above* the graphics area, click the **SOLIDWORKS Simulation** icon to show the **Simulation** tab. Near the top of the screen, click the down arrow ▾ beneath the **New Study** icon and from the pull-down menu select **New Study**. This opens the **Study** property manager.

2. In the **Type** dialogue box, click the **Buckling** icon to select a buckling analysis; in the **Name** dialogue box replace "**Buckling 1**" by typing **fixed-free ends**.

3. Click **[OK]** ✓ to close the **Study** property manager.

An outline of the buckling analysis is displayed at the bottom of the SOLIDWORKS Simulation manager tree.

Assign Material Properties to the Model

1. In the SOLIDWORKS Simulation manager right-click the model name, **Round Pin**. Then, from the pull-down menu select **Apply/Edit Material.** The **Material** window opens.

2. Next, click the > symbol next to **Steel** (if not already selected) to expand the menu and select **AISI 1020** steel from the list of available steels.

3. On the **Properties** tab, adjacent to **Units:**, select **English (IPS).**

4. Click **[Apply]** followed by **[Close]** to close the **Material** window. A check mark "✓" appears on the **Round Pin** folder and the material designation **(-[SW]AISI 1020 -)** appears next to this folder.

In the first simulation, a fixed-free end condition is specified for the pin. In the following section the bottom surface of the pin is specified as fixed, and the top surface is specified as free to move. Also, a **1.0** lb axial force is applied normal to the top surface of the pin. Please note it makes no difference which end is chosen for the 'top' or 'bottom'.

Assign Fixed-Free Fixture End Conditions to the Model

In the SOLIDWORKS Simulation manager, right-click **Fixtures** and from the pull-down menu select **Fixed Geometry**. The **Fixture** property manager opens.

1. In the **Standard (Fixed Geometry)** dialogue box, the **Fixed Geometry** icon should already be selected. The **Faces, Edges, Vertices for Fixture** field is highlighted (light blue) and is awaiting selection of the surface to be **Fixed.**

2. Rotate the model as necessary and zoom in the bottom surface using the **Zoom to Area** icon above the graphic area. Select the bottom surface. **Immovable** constraints are applied to the bottom surface of the model as seen in Fig.2.

3. Click **[OK]** ✓ (green check mark) at top of the **Fixture** property manager to accept this restraint. An icon named Fixed-1 appears beneath the **Fixtures** folder in the Simulation manager tree.

External Loads

1. Next, right-click the **External Loads** icon from the SOLIDWORKS Simulation manager and select **Force...**The **Force/Torque** property manager opens.

2. Within the **Force/Torque** dialogue box, select the **Force** icon (if not already selected) and click to select ⊙**Normal** as the direction of the force.

3. The **Face and Shell Edges for Normal Force** field is highlighted (light blue) to indicate it is active. Rotate the model and zoom in as necessary to select the top surface.

4. Verify that the **Units** field is set to **English (IPS).**

5. In the **Force Value** field, type **1.0.**

6. Click **[OK]** ✓ to close the **Force/Torque** property manager. **Force-1 (: Per item: 1 lbf:**) is now listed beneath the **External Loads** folder. The model should now appear as shown in Fig. 2.

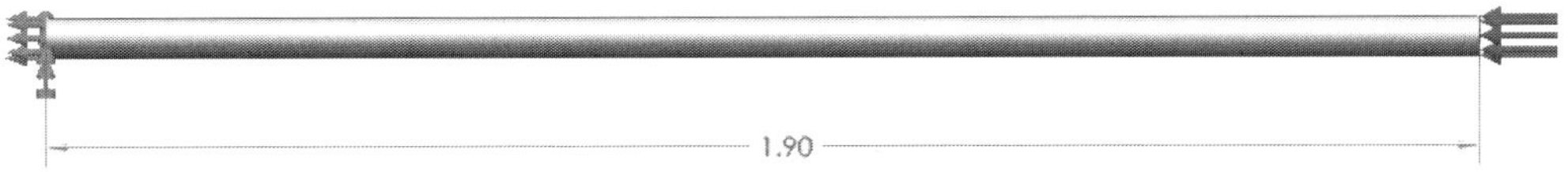

Figure 2 –Bottom surface is restrained and a **1.0** lb force applied to its top surface.

Buckling Analysis Options

1. Right-click the **fixed-free ends (-Default-)** from the SOLIDWORKS Simulation manager and select **Properties…**(see Fig.3). This opens the **Buckling** property manager.

2. Select the **Options** tab in the property manager (if not already selected), change the **Number of buckling modes** to **1,** and click to select ☑ **Automatic Solver Selection** in the **Solver** dialogue box.

3. Make no other changes in this property manager and click **[OK]** to close it.

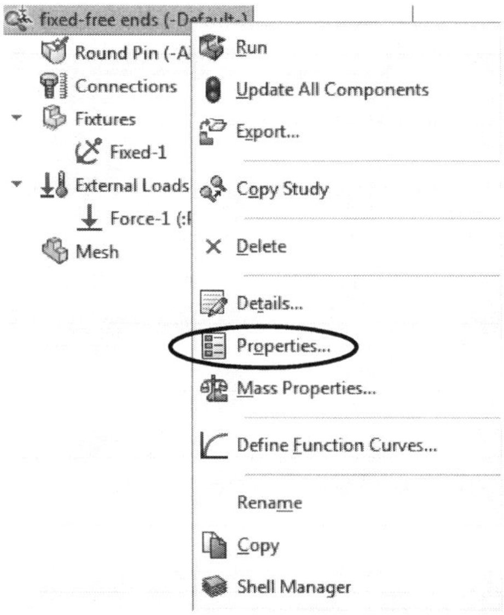

Figure 3 – SOLIDWORKS Simulation manager Properties.

> **Buckling Analysis Insight**
>
> The analysis of elastic buckling (also called linear or Euler buckling) using finite element methods is an *eigenvalue problem* with many solutions for eigenvalues and eigenvectors. The number of solutions depends on the number of degrees of freedom in the equations. The buckling force of the component is the lowest eigenvalue, and the associated eigenvector is the mode shape of the component during buckling. Thus, in elastic buckling only the first mode is useful and the higher modes do not have any practical significance.

Meshing the Model

1. Within the Simulation *tab*, select ▼ beneath the **Run this Study** (Run This Study) icon. From the pull-down menu, select the **Create Mesh** icon. The **Mesh** property manager opens as shown in Fig 4.

2. Check ✓ to turn on and open the ☑ **Mesh Parameters** dialogue box and verify that a ⊙ **Standard mesh** is selected. Accept the remaining default settings shown in this dialogue box.

3. Click the down arrow ˅ to open the **Advanced** dialogue box boxed in Fig. 4. Verify that **Jacobian points** is set at **16 points** (this setting indicates that high quality tetrahedral elements are used).

4. Finally, click **[OK]** ✓ to accept the default mesh settings and close the **Mesh** property manager.

Meshing starts automatically, and a **Mesh Progress** window appears briefly. After meshing is complete, SOLIDWORKS Simulation displays the meshed model. Also, a check mark "✓" appears on the **Mesh** icon to indicate meshing is complete.

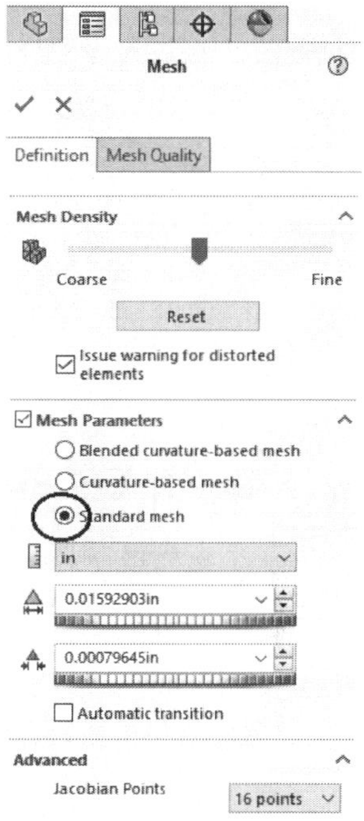

Figure 4 – **Mesh** property manager.

Solution

1. On the **Simulation** tab, click the **Run this Study** Run This Study icon to start the solution.

After a successful solution, a **Results** folder appears below the Simulation manager. This folder has the plot of the first mode shape, named **Amplitude 1 (-Res Amp – Mode Shape 1-)**, shown in Fig.5. This figure shows the shape of the buckled pin (i.e., the mode shape).

2. To find the buckling force factor of safety, right-click the **Results** folder and from the pull-down menu select **List Buckling Factor of Safety**. This opens the **List Modes** window which shows that the **Buckling Factor of safety** for **Mode No. 1** is **7.1208.** This number is also reported on the top left corner of the screen as **Load Factor** circled in Fig.6.

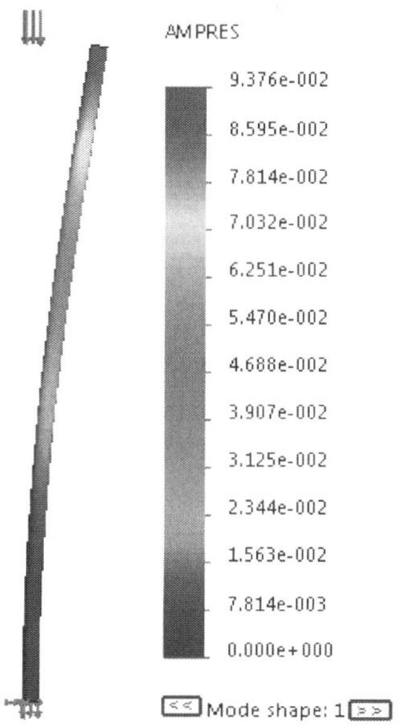

Figure 5 – First mode shape.

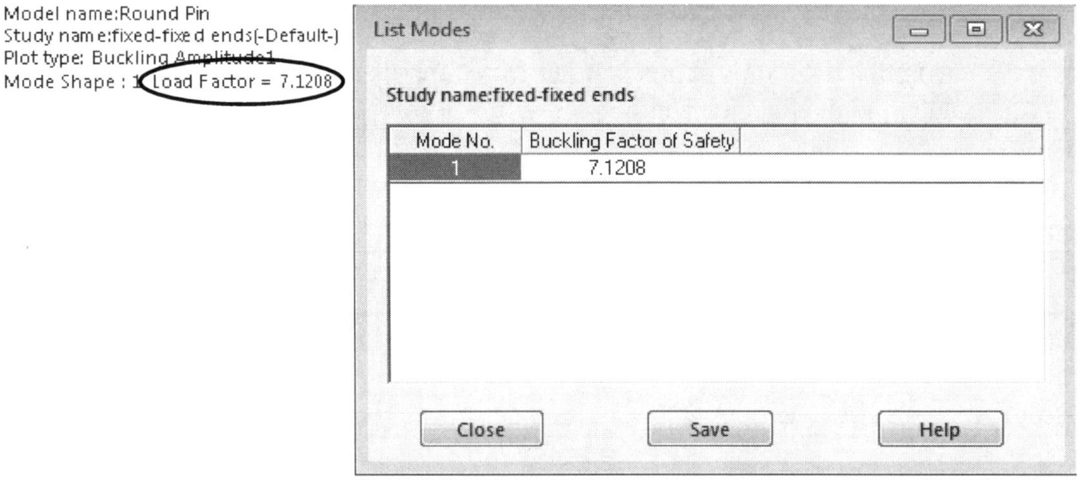

Figure 6 – **Buckling Factor of Safety** for the pin -- fixed-free end conditions.

Based on this result, for a **1.0** lb axial force the buckling factor of safety is 7.1208. Thus, the *critical* buckling force for the pin for the fixed-free end conditions is **7.1208** lb.

3. **[Close]** to exit the **List Modes** window.

ASIDE:

AISI 1020 steel has a yield strength of $\sigma_Y = 50991.06247$ psi; therefore the maximum compressive load before the pin yields is $F_Y = \sigma_Y * A = 108.29$ lb, where A =2.123e-3 in^2 is the cross-sectional area of the pin. This means the pin buckles before it yields.

Examination of Results

In elastic buckling, the theoretical critical buckling load, P_{cr}, for any type of end condition for a column with a uniform cross section area along its axis is given by the **Euler-Column** formula:

$$P_{cr} = \frac{\pi^2 E\, I}{L_e^2}$$

where E is the material modulus of elasticity, I is the 2nd area moment of inertia for the column's cross-section, and L_e is the effective length of the column. The relationship between the effective length L_e and actual length, L, is given in the table below for different end conditions.

End conditions	fixed-free	fixed-fixed	fixed-pinned	pinned-pinned
Effective Length (L_e)	$2L$	$0.5L$	$0.707L$	L

The pin under study has a diameter of $d = 0.052''$ and a length of $L = 1.9''$, a modulus of elasticity of $E = 29007547.53$ psi, and a yield strength of $\sigma_Y = 50991.06247$ psi. Thus, the theoretical critical buckling force is

$$P_{cr} = \frac{\pi^2 E\, I}{L_e^2} = \frac{\pi^2 (29007547.53 \text{ psi})(\,3.5891\text{e} - 7 \text{ in}^4)}{(3.8 \text{ in})^2} = 7.1159 \text{ lb}$$

where, $L_e = 2L = 3.8''$, and $I = \pi d^4 / 64$ =3.5891e-7 in^4.

Thus, the percent difference between the theoretical and SOLIDWORKS Simulation results is:

$$\%\text{ difference} = \left[\frac{\text{FEA result} - \text{classical result}}{\text{FEA result}}\right] 100 = \frac{7.1208 - 7.1159}{7.1208} = 0.068\%$$

Buckling Mode shape (Optional)

The mode shape plot in the buckling analysis shows the pattern of deformation of the pin when it buckles. Notice on the **mode shape** plot there are no units associated with the numbers because the displacements are relative displacements. In other words, the absolute values or the units in the **mode shape** are not important. The relative displacements are examined further by plotting the nodal displacement along a *Split Line* parallel to the axis of the pin.

1. Right-click on **Amplitude 1 (-Res Amp – Mode Shape 1-)** in the **Results** folder at bottom of the Simulation manager and, from the pull-down menu, select **Hide** Hide to hide the deformed result.

2. Click the **Features** *tab,* located *above* the graphics area. Then click the down arrow ▼ beneath the **Curves** icon Curves and from the pull-down menu select **Split Line**. This opens the **Split Line** property manager shown in Fig. 7.

3. In the **Type of Split** dialogue box, click to select ⊙ **Intersection** shown in Fig. 7.

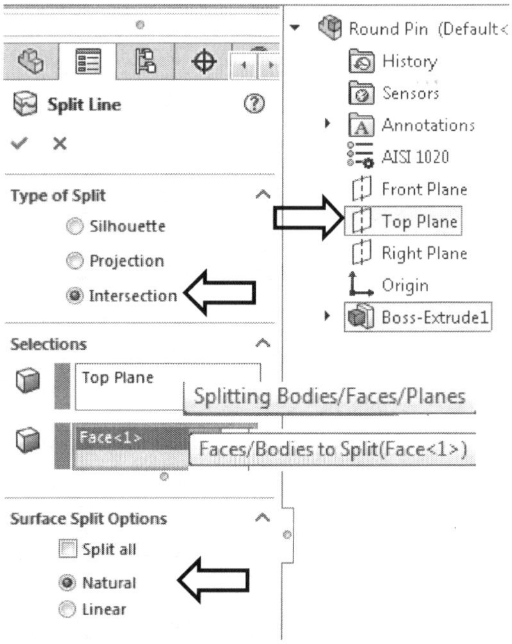

Figure 7 – **Split line** property manager.

4. In the **Selections** dialogue box, click to highlight (light blue) the **Splitting Bodies/Faces/Planes** field. Then, open the SOLIDWORKS "flyout" menu and select the **Top Plane** Top Plane.

5. Click to activate (light blue) the **Faces/Bodies to Split** field and move the cursor to select the cylindrical surface of the pin. **Face <1>** appears in the active field.

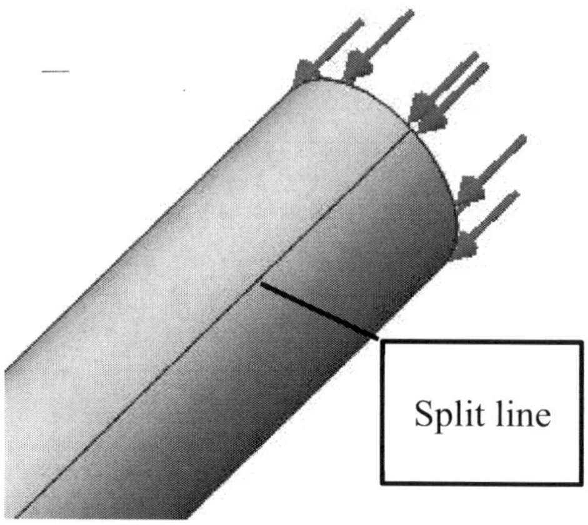

Figure 8 – Two *Split Lines* are generated on the cylindrical surface of the pin.

6. In the **Surface Split Options** dialogue box, click to select ⊙ **Natural**.

7. Click **[OK]** ✓ to close the **Split Line** property manager.

   This creates two *Split Lines* parallel to the axis of the pin (see Fig.8). Please note that since the pin model has been changed (due to addition of the *Split Lines*), SOLIDWORKS now shows warning signs ⚠ next to both the **Results** and **Mesh** folders in the Simulation manager. Ignore the warnings since the simulation result is still valid. Adding *Split Lines* does not change the mode shapes or buckling factor of safety.

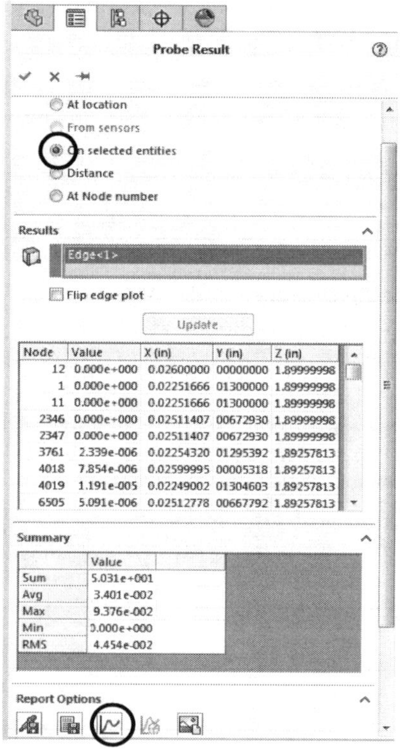

Figure 9 – **Probe Results** property manager.

8. Right-click on the **Amplitude 1 (-Res Amp – Mode Shape 1-)** in the **Results** folder in the Simulation manager and from the pull-down menu select **Show** Show to show result again.

9. Right-click on **Amplitude 1 (-Res Amp – Mode Shape 1-)** in the **Results** folder again and from the pull-down menu select **Probe** Probe to open the **Probe Result** property manager.

10. In the **Options** dialogue box, click to choose ⊙ **On selected entities**. The **Results** dialogue box expands to include a highlighted (light blue) field. This field is active and is awaiting the selection of **Faces, Edges, or Vertices** on the model.

11. In the graphics screen, move the cursor over one of the two *Split Lines* (either *Split line* is acceptable) and click to choose it. **Edge<1>** appears in the highlighted field and the **[Update]** button becomes active.

12. Click the **[Update]** button. This action fills the **Results** table with the data seen in Fig. 9.

13. In the **Report Options** dialogue box, located near the bottom of the **Probe Result** property manager, click the **Plot** icon. Immediately a graph of lateral displacement (AMPRES) along the *Split Line* (parallel to the pin axis) is displayed, as seen in Fig.10, versus the normalized length of the pin.

The magnitude of deflection (AMPRES) in this plot is irrelevant but the *relative values are important*. For instance, at 40% and 60% of the pin height, the AMPRES values are around **0.018** and **0.039**, respectively. Therefore, the relative deflection of the pin is **0.461** to **1.0** at 40% and 60% of the pin height, respectively. The SOLIDWORKS results are a close approximation to the theoretical results, since

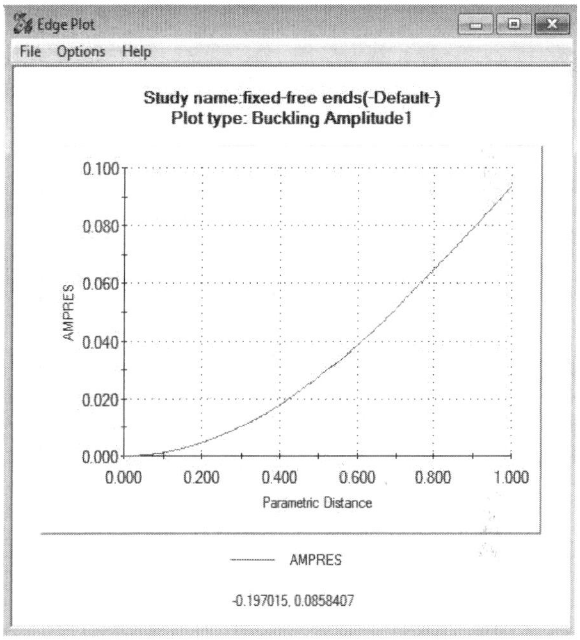

Figure 10 – Deflection (mode shape) of the fixed-free pin at buckling.

For a fixed-free column the mode shape equation is:

$$y = A\left(1 - \cos\left(\frac{\pi z}{2L}\right)\right)$$

where z is the vertical distance from the fixed end, A is an arbitrary number, and y is the deflection of the column. Therefore:

$$\frac{y_{40}}{y_{60}} = \frac{A\left(1 - \cos\left(\frac{\pi}{2}\,0.4\right)\right)}{A\left(1 - \cos\left(\frac{\pi}{2}\,0.6\right)\right)} = 0.463$$

Validity of Elastic Buckling Simulation

Elastic buckling theory assumes the member (or column) length is very large compared to its lateral dimensions. In the theory of elastic buckling, the column slenderness ratio, S_r , must be greater than a minimum slenderness ratio, S_D, for elastic buckling theory to correctly predict the buckling force. Otherwise, the analysis results are not valid and the predicted force to buckle the column using elastic theory is higher than the actual force required to buckle the member. Thus, the validity of using elastic buckling modeling to predict buckling force must be verified prior to using the analysis results.

By definition, slenderness ratio of a column is:

$$S_r = \frac{L_e}{\sqrt{\frac{I}{A}}} = \frac{2 * 1.8}{\sqrt{\left(\frac{3.589e - 7\ \text{in}^4}{2{,}123e - 3\ \text{in}^2}\right)}} = 292.3$$

where A is the area of the column cross section. Also, the lower limit for elastic buckling, S_D, is:

$$S_D = \pi\sqrt{\frac{2E}{\sigma_Y}} = \pi\sqrt{\frac{2 * 29007547.53\ \text{psi}}{50991.06247\ \text{psi}}} = 105.96$$

For the pin with fixed-free end conditions example problem, the values of the slenderness ratios are as follows: $S_r = 292.30$ and $S_D = 105.96$. Thus, the elastic buckling analysis for the pin with fixed-free end conditions is valid since $S_r > S_D$.

This concludes buckling analysis assuming for the pin with fixed-free end conditions. Next, we study the fixed-fixed end conditions.

Close the model *without saving the model.*

1. Select **File** from the main menu, followed by selecting **Close** from the pull-down menu. The SOLIDWORKS window opens and displays the message **Save modified documents.**

2. Choose → **Don't Save** to keep the **Round Pin** model intact, but to *discard changes* made to create the fixed-free end conditions simulation. The model closes.

ASIDE:

You can also use the Simulation Cleaning Utility simulation cleaning utility.exe to remove the Simulation data if the model was accidentally saved during the preceding procedure. For this purpose, run the utility from the **C:\Program Files\SolidWorks Corp\SOLIDWORKS\Simulation\Utilities** folder. The **Cleaning Utility** manager will open. Use the **Browse** button to locate the **Round Pin.SLDPRT** file and click to select **SOLIDWORKS Simulation** SOLIDWORKS Simulation. Click the **Clean File** button Clean File to remove the simulation data.

Create a Buckling Analysis Using Fixed-Fixed End Conditions

1. In the SOLIDWORKS main menu, select **File>Open...** Then, open the file named **Round Pin**.

Set up a buckling study named **fixed-fixed end conditions.** Try this on your own or follow the steps outlined below.

2. If the **Simulation** tab is not available near the top-left of the graphics area, click the <u>*name*</u> on *any tab* located *above* the graphics area. Then, from the pull-down menu, select **Simulation**. The **Simulation** *tab* is displayed.

3. Click the **Simulation** tab to display the **Simulation** toolbar and in the toolbar, click the down arrow ▼ beneath the **New Study** icon New Study. From the pull-down menu select **New Study**. This opens the **Study** property manager.

4. In the **Type** dialogue box, click **Buckling** Buckling to select a buckling analysis. In the **Name** dialogue box replace "**Buckling 1**" by typing **fixed-fixed ends**

5. Click **[OK]** ✓ to close the **Study** property manager.

You should see an outline of the buckling analysis labeled **fixed-fixed ends** at the bottom of the SOLIDWORKS Simulation manager tree.

Assign Material Properties to the Model

Assign the **AISI 1020** material to the pin and select **English** units for this study. Try this on your own or follow the steps outlined below.

1. In the SOLIDWORKS Simulation manager right-click the model name, **Round Pin**. Then, from the pull-down menu select **Apply/Edit Material ...** The **Material** window opens.

2. Next, click the > symbol next to **Steel** (if not already selected) to expand the menu and select **AISI 1020** steel from the list of available steels.

3. On the **Properties** tab, adjacent to **Units:**, select **English (IPS).**

4. Click **[Apply]** followed by **[Close]** to close the **Material** window. A check mark "✓" appears on the **Round Pin** folder and the material designation **(-[SW]AISI 1020 -)** appears next to this folder.

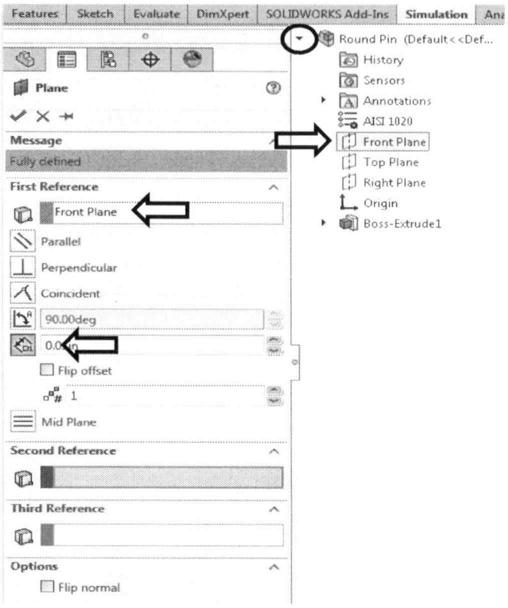

Figure 11 – The **Plane** property manager used to create a reference plane at 0.1" from the top of the pin.

Prepare the Model for Assignment of Fixed-Fixed End Conditions

In order to apply a fixed condition at the top end of the pin, it is necessary to split the cylindrical surface of the pin.

1. From the main menu, select **Insert**. Then, from successive pull-down menus make the following selections: **Reference Geometry** ► followed by **Plane...** Plane... . The **Plane** property manager opens to the left of the graphics area.

2. Within the **Plane** property manager, under **First Reference**, the field is highlighted (light blue) to indicate it is active and awaiting selection of a plane from which a *new* plane can be referenced.

3. Within the SOLIDWORKS "flyout" menu, select the **Front Plane**. The **Plane** property manager changes appearance and **Front Plane** appears in the **First Reference** dialogue box and on the model.

4. Return to the **First Reference** dialogue box and in the **Offset Distance** spin-box and type **0.1"**. This is the distance *from* the **Front Plane** to a **Reference Plane** located so that it intersects the outside cylindrical surface of the pin.

5. Click **[OK]** ✓ to close the **Plane** property manager.

The reference plane created in the previous steps is highlighted on your screen. If your model is large enough it will be labeled **Plane1**. If not, zoom-in on the top of the model. In the following steps, **Plane1** is used to create *Split Lines* near the top surface of the pin. These *Split Lines* enable us to define a small area on top of the pin to apply the fixed condition.

6. From the **Main Menu**, select **Insert**. Then, from successive pull-down menus choose: **Curve ▶** followed by **Split Line...** The **Split Line** property manager opens.

7. Beneath **Type of Split** select ⦿ **Intersection** (if not already selected).

8. In the **Selections** dialogue box, **Plane1** should already appear in the **Splitting Bodies/Faces/ Planes** field (pink color). If **Plane1** does not appear in this field, click to activate the field, then move the cursor onto the "flyout" menu and select **Plane1**. **Plane1** now appears in the upper field.

9. Next, click inside the **Faces/Bodies to Split** field. This field may already be active (light blue). Then move the cursor over the model and select anywhere on the *cylindrical surface* of the pin. Once selected, **Face<1>** appears in the active field.

10. In the **Surface Split Options** dialogue box, select ⦿ **Natural**.

11. Click **[OK]** ✓ to close the **Split Line** property manager.

Assign Fixed-Fixed Fixture to Top End of Model

1. In the SOLIDWORKS Simulation manager, right-click **Fixtures** and from the pull-down menu select **Fixed Geometry**... The **Fixture** property manager opens.

2. In the **Standard (Fixed Geometry)** dialogue box, the **Fixed Geometry** icon should already be selected. The **Faces, Edges, Vertices for Fixture** field is highlighted (light blue) and is awaiting selection of the surface to be **Fixed.**

3. Select the bottom surface. **Immovable** constraints are applied to the bottom surface of the model.

4. Click **[OK]** ✓ (green check mark) at top of the **Fixture** property manager to accept this restraint. An icon named 

appears beneath the **Fixtures** folder in the Simulation manager tree.

5. Right-click **Fixtures** again and from the pull-down menu select **Advanced Fixtures**… The **Fixture** property manager opens.

6. Within the **Standard** dialogue box, click to select **On Cylindrical Faces** icon 

. Then click to activate the **Cylindrical Faces for Fixture** (light blue) selection box (if not already selected).

7. Zoom into the top portion of the pin near the *Split Line*. Click anywhere on the cylindrical surface between the *Split Line* and top end of the pin to select it; shown shaded in Fig.12.

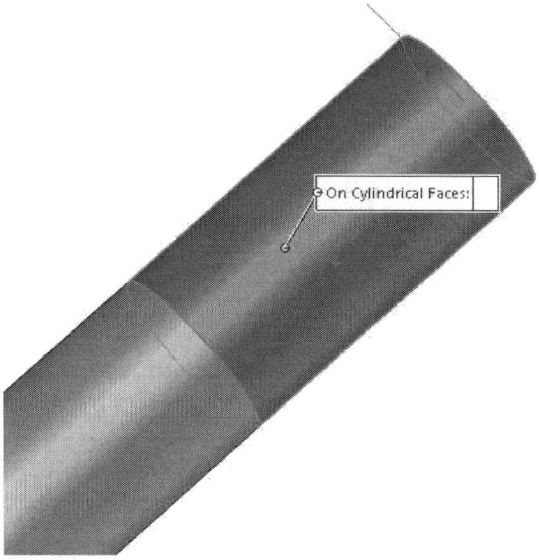

Figure 12 – Select cylindrical face at top of the pin to apply the **fixed** conditions.

8. In the **Fixture** property manager, scroll down to the **Translations** dialogue box shown in Fig. 13. Set **Unit** to **in**, then click to select the **Radial**  icon. Ensure that **0** appears in the value box. This selection sets radial displacement of the cylindrical face at the top of the pin to zero. Also, click to select the **Circumferential**  icon. Ensure that **0** appears in the value box. This selection sets rotation of the cylindrical face to zero. Do *NOT* select the **Axial**  icon. Leaving this value un-specified allows the cylindrical face to move along the center axis of the pin.

9. Click **[OK]** ✓ (green check mark) at top of the **Fixture** property manager to accept this restraint and close the property manager. The 

icon appears beneath the **Fixtures** folder in the Simulation manager tree. Pay attention to the direction of arrows on the cylindrical surface.

External Loads

Assign **1.0** lb force normal to the top surface of the pin. Try this on your own or follow the steps outlined below.

1. Right-click the **External Loads** icon from the SOLIDWORKS Simulation manager and select **Force…**The **Force/Torque** property manager opens.

2. Within the **Force/Torque** dialogue box, select the **Force** icon (if not already selected) and click to select ⊙**Normal** as the direction of the force.

3. The **Face and Shell Edges for Normal Force** field is highlighted (light blue) to indicate it is active.

4. Select the *flat* top surface on the *end* of the pin. **Face <1>** appears in the **Face and Shell Edges for Normal Force** field.

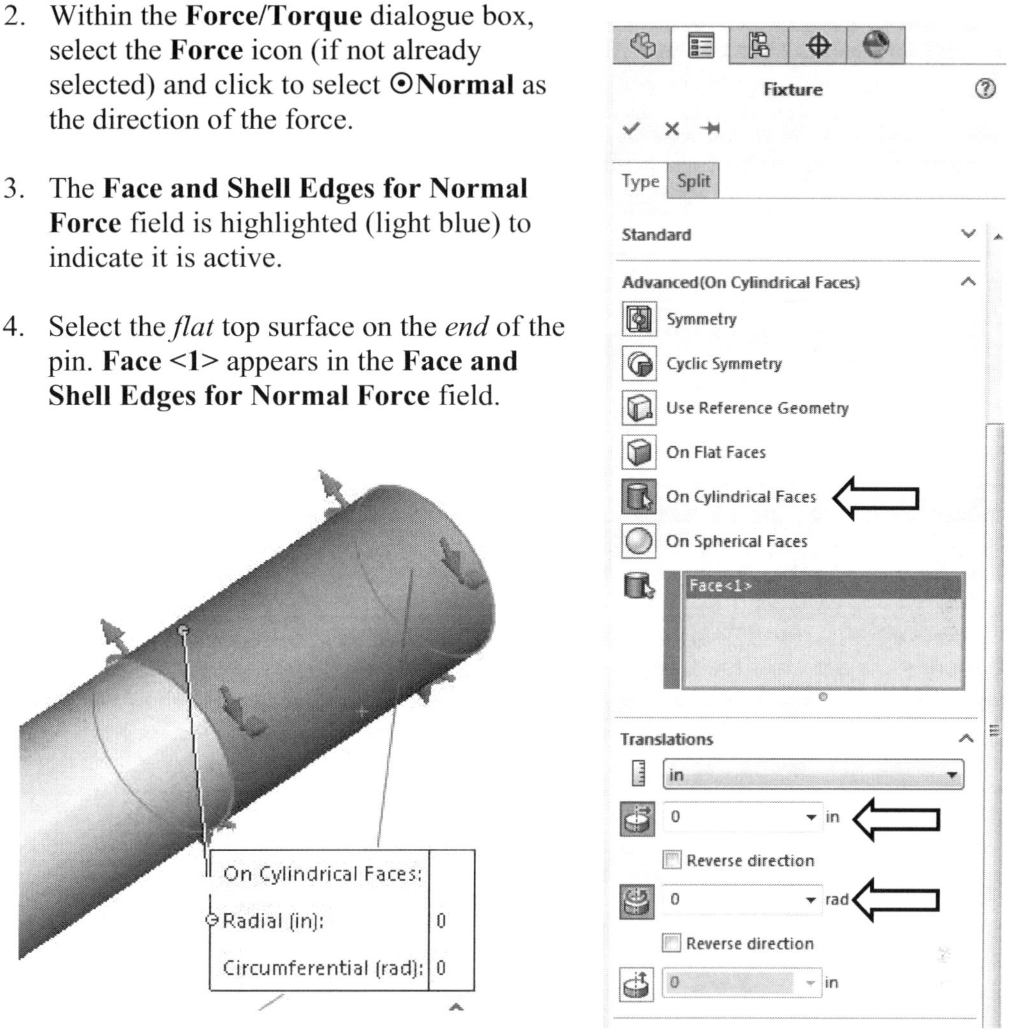

Figure 13 – The radial and circumferential translations are fixed at the top of the pin.

5. Verify that the **Units** field is set to **English (IPS).**

6. In the **Force Value** field, type **1.0**.

7. Click **[OK]** ✓ to close the **Force/Torque** property manager. **Force-1 (: Per item: 1 lbf:**) is now listed beneath the **External Loads** folder.

Buckling Analysis Options

Change the number of modes for buckling analysis to **1.0.** Try this on your own or follow the steps outlined below.

1. Right-click the **fixed-fixed ends (-Default-)** from the SOLIDWORKS Simulation manager and select **Properties...**(see Fig.3). This action opens the **Buckling** property manager.

2. Select the **Options** tab in the property manager (if not already selected). Change the **Number of buckling modes** to **1.0.**

3. Make no other changes in this property manager and click **[OK]** to close it.

Meshing and Running the Model

Use the SOLIDWORKS Simulation default mesh to mesh the model and then run the buckling analysis. Try this on your own or follow the steps outlined below.

1. In the SOLIDWORKS Simulation manager right-click the **mesh** icon 

from the pull-down menu and select **Mesh and Run...**

After a successful solution, a **Results** folder appears below the Simulation manager. This folder contains a plot of the first mode shape **Amplitude 1 (-Res Amp –Mode Shape 1-)**, shown in Fig.14. This figure shows a top view of the shape of the pin when it buckles.

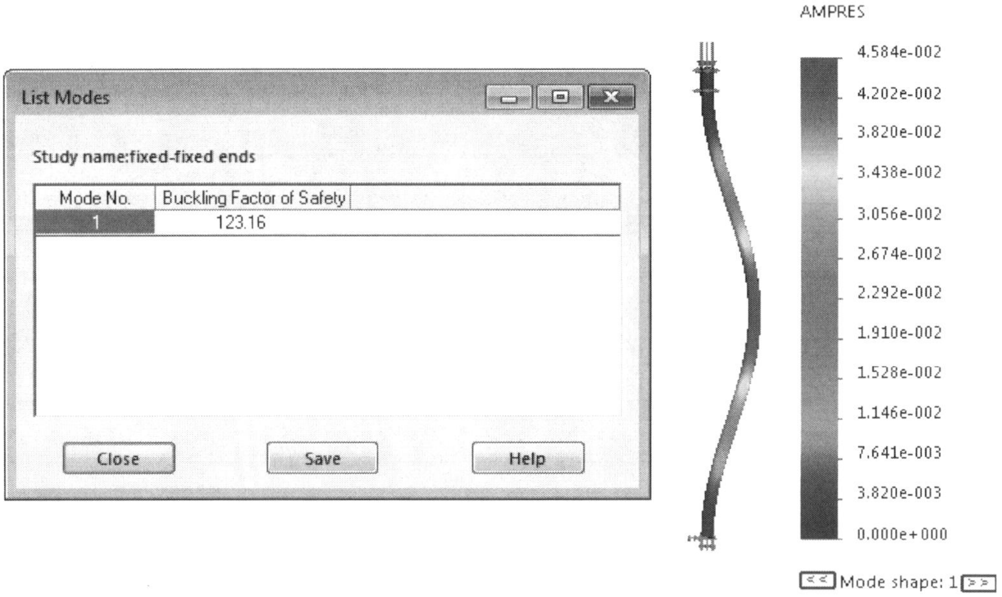

Figure 14 – **Buckling Factor of Safety** and mode shape for the pin subject to **fixed-fixed** end conditions.

2. To find the buckling force factor of safety, right-click the **Results** folder and from the pull-down menu select **List Buckling Factor of Safety**.

This opens the **List Modes** window that shows that the **Buckling Factor of safety** for **Mode No. 1** is **123.16.** This number is also reported on the top left corner of the screen as **Mode Shape: 1 Load Factor = 123.16**.

Based on this result, for a **1.0** lb axial force the buckling factor of safety is 123.16. Thus, the critical buckling force for the round pin for the fixed-fixed end conditions is **123.16** lb.

Examination of Results

Using the Euler-Column formula, the theoretical critical buckling load in elastic buckling, P_{cr}, is:

$$P_{cr} = \frac{\pi^2 E\, I}{L_e^2} = \frac{\pi^2 (29007547.53 \text{ psi})(\ 3.5891\text{e} - 7 \text{ in}^4)}{(0.5 * 1.8 \text{ in})^2} = 126.85 \text{ lb}$$

Thus, the percent difference between the theoretical and simulation results is:

$$\%\text{ difference} = \left[\frac{\text{FEA result} - \text{classical result}}{\text{FEA result}}\right] 100 = \frac{126.85 - 123.16}{123.16} = 2.99\%$$

Validity of Elastic Buckling Simulation

As previously stated, the column slenderness ratio, S_r , must be greater than a minimum slenderness ratio, S_D, in order for theory to predict the buckling force correctly. Otherwise, the results are not valid and the predicted buckling force using elastic theory is higher than the actual buckling force for a column.

The slenderness ratio of the fixed-fixed pin is:

$$S_r = \frac{L_e}{\sqrt{\frac{I}{A}}} = \frac{0.5 * 1.8 \text{ in}}{\sqrt{\frac{3.5891\text{e} - 7 \text{ in}^4}{0.002123 \text{ in}^2}}} = 69.23$$

The lower limit for elastic buckling, S_D, is:

$$S_D = \pi \sqrt{\frac{2E}{\sigma_Y}} = \pi \sqrt{\frac{2 * 29007547.53 \text{ psi}}{50991.06247 \text{ psi}}} = 105.96$$

This result shows that the elastic buckling analysis for the pin with fixed-fixed end conditions is *NOT valid* since $S_r < S_D$. In other words, the elastic buckling assumption does not apply to the pin with the fixed-fixed end conditions.

One method to determine the buckling force for this example is to use **Johnson's buckling curve**, which is based on empirical results. Figure 15 shows both the Euler's and Johnson's curves for the pin model[1]. Euler's curve is valid only for elastic buckling (i.e., $S_r > S_D$) and Johnson's curve is valid only if the buckling is not elastic (i.e., $S_r < S_D$). According to Johnson's curve, the buckling load for the pin with the fixed-fixed end conditions is **85.18** lb., which is significantly lower than the SOLIDWORK Simulation.

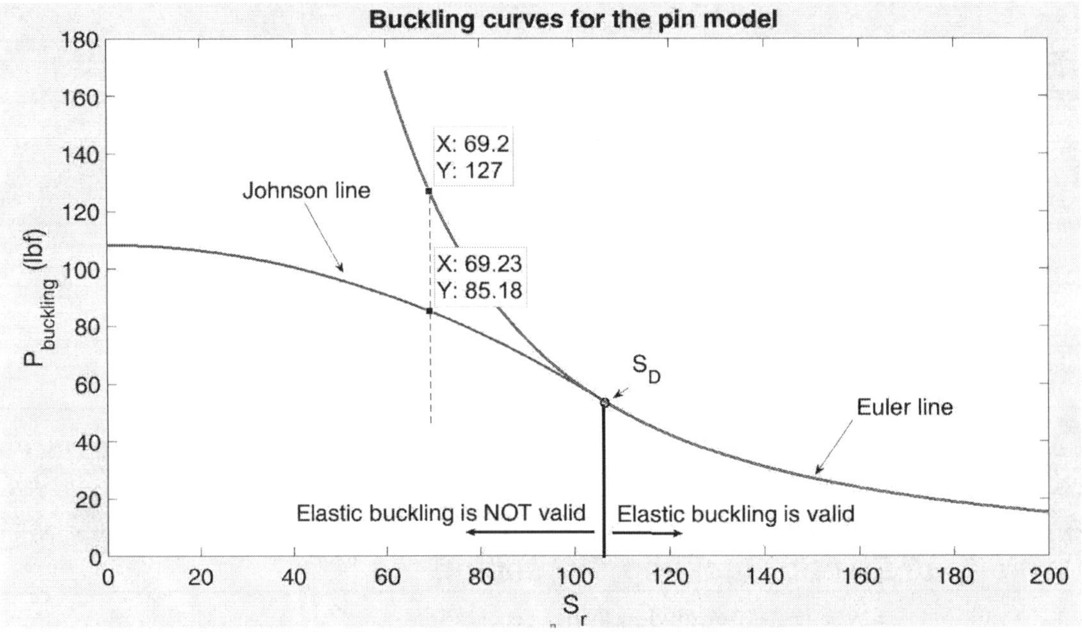

Figure 15 – Euler's and Johnson's buckling curves for the pin.

> **ASIDE:**
>
> There are two approaches to solving buckling problems using finite element analysis. The first approach is to use the elastic buckling simulation with a very conservative factor of safety (above 10), not ideal. The second approach is to carry out a nonlinear buckling analysis using the **Arc-Length** method, available in the SOLIDWORKS Simulation **Nonlinear Study**. The **Arc-Length** method works whether the buckling is elastic or not.

This concludes the buckling analysis assuming fixed-fixed end conditions for the pin model. Next, a pinned-pinned end conditions model is studied.

Close the model *without saving the model.*

[1] This figure is created using Euler and Johnson's buckling formula in MATLAB software.

Create a Buckling Analysis using Pinned-Pinned End Conditions

1. In the SOLIDWORKS main menu, select **File>Open...** Then, open the file named **Round Pin**.

Set up a buckling study named **fixed-fixed end conditions.** Try this on your own or follow the steps outlined below.

2. On the **Simulation** tab, click the down arrow ▾ beneath the **New Study** icon 

and from the pull-down menu select **New Study**. The **Study** property manager opens.

3. In the **Type** dialogue box, click on **Buckling** 

to select buckling analysis, and in the **Name** dialogue box replace "**Buckling 1**" by typing **pinned-pinned ends**.

4. Click **[OK]** ✓ to close the **Study** property manager.

An outline of the buckling analysis should appear at the bottom of the SOLIDWORKS Simulation manager tree.

Assign Material Properties to the Model

Assign **AISI 1020** material to the pin and select **English** units for this study. Try this on your own or follow the steps outlined below.

1. In the SOLIDWORKS Simulation manager right-click the model name, **Round Pin**. Then, from the pull-down menu select **Apply/Edit Material ...** The **Material** window opens.

2. Next, click the > symbol next to **Steel** (if not already selected) and select **AISI 1020** steel from the list of available steels.

3. On the **Properties** tab, adjacent to **Units:**, select **English (IPS).**

4. Click **[Apply]** followed by **[Close]** to close the **Material** window. A check mark "✓" appears on the **Round Pin** folder and the material designation **(-[SW]AISI 1020 -)** appears next to this folder.

Prepare the Model for Assignment of Pinned-Pinned End Conditions

In order to apply the pinned condition at the top and the bottom of the pin, *Split Lines* are added on both surfaces as follows.

1. From the **Main Menu**, select **Insert**. Then, from successive pull-down menus, choose **Curve ►** followed by **Split Line...** The **Split Line** property manager opens.

2. Beneath **Type of Split**, select ◉ **Intersection**.

3. In the **Selections** dialogue box, click to activate the **Splitting Bodies/Faces/Planes** field (pink color), then move the cursor onto the SOLIDWORKS "flyout" menu and select **Top Plane**. **Top Plane** now appears in the upper field.

4. Next, click inside the **Faces/Bodies to Split** field to activate it (light blue). Then move the cursor and select all three surfaces of the pin (top surface, bottom surface, and the cylindrical surface). Once selected, **Face<1>, Face<2>**, and **Face<3>** appear in the active field.

5. In the **Surface Split Options** dialogue box, select ◉ **Natural**.

6. Click **[OK]** ✓ to close the **Split Line** property manager.

Four *Split Lines* should appear on the model as follows: Two *Split Lines* on opposite sides of the cylindrical section, one on the top and one on the bottom of the pin. A pinned-pinned end conditions is next applied by using the *Split Lines* on the top and bottom surfaces of the model. *Split Lines* on the pin cylindrical surface will be used to study the buckling mode shape.

Pinned-Pinned Fixture

1. In the SOLIDWORKS Simulation manager, right-click **Fixtures** and from the pull-down menu select **Fixed Geometry**... The **Fixture** property manager opens.

2. In the **Standard (Fixed Geometry)** dialogue box, the **Fixed Geometry** icon should already be selected. The **Faces, Edges, Vertices for Fixture** field is highlighted (light blue) and is awaiting selection of the surface to be **Fixed.**
3. Select the *Split Line* on the bottom surface as shown in Fig.16. This fixture allows the bottom surface to rotate around the *Split Line* since the *Split Line* has been fixed. Thus, it creates a pinned connection.

4. Click **[OK]** ✓ (green check mark) at top of the **Fixture** property manager to accept this restraint.

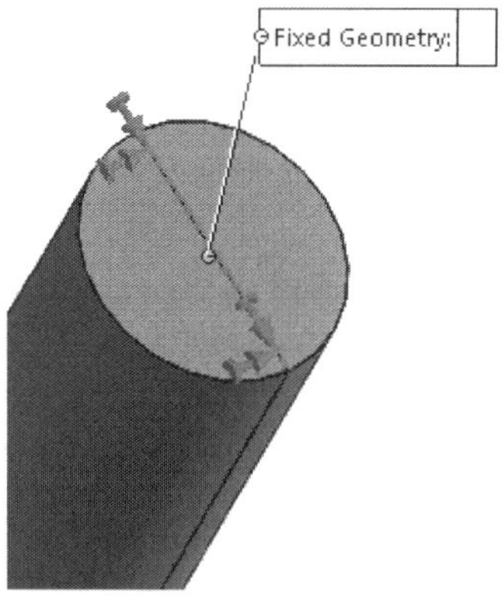

Figure 16 – Split line is fixed at the bottom surface of the pin.

5. Right-click **Fixtures** again and from the pull-down menu select **Advanced Fixtures**… The **Fixture** property manager opens.

6. Within the **Standard** dialogue box, click to select **Use Reference Geometry** icon 

. Then click to activate the **Faces, Edges, Vertices for Fixture** field (light blue). Select the *Split Line* on the top surface (see Fig.17). Next, click on the **Face, Edge, Plane, Axis for Direction** field (pink) to activate it (light blue). Move the cursor onto the "flyout" menu and select **Top Plane**. **Top Plane** now appears in the active field.

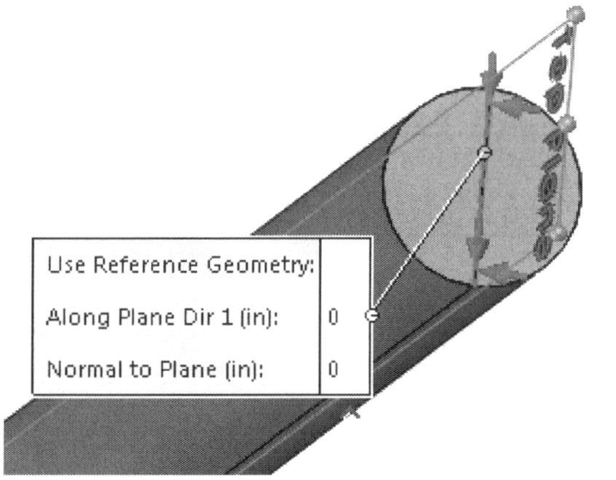
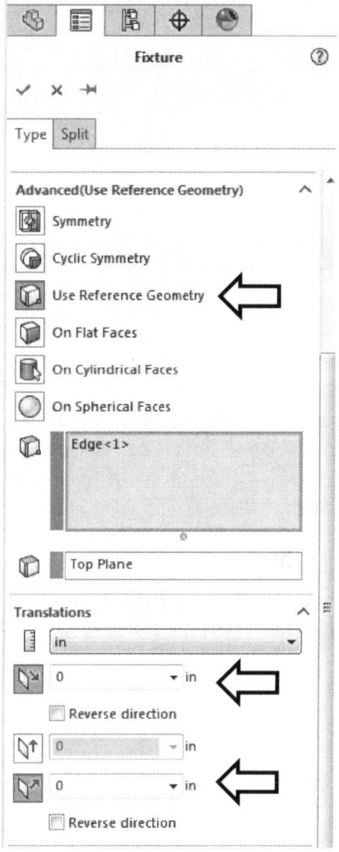

Figure 17 – **Fixture property** manager for the *Split Line* at the top of the pin.

7. In the **Fixture** property manager, scroll down to the **Translations** dialogue box. Set **Unit** to inches **in**.

8. In the **Translations** dialogue box, click to select the **Along Plane Dir 1**  icon. Ensure that **0** appears in the value box. This selection sets the lateral displacement of the *Split Line* at the top of the pin to zero. Also, click to select the **Normal to Plane**  icon. Ensure that **0** appears in the value box. This selection sets translation of the *Split Line* normal to the top plane to zero. Do NOT click to select the **Along Plane Dir 2**  icon, allowing the *Split Line* to move along the axis of the pin.

9. Click **[OK]** ✓ (green check mark) at top of the **Fixture** property manager to accept these restraints. The 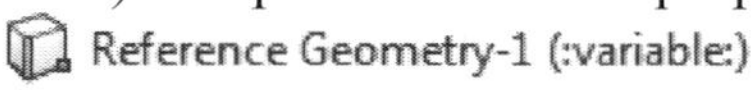

icon appears beneath the **Fixtures** folder in the Simulation manager tree. Pay attention to the direction of arrows on the cylindrical surface.

External Loads

Assign a **1.0** lb force normal to the top surface of the pin. Try this on your own or follow the steps outlined below.

1. Right-click the **External Loads** icon in the SOLIDWORKS Simulation manager and select **Force...**The **Force/Torque** property manager opens.

2. With the **Force/Torque** dialogue box, select the **Force** icon (if not already selected) and click to select ⊙**Normal** as the direction of the force.

3. The **Face and Shell Edges for Normal Force** field is highlighted (light blue) to indicate it is active. Rotate the model and zoom in as necessary to select the top surface. Note that due to the *Split Line* the top surface consists of two half-circles. Both semi-circles must be selected.

4. Verify that the **Units** field is set to **English (IPS).**

5. In the **Force Value** field, type **1.0** and click to select ⊙**Total.** (Aside: If the **Per Item** option is selected, the force on each half-circle becomes 1.0 lb. This makes a total of 2.0 lb force).

6. Click **[OK]** ✓ to close the **Force/Torque** property manager. **Force-1 (: Total: 1 lbf:)** is now listed beneath the **External Loads** folder.

Meshing and Running the Model

Use the SOLIDWORKS Simulation default mesh to mesh the model and then run the buckling analysis. Try this on your own or follow the steps outlined below.

1. In the SOLIDWORKS Simulation manager right-click the **mesh** icon Mesh from the pull-down menu and select **Mesh and Run...**

After a successful solution, a **Results** folder appears below the Simulation manager. This folder contains a plot of the first mode shape **Amplitude 1 (-Res Amp– Mode Shape 1-),** shown in Fig.18. This figure shows the shape of the pin in a side view when it buckles.

2. To find the buckling force factor of safety, right-click the **Results** folder and from the pull-down menu select **List Buckling Factor of Safety**. This action opens the **List Modes** window that shows the **Buckling Factor of Safety** for **Mode No. 1** is **28.411.** This value also appears in the plot title.

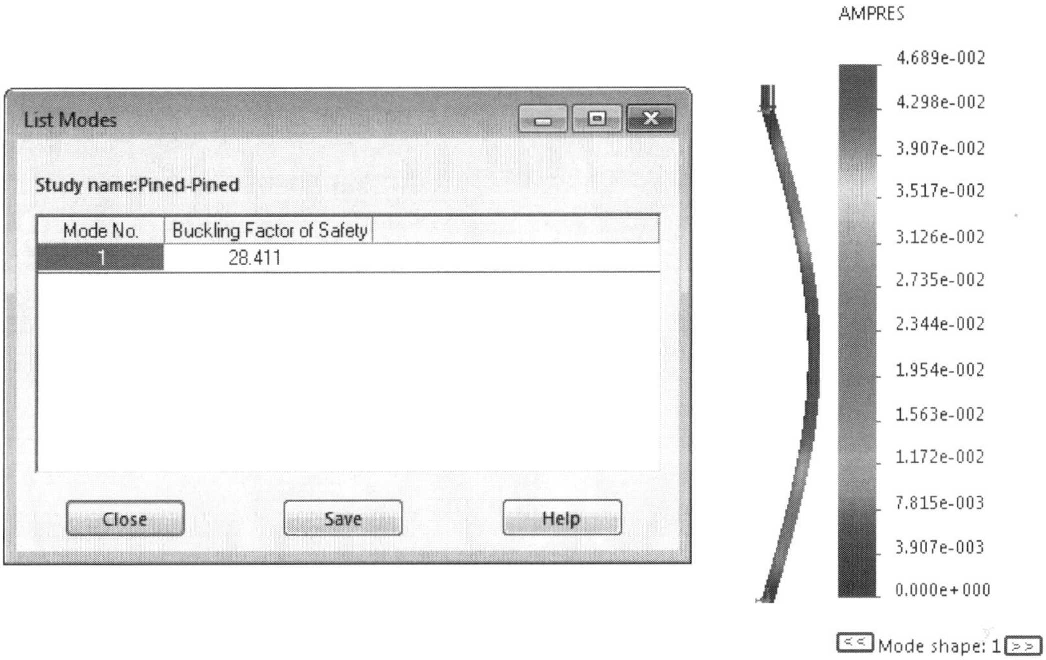

Figure 18 – **Buckling Factor of Safety** and mode shape for the pin subject to pinned-pinned end conditions.

Based on this result, for a **1.0** lb axial force, the buckling factor of safety is 28.411. Thus, the critical buckling force for the pin with the fixed-fixed end conditions is **28.411** lb.

3. Click **[Close]** to exit the **List Modes** window.

Examination of Results

Using the Euler-Column formula, the theoretical critical buckling load in elastic buckling, P_{cr}, is

$$P_{cr} = \frac{\pi^2 E\, I}{L_e^2} = \frac{\pi^2(29007547.53 \text{ psi})(\ 3.5891\text{e} - 7 \text{ in}^4)}{(1.9 \text{ in})^2} = 28.463 \text{ lb}$$

The percent difference between the theoretical and simulation results is:

$$\%\ \text{difference} = \left[\frac{\text{FEA result} - \text{classical result}}{\text{FEA result}}\right] 100 = \frac{28.463 - 28.411}{28.411} = 0.18\%$$

Buckling Mode shape (Optional)

To examine the mode shape for the pinned-pinned end column:

1. Right-click on **Amplitude 1 (-Res Amp – Mode Shape 1-)** in the **Results** folder and from the pull-down menu select **Probe** Probe to open the **Probe Result** property manager.

2. In the **Options** dialogue box, click to choose ⊙ **On selected entities**. The **Results** dialogue box expands to include a highlighted (light blue) field. This field is active and is awaiting the selection of **Faces, Edges, or Vertices** on the model.
3. In the graphics screen, move the cursor over one of the two *Split Lines* on the cylindrical surface (does not matter which one) and click to choose it. **Edge<1>** appears in the highlighted field and the **[Update]** button becomes active.

4. Click the **[Update]** button. This action fills the **Results** table.

5. In the **Report Options** dialogue box, located near the bottom of the **Probe Result** property manager, click the **Plot** icon. Immediately, a graph of lateral displacement (AMPRES) along the *Split Line* (parallel to the pin axis) is displayed (see Fig.19) versus the normalized length of the pin.

6. Click ☒ to close the **Edge Plot**.

7. Click **[OK]** ✓ to close the **Probe Result** property manager.

As expected, the mode shape is symmetrical with respect to the middle of the pin. As discussed earlier, the deflection (AMPRES) values in this plot are meaningless, but their relative values are important. For instance, at 20% and 50% of the pin height, the AMPRES values are approximately **0.0276** and **0.0468**, respectively. Therefore, the <u>relative deflection</u> of the pin is **0.589** to **1.0** at 20% and 50% of the pin height, respectively.

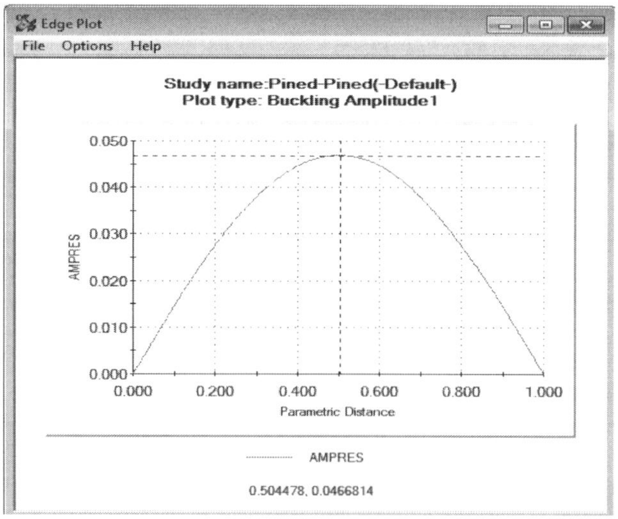

Figure 19 – Deflection (mode shape) of the pinned-pinned end connections.

This value is within 0.35 percent of the theoretical result, since, for a pinned-pinned column the expression for the mode shape is

$$y = B\sin\left(\frac{\pi z}{L}\right)$$

where z is the vertical distance from the fixed point, B is an arbitary number, and y is the deflection of the column. Therefore:

$$\frac{y_{20}}{y_{50}} = \frac{B\sin(0.2\pi)}{B\sin(0.5\pi)} = 0.587$$

Validity of Elastic Buckling Simulation

As stated before, the slenderness ratio, S_r , must be greater than a minimum slenderness ratio, S_D, in order for Euler Column theory to predict the buckling force correctly. Otherwise, the results are not valid and, in fact, the predicted buckling force based on elastic theory is higher than the actual buckling force for the structure.

The slenderness ratio of the pin with the pinned-pinned end conditions is:

$$S_r = \frac{L_e}{\sqrt{\frac{I}{A}}} = \frac{1.9\text{ in}}{\sqrt{\frac{3.5891\text{e} - 7\text{ in}^4}{0.002123\text{ in}^2}}} = 146.15$$

The lower limit for elastic buckling, S_D, is:

$$S_D = \pi\sqrt{\frac{2E}{\sigma_Y}} = \pi\sqrt{\frac{2 * 29007547.53\text{ psi}}{50991.06247\text{ psi}}} = 105.96$$

This result shows that the elastic buckling analysis for the pin with pinned-pinned end conditions is <u>*valid*</u> since $S_r > S_D$.

This concludes the buckling analysis corresponding to pinned-pinned end conditions for the pin model. At this point, the user should have all the necessary tools to carry out a buckling analysis for the pin with pinned-fixed end conditions on their own. This analysis is left as an exercise at the end of this chapter.

DO NOT CLOSE the SOLIDWORKS model at this time. The pinned-pinned end conditions model will next be used to study eccentric loading on columns.

Create a Buckling Analysis assuming an Eccentrically Loaded Pin with Pinned-Pinned End Conditions

Thus far in this chapter it has been assumed that the applied force is concentric (i.e., the load passes exactly through the pin centroid). In this section, attention is shifted to the situation in which a load is applied eccentric to the center axis of the pin. To save time, the SOLIDWORKS simulation for the pinned-pinned end connections from the previous section is modified by offsetting the applied load by the value of the eccentricity **e=0.02".**

1. Right-click on **Force-1 (:Total : 1 lbf:)** in the **External Loads** folder in the Simulation manager and from the pull-down menu select **Delete** ✕ Delete... to remove the applied load. This action opens a pop-up window. Confirm your decision by selecting **[Yes]** in this window.

2. Right-click on **Reference Geometry-1 (:variable:)** in the **Fixtures** folder in the Simulation manager and from the pull-down menu select **Delete** to remove the pinned connection at the top surface. Once again, a pop-up window opens. Confirm your decision by selecting **[Yes]** in this window.

3. Click **Amplitude1 (Res Amp – Mode Shape 1-)** and select **Hide** to hide the **Results**.

4. From the main menu, select **Insert**. Then, from succeeding pull-down menus make the following selections: **Reference Geometry ►** followed by **Plane...** Plane... . The **Plane** property manager opens to the left of the graphics area. Also, the SOLIDWORKS "flyout" menu appears at the top left of the graphics area.

5. Within the **Plane** property manager, under **First Reference**, the field is highlighted (light blue) to indicate it is active and awaiting selection of a **First Reference** plane from which a *new* plane can be referenced.

6. Begin by clicking the "▸ " sign to open the SOLIDWORKS "flyout" menu. Within the "flyout" menu select the **Top Plane**. The **Plane** property manager changes appearance and **Top Plane** appears in the **First Reference** dialogue box.

7. Return to the **First Reference** dialogue box and in the **Offset Distance** spin-box and type **0.02"**. This is the distance *from* the **Top Plane** to a **Reference Plane** located so that it intersects the cylindrical surface of the pin.

8. Click **[OK]** ✓ to close the **Plane** property manager.

The reference plane created in the previous steps appears highlighted on your screen. In the following steps, **Plane1** and the **Right Plane** are used to create two *Split Lines* at the *top* surface of the pin. The intersection of these *Split Lines* enables us to define an offset load at e=0.02". Recall that **Fixtures** were *removed* from the *top* surface.

9. From the **Main Menu**, select **Insert**. Then, from successive pull-down menus choose **Curve ►** followed by **Split Line...** The **Split Line** property manager opens.

10. Beneath **Type of Split**, select ⦿ **Intersection**.

11. Click to activate the **Splitting Bodies/Faces/ Planes** field (pink color) in the **Selections** dialogue field. Then, move the cursor onto the "flyout" menu and select both **Plane1** and **Right Plane**. **Plane1** and **Right Plane** now appear in this field. It may be necessary to scroll up or down to confirm both planes are selected.

12. Next, click inside the **Faces/Bodies to Split** field to make it active (light blue). Then move the cursor over the model and select the half-circle area at the *top surface* of the pin that intersects with **Plane 1** (see Fig.20). Once selected, **Face<1>** appears in the active field.

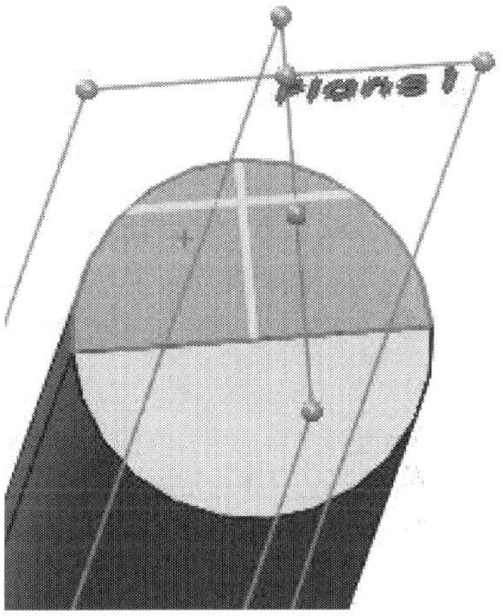

Figure 20 – **Plane 1** intersects with the half-circle area at the top surface to generate a *Split Line.*

13. In the **Surface Split Options** dialogue box, select ⦿ **Natural**.

14. Click **[OK]** ✓ to close the **Split Line** property manager.

This creates two *Split Lines* at the top surface of the pin. The intersection of these *Split Lines* defines a **vertex** that will be used to apply the eccentric load.

Pinned-Pinned Fixture

The pinned connection at the top surface was deleted to facilitate adding the two *Split Lines*. As a result, it is necessary to reapply the pinned connection on the top surface as outlined below.

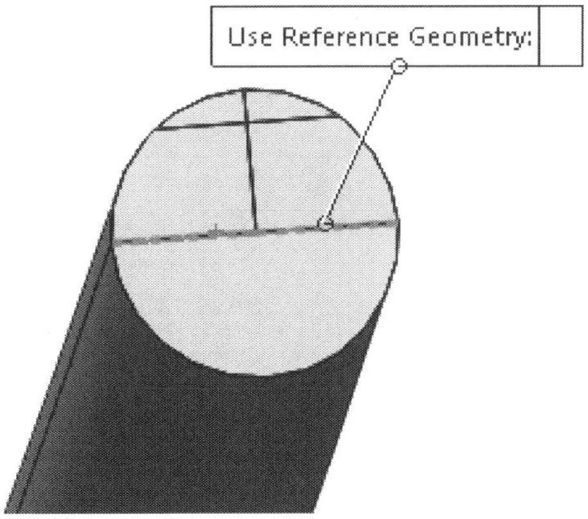

Figure 21 – The *Split Lines* at the center of the top surface.

1. Right-click **Fixtures** and from the pull-down menu select **Advanced Fixtures**... The **Fixture** property manager opens.

2. Within the **Standard** dialogue box, click to select the **Use Reference Geometry**

icon Use Reference Geometry. Then click to activate the **Faces, Edges, Vertices for Fixture** field (light blue). Select the two *segments* of the *Split Line along the middle* of the top surface labeled "**Use Reference Geometry**" in Fig. 21. Next, click on the **Face, Edge, Plane, Axis for Direction** field (pink) to activate it. Move the cursor onto the "flyout" menu and select **Top Plane**. **Top Plane** now appears in the second field.

3. In the **Fixture** property manager, scroll down to the **Translations** dialogue box. Set the **Unit** to inches **in**.

4. In the **Translations** dialogue box, click to select the **Along Plane Dir 1** icon. Ensure that **0** appears in the value box. This selection sets the lateral displacement of the Split Line at the top of the pin to zero. Also, click to select the **Normal to Plane** icon. Ensure that **0** appears in the value box. This selection sets the translation of the Split Line normal to the top plane to zero. Do NOT click to select the **Along Plane Dir 2** icon. Having this value *unspecified* allows the *Split Line* to move along the axis of the pin.

5. Click [OK] ✓ (green check mark) at top of the **Fixture** property manager to accept this restraint. The Reference Geometry-1 (:variable:) icon appears beneath the **Fixtures** folder in the Simulation manager tree.

External Loads

Assign a **1.0** lb force normal to the top surface of the pin at the intersection of the two *Split Lines* generated using the **Right Plane** and **Plane 1**.

1. Right-click the **External Loads** icon from the SOLIDWORKS Simulation manager and select **Force...**The **Force/Torque** property manager opens.

2. The **Face and Shell Edges for Normal Force** field is highlighted (light blue) to indicate it is active. Rotate the model and zoom in as necessary to select the intersection of the two Split Lines. Once selected, **Vertex<1>** appears in the active field.

3. Within the **Force/Torque** dialogue box, click to choose ⊙**Selected direction** to

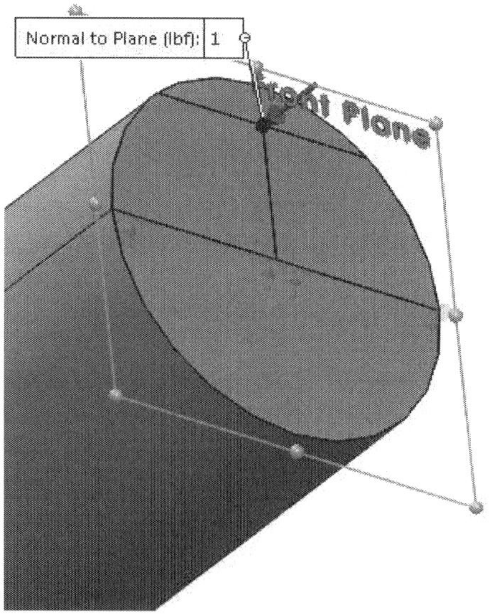

Figure 22 – A **1.0 lb** force with an offset of **0.02**" normal to the top surface of the pin.

begin defining the direction of the force. The **Face, Edge, Plane for Direction** field appears highlighted (light blue) and is awaiting selection.

4. Move the cursor onto the "flyout" menu and select **Front Plane**. **Front Plane** now appears in this field.

5. Verify that the **Units** field is set to **English (IPS).**

6. In the **Force** field, click to enable the **Normal to Plane** icon and type **1.0** for the force value. You should see a 1.0 lb force acting on the top surface as shown in Fig. 22.

7. Click **[OK]** ✓ to close the **Force/Torque** property manager. **Force-2 (: Per item: 1 lbf:)** is now listed beneath the **External Loads** folder.

Meshing and Running the Model

Use the SOLIDWORKS Simulation default mesh to mesh the model and then run the buckling analysis. Try this on your own or follow the steps outlined below.

1. In the SOLIDWORKS Simulation manager right-click the **Mesh** icon Mesh, and from the pull-down menu select **Mesh and Run…**

After a successful solution, a **Results** folder appears below the Simulation manager. This folder contains a plot of the first mode shape **Amplitude 1 (-Res Amp– Mode Shape 1-).**

2. To find the buckling force, right-click the **Results** folder and from the pull-down menu select **List Buckling Factor of Safety**. This opens the **List Modes** window that shows the **Buckling Factor of safety** for the **Mode No. 1** is **28.405.**

3. Click ☒ to close the **List Modes** window.

Therefore, the buckling load for this pin is **28.405 lb** based on the simulation results.

Examination of Results

The theoretical deflection at mid-span of a pinned-pinned end conditions column subject to an eccentric loading P is given by:

$$y_{50} = e\left[\sec\left(\frac{L}{2}\sqrt{\frac{P}{EI}}\right) - 1\right]$$

When buckling occurs, the argument of the secant is at $\pi/2$, which causes the mid-span deflection to go to infinity. Thus, the theoretical critical buckling load, P_{cr}, of an eccentrically loaded column is:

$$P_{cr} = \frac{\pi^2 E\, I}{L^2}$$

Which is the same as the critical load when the load was concentric with the column. Thus, the theoretical critical buckling load for the pin in this case is $P_{cr} = 28.463$ lb.

The percent difference between the theoretical and simulation results is:

$$\%\text{ difference} = \left[\frac{\text{FEA result} - \text{classical result}}{\text{FEA result}}\right]100 = \frac{28.463 - 28.405}{28.463} = 0.20\%$$

IMPORTANT:
It is important to note that when it comes to eccentrically loaded columns, the designer must always consider the possibility of yielding before column buckling. The maximum stress in the pin for the pinned-pinned end conditions happens at midspan and can be found using the **secant column formula:**
Insert a blank line beneath the following equation.

$$\sigma_{MAX} = \frac{P}{A}\left[1 + \frac{edA}{2I}\sec\left(L\sqrt{\frac{P}{4EI}}\right)\right]$$

By setting σ_{MAX} equal to the compressive yield strength of **AISI 1020** steel, $\sigma_Y =$ 50991.06247 psi, the maximum load for the cylindrical pin before it yields is given by:

$$P_{Max} = 13.935\ lb$$

The above result is obtained using an iterative solution where the pin parameters are:

$L = 1.9"$, $I = 3.5891\text{e-}7\ \text{in}^4$, $E = 29007547.53$ psi, $d = 0.052"$, $e = 0.02"$, and $A = 2.123\text{e-}3\ \text{in}^2$

The result for maximum axial load clearly shows that for a 0.02" eccentric load the pin will yield before experiencing buckling.

This concludes the analysis for the eccentric loading of the pin.

Summary

- Elastic buckling in SOLIDWORKS must be used with caution. The **Factor of Safety** from an elastic buckling analysis is useful in predicting the buckling load of a column as long as the slenderness ratio of the column is greater than a lower limit (S_D). Otherwise, the simulation results over-predict the **Factor of Safety** for the column. In that case, one must use a relatively large **Factor of Safety** for a design purpose. Another approach is to use a **Nonlinear Buckling** analysis or empirical results such as **Johnson's Formula** to predict the **Factor of Safety** for columns with small slenderness ratios.

- In eccentrically loaded columns, one must be very careful in determining the **Factor of Safety**. These columns could yield before they buckle, and in that case, the **Factor of Safety** from elastic buckling should not be used for design purposes. Additionally, the **Factor of Safety** from a SOLIDWORKS static analysis cannot be trusted unless the column is short since the increased bending moment due to bending deflection in long columns is not accounted for in the static analysis. In that case, one must use **Nonlinear Buckling** analysis or the **Secant Column Formula** for columns with uniform cross-sectional area.

This concludes the current chapter. Close the model (*without saving)* and exit from SOLIDWORKS.

EXERCISES

EXERCISE 1 –Buckling Analysis of the Pin with a Pinned-Fixed End Conditions

Open the file **Round Pin** (used for the examples in this chapter) and perform a linear buckling analysis.

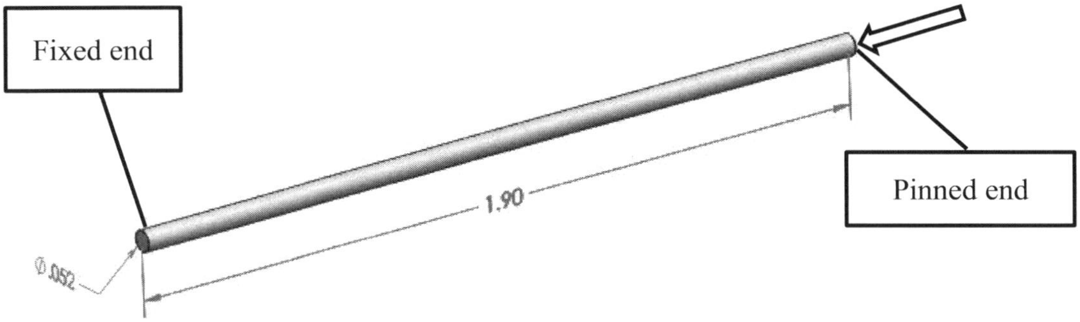

Figure E9-1 – The **pin** showing a compressive load with fixed-pinned end conditions.

- Material: **AISI 1020 steel**, round-off yield strength to nearest 1000 psi.
- Mesh: System default **Curvature based mesh.**
- Fixtures: **Fixed (immovable)** bottom surface and **Pinned** top surface.
- External Load: Apply **1.0 lb** force at the top surface.

Determine the following:

Develop a finite element analysis that includes a material specification, fixtures, external load(s), mesh, and buckling solutions.

a. Find the critical buckling load using SOLIDWORKS simulation and compare the result with the Euler column theory.

b. Optional: Plot the mode shape of the pin in an x-y graph. Use a normalized length for the x-axis and AMPRES for the y-axis.

c. Use buckling theory and verify whether or not the assumption of elastic buckling applies to this problem. If the answer is "NO," find the critical load using Johnson's buckling equation.

d. Determine if the column buckles or yields first. Show pertinent calculations/results and state the reason for your conclusion.

e. Repeat items (a) and (b) above assuming the compressive force is applied with an offset of e=0.01" with respect to the center axis of the pin.

f. Determine if the column with the eccentric load at e=0.01" buckles or yields first and state the reason for your conclusion.

g. Find the factor of safety for the column with the eccentric load at e=0.01".

EXERCISE 2 –Buckling Analysis of a Drill Bit

This exercise is based on a drill bit subject to an axial load. The goal is to simulate use in a drill press and to determine the factor of safety for the drill bit for the case in which the drill bit just begins to touch the material and is free to translate across the surface of the material at its tip. Assume the drill bit has a uniform diameter throughout its length and disregard the drill flutes.

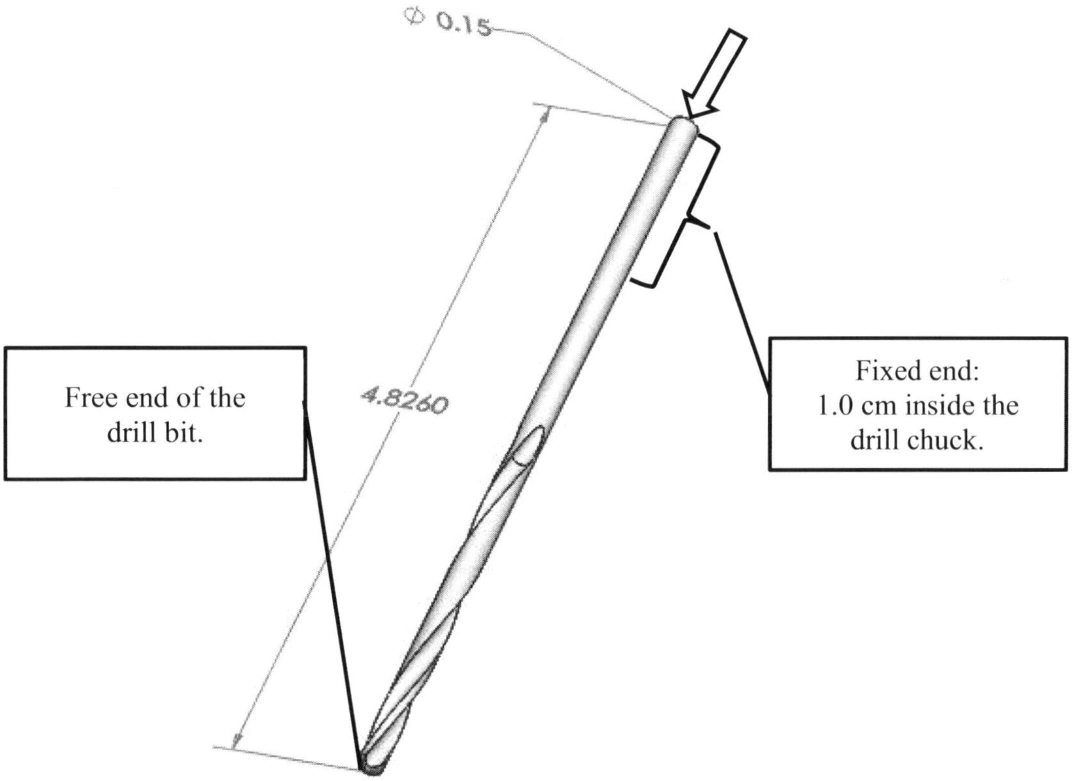

Figure E9-2 – Axially loaded **drill bit** with a fixed-free end conditions (all dimensions in "centimeters").

Open the file**: Drill Bit**

- Material: **AISI 304** steel.
- Mesh: System default **Curvature based mesh.**
- Fixtures: **Fixed (immovable)** restraints applied to top surface.
- External Load: Apply a 52 N on the top surface of the drill bit.

Determine the following:

Develop a finite element analysis that includes a material specification, fixtures, external load(s), mesh, and buckling solutions.

a. Find the critical buckling load using SOLIDWORKS Simulation. Assume the top 1.0 cm of the drill bit is fixed in the drill chuck.

b. Optional: Plot the mode shape of the pin in an x-y graph. Use a normalized length for the x-axis and AMPRES for the y-axis.

c. Use buckling theory and verify whether or not the assumption of elastic buckling applies to this problem. (HINT: Use a nominal diameter of 0.15cm for the drill bit and use classical results for columns with a uniform cross sectional area.)

d. Determine if the drill bit buckles or yields first. Show pertinent calculations/results and state the reason for your conclusion.

Solution Guidance

To create free end conditions at the tip of the drill bit, use **Front Plane**, then restrain the movement of the vertex at the drill bit tip in the plane only to lateral movements. Set the axial movement (perpendicular to the plane) to zero.

Exercise 3 – Buckling Analysis of a Bike Tire Pump

This exercise is based on a bicycle tire pump whose handle and shaft are subjected to an axial force (see E9-3). The goal is to simulate use of the pump and to determine the critical load for the shaft. As tire pressure builds up, it becomes harder to force the air into the tire. The case to be examined in this exercise is when the tire is at maximum pressure and air can no longer be forced into the tire. This situation may be modeled by assuming that the bottom of the shaft has a fixed condition. Also, assume the shaft has a uniform diameter of 3/8 inch throughout its length and disregard the stopper located 0.5 inches from the bottom.

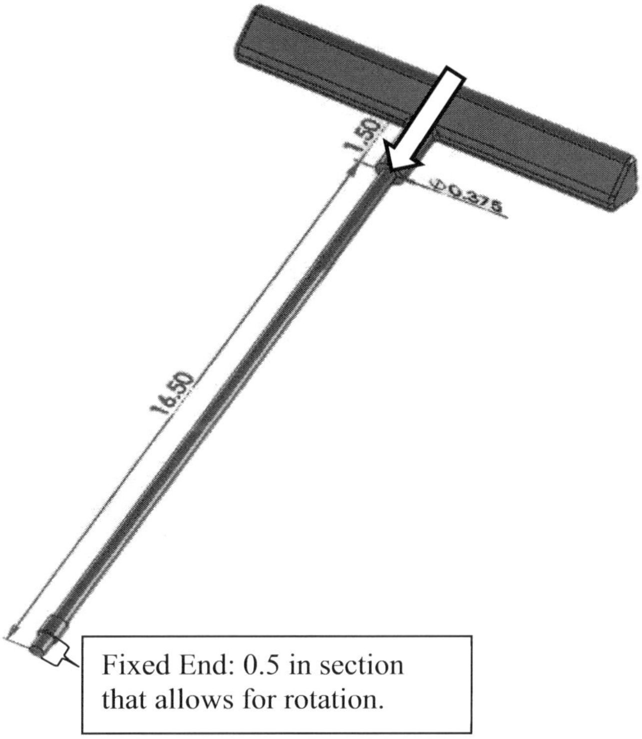

Figure E9-3 - Axially loaded **Bike Pump Handle and Shaft** with fixed-free end conditions (all dimensions are in inches).

Open the file: **Bike Pump Handle and Shaft**

- Material: **1060 Aluminum Alloy**.
- Mesh: System default, **Curvature based mesh**.
- Fixtures: **Fixed (immovable)** bottom surface and **On Cylindrical Faces** for the bottom 0.5 inches that allows for rotation.
- External Load: Apply **1.0 lb** force at the top of the shaft.

Determine the following:
Develop a finite element analysis that includes a material specification, fixtures, external load(s), mesh, and buckling solutions.

a. Find the critical buckling load using SOLIDWORKS Simulation.

b. Optional: Plot the mode shape of the **Bike Pump Handle and Shaft** in an x-y graph. Use a normalized length for the x-axis and AMPRES for the y-axis.

c. Use classical buckling theory and verify whether the assumptions of elastic buckling apply to this problem. (HINT: Use a nominal diameter of 0.375 inches for the shaft and assume the shaft has a uniform cross-sectional area. For the length of the shaft, use a value of 16 inches. This accounts for the length of the shaft between where the load is applied and where the fixture is applied). Compare the results with the results from SOLIDWORKS Simulation.

d. Determine whether the shaft buckles or yields first. Show pertinent calculations/results and state the reason for your conclusion.

Solution Guidance
To create the **On Cylindrical Faces** fixed end, use **Advanced Fixtures**, then restrain movement of the shaft to only **Circumferential** movements. Set the **Radial** and **Axial** Movement to 0.

Exercise 4 – Buckling Analysis of an I-Beam with a Fixed-Fixed End Condition

Open the file **I Beam** and perform a linear buckling analysis. The **I Beam** is fixed on the top and bottom of the member and is made of ASTM A36 steel. The top of the **I Beam** as shown in Fig. E9-4 is where the force is applied. The **I Beam** has a 1.0 lbf force acting vertically downward on the top surface.

- Material: **ASTM A36** Steel
- Mesh: System default **Standard Mesh**
- Fixtures: **Fixed (immovable)** restraints applied to the bottom and top surface.
- External Load: Apply a **1.0 lbf** on the top surface of the I-beam.

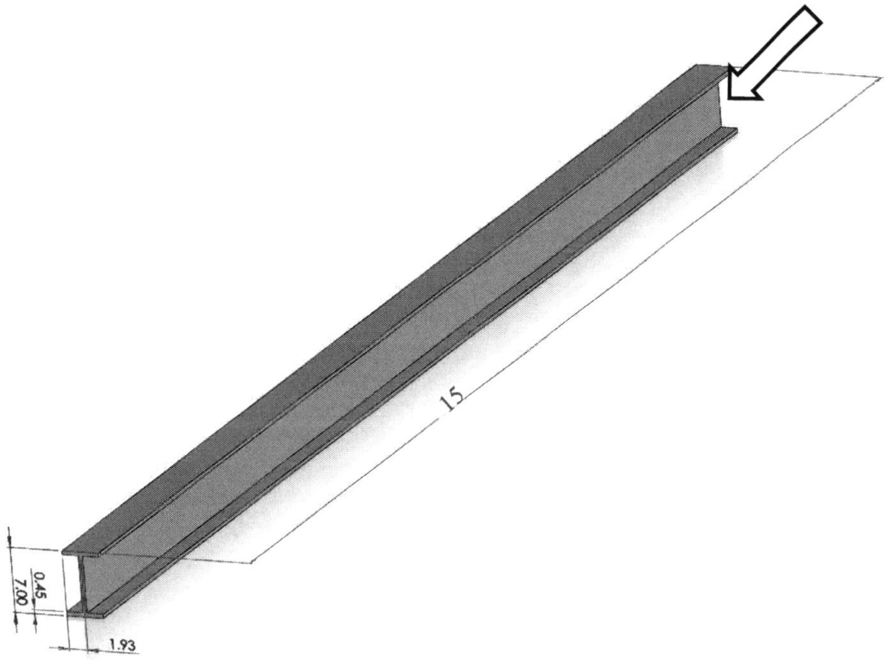

Figure E9-4- Axially loaded **I Beam** with fixed-fixed end conditions (all dimensions are in mm). It should be noted that the web thickness is equal to the flange thickness for this I-beam.

Determine the following:

Develop a finite element analysis that includes a material specification, fixtures, external load(s), mesh, and buckling solutions.

a. Find the critical buckling load using SOLIDWORKS Simulation.

b. Optional: Plot the mode shape of the **I Beam** in an x-y graph. Use a normalized length for the x-axis and AMPRES for the y-axis.

c. Use classical buckling theory and verify whether the assumptions of elastic buckling apply to this problem. Compare the results with the results from SOLIDWORKS Simulation.

d. Determine if the **I Beam** buckles or yields first. Show pertinent calculations/results and state the reason for your conclusion.

Exercise 5 – Buckling Analysis of structure with a two Pinned-Pinned End Conditions.

Open the file **Two Member Truss** and perform a linear buckling analysis. The **Two Member Truss** is subject to a 1.0 lbf acting vertically downward on the shared pin joint as shown in Fig. E9-5. The structure contains two **Fixed** wall mounts, three pins, and two rectangular members; all elements are made of 6061-T6 aluminum (see Fig. E9.6).

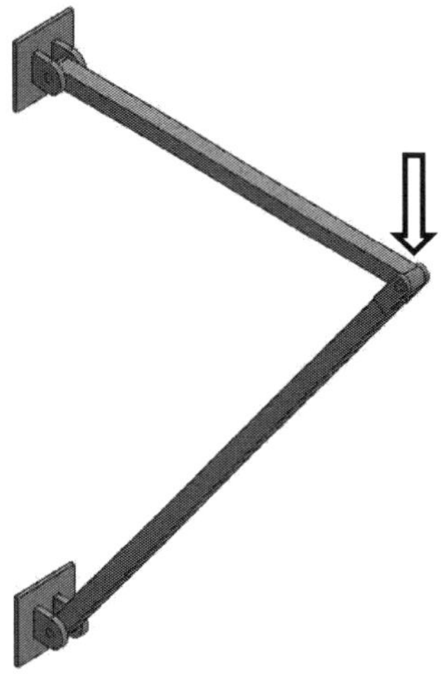

Figure E9-5- **Two Member Truss** with an applied load of 1.0 lbf, located at the pinned connection for the two members. Both members have pinned-pinned connections.

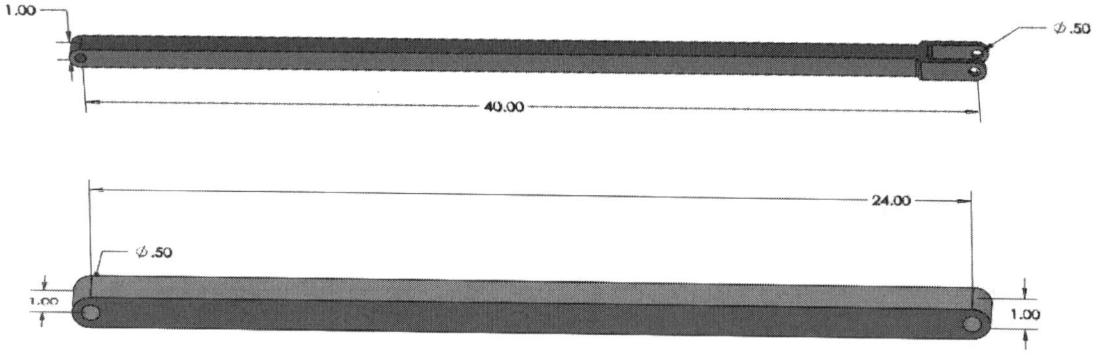

Figure E9-6- Member 1 and Member 2 of the **Two Member Truss** with dimensions shown in inches.

- Material: **6061-T6 (SS) Aluminum**
- Mesh: System default **Standard Mesh**
- Fixtures: **Fixed (immovable)** restraints applied to the back of the wall mounts. Pinned connectors need to be used at each pin joint.
- External Load: Apply a **1.0 lbf** on the bottom of the shared pin joint.

Determine the following:

Develop a finite element analysis that includes a material specification, fixtures, external load(s), mesh, and buckling solutions.

a. Find the critical buckling load using SOLIDWORKS Simulation.

b. Use classical buckling theory and verify whether the assumptions of elastic buckling apply to this problem. Compare the results with the results from SOLIDWORKS Simulation.

c. Demonstrate your understanding of SOLIDWORKS Simulation and buckling by describing why the structure deformation only shows the diagonal beam deflecting.

Solution Guidance

Due to the model being an assembly, SOLIDWORKS needs to understand how the parts are connected. This is the purpose of the **Connections** option located in the **Feature Manager Design Tree**. This assembly requires the use of 7 pin connectors. Four pin connectors are used to eliminate the pin's ability to translate and rotate. The remaining 3 pin connectors are applied to eliminate only the pin's ability to translate. It should be noted that Fig. E9-8 should be used as an aid in understanding the meaning of inner and outer pin connection, which is used in the Solution Guidance.

1) Right-click **Connectors** and select **Pin**.
2) Select **Pin B** as shown in Fig. E9-8. Select the *outer* cylindrical surface as highlighted in Fig. E9-8 and labeled as A. If the current surface cannot be clicked from your viewing angle, right click the area of interest and select **Select Other** from the pop up window.

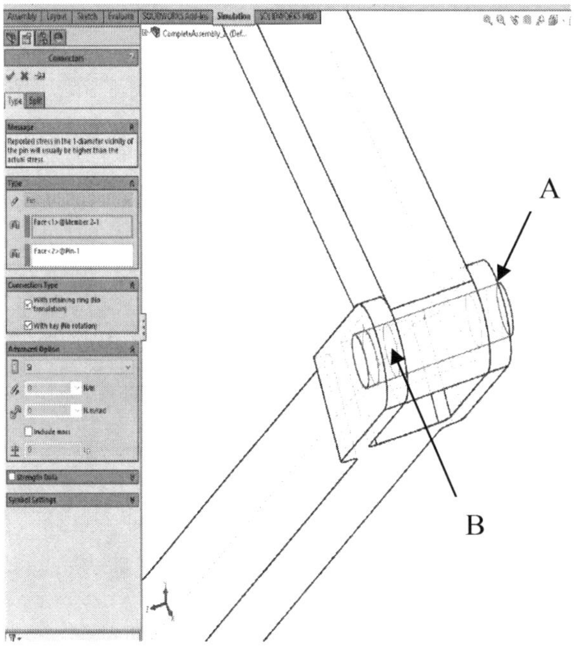

Figure E9-7 - Pin connection that eliminates a pin's ability to translate or rotate with respect to the outer pin connection.

3) Select the *inner* cylindrical face of the outer pin connection as highlighted in Fig. E9-7 and labeled as B.
4) Under **Connection Type**, check the box ☑ for "**With retaining ring (No translation)**" and for ☑"**With key (no rotation)**".
5) Your model should now look like Fig. E9-7.
6) Repeat steps 1-4 for the other two pin joints.

The fourth connection type is located at the pin joint where the two members meet.

1) Right click **Connectors** and select **Pin**.

2) This time select **Pin B** and the opposite cylindrical inner wall of the outer pin connection B that was selected earlier. Note: Figure E9-7 shows the constraining of the left side of joint B, which was done in steps 1-5 above. For this step, the right side of joint B is now being constrained.

3) Under **Connection Type** check the box ☑ for "**With retaining ring (No translation)**" and for ☑ "**With key (no rotation)**".

The remaining three **Pin Connections** will eliminate only the translation of the pin.

1) Right click **Connects** and select **Pin**.

2) Select one of the three pins: A, B, or C.

3) Select the inner cylindrical face of the inner pin connection.

4) Under **Connection Type** check the box for "**With retaining ring (No translation)**".

5) Repeat steps 1-4 for the two remaining **Pins**.

You should now have seven **Pin Connections**.

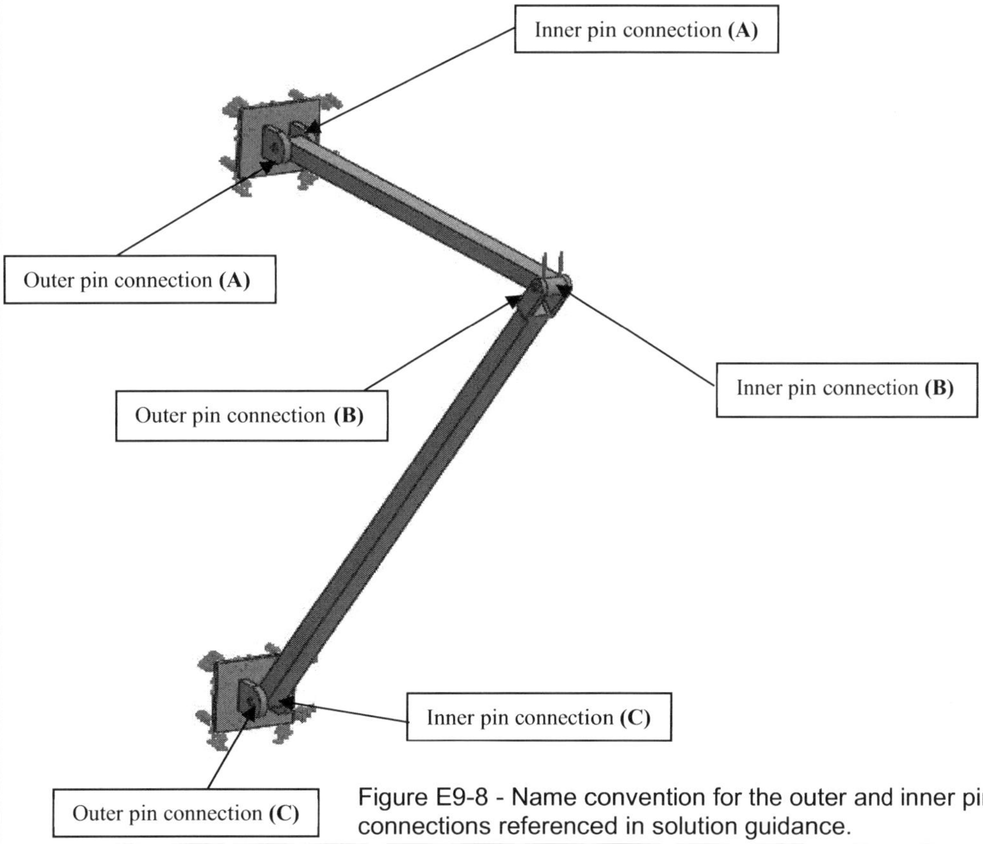

Figure E9-8 - Name convention for the outer and inner pin connections referenced in solution guidance.

NOTES:

CHAPTER #10

FATIGUE TESTING ANALYSIS

This chapter explores fatigue life of a component using stress life methods. The stress life method is commonly used when calculating fatigue life because it is applicable to a wide range of design applications. Understanding the fatigue life of a product is a critical part of the design process. This chapter focuses on the inputs needed to define a fatigue analysis in SOLIDWORKS Simulation and the boundary conditions necessary to obtain valid results. Examples in this chapter acquaint the user with both time varying axial and bending loading types.

Learning Objectives

Upon completion of these examples, users should be able to:

- Perform fatigue analysis using SOLIDWORKS Simulation.
- Apply axial and bending loading types to a fatigue analysis.
- Perform fatigue analysis for different loading combinations (fully-reversed and zero based).
- Understand the assumptions and limitations of fatigue analysis in SOLIDWORKS Simulation.

Problem-1: Fatigue Analysis of a Cylindrical Rod Subject to Reversed Bending

An AISI 1020 steel cylindrical rod (we refer it to as cylinder) with a diameter of 25mm and a length of 250mm is subject to a fully reversed bending load (see Fig.1). It is assumed that the cylinder has a polished surface finish. The goal of this example is to find the number of load cycles the cylinder can undergo before failure due to fatigue or yielding. The example will also explain the importance of the SN curve, how to generate the SN curve based on results obtained using SOLIDWORKS Simulation, and how to load the SN curve into SOLIDWORKS.

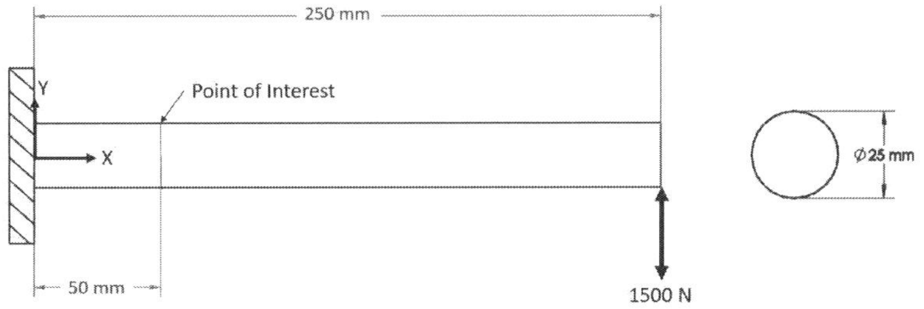

Figure 1 – Cylinder is subject to a fully reversed ±1500 N force applied in the y direction on its right end, and a *Split Line* is applied 50 mm from the left end of the component.

Creating a Static Analysis (Study)

1. Open SOLIDWORKS by making the following selections. (*NOTE:* The symbol “>” is used below to separate successive menu selections.)

2. **Start>All Programs>SOLIDWORKS 2026** (or) Click the **SOLIDWORKS 2026** icon on your screen.

3. In the SOLIDWORKS main menu, select **File > Open…** Then browse to the location where SOLIDWORKS Simulation files are stored and select the file named “**Fatigue Cylinder**;” then click **[Open]**.

4. Select **New Study** found beneath the ▼ **New Study** icon on the **Simulation** tab. Alternatively, in the main menu, select **Simulation**. Then from the pull-down menu select **Study…** Either action opens the **Study** property manager.

5. In the **Study Name** dialogue box, type **Cylinder Bending Study**.

6. Verify that a **Static** analysis is selected and click **[OK]** ✓ to close the **Study** property manager. A Study outline appears in the Simulation manager.

> **NOTE:**
> - In order to run a fatigue study, SOLIDWORKS requires there to be a static study. Stresses determined in a static study are subsequently used by a fatigue study to calculate the number of cycles to failure at each node of the model’s mesh.

Assign Material Properties to the Model

7. In the SOLIDWORKS Simulation manager right-click the model name, **Fatigue Cylinder**. Then, from the pull-down menu select **Apply/Edit Material**. The **Material** window opens.

8. Next, click the symbol next to **Steel** (if not already selected) to expand the menu and select **AISI 1020** steel from the list of available steels.

9. Click **[Apply]** followed by **[Close]** to close the **Material** window. A check mark “✓” appears on the **Fatigue Cylinder** folder and the material designation (**-AISI 1020-**) appears next to this folder.

Applying Fixtures and External Loads

The load and fixtures acting on this model include an **Immovable** restraint applied on the left-end of the cylinder and a downward acting 1500 N force applied along the right-end of the cylinder in the y-direction. Practice applying these restraints and loads on your own. After applying restraints and loads the model should appear as shown in Fig. 2. A step-by-step procedure is provided if guidance is desired.

Fixtures

10. In the SOLIDWORKS Simulation manager, right click **Fixtures,** and from the pull-down menu select **Fixed Geometry…** The **Fixture** property manager opens.

11. Within the **Standard (Fixed Geometry)** dialogue box, select the **Fixed Geometry** icon (if not already selected).

12. The **Faces, Edges, Vertices for Fixture** field is highlighted (light blue) to indicate it is active and awaiting selection of the surface to be **Fixed**. Rotate the model as necessary and select the surface on the left end of the model (closer to the *Split Line*). **Immovable** restraints are applied to the left end of the model as seen in Fig. 2.

13. Click **[OK]** ✓ (green check mark) at the top of the **Fixture** property manager to accept this restraint. An icon named Fixed-1 appears beneath the **Fixtures** folder in the Simulation manager tree.

Applying External Load(s)

14. In the Simulation manager, right-click the **External Loads** icon, and from the pop-up menu select **Force…** The **Force/Torque** property manager opens.

15. Within the **Force/Torque** dialogue box, select the **Force** icon (if not already selected).

16. The **Faces, Edges, Vertices, Reference Points for Force** field is highlighted (light blue) to indicate it is active. Rotate the model and zoom in as necessary to select the right face of the cylinder.

17. Click **Selected Direction** as the direction of the force.

18. The **Face, Edge, Plane for Direction** is highlighted (blue color) to indicate it is active. Rotate the model and zoom in as necessary to select the left face of the cylinder.

19. Verify that the **Units** field is set to **SI.**

20. In the **Force Value** field, select the **Along Plane Dir 1** option and enter 1500.

21. Because the default orientation for forces applied on a surface is in the positive direction, it is necessary to check ☑ **Reverse direction** to apply the intended downward bending load.

22. Click **[OK]** ✓ (green check mark) at the top of the **Force/Torque** property manager to accept this force. An icon named Force-1 (:Per item: -1500 N:) appears beneath the **External Loads** folder in the Simulation manager tree.

Figure 2 – Fatigue Cylinder restrained on its left end with a downward -1500 N force applied in the y direction on its right end.

Meshing the Model

23. Right-click the **Mesh** folder, and from the pull-down menu select **Create Mesh…**

24. Set the **Mesh Density** to **Fine** and check ✓ to open the ☑ **Mesh Parameters** dialogue box and verify that a ⊙ **Standard mesh** is selected. Set the **Unit** field to **mm** (if not already selected). Accept the remaining default settings (i.e., mesh **Global Size** and **Tolerance**).
25. Finally, click **[OK]** ✓ to accept the default mesh settings and close the **Mesh** property manager.

MESH SIZE:

- When doing fatigue analysis in SOLIDWORKS it is important to set the mesh size to **Fine** to ensure accurate results. A small change in stress results in a large change in the number of cycles to failure. This is due to the log-log scale used to interpolate the SN-Curve within SOLIDWORKS.

Static Solution

26. On the **Simulation** tab click the **Run this Study** Run This Study icon to start calculating the solution. It will take around a minute before SOLIDWORKS populates the **Results** folder. In this study, the maximum Von Mises stress and displacement should be approximately 235 MPa and 2.04 mm, respectively.

Fatigue Study

After a static study is successfully run, the next step is to begin the fatigue analysis in SOLIDWORKS. The same settings defined in the static study will be used for the fatigue analysis.

27. Select **New Study** found beneath the ▼ **New Study** icon on the **Simulation** tab. Alternatively, in the main menu, select **Simulation**. Then from the pull-down menu select **Study…** Either action opens the **Study** property manager.

28. In the **Name** dialogue box type **Cylinder Fatigue Study**.

29. From the pull-down menu under **Advanced Simulation** select **Fatigue** as the study type. Below the fatigue icon select **Constant amplitude events with defined cycles** for the fatigue type analysis. Click **[OK]** ✓ to close the **Study** property manager. A Study outline appears in the Simulation manager.

Add Event

30. In the Simulation manager, right click **Loading (-Constant Amplitude-)** and select **Add Event…** Add Event...

31. Under **Loading Type** click the pull-down arrow ▼ and select **Fully Reversed (LR= -1).** Leave the **number of cycles** and **stress Scale** set to the default value of 1000 cycles and 1, respectively.

32. Under **Study** click the pull-down arrow ▼ and select "Cylinder Bending Study" (see Fig. 3).

33. Click **[OK]** ✓ to close the **Add Event** property manager.

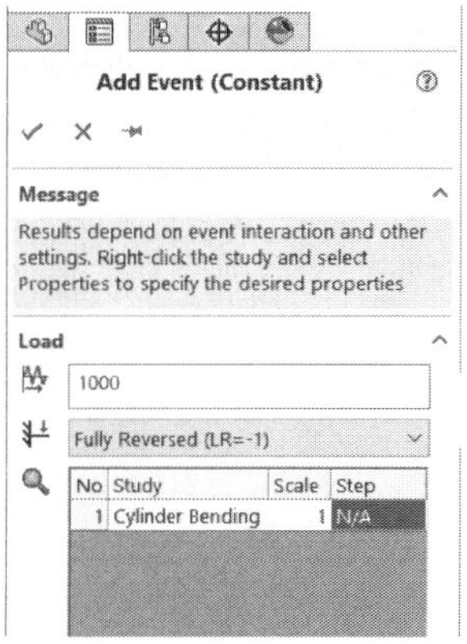

Figure 3 – Fatigue event property manager settings

The above settings for the fatigue event imply all the loads and hence stress components reverse their directions simultaneously for the specified number of cycles in this event.

For the different loading types' description in SOLIDWORKS Simulation fatigue analysis refer to the table below.

Table-1: Fatigue Event Loading Type

Type	Descriptions	
Fully Reversed (LR=-1)	All the loads, and hence stress components, reverse their directions simultaneously for the specified number of cycles in the event.	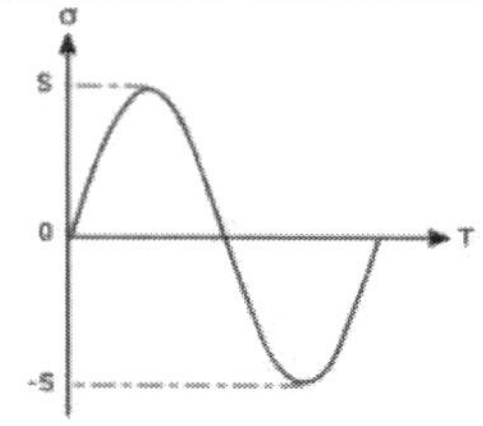
Zero Based (LR=0)	All loads, and hence stress components, change their magnitudes from their maximum values to zero for the specified number of cycles in the event.	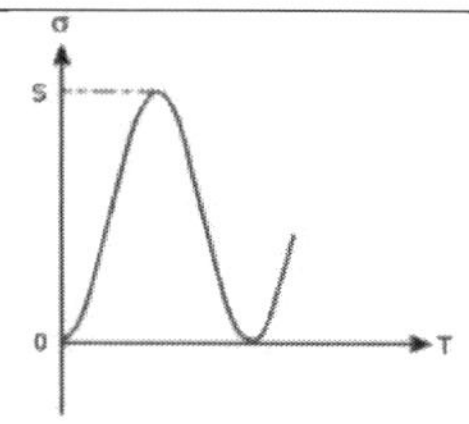
Loading Ratio	Each load, and hence each stress component, changes its magnitude proportionally from its maximum value (S_{max}) to a minimum value defined by $R*S_{max}$, where R is the load ratio. A negative ratio indicates reversal of the load direction for the specified number of cycles in the event.	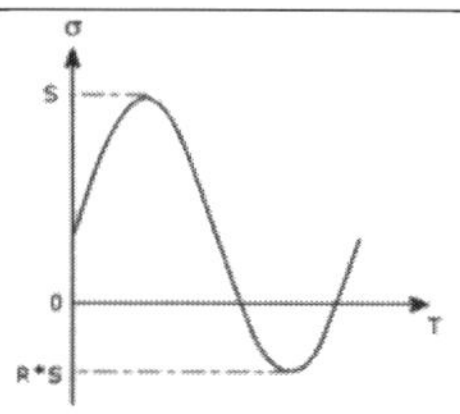
Find Cycle Peaks	The fatigue event is based on several load cases. The program calculates the alternating stresses for each node by considering the combination of peaks from different fatigue loads. It then determines the combination of loads that produces the largest stress.	

Generating the SN-Curve

In order to solve a fatigue study, SOLIDWORKS requires the user to input a Stress versus number of Cycles, or (SN)-curve, for the material. This is due to the large dependency of the fatigue life of a part on the material condition, part size, and loading type. SN-curves can either be found experimentally or by analytical expressions. For best results it is suggested that the SN-curve be experimentally determined for the material properties and conditions of interest. For purposes of this text, however, a SN-curve calculator is included to assist in generating the SN-curve[1]. The calculator utilizes the stress-life method to approximate the SN-curve based on material properties and various part or

[1] The calculator is adapted from SOLIDWORKS Support Solution ID: S-018810 "Fatigue curve calculation for steels"

loading conditions. With the provided inputs the SN-curve calculator will generate 12 points representing the low and high cycle portions of a SN-curve as shown in Fig. 4 below.

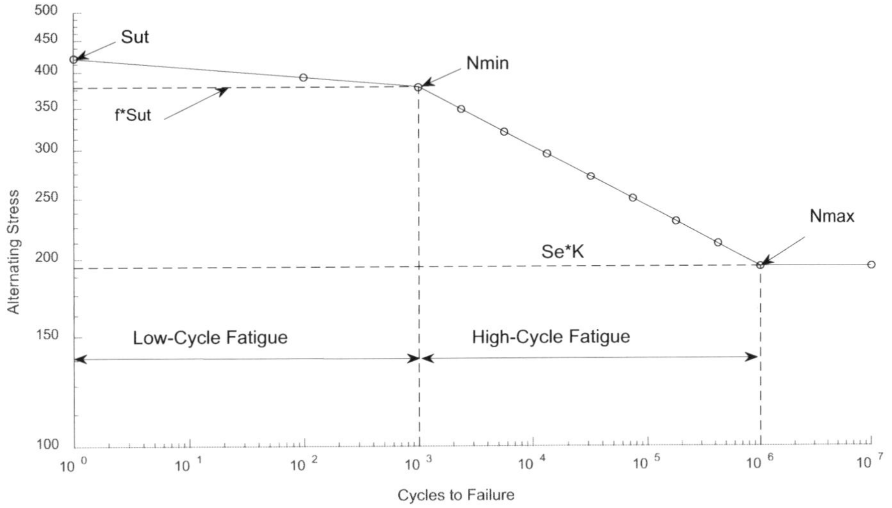

Figure 4 – Depiction of the SN-curve generated by the included SN-curve calculator.

Navigating the SN-Curve Calculator

The SN-curve calculator is a Microsoft Excel® sheet **(SnCalculator.xlsx)** which needs to be downloaded from the publisher's web site. Save the file in your project folder. To open the sheet:

Launch Excel 2013 (or newer version) from your computer's startup menu.

34. In the Excel main menu, select **File > Open...** Then browse to the location where **SnCalculator.xlsx** file is stored and click **[Open]**. The calculator should appear as shown in Fig. 5.

There are six main inputs to the SN-Curve calculator located in Cells C22:C27. Figure 4 is useful in understanding how the different inputs of the SN-Curve calculator affect the SN-Curve. Those inputs are described below.

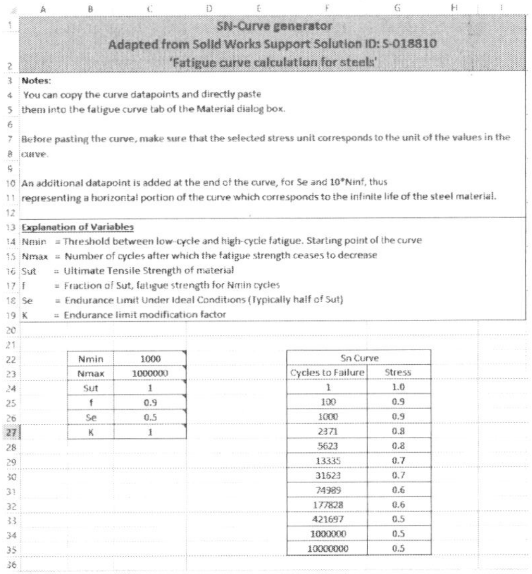

SN-Curve generator
Adapted from Solid Works Support Solution ID: S-018810
'Fatigue curve calculation for steels'

Notes:
You can copy the curve datapoints and directly paste
them into the fatigue curve tab of the Material dialog box.

Before pasting the curve, make sure that the selected stress unit corresponds to the unit of the values in the curve.

An additional datapoint is added at the end of the curve, for Se and 10*Ninf, thus
representing a horizontal portion of the curve which corresponds to the infinite life of the steel material.

Explanation of Variables
Nmin = Threshold between low-cycle and high-cycle fatigue. Starting point of the curve
Nmax = Number of cycles after which the fatigue strength ceases to decrease
Sut = Ultimate Tensile Strength of material
f = Fraction of Sut, fatigue strength for Nmin cycles
Se = Endurance Limit Under Ideal Conditions (Typically half of Sut)
K = Endurance limit modification factor

Nmin	1000
Nmax	1000000
Sut	1
f	0.9
Se	0.5
K	1

Sn Curve	
Cycles to Failure	Stress
1	1.0
100	0.9
1000	0.9
2371	0.8
5623	0.8
13335	0.7
31623	0.7
74989	0.6
177828	0.6
421697	0.5
1000000	0.5
10000000	0.5

Figure 5 – Example setup for SN-Curve calculator in Microsoft Excel ®.

Nmin – The value located in Cell C22 represents the threshold between low-cycle and high-cycle fatigue. It is commonly assumed to be 10^3 cycles

Nmax – The value located in Cell C23, represents the number of cycles after which the fatigue strength ceases to decrease.

Sut – The value located in Cell C24 is the ultimate tensile strength of the material, or **Tensile Strength** property, found in SOLIDWORKS **Material Dialog Box - Properties Tab**.

f – The value located in Cell C25 represents the fraction of **Sut** that corresponds to the fatigue strength at **Nmin** cycles.

Se – The value located in Cell C26 represents the endurance limit for the selected material. The endurance limit input by default is automatically calculated to be half of Sut; however, this can be changed by the user if desired.

K – The value located in Cell C27 represents the product of all the endurance limit modification factors. These modification factors take into account different material and part conditions such as the surface finish, size, loading conditions, and the temperature of the part.

For the **Low-Cycle** portion of the SN-Curve the SN-Curve calculator generates three logarithmically spaced points including and between 1 and **Nmin** cycles. For each cycle point the respective alternating stress, utilizing the user inputs and a straight line, is placed on the log-log plot between the points (1, **Sut**) and (**Nmin**, **f*sut**) as shown in Fig. 4. Similarly, the **High-Cycle** portion of the SN-Curve is found by analyzing nine logarithmically spaced points between, and including, 1000 and 1000000 cycles. The alternating stress for each point is again calculated for each cycle point by utilizing the user inputs and a straight-line interpolation of the curve on a log-log plot as shown in Fig. 4. One additional located point at (10^7, **Se*K**) is added to the end of the curve. This accounts for the endurance limit modification factor. The point at 10^7 cycles represents the infinite cycles to failure that SOLIDWORKS will report if the alternating stress is less than or equal to **Se*K**.

Endurance Limit (K):

- It should be noted that this text utilizes the Marin Factors outlined in the 10th edition of *Shigley's Mechanical Engineering Design* textbook for the endurance limit modification factors.

The steps for generating an SN-Curve using the included **SnCalculator.xlsx** file are outlined below. Before the calculator is used, several material parameters are needed in order to extract for the SN-Curve.

35. In the SOLIDWORKS Simulation manager, right-click **Fatigue Cylinder** ... then from the pop-up menu select the **Material** icon and select the **Apply/Edit Fatigue Data.**

36. In the **Materials** window, select the **Properties** tab and locate the material property **Tensile Strength**. For **AISI 1020 Steel** the tensile strength is 420507000 N/m^2 shown circled in Fig. 6.

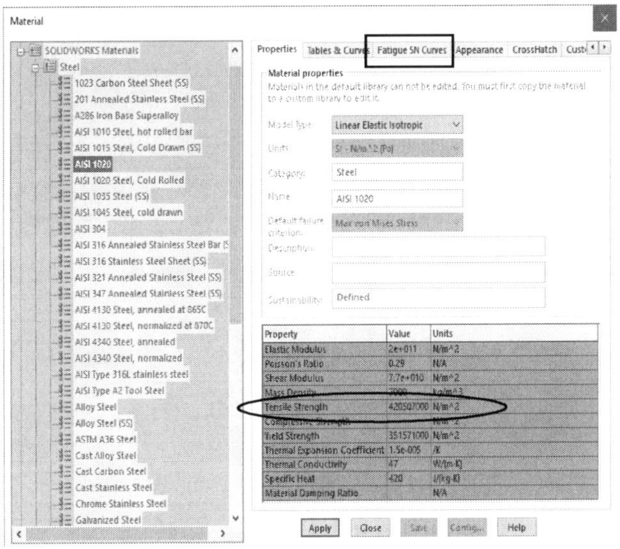

Figure 6 – Location of material tensile strength in the SOLIDWORKS **Material** window.

37. In the **Material** window, return to the **Fatigue SN Curves** tab. Before any calculations are performed, ensure that the units drop-down menu in the **Table Data**, circled in Fig. 7, matches the units of the **Tensile Strength** units found in Fig. 6.

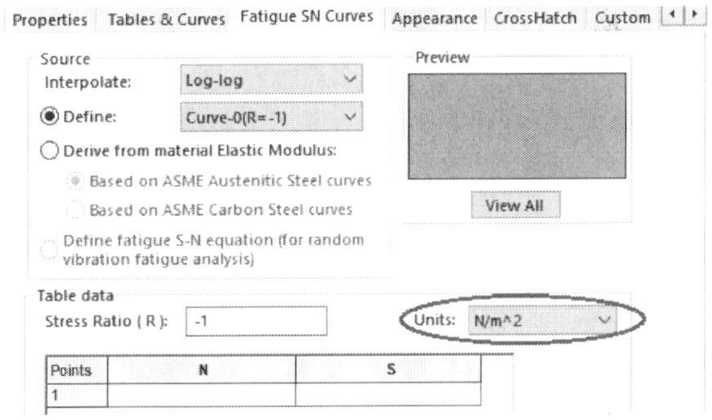

Figure 7 – **Fatigue SN Curves** tab.

38. Without closing SOLIDWORKS, locate and open the '**SnCalculator.xlsx**' file.

39. In cell **C24**, enter the material tensile strength, **Sut**, of 420507000 N/m^2. This action causes the endurance limit, **Se** in cell **C26** to be updated to half of the **Sut** value.

40. In cell **C27** enter the endurance limit modification factor, **K**, of 0.7854. This value accounts for a polished surface finish and the size of the cylinder. Leave **Nmin** at 1000 cycles, **Nmax**=1000000 cycles, and f=0.9 in the sheet.

41. Left-click and hold cell **F24**. While still holding the keys, drag (your mouse point) OR drag the cursor to cell **G36** to highlight the values generated to plot the SN-Curve in the sheet (see Fig. 8).

42. Next, right-click the highlighted area in Excel and select **copy**.

43. Return to the SOLIDWORKS **Fatigue SN Curve** tab and select the first Cell **1N**.

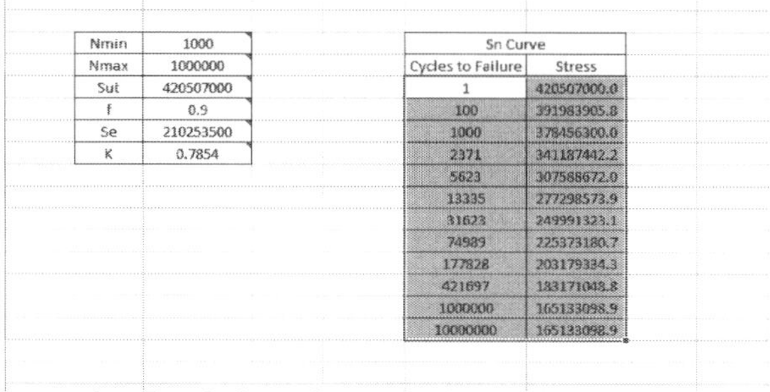

Figure 8 – Depiction of selected cells in the Excel spreadsheet required to produce a SN curve.

44. Using the keyboard shortcut, **Ctrl+V**, paste the SN-Curve into the table. Note the **Material** window should match what is shown in Fig. 9. It is important that the **Units** drop down menu in the **Material** tab matches units used for the **Sut** variable in Excel.

45. Finally, click **Apply**, and close the **Material** property manager.

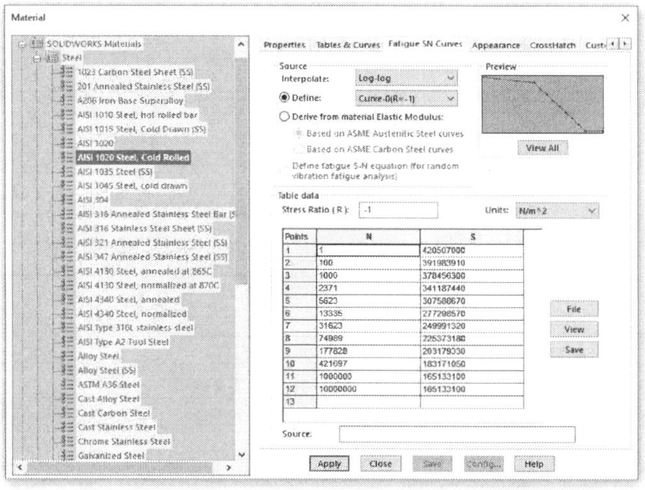

Figure 9 – SN curve pasted into SOLIDWORKS.

Setting Fatigue Study Parameters

46. In the Simulation manager, right-click **Cylinder Fatigue Study**, and select **Properties**. The **Fatigue - Constant Amplitude** window should appear as shown in Fig. 10.

47. Under the **Computing alternating stress using** heading, select ⊙**Equivalent Stress (von Mises)**. This sets to **von Mises** the type of stress used to calculate the equivalent alternating stresses for extracting the number of cycles from the SN- Curve. Von Mises stress is selected because it is assumed the cylinder is ductile.

Figure 10 – **Fatigue-Constant Amplitude** properties manager.

48. Leave the remaining settings as default. Click **Apply** and close the **Fatigue Study** property manager.

When to Use the Different Stress Options in Fatigue Analysis:

- **Stress intensity (P1-P3):** can be used for ductile materials. It is a more conservative theory thereby resulting in lower predicted safety factors.
- **Equivalent stress (von Mises):** can also be used for ductile materials. It is considered the best predictor of actual failure in ductile materials.
- **Max. absolute principal (P1):** should be used for brittle materials only.

Fatigue Study Solution

49. On the **Simulation** tab, click the **Run this Study** 

icon to start the Solution.

50. It takes a few seconds before the simulation is complete and the **Results** folder in the Simulation manager includes the **-Damage-** plot.

51. Right click the **Results1 (-Damage-)** and select **Edit-Definition** to change the plot type.

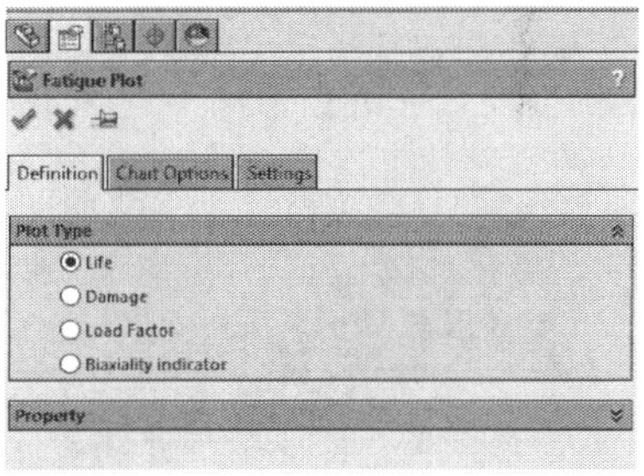

Figure 11 – **Fatigue Plot** property manager.

52. The **Fatigue Plot** property manager opens as shown in Fig. 11. Select ⊙ **Life** for the **Plot Type** and select **[OK]** to exit.

A description of each Fatigue Study Plot is provided below:

- **Life** – Shows the number of cycles to failure at each location on the part. The number of cycles is based on the SN-Curve and the alternating stress at each location.
  Yellow indicates suggested **Bold Font**.
- **Damage** – Shows what percent of life the applied loads have expended.
- **Load Factor** – Shows the load factor of safety at each location.
- **Biaxiality Indicator** – Plots the ratio of the smaller alternating principal stresses to the larger alternating principal stress. A value of -1.0 indicates pure shear and a value of 1.0 indicates a pure biaxial state.

53. Right-click the **Results1 (-Life-)** plot and select **List Selected**. This should open the **Probe Result** property manager.

54. Choose ⊙ **On selected entities** for the probe **Options.**

55. The **Faces, Edges, or Vertices** box should be highlighted blue. On the model, click on *Split Line 1* shown in Fig. 12.

56. Next in the **Results** dialogue box, click the **[Update]** button in the **Probe Result** property manager. Immediately the table is populated with data occurring at every node located on the *Split Line 1*. The **Value (cycle)** column contains values of the fatigue cycles to failure required at the nodes located on *Split Line 1* of the **Fatigue Cylinder** part.

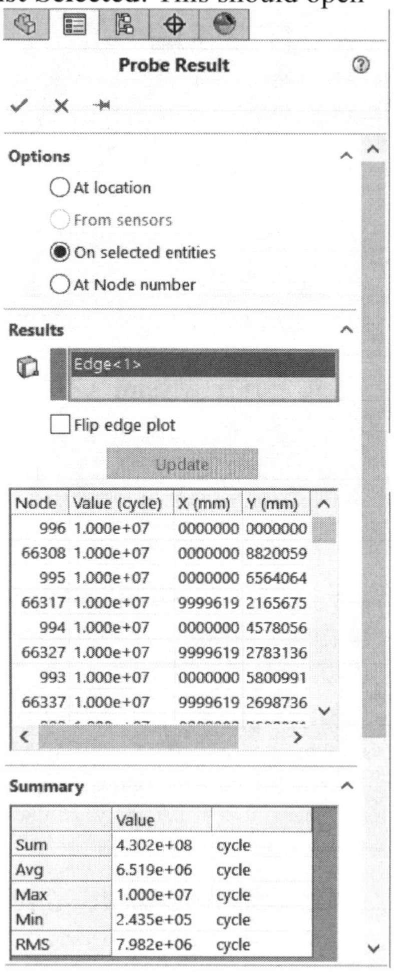

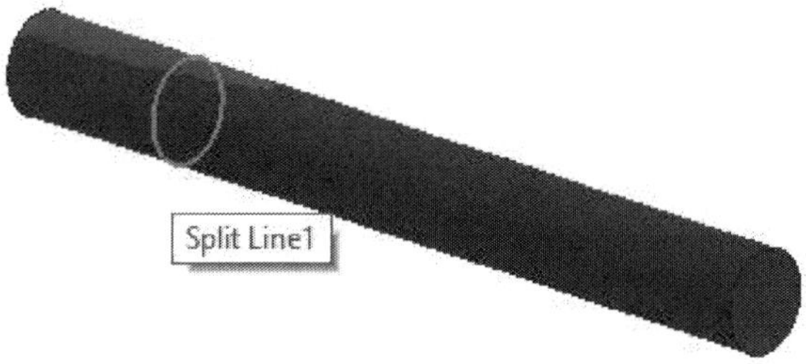

Figure 12 – The split line and the life cycle results at this location.

In the **Summary** dialogue box, located near the bottom of the **Probe Result** property manager, observe that the cycle values on *Split Line 1* are summarized in several different forms. For our analysis we are interested in the minimum cycles to failure at the *Split Line 1* location. For this example, consider **Min Value** of **2.435e+05 cycle** (numbers may vary a little). This value corresponds to the location on the *Split Line 1* with the largest stress.

Verification of Results

Consistent with previous examples in this text, a check is performed to ensure the validity of results in the current numerical analysis. Classical equations were used to find the reversing stress at the point of interest on the **Fatigue Cylinder** part.

From the elastic beams bending equation, the maximum stress σ_x along the cylinder axis at an arbitrary location *x* is:

$$\sigma_x = \frac{M * \frac{D}{2}}{I_{zz}} = \frac{F_y * (L - x) * \frac{D}{2}}{\frac{\pi * D^4}{64}} \qquad [1]$$

in which *M* is the bending moment, *x* is the location of Split Line, *D* is the cylinder diameter, I_{zz} is the surface moment of inertia along the z-axis, F_y is the load in *-y* direction, and *L* is the cylinder length. Substituting for these parameters from data given in Fig.1 yields:

$$\sigma_x = \frac{1500\ \mathrm{N} * (0.250\mathrm{m} - 0.05\mathrm{m}) * \left(\frac{0.025\mathrm{m}}{2}\right)}{\frac{\pi * (0.025\mathrm{m})^4}{64}} * \frac{1\mathrm{MPa}}{1\mathrm{e} + 6\ \frac{\mathrm{N}}{\mathrm{m}^2}} \qquad [2]$$

$$\sigma_x = 195.6\ \mathrm{MPa}$$

Since $\sigma_y = \tau_{xy} = 0$, Von Mises stress, σ', is the same as σ_x.

$$\sigma' = \sqrt{\sigma_x{}^2 + \sigma_x\sigma_y + \sigma_y{}^2 + 3 * \tau_{xy}{}^2} = \sigma_x \qquad [3]$$

The loading case was set as fully reversed $\sigma'_{Max} = -\sigma'_{Min}$. Thus, the alternating (σ'_A) and mid-range (σ'_M) Von Mises stresses are:

$$\sigma'_A = \frac{(\sigma'_{Max} - \sigma'_{Min})}{2} = \frac{(195.569\ \mathrm{MPa} - -195.569\ \mathrm{MPa})}{2} = 195.6\ \mathrm{MPa} \qquad [4]$$

$$\sigma'_M = \frac{(\sigma'_{Max} + \sigma'_{Min})}{2} = \frac{(195.569\ \mathrm{MPa} + -195.569\ \mathrm{MPa})}{2} = 0\ \mathrm{Mpa} \qquad [5]$$

At this point it is important to remember to check for localized yield before calculating the cycles to failure. For our example, localized yielding does not occur as shown in equation [6].

$$\sigma'_A + \sigma'_M \leq Sy\ (\text{yield stress}) \qquad [6]$$

$$195.6\ \mathrm{Mpa} + 0 \leq 351.571\ \mathrm{MPa}$$

Finally, the calculation of the cycles to failure using the Stress-Life method is given by:

$$a = \frac{(f * S_{ut})^2}{S_e\ (= K * 0.5 * S_{ut})} = \frac{(0.9 * 420.507\ \text{MPa})^2}{0.7854 * 0.5 * 420.507\ \text{MPa}} = 867.3\ \text{Mpa} \qquad [7]$$

$$b = -\frac{1}{3}\log_{10}\left(\frac{f * S_{ut}}{S_e}\right) = -\frac{1}{3}\log_{10}\left(\frac{.9 * 420.507\ \text{MPa}}{0.7854 * 0.5 * 420.507\ \text{MPa}}\right) = -0.1201 \qquad [8]$$

where a , b are the two constants of the Stress-Life equation (see Eq. 9).

Thus, the theoretical number of cycles to failure is given by:

$$N = \left(\frac{\sigma'_{rev}}{a}\right)^{\frac{1}{b}} = \left(\frac{195.6\ \text{MPa}}{867.3}\right)^{\frac{1}{-0.1201}} = 244389\ \text{Cycles} \qquad [9]$$

This result is in strong agreement with the FEA results model and yields a percent difference of 0.22%.

$$\%\ \text{Difference} = \left[\frac{\text{FEA Result} - \text{Classical Result}}{\text{FEA Result}}\right] * 100 = \left[\frac{244350 - 244900}{244350}\right] * 100 = 0.22\%$$

Save and Log Out of the Current Analysis

The preceding problem will be used again in the next example, so it is important to save your work.

57. On the **Main Menu**, click **File** followed by choosing **Close**.
58. The SOLIDWORKS window should appear; click **Save**. Save the file to a local directory where it can be retrieved for the second example.

Next, the same cylinder, subject to combined axial and bending loads, is explored using fatigue analysis in SOLIDWORKS.

Problem-2: Fatigue Analysis of a Cylinder Subject to a Combined Loading

The AISI 1020 steel cylinder with a diameter of 25mm and a length of 250mm is shown in Fig. 13; it serves as the model for this example. The surface of the cylinder is machine finished and the cylinder is subject to a zero based (see Table-1) combined loading consisting of an axial and bending load. The endurance limit modification factor has also changed to K=0.9240 due to a different component surface finish than Problem-1. Also, the bending force in this problem is changed arbitrarily to 1350N (from 1500N). The objective of this example is to find the number of loading cycles the cylinder can undergo before failure due to fatigue or yielding.

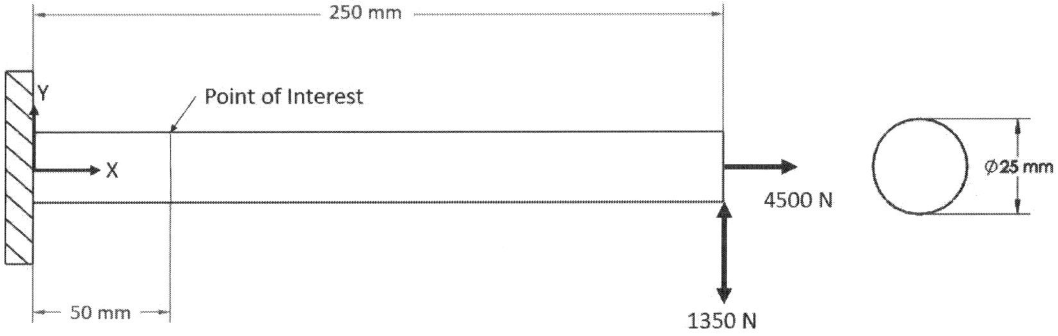

Figure 13 – Three-dimensional model of the cylinder with a combined loading (dimensions are in "millimeters")

Opening Previous Example

1. Locate and open the **Fatigue Cylinder** model file used in the previous example.

Duplicating the Static Analysis (Study) and Fatigue Studies

2. At the bottom of the screen, right click on **Cylinder Bending** and select **Copy Study**. This opens the **Copy Study** menu.

3. Under **Study Name:** enter **Combined Loading Cylinder**. Do not change any other settings and click **[OK]** ✓ to close the window. This action duplicates the study.

4. Repeat Steps 1-2 for the **Cylinder Fatigue Study**; rename it **Combined Cylinder Fatigue Study**.

Copy Study copies the study selected, which includes all the previous settings (i.e., Mesh settings, External Loads, Fixtures, and Material specification). This feature is very useful when performing fatigue studies because extensive time is required to set up static studies that are needed for each fatigue test. After duplicating the first static study, only minor adjustments are needed before running a revised study.

Modifying External Load(s)

Only two modifications are needed for the external loads of the combined study. The first modification is to add a 45000 N force perpendicular to the **Fatigue Cylinder's** right face in the positive x direction. The second modification is to apply the bending force in example 1 of 1350 N. Try this on your own, or follow the steps outlined below.

5. Left-click the **Combined Loading Cylinder** static study on the bottom of the screen.

6. Right-click the **External Loads** icon, and from the pop-up menu select **Force...** The **Force/Torque** property manager opens.

7. Within the **Force/Torque** dialogue box, select the **Force** icon (if not already selected).

8. The **Faces and Shell Edges for Normal Force** field is highlighted (light blue) to indicate it is active. Rotate the model and zoom in as necessary to select the right face of the cylinder.

9. Verify that the **Units** field is set to **SI**.

10. In the **Force Value** field type 45000 N.

11. Ensure that the resulting force is in the positive x direction. The right end of the model should match Fig. 14.

12. Click **[OK]** ✓ (green check mark) at the top of the **Force/Torque** property manager to accept this force. An icon named Force-2 (:Per item: -45000 N:) appears beneath the **External Loads** folder in the Simulation manager tree.

13. Right-click the **Force-1 (:Per item: -1500 N :)** icon, and from the pop-up menu select **Edit Definition...** The **Force/Torque** property manager opens.

14. In the **Force Value** field type 1350 N.

15. Click **[OK]** ✓ (green check mark) at the top of the **Force/Torque** property manager to accept this force. An icon named Force-1 (:Per item: -1350 N:) appears beneath the **External Loads** folder in the Simulation manager tree.

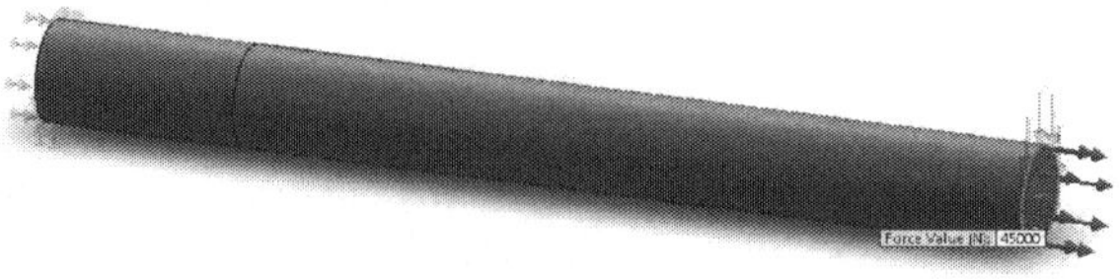

Figure 14 – Depiction of properly applied fixtures and loads

Modifying Fatigue Study Parameters

Because the part is now undergoing a zero based loading and has an additional axial load applied, the fatigue event will have to be adjusted accordingly.

Edit Fatigue Event

16. Left-click the **Combined Cylinder Fatigue Study.**

17. Left-click the ‣ next to the **Loading (-Constant Amplitude-)** icon to expand the fatigue events, if not already expanded.

18. Right-click **Event-1** and select edit definition. The **Add Event (Constant)** property manager should appear as shown in Fig. 15.

19. Left-click on ⌄ **the Loading Type** menu and select **Zero Based (LR=0)** from the list. This sets the loading type to a zero based event where the minimum stress is equal to zero.

20. Next, in the study association area, left-click ⌄ on the **Study** tab dropdown menu and select **Combined Loading Cylinder.**

21. Before closing the **Add Event** property manager, check to ensure that entries match those shown in Fig. 15.

22. Click **[OK]** ✓ (green check mark) at the top of the **Add Event** property manager to accept these settings.

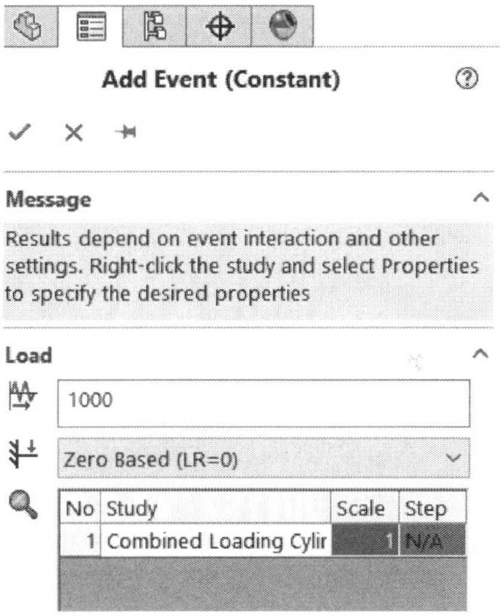

Figure 15 – **Add Event** property manager proper setup.

Setting Fatigue Study Parameters

For this fatigue study, because the part is not under a fully reversed load type it is important that the reversing stress be corrected. For this analysis the Goodman stress correction will be used. The Goodman model is one of the most widely accepted methods for studying fatigue problems involving nonzero mean stress. The descriptions of other empirical models used in SOLIDWORKS for fatigue analysis with a nonzero mean stress are summarized in Table-2.

Table-2: Imperial Fatigue analysis models for nonzero mean stress

Goodman Line	The Goodman stress correction is an empirical model that relates alternating stress to mean stress using a straight line that connects the endurance limit, σ_e', on the alternating stress axis to the ultimate strength, S_{ut}, on the mean stress axis.	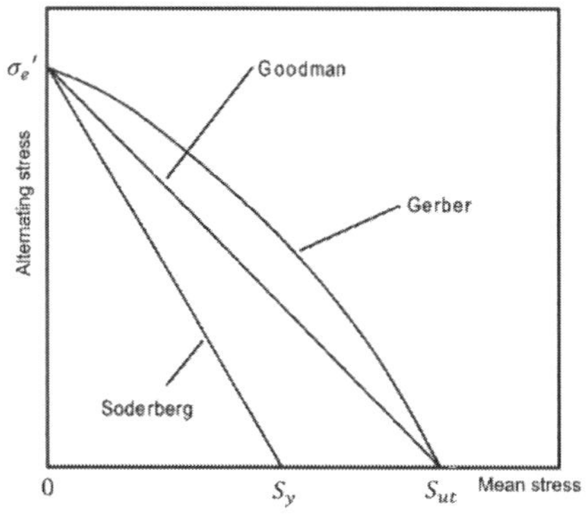
Gerber Line	The Gerber Line has the same end points as Goodman, but it uses a parabola (instead of a straight line) between the endurance limit and ultimate strength.	
Soderberg Line	The Soderberg line has the same form as the Goodman model but instead of the ultimate strength uses the yield strength, S_y, on the mean stress axis. This model is the most conservative model.	

23. Right-click **Combined Cylinder Fatigue Study** in the Simulation manager and select **Properties**. The **Fatigue-Constant Amplitude** window should appear.

24. Under the **Mean Stress Correction** block select **Goodman.** This sets the mean stress correction method to use Goodman.

25. Make sure Von Mises is chosen for **Computing alternating stress** and set **Fatigue Strength reduction factor (K_f)** to 1.0. SOLIDWORKS Simulation divides the alternating stress by this factor before reading the corresponding number of cycles from the SN-Curve.

26. Leave the remaining settings as default. Click **Apply** and close the **Fatigue Study** property manager.

Modifying the SN-Curve

27. In the SOLIDWORKS Simulation manager, right-click on the **Fatigue Cylinder-Copy (-User Defined-)** and select **Apply/Edit Fatigue Data**.

28. In the **materials** window, select the **properties** tab and locate the material property **tensile strength**. For **AISI 1020** Steel the **Tensile Strength** is 420507000 N/m^2.

29. At the top of the **Material** window, select the **Fatigue SN Curves** tab. Before any calculations are performed ensure that the **units** drop down menu in the **Table data** section is set to N/m^2.

30. Without closing SOLIDWORKS, locate and open the **SnCalculator.xlsx** file.

31. In cell **C24** enter the material tensile strength, **Sut**, of 420507000 N/m^2.

32. In cell **C27** enter the endurance limit modification factor, **K,** of 0.9240. This accounts for the different surface finish and size of the part. Before proceeding compare your SN-Curve data in the Excel file with data shown in Fig. 16.

33. Left-click and hold the key while selecting cell **F24** and while still holding, drag the cursor to cell **G35.** This action highlights all **Stress** and number of **Cycles to Failure** in the Excel file.

SN-Curve	
Cycles to Failure	Stress
1	420507000.0
100	391983905.8
1000	378456300.0
2371	348189501.6
5623	320343270.9
13335	294724024.5
31623	271153660.8
74989	249468321.8
177828	229517253.7
421697	211161759.5
1000000	194274234.0
10000000	194274234.0

Figure 16 – SN curve data generated in the SN-Curve calculator sheet.

34. Highlight the SN-Curve results in Excel and select **copy**.

35. Return to the SOLIDWORKS **material** tab.

36. Left-click and hold the key while selecting cell **1N.** While still holding the key, drag the cursor to cell **S12** and press the **[Delete]** key to erase the S-N data from Problem-1.

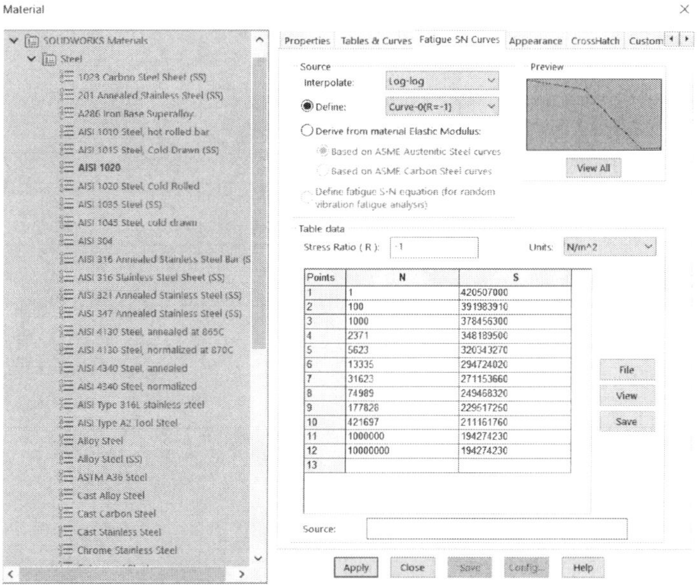

Figure 17 – Depiction of the selected cells on the **Materials Properties** menu.

37. Select the first cell, **1N**, and using the keyboard shortcut, **Ctrl+V**, paste the SN-Curve data into the table. Note the **Material** window should match that shown in Fig. 17. It is important that the **Units** drop down menu in the **Material** window matches the units used for **Sut** variable in Excel.

38. Finally, click **[Apply]**, and close the **Material** property manager.

Fatigue Study Solution

39. On the **Simulation** tab click the **Run this Study** 

icon to start the solution.

40. If not already active, double-click the **Results1(-Life-)** plot.

41. Right-click the **Results2 (-Life-)** plot and choose **List Selected**. This should open the **Probe Result** property manager.

42. The **Faces, Edges, or Vertices** box should be highlighted blue. On the model, left-click **1** *Split Line1*.

43. Next, in the **Results** dialogue box, click the **[Update]** button in the **Probe Result** property manager.

Immediately the table is populated with data occurring at every node located on the *Split Line*. The **Value (Cycle)** column contains values of the number of cycles to failure required at nodes located on the *Split Line* of the **Fatigue Cylinder** part. Values and their X, Y coordinates are listed in Fig. 18.

In the **Summary** dialogue box, the **Min** number of cycles to failure of 8.931e+5 **cycle** (numbers will vary) appears. This value corresponds to the location on the *Split Line* with the largest stress.

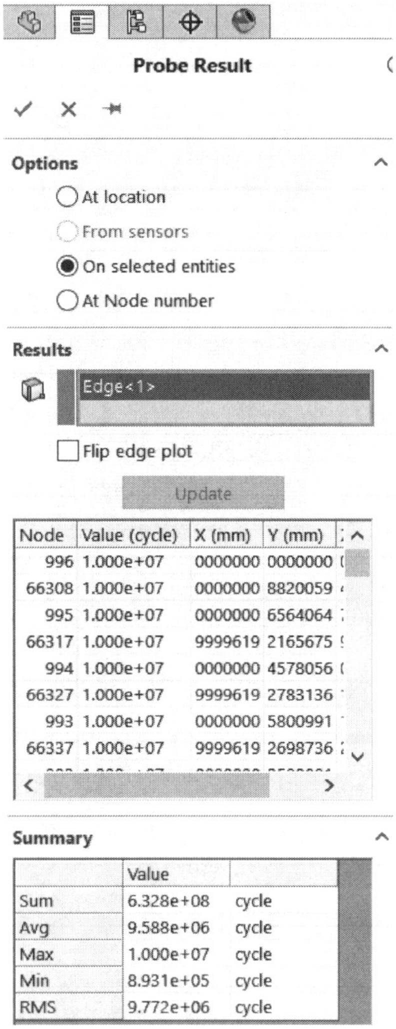

Figure 18 – Life cycle results at the split line.

Verification of Results

Consistent with previous examples in the text, a check is made to ensure the validity of results in the current analysis. Classical equations were utilized to calculate the reversing stress at the point of interest on the **Fatigue Cylinder** part. It is again important to remember to check for localized yielding around the area of fatigue.

Combining the stresses along the *x*-axis due to a bending moment caused by the force $F_y = 1350\ N$ and tensile stress due to the force of $F_x = 45000\ N,$ the maximum stress σ_x along the cylinder axis at location *x* is:

$$\sigma_x = \frac{F_y * (L - x) * \frac{D}{2}}{\frac{\pi * D^4}{64}} + \frac{F_x}{\frac{\pi * D^2}{4}} \qquad [1]$$

In which *x*=0.05m is the *Split Line* location. Substituting values into this equation using the parameters given in problem-2 statement yields:

$$\sigma_x = \left(\frac{1350\text{ N} * (0.250\text{m} - 0.05\text{m}) * \left(\frac{0.025\text{m}}{2}\right)}{\frac{\pi * (0.025\text{m})^4}{64}} + \frac{45000}{\frac{\pi * (0.025\text{m})^2}{4}} \right) \frac{1\text{MPa}}{1\text{e} + 6\ \frac{\text{N}}{\text{m}^2}} \qquad [2]$$

or

$$\sigma_x = 267.68\text{ Mpa}$$

Since $\sigma_y = \tau_{xy} = 0,$ Von Mises stress, σ', is the same as σ_x.

The load case was set as a zero base. Thus $\sigma'_{Max} = \sigma_x$ and $\sigma'_{Min} = 0$. Thus, the alternating and mid-range Von Mises stresses are:

$$\sigma'_A = \frac{(\sigma'_{Max} - \sigma'_{Min})}{2} = \frac{(267.68\text{ MPa} - 0\text{ MPa})}{2} = 133.84\text{ MPa} \qquad [3]$$

$$\sigma'_M = \frac{(\sigma'_{Max} + \sigma'_{Min})}{2} = \frac{(267.68\text{ MPa} + 0\text{ MPa})}{2} = 133.84\text{ Mpa} \qquad [4]$$

It is very important to check for localized yield before calculating the cycles to failure in fatigue analysis. In this example, localized yielding does not occur since

$$\sigma'_A + \sigma'_M \leq Sy\ \text{(yield stress)} \qquad [5]$$

$$133.84\text{ Mpa} + 133.84 \leq 351.57\text{ MPa}$$

Next, using the Goodman empirical line to estimate mean stress effects, σ_e', on fatigue life results in:

$$\frac{\sigma_A'}{\sigma_e'} + \frac{\sigma_M'}{S_{ut}} = 1 \qquad [6]$$

$$\frac{133.84}{\sigma_e'} + \frac{133.84}{420.507} = 1 \rightarrow \sigma_e' = 196.33 \text{ Mpa}$$

Finally, the Stress-Life method is used to calculate the number of cycles to failure.

$$a = \frac{(f * S_{ut})^2}{S_e} = \frac{(0.9 * 420.507 \text{ MPa})^2}{0.924 * 0.5 * 420.507 \text{ MPa}} = 737.252 \text{ Mpa} \qquad [7]$$

$$b = -\frac{1}{3}\log_{10}\left(\frac{f * S_{ut}}{S_e}\right) = -\frac{1}{3}\log_{10}\left(\frac{0.9 * 420.507 \text{ MPa}}{0.924 * 0.5 * 420.507 \text{ MPa}}\right) = -0.0965 \qquad [8]$$

$$N = \left(\frac{\sigma_e'}{a}\right)^{\frac{1}{b}} = \left(\frac{196.33 \text{ MPa}}{737.252}\right)^{\frac{1}{-0.0965}} = 896804 \text{ Cycles} \qquad [9]$$

This result is in strong agreement with the FEA results model and yields a percent difference of 0.41%.

$$\% \text{ Difference} = \left[\frac{\text{FEA Result} - \text{Classical Result}}{\text{FEA Result}}\right] * 100 = \left[\frac{893100 - 896804}{893100}\right] * 100 = 0.41\%$$

EXERCISES

End of chapter exercises are intended to provide additional practice using principles introduced in the current chapter plus capabilities mastered in preceding chapters. Most exercises include multiple parts. In an academic setting, it is likely that parts of problems may be assigned or modified to suit specific course goals.

╬ ***Designates problems that introduce new concepts. Solution guidance is provided for these problems.***

╬ EXERCISE 1 – Study of Specimen Undergoing a Fatigue Test (Special Topic: *Pure Bending)*

Understanding how to design to mitigate fatigue or predict when a product or part will fail due to fatigue is very important. Fatigue failure is often sudden and unexpected and, therefore, can be very dangerous. For these reasons, when applications have time-varying loads, the materials are tested to determine their fatigue life subject to various loading situations. A variety of fatigue testing machines are required to test parts subject to time-varying axial, bending, and torsional loads. A standard rotating beam fatigue testing machine is shown in Fig. E10-1. It applies reversed bending loads to standardized or custom fatigue specimens.

The rotating beam fatigue testing machine, shown in Fig. E10-2, has a 200-inch pound maximum capacity. However, in this exercise the sample specimen is subject to an 85-inch pounds bending moment. Assume the following:

Open file: **Test Specimen**

- Material: **Plain Carbon Steel** with a machined surface finish.
- Marin Factors: Apply modification factor(s) for surface finish and size.
- Mesh: In the **Mesh** property manager, select **Standard mesh**; use a **Fine** mesh size.
- Fixture: **Fixed** at each end of the cylinder along the *Splits Lines.*
- External Load: 85 lbf.in moment applied to the left and right faces of the specimen.

Figure E10-1 Variety of standard rotating beam fatigue specimens; note that specimen size and surface finish may differ.

Figure E10-2 - RBF-200 Rotating Beam Fatigue Testing Machine located in many universities and industrial materials testing laboratories.

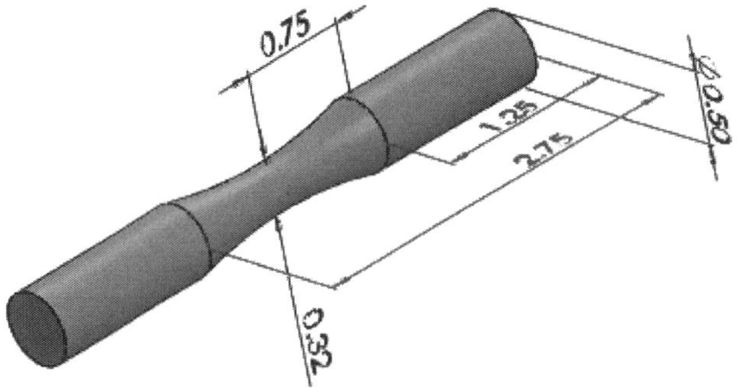

Figure E10-3 -Typical test specimen used in the fatigue testing machine. Dimensions are in inches.

Solution Guidance
It is assumed that the user has opened the model file and started a Study in SOLIDWORKS Simulation. The following instructions are to serve as a "guide"; they are less detailed than the step-by-step procedure found in example problems.

Split Lines and Axes

- Use the **Curve commands** found on the **Features** tab to create two *Split Lines*.
  - Place a **Split Line** on each end of the specimen along the **Top Plane**.
- Use the **Reference Geometry** commands found on the **Features** tab to create two axes.
  - Select **Two Planes** under the **Selections** tab.
  - Select the **Top Plane** and the two end faces of the specimen to properly place the axes.

Fixture

- Open the **Fixture** window by right-clicking the **Fixtures** folder and select **Fixed Geometry…**
  - Highlight the **Faces, Edges, and Vertices for Fixtures** field and select both *Split Lines* on the specimen ends.

Applying a Pure Bending Load

- Open the **Force/Torque** window by right-clicking the **External Loads** folder and select **Torque…**
- Highlight the **Faces for Torque** field and select both the top and bottom faces on the left side of the specimen.
- Highlight the **Axis, Cylindrical Face for Direction** field and select the axis on the left face.
- Make sure the units are in **English (IPS)** and enter 85 lbf.in as the **Torque Value**.
- Select **Total** in the **Force/Torque** property manager.
- Repeat the above five steps for the right end of the specimen.

Determine the following:

a. Find cycles to failure using a **Fatigue Study** in SOLIDWORKS. Results should be found on the *Split Line* located in the center of the specimen.

b. Perform theoretical calculations to determine the number of cycles to failure. Clearly label and organize all calculations.

c. Compare simulated and theoretical results and give reasons for any differences.

EXERCISE 2 – Fatigue Failure of a Pressure Vessel

The paintball tank (pressure vessel) shown in Fig E10-4 is subject to an internally applied force that is zero based. A pressure vessel undergoes one fatigue cycle each time the pressure is increased and decreased within the vessel. A $1/8^{th}$ model of this part is available with the file name: **Fatigue_Pressure_Vessel**. Apply a 2200 psi internal pressure to the wall of the pressure vessel. Assume the following:

- Material: **Plain Carbon Steel** with a forged surface finish.
- Marin Factors: Apply modification factor(s) for surface finish.
- Mesh: In the **Mesh** property manager, select **Standard mesh**; use a **Fine** mesh size.
- Fixture: Normal to the plane of symmetry **Fixture**
- Internal Load: 2200 psi

Solution Guidance

- For guidance on how to properly restrain the pressure vessel refer to Chapter 4 regarding Thin and Thick Wall Pressure Vessels. This chapter provides information on how to apply restraints to a thick-walled pressure vessel and an explanation of the steps.
- When determining the cycles to failure use the **Probe** tool in the **Life Results** and select 10 or more points that are on the inside cylindrical face and significantly far away from the edges.

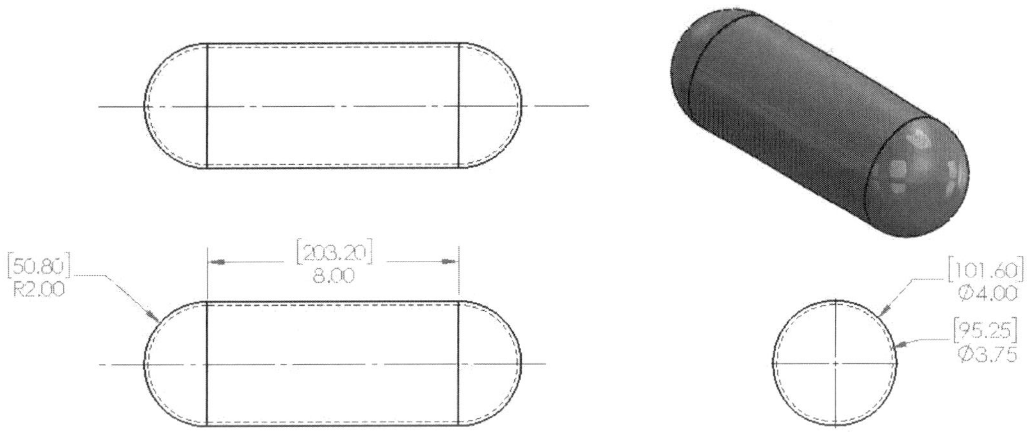

Figure E10-4 - Dimensioned pressure vessel. Dimensions are shown in both inches and mm. Note the SOLIDWORKS file provided is already cut as shown in Fig. E10-4.

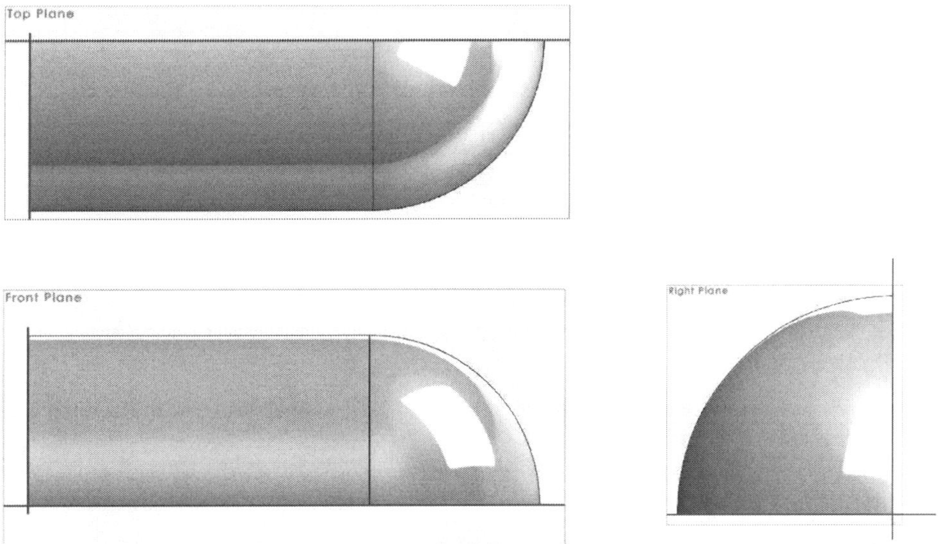

Figure E10-4 - Depiction of how the pressure vessel was cut to enable proper fixing.

Determine the following:

a. Find number of cycles to failure using a **Fatigue Study** in SOLIDWORKS.

b. Perform theoretical calculations to determine the number of cycles to failure. Clearly label and organize all calculations.

c. Compare simulated and theoretical results and give reasons for any differences.

╬ EXERCISE 3 – Fatigue Failure of a Bent Cylinder (Special Topic: Find-Cycle-Peaks)

This example will instruct the user regarding how to perform a fatigue study using the **Find-Cycle-Peaks** event type in SOLIDWORKS. This event type calculates alternating stresses at each node by considering the combination of peaks from different fatigue loads. This approach can be useful, for example, when the stress in a part is dependent on loading that varies in direction. The bent cylinder shown in Fig. E10-5 is subject to various bending loads that are applied in four different orientations. SOLIDWORKS Fatigue Simulation will be used to determine the worst loading condition and the resulting number of cycles to failure. A model of this part is available with file name: **Bent-Cylinder**. Apply four separate 10,000 N force loading conditions as shown in Fig. E10-7. Assume the following:

- Material: **AISI 1020** with a machined surface finish.
- Marin Factors: Apply the modification factor(s) for surface finish.
- Mesh: In the **Mesh** property manager, select **Standard mesh**; use a **Fine** mesh size.
- Fixture: **Fixed** on the bottom face of the cylinder as shown in Fig. E10-7.
- External Load: 10,000 N bending load in 90-degree increments.

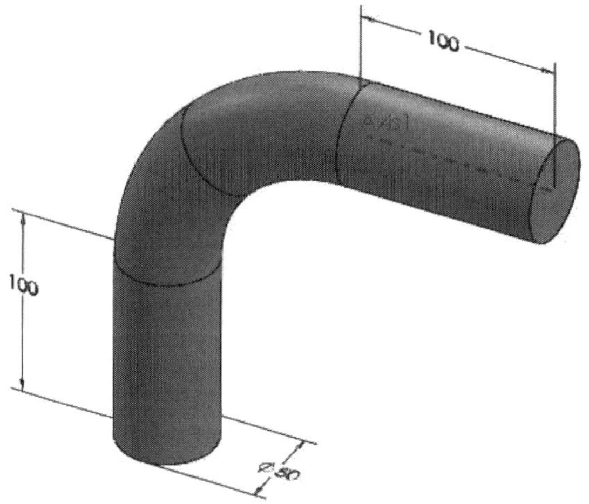

Figure E10-5 – Bent Cylinder with dimensions shown in mm.

Solution Guidance

It is assumed that the user has opened the model file and started a Study in SOLIDWORKS Simulation. The following instructions are to serve as a "guide"; they are less detailed than the step-by-step procedure found in example problems.

Add Fixture to Bottom Surface of the Bent Cylinder

- Apply **Fixed** geometry on the bottom cylinder face.

Creation of Four static studies

Create an external force of 10,000N acting at 0 degree on the free end of the Bent Cylinder model shown in Fig. E10-7(a).

- To properly apply the force, select the flat circular face on the "free end" of the Bent Cylinder. In the property manager, select the **Faces, Edges, Vertices, Reference Points for Force** field.
- Under the **Face, Edge, Plane for Direction** field select Plane1.
- Enter 10,000 N **Along Plane Dir 2**.

- To create the 90-degree loading condition duplicate the 0-degree static study.
- Change Plane1 in the **Face, Edge, Plane for Direction** field to Plane2 and refer to Fig. E10-7(b).
- To create the 180-degree loading condition duplicate steps in the 0-degree static study.
  - Under the **Along Plane Dir 2** select **Reverse direction**.
- To create the 270-degree loading condition duplicate the 90-degree static study.
  - Under the **Along Plane Dir 2** select **Reverse direction**.

Adding Fatigue Events

- In the **Add Event (Constant)** property manager, under **Loading Type** select **Find Cycle Peaks**.
    - Add the 0-degree, 90-degree, 180-degree, and 270-degree static studies as new events. The **Add Event** property manager should look like Fig. E10-6.

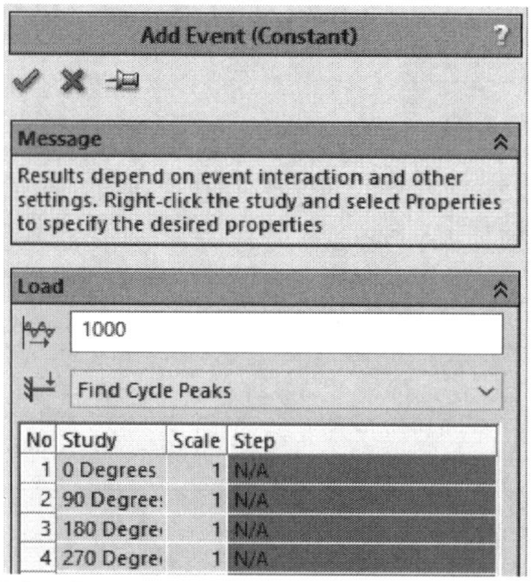

Figure E10-6 – Proper set-up of events for Fatigue study.

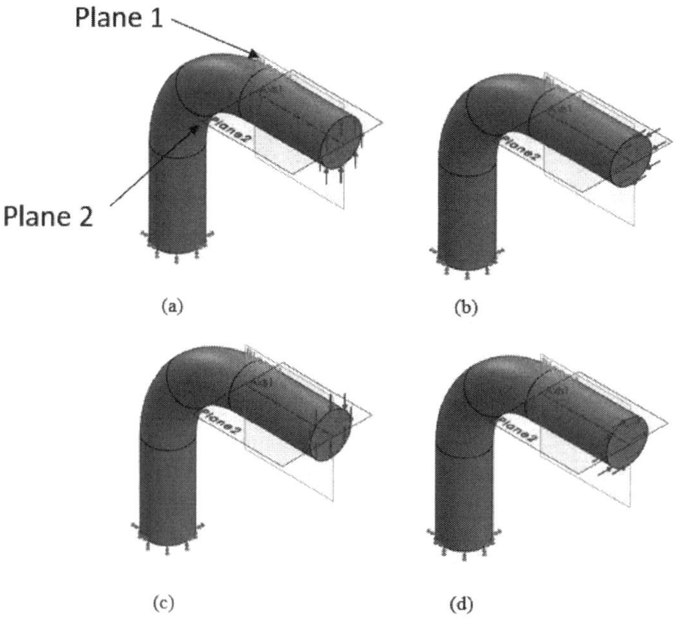

Figure E10-7 - Depiction of the four loading conditions each with a 10,000 N applied force. (a) is 0-degree loading, (b) is 90-degree loading, (c) is 180-degree loading, and (d) is 270-degree loading.

Determine the following:

a. Find the number of cycles to failure using a **Fatigue Study** in SOLIDWORKS. Results should be approximately 50 mm from the fixed face of the part on the inside of the Bend as shown in Fig. E10-8.

b. Perform theoretical calculations to determine the number of cycles to failure at a point 50 mm above the fixed end on the inside of the bent cylinder.

c. Compare simulated and theoretical results and give reasons for any differences.

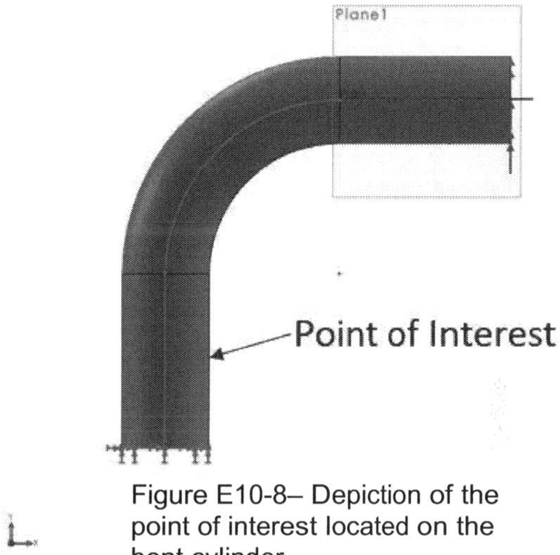

Figure E10-8– Depiction of the point of interest located on the bent cylinder

NOTES:

CHAPTER #11

Thermal Stress Analysis

Temperature changes or gradients within mechanical, electrical, or even biological entities can lead to thermally induced stresses that engineers must account for in various design situations. Thermal stress is particularly prevalent in material that is rapidly cooled or heated due to temperature differences between internal and external surfaces. Consider, for example, the engineering challenges for materials used in aircraft design. Presume that a jet that takes-off from a Phoenix, Arizona, airport where summer temperatures on the field are 105 °F (41 °C) and the plane rapidly climbs to 35,000 feet, where the outside air temperature is -60 °F (-54 °C). Also consider the many different materials used in aircraft construction and the different coefficients of thermal expansion of each. Add to that consideration of the temperature gradient between the exterior and interior of the aircraft cabin. This brief example should provide ample justification for the consideration of thermally induced stress that must be accounted for in various design situations.

Thermal stresses in SOLIDWORKS can be modeled using two different methods. One method is to apply a specified temperature profile by prescribing temperature boundary conditions (or loads) to components, faces, and vertices in a Static Study. However, this method is not very practical if different modes of heat transfer (conduction, convection, or radiation) are involved in the problem. The second method is a two-step process. In the first step, a steady-state or transient Thermal Study is carried out and then, the results of the thermal study are used as thermal loads to solve the thermal stress problem in a Static Study. Throughout this chapter, these options will be explored briefly, along with an extensive look at how to properly set up thermal stress problems.

Learning Objectives

Upon completion of this example, users should be able to:

- Utilize SOLIDWORKS *static simulation* to determine thermal stresses in parts because of a temperature change.
- Apply appropriate boundary or end conditions in thermal stress analysis.
- Apply a temperature and thermal study in order to complete a static (stress) analysis.

Problem Statement

A solid **Aluminum Alloy** shaft with a diameter of 300 mm and a length of 5000 mm is surrounded by a shaft collar made from **Alloy Steel** along its entire length. The collar has an inner diameter of 300 mm and an outer diameter of 500 mm. The goal of this example is to determine the stress distribution throughout assembly due to a uniform 20 °C increase in the surrounding temperature.

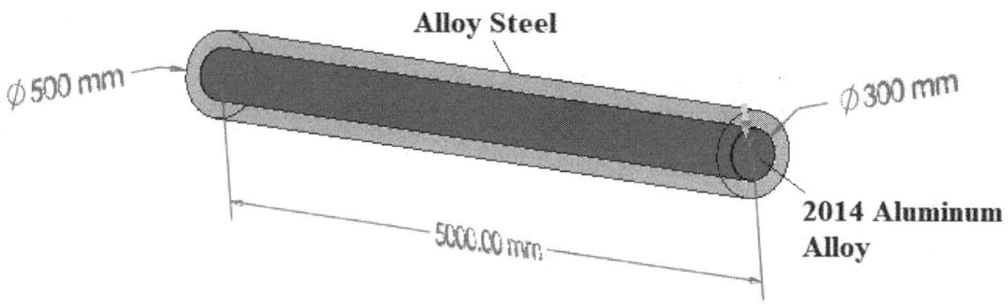

Figure 1 – An aluminum shaft with a steel collar

Static Analysis

Begin by setting up a static analysis for the assembly. Proceed as follows:

1. In the SOLIDWORKS 2026 main menu, select **File>Open...** Then, open the file named **Collar and Shaft Assembly**.

2. In the **Simulation** *tab*, click the **New Study** icon New Study. This enables the simulation study *tab*.

3. In the **Type** dialogue box, click the **Static** icon Static to select a static analysis. In the **Name** dialogue box replace "**Static 1**" by typing **Thermal Stress.**

4. Click **[OK]** ✓ to close the **Study** property manager.

5. **Thermal Stress (-Default-)** should appear in the Simulation manager at the top-left of the graphics window.

Material Properties Applied to the Model

1. In the SOLIDWORKS Simulation manager, right-click the model name, **Shaft Collar-1** under **Parts**. Then select **Apply/Edit Material.** The **Material** window opens.

2. Next, click the > symbol next to **Steel** (if not already selected) to expand the menu and select **Alloy Steel** from the list of available steels.

3. Click **[Apply]** followed by **[Close]** to close the **Material** window. A check mark "✓" appears on the **Shaft Collar-1** folder and the material designation **(-Alloy Steel-)** appears next to this folder.

4. Repeat steps 1 to 3 for **Shaft2-1,** but choose **2014 Alloy** for the shaft collar under the **Aluminum Alloys** folder.

Assign Connection in the Model

Next, define the type of connection between the shaft and the shaft collar. Because there are only two components in this assembly, it is possible to define contact between mating surfaces by applying a *Global* contact. Specifying *Global* contact applies the same contact condition to all contacting surfaces in an assembly.

1. In the Simulation manager tree, double click the **Connections** folder to open the **Component Interactions.**

2. Double click the **Component Interactions** folder to open the **Global Interaction (-Bonded- Meshed independently-**).

3. Right-click **Global Interaction (-Bonded- Meshed independently-**) and select **Edit Definition…** . This opens the **Component Interaction** property manager shown in Fig. 2.

4. Within the **Component Contact** property manager, under **Contact Type**, select the ⊙**Contact** button.

5. Make sure that in the **Components** section, ☑**Global Contact** is also checked.

6. Click **[OK]** ✓ to close the **Component Contact** property manager. **Global Interaction (-Contact-**) should appear for the **Component Contact** in the Simulation manager tree.

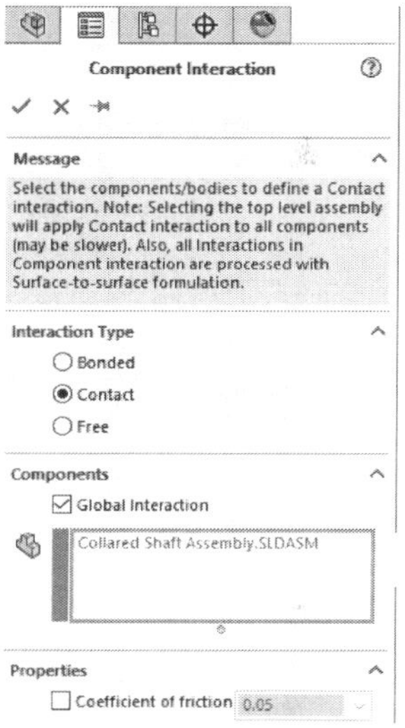

Figure 2 – Component Contact Property

Note:

Bonded components behave as if they were welded (or glued) together during simulation (i.e., no gap or penetration is allowed between the connecting surfaces). **Contact or No Penetration** components do not penetrate each other during simulation but gap distance between the components is allowed. In this study the shaft and the collar can expand axially (along their lengths) freely without interfering with each other and thus the **No Penetration** is selected. **Free** allows penetration between the surfaces.

Assign Fixtures to the Model

1. In the Simulation manager right-click **Fixtures** and select **Advanced Fixtures….** The **Fixture** property manager opens.

2. Click the down arrow ˅ to open the **Advanced** dialogue box. Then, select the **Use Reference Geometry** icon 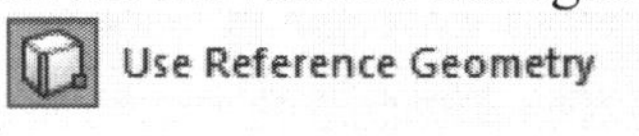 as shown in Fig. 3. Next, click to activate the **Face, Vertices, and Edges for Fixture** (light blue) selection box (if not already selected).

3. Zoom in on the end of the assembly (either right or left end). Click to select the ends of both the shaft and the collar as shown in Fig.3. **Face<1> @ Shaft Collar-1** and **Face<2> @ Shaft2-1** should be listed in the **Face, Vertices, and Edges for Fixture** field.

4. Next, click to activate the **Face, Edge, Plane, and Axis for Direction** (pink) selection box (if not already selected). Select **Axis 1** of Shaft2 shown circled in the fly-out menu of Fig. 3

5. In the **Fixture** property manager, scroll down to the **Translations** dialogue box and set the **Unit** to **mm,** then click to select the **Circumferential** icon and ensure that **0** appears in the value box. This selection sets rotation of the cylindrical face to **0.** Finally, select the **Axial** icon and make sure that 0 appears in the value box. Press OK.

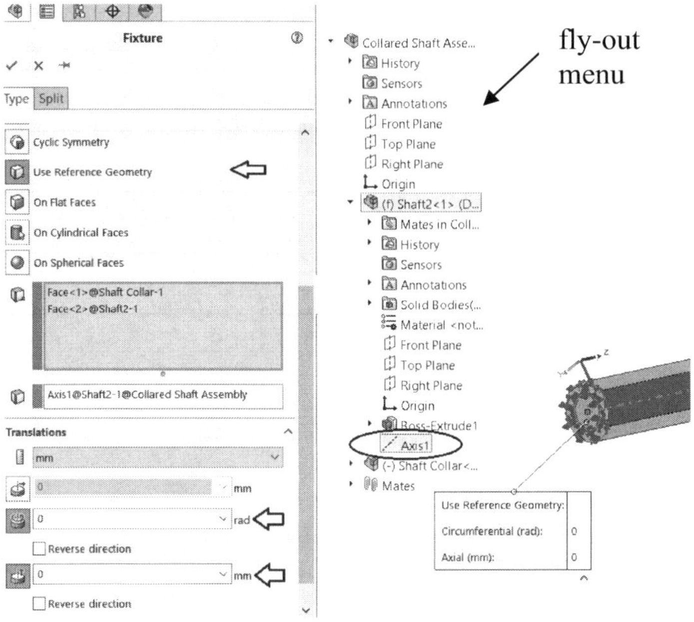

Figure 3 – Fixture Property Manager.

The above selections allow the assembly to expand both radially and axially away from the fixed end.

External Loads (Method -1)

There are two ways to apply a temperature change to the assembly. In the first method (Method-1), temperature boundary conditions can be applied using the **Temperature** property manager found in the Simulation manager tree. Proceed as follows.

1. Right-click **External Loads** from the Simulation manager and select **Temperature ....** The **Temperature** property manager opens as seen in Fig. 5.

2. In the **Temperature** property manager click to highlight the **Faces, Edges, Vertices, and Components for Temperature**. Light-blue indicates the field is active and awaiting user input.

3. If the SOLIDWORKS **Selection Filters Toolbar**  is not enabled, press F5 on your keyboard to turn the toolbar on. This filter is located on the **Toolbar** *tab*.

4. It is important to select the shaft and the collar solid bodies (not their surfaces) to assign the temperature. For this purpose, click to select **Filter Solid Bodies**  from the **Selection Filters Toolbar** shown circled in Fig. 4.

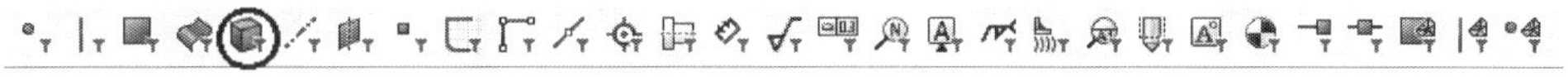

Figure 4 – Selection Filters Toolbar.

5. Expand the SOLIDWORKS flyout menu and select **Boss-Extrude1** under **Solid Bodies (1)** folder for both **Shaft2** and **Shaft Collar-1**. You should see that **Boss-Extrude1@ Shaft Collar-1@ Collared Shaft Assembly** and **Boss-Extrude1@ Shaft2-1@ Collared Shaft Assembly** are selected as shown in Fig. 5.

6. Type **298.15+20** for the **Temperature** input and make sure **Kelvin (K)** is selected from the unit dropdown. 298.15 K is the SOLIDWORKS default temperature.

CAUTION:

In SOLIDWORKS one must be very careful when applying external loads caused by temperature. It is very easy (and incorrect) to only apply temperatures to the face of parts instead of the solid body. SOLIDWORKS default temperature at zero strain for all parts and surfaces is 298.15 K.

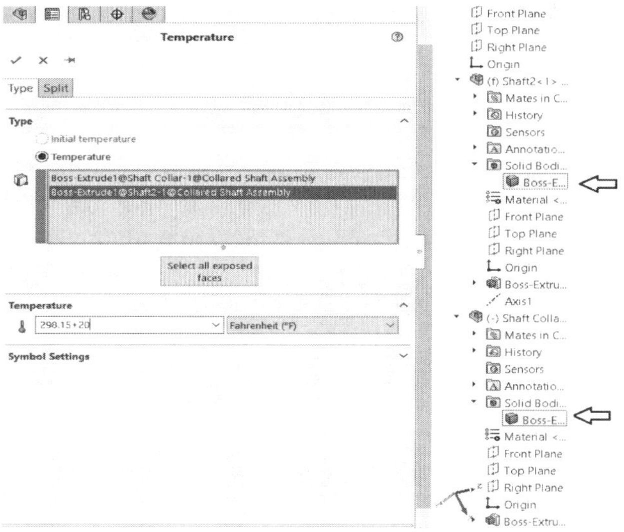

Figure 5 – Temperature Property Manager.

External Loads (Method-2)

In the second method, a **Thermal Study** is performed first to determine the temperature of the assembly. Then those results are applied as external loads in a static simulation. Proceed as follows.

1. In the **Simulation** *tab*, click the **New Study** icon.
2. Select **Thermal** from within the **Advanced Simulation** dropdown menu and rename the study **Temperature Profiles.**
3. Click **[OK]** ✓ to close the **Study** property manager.
4. **Temperature Profiles (-Default-)** should now appear at the top of the Simulation manager tree to the left of the graphics window.

Material Properties Applied to the Model

1. In the SOLIDWORKS Simulation manager**,** right-click the model name, **Shaft Collar-1** under **Parts**. Then select **Apply/Edit Material.** The **Material** window opens.
2. In the Materials window, assign **Alloy Steel** from the list of available steels. Similarly, assign **2014 Alloy Aluminum** for **Shaft2-1** material.

Applying Thermal Loads for Uniform Temperature

1. In the Simulation manager, right click **Thermal Loads**, then from the pull-down menu select **Temperature**. This action opens the **Temperature** property manager to permit application of temperature conditions.
2. The **Faces, Edges, Vertices, and Components for Temperature** box should be highlighted (light blue). Proceed to manually select all exposed surfaces or click the **[Select all exposed faces]** button to select the exposed surfaces. Ensure that "**Face<1>@Shaft Collar-1**", "**Face<2>@ Shaft Collar-1**", "**Face<3>@ Shaft Collar-1**", "**Face<4>@Shaft2-1**", and "**Face<5>@Shaft2-1**", appear in this box as shown in Fig. 6.

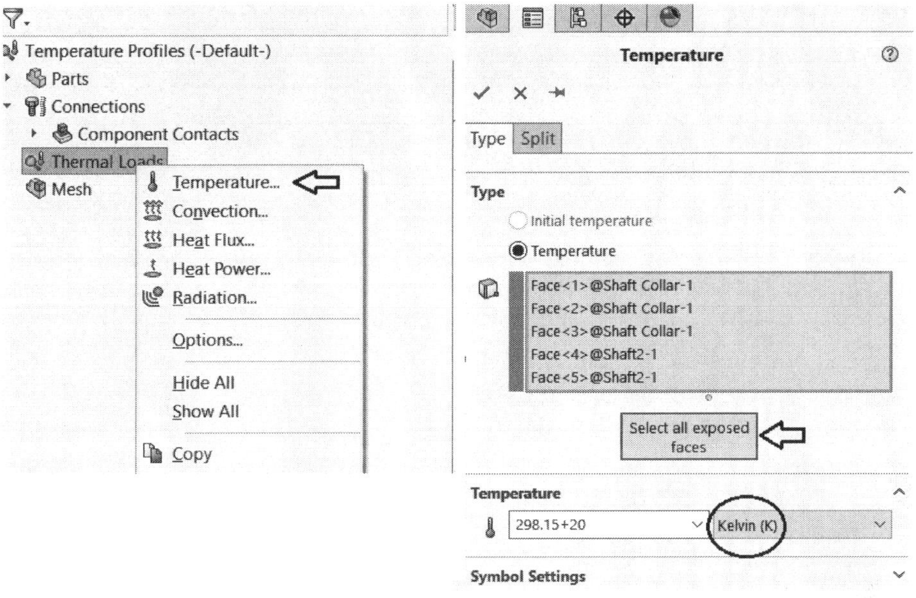

Figure 6 – Temperature Property Manager.

3. Within the **Temperature** dropdown, type **298.15+20** as the temperature, and ensure **Kelvin (K)** is selected from the unit dropdown.
4. Click **[OK] ✓** to close the **Temperature** property manager.

5. Right click **Temperature Profiles (-Default-)** from the Simulation manager tree and select **Properties** from the drop-down menu.

6. Once in the **Thermal Properties** menu, ensure that the **Steady state** button is selected as circled in Fig.7.

7. Click **OK** to exit.

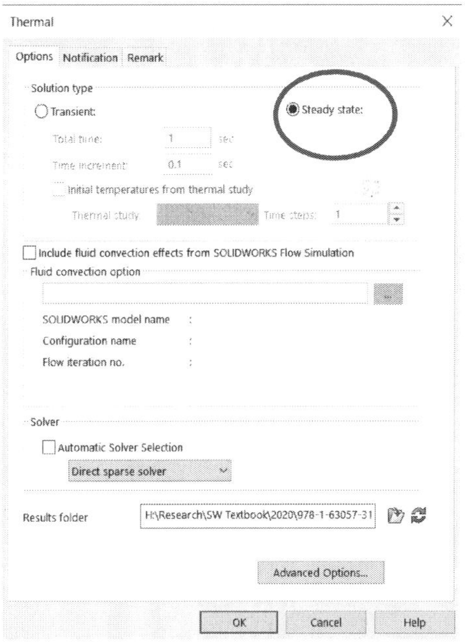

Figure 7 - Thermal Study setup.

Solve the Thermal Study and Apply the Solution

1. In the Simulation manager right-click **Mesh** and select **Mesh and Run** to display temperature profiles for the shaft and the collar. Since all surfaces are set to 318.15 K (i.e., 298.15+20 K), the temperature study results in 318.15 K for the temperature of all nodes.

At this point the **Thermal Study** is complete. However, *do NOT close the* **Thermal Study** model.

2. At bottom of the screen, click to select the Simulation Study *tab* named **Thermal Stress.**

3. Right-click **External Loads** from the Simulation manager tree and select **Thermal Effects…**

4. The **Flow/Thermal Effects** *tab* should open from within the **Static** properties window.

5. Select ⊙**Temperatures from thermal study**. Next, **Temperature Profiles** should be selected from the **Thermal study** dropdown menu shown in Fig.8.

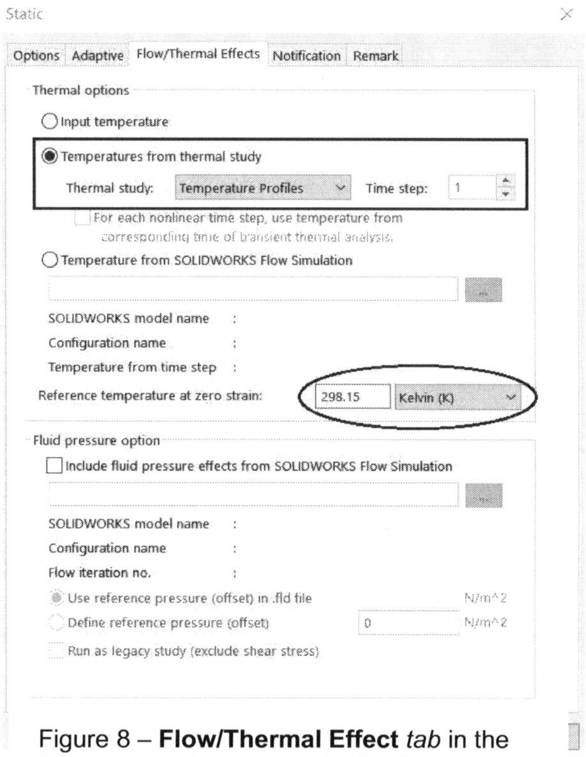

Figure 8 – **Flow/Thermal Effect** *tab* in the **Static** property manager Static Property Manager.

6. Ensure that **Reference temperature at zero strain:** is set to **298.15** and the units are in **Kelvin (K)**. This step is important because it sets the temperature of the assembly when no thermal strain was present. **298.15** is the reference used to determine the temperature change ΔT in the SOLIDWORKS solver.

7. Click **[OK]** to exit the **Static** properties window.

8. Under **External Loads** a new load called **Thermal** should appear now.

NOTE: Using the Thermal study approach (i.e., Method-2), it is possible to apply different types of thermal loads and boundary conditions (i.e., convection, radiation, heat flux, ...) to the model depending on the problem. However, Method-1 offers only temperature change within the Static Analysis for boundary conditions.

NOTE: Before proceeding to mesh and solve the static model, it is necessary to disable one of the **External loads** inputs because two identical thermal loads were created when using Method-1 and Method-2.

9. To disable the Method-1 entry, simply right-click on the **Temperature-1 (: 318.15 Kelvin)** and select **Suppress.** To disable the Method-2 entry, right-click and select **Edit Definition...** to open the **Flow/Thermal Effects** *tab*. Select the ⊙**Input Temperature** and press **OK.**

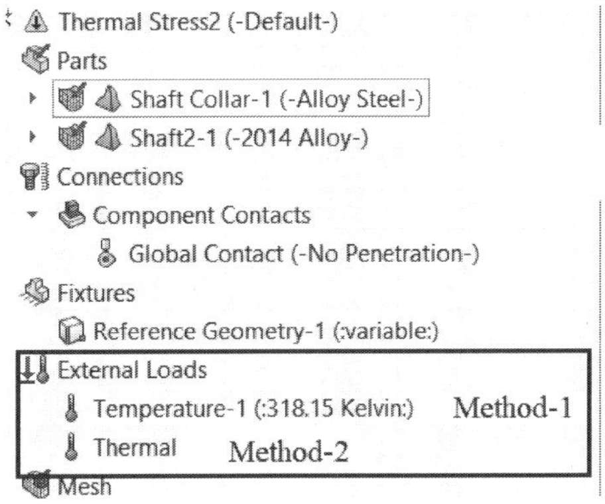

Figure 9 – **External Loads** inputs from Method-1 and Method-2.

NOTE: There is no preference for which input is selected to be disabled. Thus, arbitrarily, Method-2 input is disabled for the remainder of this study.

The **Thermal Stress** model is now ready to solve. However, before meshing and running the model, the shaft and collar are separated in an exploded view to facilitate observing results on their respective cylindrical surfaces. These components are separated by creating an exploded view as follows.

10. From the Main menu select **Insert**. Then from the pull-down menu select **Exploded View...** A portion of the **Explode** property manager is seen in Fig. 10.

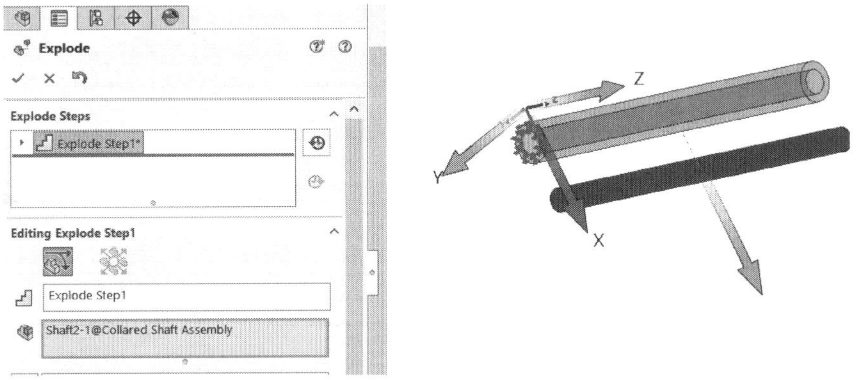

Figure 10 – Manually creating an exploded view of the assembly.

11. In the **Explode Step Type** dialogue box, select the **Regular step (translate and rotate)** icon (if not already selected).

12. For this example, move the cursor onto the graphics screen and click to select the *shaft*. Immediately, an X, Y, Z coordinate triad and three rings appear to "float" on the shaft. Click-and-drag the vector aligned with the X axis and drag the shaft away from the collar as illustrated in Fig. 10. This action is recorded in the **Explode Steps** dialogue box as **Explode Step1**.

13. Click **[OK]** ✓ to close the **Explode** property manager. NOTE: Either component could be moved in any direction to create an acceptable exploded view. The exploded view will be used for the rest of this chapter.

Apply Mesh for Thermal Study

1. Right-click **Mesh** from the Simulation manager and select **Create Mesh….** To open **Mesh** property window.

2. In this window, move the **Mesh Density** slider all the way to the right to generate **Fine** mesh. This improves accuracy of the solution.

3. Check the **Mesh Parameters box** and select ⊙ **Curved-based mesh** for the **Mesh Parameters**. Select **mm** for the mesh **Unit.**

4. Click the down arrow ˅ to open the **advanced** dialogue box. Verify that **Jacobian points** is set at **16 points.**

5. Click **[OK]** ✓ to close the **Mesh** property manager.

Meshing starts automatically and a **Mesh Progress** window appears briefly. After meshing is complete, SOLIDWORKS Simulation displays the meshed model. Also, a check mark "✓" appears on the **Mesh** icon to indicate meshing is complete.

Reference Temperature at Zero Strain

1. From the Simulation manager, right-click **Thermal Stress (-Default-)** and select **Properties…** This opens the **Static** property manager.
2. Next, click to open the **Flow/Thermal Effects** *tab* located at top of the **Static** properties window.

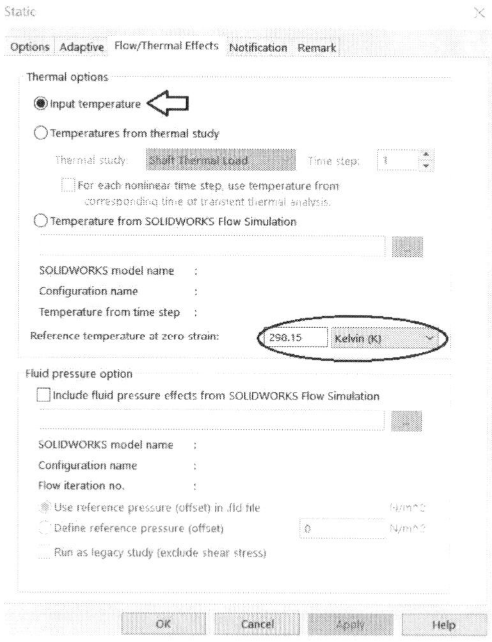

Figure 11 – Static Analysis property manager.

3. Within the **Thermal options**, select ⊙**Input temperature.**

4. Make sure the reference temperature at zero strain is set to 298.15 K as circled in Fig.11.

5. Click **Run This Study** from the Simulation *tab* and wait for the simulation to complete. After a successful solution, a **Results folder** appears below the Simulation manager. This folder contains three plots that are titled **Stress 1 (-vonMises-), Displacement1 (-Res disp-), Strain1 (-Equivalent-).**

Examination of Results

Default Stress Plot

Begin by examining the vonMises stress plot shown in Fig. 12 to gain an overview of results. Desired appearance attributes for this plot are defined below so that they can be copied when producing additional plots.

1. If necessary, click the " ▸ " symbol adjacent to the **Results** folder to display a list of the three default plots, **Stress1**, **Displacement1**, and **Strain1**.

2. If necessary, double-click the **Stress1 (-vonMises-)** *icon* to display this plot.

3. Right-click **Stress1 (-vonMises-)**, and from the pop-up menu select **Edit Definition…** The **Stress Plot** property manager opens.

4. In the **Display** dialogue box, change **Units** to **N/m^2**.

5. Check "✓" to open the ☑ **Deformed Shape** dialogue box (if not already open). Within this dialogue box, select ⊙ **Automatic**. Then click **[OK]** ✓ to close the **Stress Plot** property manager. The system default, exaggerated deformation scale, is applied to the exploded view of the model shown in Fig.12.

6. Click ˅ to open the **Advanced Options** dialogue box. Then, click to *clear* the check from ☐ **Average results across boundary for parts**. This action is important because parts of this assembly are made of two *different materials*.

Figure 12 – vonMises stress plot for the assembly due to a 20 °C increase of temperature.

7. On the **Simulation** *tab* located above the graphics area, click the  **Deformed Result** icon.

The VonMises stress on the surface of the shaft shows an approximate value of 9.64 MPa.

Stress Plots in a Cylindrical Coordinate System

Radial Stress

Because traditional stresses like σ_x, σ_y, σ_z, σ_1, σ_2, σ_3, τ_{xy}, τ_{yz}, τ_{zx}, etc., in a Cartesian (X, Y, Z) coordinate system are not conducive for representing radial stress in cylindrical parts, a cylindrical coordinate system is introduced below to facilitate the examination of results.

When establishing a cylindrical coordinate system, *any* axis can be used to define the axis of a local cylindrical coordinate system. However, this axis must be chosen wisely because once an axis is selected, stresses usually associated with SX = σ_x, SY = σ_y, and SZ = σ_z take on new meanings as summarized in Table 1.

In the following discussion, "reference axis" refers to an axis aligned with the centerline of a cylindrical coordinate system.

Table 1 – Correspondence between stresses in a Cartesian coordinate system and their equivalents in a cylindrical coordinate system.

Original Meaning of Stress	**New Meaning in the Cylindrical Coordinate System**
SX = stress in X-direction σ_x.	SX = now denotes stress in the *radial* direction (σ_r) relative to the selected reference axis.
SY = stress in Y-direction σ_y.	SY = denotes stress in the *circumferential* or *tangential* direction (σ_t) relative to the selected reference axis.
SZ = stress in Z-direction σ_z.	SZ = denotes stress in the *axial* direction (σ_a) relative to the selected reference axis.

In brief, no matter what axis is chosen to be the reference axis[1] of a cylindrical coordinate system, the correspondence between radial, circumferential, and axial stresses defined in Table 1 remains valid. Thus, a reference axis is selected consistent with the above criteria.

Before selecting an axis to define a cylindrical coordinate system, a *copy* of the existing vonMises stress plot is made. The primary reason for making a copy of this plot is to save the time it would take to recreate all of the graphic settings defined earlier. Copy the plot as follows.

1. Right-click **Stress1 (-vonMises-)** and from the pop-up menu select **Copy**.

[1] Reference axis refers to an axis aligned with the centerline of the cylindrical coordinate system.

2. Right-click the **Results** folder and from the pop-up menu select **Paste**. A plot named **Copy[1] Stress1 (-vonMises-)** is added to the list of plots beneath the **Results** folder.

3. Double-click **Copy[1] Stress1 (-vonMises-)** to display an *identical* plot of the vonMises stress that includes all previously defined display options.

Next, a cylindrical coordinate system is defined. **Axis1**, aligned with the shaft centerline, is the *only logical choice* for the axis of a cylindrical coordinate system. However, since the goal is to display radial stress in the cylindrical coordinate system, two changes must be made to the *copied* plot. First, **SX** must be specified as the stress to be viewed in this plot because, according to Table 1, **SX** = *radial* stress in a cylindrical coordinate system. And second, **Axis1** must be defined as the axis of a cylindrical coordinate system. Proceed as follows to alter the copied plot.

4. Right-click **Copy[1] Stress1 (-vonMises-)** and from the pop-up menu select **Edit Definition…** The **Stress Plot** property manager opens as shown in Fig.13.

5. In the **Display** dialogue box, click ▼ to open the stress  **Component** pull-down menu and change it to **SX: X Normal Stress**. This action also opens the **Advanced Options** dialogue.

6. Move the cursor over the top field in the **Advanced Options** dialogue box to identify it as the **Plane, Axis, or Coordinate System**. Click to highlight this field (light blue) to indicate it is active and awaiting user input (if not already selected).

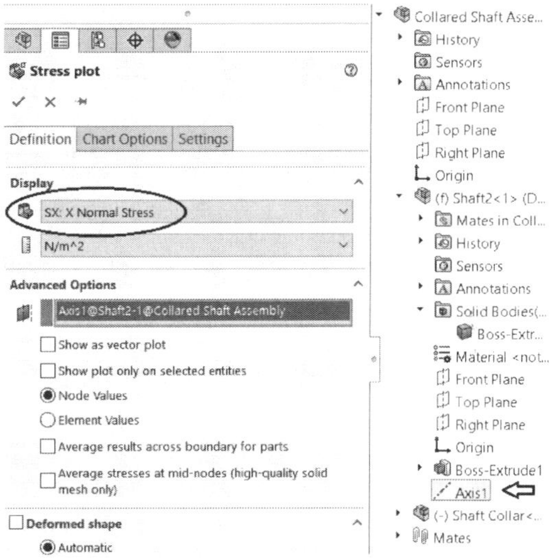

Figure 13 – Selections to define a cylindrical coordinate system and radial stress.

7. In the graphics screen, either click to select the centerline of the shaft axis (or) click to select **Axis1** in the SOLIDWORKS flyout menu shown in Fig. 13. Either selection establishes **Axis1** as the reference axis of a cylindrical coordinate system, and the name **Axis1@ Shaft2-1@Collared Shaft Assembly** appears in the currently active field.

8. Verify that ⊙ **Node Values** is selected and click **[OK]** ✓ to close the **Stress Plot** property manager and the model appears as an exploded view.

9. Move the cursor onto **Copy[1] Stress1 (-X normal-)** and click-*pause* to select this 'name.' Then within the name field, type "**Radial Stress**" and press **[Enter]**. The plot name is changed to **Radial Stress (-X normal-)**.

Now back to our investigation of radial stress on the contacting surfaces.

10. In the Simulation manager, right-click **Radial Stress (-X normal-)** and from the pull-down menu choose **List Selected**. The **Probe Result** window opens as shown in Fig. 14.

11. In the **Options** dialogue box, choose ⊙ **On selected entities** (if not already selected).

12. In the **Results** dialogue box the **Faces, Edges, or Vertices** field is highlighted (light blue) and awaits selection of the item for which results are to be displayed. On the graphics screen, select the outer cylindrical surface of the shaft, then click to select it. **Face<1>@Shaft2-1** appears in the active field.

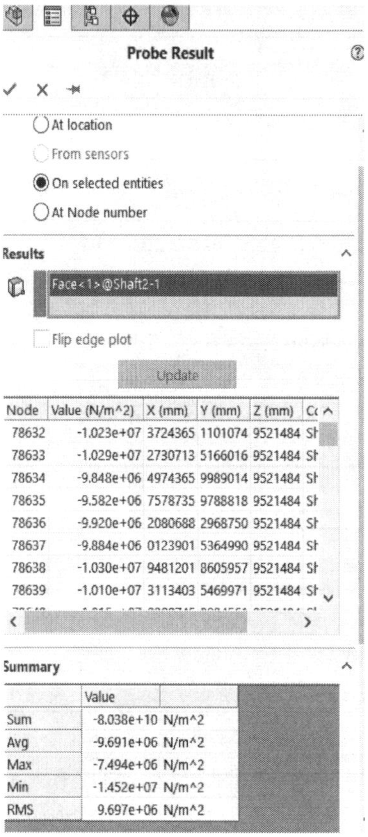

Figure 14 – Summary of the **Probe Results** for radial stresses on the outer surface of the shaft.

13. Next, in the **Results** dialogue box, click the **[Update]** button.

14. Immediately the table is populated with data occurring at every node on the selected surface. The **Value (N/m^2)** column contains values of *radial* stress at all nodes on the cylindrical surface of the shaft. Also included are node numbers and X, Y, Z coordinates of each data point on the selected surface, and a column identifying the **Components**, in this case **Shaft2-1**, to which the data applies.

NOTE: To accurately view tabulated data, it may be necessary to click-and-drag the right margin of the Simulation manager tree as well as column-edges within the table to increase their width.

Observation of Fig. 14 reveals that average stress level at the shaft cylindrical surface is approximately -9.691 Mpa (m*ay vary a little*). The **Min** and **Max** values of the radial stress in Fig.14 are associated with the nodes close to the fixed end, and thus they are not useful. Note that the negative sign for these results reveals that the shaft is subject to compression due to the 20 ºC temperature change.

Next, axial displacement of the shaft is examined.

15. In the Simulation manager, right-click **Displacement1 (-Res disp-),** and from the pull-down menu select **Show**. The **Displacement** plot is displayed.

16. Again, right-click **Displacement1 (-Res disp-)**, and from the pull-down menu select **Edit Definition…** The **Displacement Plot** property manager opens.

17. In the **Component** field of the **Display** dialogue box, select **UZ: Z Displacement**. According to Table 1, **UZ: Z Displacement** corresponds to *axial* displacement in a cylindrical coordinate system.

18. Also, in the **Display** dialogue box, verify that **Units** are set to **mm** and that ⊙ **Automatic** is selected in the ☑ **Deformed Shape** dialogue box.

19. Click ˅ to open the **Advanced Options** dialogue box. Click to activate (light blue) the **Plane, Axis or Coordinate System** field. It now awaits selection of an axis to define a cylindrical coordinate system.

20. On the model, select **Axis1** on the shaft centerline as the reference axis for a cylindrical coordinate system. Alternately, near the bottom of the SOLIDWORKS flyout menu, select **Axis1**. **Axis1@Shaft2-1@Collared Shaft Assembly** should appear in the highlighted field.

21. Click **[OK]** ✓ to close the **Displacement plot** property manager.

22. If the plot produced in the preceding step does not appear on the graphics screen, double-click **Displacement1 (-Z disp-)** to display the plot.

23. Finally, from the **View Setting** toolbar pick the top view orientation for the display. Figure-15 shows displacement of the collar and shaft in the axial (Z) direction.

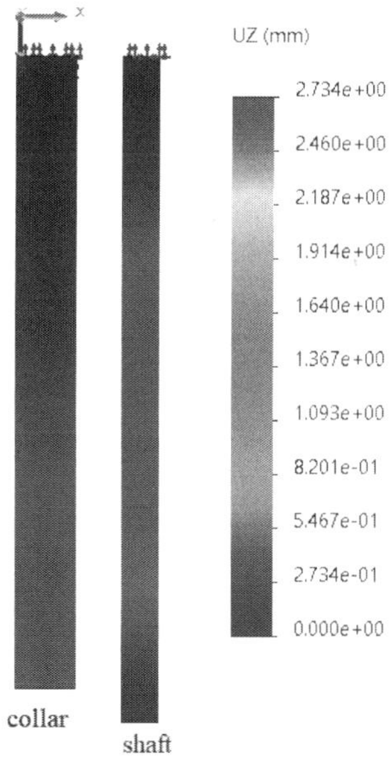

Figure 15 – Axial displacement (Uz) of the shaft and the shaft collar.

24. Clearly the aluminum shaft expands more than the steel collar since the aluminum has a larger thermal expansion coefficient than steel (2.3e-5 /°C vs. 1.3e-5 /°C). This plot also shows why **No Penetration** was selected for the connection type between the shaft and the collar. The shaft and the collar can move independently in the axial direction. However, if **Bonded** were selected for the connection type, both the shaft and the collar would displace equally in the axial direction since they would be considered bonded or glued together.

Validation of Radial Stress Results

The theoretical radial stress, $\sigma_{thermal}$ for a press fit on the shaft due to thermal expansion is calculated using the following equations:

$$\sigma_{thermal} = p * \frac{(R^2 + r_i^2)}{(R^2 - r_i^2)}$$

In which,

$$p = \frac{\delta = R(\alpha_s - \alpha_{sc})\Delta T}{R\left(\frac{1}{E_o} * \left(\frac{r_o^2 + R^2}{r_o^2 - R^2} + v_o\right) + \frac{1}{E_i} * \left(\frac{(R^2 + r_i^2)}{(R^2 - r_i^2)} - v_i\right)\right)}$$

where, r_i is the inner radius of the shaft (which in this case is $0\ mm$), r_o is the outer radius of the shaft collar, R is the radius of the point of contact between the shaft and the shaft collar, δ is the radial interference between the two parts after they have expanded, p is the pressure caused by the shrink fit, E_i is the modulus of elasticity of the inner component, E_o is the modulus of elasticity of the outer component, v_i is Poisson's ratio of the shaft, α is the thermal expansion coefficient and v_o is Poisson's ratio of the shaft collar.

For this example $r_i = 0$ mm , $r_o = 250$ mm, $R = 150$ mm, $\Delta T = 20$ °C, α_{sc}= 1.3e-5 /°C , α_s= 2.3e-5 / °C, $E_o = 2.1e11\ \mathrm{N/m^2}$, $E_i = 7.3e10\ \mathrm{N/m^2}$, $v_o = 0.28$, $v_i = 0.33$,.

Thus, the theoretical p is

$$p = \frac{(\alpha_s - \alpha_{sc})\Delta T}{\frac{1}{E_o} * \left(\frac{r_o^2 + R^2}{r_o^2 - R^2} + v_o\right) + \frac{1}{E_i} * \left(\frac{(R^2 + r_i^2)}{(R^2 - r_i^2)} - v_i\right)}$$

$$p = \frac{(1.2 - 2.3)10^{-5}\ 20}{\frac{1}{2.1e11\frac{N}{m^2}} * \left(\frac{(0.25\ m)^2 + (0.15\ m)^2}{(0.25\ m)^2 - (0.15\ m)^2} + 0.28\right) + \frac{1}{7.3e10\frac{N}{m^2}} * \left(\frac{(0.15\ m)^2 + 0}{(0.15\ m)^2 - 0} - 0.33\right)}$$

$$p = -9.6944e + 06\ \mathrm{N}/m^2$$

The resulting p value is substituted into the thermal stress equation.

$$\sigma_{thermal} = p * \frac{(R^2 + r_i^2)}{(R^2 - r_i^2)} = 9.6944e6\ \mathrm{N/m^2} * \frac{(0.15\ m)^2 + 0}{(0.15\ m)^2 - 0} = -9.6944e6\ \mathrm{N/m^2}$$

Thus, the percent difference between the theoretical and SOLIDWORKS Simulation results is:

$$\%\text{difference} = \left[\frac{\text{FEA result} - \text{classical result}}{\text{FEA result}}\right]100 = \frac{-9.691e6 + (9.6944e6)}{-9.691e6} * 100$$
$$= 0.04\%$$

Validation of Axial Displacement Results

The theoretical axial displacement for the shaft and the collar is

$$\Delta L = L\,\alpha\,\Delta T$$

where L is the length of the shaft (or collar). Aluminum shaft has a thermal expansion coefficient of $\alpha_s = 2.3e - 5/\,°\text{C}$, and the steel collar thermal expansion coefficient is $\alpha_{sc} = 1.3e - 5/\,°\text{C}$. As a result:

$\Delta L_s = L\,\alpha_s\,\Delta T$ = 5000 * 2.3e-5 * 20 = 2.3 mm (differ by 15% vs. 2.73 mm from Simulation)

$\Delta L_{sc} = L\,\alpha_{sc}\,\Delta T$ = 5000 * 1.3e-5 * 20 = 1.3 mm (differ by 5% vs, 1.23 mm from Simulation)

Logging Out of the Current Analysis

This concludes the thermal stress analysis. It is suggested that the open files *not* be saved. Proceed as follows.

1. On the **Main Menu**, select **File** followed by choosing **Close**.

The **SOLIDWORKS** window opens and provides the options of either saving the current analysis or not. Select **[Don't Save]** for all the open files.

EXERCISES

EXERCISE 1 –Thermal Stress on an I-Beam

Open the assembly file **I-Beam** and perform a thermal stress analysis

- Material: **AISI 1010 Steel, hot rolled bar**
- Mesh: Use the default mesh
- Fixtures: **Fixed (immovable)** top and bottom.
- External Load: 80 K body temperature change and a 1000 N force to the top center of the beam.

Determine the following:

Develop a finite element analysis that includes a material specification, fixtures, external load(s), mesh, and thermal stress solutions.

a. Find the average thermal stress using SOLIDWORKS simulation and compare the result with the thermal stress theory.

b. Determine if the column yields. Show pertinent calculations/results and state the reason for your conclusion.

c. Determine the temperature at which the I-Beam has a minimum factor of safety of 2 and state the reason for your conclusion.

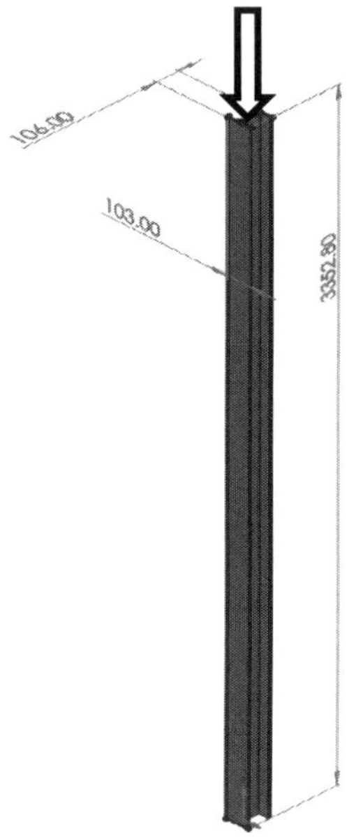

Figure E11 -1 - I-beam on which thermal and axial stresses applied.

EXERCISE 2 –Thermal Stress of a Drill Bit

This exercise is based on a drill bit exposed to a thermal load, with an axial force applied normal to the bottom of the hole it is cutting

Open the file: **56_Drill_Bit**

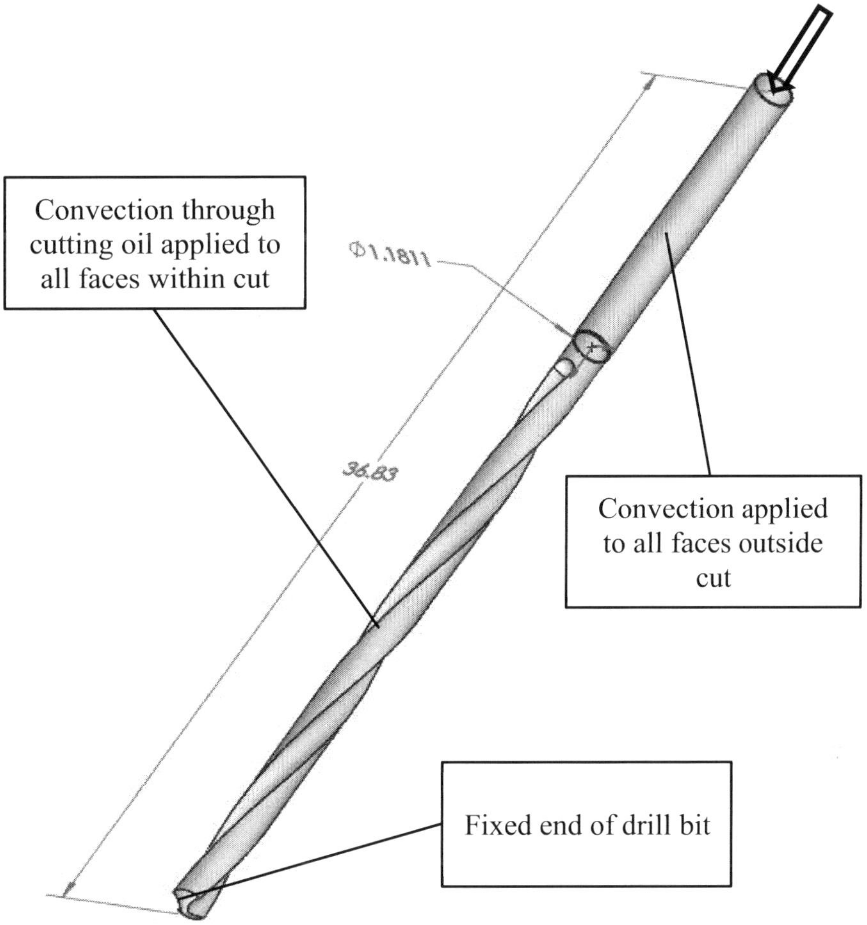

Figure E11-2 - Thermally and axially loaded #56 drill-bit (all dimensions expressed in mm).

- Material: **Titanium Ti-13V-11Cr-3Al Solution Treated** (both analyses)
- Mesh: **Blended curvature-based mesh** (both analyses)
- Fixtures: **Fixed (immovable)** restraints applied to drill tip. (Static analysis)
- External Load:
    - Thermal Analysis: **Convection 1** of **20 W/m^2.K**, **Tamb=298 K** applied to smooth cylindrical surface, **Convection 2** of **250 W/m^2.K, Tamb=350 K** applied to all surfaces within cut.
    - Static Analysis: **Force** of **25 N** applied to flat end of drill-bit in direction of cut, **Thermal Analysis** results imported with **Tref=298 K**.

Determine the following:

Develop a finite element analysis that includes material specification, fixtures, external load(s), mesh, and buckling solutions.

a. Find the maximum temperature of the drill bit.

b. Look for and determine any radial deformation that occurs within the portion of the drill bit submerged in the cut.

c. Determine the minimum Factor of Safety throughout the drill bit based on **Max von Mises Stress** criteria. Is the drill bit predicted to fail? Provide specific reasons for your answer and refer to values upon which your conclusion is based.

EXERCISE 3 –Thermal Study of Stress in a Connecting Rod

This exercise is based on the connecting rod of an engine exposed to convection heat transfer.

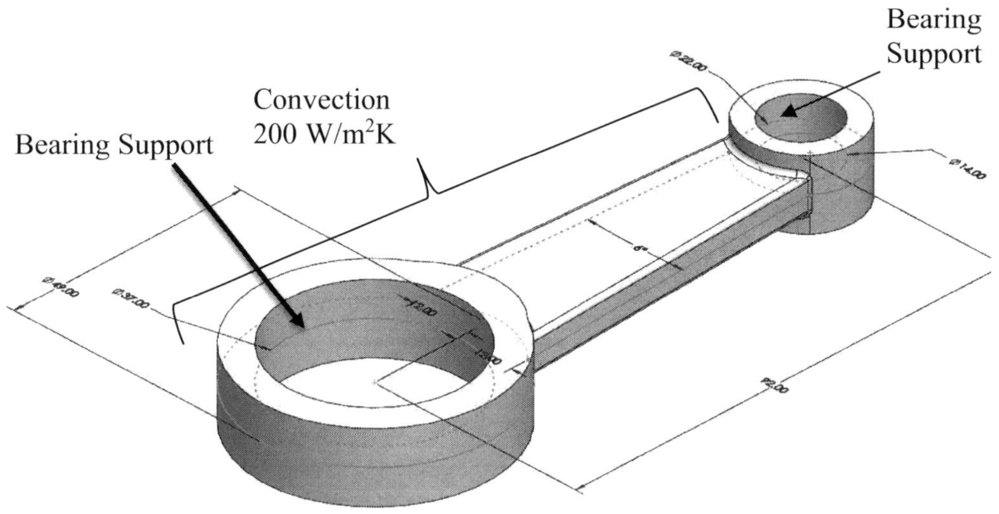

Figure E11-3 - Thermally loaded Connecting Rod (all dimensions expressed in mm).

Open the file: **Connecting_Rod_Exercise_3**

- Material: **Cast Alloy** (both analyses)
- Mesh: **Blended curvature-based mesh** (both analyses)
- Fixtures: **Bearing Supports for both the connecting ends**

- External Load:
  - Thermal Analysis: **Convection of 200 W/m²K, T_{amb}=305 K** applied to all surfaces except the inner and outer cylindrical surfaces on the smaller end of the rod, **Convection 2** of **15 W/m²K, T_{amb}=350 K** applied to the outer circumference of the smaller end of the connecting rod. Assume the inner circumference of the smaller bearing support is adiabatic.

Determine the following:

Develop a finite element analysis that includes a material specification, fixtures, external load(s), mesh, and buckling solutions.

a. Find the maximum temperature of the connecting rod via a thermal study.

b. What is the maximum stress and minimum factor of safety of this part?

EXERCISE 4 –Thermal Study and Stress of an Axial Expansion Joint

This exercise is based on a stainless-steel axial expansion joint in a pipeline exposed to convection heat transfer.

Open the file: **Axial_Expansion_Joint**

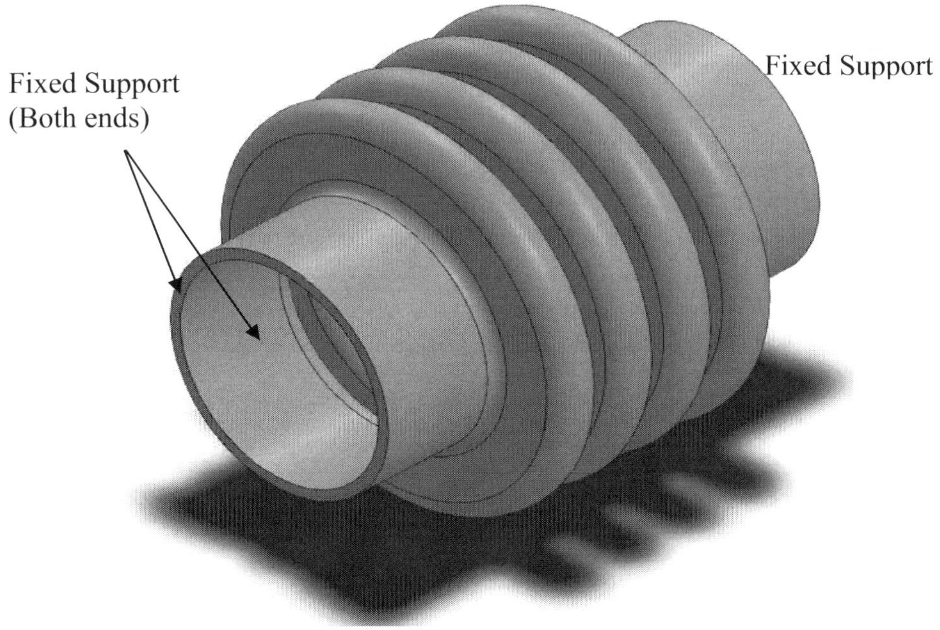

Figure E11-4 - Thermally loaded Axial Expansion Joint.

- Material: **AISI Type 316L stainless Steel**
- Mesh: **Blended curvature-based mesh**
- Fixtures: **Fixed (immovable)** restraints applied to both ends of the joint
- External Load:
    - Thermal Analysis: **Convection 1 of 100 W/m²K, T_{amb}=310 K** applied to all outer surfaces of the joint, **Convection 2** of **2500 W/m²K, T_{amb}=500 K** applied to all inner surfaces of the joint.

Determine the following:

Develop a finite element analysis that includes a material specification, fixtures, external load(s), mesh, and thermal stress solutions.

a. Find the maximum temperature of the axial expansion joint via a thermal study.

b. What are the maximum von Mises stresses and minimum factor of safety of this part?

APPENDIX A

ORGANIZING ASSIGNMENTS USING MS WORD®

This appendix is included to offer guidance in the use of Microsoft Word® for the preparation of deliverables associated with end of chapter exercises. It is assumed that users are familiar with Word® or some other word processor. However, a few procedures outlined below might be new even to seasoned Word® users. Although Chapter 5 demonstrates a semi-automated means to generate a **Report** using features embedded within the Simulation software, this section provides guidance for users desiring to output into a neat, customized report, *only* those items requested in end of chapter exercises. An added benefit of this approach is that, in addition to a professional looking assignment, the report (a) can be prepared simultaneously while working an exercise, and (b) can be printed on fewer pages, a real plus for students on a tight print quota.

The goal of this section is to show, through example, how to combine features of Word® with capabilities of SOLIDWORKS Simulation to produce a concise and well-organized report. Techniques described herein are the same procedures used to create and format text and images in this book. An example of the "final report" created below can be found beginning on page A-13. Be advised that *only the basics* of incorporating screen images into a document are described here.

Learning Objectives

Upon completion of this unit, users should be able to:

- *Copy and paste* images from SOLIDWORKS Simulation into a word processor document. (It is presumed users already possess copy and paste capability.)
- *Crop* and *Re-size* images extracted from SOLIDWORKS Simulation.
- Apply *Text Wrapping* around images copied from SOLIDWORKS Simulation into a Word® document.
- *Extract data* from **Probe Results** tables and include it in a document as an Excel® *spreadsheet* table.
- Append *Callouts* to images to label significant aspects of a model or results.

Problem Statement

The problem used in this example is based on the cam follower analysis performed in Chapter 1. As such, users should be familiar with technical aspects of the analysis, thereby allowing us to focus attention solely upon how results of that problem might be presented in a report. Assume the following items are requested as part of the finite element analysis.

Deliverables:

a. Within a report, produce an image that documents **Fixtures** and **External Loads** applied to the model. Label applied force magnitudes on this image.

b. On the same page as part (a) create a plot of the most appropriate stress in the cam follower. See item (c) below for *where* on the model stresses are to be plotted.

c. Plot a graph of the most appropriate stress at one inch below the top end of the cam follower. On this graph include descriptive titles and axis labels.

d. On the same page as the graph in part (c), include an Excel table of stress values determined using the **Probe** tool for the graph of the previous step.

> **Software Version**
>
> Based on wide adoption of Windows7® and Windows8® and upgraded versions of Word® and Excel®, instructions below are based on Word 2010® or Word 2013® or Word 365®.

Setting Up the Necessary Editing Tools

WORD 2010® / WORD 2013® / WORD 365®

Before demonstrating how to create an organized report, the necessary Word® editing tools must be placed on the screen. These tools are placed on the **Quick Access Toolbar**. A brief review of the Word ® toolbars is included below for those unfamiliar with its organization.

In Word 2010® (and newer editions) two menu bars are located at the top of the screen. The larger menu, called the "**Ribbon**," contains many familiar commands, which are organized beneath different *tabs*. Related items are grouped together within a single tab. A portion of the **Home** tab is illustrated in Fig. 1. Located just above the ribbon (default location) or below the ribbon, as shown in Fig. 1, is what is called the "**Quick access toolbar**." This *customizable* toolbar is where commands frequently used to edit and create a report are placed. Various parts of the Word® user interface are labeled in Fig. 1. NOTE: For many items demonstrated below there exist alternative ways to accomplish the same tasks. However, for the sake of brevity, only one method is shown.

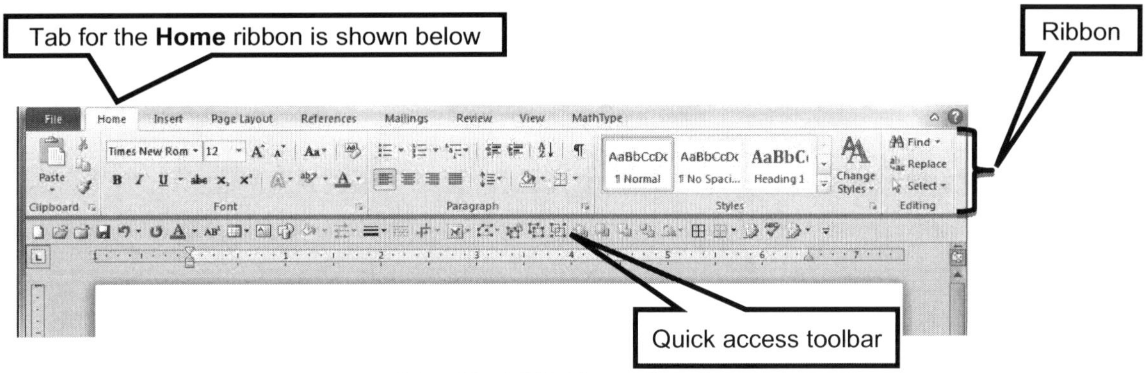

Figure 1 – Upper portion of the Word 2010® user interface.

1. To move the **Quick Access Toolbar** beneath the ribbon, right-click the **Quick Access Toolbar** (in its default location above the ribbon) and from the pop-up menu shown in Fig. 2, select **#1**, **Show Quick Access Toolbar Below the Ribbon**.

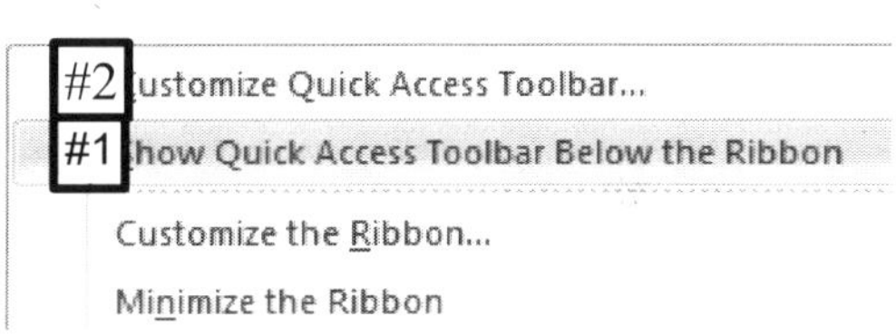

Figure 2 – Relocating and customizing the **Quick Access Toolbar** beneath the **Ribbon**.

Location of the **Quick Access Toolbar** is a user preference. However, the author finds it "closer to the action" and hence more convenient in the lower position. Next proceed to add the necessary icons to this toolbar. Although most icons are located beneath the various ribbon tabs, it is convenient to have the frequently used icons located where they are easily accessible. Proceed as follows.

2. Right-click the **Quick Access Toolbar**, and from the pull-down menu select **Customize Quick Access Toolbar…** shown at **#2** in Fig. 2. The **Word Options** window opens as shown in Fig. 3.

3. Beneath **Choose commands from:** located above the left-hand column, select **Popular Commands** from the pull-down menu. See arrow in Fig. 3.

4. Scroll down the alphabetical listing of commands in the left-hand column and select **Shapes** highlighted in Fig. 3. Then click the **[Add >>]** button, circled in Fig. 3, to move this selection into the right-hand column labeled **Customize Quick Access Toolbar:**.

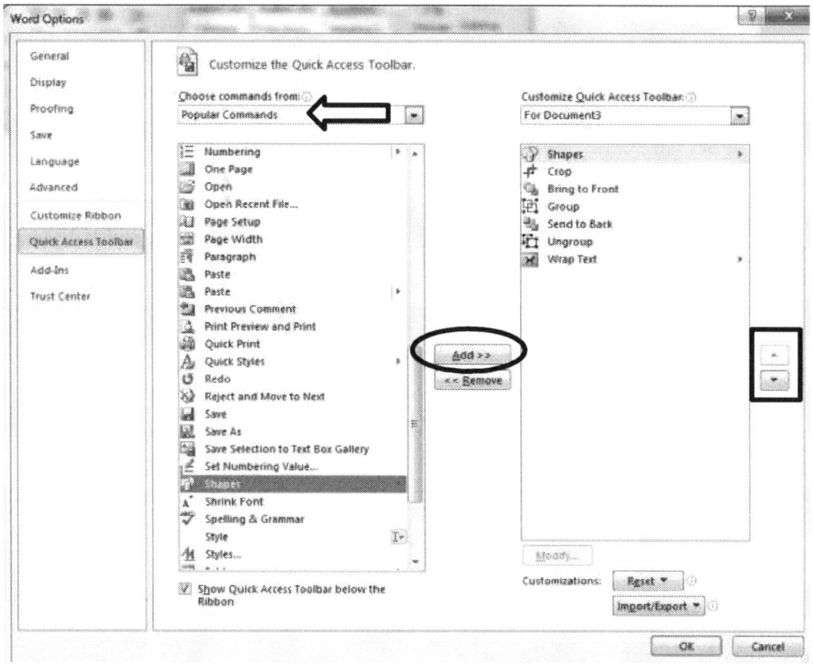

Figure 3 – Selecting commands to be added to the **Quick Access Toolbar**.

5. Return to the pull-down menu beneath **Choose commands from:** at top of the left-hand column and from the pull-down menu select **Picture Tools | Format Tab**.

6. Scroll down the alphabetical listing to select the remaining commands, shown in Fig. 4, and [**Add** >>] each command to the right-hand column.

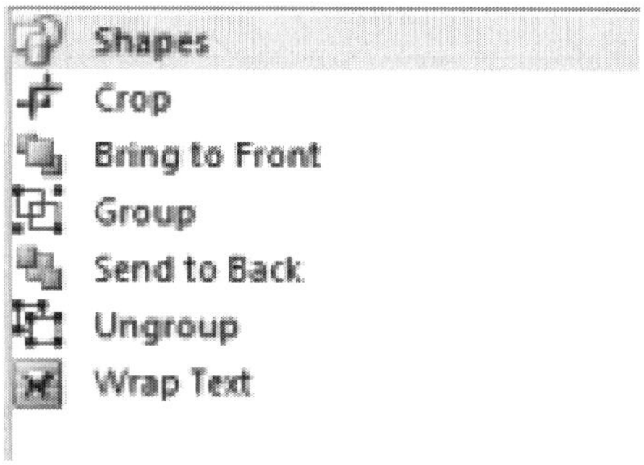

Figure 4 – Commands selected for addition to the **Quick Access Toolbar**.

7. Commands in the right-hand column can be arranged in any desired order by selecting an item and then clicking the up ▲ or down ▼ arrows shown boxed in Fig. 3.

8. Click **[OK]** to close the **Word Options** window and the selected commands appear in the **Quick access Toolbar**.

You are now ready to begin creating a report containing customized graphic images extracted from SOLIDWORKS Simulation.

Creating a Custom Report (a demonstration)

Incorporating Images into a Word Document

Begin by assuming that both SOLIDWORKS Simulation *and* a Word document are open, side-by-side on the screen. Both these windows must be sized to fit on the monitor. *NOTE: It is also possible to switch from window to window by using the* ***Minimize*** *and* ***Restore*** *buttons located at the top right of each window.* As larger monitors become more common, having two windows open simultaneously is less of a hassle. Dual monitors can also be used with SOLIDWORKS on one screen and Word® on the other.

Because it can be tricky to place text onto a page *after* an image is placed on the page, it is a good practice to type your name, date, and exercise number at the top of a blank sheet in Word® before adding images.

There are three ways to incorporate images into a Word® document. For all three methods, assume that the cam follower of Chapter 1 is displayed in the SOLIDWORKS simulation graphics area with **Fixtures** and **External Loads** applied to the model as shown in Fig. 5. The easiest method is described first. This method works for all versions of Word®, but only captures images *within the graphics portion* of the SOLIDWORKS screen.

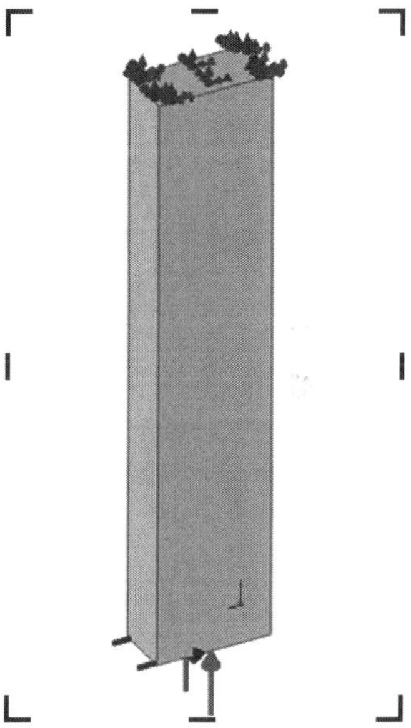

Figure 5 – Image to be pasted into a Word document. Note **Crop** marks around the image.

Before performing any of the steps below, choose a view of the model, plot, or graph that best displays the attributes you want to show.

METHOD 1 - Using SOLIDWORKS Simulation "Screen Capture"

1. To add **Screen Capture** permanently to menus at the top of your SOLIDWORKS screen, right-click anywhere on the menus and from the pull-down menu select **Toolbars > Screen Capture** 

. The screen capture toolbar, shown in Fig. 6, is added to the menu. To use this feature, simply click the camera  icon to capture an image in the *graphics area* of the screen and place it on the clipboard.

Figure 6 – Using the **Screen Capture** capability built into SOLIDWORKS.

2. Next, move the cursor to the desired location within a Word® document and select **Paste** from the Word® menu. A *full size* image, shown cropped and downsized in Fig. 5, is placed into the current document. Methods for cropping, resizing, and placing this image on a page are described later.

The following sections describe two alternate methods of placing SOLIDWORKS Simulation images into Word® documents.

METHOD 2 – Using "Screenshot" in Word®

1. In the Word ® ribbon, select the **Insert** *tab*, and within the **Illustrations** sub-group, select the ▼ symbol adjacent to **Screenshot** . Any other currently *open* windows appear as thumbnail images as illustrated in Fig. 7. This feature does not display windows that are minimized to the taskbar.

Figure 7 shows that SOLIDWORKS Simulation is the only other open window on the screen. If multiple windows are open, select the SOLIDWORKS window containing the desired image.

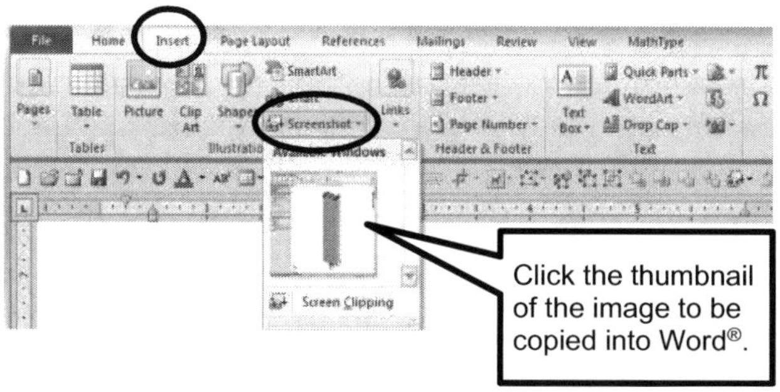

Figure 7 – Copying the contents of any open window into a Word document using the **Screenshot** capability.

2. Click the thumbnail image of the window to be copied and a full-size **Screenshot** of the image appears in the current Word® document as shown in Fig. 8.

Observe the difference between the image in Fig. 8 and the image in Fig. 5. Figure 5 shows *only the model within the graphics area of the screen* while Fig. 8 includes the *entire* SOLIDWORKS screen. Occasionally the entire screen image is desired in order to show additional details of the analysis included within either the SOLIDWORKS manager tree or the Simulation manager tree. However, if only an image of the model is desired, then the **Screen Capture** capability within SOLIDWORKS might be preferred. Both Figs. 5 and 8 require additional cropping and resizing as described later.

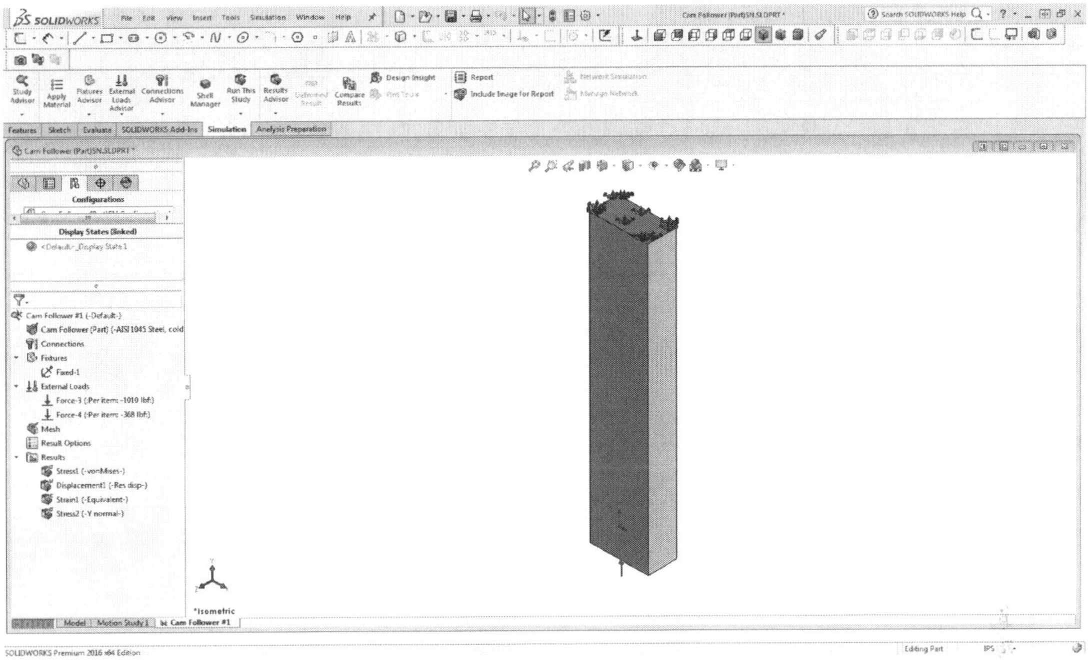

Figure 8 – Full-size image obtained using the **Screenshot** option within Word®. No size alterations were applied to this image.

METHOD 3 – Using "[Ctrl] + [Print Screen]" Available in All Word Versions

1. By simultaneously pressing the **[Ctrl]** + **[Print Screen]** buttons on the keyboard, the *entire screen image* is copied to the clipboard. The image shown in Fig. 9 reveals that *both* the SOLIDWORKS Simulation model *and* the currently open Word® document are copied. This approach can be used with all versions of Word®.

2. Next, move the cursor into the currently open Word® document and select **Paste**. The entire image is placed into the open document.

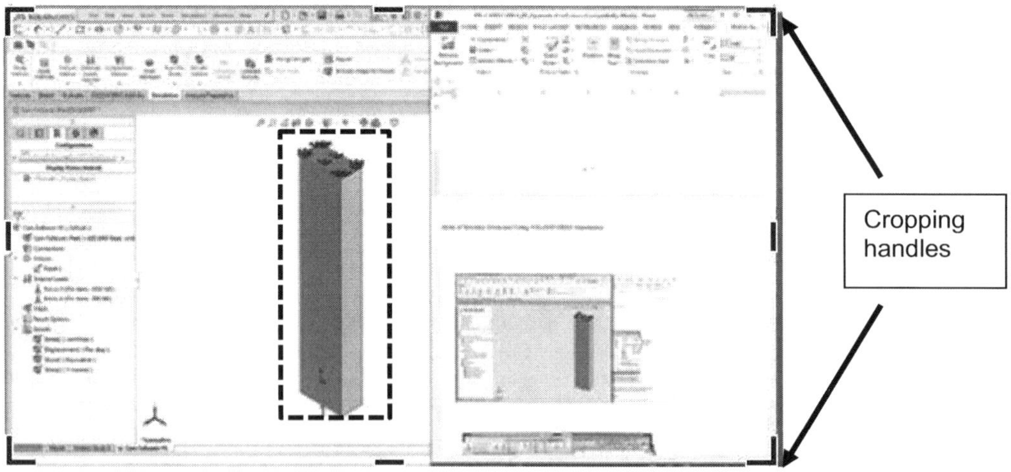

Figure 9 – The result of pressing the **[Ctrl] + [Print Screen]** buttons is to capture an image of the entire screen. If both SOLIDWORKS and Word are open on your screen, then images of both are pasted into the current document.

No matter what method is used to copy a screen image into a Word document that image typically *must* be further edited by either cropping or re-sizing the image, or both.

Editing Images Within a Word Document

This section outlines how images are cropped and resized using the editing commands that were added to the **Quick Access Toolbar**. Although reference is made only to the image in Fig. 9, the same editing process can be applied to images copied by any of the methods outlined above.

Cropping and Sizing Images

1. Within the Word document, begin by clicking the image to select it. When selected, "handles" (tiny circles) appear at each corner and tiny squares appear on each mid-side of the image. If desired, resize the image by clicking and dragging these handles.

2. Because the hypothetical 'assignment' requests only an image of the model and its **Fixtures** and **External Loads**, the image is next cropped by selecting the **Crop** tool. It should be found on the **Quick Access Toolbar**. Once selected, the **Crop** tool replaces the cursor and bold corners and short dashes appear at the corners and mid-section on each edge of the selected image as shown in Figs. 5 and 9. Cropping handles are shown on Fig. 9 above.

3. Using the **Crop** tool, click and drag any of the "corners" or dark bars appearing on the image boundaries to crop the image to the approximate size shown by bold dashed lines in Fig. 9. Click anywhere outside the image to end cropping. *NOTE: Dashed lines shown around the model in Fig. 9 do not appear.*

4. If after cropping, the image needs to be resized, click the image again to select it. The "handles" reappear. Click and drag any of these handles to re-size the image as desired. Because cropping occurs in finite steps, it is often helpful to enlarge the image, crop it again, and then return the image to its desired size.

NOTE: After cropping, the image will probably *not* appear at its desired location on the page. An image may jump to a random location on the page or even a different page. If the image is difficult to locate, typically look *above* the location where you clicked to paste it. Placing an image *and* text together at desired locations on a page is described in the **Text Wrapping** section on the next page.

Adding Labels to Images

Part (a) of the problem statement also requests that magnitudes of the force components be labeled. Labeling can be done manually in Word® or as outlined below.

1. On the main **Ribbon** in Word®, select the **Insert** *tab*. Next, click ▼ below the **Shapes**  icon and from the pull-down menu, beneath **Callouts**, select the callout of your choice. Alternatively, in the **Quick Access Toolbar**, select the **Insert Shapes**  icon and from the pull-down menu select the **Callout** of your choice. A rectangular callout is used in this example.

2. In Word®, move the cursor near where the force component is to be labeled. The cursor symbol changes to a "+" sign. Click-and-drag the cursor to create a small **Callout** text box. This box can be resized as needed by dragging its handles.

3. Click inside the **Callout** box and type a label for the X-component of force. Font style and font size can be changed by right clicking the **Callout** boundary in Word® for access to font style and size options. Finally, drag the "pointer" on the **Callout** box to attach it to the force component to be labeled as shown in Fig. 10.

4. An identical procedure is used to label the Y-force component. It is not repeated here.

Grouping Images

To finalize this image, two additional steps are necessary. First, it is necessary to **Group** the image and its label. Grouping is necessary because the model and its force label are two different entities. As such, they will move independently and might become separated during subsequent editing of the document. Any such movement will separate the label from the force vector, thereby rendering it meaningless. Proceed as follows to **Group** these items. Items can be un-grouped and positions changed at a later time if desired. However, un-grouping can get messy.

5. Simultaneously hold down the **[Shift]** key while clicking to select the **Callout** and then the model image. Selection handles appear around each object as shown in Fig. 10. Then in the **Quick Access Toolbar**, select the **Group** icon. Selected items now move as one.

Text Wrapping

A second step is required to finalize the image location whenever typed text accompanies an image, such as Fig. 10. Text can be placed in several different locations relative to the image. In this book, the most typical arrangement is for text to appear adjacent to the image, like this paragraph *and* the image in Fig. 10 at right. A second option is for text to appear above and below an image as illustrated in Fig. 12. Either selection is made by choosing the **Text Wrapping** icon and selecting either **Tight** or **Top and Bottom** from the pop-up menu. *NOTE: An image must first be selected in order for the* ***Text Wrapping*** *icon to be active.* Select an image in your Word document and then click the **Text Wrapping** icon now to view these and other options available for placing an image onto a page with text. Figure 10, with text appearing *adjacent* to the image, was accomplished by selecting the **Tight** option from the **Text Wrapping** pull-down menu.

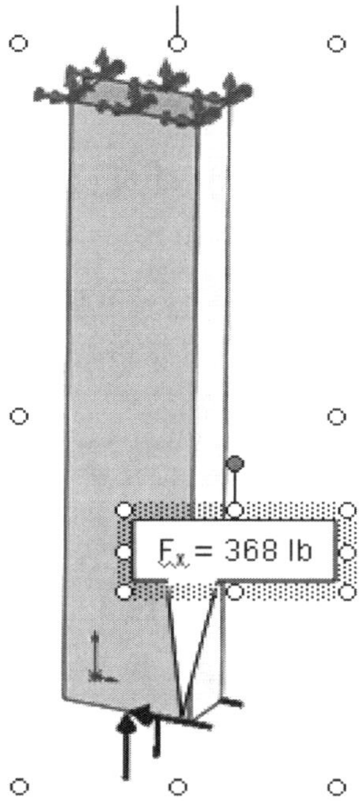

Figure 10 – Placing a label on an image and grouping the entities to effectively "lock" them together.

After applying **Text Wrapping** it is typically necessary to click the image and drag it to re-size it and to place it at its desired location on a page. Important reminder, *if* various parts of an image are not **Grouped** together, then each part will need to be moved one-at-a-time and re-organized in its final position. Grouping eliminates this extra task. Occasionally the **Bring to Front** or **Send to Back** icons must be used to show all important parts of an image. For example, if the force label **Callout** in Fig. 10 is hidden behind the model image, we could either apply **Bring to Front** to the **Callout** or apply **Send to Back** to the model image. Either action results in properly "stacked" images so that the most visible item appears "in front."

A Word of Caution and Encouragement

Using the cut, paste, crop, callout, and group commands takes some getting used to. It easily frustrates individuals with a low tolerance for ambiguity. In other words, all kinds of unexpected things can happen. For example, after grouping items together, it is common for typed text to overlap the image. Don't panic, simply make a selection using the **Text Wrapping** tool and the text will nicely organize itself around (or) above and below the image. Using **Ungroup** causes similar problems.

The procedures to cut and paste images from SOLIDWORKS Simulation into a Word® document, to re-size those images, and to document them by the addition of labels is demonstrated above. Although this procedure may seem unnecessarily tedious, after a few trials, these tasks can be accomplished in 30 seconds or less. The procedure outlined above can be used to copy an image of the *most appropriate stress* [requested in part (b) of the problem statement] onto the same page as the image in Fig. 10. These two images are shown together in Fig. 12 where a "sample" report is illustrated.

Incorporating an Excel Spreadsheet into a Word Document

Parts (c) and (d) of the problem statement request that a graph of the most appropriate stress (σ_Y) be placed onto the same page with an Excel® spreadsheet that contains data used to produce the graph. Therefore, the last item to be demonstrated here is to capture data from the **Probe Results** table, to export it into an Excel® spreadsheet, and finally to insert the spreadsheet into a Word document. The procedure to accomplish this is outlined next.

Capturing Probe Results Data and Exporting it to an Excel Spreadsheet

The following steps assume that the **Probe** tool is used to select nodes from left to right across the model at a location 1 inch below the top (fixed) end of the cam follower. It is also assumed that the **Probe Result** property manager is open and that stress values at each node location are stored in the **Results** table as shown in Fig. 11. One problem with the **Results** table is that, without resorting to scrolling through the data, its small size often prevents display of *all* values determined when using the **Probe** tool. This shortcoming is overcome by saving and displaying *all* the data in an Excel® spreadsheet. To capture this data into a spreadsheet, proceed as follows.

1. In the **Report Options** dialogue box, at bottom of the **Probe Results** property manager, click the **Save** icon circled in Fig. 11. Immediately the **Save As** window opens and the **File name:** field contains the name assigned to the current Study. It is best to assign a descriptive name associated with this file such as "**Cam Follower Data**." Then save this file to an easy to find location on the hard drive such as **C: \My Excel\Cam Follower Data.csv**. Also, at the bottom of this window note that the **Save as type:** field shows **Excel File (*.csv)**. Finally, click the **[Save]** button.

2. Also, click **[OK]** ✓ to close the **Probe Result** property manager.

3. Next, open the file in Excel® and copy the data by clicking and dragging over it to select it and then selecting **Copy**. Carefully note the number of rows and columns of data.

4. Return to the Word® document and insert the Excel® file by clicking **Paste** and sizing the spreadsheet using its drag handles much like sizing an image.

5. Within the Word document, begin by placing the data table and then the **Probe** graph in their desired locations on a page by selecting them one item at a time. For example, select the Excel® data table in Fig. 13 and then choose the desired **Text Wrapping** option (**Tight** is used in Fig. 13) and finally click to place and size the data table in a Word® document.

6. Repeat step 5 to paste an image of the **Probe** graph at the desired location in your Word® document. The final result is shown in the Sample Report on pg. A-14.

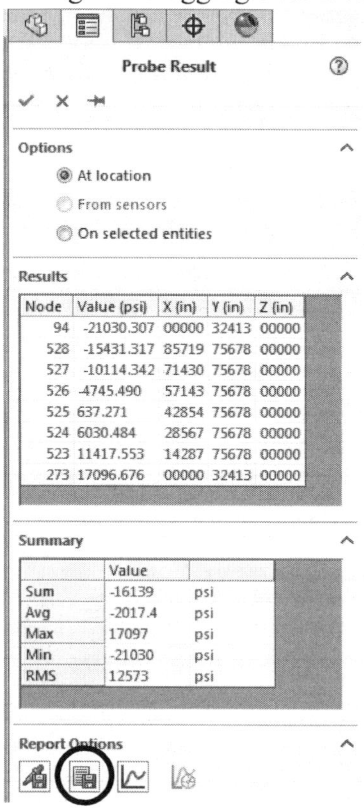

Figure 11 – The **Probe Result** table populated with **SY** stress values sampled across the cam follower face.

Exhibits of two pages of an "example report" are shown on the following pages.

EXAMPLE REPORT

Exercise 1, Chapter #1 NAME: YOUR NAME

Below are examples of figures requested in parts (a) and (b) of the example exercise used to demonstrate report preparation by copying, pasting, cropping, labeling, and grouping multiple images from SOLIDWORKS Simulation onto a single page in a Word® document. In an actual end-of-chapter Exercise, this first paragraph would be used to describe technical aspects about the finite element models shown below.

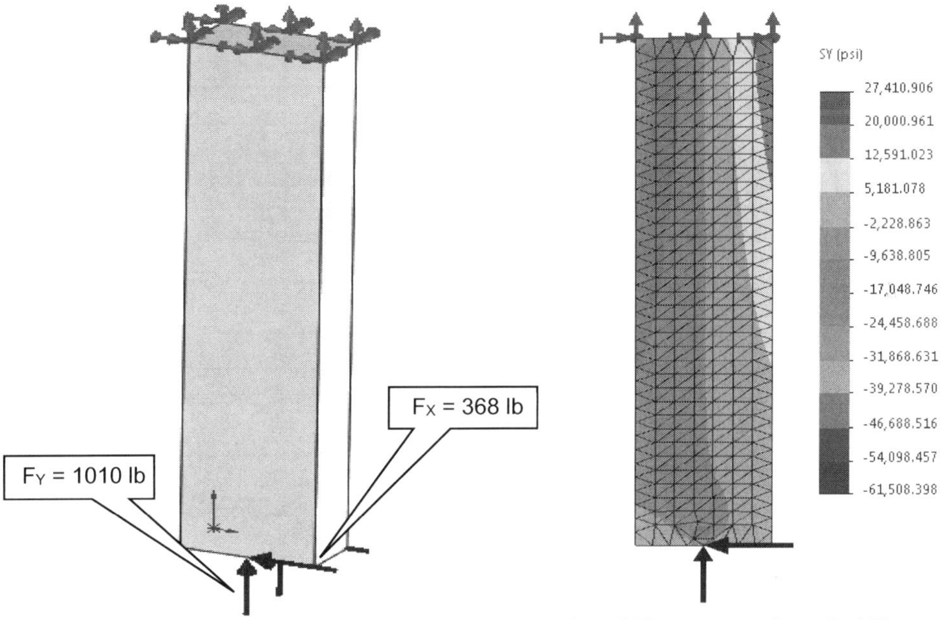

Figure 12 - Figure (a) shows the cam follower and its associated **Fixtures** and applied **External Loads**. Figure (b) shows a plot of σ_y due to combined axial and bending stress in the cam follower.

A descriptive figure caption can be placed beneath the figures and answers to questions about the model can be typed in available space on the page adjacent to the images or above and below the image as shown on this page. The above figures were cut and pasted from SOLIDWORKS Simulation. Then, labels were added and all items were grouped together using techniques demonstrated in this Appendix. Finally the **Text Wrapping** tool  was used to specify that figures would be placed on a page such that text could be placed above and below the images (using the **Top and Bottom** option) as illustrated above.

EXAMPLE REPORT (continued)

The spreadsheet in Fig. 13 at right contains all **Results** data found using the **Probe** tool. In spreadsheet format, it is possible to compare stress magnitudes on both left and right sides of the cam follower with values calculated using classical stress equations. See below for explanatory "notes" added to the Excel spreadsheet.

Node	Value (psi)	X (in)	Y (in)	Z (in)
94	-21030.307	0	4.324324	0.5
528	-15431.317	0.142857	4.256757	0.5
527	-10114.342	0.285714	4.256757	0.5
526	-4745.49	0.428571	4.256757	0.5
525	637.271	0.571429	4.256757	0.5
524	6030.484	0.714286	4.256757	0.5
523	11417.553	0.857143	4.256757	0.5
273	17096.676	1	4.324324	0.5

Maximum compressive stress on top left side of the cam follower at 1" below the top of the model.

Maximum tensile stress on right side of the cam follower at 1" below top of the model.

Figure 13 – Data from the **Probe Result** table that was saved into an Excel® Spreadsheet and subsequently inserted into a Word® document.

In an actual report, this space can be used to discuss stress trends observed on the graph in Fig. 14 or values determined using the **Probe** tool.

Additionally, calculations of stress determined using classical stress equations can be included here and compared with finite element results.

All this can be accomplished in the neat and concise report format illustrated here.

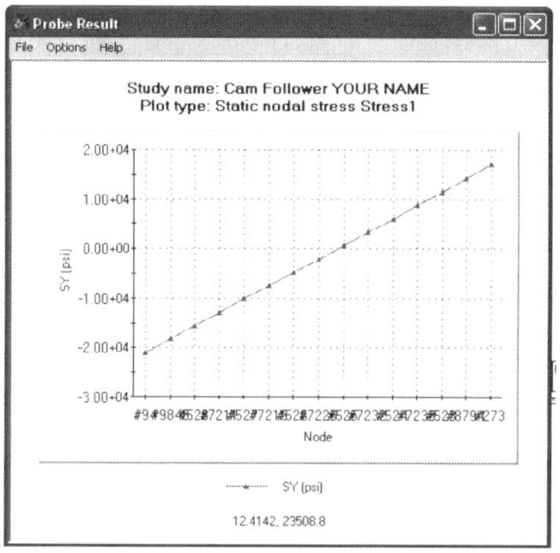

Figure 14 – Graph of combined axial compressive stress and bending stress across the face of the cam follower at 1″ below the top (fixed) end.

APPENDIX B

Alternate Method to Change Screen Background Color

This section describes an alternate method of changing the graphics area background color to white. The method outlined below often works for computers that do not have the exact graphics board recommended for use with SOLIDWORKS. Give it a try and if it works, so much the better. The procedure below assumes SOLIDWORKS or SOLIDWORKS Simulation is open and a new part or assembly is displayed on the screen. Note the default gray shading in the graphics area of Fig. 1.

1. At the top of the SOLIDWORKS feature manager tree, click the **Display Manager** icon shown circled in Fig. 1.

2. Next, adjacent to the arrow in Fig. 1, click the **View Scene, Lights, and Cameras** icon also located near the top of the **Display Manager**. The screen should now appear as shown in Fig. 1

Figure 1 – Accessing the **View Scene, Lights, and Cameras** icon on the **Display Manager** tab.

3. Within the **Scene, Lights, and Cameras** display manager tree, click the "▶" symbol adjacent to **Scene (3 Point Faded*)**. This action reveals sub-menu choices shown in Fig. 2.

4. From this sub-menu, double-click **Background (softbox)** to open the **Edit Scene** property manager which is partially shown in Fig. 3.

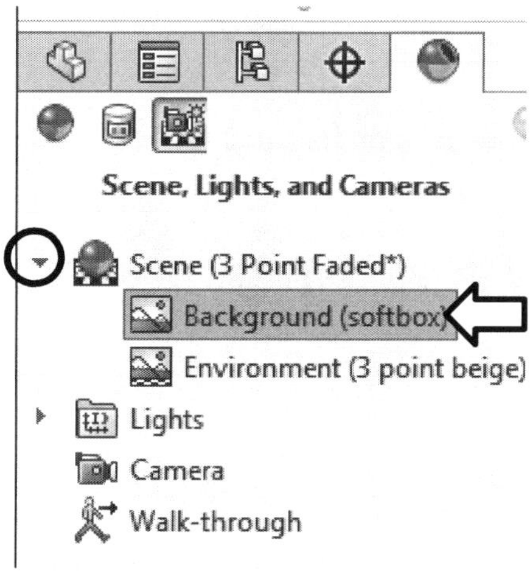

Figure 2 – Accessing the **Background (Gradient)** option.

5. Within the **Background** dialogue box, click ▼ to open the **Background Type** drop down menu, shown boxed in Fig. 3, and from the menu select **Gradient**.

6. Also, within the **Background** dialogue box the **Top gradient color:** field should appear white by default. If not, click the field to open the **Color** window shown to the right in Fig. 3.

7. In the **Color** window, select the color white, circled in Fig. 3, and click **[OK]**.

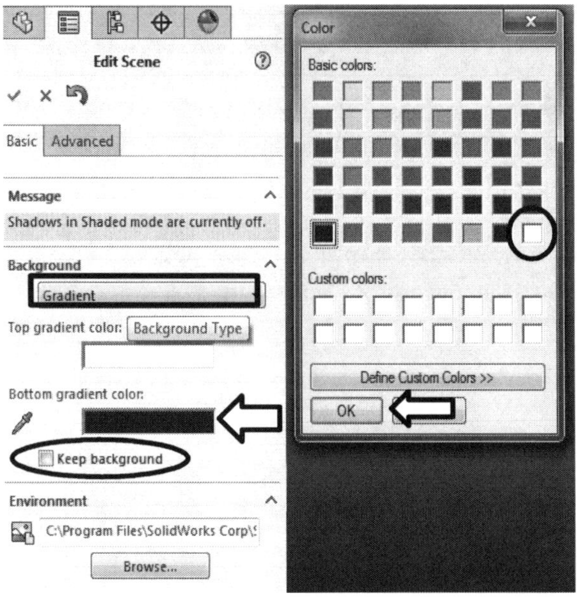

Figure 3 – Sequence of steps to change the background color to white.

8. Repeat steps 6 and 7 to change the color of the **Bottom gradient color:** field to white.

9. Next, within the **Background** dialogue box, check "✓" the ☑ **Keep background** in the oval on Fig. 3. This action *should* retain this setting during future SOLIDWORKS Simulation sessions. *However, be prepared to repeat this simple procedure if the shaded background appears again.*

10. Finally, click **[OK]** ✓ (green check mark) to close the **Edit Scene** property manager and, if successful, the graphics area should now appear white. If not, the SOLIDWORKS default display (gradient color) must be used.

11. Return to the **SOLIDWORKS Feature Manager Design Tree** by clicking its icon located at top of the Feature Manager tree circled in Fig. 4.

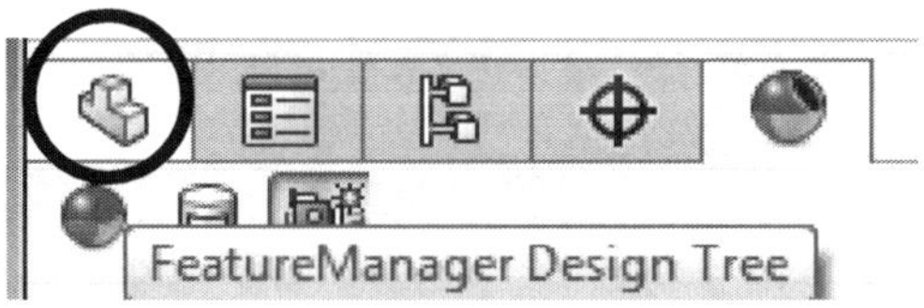

Figure 4 – Select the SOLIDWORKS Feature Manager Design tree icon to return to SOLIDWORKS Simulation.